SECRET SIX

VOLUME 4

CAUTION TO THE WIND

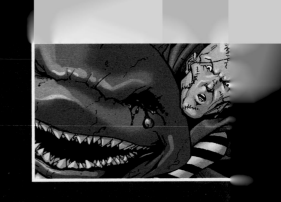

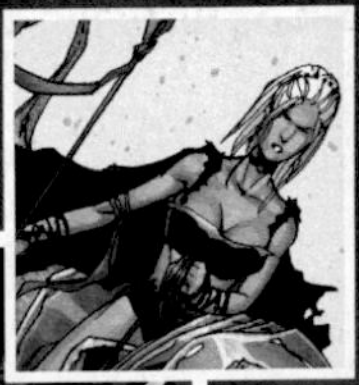

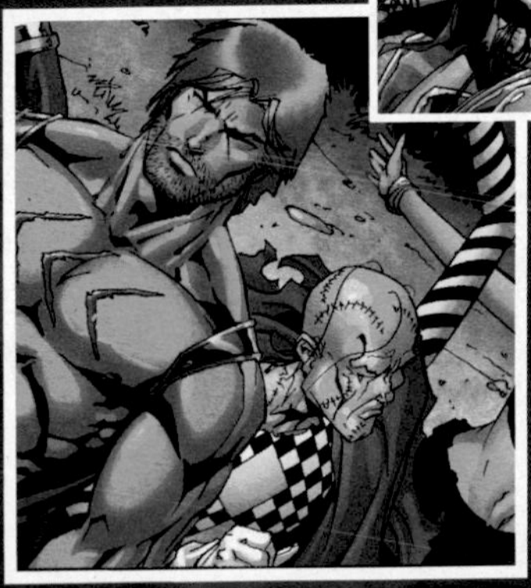

SECRET SIX

VOLUME 4
CAUTION TO THE WIND

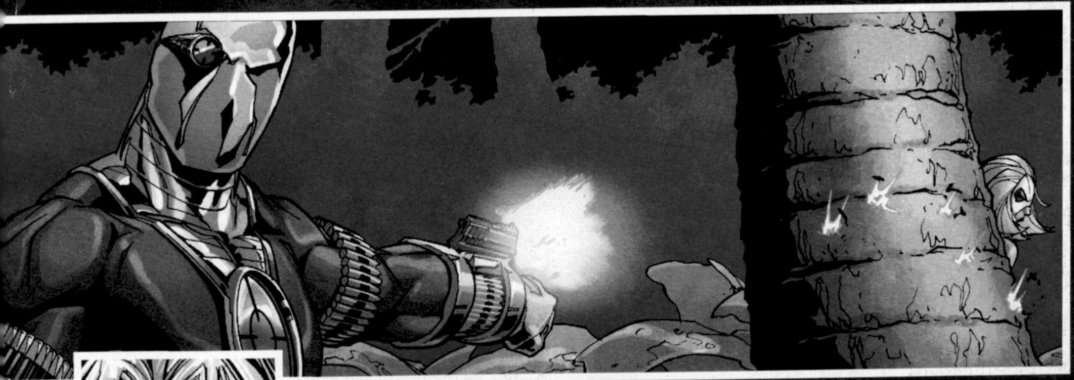

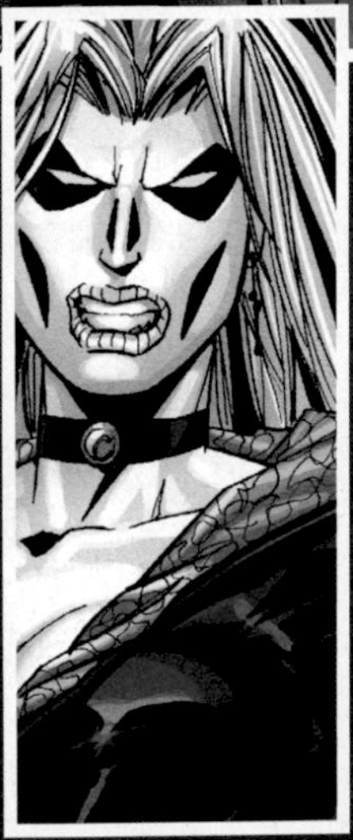

Gail Simone
Paul Cornell
Keith Giffen
writers

J. Calafiore
Pete Woods
Marcos Marz
Luciana Del Negro
Matthew Clark
Ron Randall
Art Thibert
Sean Parsons
artists

Jason Wright
John Kalisz
Brad Anderson
Guy Major
colorists

Travis Lanham
Rob Leigh
Pat Brosseau
letterers

Daniel LuVisi
collection cover artist

SUPERMAN created by
Jerry Siegel and Joe Shuster
By special arrangement
with the Jerry Siegel family

DEADSHOT co-created by
LEW SAYRE SCHWARTZ

DOOM PATROL created by
ARNOLD DRAKE

SEAN RYAN RACHEL GLUCKSTERN MATT IDELSON ELISABETH V. GEHRLEIN	Editors – Original Series
WIL MOSS	Associate Editor – Original Series
RICKEY PURDIN SIMONA MARTORE	Assistant Editors – Original Series
JEB WOODARD	Group Editor – Collected Editions
ROBIN WILDMAN	Editor – Collected Edition
STEVE COOK	Design Director – Books
SARABETH KETT	Publication Design
BOB HARRAS	Senior VP – Editor-in-Chief, DC Comics
DIANE NELSON	President
DAN DIDIO AND JIM LEE	Co-Publishers
GEOFF JOHNS	Chief Creative Officer
AMIT DESAI	Senior VP – Marketing & Global Franchise Management
NAIRI GARDINER	Senior VP – Finance
SAM ADES	VP – Digital Marketing
BOBBIE CHASE	VP – Talent Development
MARK CHIARELLO	Senior VP – Art, Design & Collected Editions
JOHN CUNNINGHAM	VP – Content Strategy
ANNE DEPIES	VP – Strategy Planning & Reporting
DON FALLETTI	VP – Manufacturing Operations
LAWRENCE GANEM	VP – Editorial Administration & Talent Relations
ALISON GILL	Senior VP – Manufacturing & Operations
HANK KANALZ	Senior VP – Editorial Strategy & Administration
JAY KOGAN	VP – Legal Affairs
DEREK MADDALENA	Senior VP – Sales & Business Development
JACK MAHAN	VP – Business Affairs
DAN MIRON	VP – Sales Planning & Trade Development
NICK NAPOLITANO	VP – Manufacturing Administration
CAROL ROEDER	VP – Marketing
EDDIE SCANNELL	VP – Mass Account & Digital Sales
COURTNEY SIMMONS	Senior VP – Publicity & Communications
JIM (SKI) SOKOLOWSKI	VP – Comic Book Specialty & Newsstand Sales
SANDY YI	Senior VP – Global Franchise Management

SECRET SIX VOL. 4: CAUTION TO THE WIND

DC Comics, 2900 West Alameda Avenue, Burbank, CA 91505
Printed by RR Donnelley, Salem, VA, USA. 3/18/16. First Printing.
ISBN: 978-1-4012-6090-3

Library of Congress Cataloging-in-Publication Data is Available.

PEFC Certified
Printed on paper from sustainably managed forests and controlled sources
PEFC™
PEFC/29-31-75
www.pefc.org

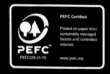

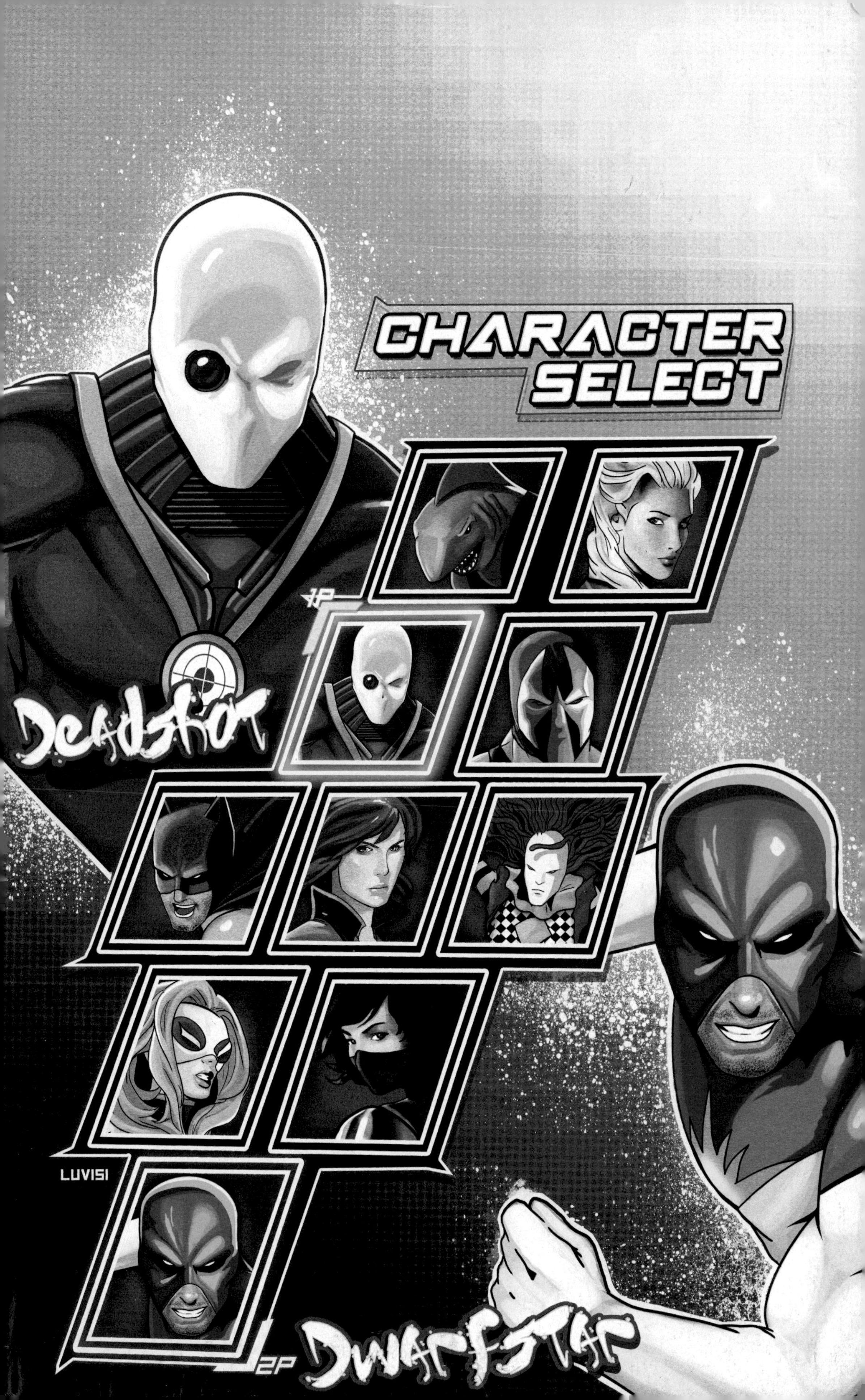

CHARACTER SELECT
1P
Deadshot
LUVISI
2P
Dwarfstar

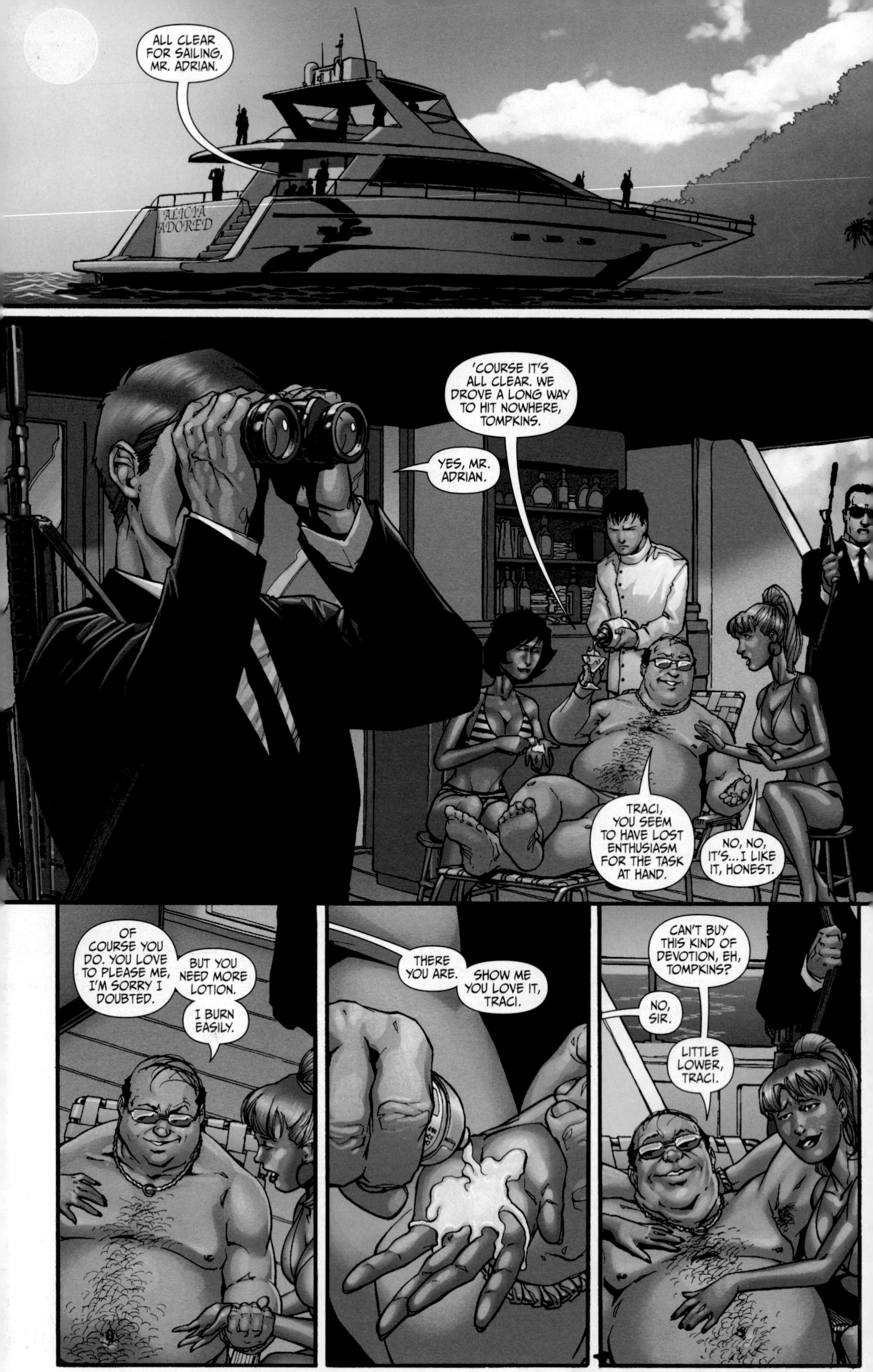
ALL CLEAR FOR SAILING, MR. ADRIAN.
ALICIA ADORED
'COURSE IT'S ALL CLEAR. WE DROVE A LONG WAY TO HIT NOWHERE, TOMPKINS.
YES, MR. ADRIAN.
TRACI, YOU SEEM TO HAVE LOST ENTHUSIASM FOR THE TASK AT HAND.
NO, NO, IT'S...I LIKE IT, HONEST.
OF COURSE YOU DO. YOU LOVE TO PLEASE ME, I'M SORRY I DOUBTED.
BUT YOU NEED MORE LOTION.
I BURN EASILY.
THERE YOU ARE.
SHOW ME YOU LOVE IT, TRACI.
CAN'T BUY THIS KIND OF DEVOTION, EH, TOMPKINS?
NO, SIR.
LITTLE LOWER, TRACI.

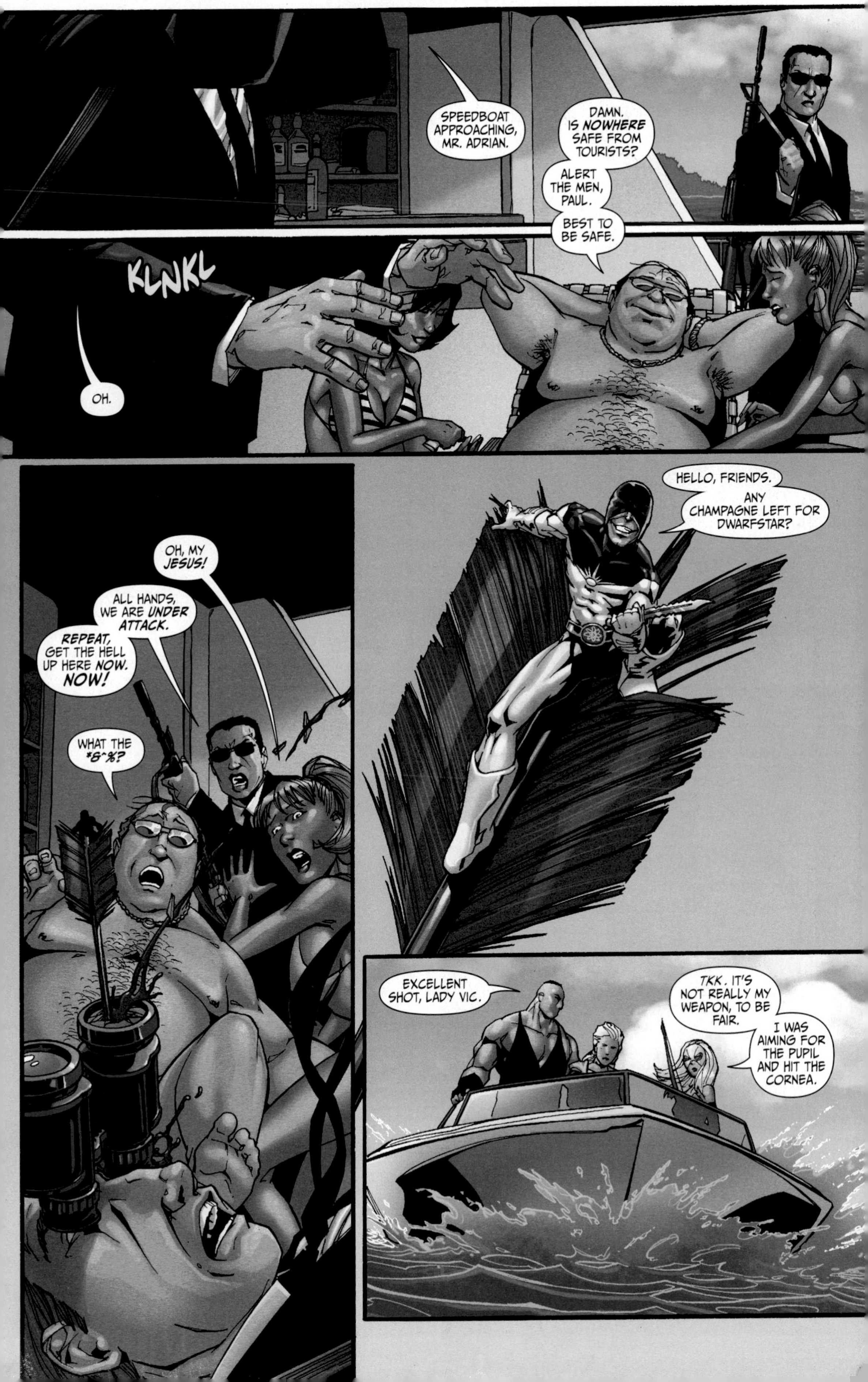
SPEEDBOAT APPROACHING, MR. ADRIAN.
DAMN. IS NOWHERE SAFE FROM TOURISTS?
ALERT THE MEN, PAUL.
BEST TO BE SAFE.
KLNKL
OH.
OH, MY JESUS!
ALL HANDS, WE ARE UNDER ATTACK.
REPEAT, GET THE HELL UP HERE NOW. NOW!
WHAT THE *&^%?
HELLO, FRIENDS.
ANY CHAMPAGNE LEFT FOR DWARFSTAR?
EXCELLENT SHOT, LADY VIC.
TKK. IT'S NOT REALLY MY WEAPON, TO BE FAIR.
I WAS AIMING FOR THE PUPIL AND HIT THE CORNEA.

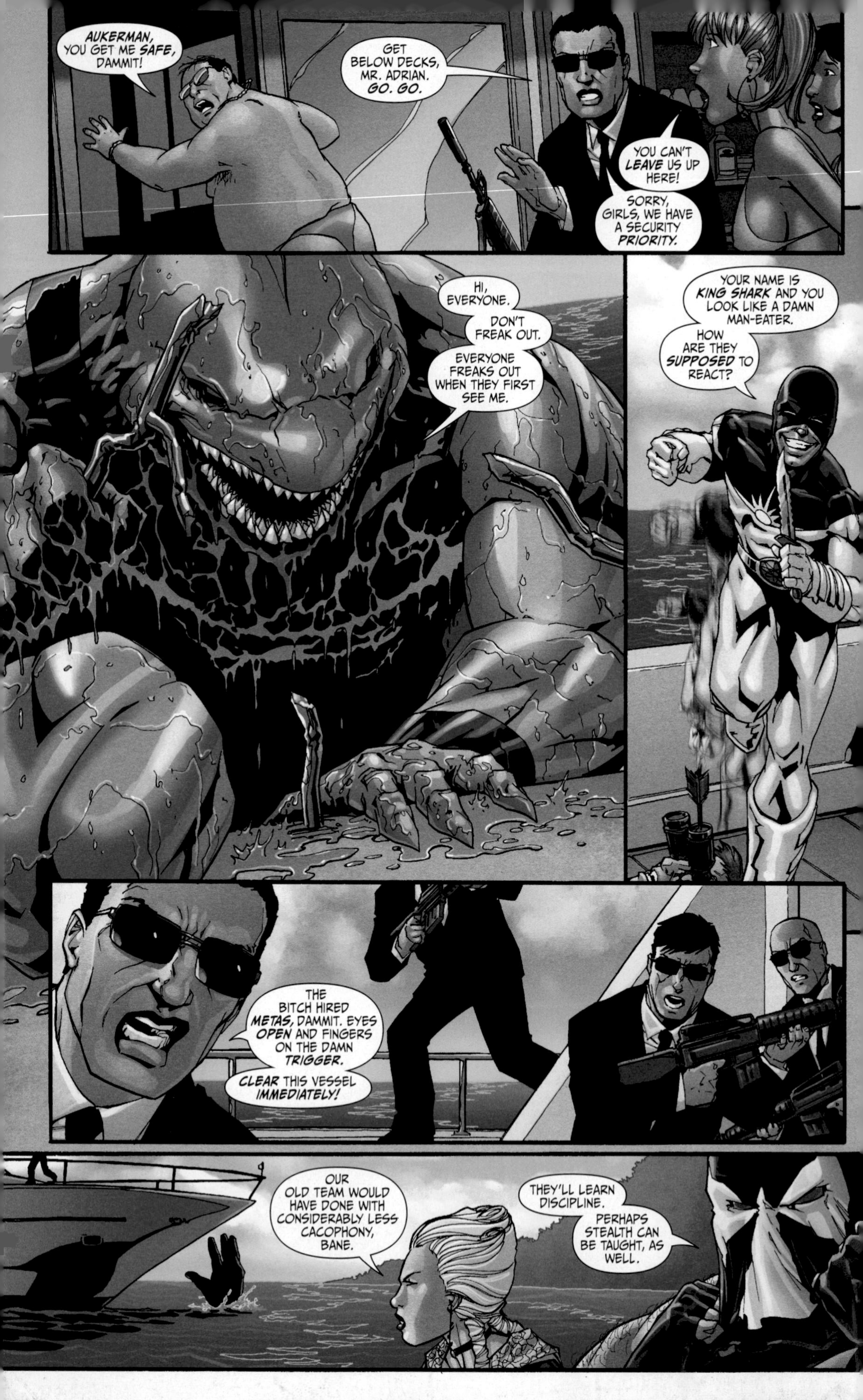
AUKERMAN, YOU GET ME SAFE, DAMMIT!
GET BELOW DECKS, MR. ADRIAN. GO. GO.
YOU CAN'T LEAVE US UP HERE!
SORRY, GIRLS, WE HAVE A SECURITY PRIORITY.
HI, EVERYONE.
DON'T FREAK OUT.
EVERYONE FREAKS OUT WHEN THEY FIRST SEE ME.
YOUR NAME IS KING SHARK AND YOU LOOK LIKE A DAMN MAN-EATER.
HOW ARE THEY SUPPOSED TO REACT?
THE BITCH HIRED METAS, DAMMIT. EYES OPEN AND FINGERS ON THE DAMN TRIGGER.
CLEAR THIS VESSEL IMMEDIATELY!
OUR OLD TEAM WOULD HAVE DONE WITH CONSIDERABLY LESS CACOPHONY, BANE.
THEY'LL LEARN DISCIPLINE.
PERHAPS STEALTH CAN BE TAUGHT, AS WELL.

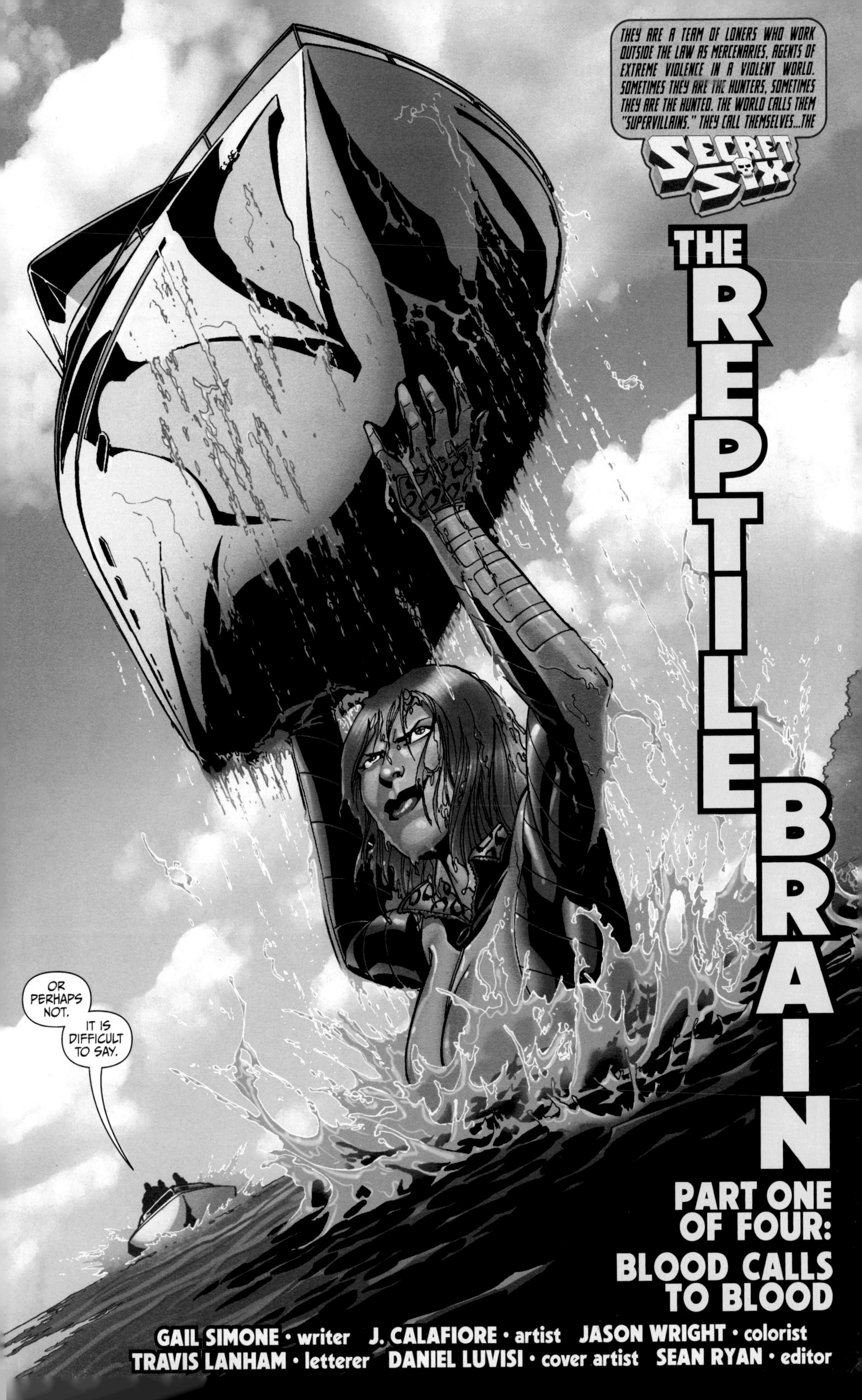
THEY ARE A TEAM OF LONERS WHO WORK OUTSIDE THE LAW AS MERCENARIES, AGENTS OF EXTREME VIOLENCE IN A VIOLENT WORLD. SOMETIMES THEY ARE THE HUNTERS, SOMETIMES THEY ARE THE HUNTED. THE WORLD CALLS THEM "SUPERVILLAINS." THEY CALL THEMSELVES...THE
SECRET SIX
THE REPTILE BRAIN
PART ONE OF FOUR: BLOOD CALLS TO BLOOD
OR PERHAPS NOT.
IT IS DIFFICULT TO SAY.
GAIL SIMONE • writer J. CALAFIORE • artist JASON WRIGHT • colorist
TRAVIS LANHAM • letterer DANIEL LUVISI • cover artist SEAN RYAN • editor

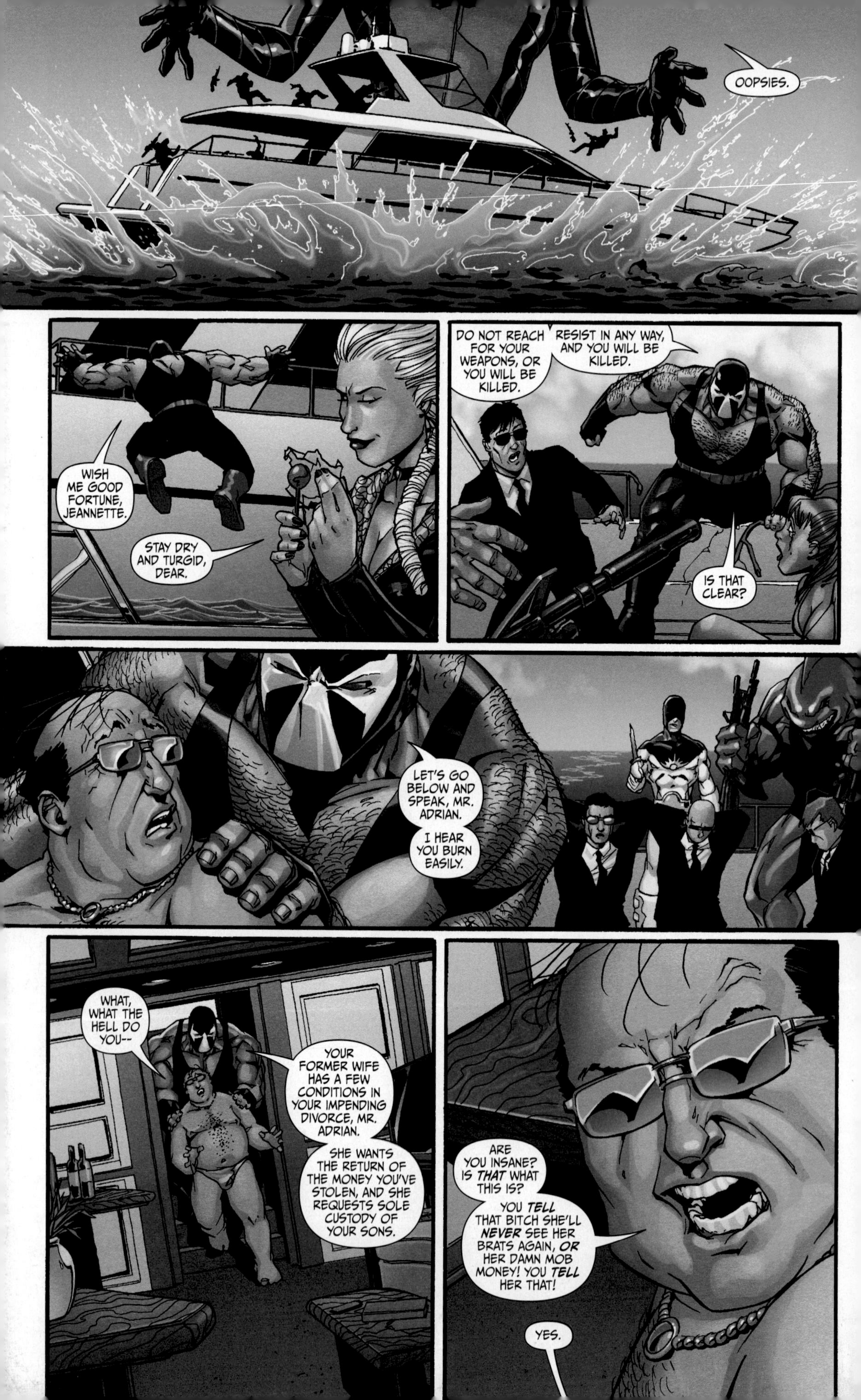
OOPSIES.
WISH ME GOOD FORTUNE, JEANNETTE.
STAY DRY AND TURGID, DEAR.
DO NOT REACH FOR YOUR WEAPONS, OR YOU WILL BE KILLED.
RESIST IN ANY WAY, AND YOU WILL BE KILLED.
IS THAT CLEAR?
LET'S GO BELOW AND SPEAK, MR. ADRIAN.
I HEAR YOU BURN EASILY.
WHAT, WHAT THE HELL DO YOU--
YOUR FORMER WIFE HAS A FEW CONDITIONS IN YOUR IMPENDING DIVORCE, MR. ADRIAN.
SHE WANTS THE RETURN OF THE MONEY YOU'VE STOLEN, AND SHE REQUESTS SOLE CUSTODY OF YOUR SONS.
ARE YOU INSANE? IS *THAT* WHAT THIS IS?
YOU *TELL* THAT BITCH SHE'LL *NEVER* SEE HER BRATS AGAIN, *OR* HER DAMN MOB MONEY! YOU *TELL* HER THAT!
YES.

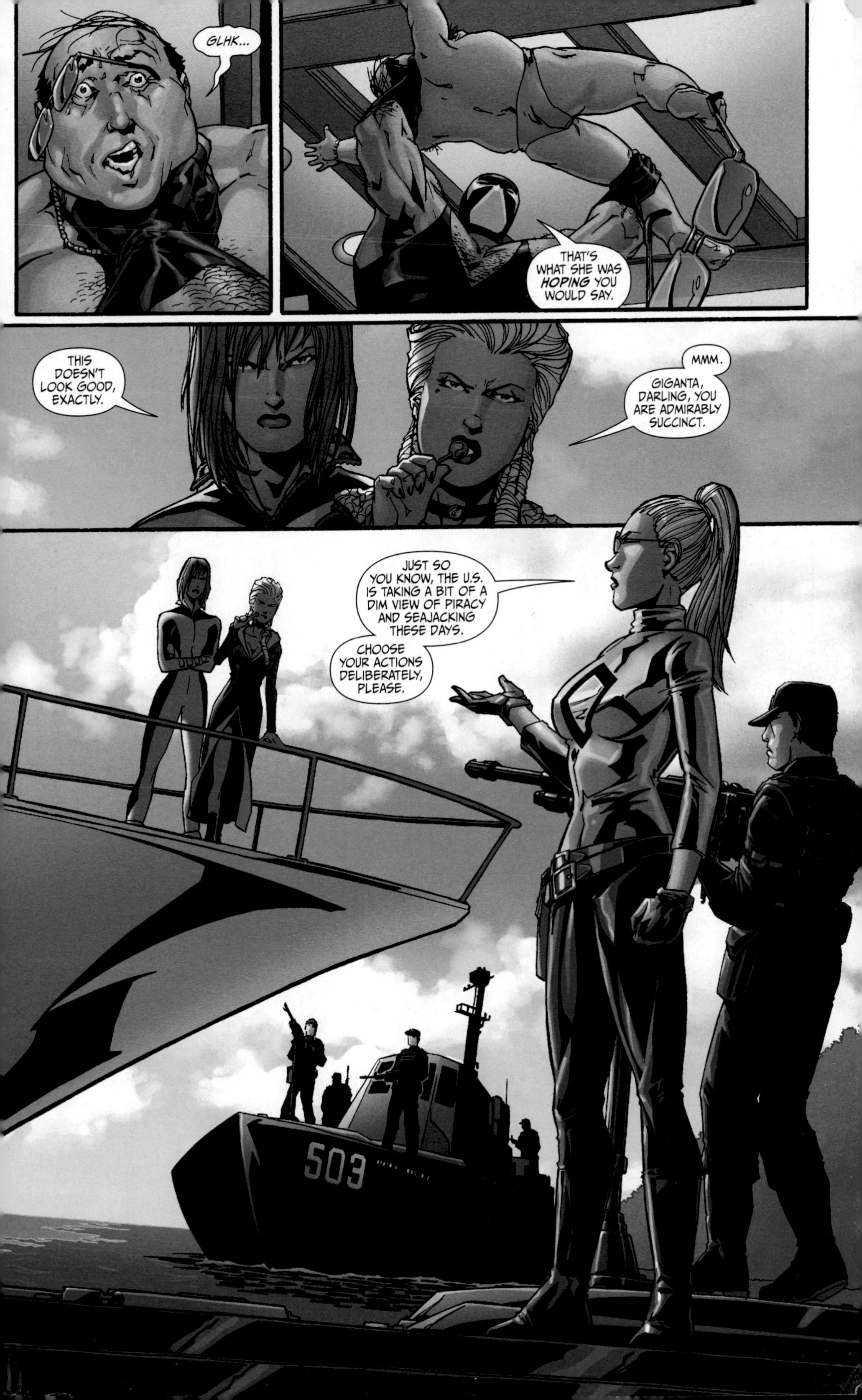
GLHK...
THAT'S WHAT SHE WAS *HOPING* YOU WOULD SAY.
THIS DOESN'T LOOK GOOD, EXACTLY.
MMM.
GIGANTA, DARLING, YOU ARE ADMIRABLY SUCCINCT.
JUST SO YOU KNOW, THE U.S. IS TAKING A BIT OF A DIM VIEW OF PIRACY AND SEAJACKING THESE DAYS.
CHOOSE YOUR ACTIONS DELIBERATELY, PLEASE.
503

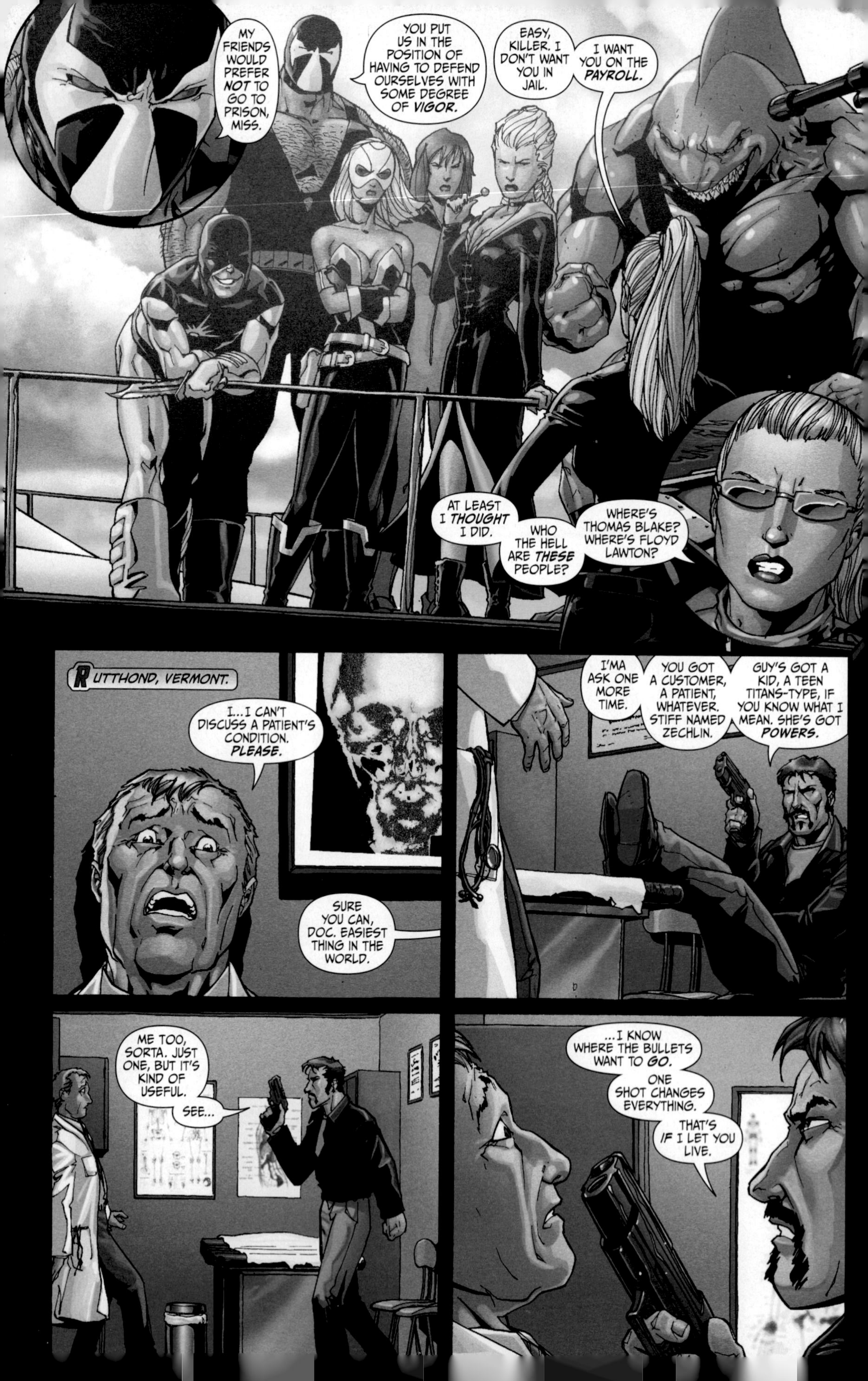
MY FRIENDS WOULD PREFER NOT TO GO TO PRISON, MISS.
YOU PUT US IN THE POSITION OF HAVING TO DEFEND OURSELVES WITH SOME DEGREE OF VIGOR.
EASY, KILLER. I DON'T WANT YOU IN JAIL.
I WANT YOU ON THE PAYROLL.
AT LEAST I THOUGHT I DID.
WHO THE HELL ARE THESE PEOPLE?
WHERE'S THOMAS BLAKE? WHERE'S FLOYD LAWTON?
RUTTHOND, VERMONT.
I...I CAN'T DISCUSS A PATIENT'S CONDITION. PLEASE.
SURE YOU CAN, DOC. EASIEST THING IN THE WORLD.
I'MA ASK ONE MORE TIME.
YOU GOT A CUSTOMER, A PATIENT, WHATEVER. STIFF NAMED ZECHLIN.
GUY'S GOT A KID, A TEEN TITANS-TYPE, IF YOU KNOW WHAT I MEAN. SHE'S GOT POWERS.
ME TOO, SORTA. JUST ONE, BUT IT'S KIND OF USEFUL.
SEE...
...I KNOW WHERE THE BULLETS WANT TO GO.
ONE SHOT CHANGES EVERYTHING.
THAT'S IF I LET YOU LIVE.

LORI? SHE *SAID* SHE HAD POWERS, I DON'T BELIEVE IT.

DOESN'T *MATTER* IF YOU BELIEVE IT. SAY SHE COULD GET INSIDE SOMEONE'S BODY, AND DIDN'T KNOW HER OWN... TALENTS.

COULD SHE HAVE GIVEN HER OLD MAN CANCER?

I...

DOC...

I DON'T *KNOW.* HOW COULD I *KNOW?*

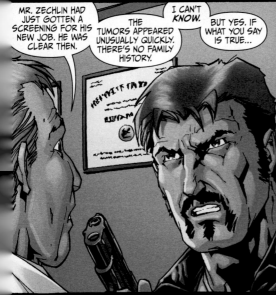

MR. ZECHLIN HAD JUST GOTTEN A SCREENING FOR HIS NEW JOB. HE WAS CLEAR THEN.

THE TUMORS APPEARED UNUSUALLY QUICKLY. THERE'S NO FAMILY HISTORY.

I CAN'T *KNOW.*

BUT YES. IF WHAT YOU SAY IS TRUE...

...IT WOULD EXPLAIN SOME THINGS.

AND HIS CHANCES ARE...?

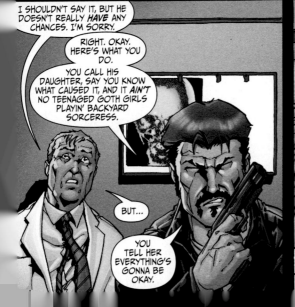

I SHOULDN'T SAY IT, BUT HE DOESN'T REALLY *HAVE* ANY CHANCES. I'M SORRY.

RIGHT. OKAY. HERE'S WHAT YOU DO.

YOU CALL HIS DAUGHTER, SAY YOU KNOW WHAT CAUSED IT, AND IT *AIN'T* NO TEENAGED GOTH GIRLS PLAYIN' BACKYARD SORCERESS.

BUT...

YOU TELL HER EVERYTHING'S GONNA BE OKAY.

I CAN'T *DO* THAT.

OH, I THINK YOU CAN. I *KNOW* YOU DAMN WELL CAN.

AND DOCTOR...

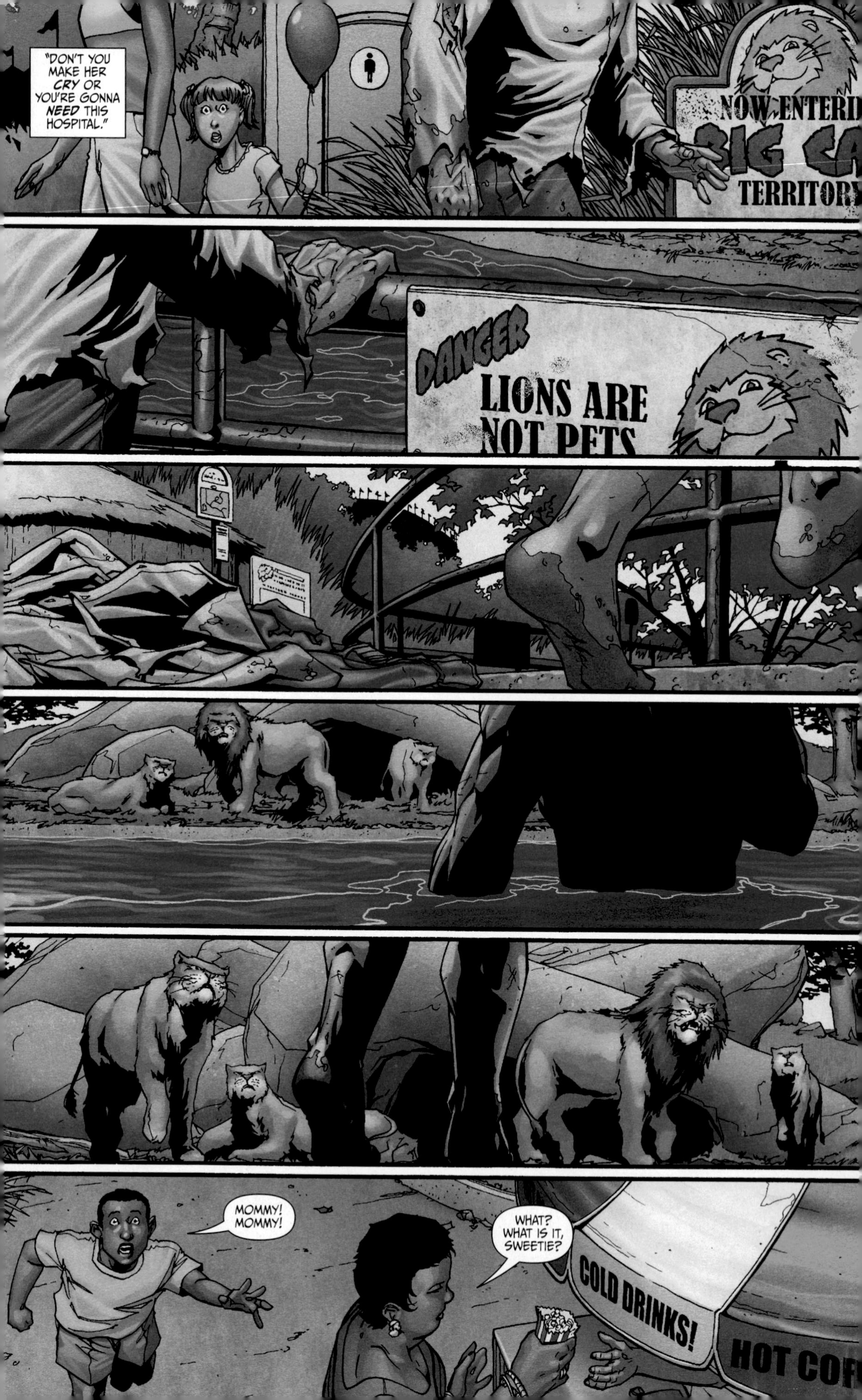
"DON'T YOU MAKE HER CRY OR YOU'RE GONNA NEED THIS HOSPITAL."
NOW ENTERI
TERRITORY
DANGER
LIONS ARE NOT PETS
MOMMY! MOMMY!
WHAT? WHAT IS IT, SWEETIE?
COLD DRINKS!
HOT CO

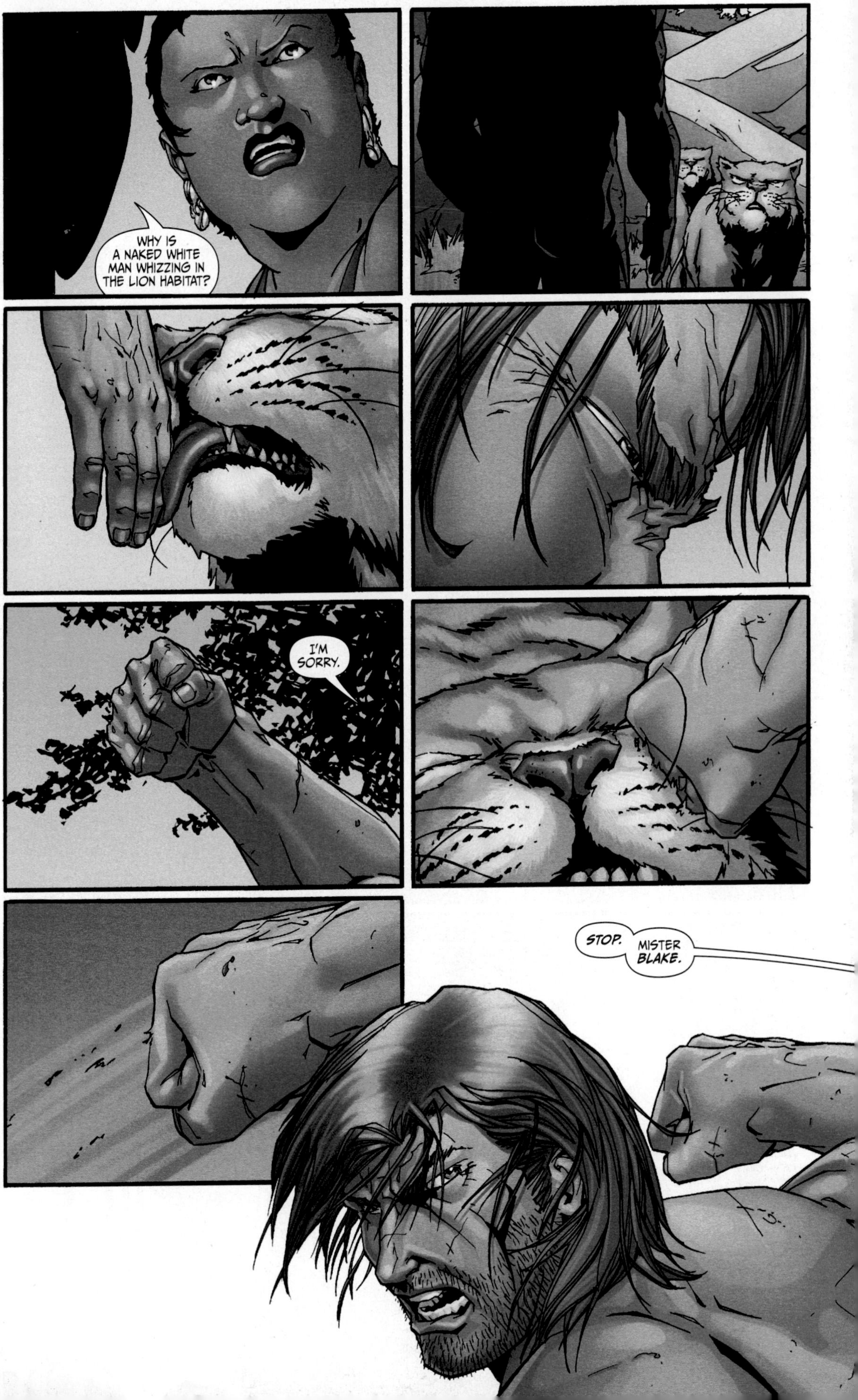
WHY IS A NAKED WHITE MAN WHIZZING IN THE LION HABITAT?
I'M SORRY.
STOP.
MISTER BLAKE.

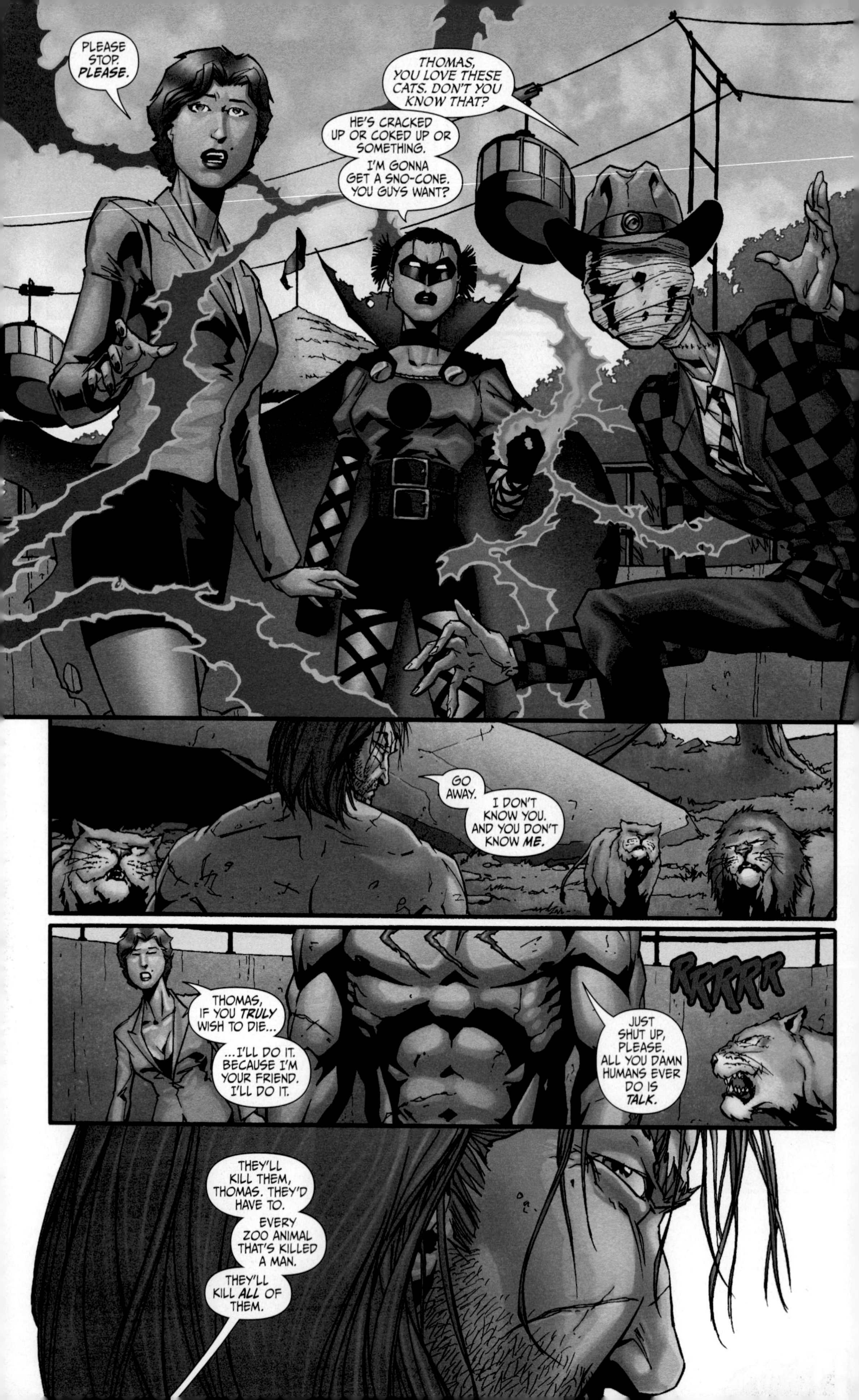
PLEASE STOP. PLEASE.
THOMAS, YOU LOVE THESE CATS. DON'T YOU KNOW THAT?
HE'S CRACKED UP OR COKED UP OR SOMETHING.
I'M GONNA GET A SNO-CONE. YOU GUYS WANT?
GO AWAY.
I DON'T KNOW YOU. AND YOU DON'T KNOW ME.
THOMAS, IF YOU TRULY WISH TO DIE...
...I'LL DO IT. BECAUSE I'M YOUR FRIEND. I'LL DO IT.
RRRRR
JUST SHUT UP, PLEASE. ALL YOU DAMN HUMANS EVER DO IS TALK.
THEY'LL KILL THEM, THOMAS. THEY'D HAVE TO.
EVERY ZOO ANIMAL THAT'S KILLED A MAN.
THEY'LL KILL ALL OF THEM.

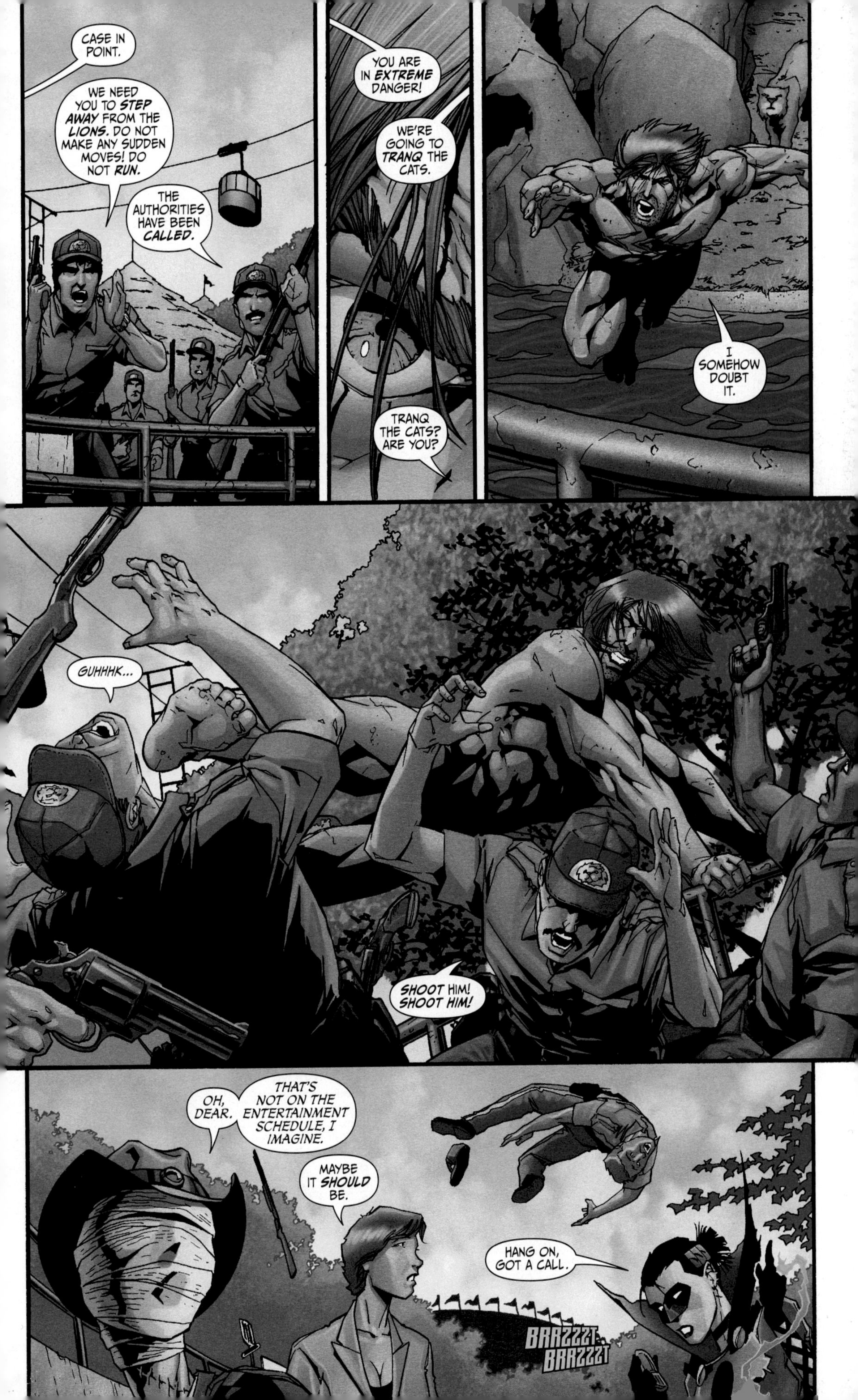
CASE IN POINT.
WE NEED YOU TO STEP AWAY FROM THE LIONS. DO NOT MAKE ANY SUDDEN MOVES! DO NOT RUN.
THE AUTHORITIES HAVE BEEN CALLED.
YOU ARE IN EXTREME DANGER!
WE'RE GOING TO TRANQ THE CATS.
TRANQ THE CATS? ARE YOU?
I SOMEHOW DOUBT IT.
GUHHHK...
SHOOT HIM! SHOOT HIM!
OH, DEAR.
THAT'S NOT ON THE ENTERTAINMENT SCHEDULE, I IMAGINE.
MAYBE IT SHOULD BE.
HANG ON, GOT A CALL.
BRRZZZT BRRZZZT

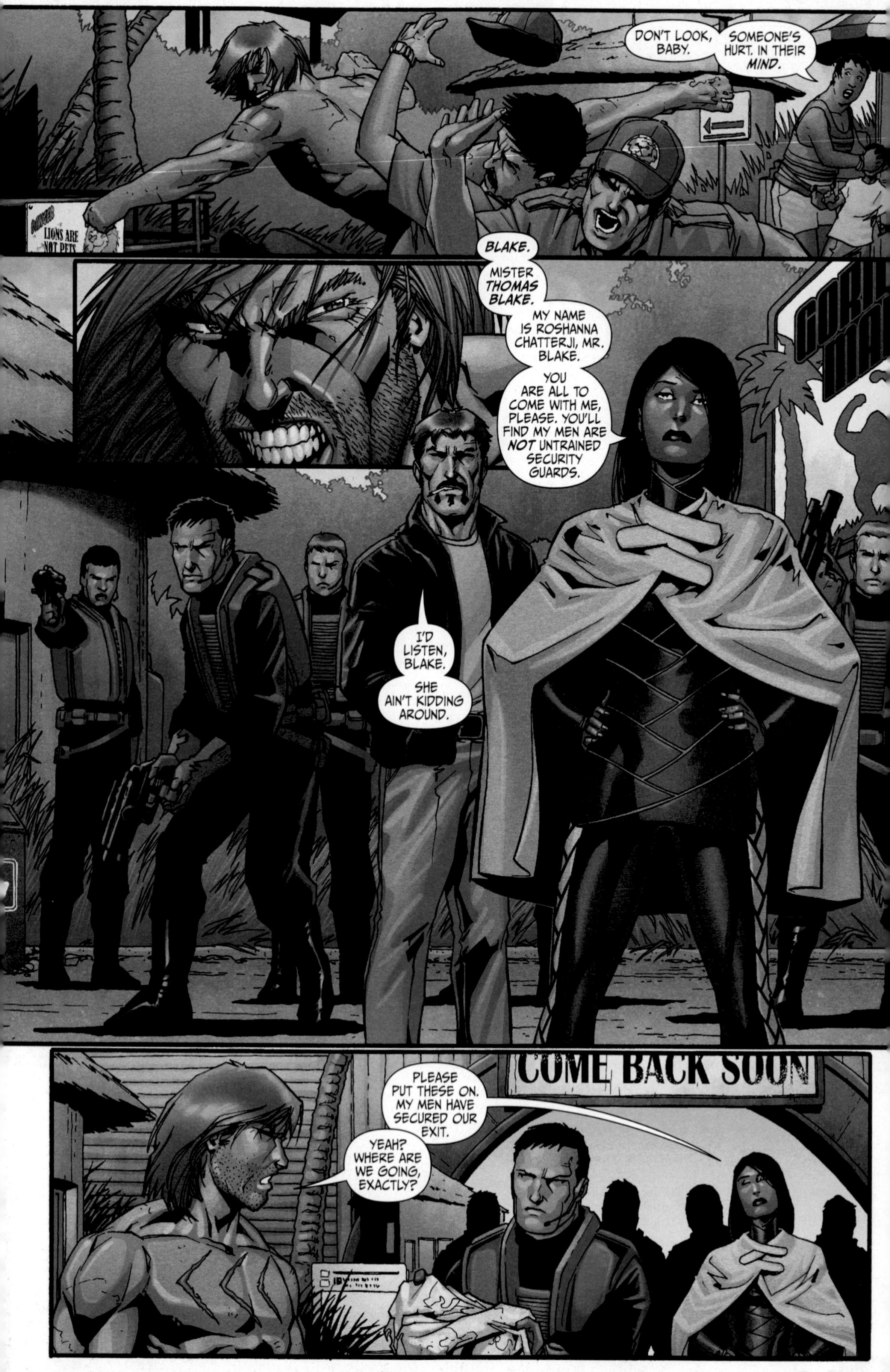
DANGER
LIONS ARE NOT PETS
DON'T LOOK, BABY.
SOMEONE'S HURT. IN THEIR *MIND.*
BLAKE.
MISTER *THOMAS BLAKE.*
MY NAME IS ROSHANNA CHATTERJI, MR. BLAKE.
YOU ARE ALL TO COME WITH ME, PLEASE. YOU'LL FIND MY MEN ARE ***NOT*** UNTRAINED SECURITY GUARDS.
I'D LISTEN, BLAKE.
SHE AIN'T KIDDING AROUND.
COME BACK SOON
PLEASE PUT THESE ON. MY MEN HAVE SECURED OUR EXIT.
YEAH? WHERE ARE WE GOING, EXACTLY?

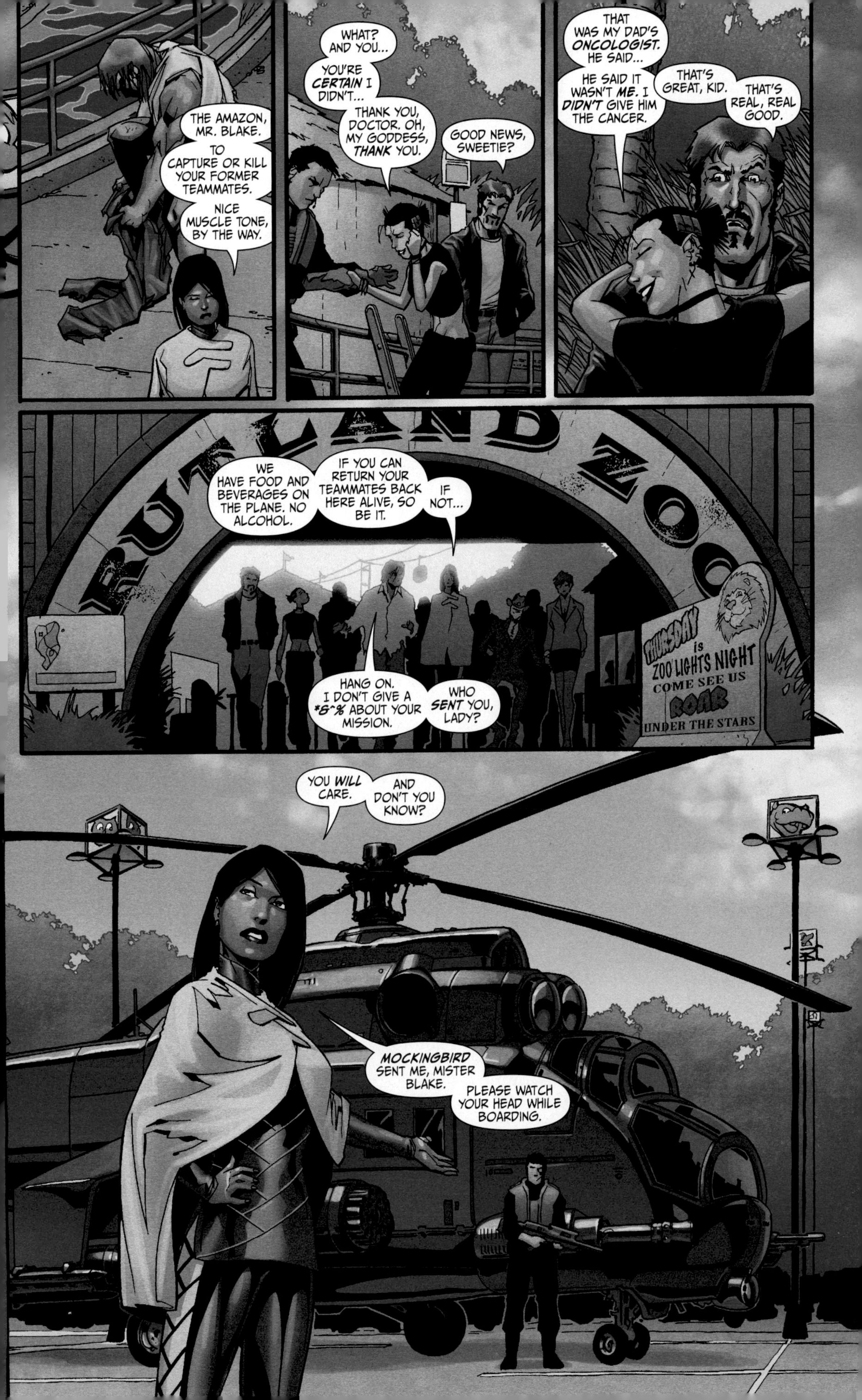
THE AMAZON, MR. BLAKE.
TO CAPTURE OR KILL YOUR FORMER TEAMMATES.
NICE MUSCLE TONE, BY THE WAY.
WHAT? AND YOU...
YOU'RE CERTAIN I DIDN'T...
THANK YOU, DOCTOR. OH, MY GODDESS, THANK YOU.
GOOD NEWS, SWEETIE?
THAT WAS MY DAD'S ONCOLOGIST. HE SAID...
HE SAID IT WASN'T ME. I DIDN'T GIVE HIM THE CANCER.
THAT'S GREAT, KID.
THAT'S REAL, REAL GOOD.
RUTLAND ZOO
WE HAVE FOOD AND BEVERAGES ON THE PLANE. NO ALCOHOL.
IF YOU CAN RETURN YOUR TEAMMATES BACK HERE ALIVE, SO BE IT.
IF NOT...
HANG ON. I DON'T GIVE A *&^% ABOUT YOUR MISSION.
WHO SENT YOU, LADY?
THURSDAY is ZOO LIGHTS NIGHT
COME SEE US
ROAR
UNDER THE STARS
YOU WILL CARE.
AND DON'T YOU KNOW?
MOCKINGBIRD SENT ME, MISTER BLAKE.
PLEASE WATCH YOUR HEAD WHILE BOARDING.

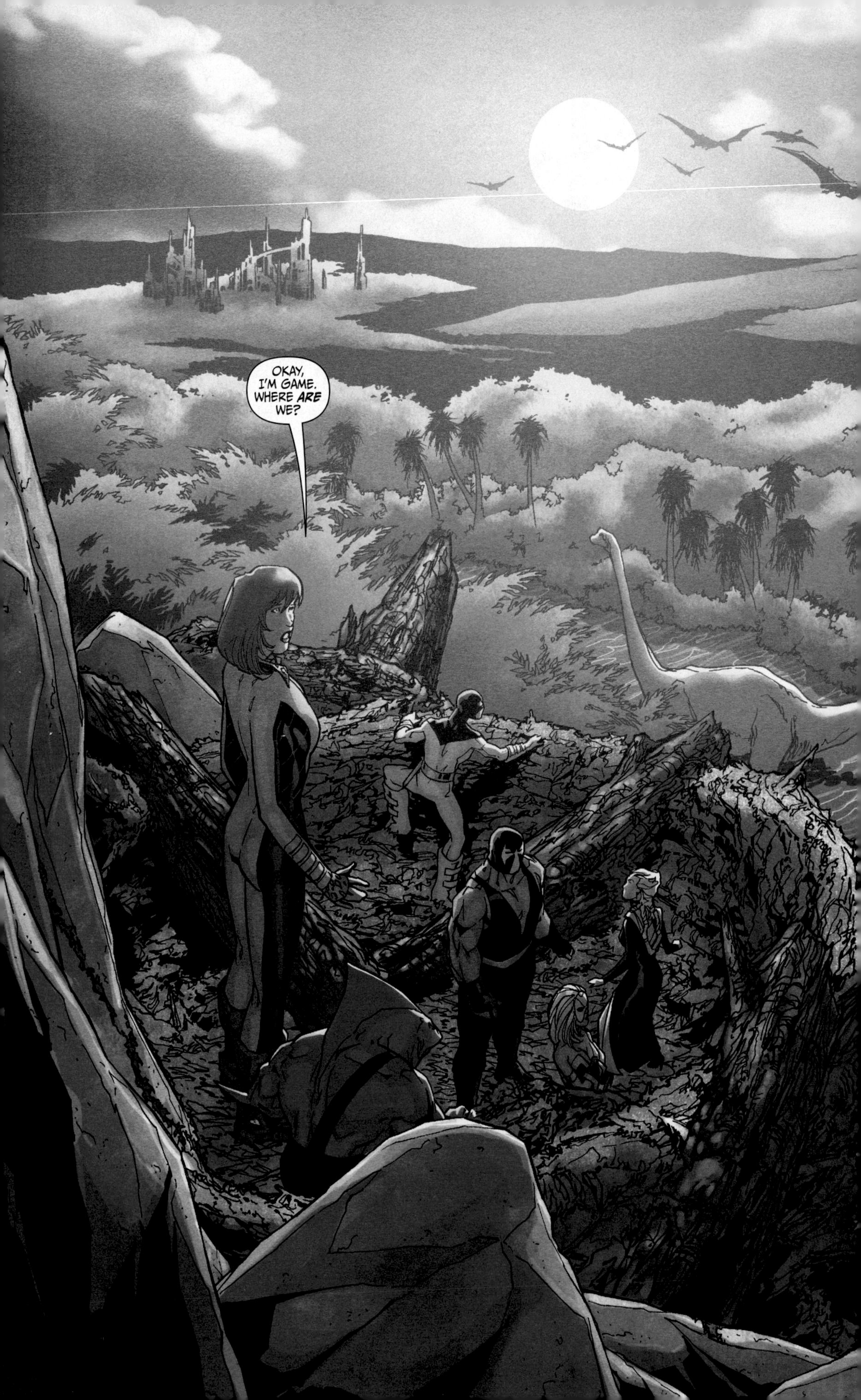
OKAY, I'M GAME. WHERE *ARE* WE?

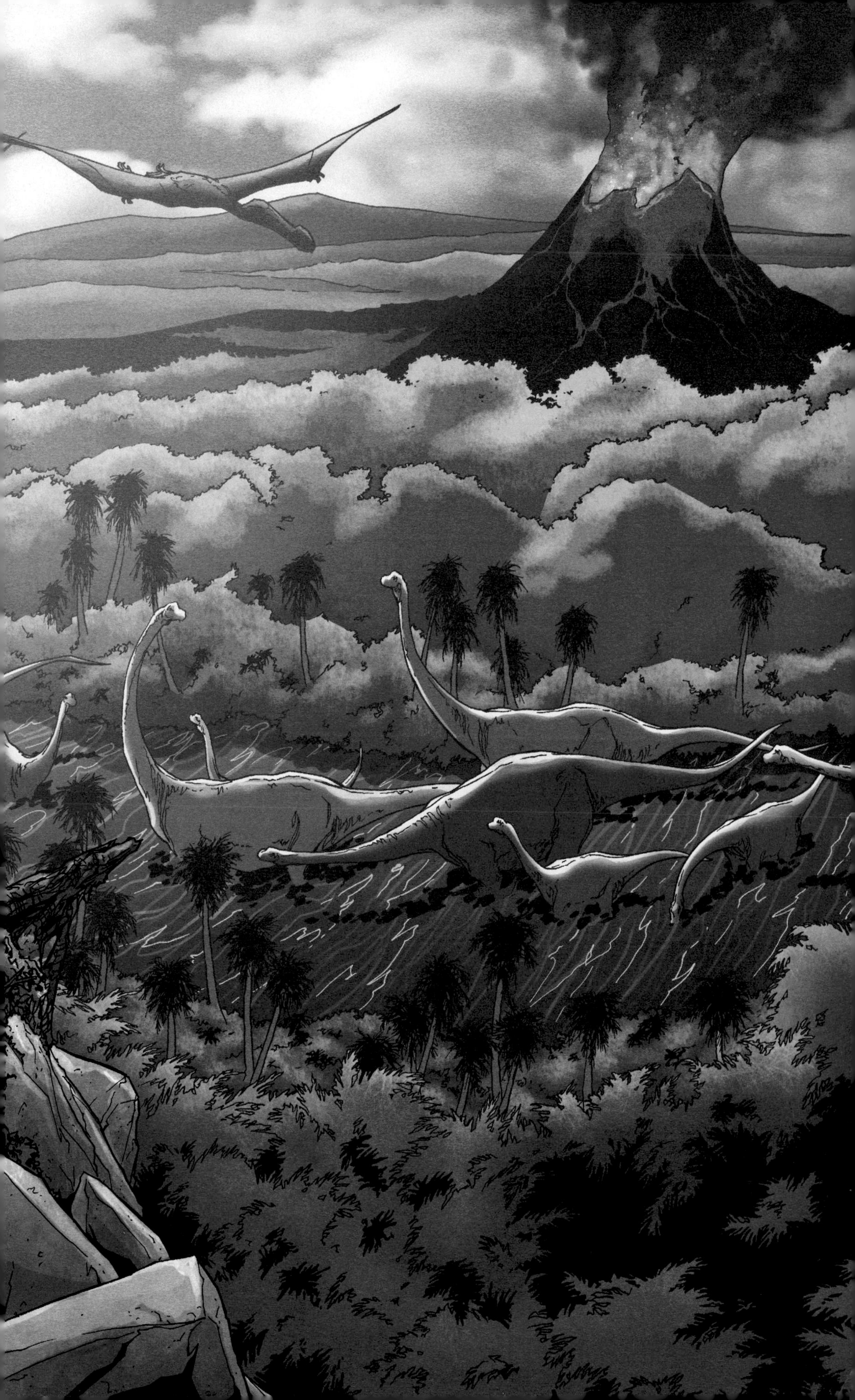

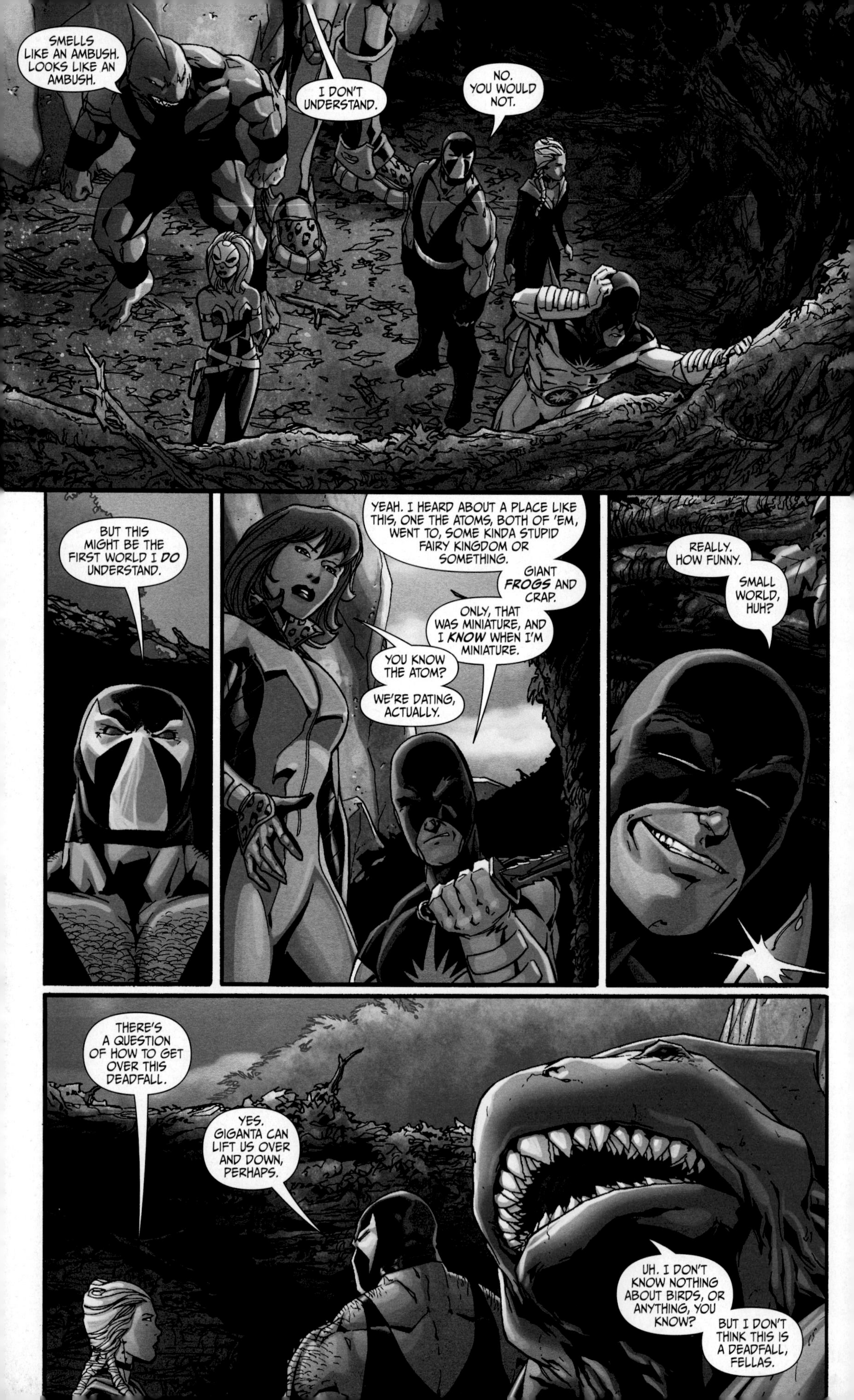
SMELLS LIKE AN AMBUSH. LOOKS LIKE AN AMBUSH.
I DON'T UNDERSTAND.
NO. YOU WOULD NOT.
BUT THIS MIGHT BE THE FIRST WORLD I *DO* UNDERSTAND.
YEAH. I HEARD ABOUT A PLACE LIKE THIS, ONE THE ATOMS, BOTH OF 'EM, WENT TO, SOME KINDA STUPID FAIRY KINGDOM OR SOMETHING.
GIANT *FROGS* AND CRAP.
ONLY, THAT WAS MINIATURE, AND I *KNOW* WHEN I'M MINIATURE.
YOU KNOW THE ATOM?
WE'RE DATING, ACTUALLY.
REALLY. HOW FUNNY.
SMALL WORLD, HUH?
THERE'S A QUESTION OF HOW TO GET OVER THIS DEADFALL.
YES. GIGANTA CAN LIFT US OVER AND DOWN, PERHAPS.
UH. I DON'T KNOW NOTHING ABOUT BIRDS, OR ANYTHING, YOU KNOW?
BUT I DON'T THINK THIS IS A DEADFALL, FELLAS.

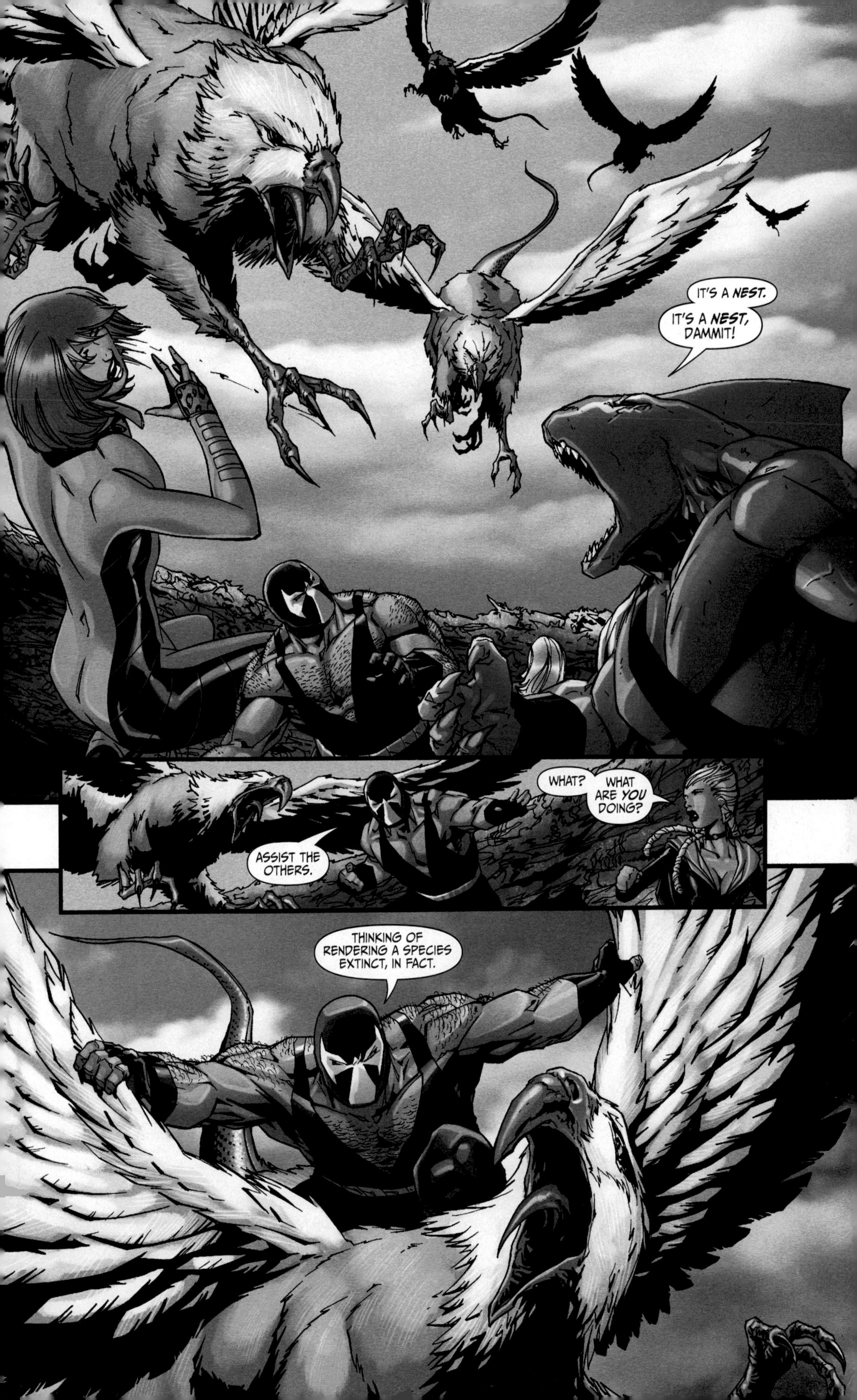
IT'S A NEST.
IT'S A NEST, DAMMIT!
WHAT?
WHAT ARE YOU DOING?
ASSIST THE OTHERS.
THINKING OF RENDERING A SPECIES EXTINCT, IN FACT.

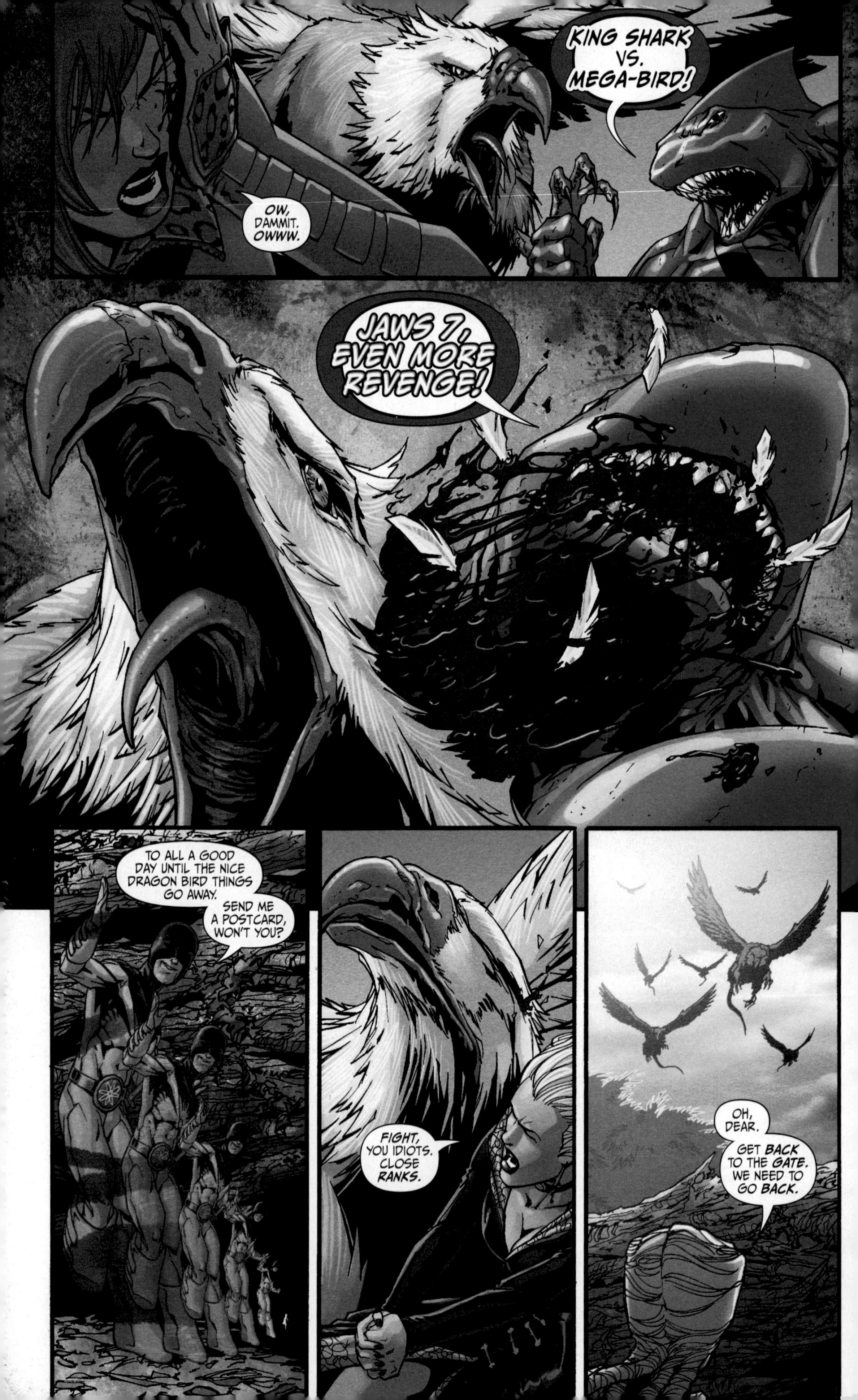
KING SHARK VS. MEGA-BIRD!
OW, DAMMIT. OWWW.
JAWS 7, EVEN MORE REVENGE!
TO ALL A GOOD DAY UNTIL THE NICE DRAGON BIRD THINGS GO AWAY.
SEND ME A POSTCARD, WON'T YOU?
FIGHT, YOU IDIOTS. CLOSE RANKS.
OH, DEAR.
GET BACK TO THE GATE. WE NEED TO GO BACK.

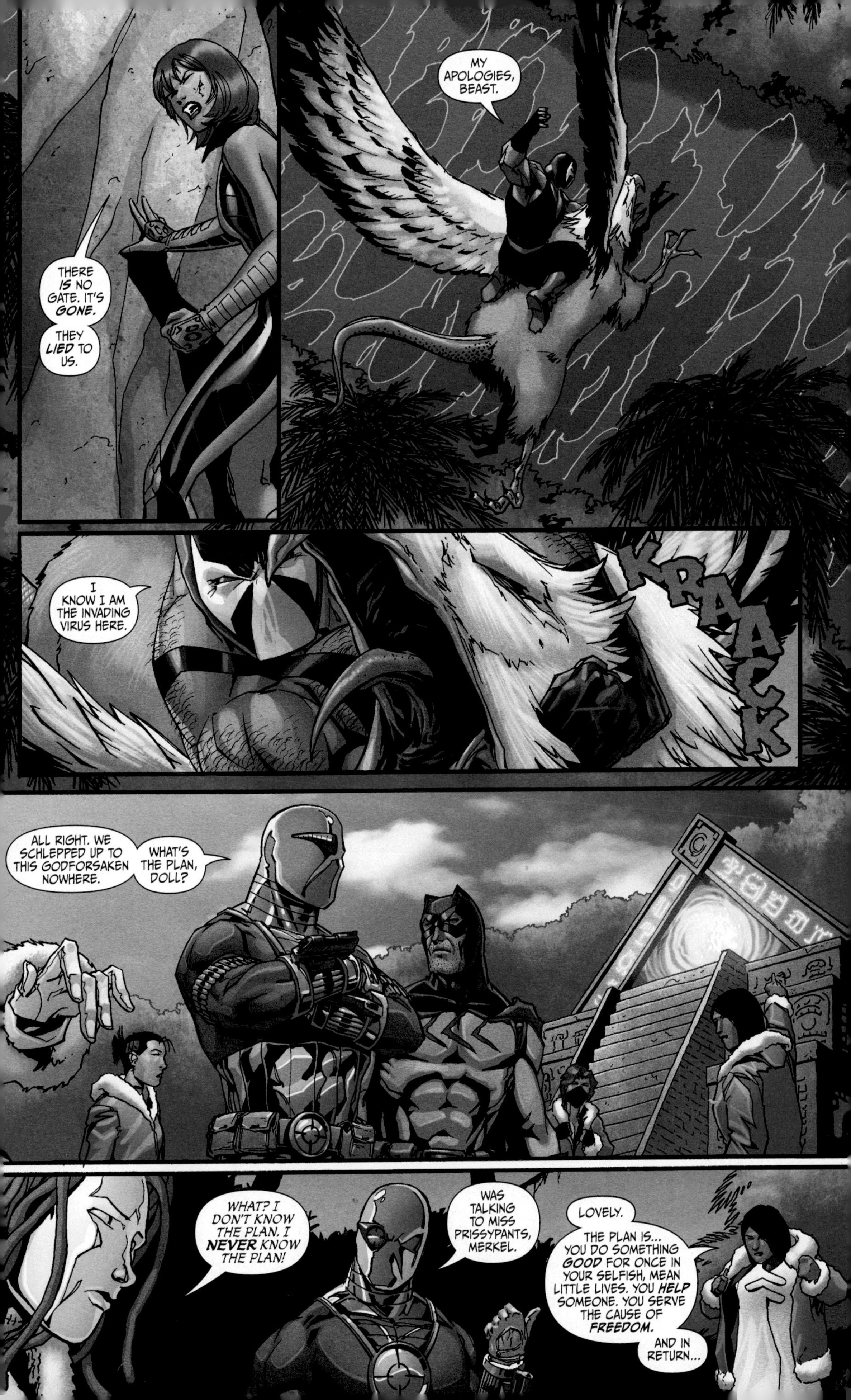
THERE IS NO GATE. IT'S GONE.
THEY LIED TO US.
MY APOLOGIES, BEAST.
I KNOW I AM THE INVADING VIRUS HERE.
KRAAACK
ALL RIGHT. WE SCHLEPPED UP TO THIS GODFORSAKEN NOWHERE.
WHAT'S THE PLAN, DOLL?
WHAT? I DON'T KNOW THE PLAN. I NEVER KNOW THE PLAN!
WAS TALKING TO MISS PRISSYPANTS, MERKEL.
LOVELY.
THE PLAN IS... YOU DO SOMETHING GOOD FOR ONCE IN YOUR SELFISH, MEAN LITTLE LIVES. YOU HELP SOMEONE. YOU SERVE THE CAUSE OF FREEDOM.
AND IN RETURN...

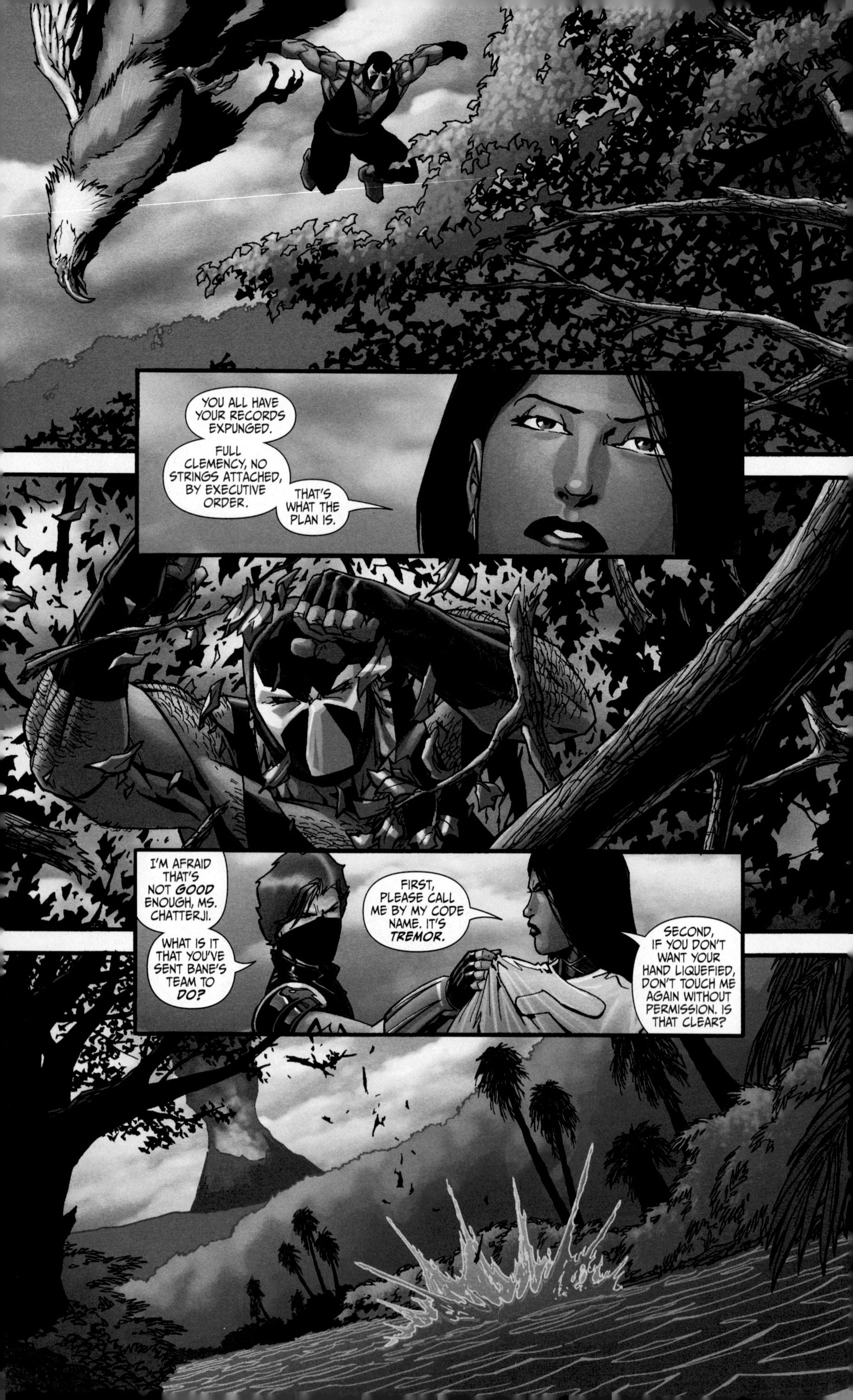
YOU ALL HAVE YOUR RECORDS EXPUNGED.
FULL CLEMENCY, NO STRINGS ATTACHED, BY EXECUTIVE ORDER.
THAT'S WHAT THE PLAN IS.
I'M AFRAID THAT'S NOT GOOD ENOUGH, MS. CHATTERJI.
WHAT IS IT THAT YOU'VE SENT BANE'S TEAM TO DO?
FIRST, PLEASE CALL ME BY MY CODE NAME. IT'S TREMOR.
SECOND, IF YOU DON'T WANT YOUR HAND LIQUEFIED, DON'T TOUCH ME AGAIN WITHOUT PERMISSION. IS THAT CLEAR?

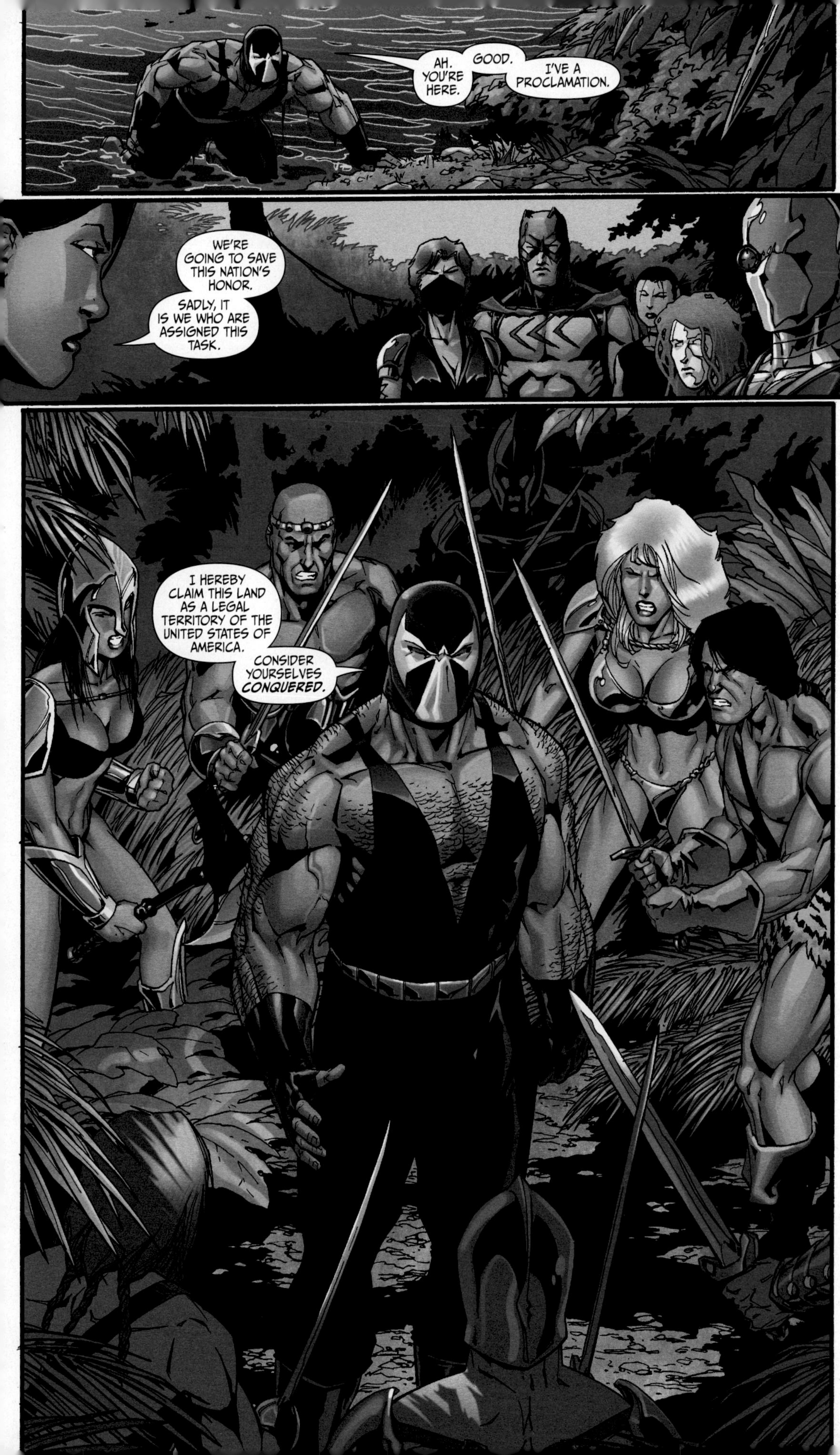
AH. YOU'RE HERE.
GOOD.
I'VE A PROCLAMATION.
WE'RE GOING TO SAVE THIS NATION'S HONOR.
SADLY, IT IS WE WHO ARE ASSIGNED THIS TASK.
I HEREBY CLAIM THIS LAND AS A LEGAL TERRITORY OF THE UNITED STATES OF AMERICA.
CONSIDER YOURSELVES CONQUERED.

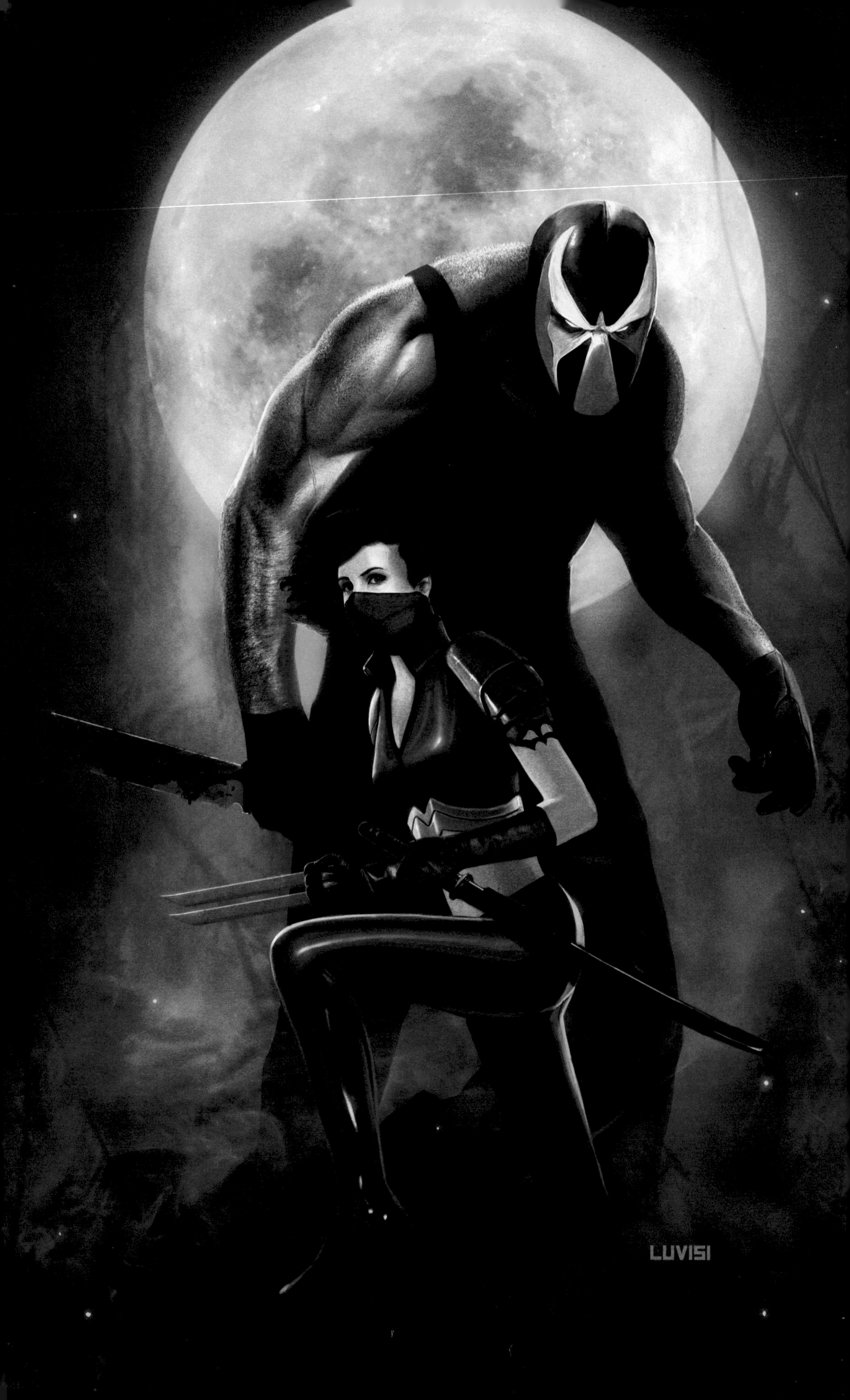
LUVISI

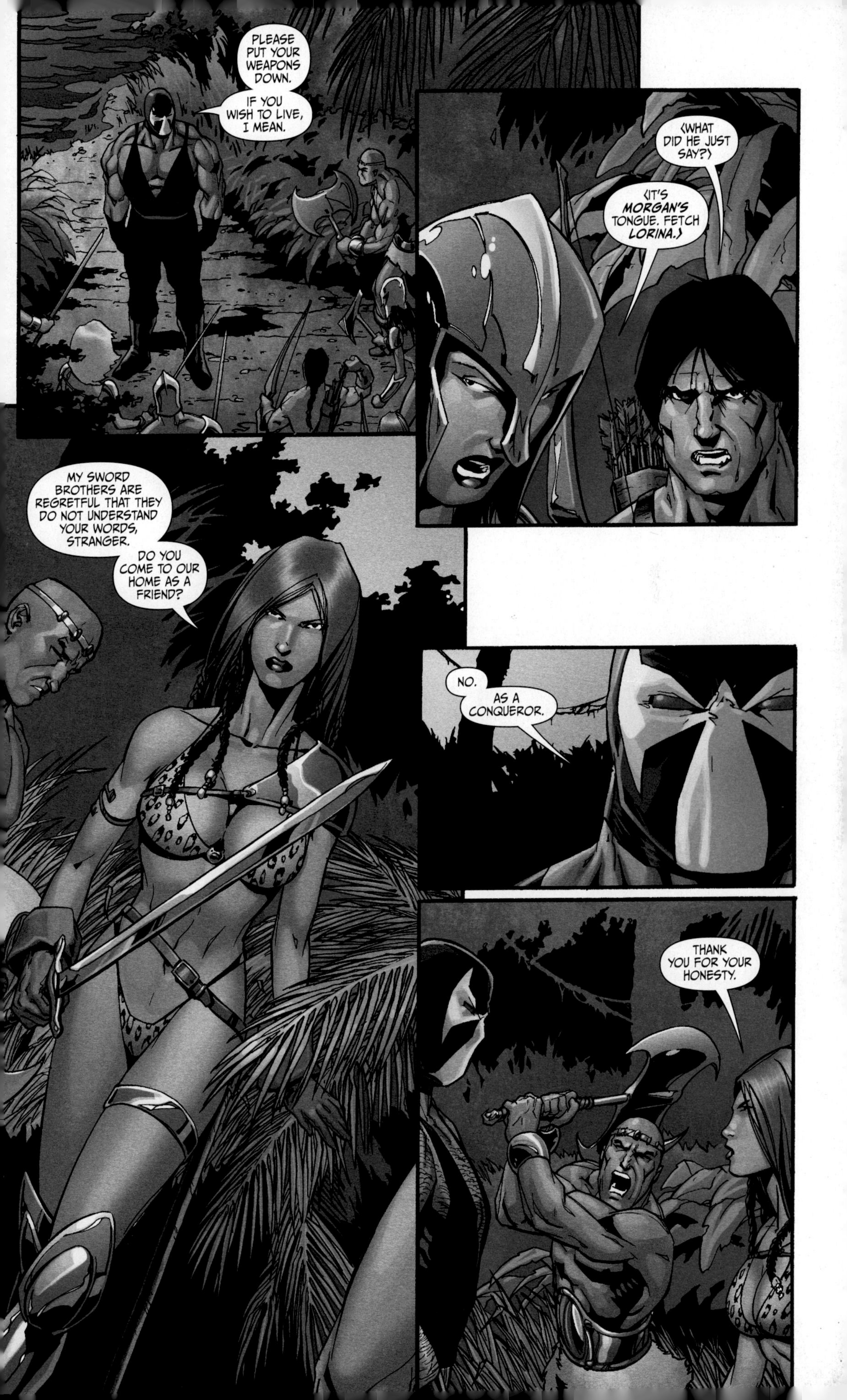
PLEASE PUT YOUR WEAPONS DOWN.
IF YOU WISH TO LIVE, I MEAN.
‹WHAT DID HE JUST SAY?›
‹IT'S MORGAN'S TONGUE. FETCH LORINA.›
MY SWORD BROTHERS ARE REGRETFUL THAT THEY DO NOT UNDERSTAND YOUR WORDS, STRANGER.
DO YOU COME TO OUR HOME AS A FRIEND?
NO.
AS A CONQUEROR.
THANK YOU FOR YOUR HONESTY.

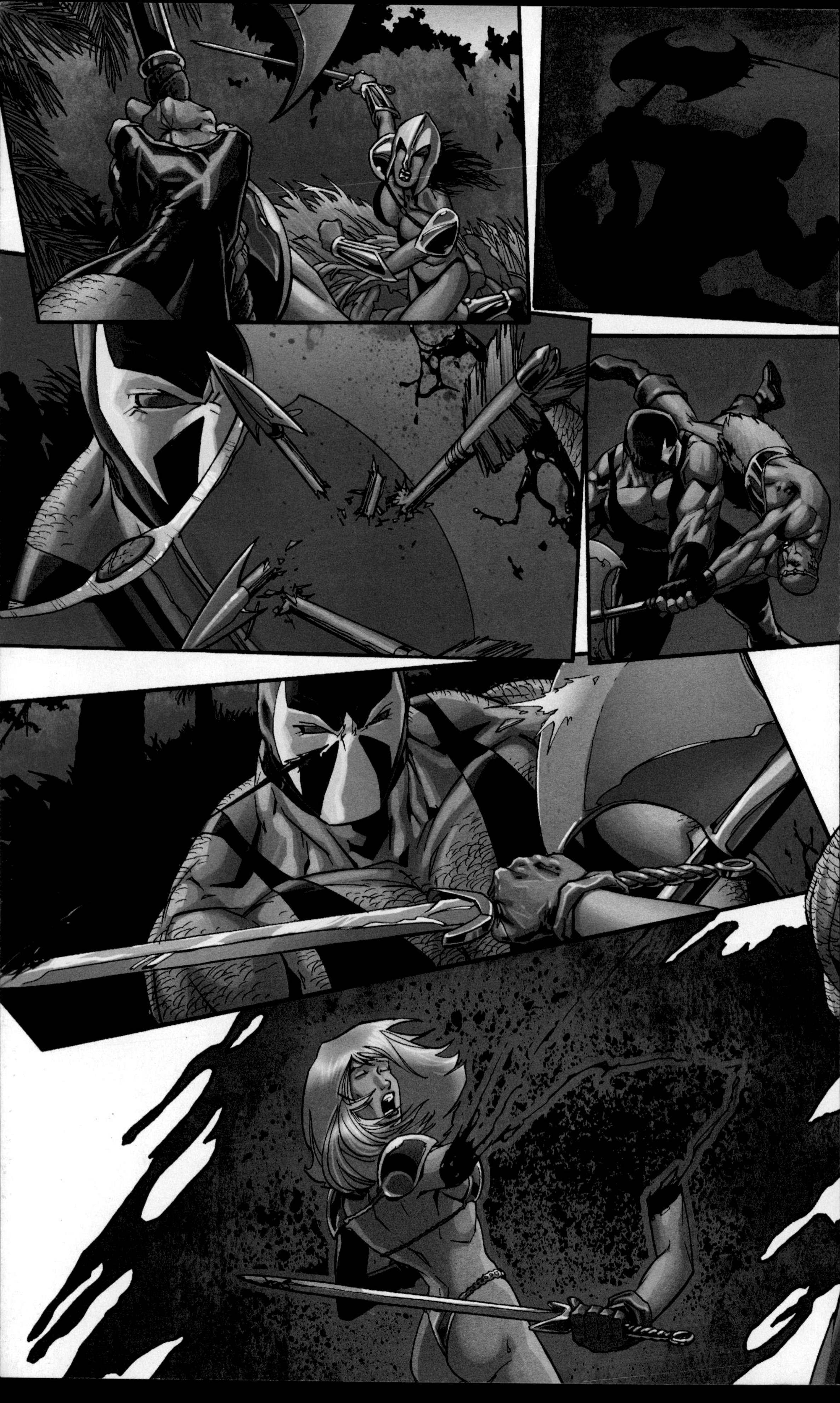

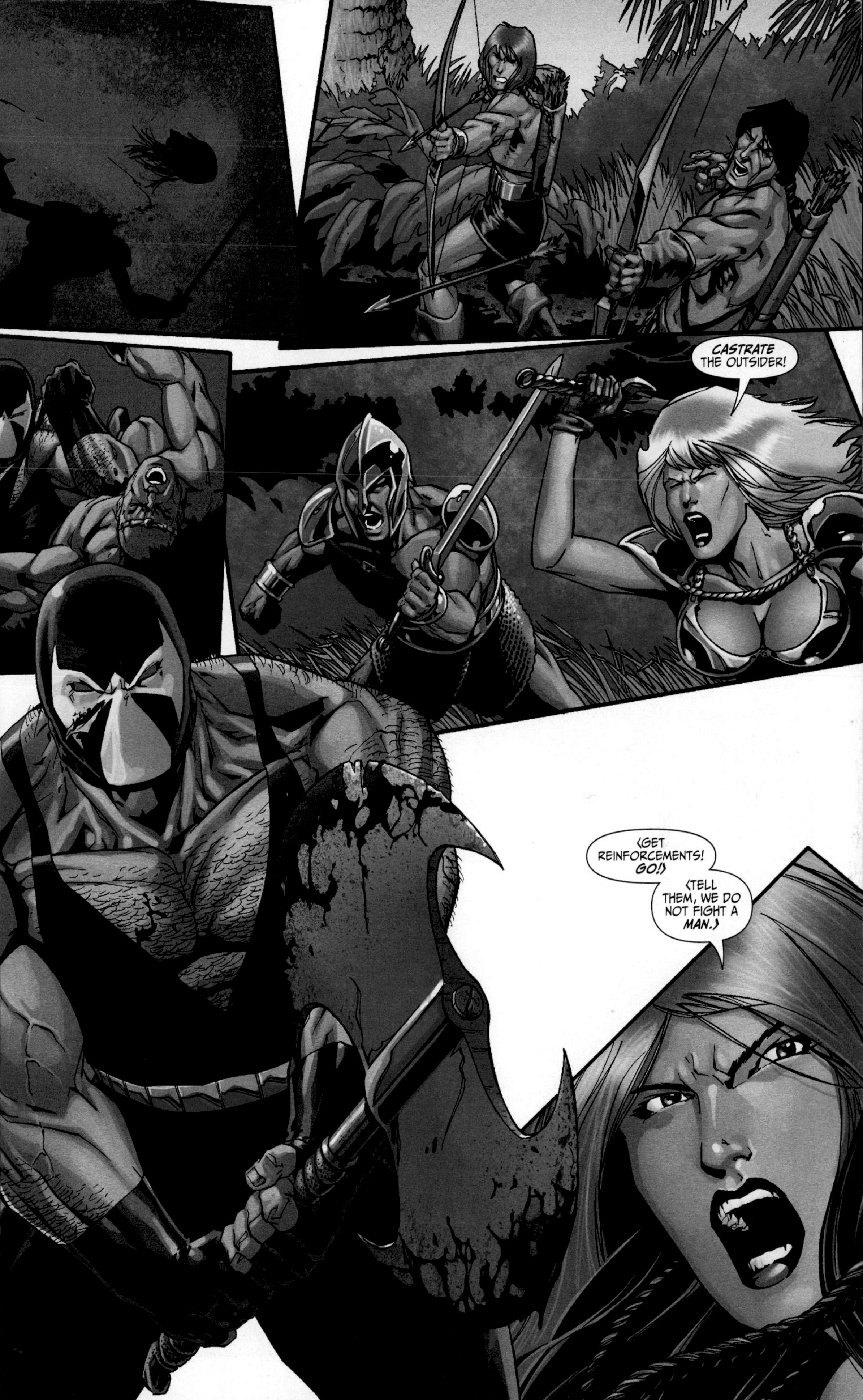
CASTRATE THE OUTSIDER!
‹GET REINFORCEMENTS! GO!›
‹TELL THEM, WE DO NOT FIGHT A MAN.›

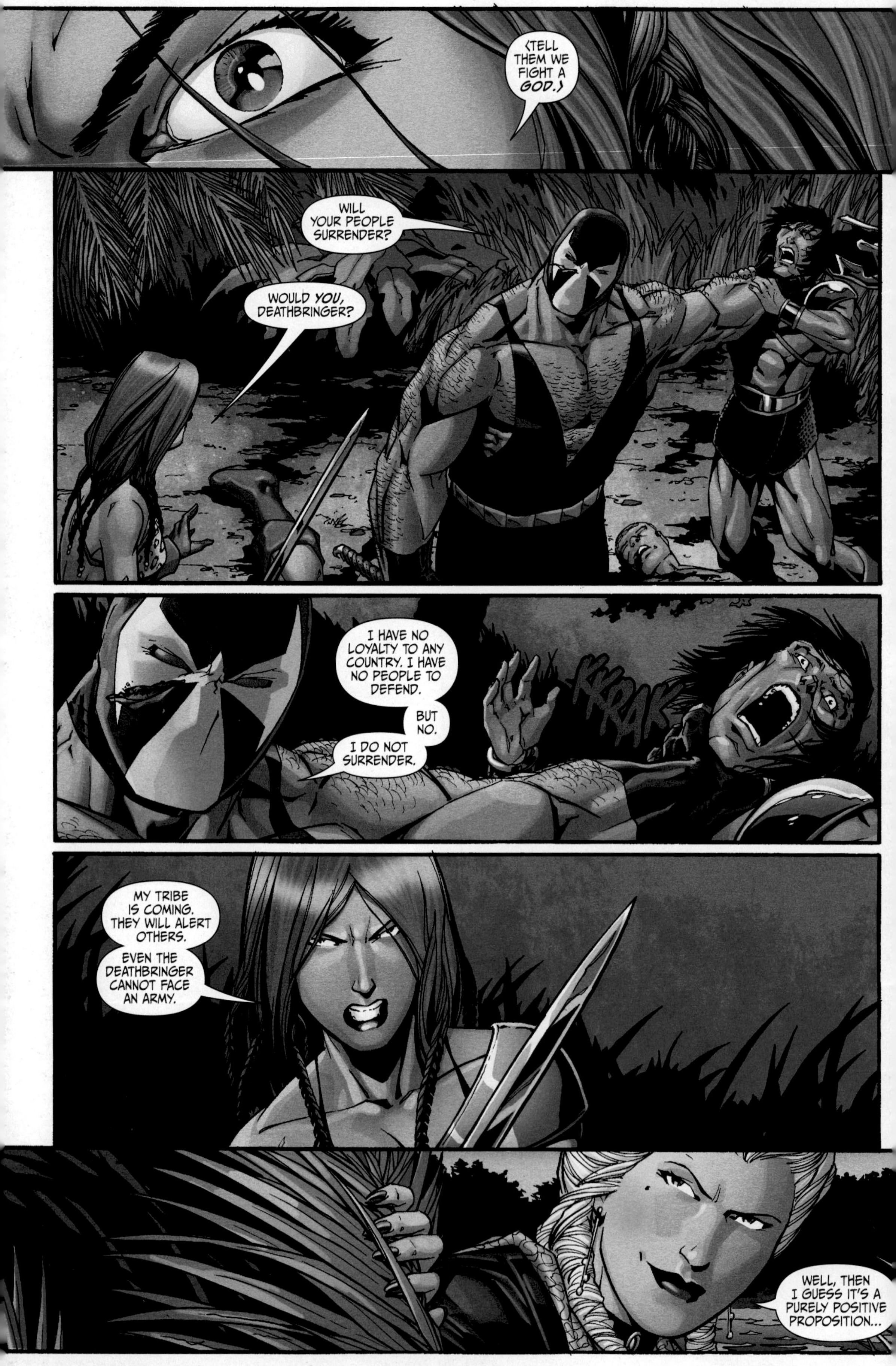
⟨TELL THEM WE FIGHT A GOD.⟩
WILL YOUR PEOPLE SURRENDER?
WOULD YOU, DEATHBRINGER?
I HAVE NO LOYALTY TO ANY COUNTRY. I HAVE NO PEOPLE TO DEFEND.
BUT NO.
I DO NOT SURRENDER.
KKRAK
MY TRIBE IS COMING. THEY WILL ALERT OTHERS.
EVEN THE DEATHBRINGER CANNOT FACE AN ARMY.
WELL, THEN I GUESS IT'S A PURELY POSITIVE PROPOSITION...

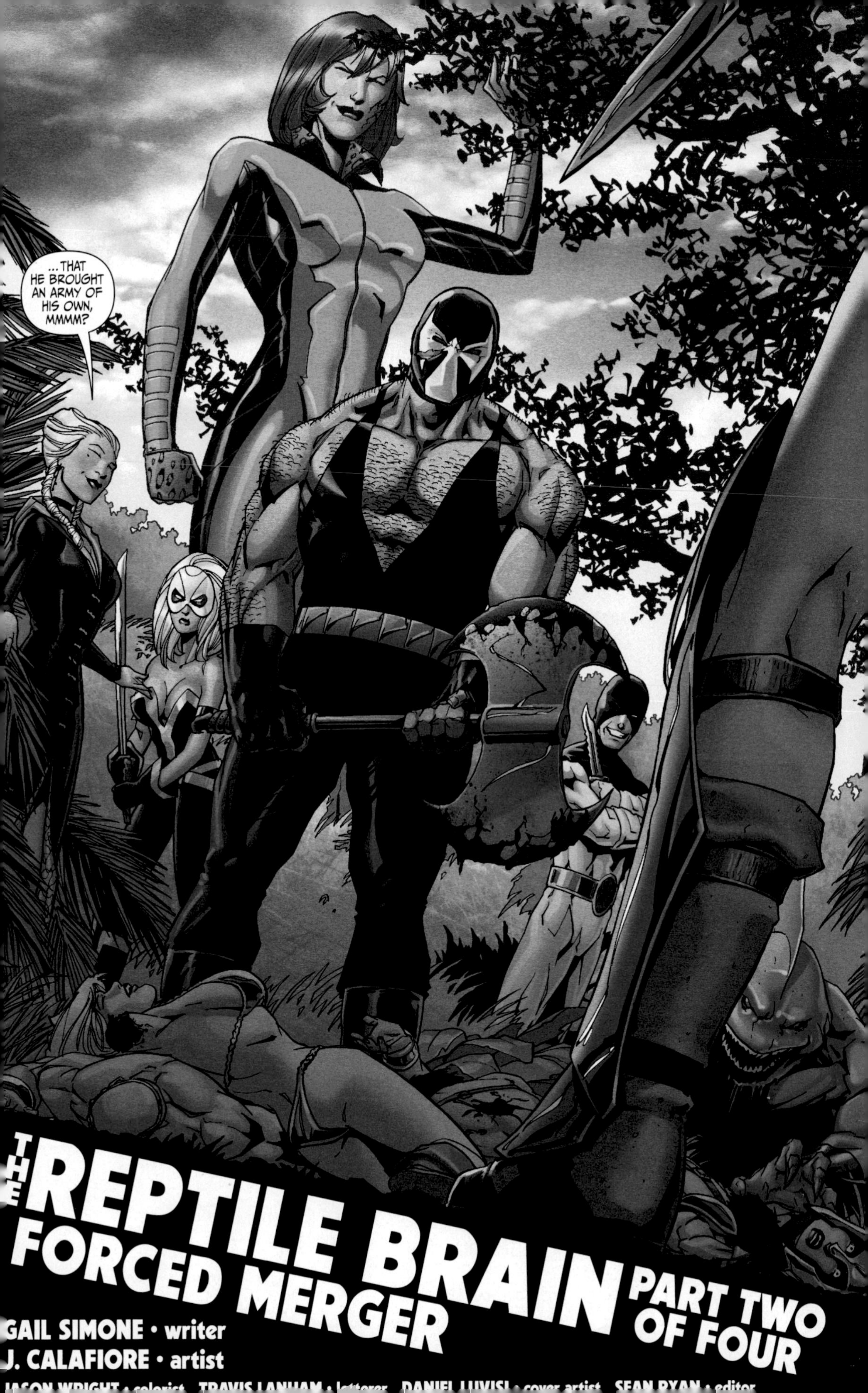
...THAT HE BROUGHT AN ARMY OF HIS OWN, MMMM?
THE REPTILE BRAIN
FORCED MERGER
PART TWO OF FOUR
GAIL SIMONE • writer
J. CALAFIORE • artist
JASON WRIGHT • colorist TRAVIS LANHAM • letterer DANIEL LUVISI • cover artist SEAN RYAN • editor

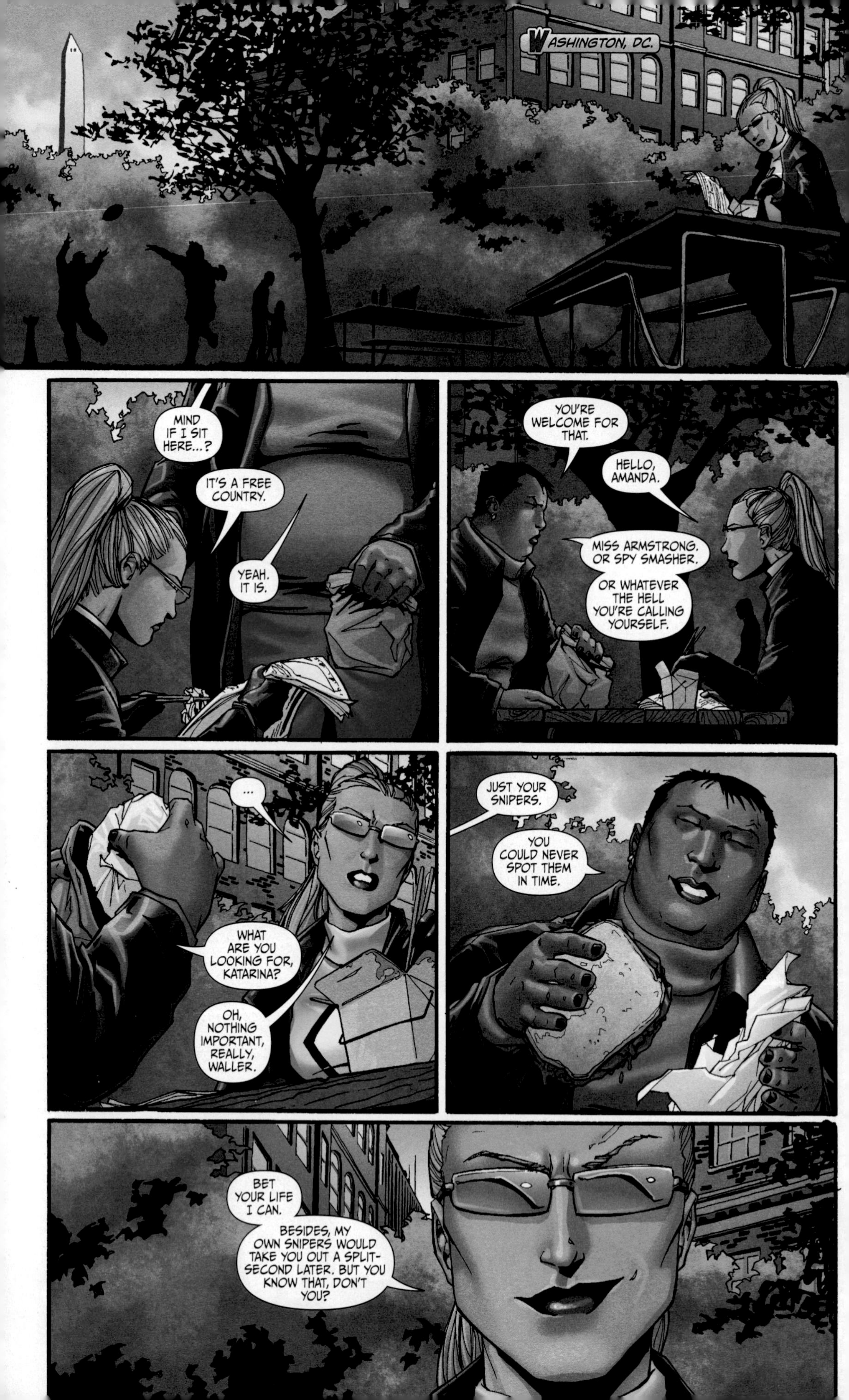
WASHINGTON, DC.
MIND IF I SIT HERE...?
IT'S A FREE COUNTRY.
YEAH. IT IS.
YOU'RE WELCOME FOR THAT.
HELLO, AMANDA.
MISS ARMSTRONG. OR SPY SMASHER.
OR WHATEVER THE HELL YOU'RE CALLING YOURSELF.
...
WHAT ARE YOU LOOKING FOR, KATARINA?
OH, NOTHING IMPORTANT, REALLY, WALLER.
JUST YOUR SNIPERS.
YOU COULD NEVER SPOT THEM IN TIME.
BET YOUR LIFE I CAN.
BESIDES, MY OWN SNIPERS WOULD TAKE YOU OUT A SPLIT-SECOND LATER. BUT YOU KNOW THAT, DON'T YOU?

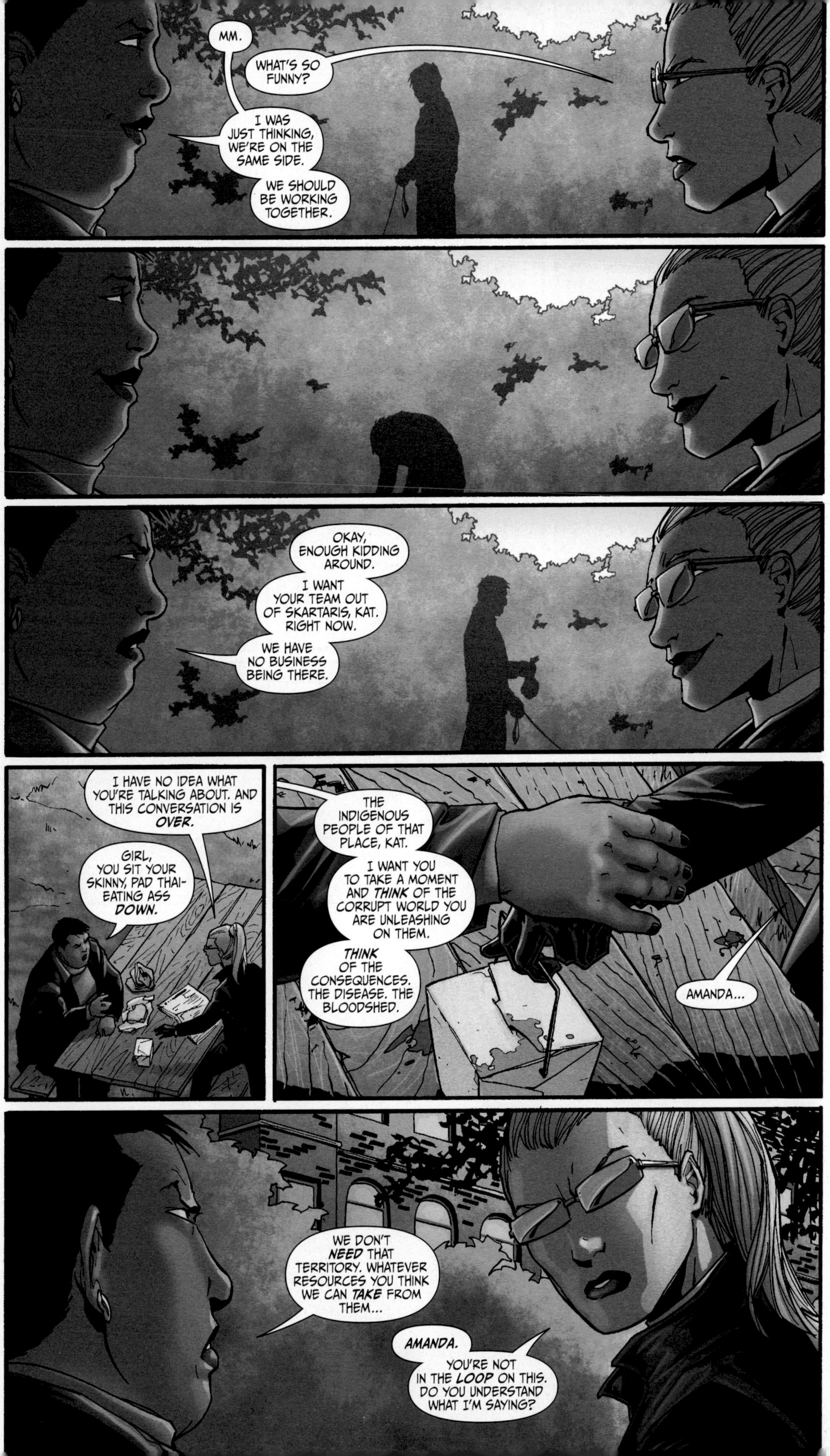
MM.
WHAT'S SO FUNNY?
I WAS JUST THINKING, WE'RE ON THE SAME SIDE.
WE SHOULD BE WORKING TOGETHER.
OKAY, ENOUGH KIDDING AROUND.
I WANT YOUR TEAM OUT OF SKARTARIS, KAT. RIGHT NOW.
WE HAVE NO BUSINESS BEING THERE.
I HAVE NO IDEA WHAT YOU'RE TALKING ABOUT. AND THIS CONVERSATION IS *OVER.*
GIRL, YOU SIT YOUR SKINNY, PAD THAI-EATING ASS *DOWN.*
THE INDIGENOUS PEOPLE OF THAT PLACE, KAT.
I WANT YOU TO TAKE A MOMENT AND *THINK* OF THE CORRUPT WORLD YOU ARE UNLEASHING ON THEM.
THINK OF THE CONSEQUENCES. THE DISEASE. THE BLOODSHED.
AMANDA...
WE DON'T *NEED* THAT TERRITORY. WHATEVER RESOURCES YOU THINK WE CAN *TAKE* FROM THEM...
AMANDA.
YOU'RE NOT IN THE *LOOP* ON THIS. DO YOU UNDERSTAND WHAT I'M SAYING?

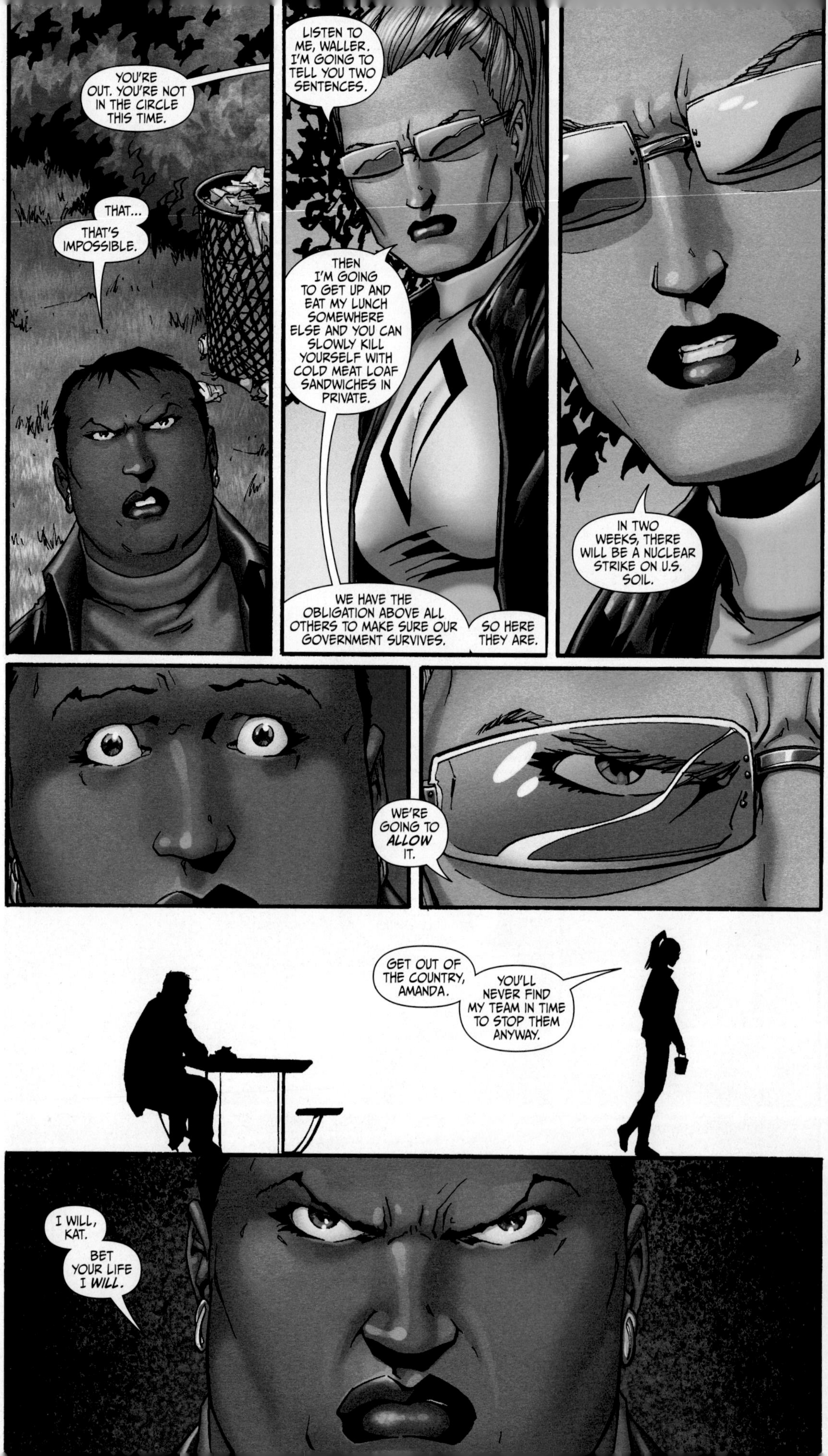

YOU'RE OUT. YOU'RE NOT IN THE CIRCLE THIS TIME.
THAT...
THAT'S IMPOSSIBLE.
LISTEN TO ME, WALLER. I'M GOING TO TELL YOU TWO SENTENCES.
THEN I'M GOING TO GET UP AND EAT MY LUNCH SOMEWHERE ELSE AND YOU CAN SLOWLY KILL YOURSELF WITH COLD MEAT LOAF SANDWICHES IN PRIVATE.
WE HAVE THE OBLIGATION ABOVE ALL OTHERS TO MAKE SURE OUR GOVERNMENT SURVIVES.
SO HERE THEY ARE.
IN TWO WEEKS, THERE WILL BE A NUCLEAR STRIKE ON U.S. SOIL.
WE'RE GOING TO *ALLOW* IT.
GET OUT OF THE COUNTRY, AMANDA.
YOU'LL NEVER FIND MY TEAM IN TIME TO STOP THEM ANYWAY.
I WILL, KAT.
BET YOUR LIFE I *WILL*.

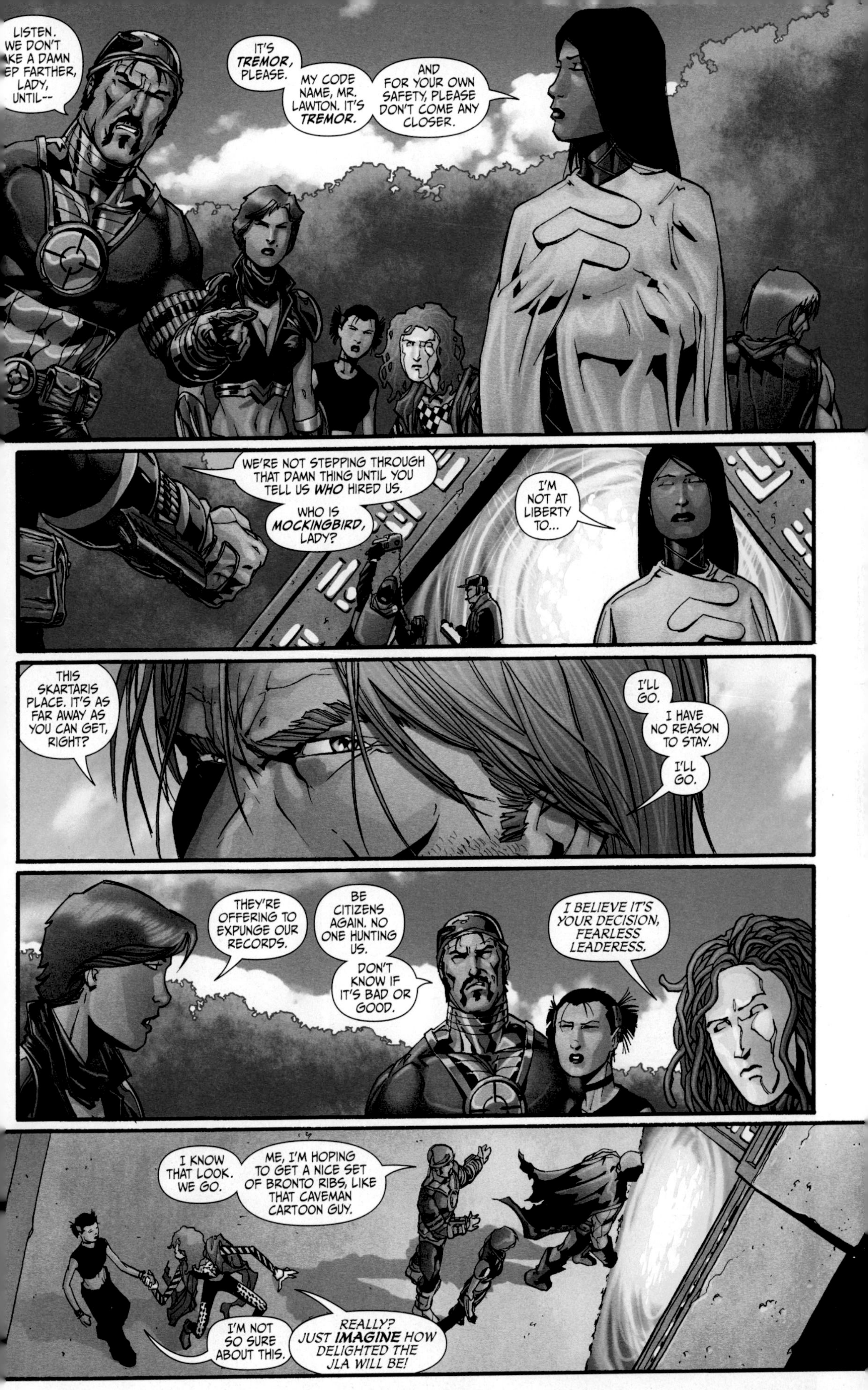
LISTEN. WE DON'T AKE A DAMN EP FARTHER, LADY, UNTIL--
IT'S TREMOR, PLEASE.
MY CODE NAME, MR. LAWTON. IT'S TREMOR.
AND FOR YOUR OWN SAFETY, PLEASE DON'T COME ANY CLOSER.
WE'RE NOT STEPPING THROUGH THAT DAMN THING UNTIL YOU TELL US WHO HIRED US.
WHO IS MOCKINGBIRD, LADY?
I'M NOT AT LIBERTY TO...
THIS SKARTARIS PLACE. IT'S AS FAR AWAY AS YOU CAN GET, RIGHT?
I'LL GO.
I HAVE NO REASON TO STAY.
I'LL GO.
THEY'RE OFFERING TO EXPUNGE OUR RECORDS.
BE CITIZENS AGAIN. NO ONE HUNTING US.
DON'T KNOW IF IT'S BAD OR GOOD.
I BELIEVE IT'S YOUR DECISION, FEARLESS LEADERESS.
I KNOW THAT LOOK. WE GO.
ME, I'M HOPING TO GET A NICE SET OF BRONTO RIBS, LIKE THAT CAVEMAN CARTOON GUY.
I'M NOT SO SURE ABOUT THIS.
REALLY? JUST IMAGINE HOW DELIGHTED THE JLA WILL BE!

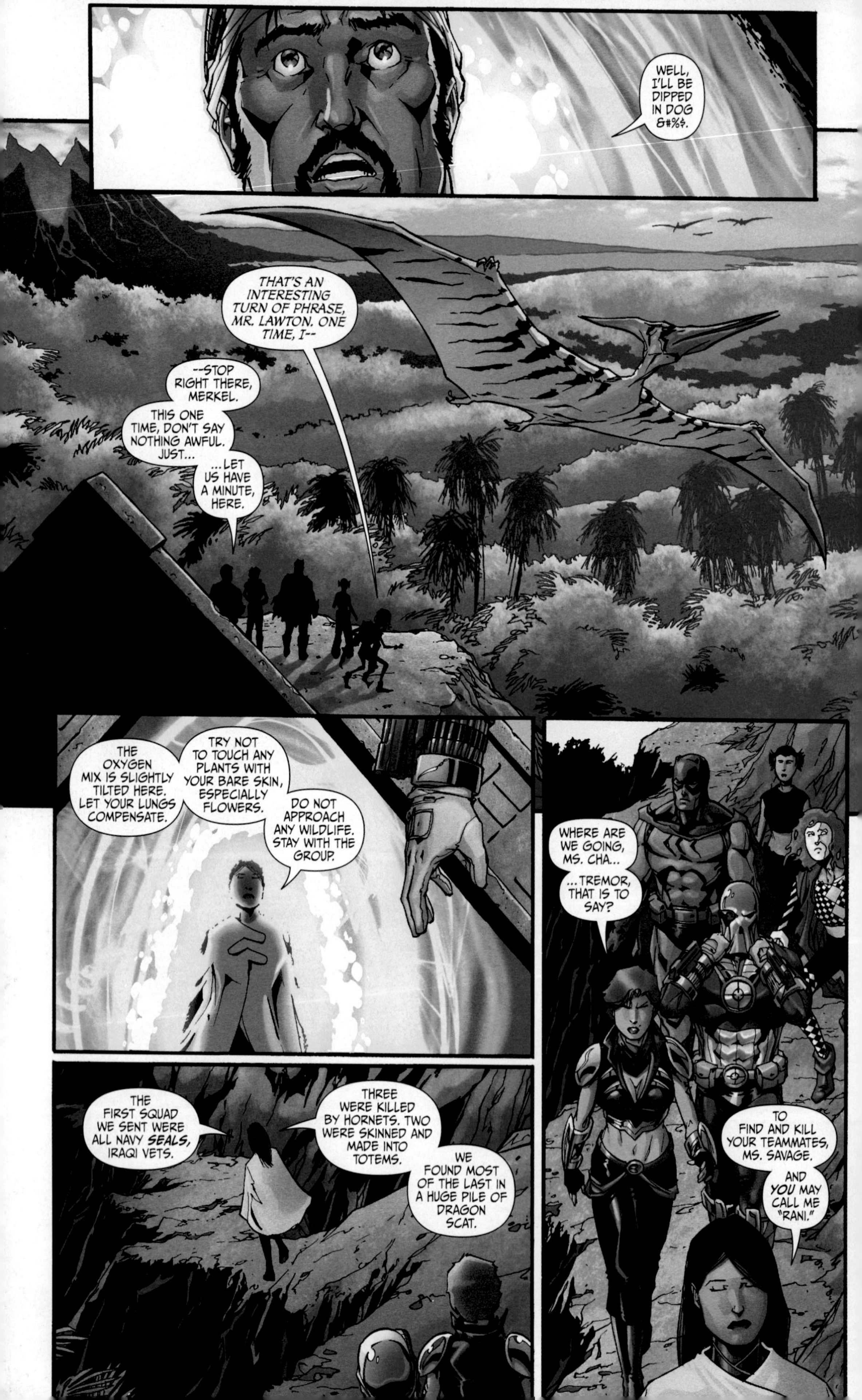
WELL, I'LL BE DIPPED IN DOG &#%$.
THAT'S AN INTERESTING TURN OF PHRASE, MR. LAWTON. ONE TIME, I--
--STOP RIGHT THERE, MERKEL.
THIS ONE TIME, DON'T SAY NOTHING AWFUL. JUST...
...LET US HAVE A MINUTE, HERE.
THE OXYGEN MIX IS SLIGHTLY TILTED HERE. LET YOUR LUNGS COMPENSATE.
TRY NOT TO TOUCH ANY PLANTS WITH YOUR BARE SKIN, ESPECIALLY FLOWERS.
DO NOT APPROACH ANY WILDLIFE. STAY WITH THE GROUP.
WHERE ARE WE GOING, MS. CHA...
...TREMOR, THAT IS TO SAY?
TO FIND AND KILL YOUR TEAMMATES, MS. SAVAGE.
AND YOU MAY CALL ME "RANI."
THE FIRST SQUAD WE SENT WERE ALL NAVY SEALS, IRAQI VETS.
THREE WERE KILLED BY HORNETS. TWO WERE SKINNED AND MADE INTO TOTEMS.
WE FOUND MOST OF THE LAST IN A HUGE PILE OF DRAGON SCAT.

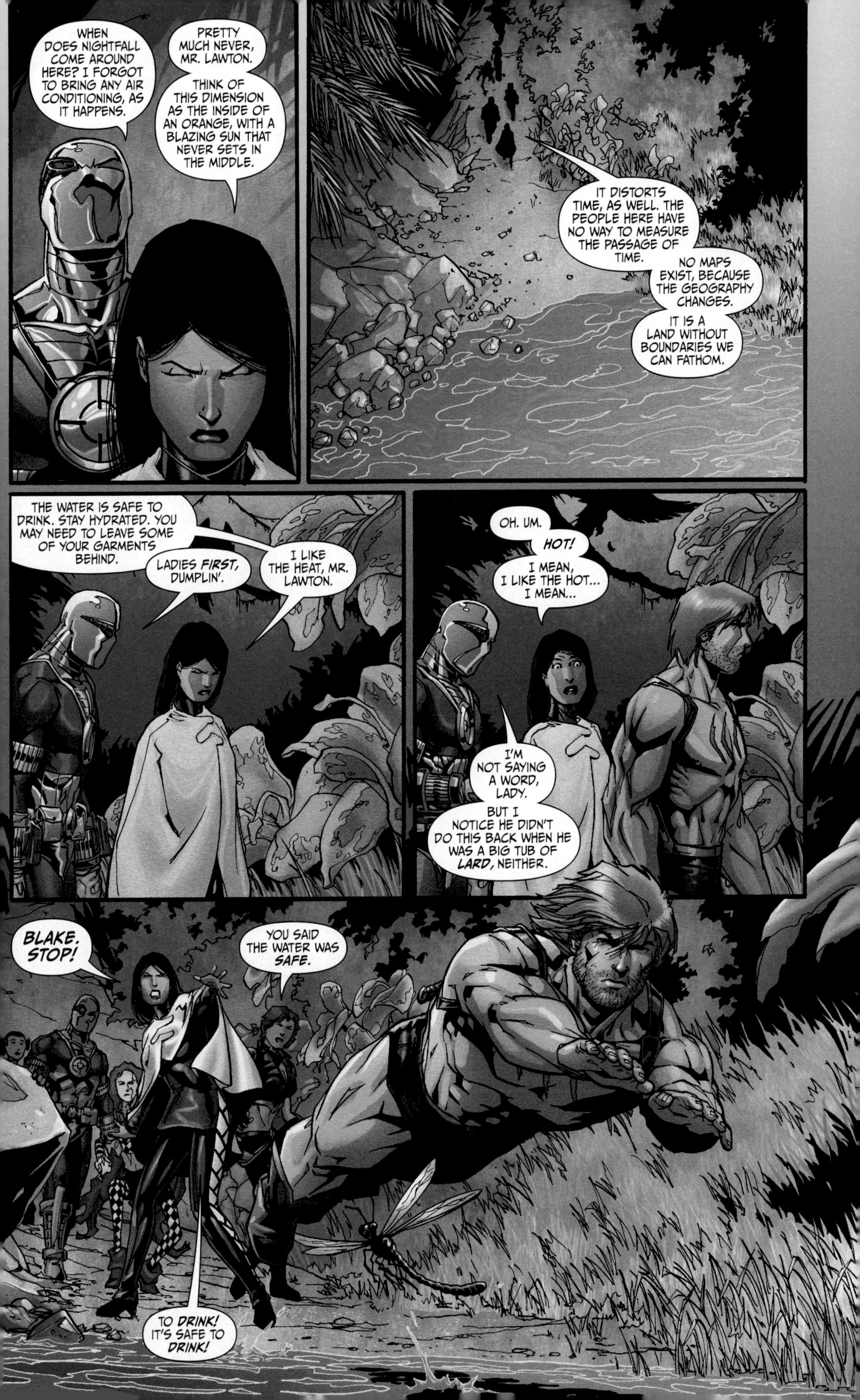
WHEN DOES NIGHTFALL COME AROUND HERE? I FORGOT TO BRING ANY AIR CONDITIONING, AS IT HAPPENS.
PRETTY MUCH NEVER, MR. LAWTON.
THINK OF THIS DIMENSION AS THE INSIDE OF AN ORANGE, WITH A BLAZING SUN THAT NEVER SETS IN THE MIDDLE.
IT DISTORTS TIME, AS WELL. THE PEOPLE HERE HAVE NO WAY TO MEASURE THE PASSAGE OF TIME.
NO MAPS EXIST, BECAUSE THE GEOGRAPHY CHANGES.
IT IS A LAND WITHOUT BOUNDARIES WE CAN FATHOM.
THE WATER IS SAFE TO DRINK. STAY HYDRATED. YOU MAY NEED TO LEAVE SOME OF YOUR GARMENTS BEHIND.
LADIES FIRST, DUMPLIN'.
I LIKE THE HEAT, MR. LAWTON.
OH. UM.
HOT!
I MEAN, I LIKE THE HOT... I MEAN...
I'M NOT SAYING A WORD, LADY.
BUT I NOTICE HE DIDN'T DO THIS BACK WHEN HE WAS A BIG TUB OF LARD, NEITHER.
BLAKE. STOP!
YOU SAID THE WATER WAS SAFE.
TO DRINK! IT'S SAFE TO DRINK!

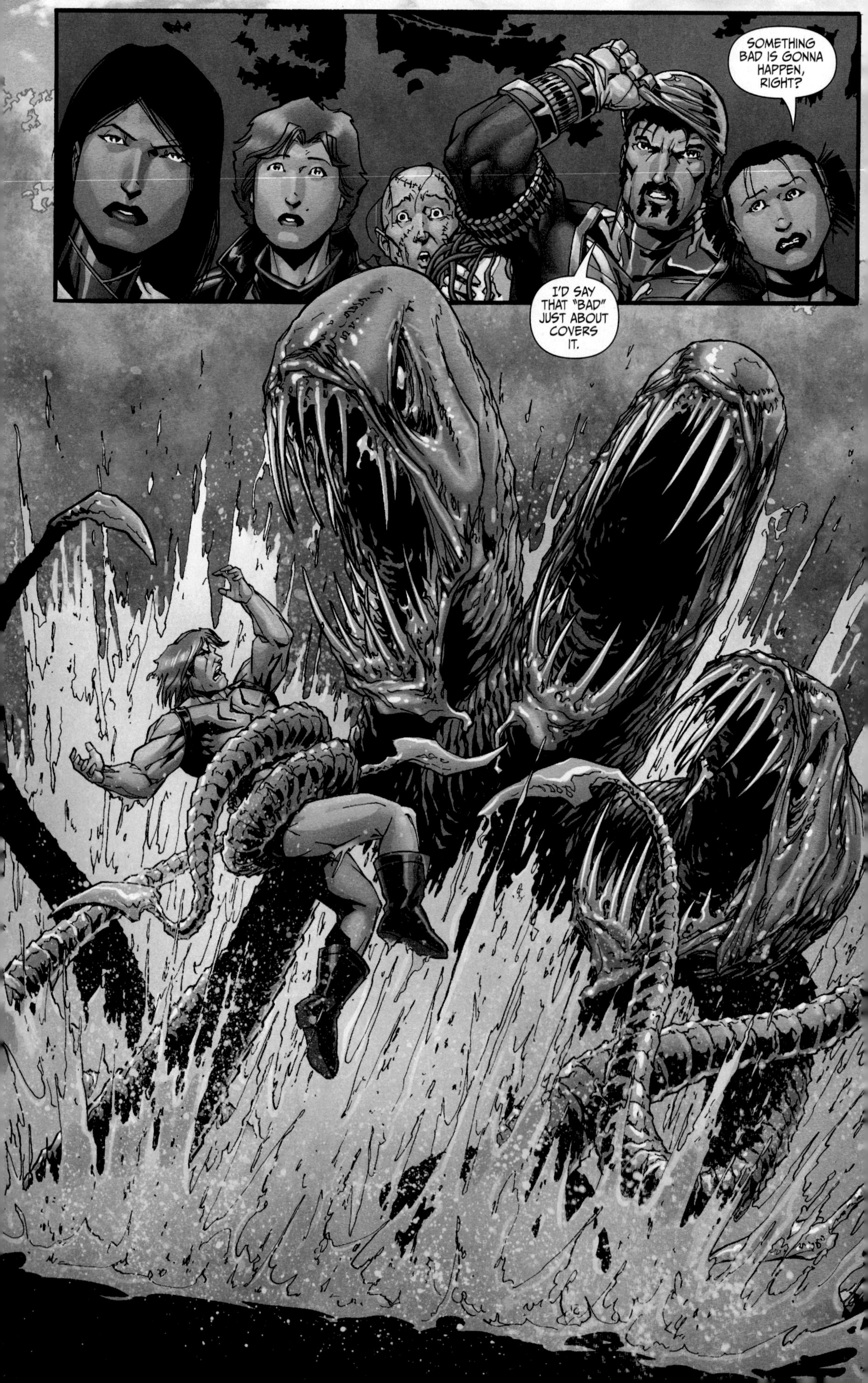
SOMETHING BAD IS GONNA HAPPEN, RIGHT?
I'D SAY THAT "BAD" JUST ABOUT COVERS IT.

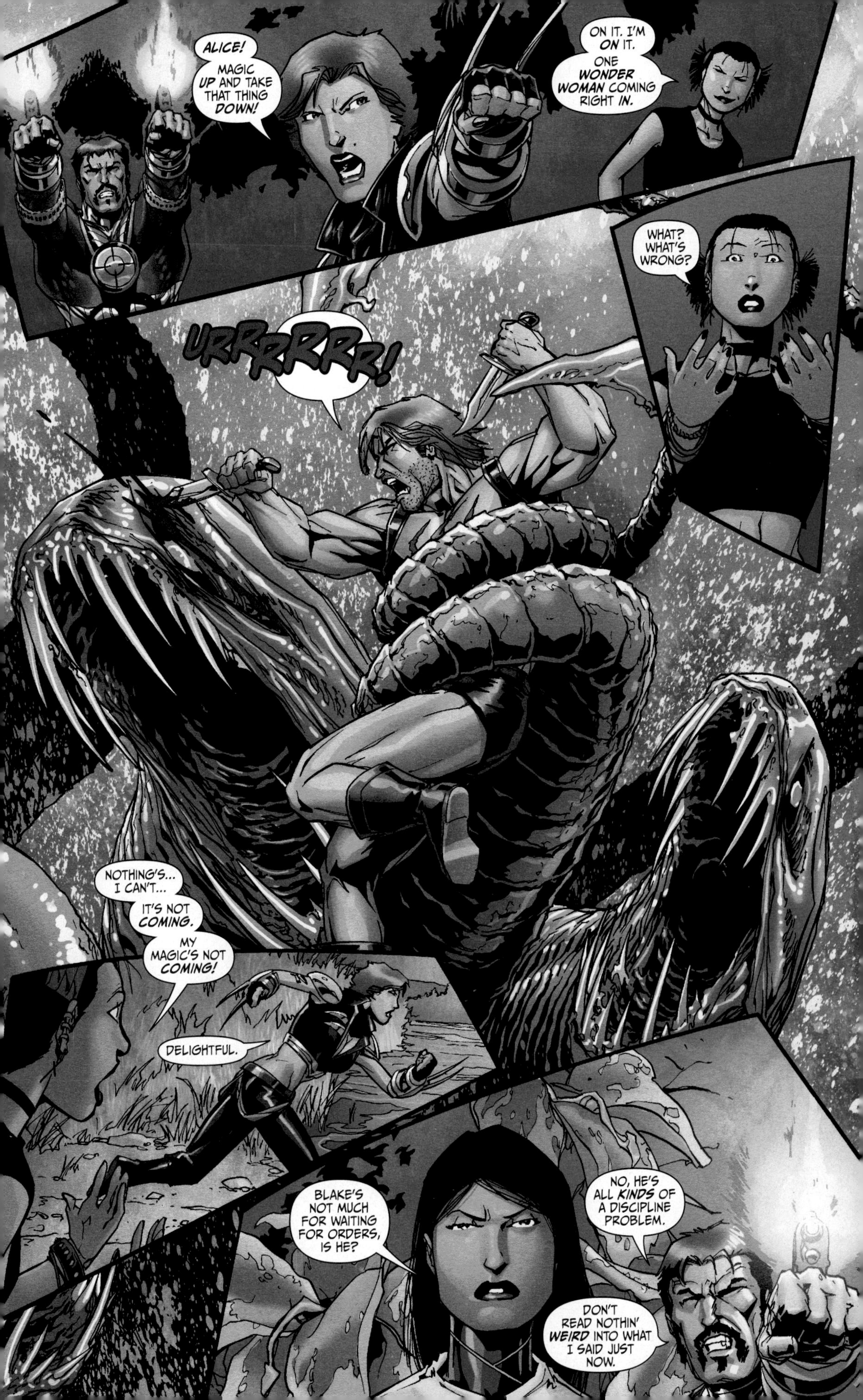
ALICE!
MAGIC UP AND TAKE THAT THING DOWN!
ON IT. I'M ON IT.
ONE WONDER WOMAN COMING RIGHT IN.
WHAT? WHAT'S WRONG?
URRRRRRR!
NOTHING'S... I CAN'T...
IT'S NOT COMING.
MY MAGIC'S NOT COMING!
DELIGHTFUL.
BLAKE'S NOT MUCH FOR WAITING FOR ORDERS, IS HE?
NO, HE'S ALL KINDS OF A DISCIPLINE PROBLEM.
DON'T READ NOTHIN' WEIRD INTO WHAT I SAID JUST NOW.

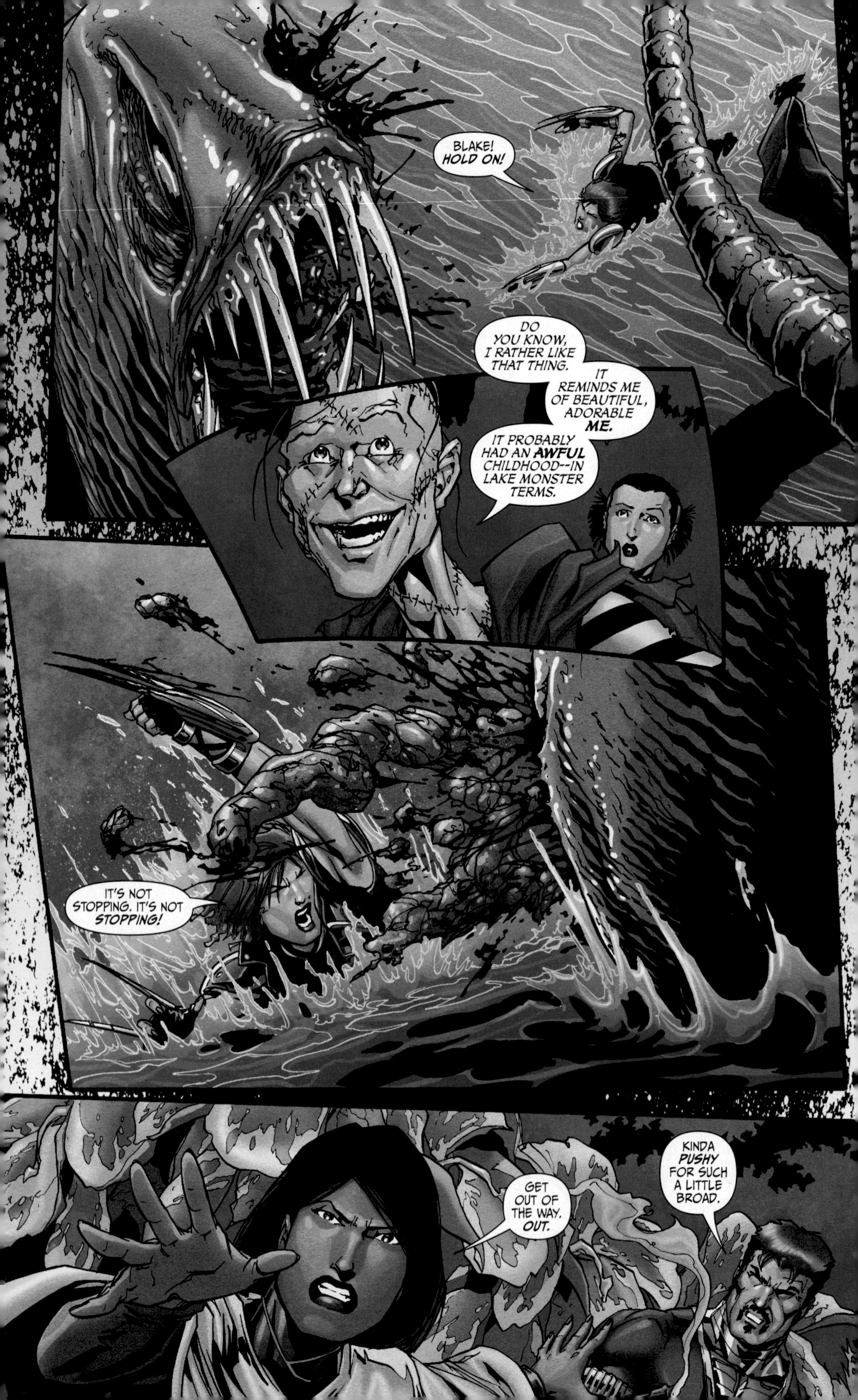
BLAKE! HOLD ON!
DO YOU KNOW, I RATHER LIKE THAT THING.
IT REMINDS ME OF BEAUTIFUL, ADORABLE ME.
IT PROBABLY HAD AN AWFUL CHILDHOOD--IN LAKE MONSTER TERMS.
IT'S NOT STOPPING. IT'S NOT STOPPING!
GET OUT OF THE WAY. OUT.
KINDA PUSHY FOR SUCH A LITTLE BROAD.

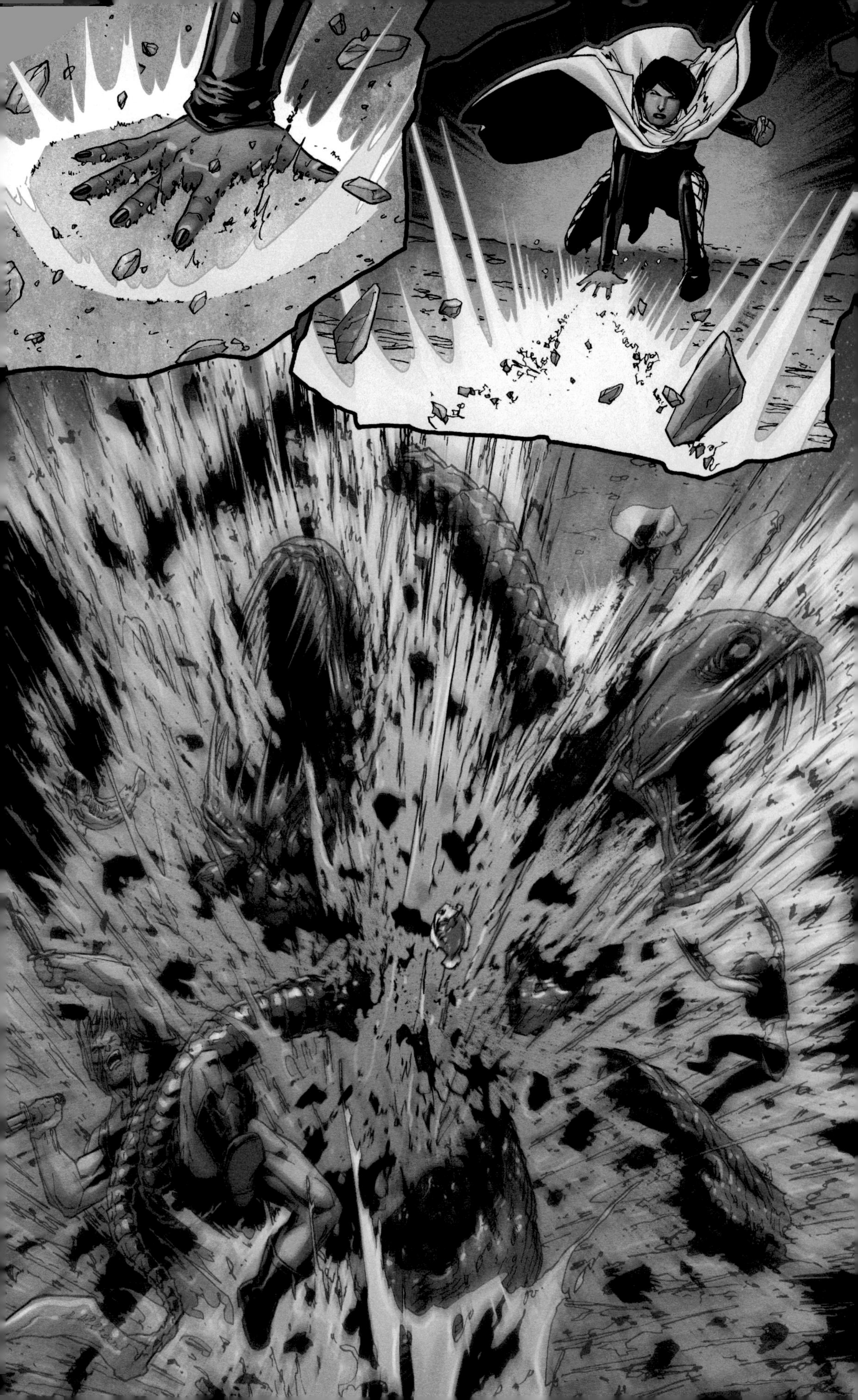

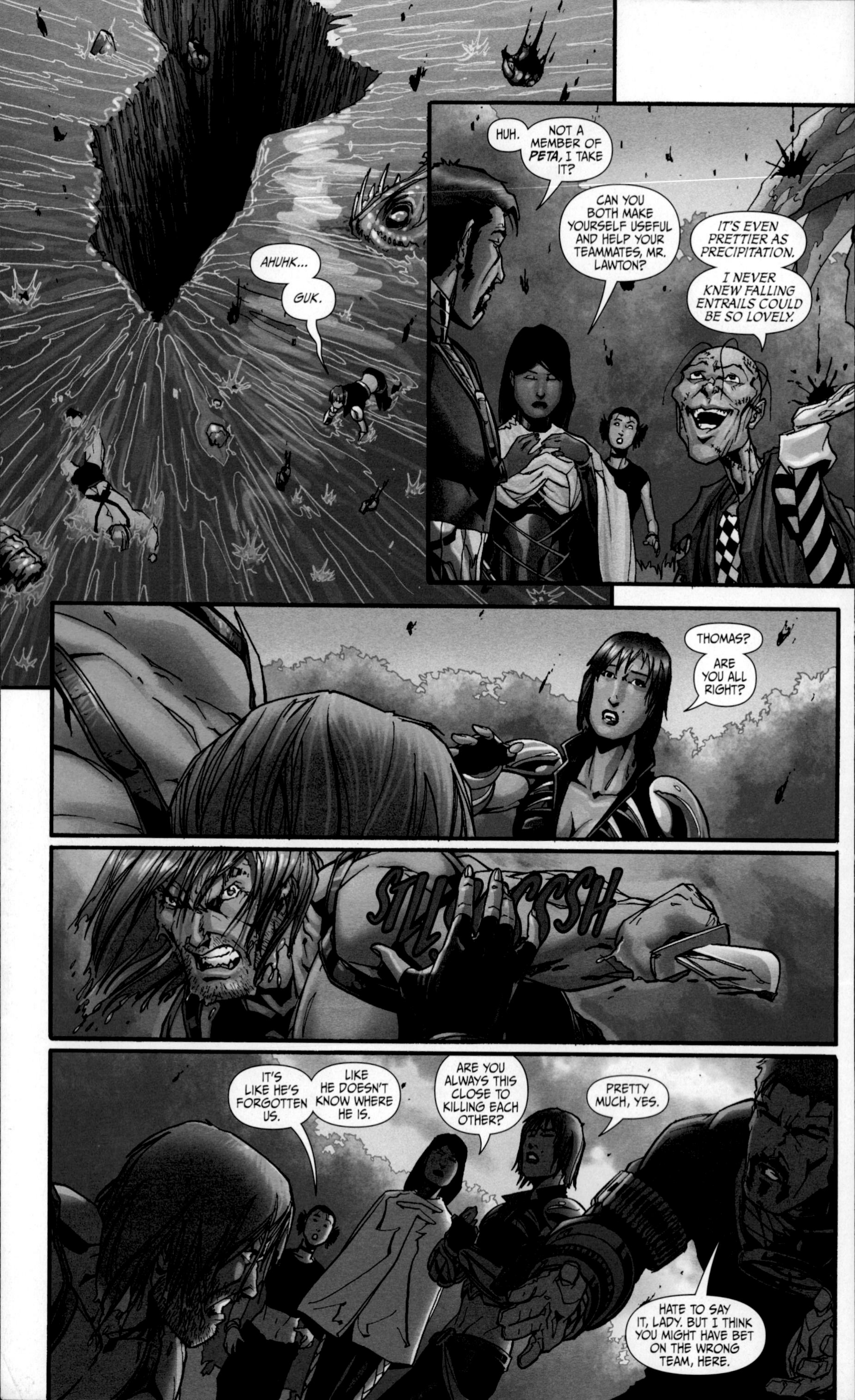
AHUHK...
GUK.
HUH.
NOT A MEMBER OF PETA, I TAKE IT?
CAN YOU BOTH MAKE YOURSELF USEFUL AND HELP YOUR TEAMMATES, MR. LAWTON?
IT'S EVEN PRETTIER AS PRECIPITATION.
I NEVER KNEW FALLING ENTRAILS COULD BE SO LOVELY.
THOMAS?
ARE YOU ALL RIGHT?
SHHHCSSH
IT'S LIKE HE'S FORGOTTEN US.
LIKE HE DOESN'T KNOW WHERE HE IS.
ARE YOU ALWAYS THIS CLOSE TO KILLING EACH OTHER?
PRETTY MUCH, YES.
HATE TO SAY IT, LADY. BUT I THINK YOU MIGHT HAVE BET ON THE WRONG TEAM, HERE.

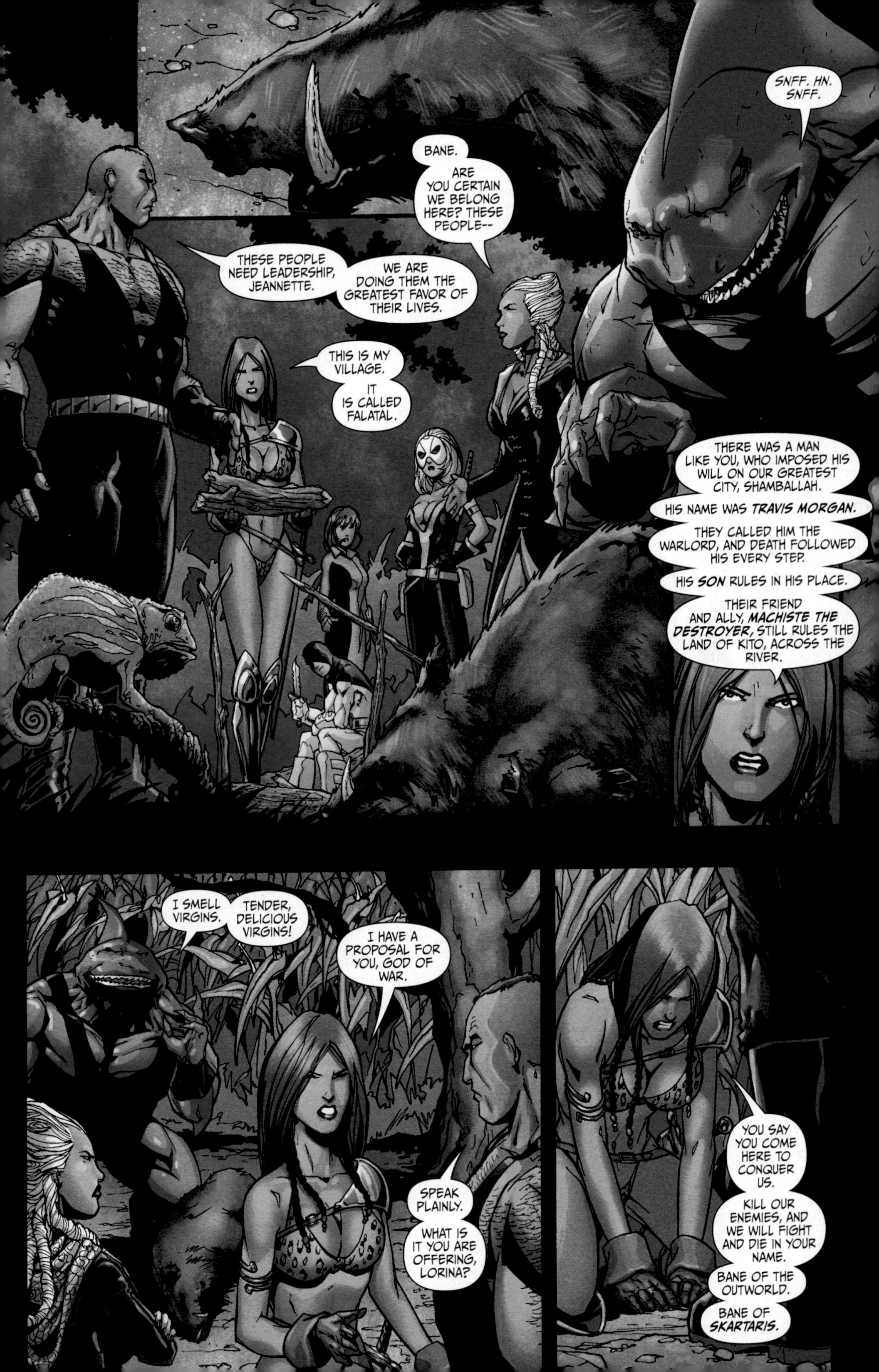
SNFF. HN. SNFF.
BANE.
ARE YOU CERTAIN WE BELONG HERE? THESE PEOPLE--
THESE PEOPLE NEED LEADERSHIP, JEANNETTE.
WE ARE DOING THEM THE GREATEST FAVOR OF THEIR LIVES.
THIS IS MY VILLAGE.
IT IS CALLED FALATAL.
THERE WAS A MAN LIKE YOU, WHO IMPOSED HIS WILL ON OUR GREATEST CITY, SHAMBALLAH.
HIS NAME WAS TRAVIS MORGAN.
THEY CALLED HIM THE WARLORD, AND DEATH FOLLOWED HIS EVERY STEP.
HIS SON RULES IN HIS PLACE.
THEIR FRIEND AND ALLY, MACHISTE THE DESTROYER, STILL RULES THE LAND OF KITO, ACROSS THE RIVER.
I SMELL VIRGINS.
TENDER, DELICIOUS VIRGINS!
I HAVE A PROPOSAL FOR YOU, GOD OF WAR.
SPEAK PLAINLY.
WHAT IS IT YOU ARE OFFERING, LORINA?
YOU SAY YOU COME HERE TO CONQUER US.
KILL OUR ENEMIES, AND WE WILL FIGHT AND DIE IN YOUR NAME.
BANE OF THE OUTWORLD.
BANE OF SKARTARIS.

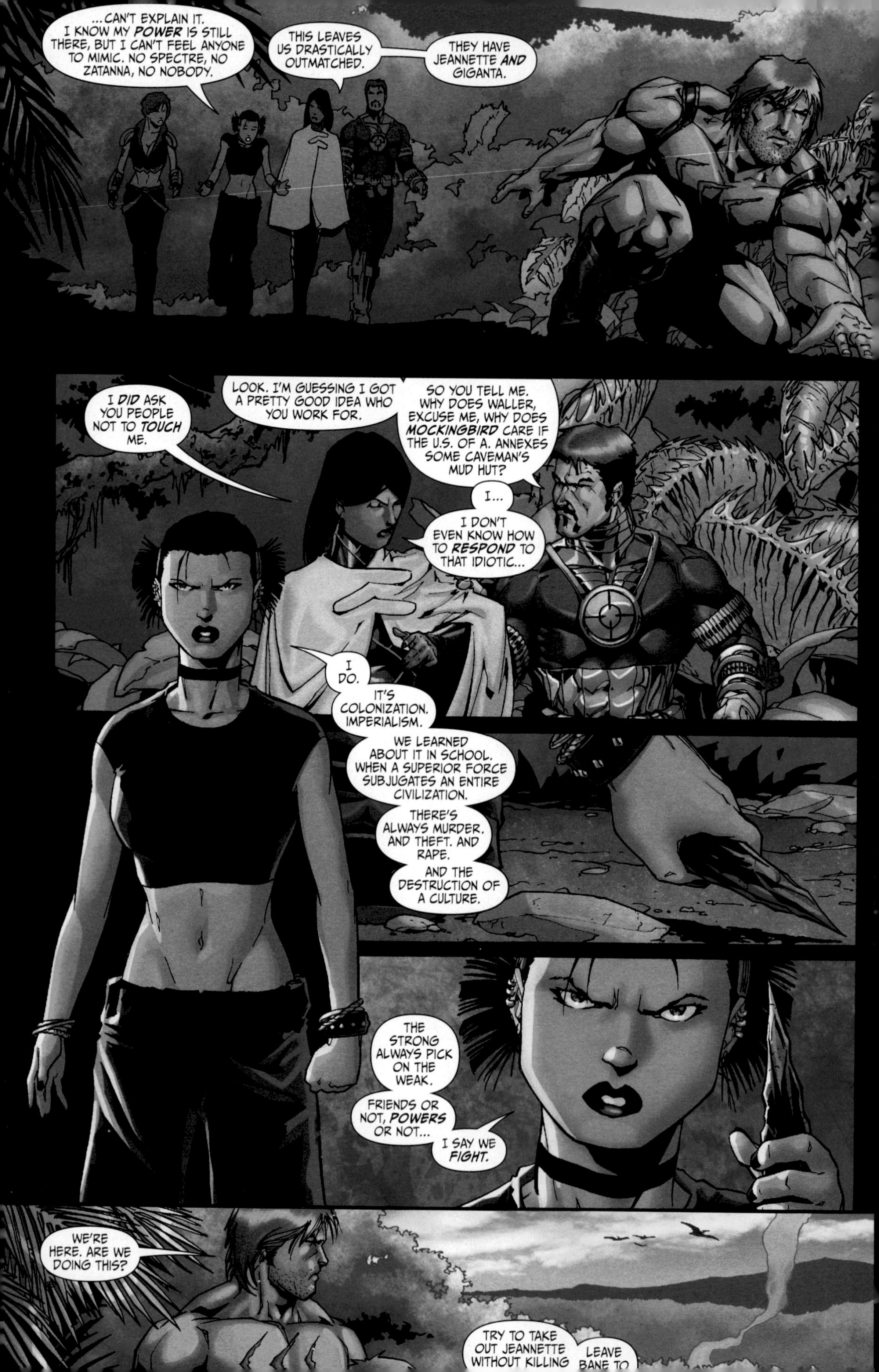
...CAN'T EXPLAIN IT. I KNOW MY *POWER* IS STILL THERE, BUT I CAN'T FEEL ANYONE TO MIMIC. NO SPECTRE, NO ZATANNA, NO NOBODY.
THIS LEAVES US DRASTICALLY OUTMATCHED.
THEY HAVE JEANNETTE *AND* GIGANTA.
I *DID* ASK YOU PEOPLE NOT TO *TOUCH* ME.
LOOK. I'M GUESSING I GOT A PRETTY GOOD IDEA WHO YOU WORK FOR.
SO YOU TELL ME. WHY DOES WALLER, EXCUSE ME, WHY DOES *MOCKINGBIRD* CARE IF THE U.S. OF A. ANNEXES SOME CAVEMAN'S MUD HUT?
I...
I DON'T EVEN KNOW HOW TO *RESPOND* TO THAT IDIOTIC...
I DO.
IT'S COLONIZATION. IMPERIALISM.
WE LEARNED ABOUT IT IN SCHOOL. WHEN A SUPERIOR FORCE SUBJUGATES AN ENTIRE CIVILIZATION.
THERE'S ALWAYS MURDER. AND THEFT. AND RAPE.
AND THE DESTRUCTION OF A CULTURE.
THE STRONG ALWAYS PICK ON THE WEAK.
FRIENDS OR NOT, *POWERS* OR NOT...
I SAY WE *FIGHT*.
WE'RE HERE. ARE WE DOING THIS?
TRY TO TAKE OUT JEANNETTE WITHOUT KILLING
LEAVE BANE TO

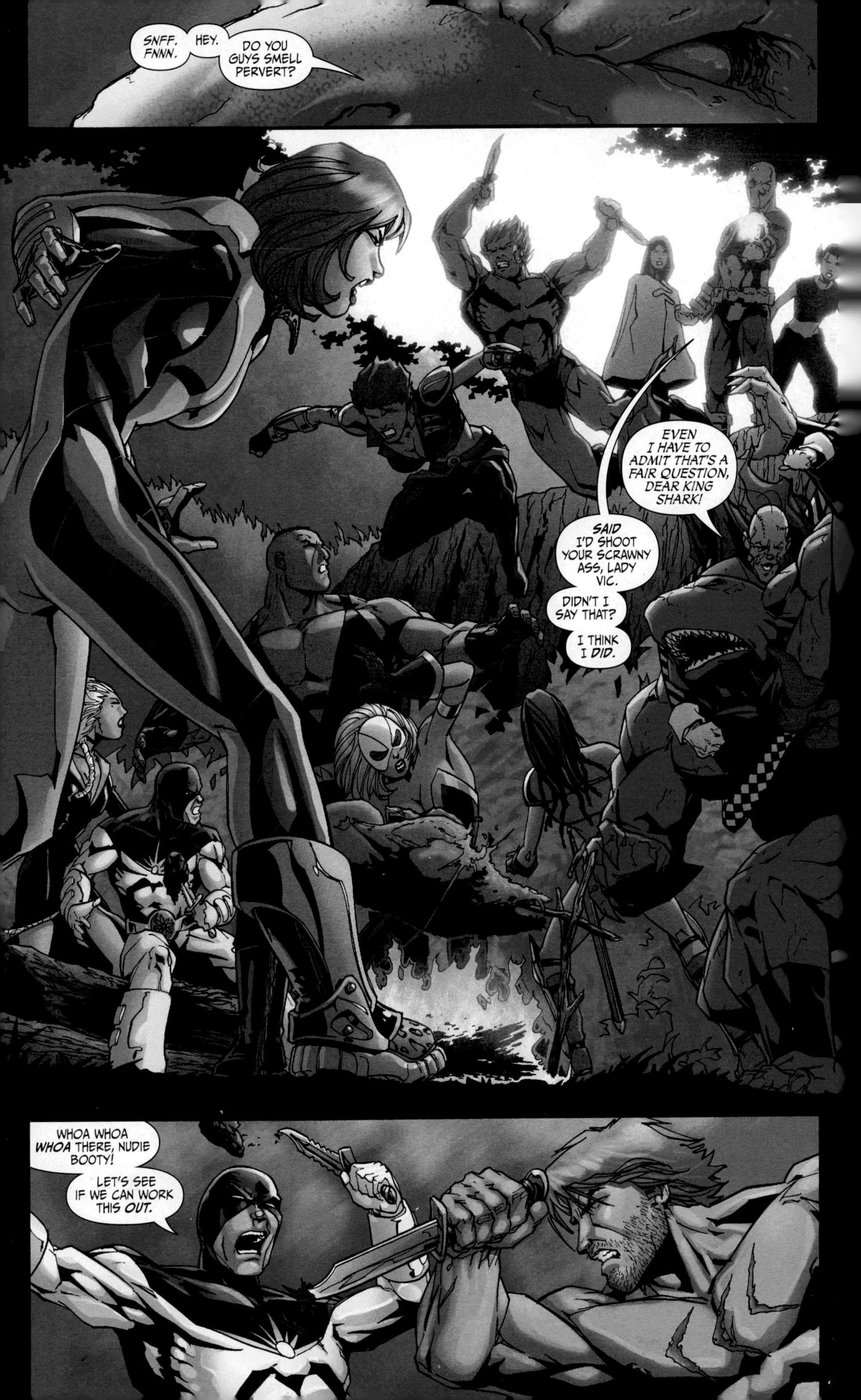
SNFF. FNNN.
HEY.
DO YOU GUYS SMELL PERVERT?
EVEN I HAVE TO ADMIT THAT'S A FAIR QUESTION, DEAR KING SHARK!
SAID I'D SHOOT YOUR SCRAWNY ASS, LADY VIC.
DIDN'T I SAY THAT?
I THINK I DID.
WHOA WHOA WHOA THERE, NUDIE BOOTY!
LET'S SEE IF WE CAN WORK THIS OUT.

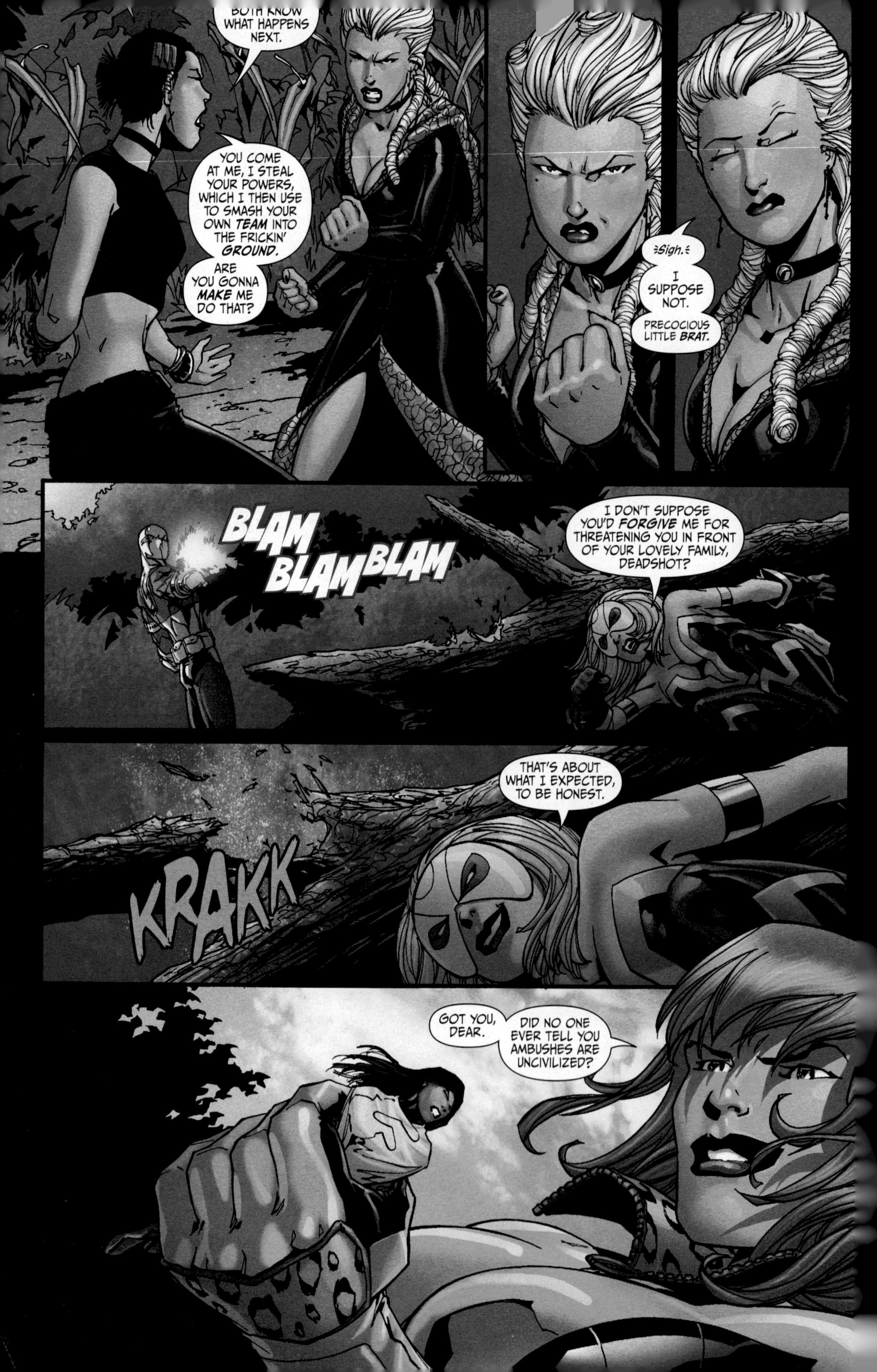
BOTH KNOW WHAT HAPPENS NEXT.
YOU COME AT ME, I STEAL YOUR POWERS, WHICH I THEN USE TO SMASH YOUR OWN TEAM INTO THE FRICKIN' GROUND.
ARE YOU GONNA MAKE ME DO THAT?
Sigh.
I SUPPOSE NOT.
PRECOCIOUS LITTLE BRAT.
BLAM
BLAM BLAM
I DON'T SUPPOSE YOU'D FORGIVE ME FOR THREATENING YOU IN FRONT OF YOUR LOVELY FAMILY, DEADSHOT?
THAT'S ABOUT WHAT I EXPECTED, TO BE HONEST.
KRAKK
GOT YOU, DEAR.
DID NO ONE EVER TELL YOU AMBUSHES ARE UNCIVILIZED?

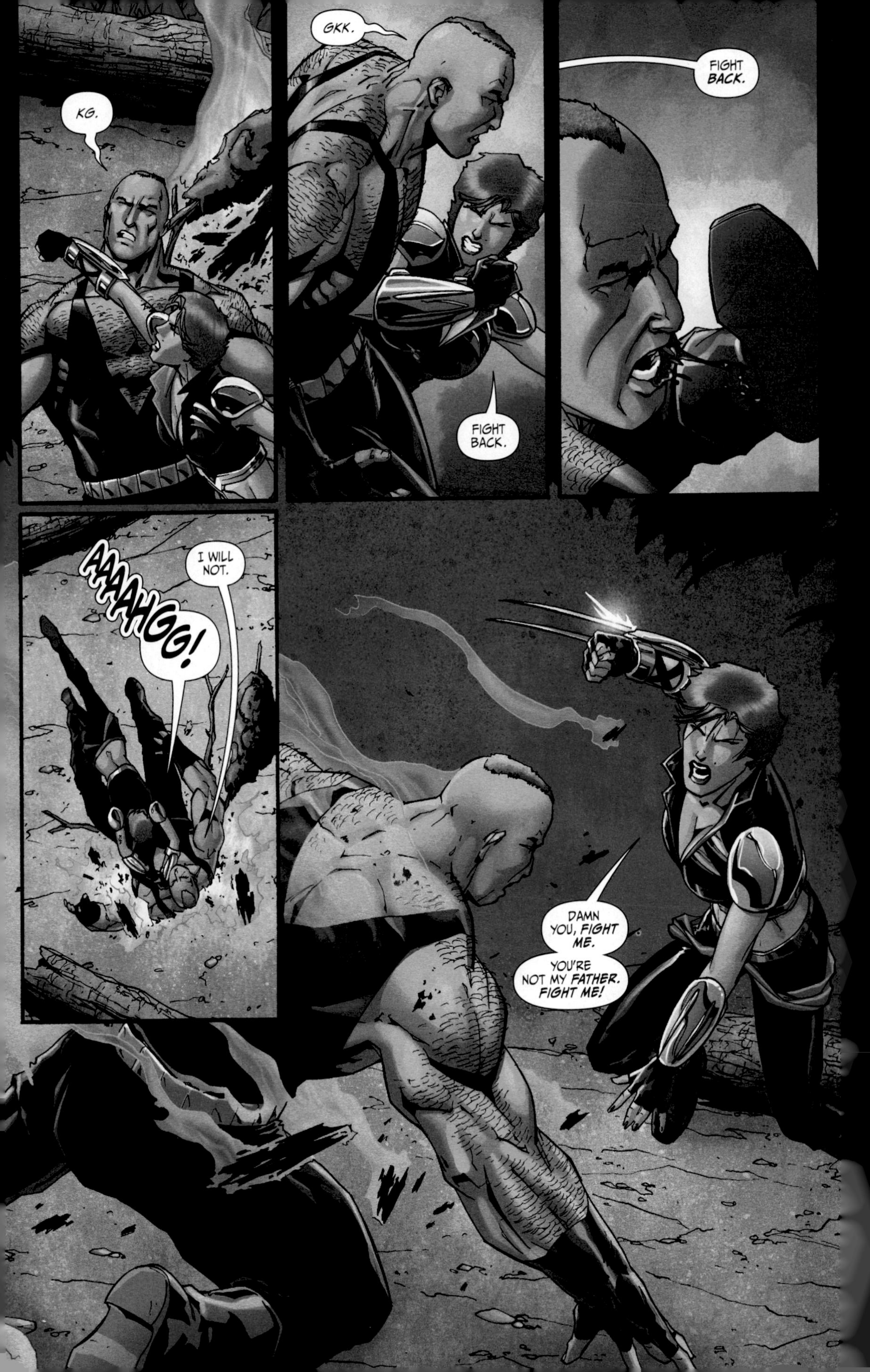
KG.
GKK.
FIGHT BACK.
FIGHT BACK.
AAAAHGG!
I WILL NOT.
DAMN YOU, FIGHT ME.
YOU'RE NOT MY FATHER. FIGHT ME!

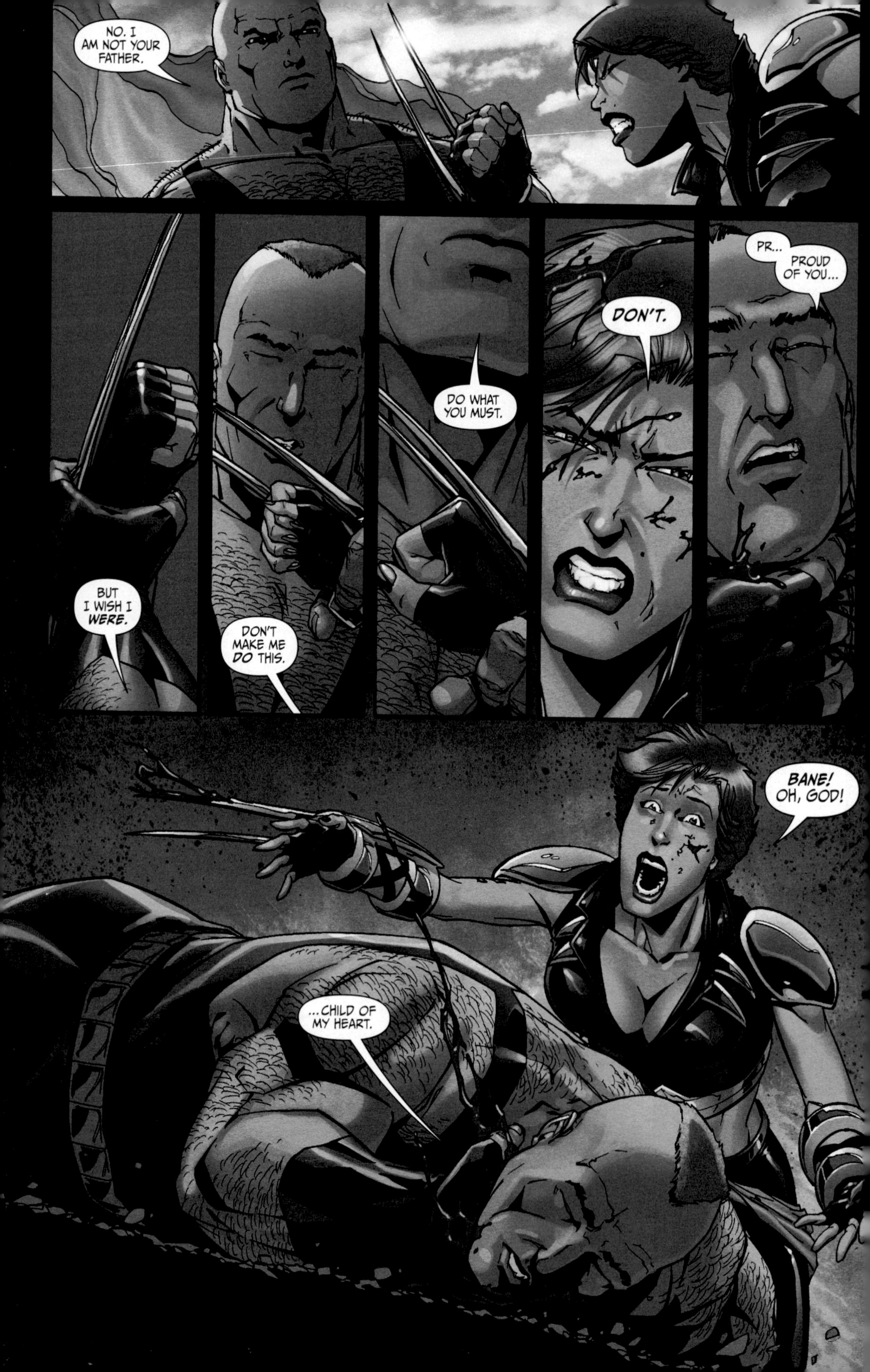
NO. I AM NOT YOUR FATHER.
BUT I WISH I *WERE.*
DON'T MAKE ME *DO* THIS.
DO WHAT YOU MUST.
DON'T.
PR...
PROUD OF YOU...
BANE! OH, GOD!
...CHILD OF MY HEART.

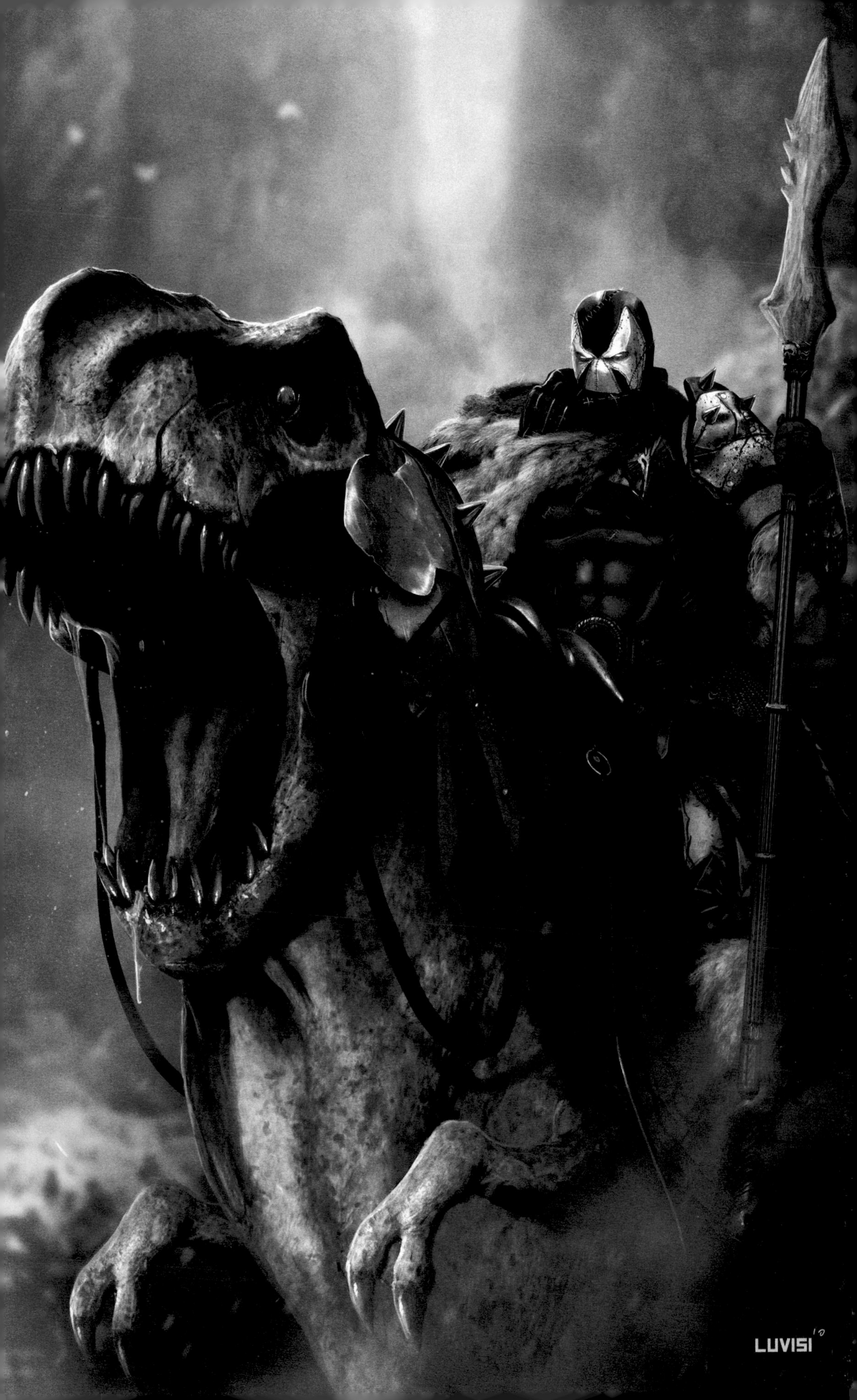
LUVISI '10

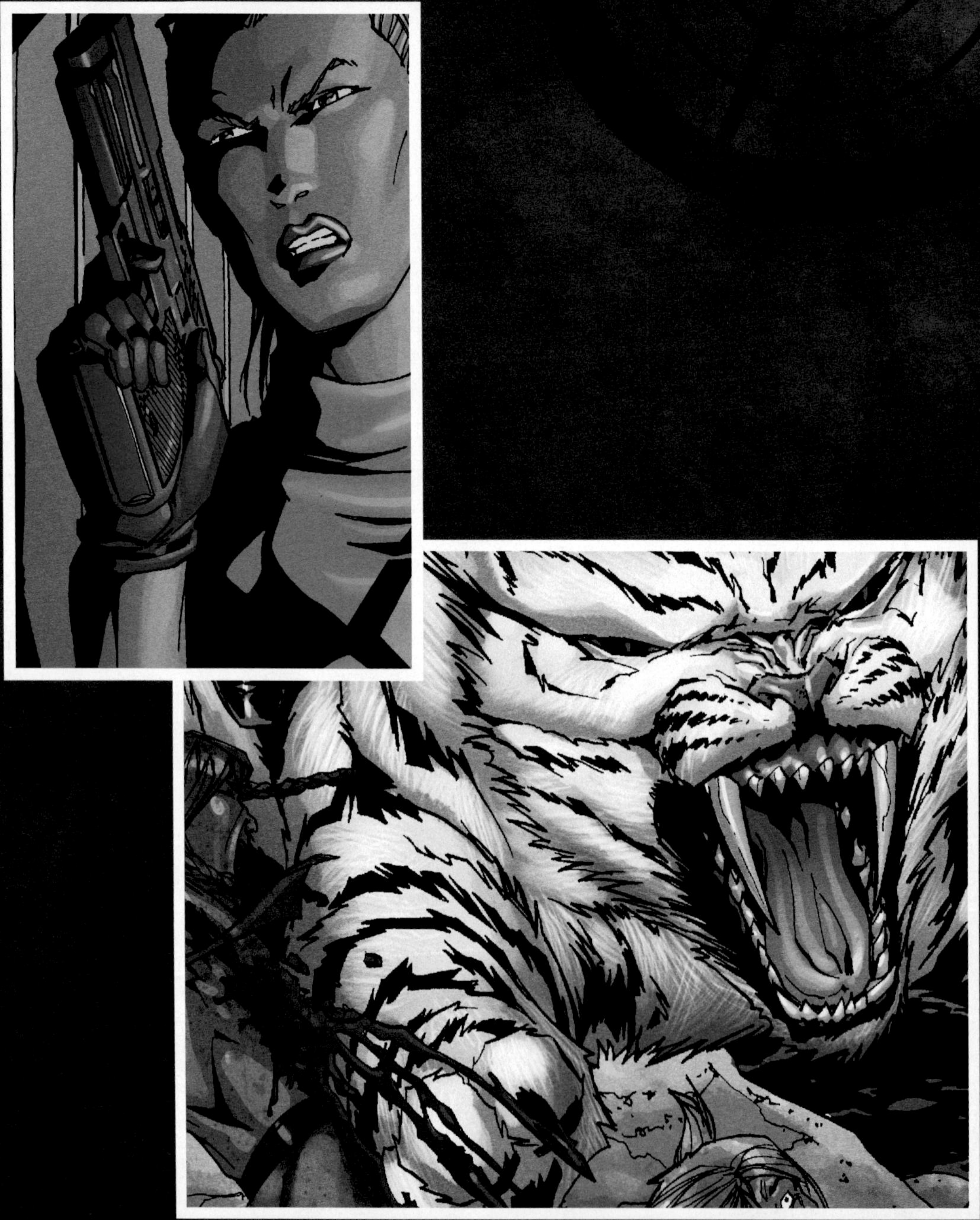

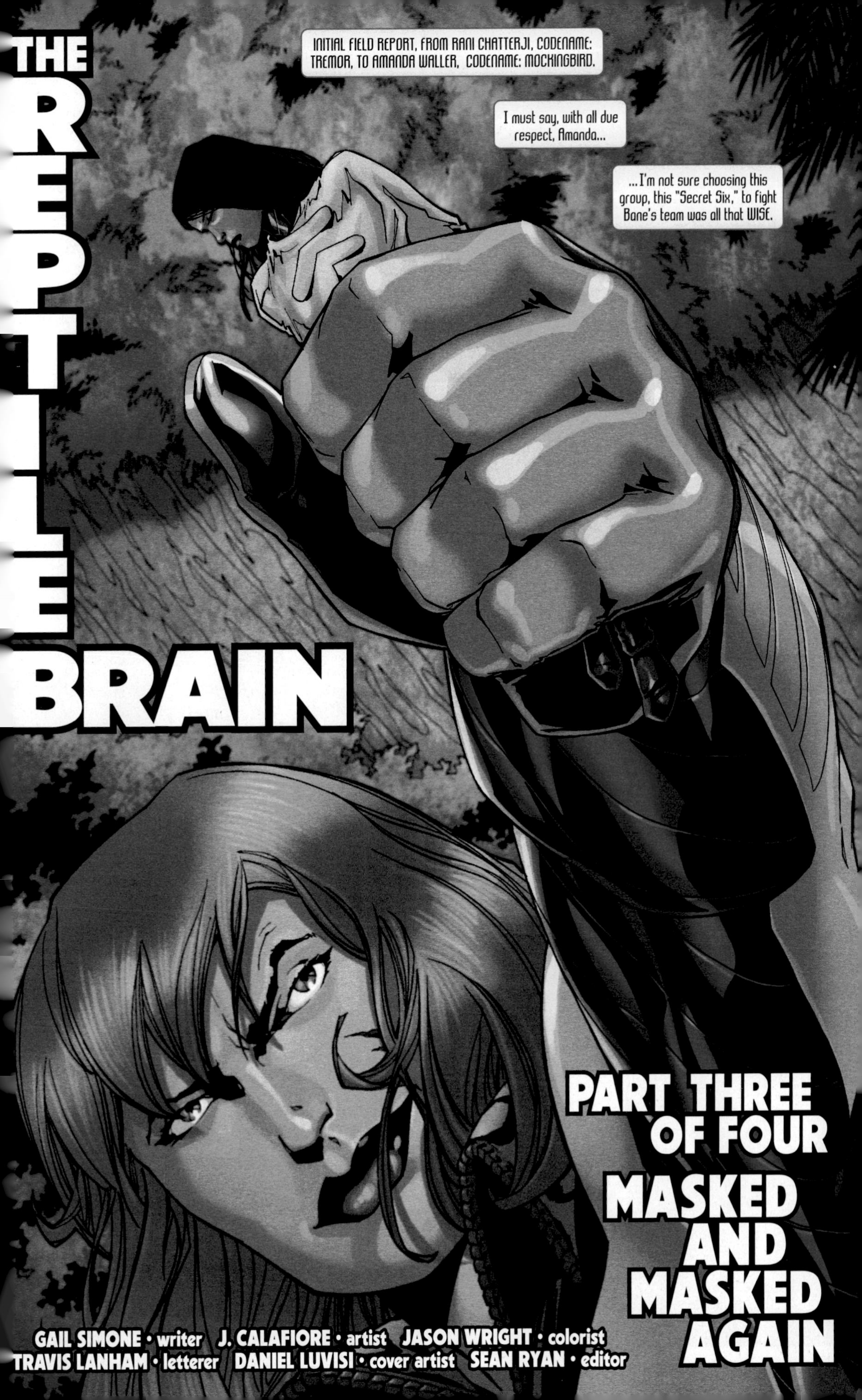
THE REPTILE BRAIN
INITIAL FIELD REPORT, FROM RANI CHATTERJI, CODENAME: TREMOR, TO AMANDA WALLER, CODENAME: MOCKINGBIRD.
I must say, with all due respect, Amanda...
...I'm not sure choosing this group, this "Secret Six," to fight Bane's team was all that WISE.
PART THREE OF FOUR
MASKED AND MASKED AGAIN
GAIL SIMONE • writer J. CALAFIORE • artist JASON WRIGHT • colorist
TRAVIS LANHAM • letterer DANIEL LUVISI • cover artist SEAN RYAN • editor

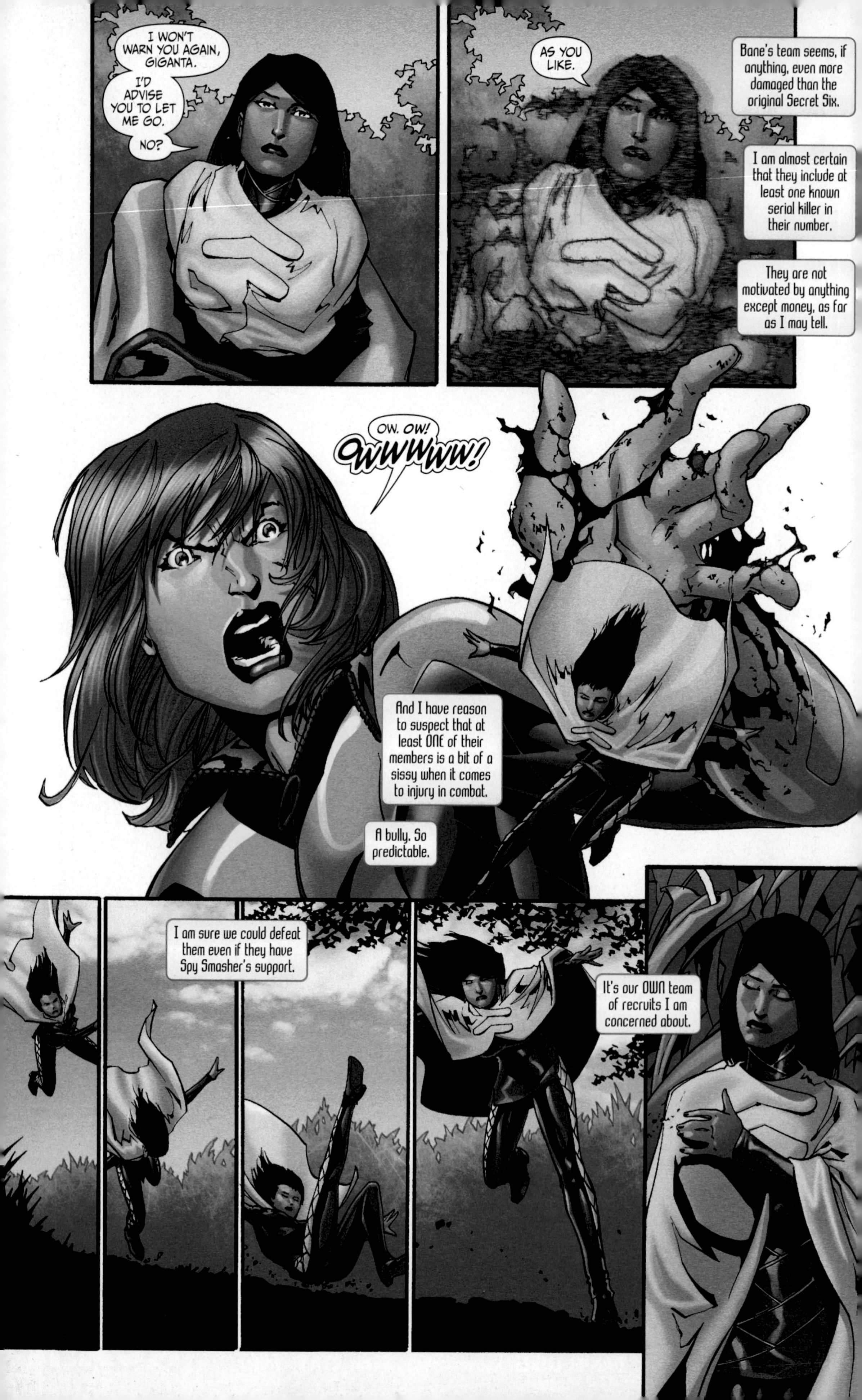
I WON'T WARN YOU AGAIN, GIGANTA.
I'D ADVISE YOU TO LET ME GO.
NO?
AS YOU LIKE.
Bane's team seems, if anything, even more damaged than the original Secret Six.
I am almost certain that they include at least one known serial killer in their number.
They are not motivated by anything except money, as far as I may tell.
OW. OW! OWWWWW!
And I have reason to suspect that at least ONE of their members is a bit of a sissy when it comes to injury in combat.
A bully. So predictable.
I am sure we could defeat them even if they have Spy Smasher's support.
It's our OWN team of recruits I am concerned about.

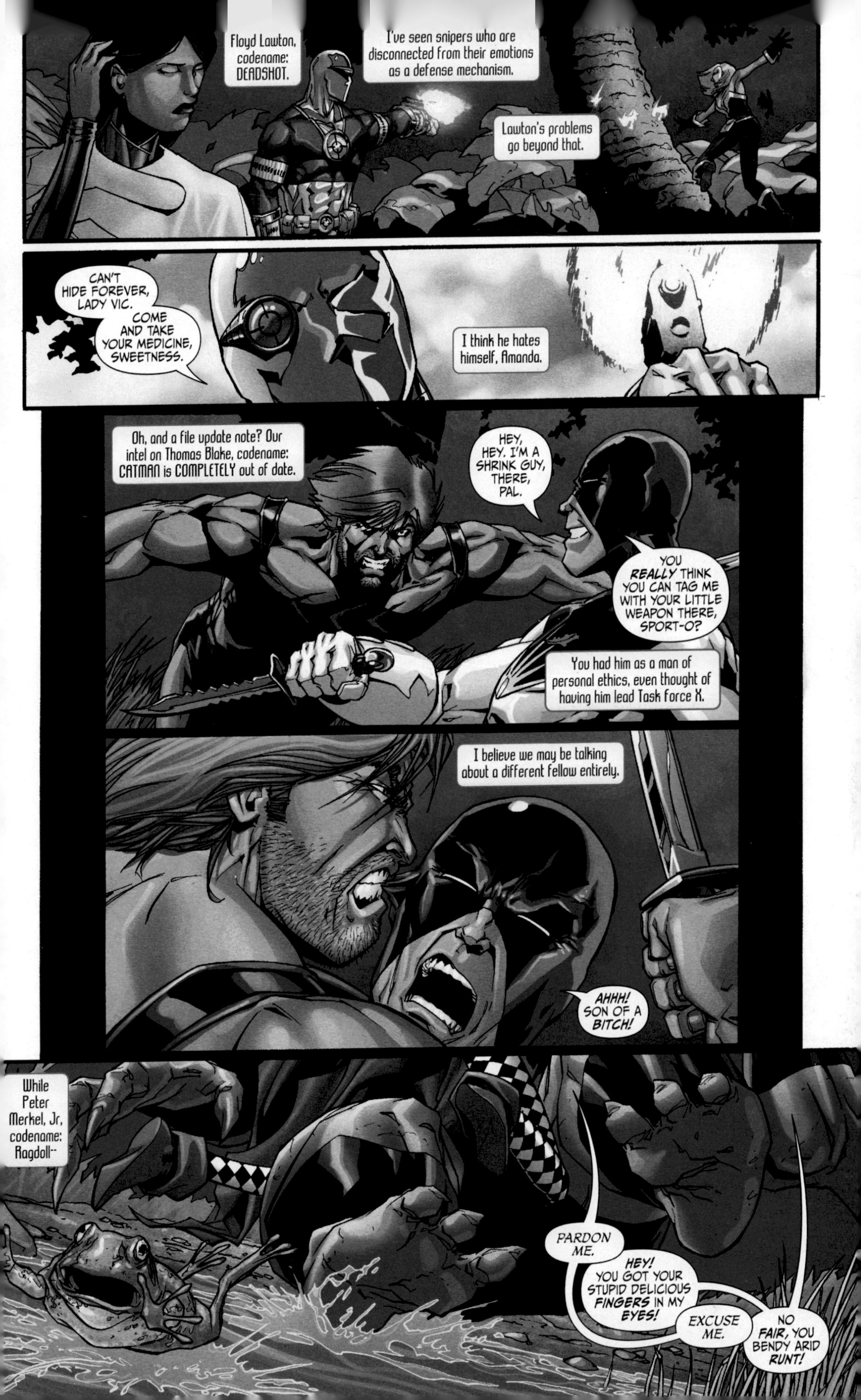
Floyd Lawton, codename: DEADSHOT.
I've seen snipers who are disconnected from their emotions as a defense mechanism.
Lawton's problems go beyond that.
CAN'T HIDE FOREVER, LADY VIC.
COME AND TAKE YOUR MEDICINE, SWEETNESS.
I think he hates himself, Amanda.
Oh, and a file update note? Our intel on Thomas Blake, codename: CATMAN is COMPLETELY out of date.
HEY, HEY. I'M A SHRINK GUY, THERE, PAL.
YOU REALLY THINK YOU CAN TAG ME WITH YOUR LITTLE WEAPON THERE, SPORT-O?
You had him as a man of personal ethics, even thought of having him lead Task Force X.
I believe we may be talking about a different fellow entirely.
AHHH! SON OF A BITCH!
While Peter Merkel, Jr, codename: Ragdoll--
PARDON ME.
HEY! YOU GOT YOUR STUPID DELICIOUS FINGERS IN MY EYES!
EXCUSE ME.
NO FAIR, YOU BENDY ARID RUNT!

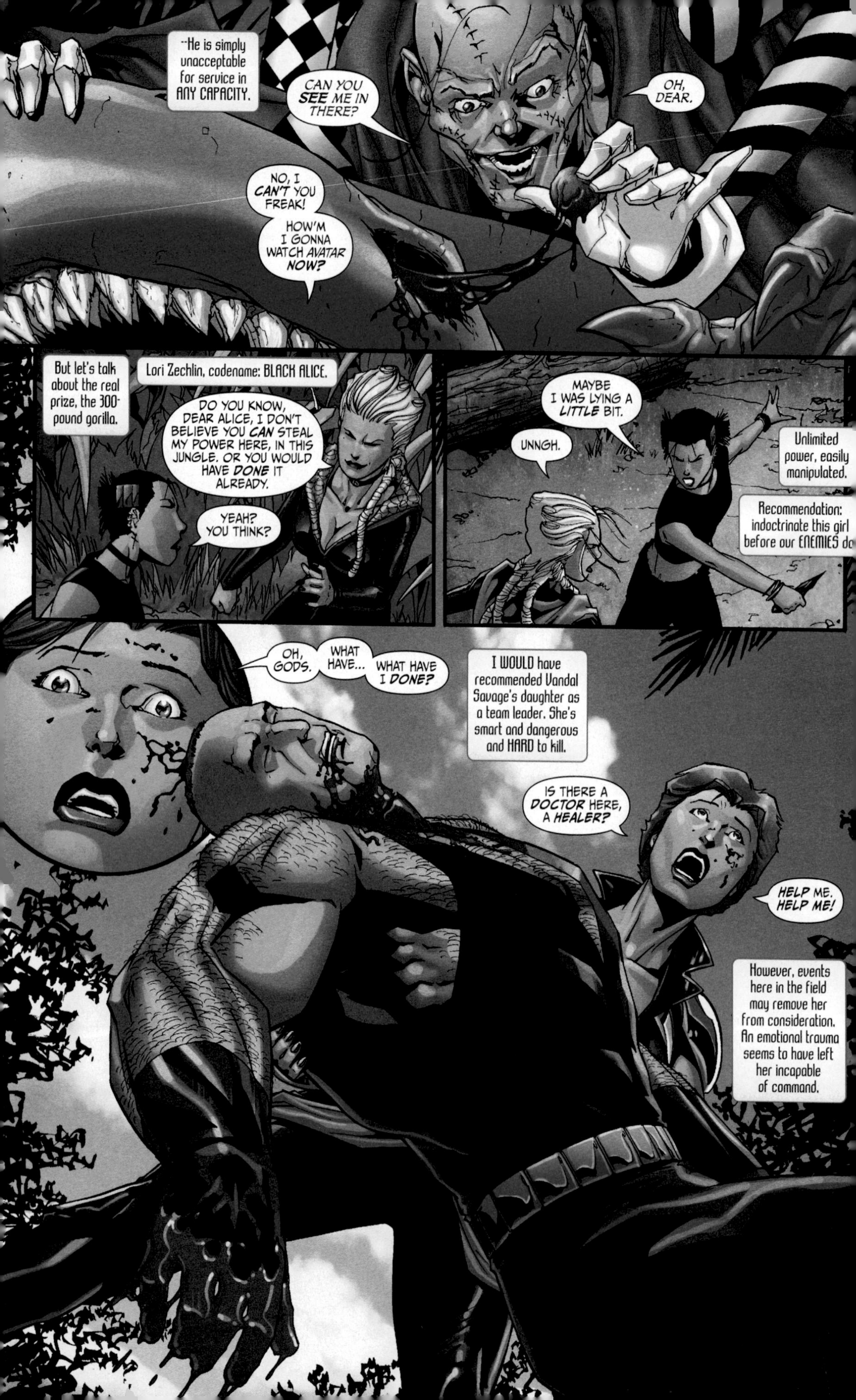
--He is simply unacceptable for service in ANY CAPACITY.
CAN YOU SEE ME IN THERE?
OH, DEAR.
NO, I CAN'T YOU FREAK!
HOW'M I GONNA WATCH AVATAR NOW?
But let's talk about the real prize, the 300-pound gorilla.
Lori Zechlin, codename: BLACK ALICE.
DO YOU KNOW, DEAR ALICE, I DON'T BELIEVE YOU CAN STEAL MY POWER HERE, IN THIS JUNGLE. OR YOU WOULD HAVE DONE IT ALREADY.
YEAH? YOU THINK?
UNNGH.
MAYBE I WAS LYING A LITTLE BIT.
Unlimited power, easily manipulated.
Recommendation: indoctrinate this girl before our ENEMIES do
OH, GODS.
WHAT HAVE...
WHAT HAVE I DONE?
I WOULD have recommended Vandal Savage's daughter as a team leader. She's smart and dangerous and HARD to kill.
IS THERE A DOCTOR HERE, A HEALER?
HELP ME. HELP ME!
However, events here in the field may remove her from consideration. An emotional trauma seems to have left her incapable of command.

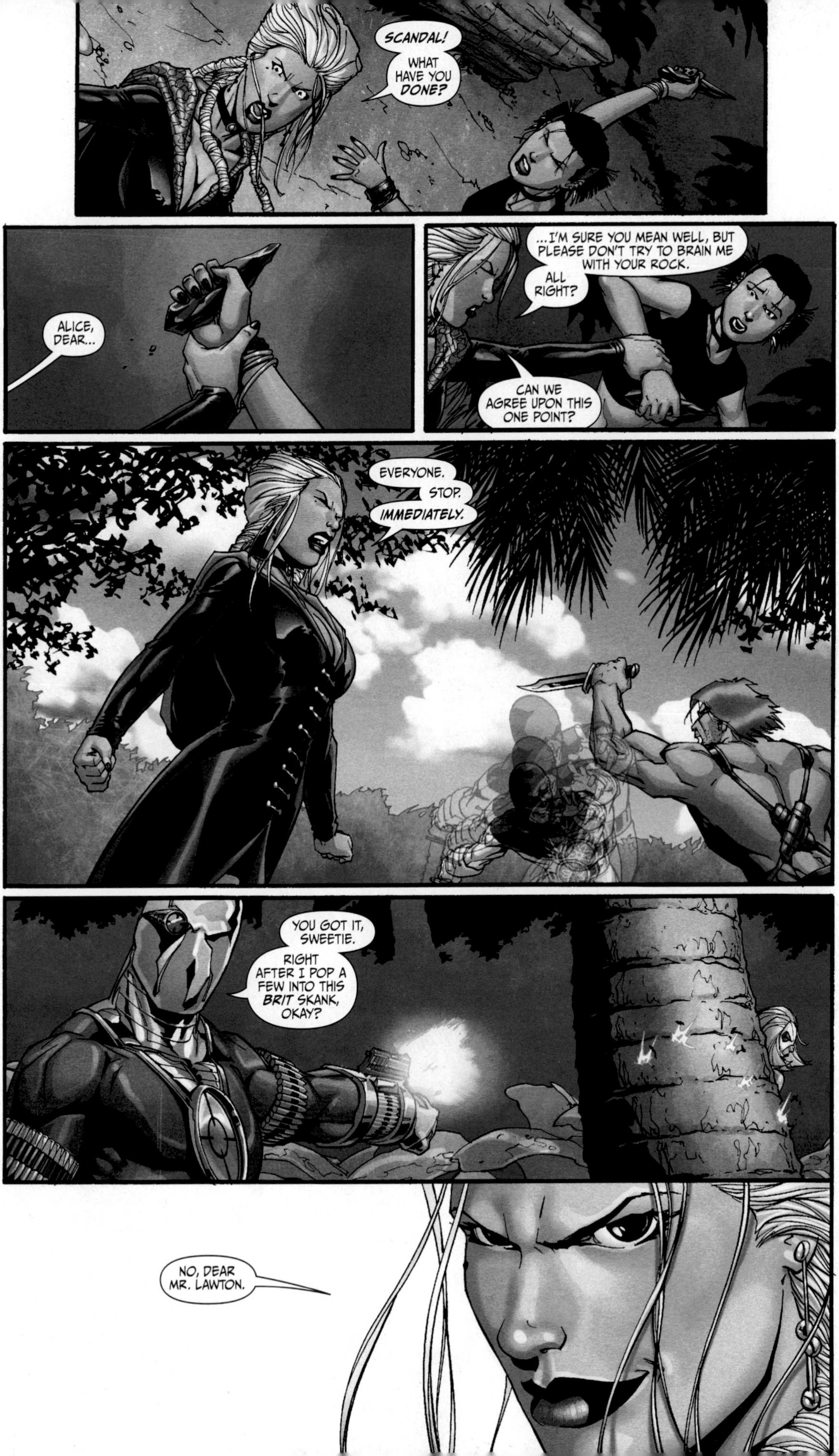

SCANDAL! WHAT HAVE YOU DONE?
ALICE, DEAR...
...I'M SURE YOU MEAN WELL, BUT PLEASE DON'T TRY TO BRAIN ME WITH YOUR ROCK.
ALL RIGHT?
CAN WE AGREE UPON THIS ONE POINT?
EVERYONE. STOP. IMMEDIATELY.
YOU GOT IT, SWEETIE.
RIGHT AFTER I POP A FEW INTO THIS BRIT SKANK, OKAY?
NO, DEAR MR. LAWTON.

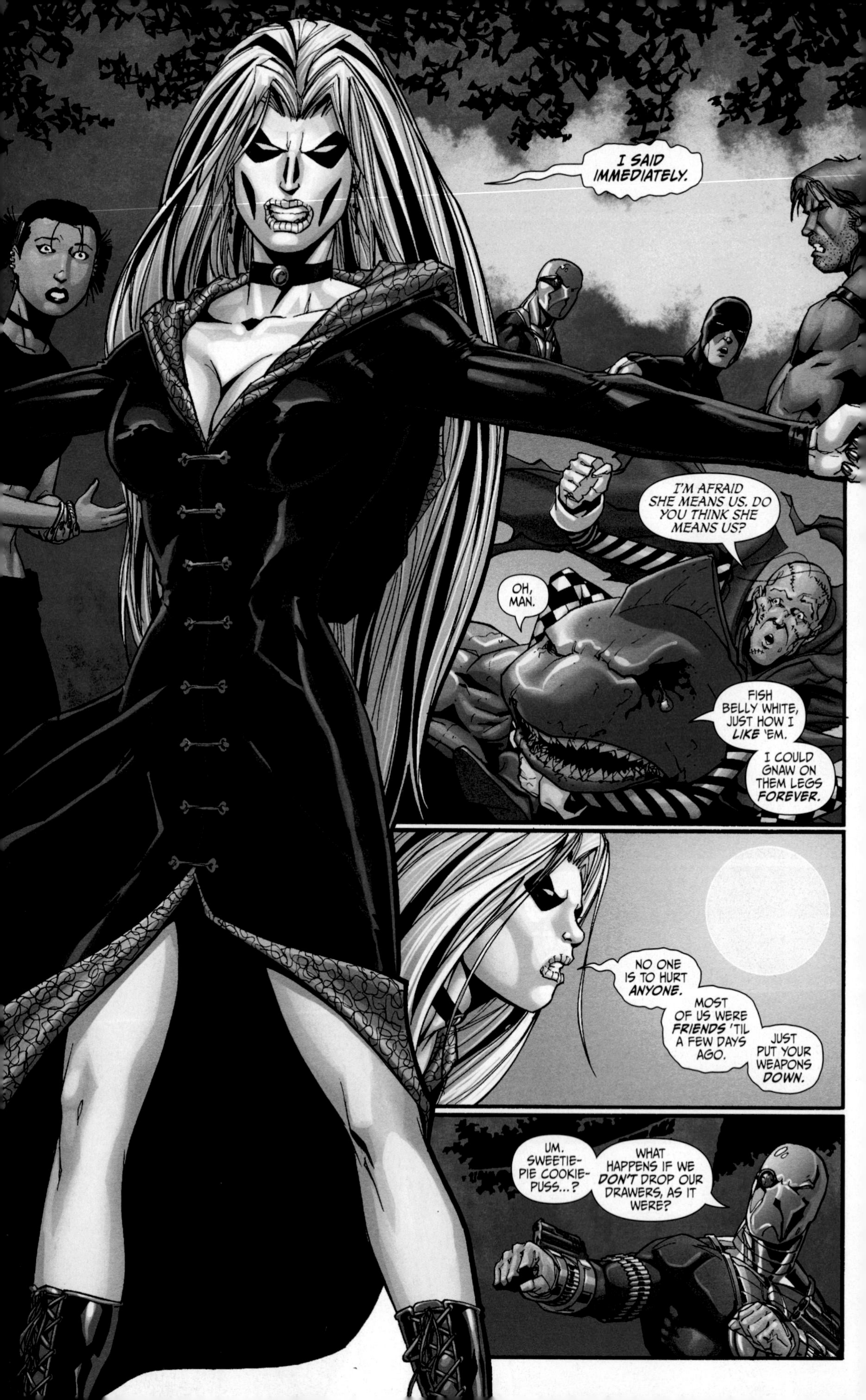
I SAID IMMEDIATELY.
I'M AFRAID SHE MEANS US. DO YOU THINK SHE MEANS US?
OH, MAN.
FISH BELLY WHITE, JUST HOW I LIKE 'EM.
I COULD GNAW ON THEM LEGS FOREVER.
NO ONE IS TO HURT ANYONE.
MOST OF US WERE FRIENDS 'TIL A FEW DAYS AGO.
JUST PUT YOUR WEAPONS DOWN.
UM. SWEETIE-PIE COOKIE-PUSS...?
WHAT HAPPENS IF WE DON'T DROP OUR DRAWERS, AS IT WERE?

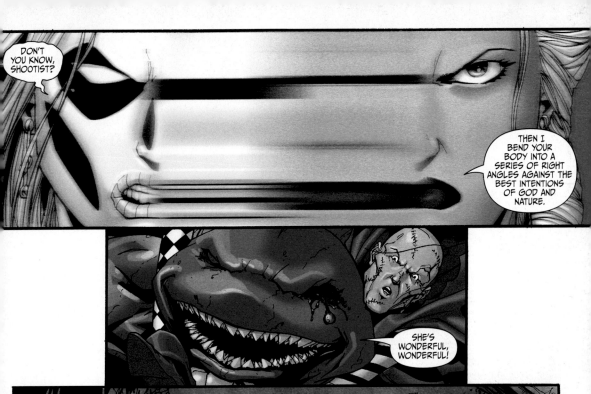

DON'T YOU KNOW, SHOOTIST?

THEN I BEND YOUR BODY INTO A SERIES OF RIGHT ANGLES AGAINST THE BEST INTENTIONS OF GOD AND NATURE.

SHE'S WONDERFUL, WONDERFUL!

SCANDAL SAVAGE, DON'T YOU KNOW THE RULES OF THESE THINGS?

NO ONE IS SUPPOSED TO DIE.

I KNOW! I KNOW!

I...HE SOUNDED SO MUCH LIKE MY REAL FATHER FOR A MOMENT...

I FLASHED BACK TO MY "TRAINING."

MY PARENTS ESSENTIALLY SOLD ME TO A SERIAL KILLER BARONESS AND I THINK I RESENT THEM LESS THAN YOU DO THAT BEARDED CAVEMAN OF YOURS.

GET HELP, JEANNETTE.

IF WE WERE EVER FRIENDS, IF YOU EVER LOVED ME, PLEASE, GET HELP.

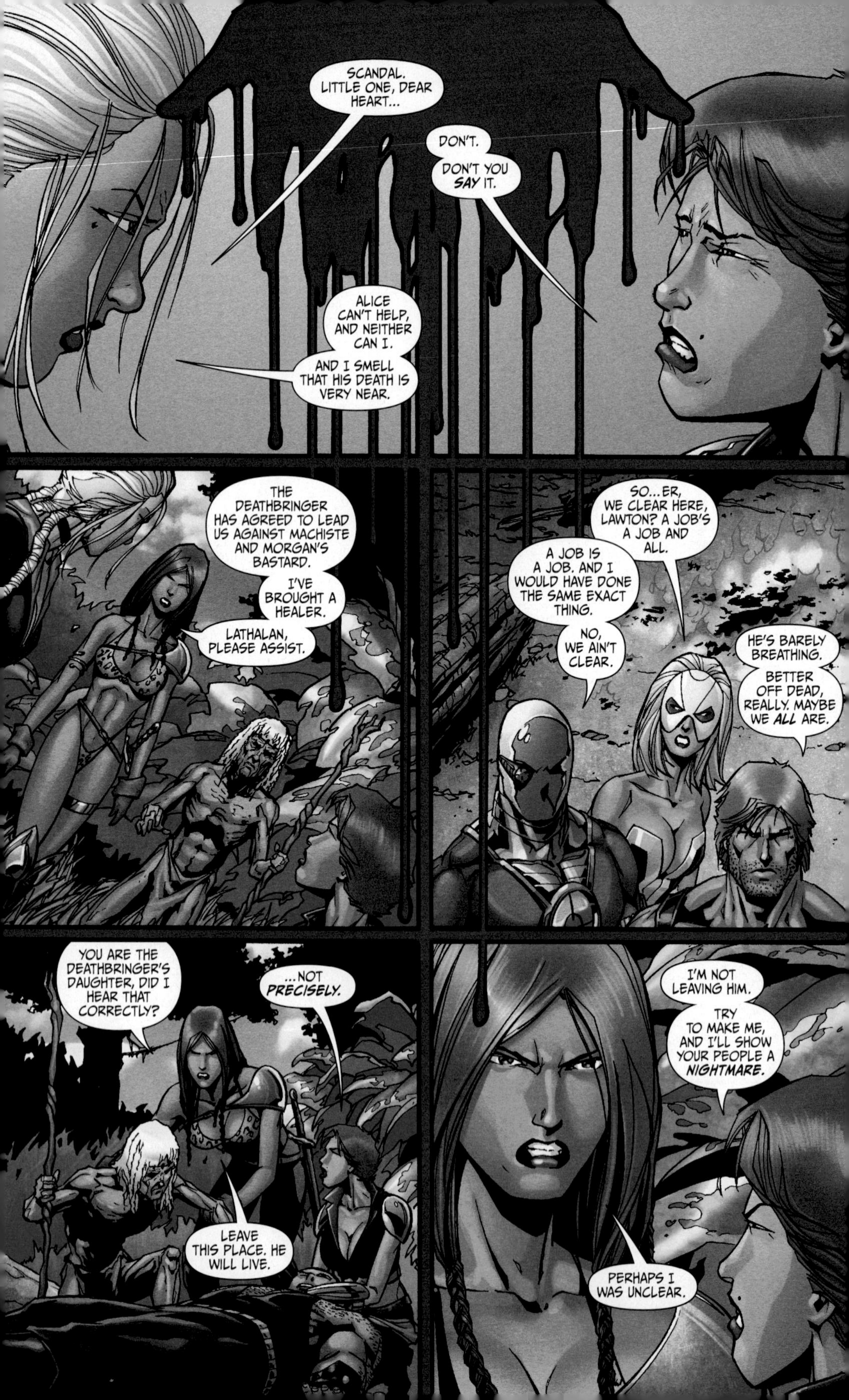
SCANDAL. LITTLE ONE, DEAR HEART...
DON'T.
DON'T YOU SAY IT.
ALICE CAN'T HELP, AND NEITHER CAN I.
AND I SMELL THAT HIS DEATH IS VERY NEAR.
THE DEATHBRINGER HAS AGREED TO LEAD US AGAINST MACHISTE AND MORGAN'S BASTARD.
I'VE BROUGHT A HEALER.
LATHALAN, PLEASE ASSIST.
SO...ER, WE CLEAR HERE, LAWTON? A JOB'S A JOB AND ALL.
A JOB IS A JOB. AND I WOULD HAVE DONE THE SAME EXACT THING.
NO, WE AIN'T CLEAR.
HE'S BARELY BREATHING.
BETTER OFF DEAD, REALLY. MAYBE WE ALL ARE.
YOU ARE THE DEATHBRINGER'S DAUGHTER, DID I HEAR THAT CORRECTLY?
...NOT PRECISELY.
LEAVE THIS PLACE. HE WILL LIVE.
I'M NOT LEAVING HIM.
TRY TO MAKE ME, AND I'LL SHOW YOUR PEOPLE A NIGHTMARE.
PERHAPS I WAS UNCLEAR.

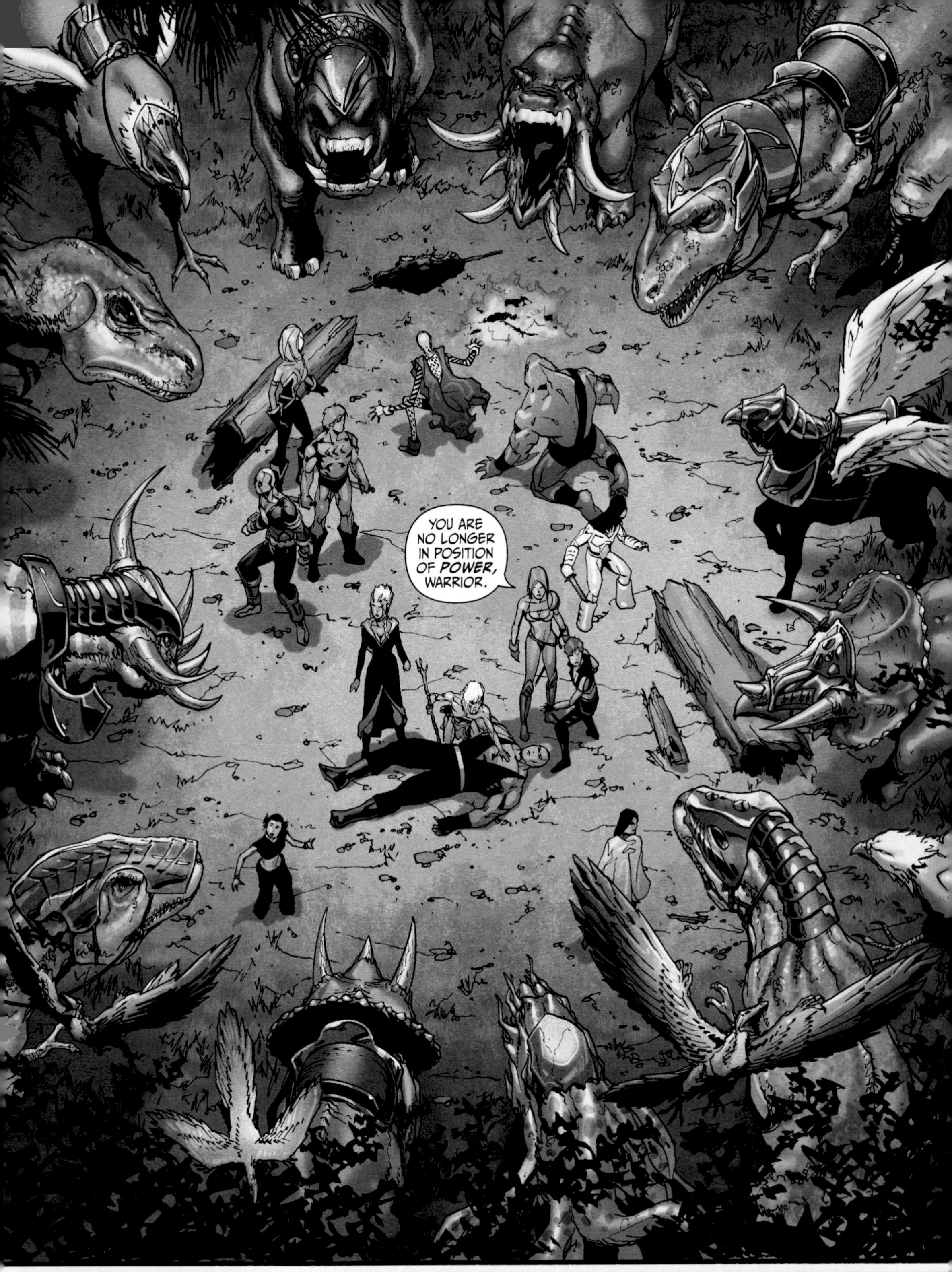
YOU ARE NO LONGER IN POSITION OF POWER, WARRIOR.

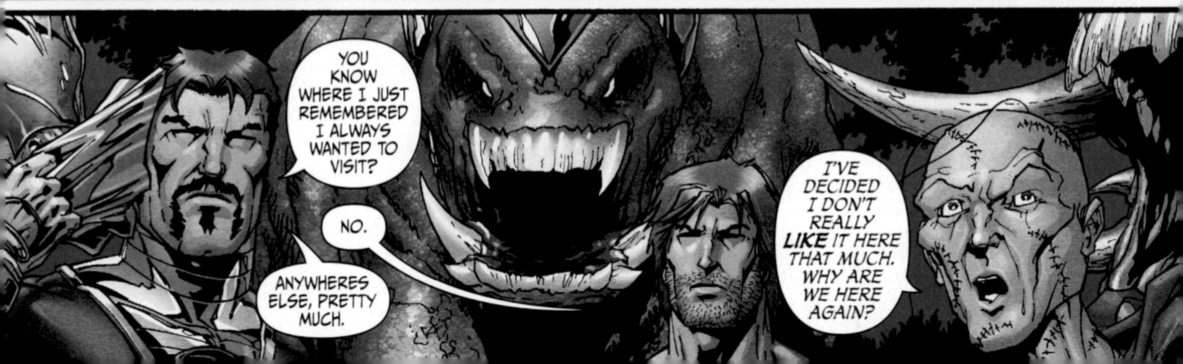
YOU KNOW WHERE I JUST REMEMBERED I ALWAYS WANTED TO VISIT?
NO.
ANYWHERES ELSE, PRETTY MUCH.
I'VE DECIDED I DON'T REALLY LIKE IT HERE THAT MUCH. WHY ARE WE HERE AGAIN?

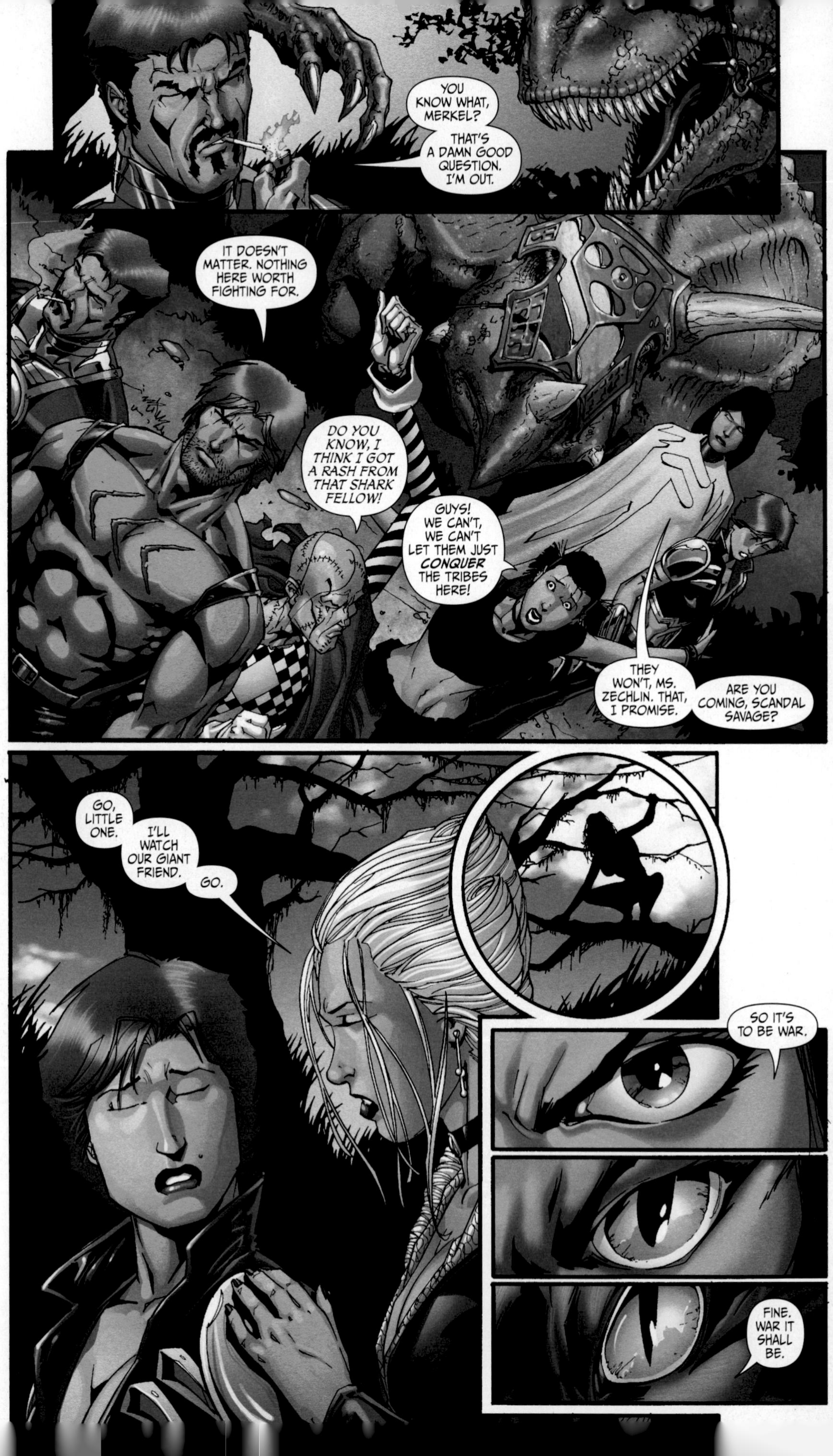
YOU KNOW WHAT, MERKEL?
THAT'S A DAMN GOOD QUESTION. I'M OUT.
IT DOESN'T MATTER. NOTHING HERE WORTH FIGHTING FOR.
DO YOU KNOW, I THINK I GOT A RASH FROM THAT SHARK FELLOW!
GUYS! WE CAN'T, WE CAN'T LET THEM JUST ***CONQUER*** THE TRIBES HERE!
THEY WON'T, MS. ZECHLIN. THAT, I PROMISE.
ARE YOU COMING, SCANDAL SAVAGE?
GO, LITTLE ONE.
I'LL WATCH OUR GIANT FRIEND.
GO.
SO IT'S TO BE WAR.
FINE. WAR IT SHALL BE.

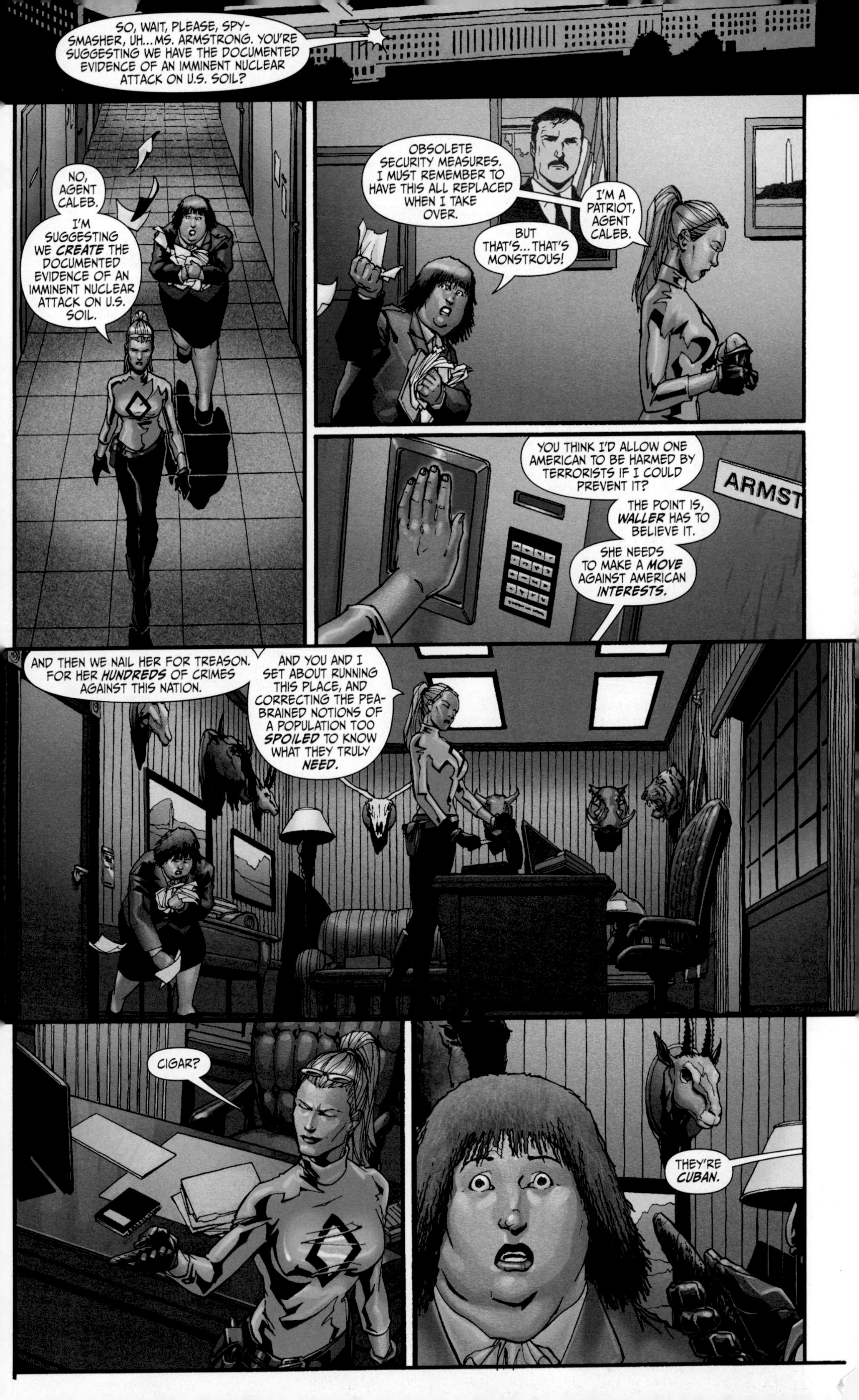
SO, WAIT, PLEASE, SPY-SMASHER, UH...MS. ARMSTRONG. YOU'RE SUGGESTING WE HAVE THE DOCUMENTED EVIDENCE OF AN IMMINENT NUCLEAR ATTACK ON U.S. SOIL?
NO, AGENT CALEB.
I'M SUGGESTING WE CREATE THE DOCUMENTED EVIDENCE OF AN IMMINENT NUCLEAR ATTACK ON U.S. SOIL.
OBSOLETE SECURITY MEASURES. I MUST REMEMBER TO HAVE THIS ALL REPLACED WHEN I TAKE OVER.
BUT THAT'S...THAT'S MONSTROUS!
I'M A PATRIOT, AGENT CALEB.
YOU THINK I'D ALLOW ONE AMERICAN TO BE HARMED BY TERRORISTS IF I COULD PREVENT IT?
ARMST
THE POINT IS, WALLER HAS TO BELIEVE IT.
SHE NEEDS TO MAKE A MOVE AGAINST AMERICAN INTERESTS.
AND THEN WE NAIL HER FOR TREASON. FOR HER HUNDREDS OF CRIMES AGAINST THIS NATION.
AND YOU AND I SET ABOUT RUNNING THIS PLACE, AND CORRECTING THE PEA-BRAINED NOTIONS OF A POPULATION TOO SPOILED TO KNOW WHAT THEY TRULY NEED.
CIGAR?
THEY'RE CUBAN.

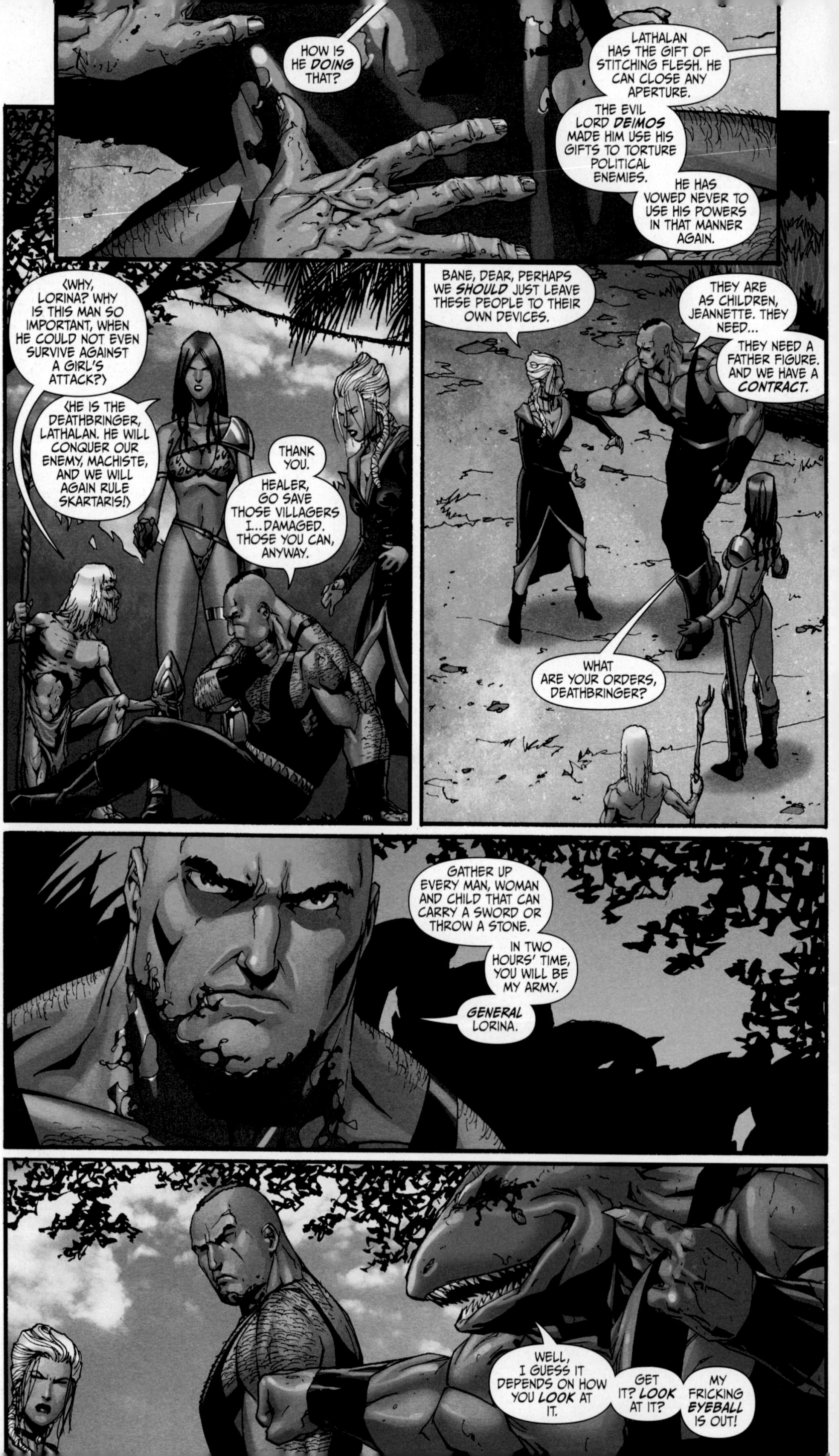
HOW IS HE *DOING* THAT?
LATHALAN HAS THE GIFT OF STITCHING FLESH. HE CAN CLOSE ANY APERTURE.
THE EVIL LORD *DEIMOS* MADE HIM USE HIS GIFTS TO TORTURE POLITICAL ENEMIES.
HE HAS VOWED NEVER TO USE HIS POWERS IN THAT MANNER AGAIN.
‹WHY, LORINA? WHY IS THIS MAN SO IMPORTANT, WHEN HE COULD NOT EVEN SURVIVE AGAINST A GIRL'S ATTACK?›
‹HE IS THE DEATHBRINGER, LATHALAN. HE WILL CONQUER OUR ENEMY, MACHISTE, AND WE WILL AGAIN RULE SKARTARIS!›
THANK YOU.
HEALER, GO SAVE THOSE VILLAGERS I...DAMAGED. THOSE YOU CAN, ANYWAY.
BANE, DEAR, PERHAPS WE *SHOULD* JUST LEAVE THESE PEOPLE TO THEIR OWN DEVICES.
THEY ARE AS CHILDREN, JEANNETTE. THEY NEED...
THEY NEED A FATHER FIGURE. AND WE HAVE A *CONTRACT.*
WHAT ARE YOUR ORDERS, DEATHBRINGER?
GATHER UP EVERY MAN, WOMAN AND CHILD THAT CAN CARRY A SWORD OR THROW A STONE.
IN TWO HOURS' TIME, YOU WILL BE MY ARMY.
GENERAL LORINA.
WELL, I GUESS IT DEPENDS ON HOW YOU *LOOK* AT IT.
GET IT? *LOOK* AT IT?
MY FRICKING *EYEBALL* IS OUT!

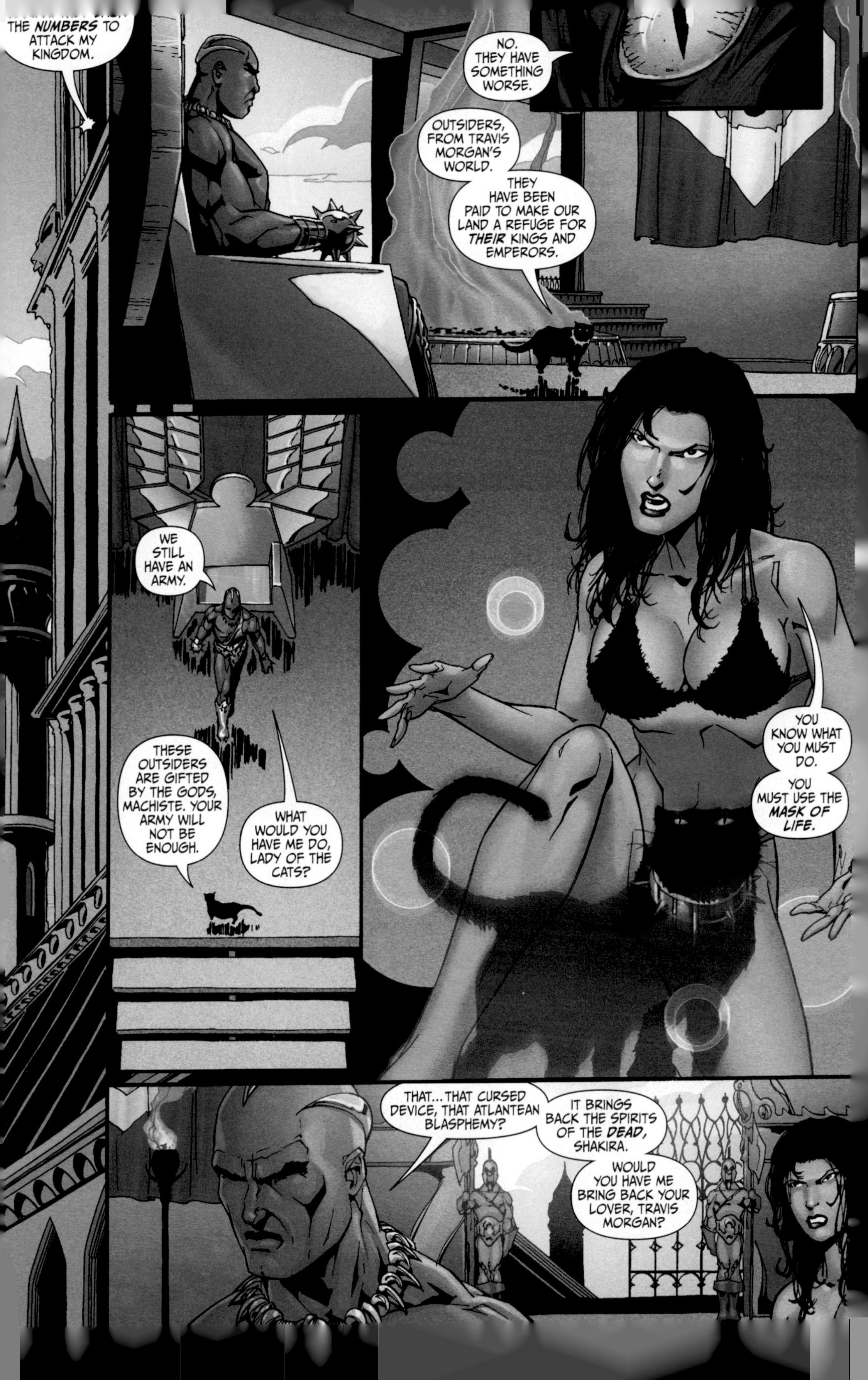
THE NUMBERS TO ATTACK MY KINGDOM.
NO. THEY HAVE SOMETHING WORSE.
OUTSIDERS, FROM TRAVIS MORGAN'S WORLD.
THEY HAVE BEEN PAID TO MAKE OUR LAND A REFUGE FOR THEIR KINGS AND EMPERORS.
WE STILL HAVE AN ARMY.
THESE OUTSIDERS ARE GIFTED BY THE GODS, MACHISTE. YOUR ARMY WILL NOT BE ENOUGH.
WHAT WOULD YOU HAVE ME DO, LADY OF THE CATS?
YOU KNOW WHAT YOU MUST DO.
YOU MUST USE THE MASK OF LIFE.
THAT... THAT CURSED DEVICE, THAT ATLANTEAN BLASPHEMY?
IT BRINGS BACK THE SPIRITS OF THE DEAD, SHAKIRA.
WOULD YOU HAVE ME BRING BACK YOUR LOVER, TRAVIS MORGAN?

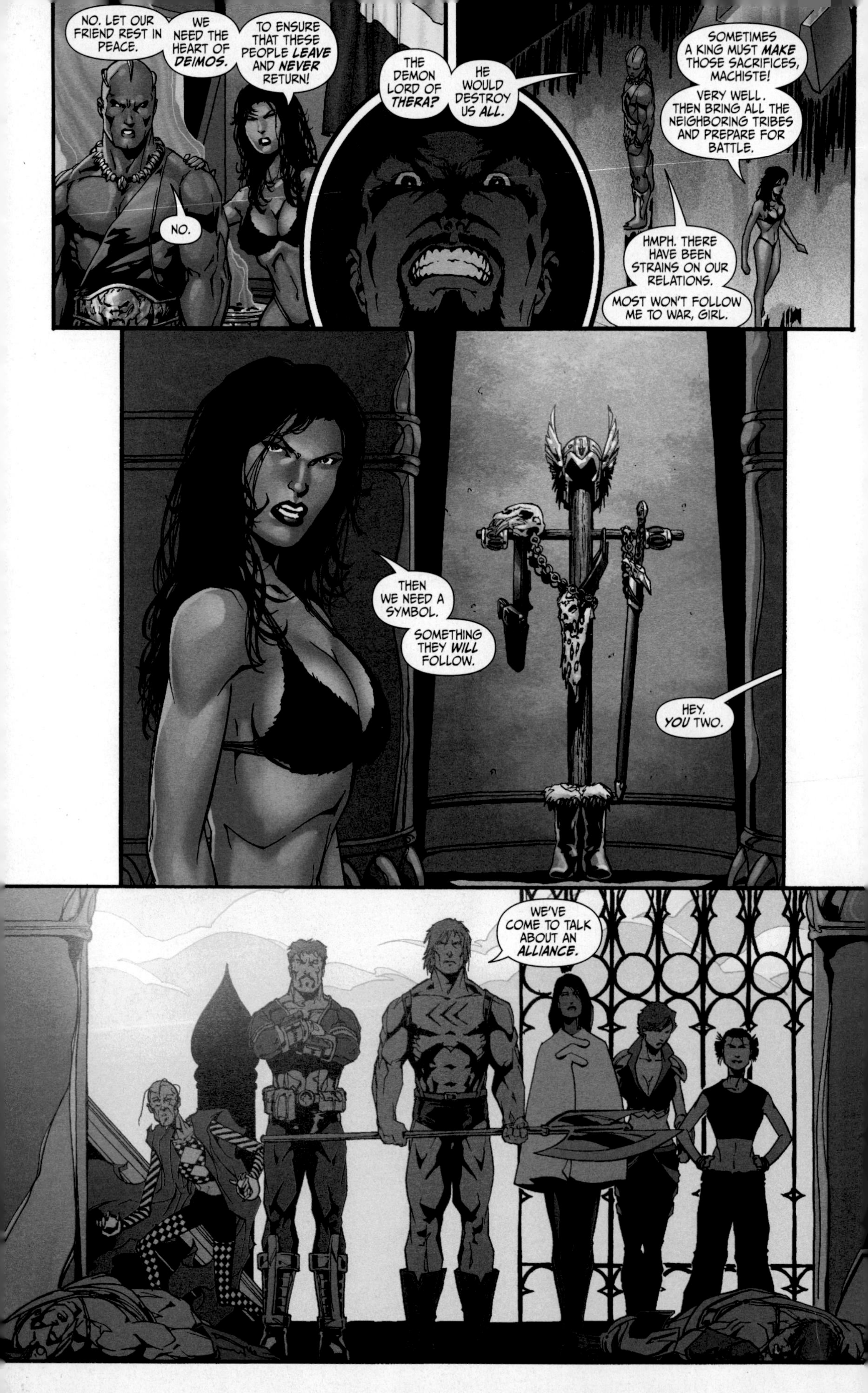
NO. LET OUR FRIEND REST IN PEACE.
WE NEED THE HEART OF DEIMOS.
TO ENSURE THAT THESE PEOPLE LEAVE AND NEVER RETURN!
NO.
THE DEMON LORD OF THERA?
HE WOULD DESTROY US ALL.
SOMETIMES A KING MUST MAKE THOSE SACRIFICES, MACHISTE!
VERY WELL. THEN BRING ALL THE NEIGHBORING TRIBES AND PREPARE FOR BATTLE.
HMPH. THERE HAVE BEEN STRAINS ON OUR RELATIONS.
MOST WON'T FOLLOW ME TO WAR, GIRL.
THEN WE NEED A SYMBOL.
SOMETHING THEY WILL FOLLOW.
HEY. YOU TWO.
WE'VE COME TO TALK ABOUT AN ALLIANCE.

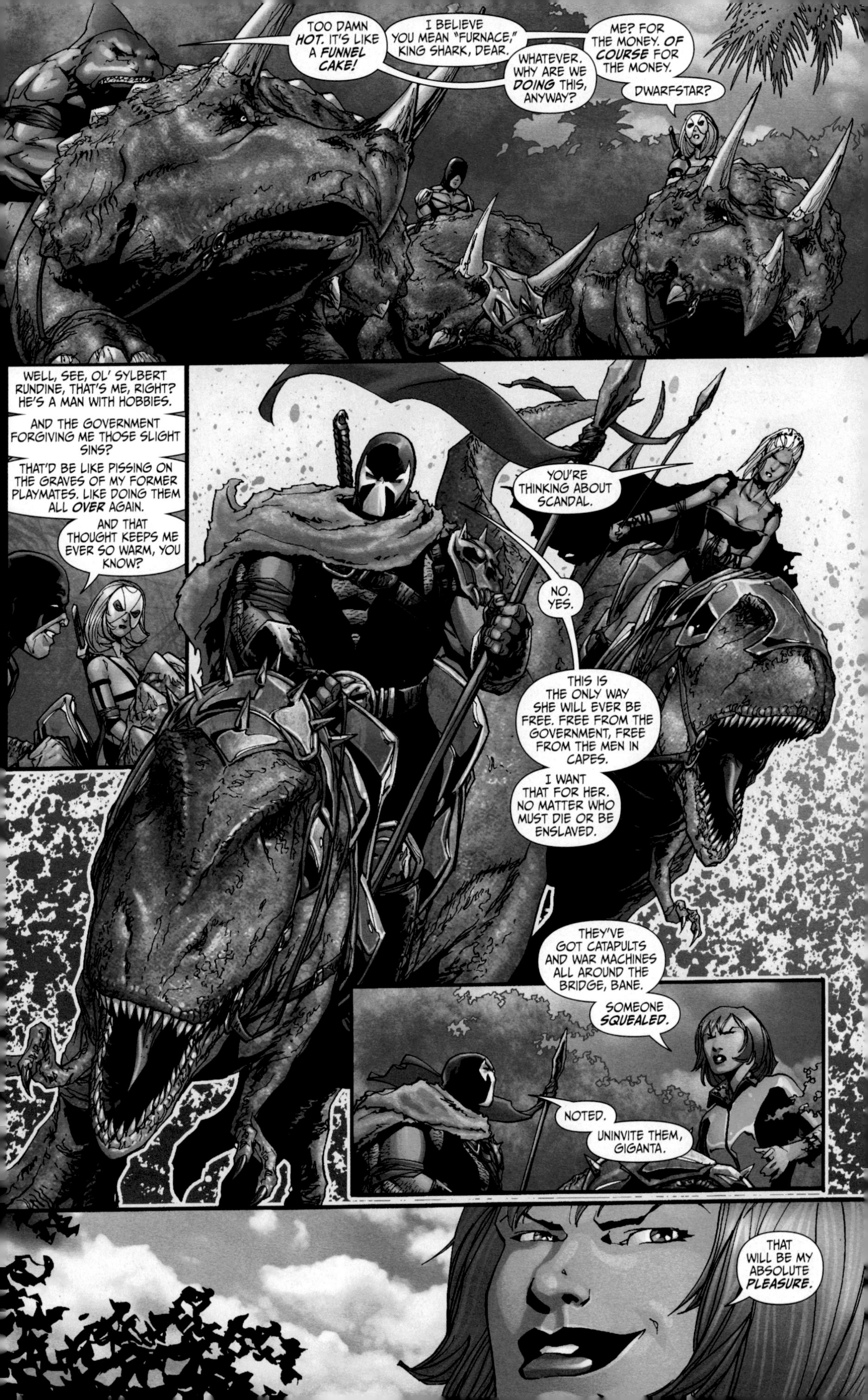
TOO DAMN HOT. IT'S LIKE A FUNNEL CAKE!
I BELIEVE YOU MEAN "FURNACE," KING SHARK, DEAR.
WHATEVER. WHY ARE WE DOING THIS, ANYWAY?
ME? FOR THE MONEY. OF COURSE FOR THE MONEY.
DWARFSTAR?
WELL, SEE, OL' SYLBERT RUNDINE, THAT'S ME, RIGHT? HE'S A MAN WITH HOBBIES.
AND THE GOVERNMENT FORGIVING ME THOSE SLIGHT SINS?
THAT'D BE LIKE PISSING ON THE GRAVES OF MY FORMER PLAYMATES. LIKE DOING THEM ALL OVER AGAIN.
AND THAT THOUGHT KEEPS ME EVER SO WARM, YOU KNOW?
YOU'RE THINKING ABOUT SCANDAL.
NO. YES.
THIS IS THE ONLY WAY SHE WILL EVER BE FREE. FREE FROM THE GOVERNMENT, FREE FROM THE MEN IN CAPES.
I WANT THAT FOR HER. NO MATTER WHO MUST DIE OR BE ENSLAVED.
THEY'VE GOT CATAPULTS AND WAR MACHINES ALL AROUND THE BRIDGE, BANE.
SOMEONE SQUEALED.
NOTED.
UNINVITE THEM, GIGANTA.
THAT WILL BE MY ABSOLUTE PLEASURE.

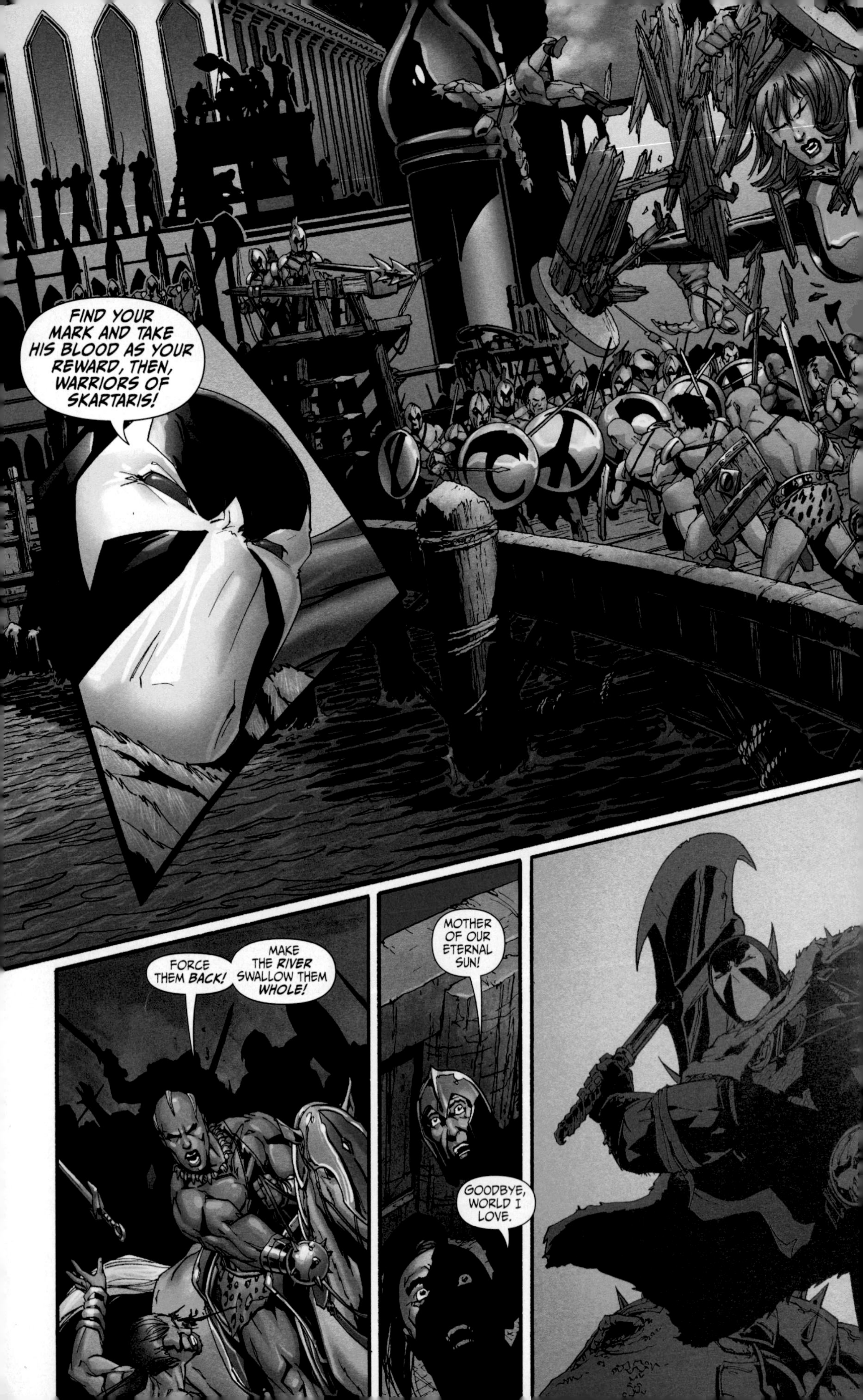
FIND YOUR MARK AND TAKE HIS BLOOD AS YOUR REWARD, THEN, WARRIORS OF SKARTARIS!
FORCE THEM BACK!
MAKE THE RIVER SWALLOW THEM WHOLE!
MOTHER OF OUR ETERNAL SUN!
GOODBYE, WORLD I LOVE.

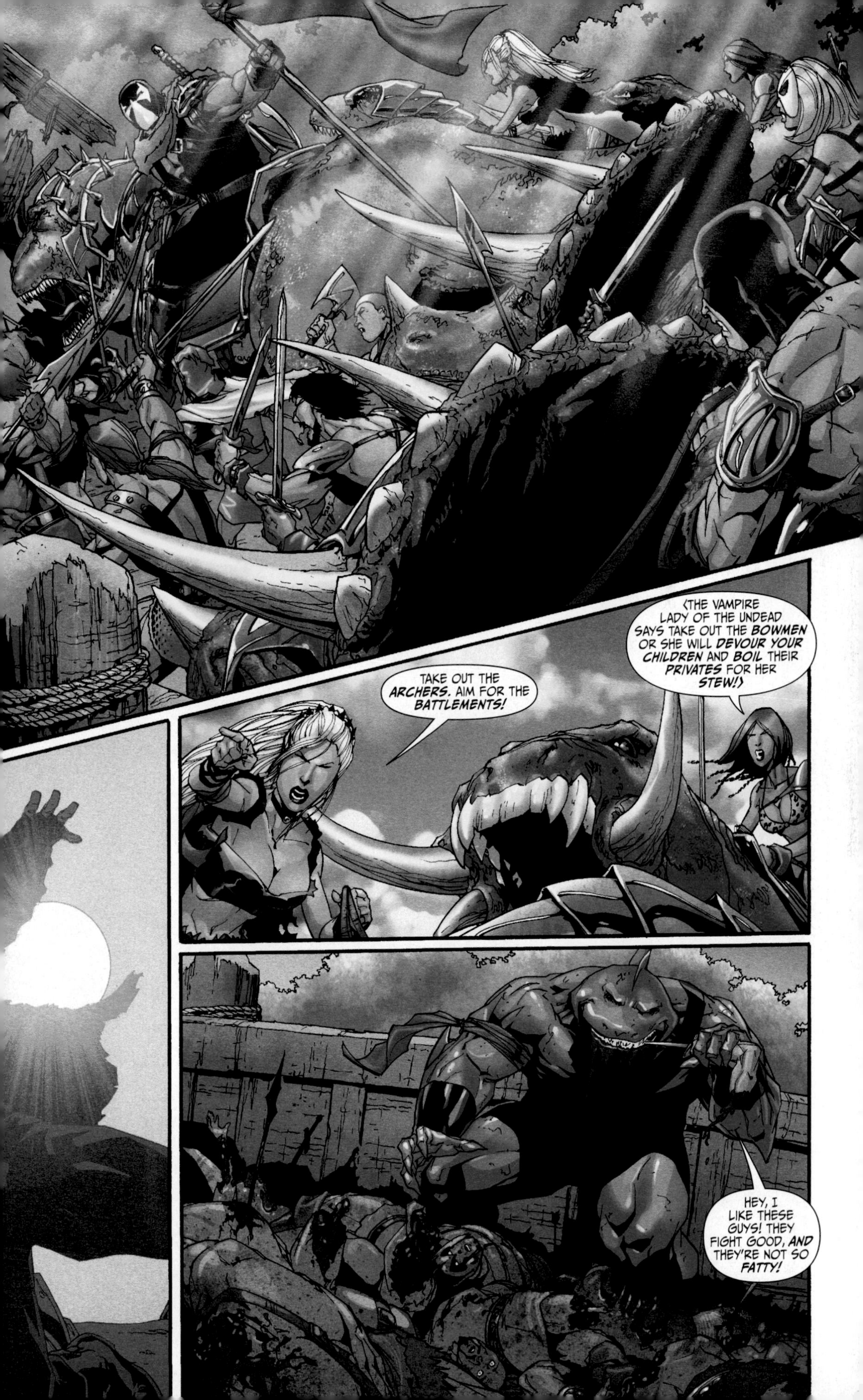
TAKE OUT THE ARCHERS. AIM FOR THE BATTLEMENTS!
<THE VAMPIRE LADY OF THE UNDEAD SAYS TAKE OUT THE BOWMEN OR SHE WILL DEVOUR YOUR CHILDREN AND BOIL THEIR PRIVATES FOR HER STEW!>
HEY, I LIKE THESE GUYS! THEY FIGHT GOOD, AND THEY'RE NOT SO FATTY!

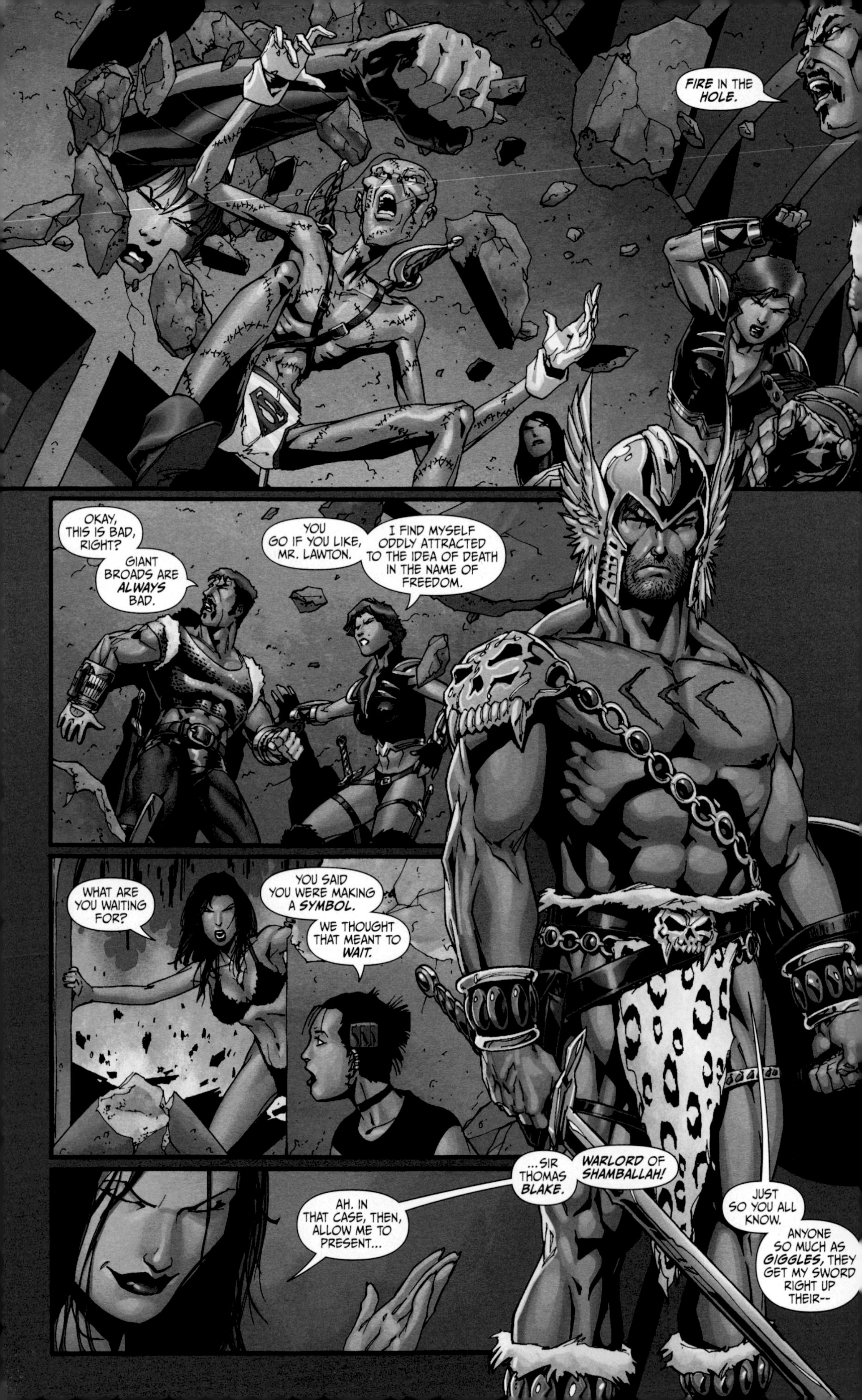
FIRE IN THE HOLE.
OKAY, THIS IS BAD, RIGHT?
GIANT BROADS ARE ALWAYS BAD.
YOU GO IF YOU LIKE, MR. LAWTON.
I FIND MYSELF ODDLY ATTRACTED TO THE IDEA OF DEATH IN THE NAME OF FREEDOM.
WHAT ARE YOU WAITING FOR?
YOU SAID YOU WERE MAKING A SYMBOL.
WE THOUGHT THAT MEANT TO WAIT.
AH. IN THAT CASE, THEN, ALLOW ME TO PRESENT...
...SIR THOMAS BLAKE.
WARLORD OF SHAMBALLAH!
JUST SO YOU ALL KNOW.
ANYONE SO MUCH AS GIGGLES, THEY GET MY SWORD RIGHT UP THEIR--

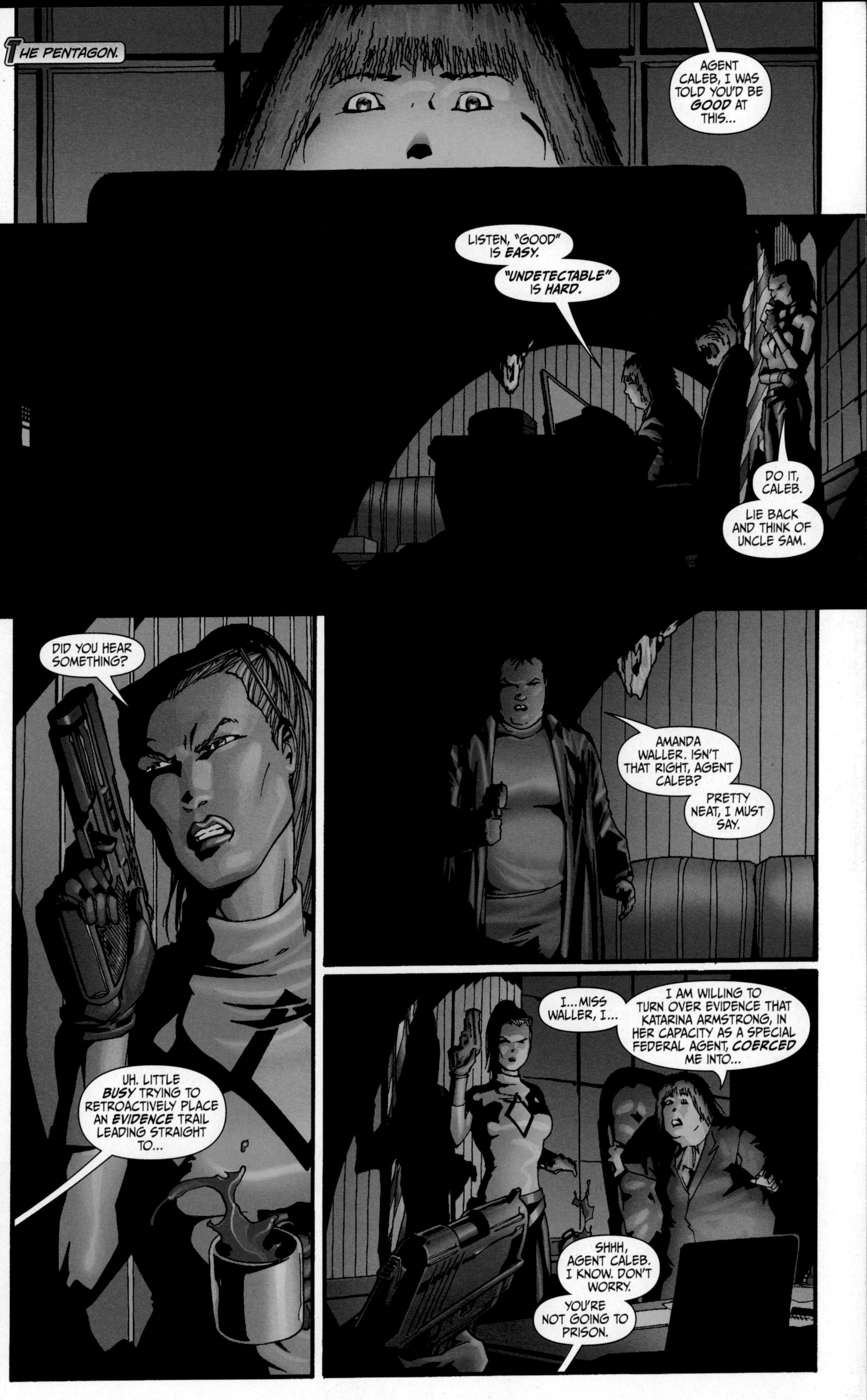
THE PENTAGON.
AGENT CALEB, I WAS TOLD YOU'D BE GOOD AT THIS...
LISTEN, "GOOD" IS EASY.
"UNDETECTABLE" IS HARD.
DO IT, CALEB.
LIE BACK AND THINK OF UNCLE SAM.
DID YOU HEAR SOMETHING?
UH. LITTLE BUSY TRYING TO RETROACTIVELY PLACE AN EVIDENCE TRAIL LEADING STRAIGHT TO...
AMANDA WALLER. ISN'T THAT RIGHT, AGENT CALEB?
PRETTY NEAT, I MUST SAY.
I...MISS WALLER, I...
I AM WILLING TO TURN OVER EVIDENCE THAT KATARINA ARMSTRONG, IN HER CAPACITY AS A SPECIAL FEDERAL AGENT, COERCED ME INTO...
SHHH, AGENT CALEB. I KNOW. DON'T WORRY.
YOU'RE NOT GOING TO PRISON.

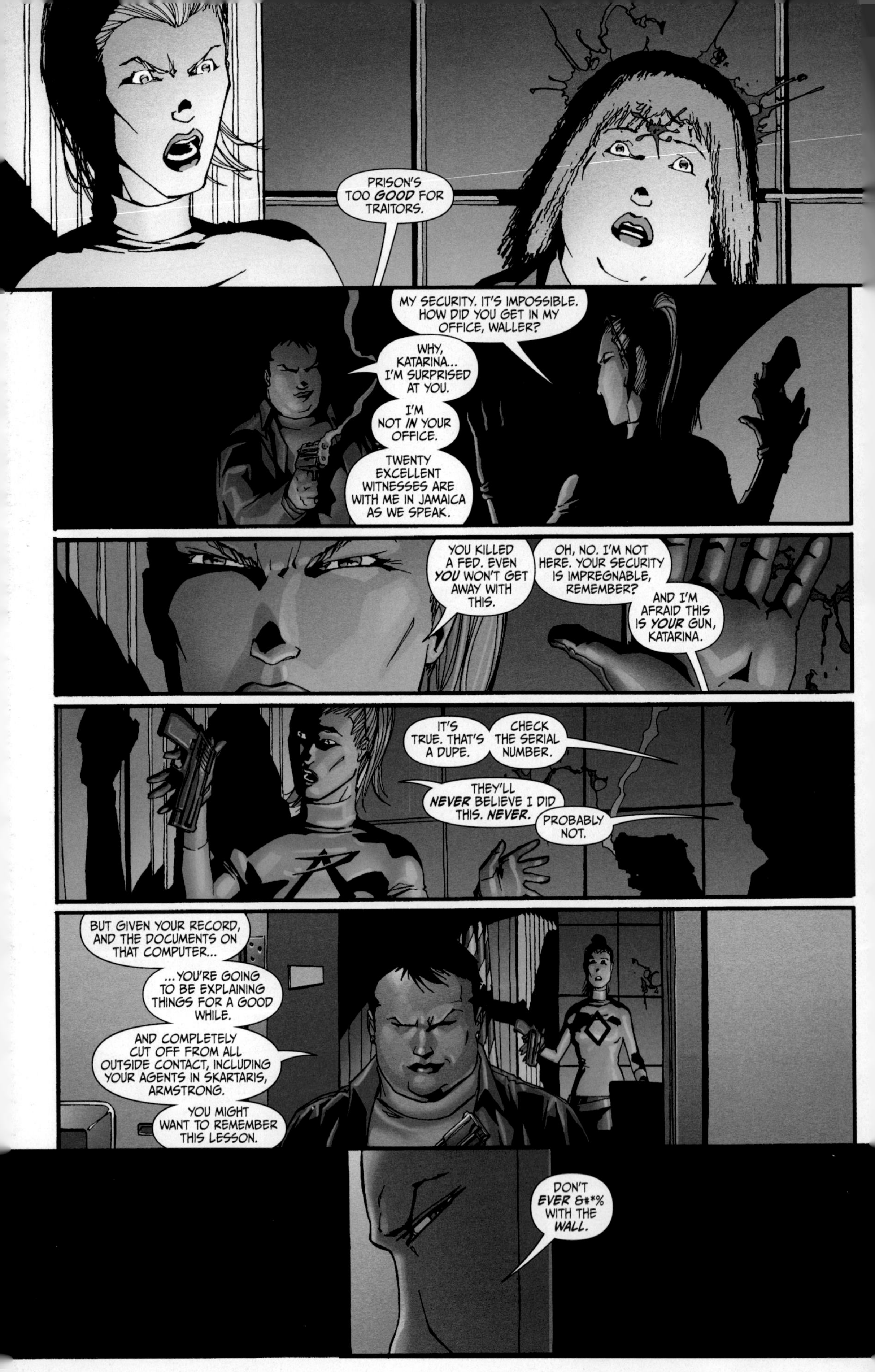
PRISON'S TOO GOOD FOR TRAITORS.
MY SECURITY. IT'S IMPOSSIBLE. HOW DID YOU GET IN MY OFFICE, WALLER?
WHY, KATARINA... I'M SURPRISED AT YOU.
I'M NOT IN YOUR OFFICE.
TWENTY EXCELLENT WITNESSES ARE WITH ME IN JAMAICA AS WE SPEAK.
YOU KILLED A FED. EVEN YOU WON'T GET AWAY WITH THIS.
OH, NO. I'M NOT HERE. YOUR SECURITY IS IMPREGNABLE, REMEMBER?
AND I'M AFRAID THIS IS YOUR GUN, KATARINA.
IT'S TRUE. THAT'S A DUPE.
CHECK THE SERIAL NUMBER.
THEY'LL NEVER BELIEVE I DID THIS. NEVER.
PROBABLY NOT.
BUT GIVEN YOUR RECORD, AND THE DOCUMENTS ON THAT COMPUTER...
...YOU'RE GOING TO BE EXPLAINING THINGS FOR A GOOD WHILE.
AND COMPLETELY CUT OFF FROM ALL OUTSIDE CONTACT, INCLUDING YOUR AGENTS IN SKARTARIS, ARMSTRONG.
YOU MIGHT WANT TO REMEMBER THIS LESSON.
DON'T EVER &#*% WITH THE WALL.

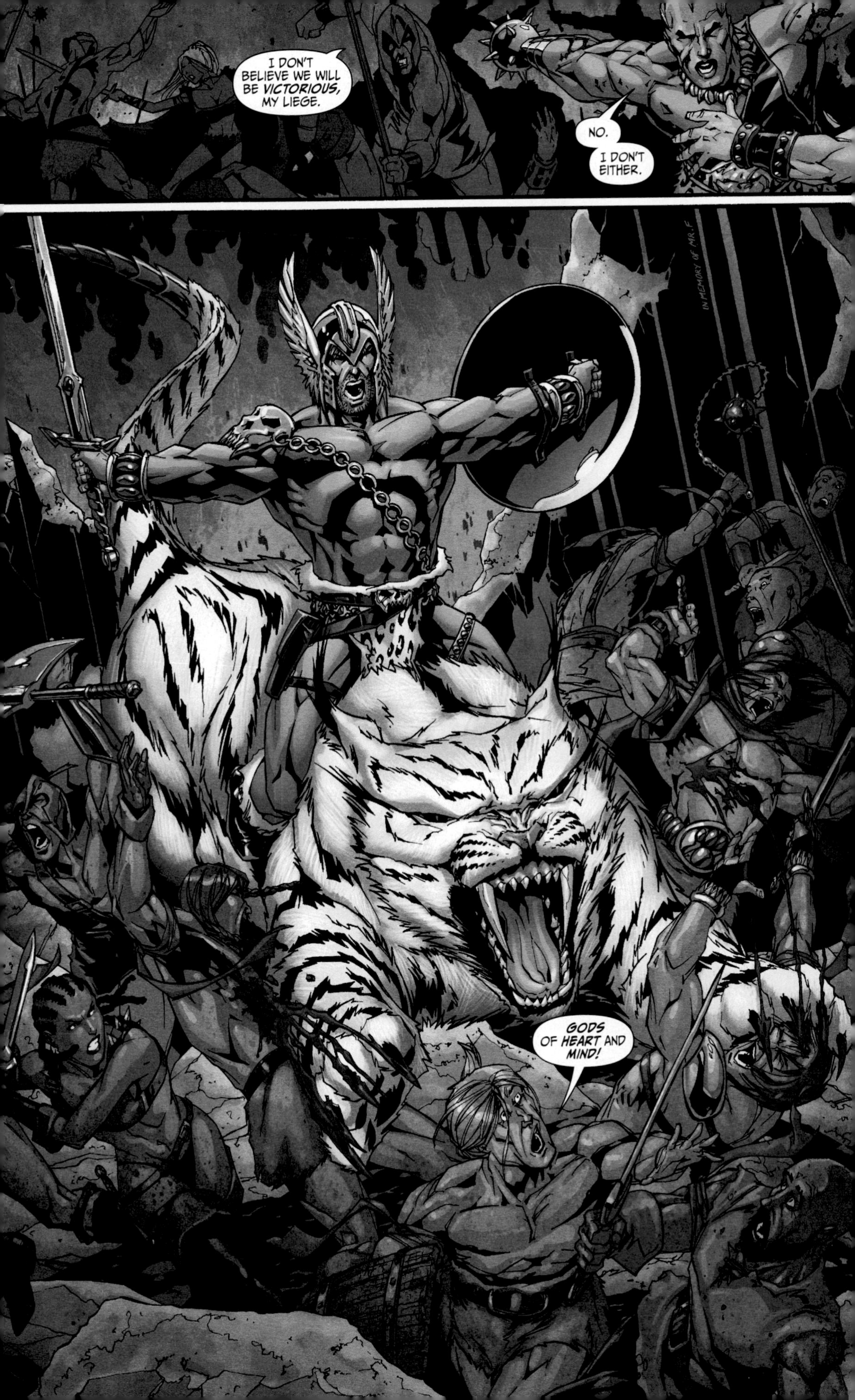
I DON'T BELIEVE WE WILL BE VICTORIOUS, MY LIEGE.
NO.
I DON'T EITHER.
IN MEMORY OF MR. F
GODS OF HEART AND MIND!

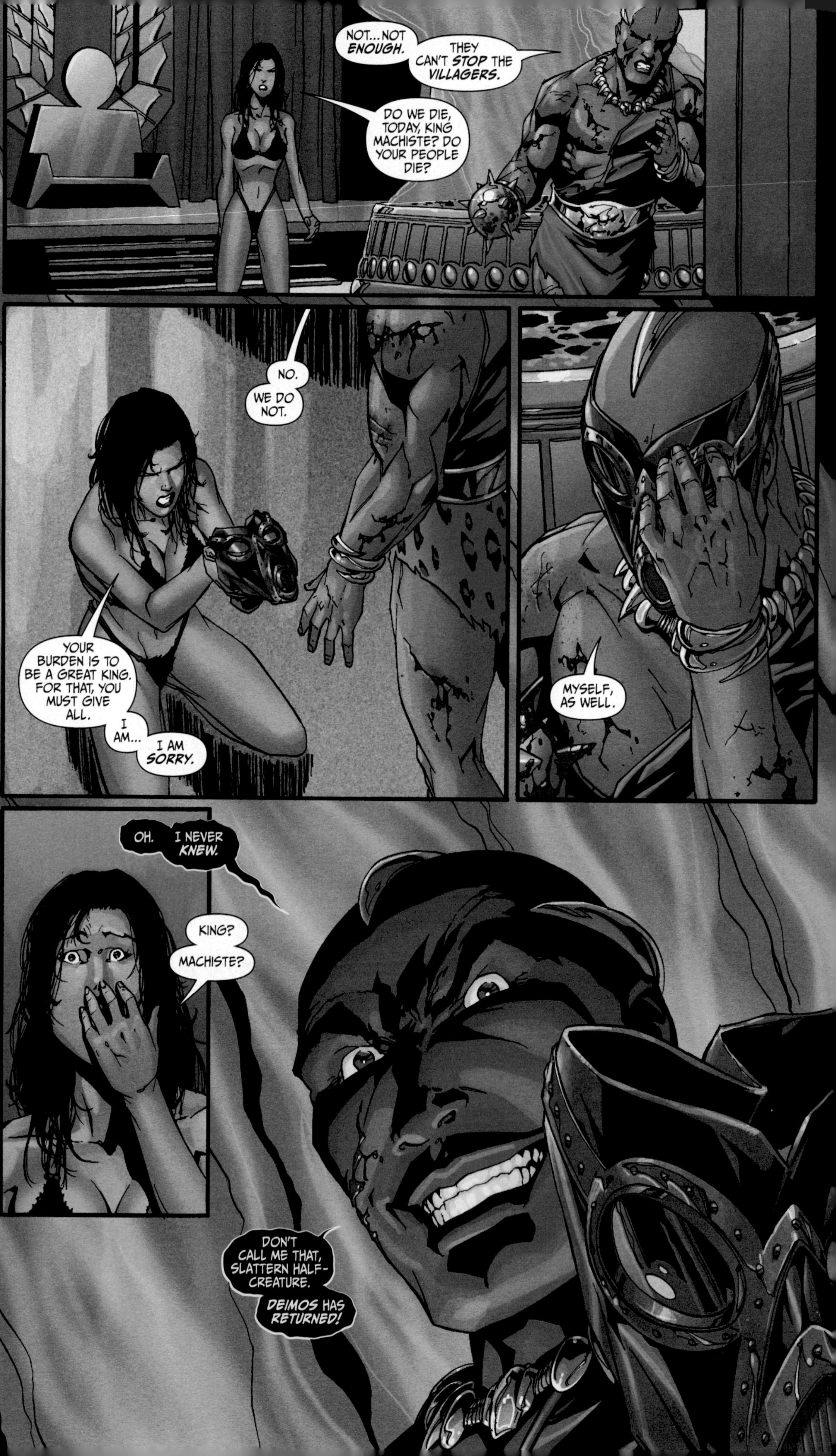
NOT...NOT ENOUGH.
THEY CAN'T STOP THE VILLAGERS.
DO WE DIE, TODAY, KING MACHISTE? DO YOUR PEOPLE DIE?
NO. WE DO NOT.
YOUR BURDEN IS TO BE A GREAT KING. FOR THAT, YOU MUST GIVE ALL.
I AM...
I AM SORRY.
MYSELF, AS WELL.
OH.
I NEVER KNEW.
KING?
MACHISTE?
DON'T CALL ME THAT, SLATTERN HALF-CREATURE.
DEIMOS HAS RETURNED!

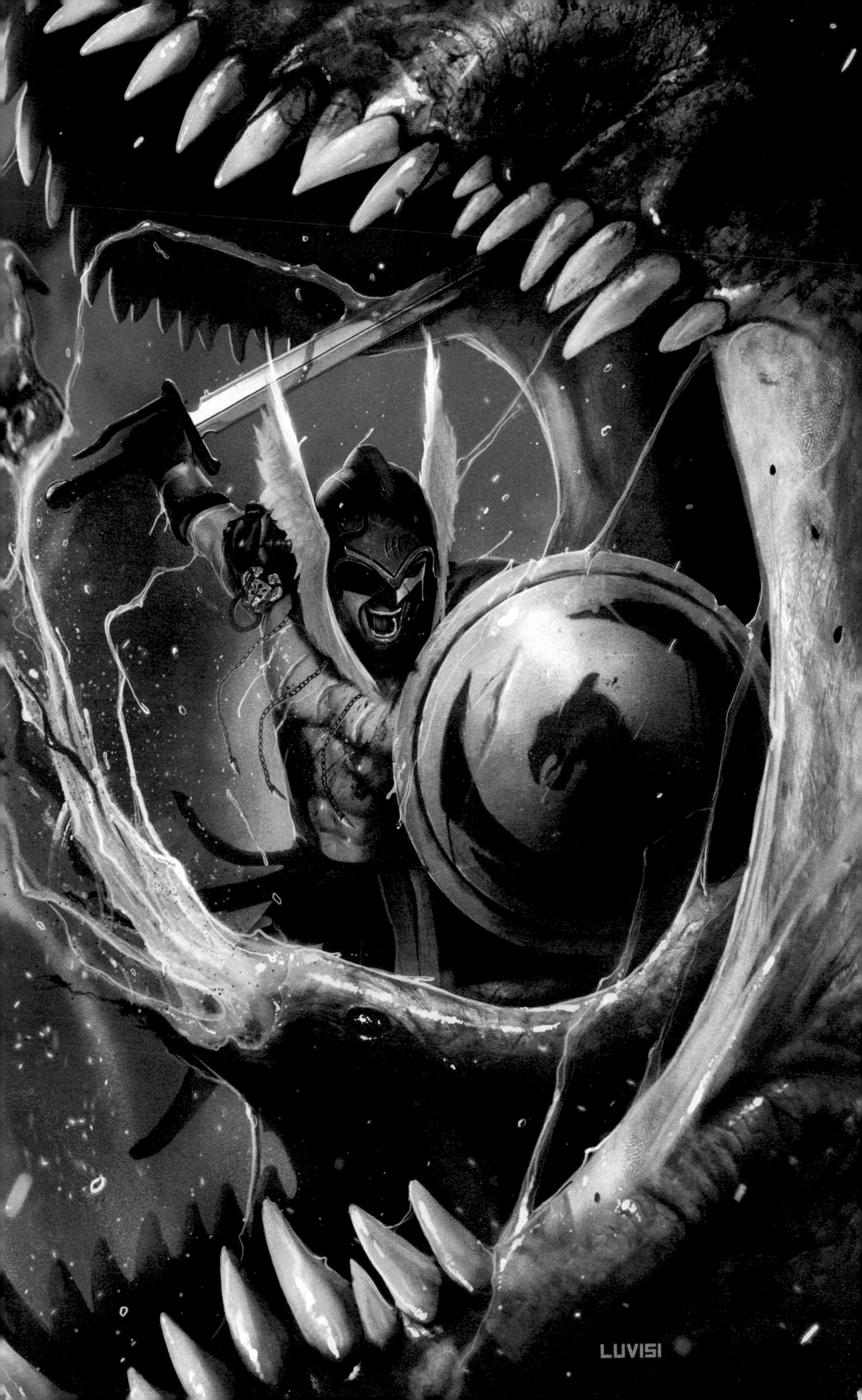
LUVISI

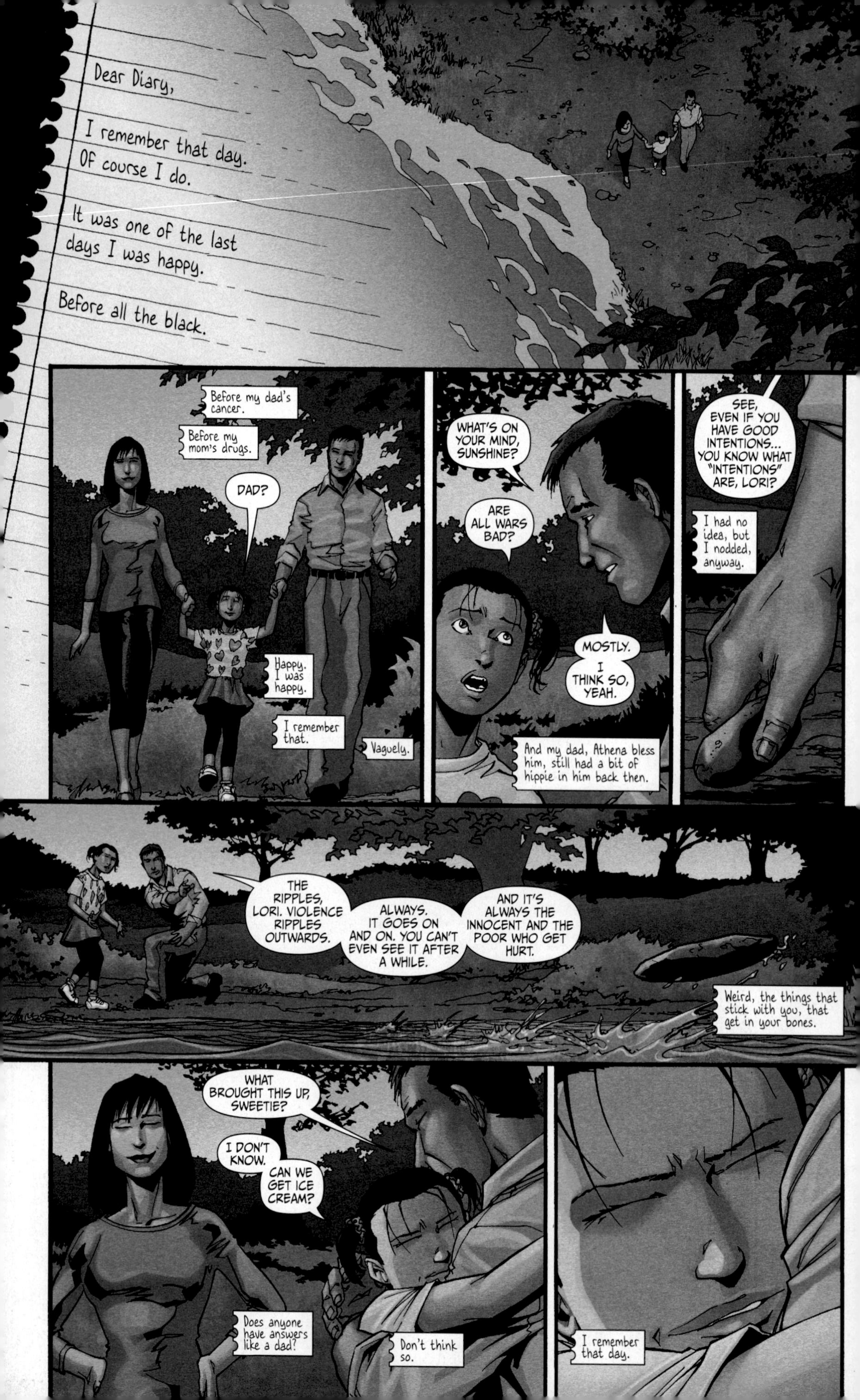
Dear Diary,
I remember that day. Of course I do.
It was one of the last days I was happy.
Before all the black.
Before my dad's cancer.
Before my mom's drugs.
DAD?
Happy. I was happy.
I remember that.
Vaguely.
WHAT'S ON YOUR MIND, SUNSHINE?
ARE ALL WARS BAD?
MOSTLY. I THINK SO, YEAH.
And my dad, Athena bless him, still had a bit of hippie in him back then.
SEE, EVEN IF YOU HAVE GOOD INTENTIONS... YOU KNOW WHAT "INTENTIONS" ARE, LORI?
I had no idea, but I nodded, anyway.
THE RIPPLES, LORI. VIOLENCE RIPPLES OUTWARDS.
ALWAYS. IT GOES ON AND ON. YOU CAN'T EVEN SEE IT AFTER A WHILE.
AND IT'S ALWAYS THE INNOCENT AND THE POOR WHO GET HURT.
Weird, the things that stick with you, that get in your bones.
WHAT BROUGHT THIS UP, SWEETIE?
I DON'T KNOW.
CAN WE GET ICE CREAM?
Does anyone have answers like a dad?
Don't think so.
I remember that day.

THE REPTILE BRAIN
PART FOUR OF FOUR
THE SKULL JUST BENEATH THE FLESH
The last time I was HAPPY.
GAIL SIMONE writer
JIM CALAFIORE artist
JASON WRIGHT colorist TRAVIS LANHAM letterer
DANIEL LUVISI cover artist SEAN RYAN editor
And a huge THANK YOU to the legendary MIKE GRELL, creator of Skartaris, for his generous support, help and encouragement!

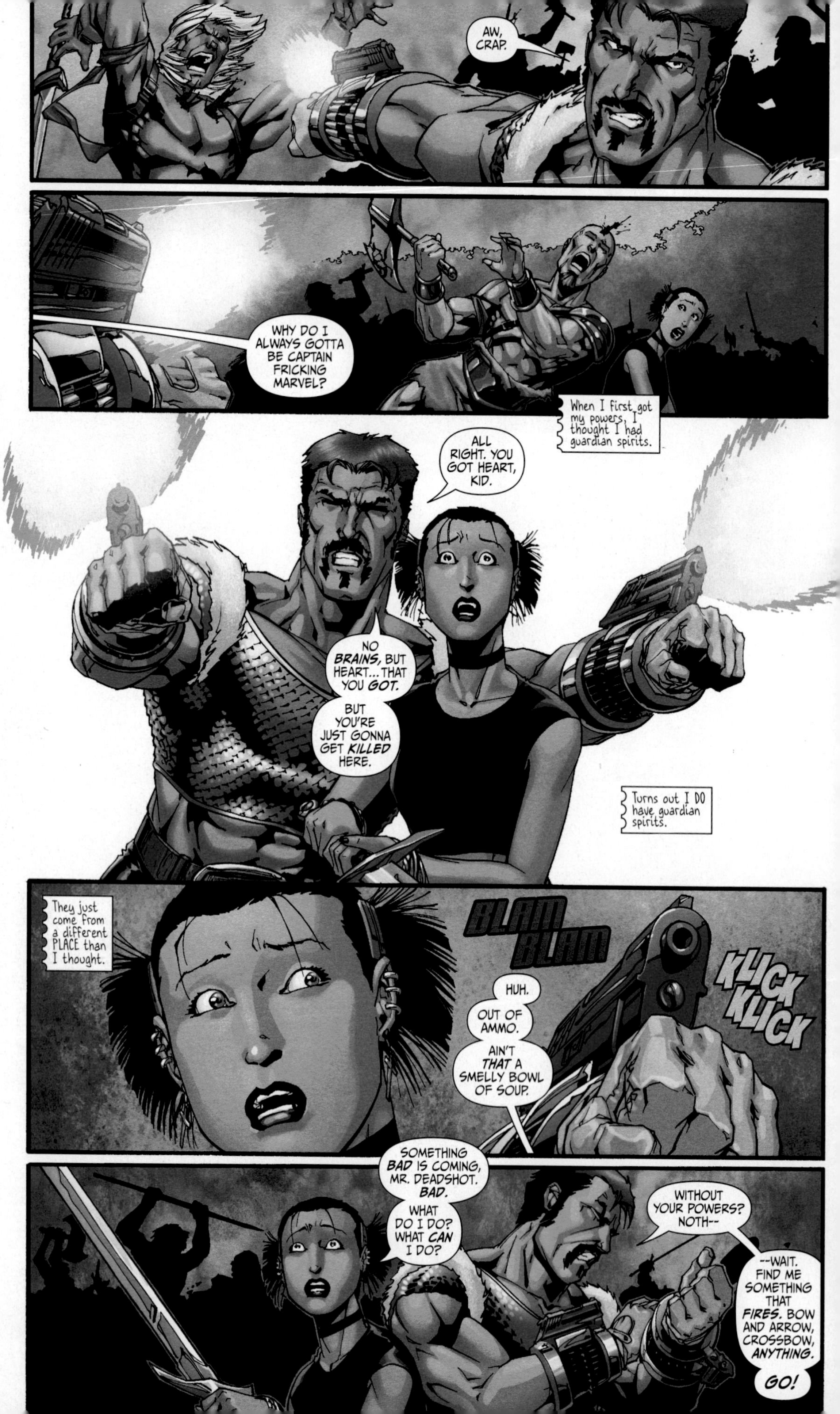
AW, CRAP.
WHY DO I ALWAYS GOTTA BE CAPTAIN FRICKING MARVEL?
When I first got my powers, I thought I had guardian spirits.
ALL RIGHT. YOU GOT HEART, KID.
NO BRAINS, BUT HEART... THAT YOU GOT.
BUT YOU'RE JUST GONNA GET KILLED HERE.
Turns out I DO have guardian spirits.
They just come from a different PLACE than I thought.
BLAM BLAM
KLICK KLICK
HUH.
OUT OF AMMO.
AIN'T THAT A SMELLY BOWL OF SOUP.
SOMETHING BAD IS COMING, MR. DEADSHOT. BAD.
WHAT DO I DO? WHAT CAN I DO?
WITHOUT YOUR POWERS? NOTH--
--WAIT. FIND ME SOMETHING THAT FIRES. BOW AND ARROW, CROSSBOW, ANYTHING.
GO!

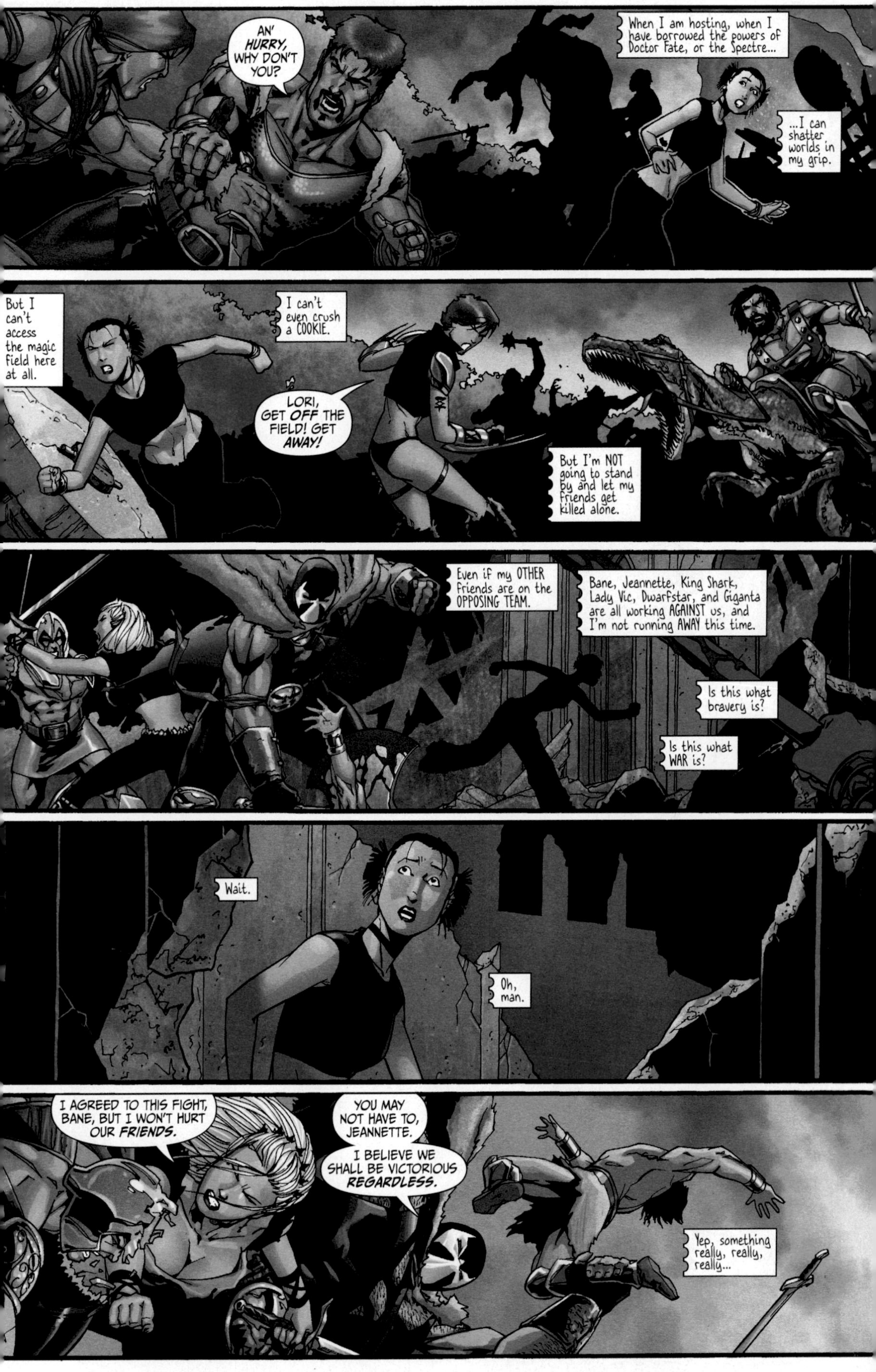
AN' HURRY, WHY DON'T YOU?
When I am hosting, when I have borrowed the powers of Doctor Fate, or the Spectre...
...I can shatter worlds in my grip.
But I can't access the magic field here at all.
I can't even crush a COOKIE.
LORI, GET OFF THE FIELD! GET AWAY!
But I'm NOT going to stand by and let my friends get killed alone.
Even if my OTHER friends are on the OPPOSING TEAM.
Bane, Jeannette, King Shark, Lady Vic, Dwarfstar, and Giganta are all working AGAINST us, and I'm not running AWAY this time.
Is this what bravery is?
Is this what WAR is?
Wait.
Oh, man.
I AGREED TO THIS FIGHT, BANE, BUT I WON'T HURT OUR FRIENDS.
YOU MAY NOT HAVE TO, JEANNETTE.
I BELIEVE WE SHALL BE VICTORIOUS REGARDLESS.
Yep, something really, really, really...

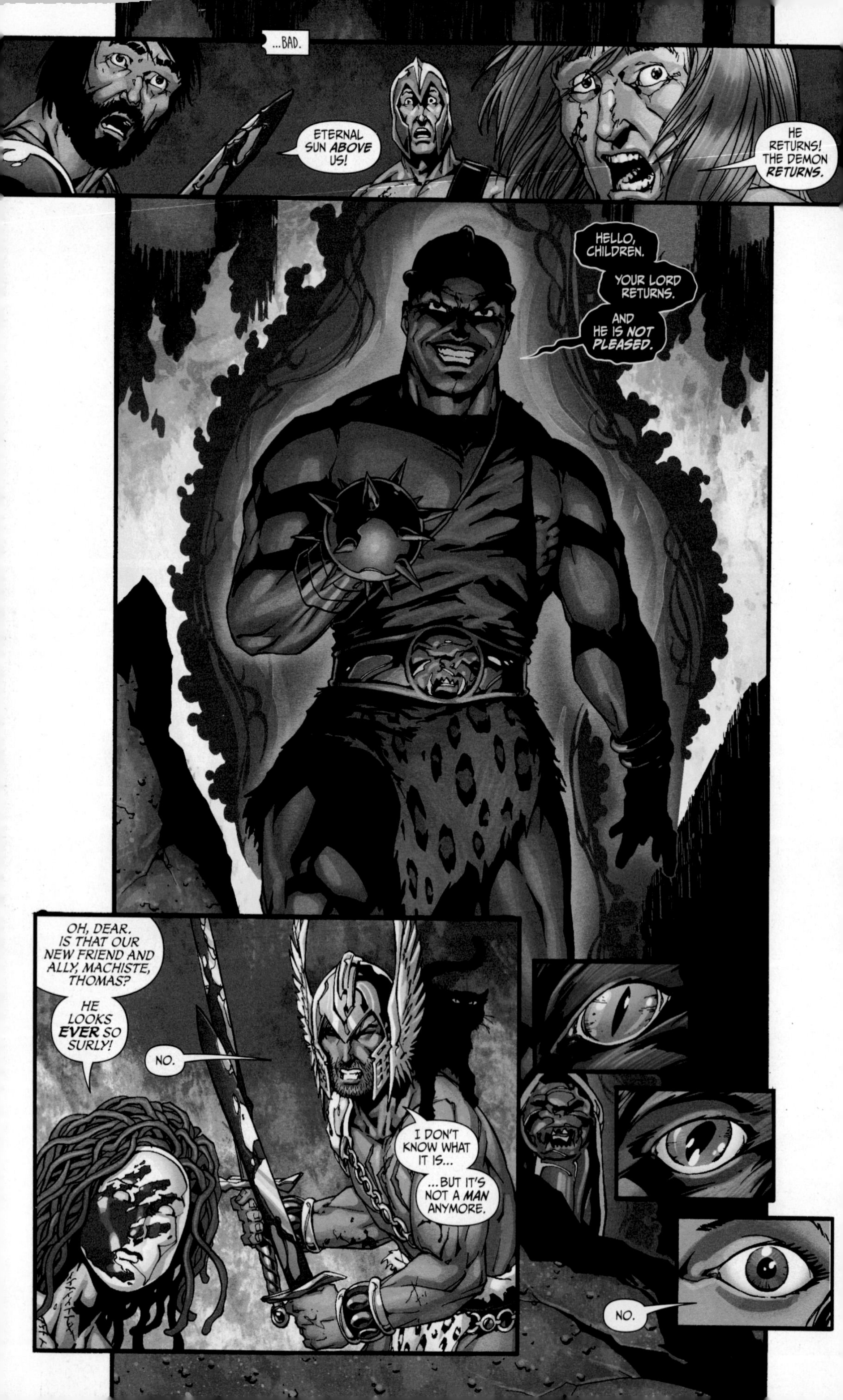
...BAD.
ETERNAL SUN ABOVE US!
HE RETURNS! THE DEMON RETURNS.
HELLO, CHILDREN.
YOUR LORD RETURNS.
AND HE IS NOT PLEASED.
OH, DEAR. IS THAT OUR NEW FRIEND AND ALLY, MACHISTE, THOMAS?
HE LOOKS EVER SO SURLY!
NO.
I DON'T KNOW WHAT IT IS...
...BUT IT'S NOT A MAN ANYMORE.
NO.

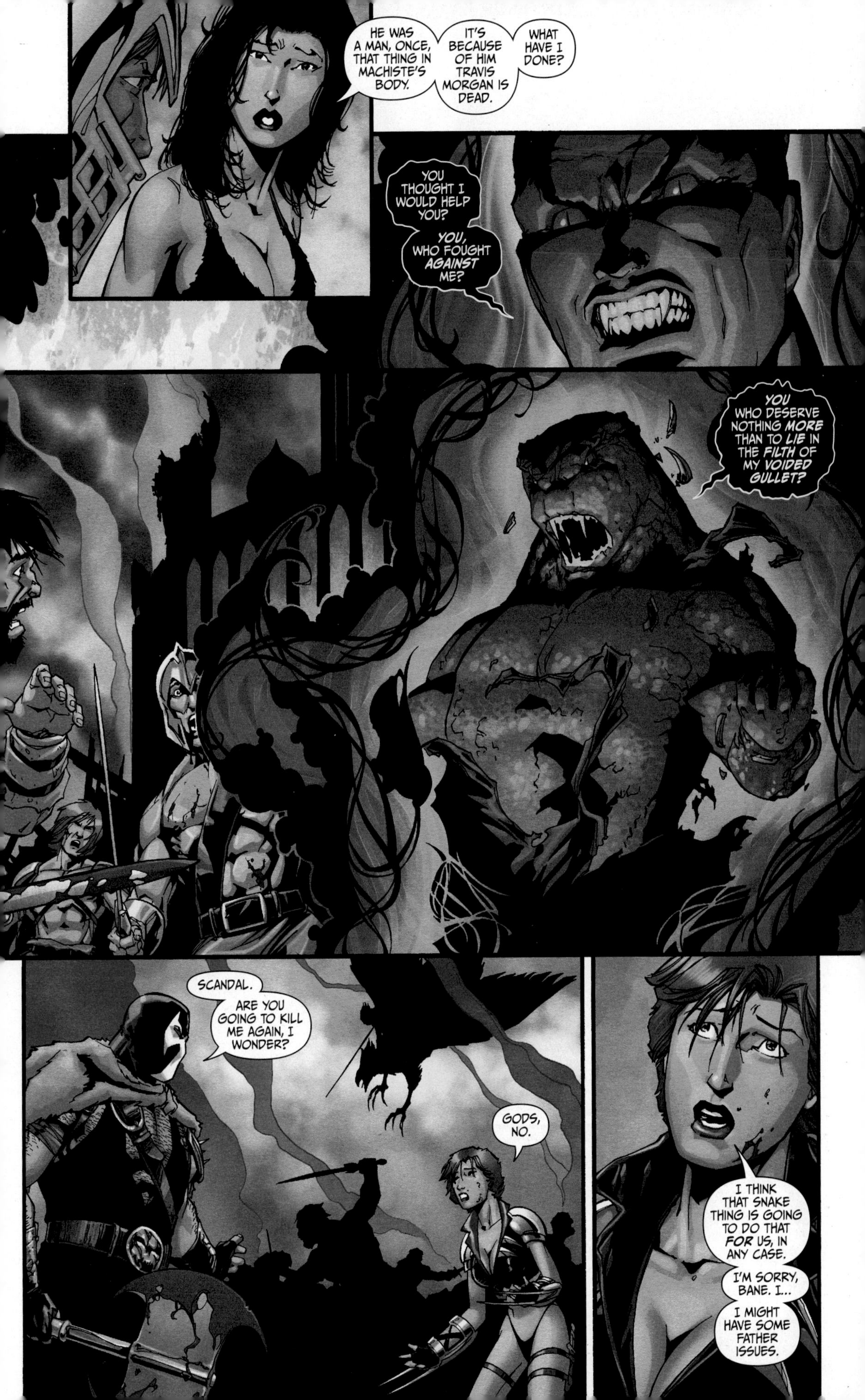
HE WAS A MAN, ONCE, THAT THING IN MACHISTE'S BODY.
IT'S BECAUSE OF HIM TRAVIS MORGAN IS DEAD.
WHAT HAVE I DONE?
YOU THOUGHT I WOULD HELP YOU?
YOU, WHO FOUGHT AGAINST ME?
YOU WHO DESERVE NOTHING MORE THAN TO LIE IN THE FILTH OF MY VOIDED GULLET?
SCANDAL.
ARE YOU GOING TO KILL ME AGAIN, I WONDER?
GODS, NO.
I THINK THAT SNAKE THING IS GOING TO DO THAT FOR US, IN ANY CASE.
I'M SORRY, BANE. I...
I MIGHT HAVE SOME FATHER ISSUES.

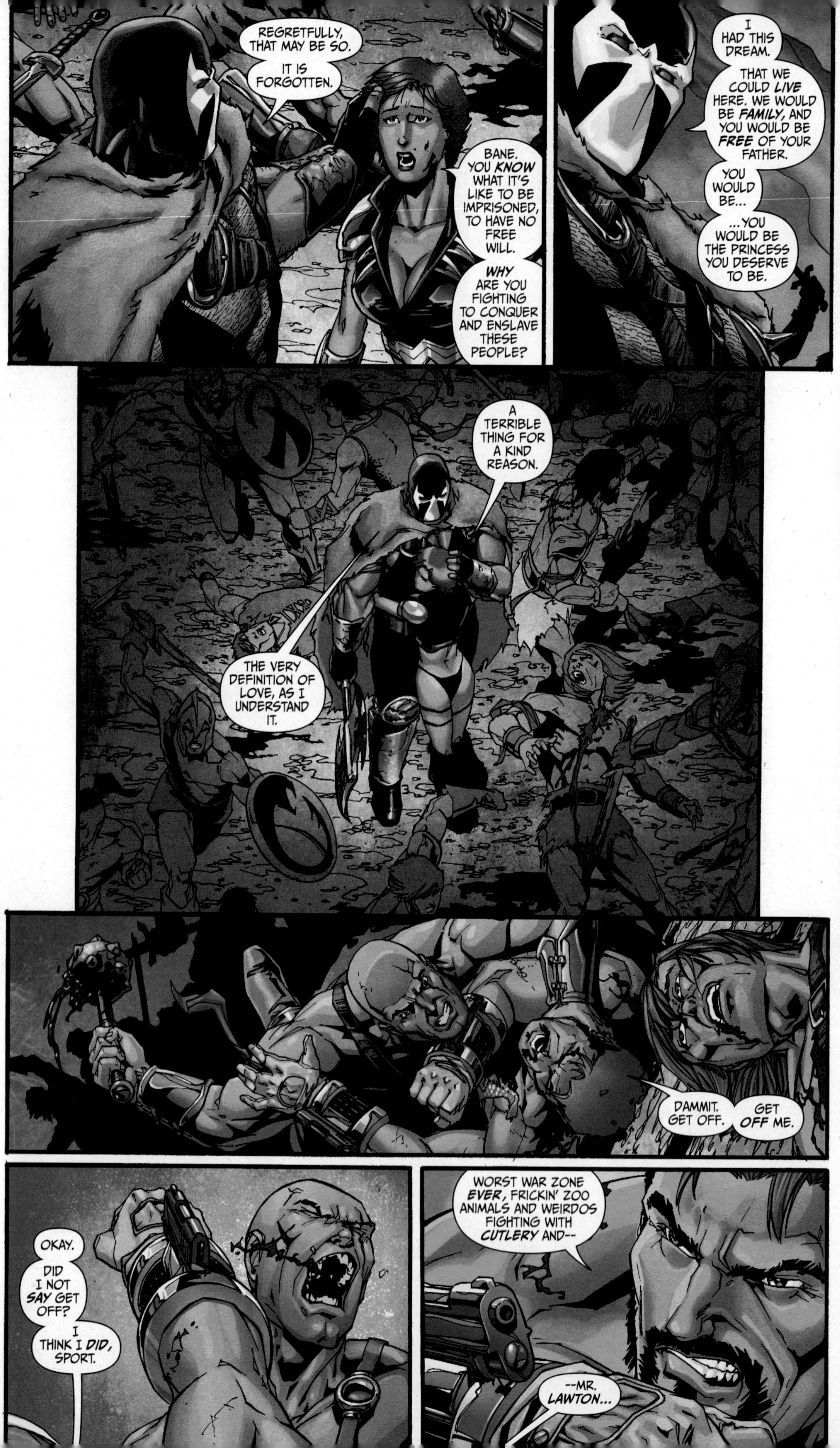
REGRETFULLY, THAT MAY BE SO.
IT IS FORGOTTEN.
BANE. YOU KNOW WHAT IT'S LIKE TO BE IMPRISONED, TO HAVE NO FREE WILL.
WHY ARE YOU FIGHTING TO CONQUER AND ENSLAVE THESE PEOPLE?
I HAD THIS DREAM.
THAT WE COULD LIVE HERE. WE WOULD BE FAMILY, AND YOU WOULD BE FREE OF YOUR FATHER.
YOU WOULD BE...
...YOU WOULD BE THE PRINCESS YOU DESERVE TO BE.
A TERRIBLE THING FOR A KIND REASON.
THE VERY DEFINITION OF LOVE, AS I UNDERSTAND IT.
DAMMIT. GET OFF.
GET OFF ME.
OKAY.
DID I NOT SAY GET OFF?
I THINK I DID, SPORT.
WORST WAR ZONE EVER, FRICKIN' ZOO ANIMALS AND WEIRDOS FIGHTING WITH CUTLERY AND--
--MR. LAWTON...

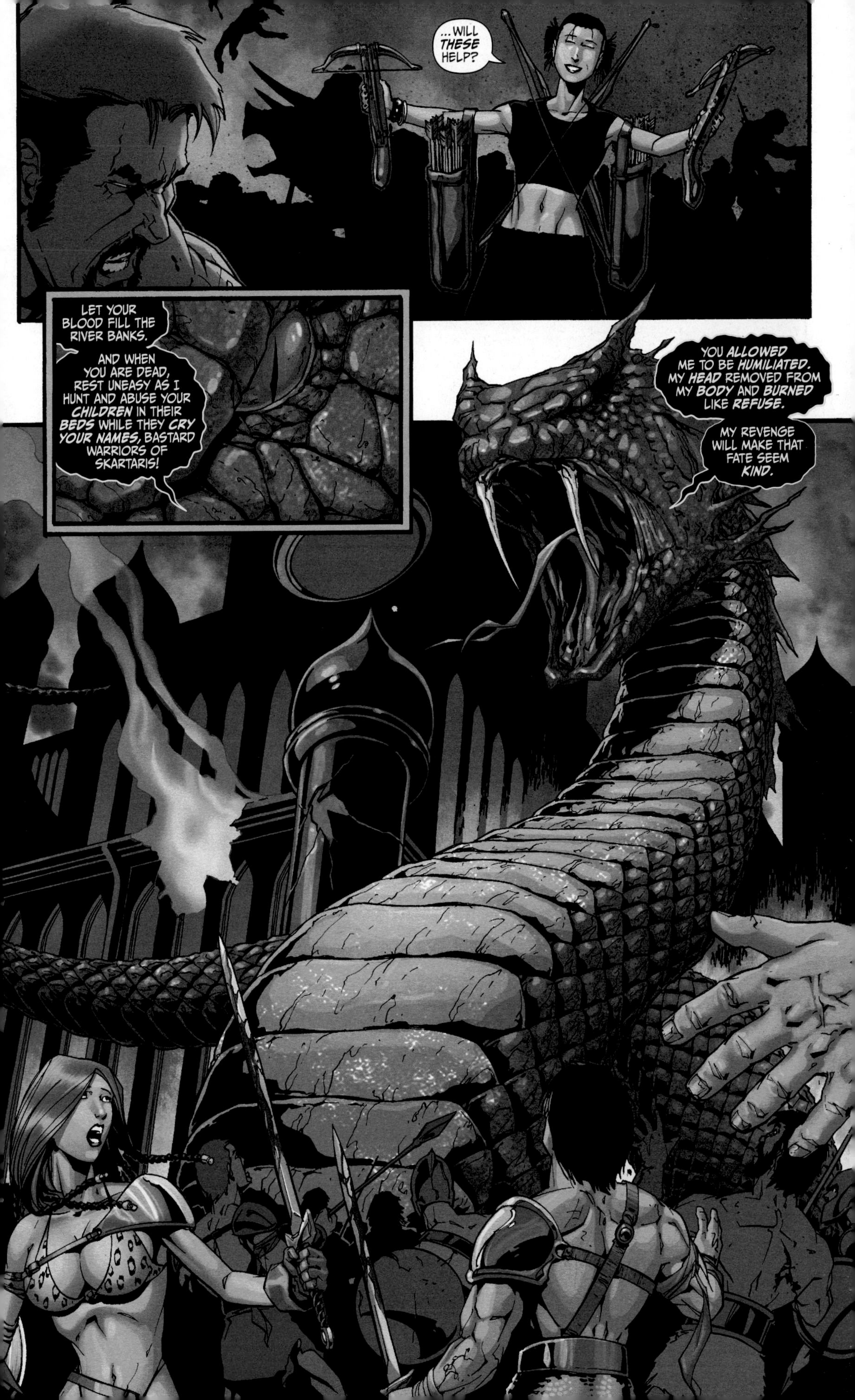
...WILL THESE HELP?
LET YOUR BLOOD FILL THE RIVER BANKS.
AND WHEN YOU ARE DEAD, REST UNEASY AS I HUNT AND ABUSE YOUR CHILDREN IN THEIR BEDS WHILE THEY CRY YOUR NAMES, BASTARD WARRIORS OF SKARTARIS!
YOU ALLOWED ME TO BE HUMILIATED. MY HEAD REMOVED FROM MY BODY AND BURNED LIKE REFUSE.
MY REVENGE WILL MAKE THAT FATE SEEM KIND.

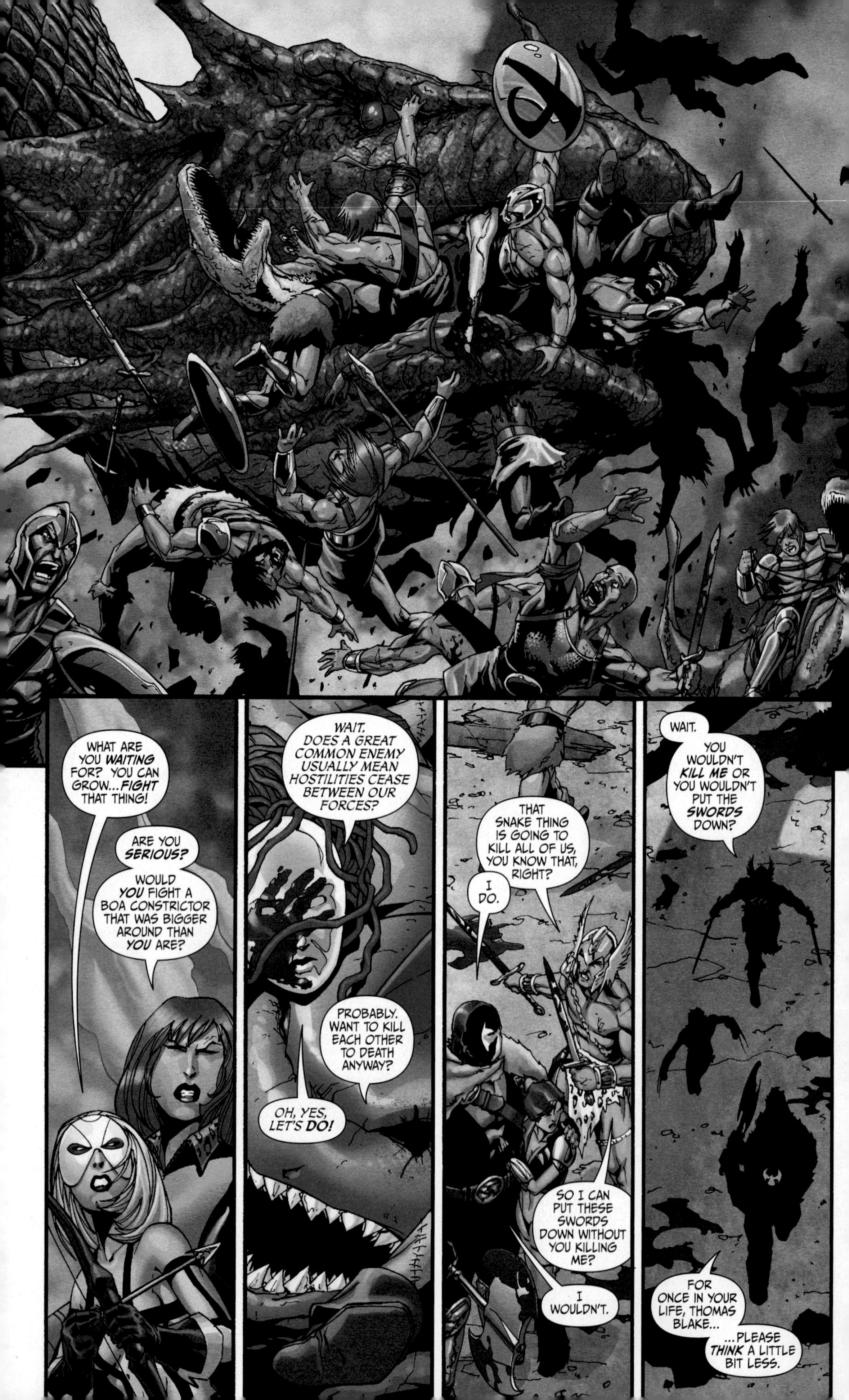
WHAT ARE YOU WAITING FOR? YOU CAN GROW... FIGHT THAT THING!
ARE YOU SERIOUS?
WOULD YOU FIGHT A BOA CONSTRICTOR THAT WAS BIGGER AROUND THAN YOU ARE?
WAIT. DOES A GREAT COMMON ENEMY USUALLY MEAN HOSTILITIES CEASE BETWEEN OUR FORCES?
PROBABLY. WANT TO KILL EACH OTHER TO DEATH ANYWAY?
OH, YES, LET'S DO!
THAT SNAKE THING IS GOING TO KILL ALL OF US, YOU KNOW THAT, RIGHT?
I DO.
SO I CAN PUT THESE SWORDS DOWN WITHOUT YOU KILLING ME?
I WOULDN'T.
WAIT.
YOU WOULDN'T KILL ME OR YOU WOULDN'T PUT THE SWORDS DOWN?
FOR ONCE IN YOUR LIFE, THOMAS BLAKE...
...PLEASE THINK A LITTLE BIT LESS.

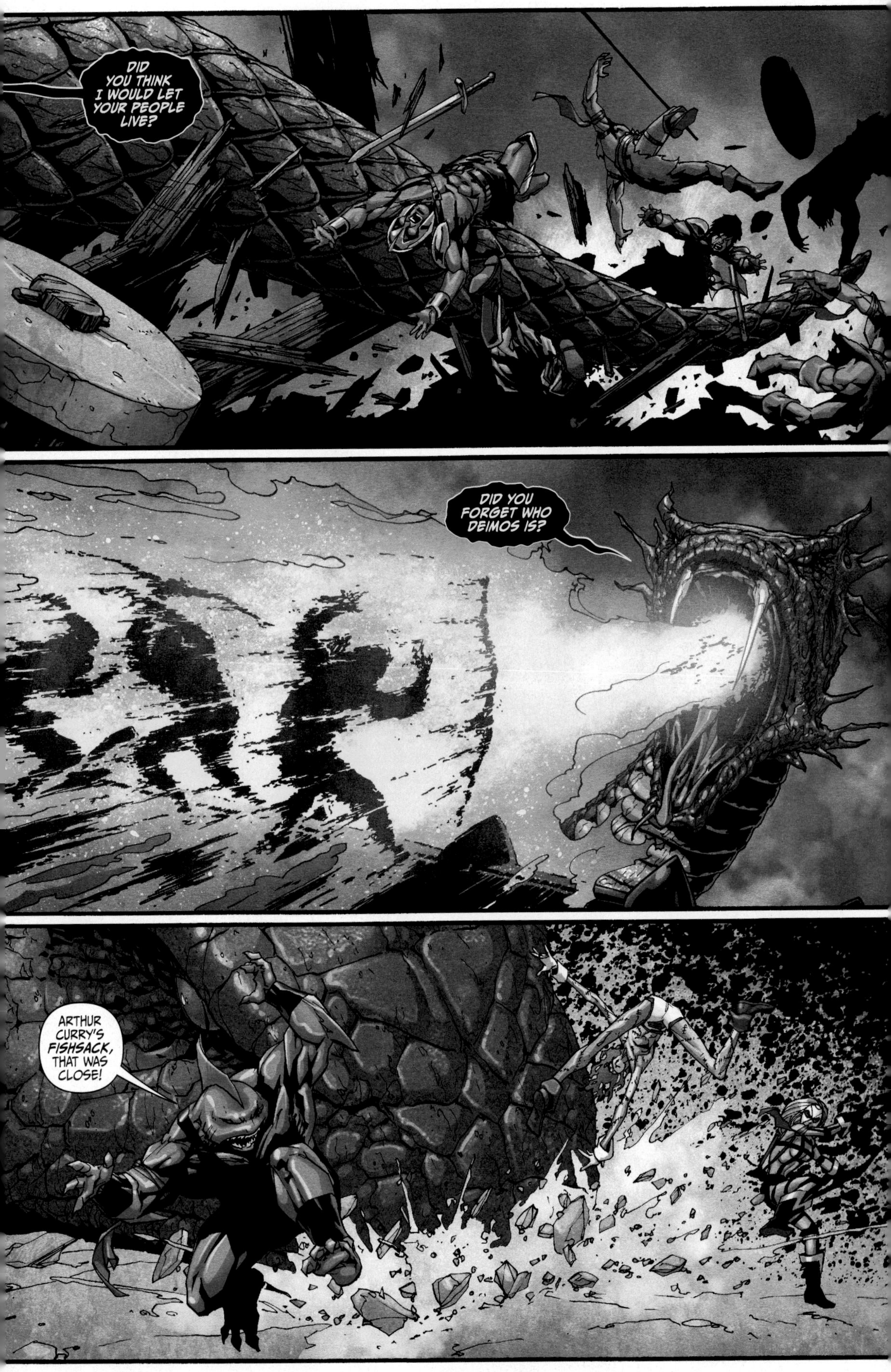
DID YOU THINK I WOULD LET YOUR PEOPLE LIVE?
DID YOU FORGET WHO DEIMOS IS?
ARTHUR CURRY'S FISHSACK, THAT WAS CLOSE!

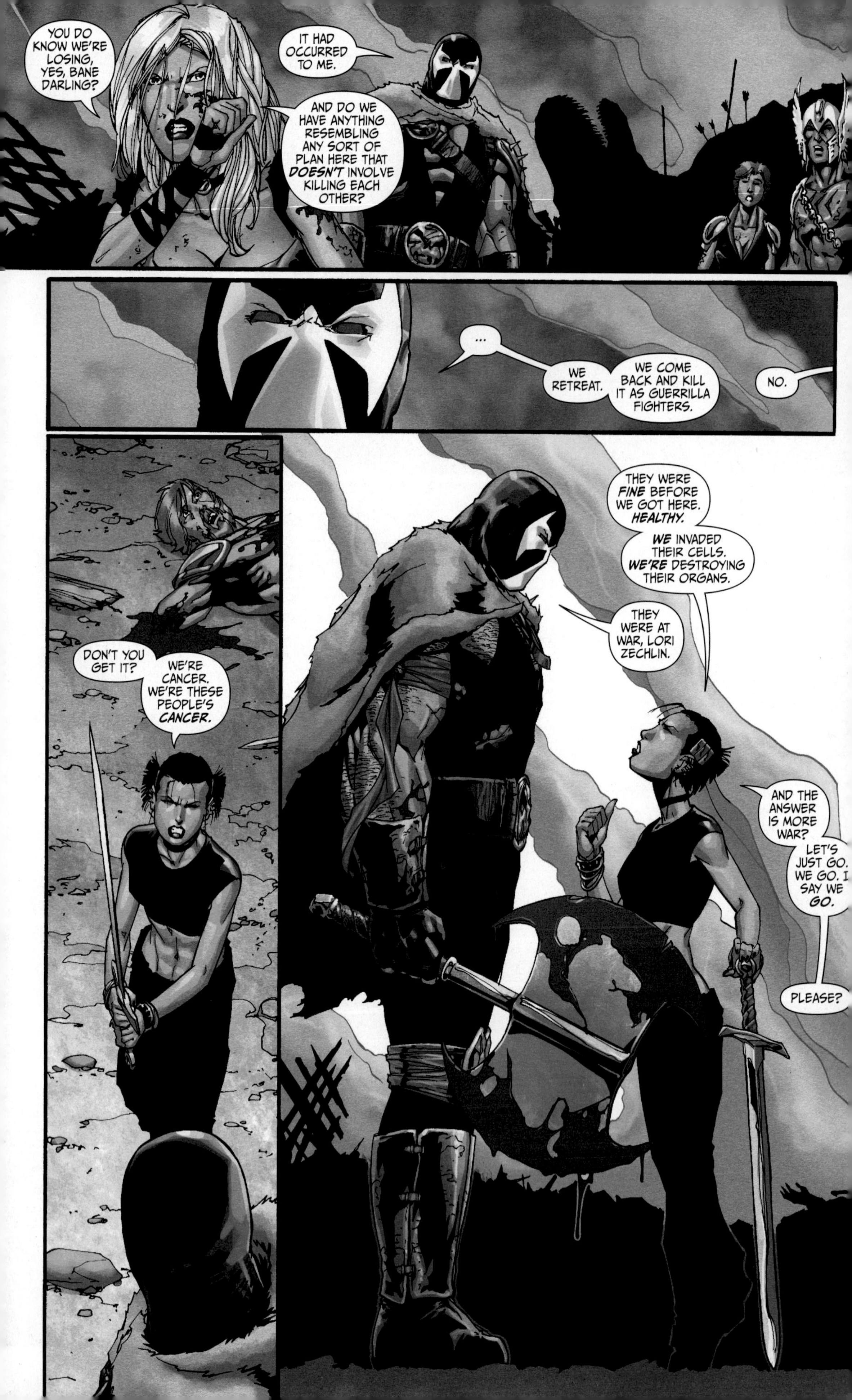
YOU DO KNOW WE'RE LOSING, YES, BANE DARLING?
IT HAD OCCURRED TO ME.
AND DO WE HAVE ANYTHING RESEMBLING ANY SORT OF PLAN HERE THAT DOESN'T INVOLVE KILLING EACH OTHER?
...
WE RETREAT.
WE COME BACK AND KILL IT AS GUERRILLA FIGHTERS.
NO.
DON'T YOU GET IT?
WE'RE CANCER. WE'RE THESE PEOPLE'S CANCER.
THEY WERE FINE BEFORE WE GOT HERE. HEALTHY.
WE INVADED THEIR CELLS. WE'RE DESTROYING THEIR ORGANS.
THEY WERE AT WAR, LORI ZECHLIN.
AND THE ANSWER IS MORE WAR?
LET'S JUST GO. WE GO. I SAY WE GO.
PLEASE?

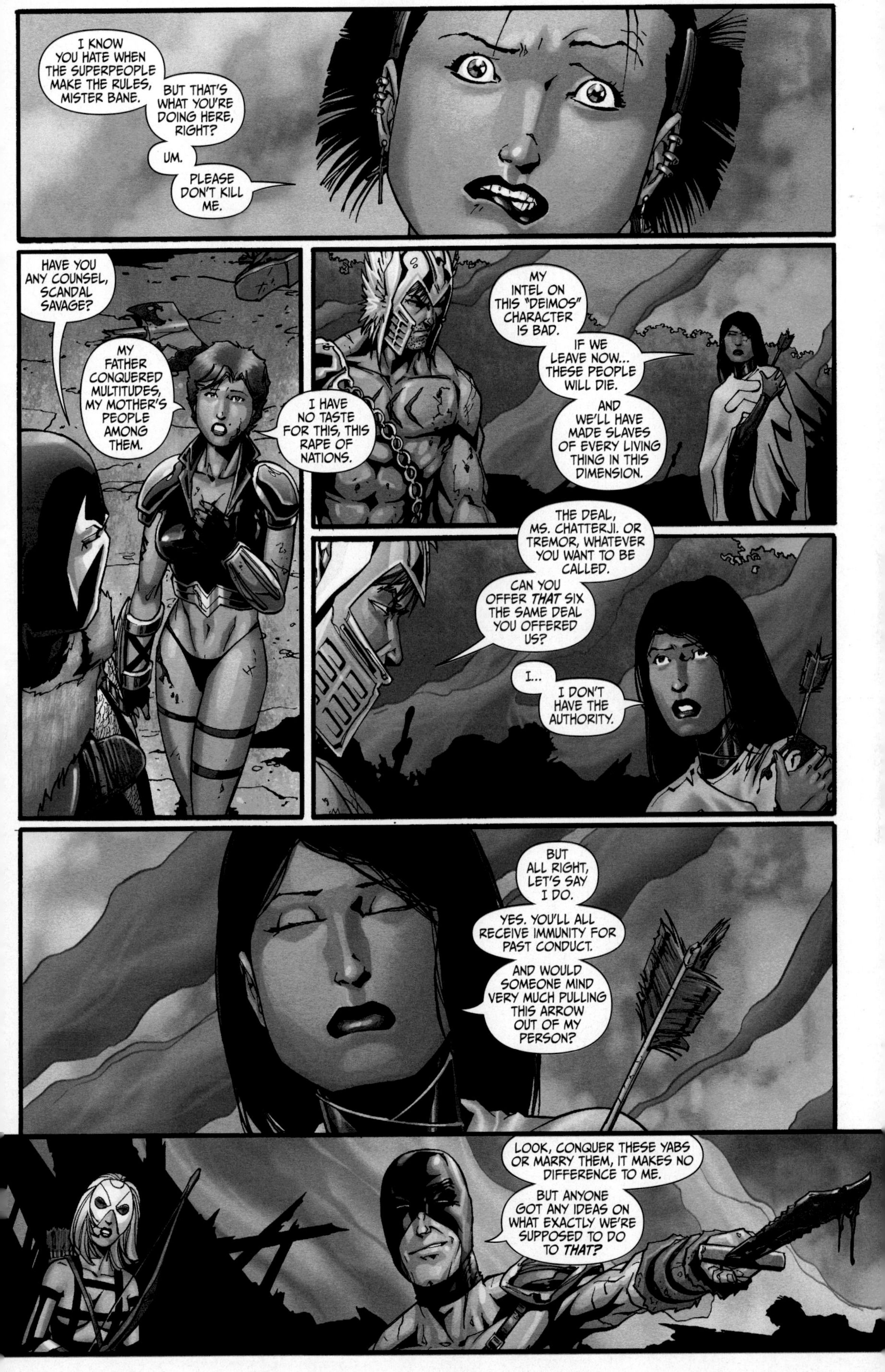

I KNOW YOU HATE WHEN THE SUPERPEOPLE MAKE THE RULES, MISTER BANE.
BUT THAT'S WHAT YOU'RE DOING HERE, RIGHT?
UM.
PLEASE DON'T KILL ME.
HAVE YOU ANY COUNSEL, SCANDAL SAVAGE?
MY FATHER CONQUERED MULTITUDES, MY MOTHER'S PEOPLE AMONG THEM.
I HAVE NO TASTE FOR THIS, THIS RAPE OF NATIONS.
MY INTEL ON THIS "DEIMOS" CHARACTER IS BAD.
IF WE LEAVE NOW... THESE PEOPLE WILL DIE.
AND WE'LL HAVE MADE SLAVES OF EVERY LIVING THING IN THIS DIMENSION.
THE DEAL, MS. CHATTERJI. OR TREMOR, WHATEVER YOU WANT TO BE CALLED.
CAN YOU OFFER *THAT* SIX THE SAME DEAL YOU OFFERED US?
I...
I DON'T HAVE THE AUTHORITY.
BUT ALL RIGHT, LET'S SAY I DO.
YES. YOU'LL ALL RECEIVE IMMUNITY FOR PAST CONDUCT.
AND WOULD SOMEONE MIND VERY MUCH PULLING THIS ARROW OUT OF MY PERSON?
LOOK, CONQUER THESE YABS OR MARRY THEM, IT MAKES NO DIFFERENCE TO ME.
BUT ANYONE GOT ANY IDEAS ON WHAT EXACTLY WE'RE SUPPOSED TO DO TO *THAT?*

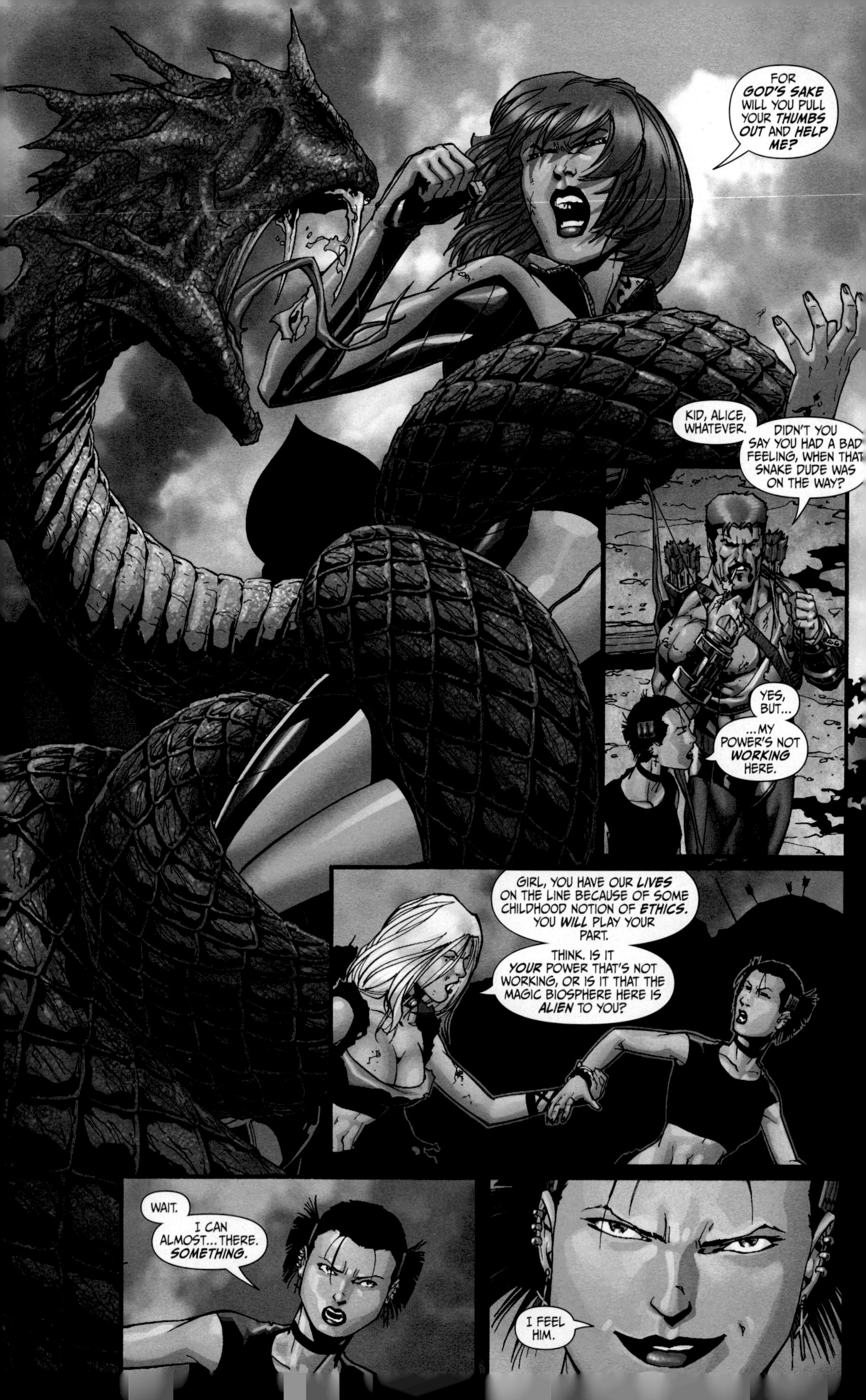
FOR GOD'S SAKE WILL YOU PULL YOUR THUMBS OUT AND HELP ME?
KID, ALICE, WHATEVER.
DIDN'T YOU SAY YOU HAD A BAD FEELING, WHEN THAT SNAKE DUDE WAS ON THE WAY?
YES, BUT...
...MY POWER'S NOT WORKING HERE.
GIRL, YOU HAVE OUR LIVES ON THE LINE BECAUSE OF SOME CHILDHOOD NOTION OF ETHICS. YOU WILL PLAY YOUR PART.
THINK. IS IT YOUR POWER THAT'S NOT WORKING, OR IS IT THAT THE MAGIC BIOSPHERE HERE IS ALIEN TO YOU?
WAIT.
I CAN ALMOST... THERE. SOMETHING.
I FEEL HIM.

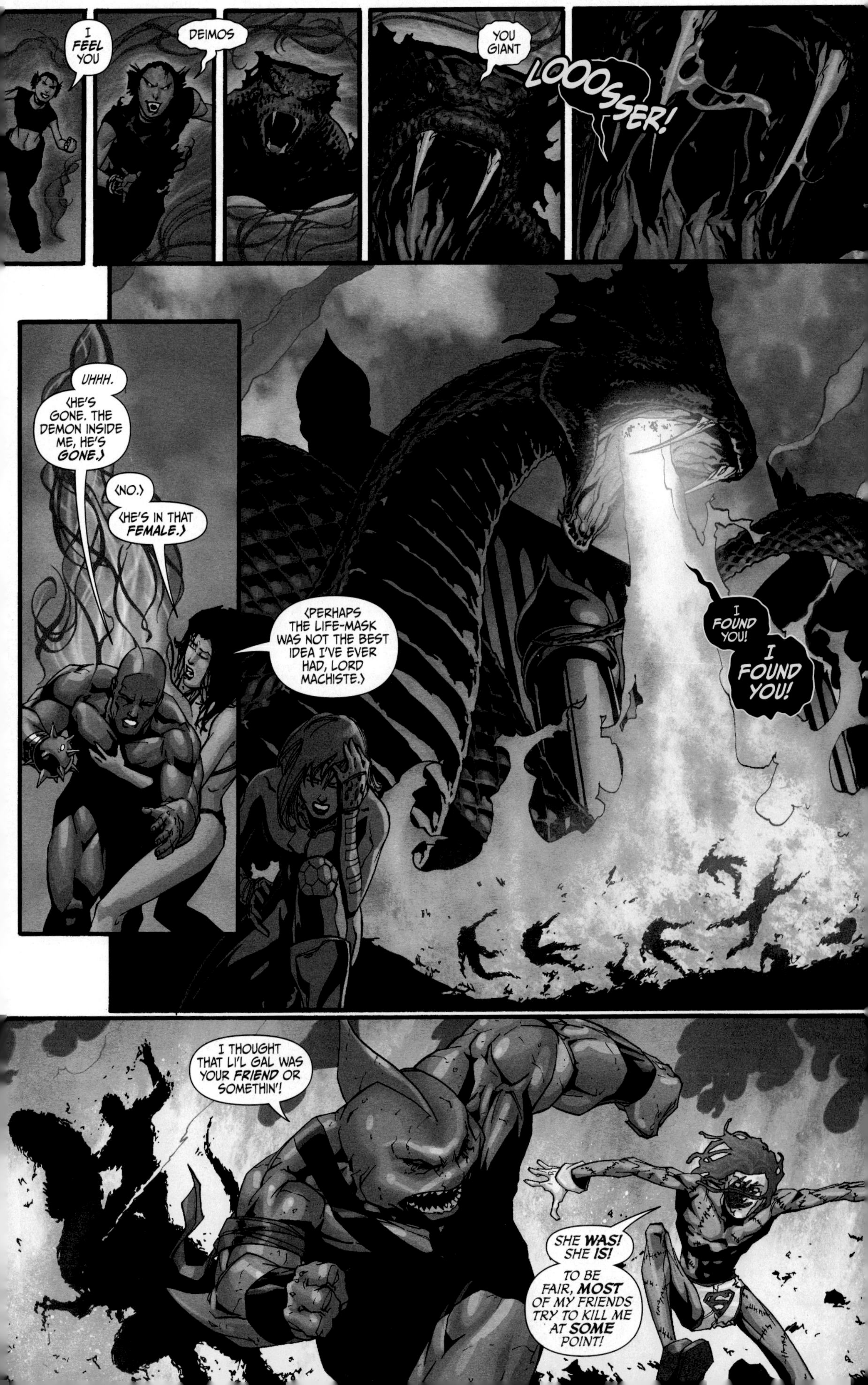
I FEEL YOU
DEIMOS
YOU GIANT
LOOOSSER!
UHHH.
‹HE'S GONE. THE DEMON INSIDE ME, HE'S GONE.›
‹NO.›
‹HE'S IN THAT FEMALE.›
‹PERHAPS THE LIFE-MASK WAS NOT THE BEST IDEA I'VE EVER HAD, LORD MACHISTE.›
I FOUND YOU!
I FOUND YOU!
I THOUGHT THAT LI'L GAL WAS YOUR FRIEND OR SOMETHIN'!
SHE WAS! SHE IS!
TO BE FAIR, MOST OF MY FRIENDS TRY TO KILL ME AT SOME POINT!

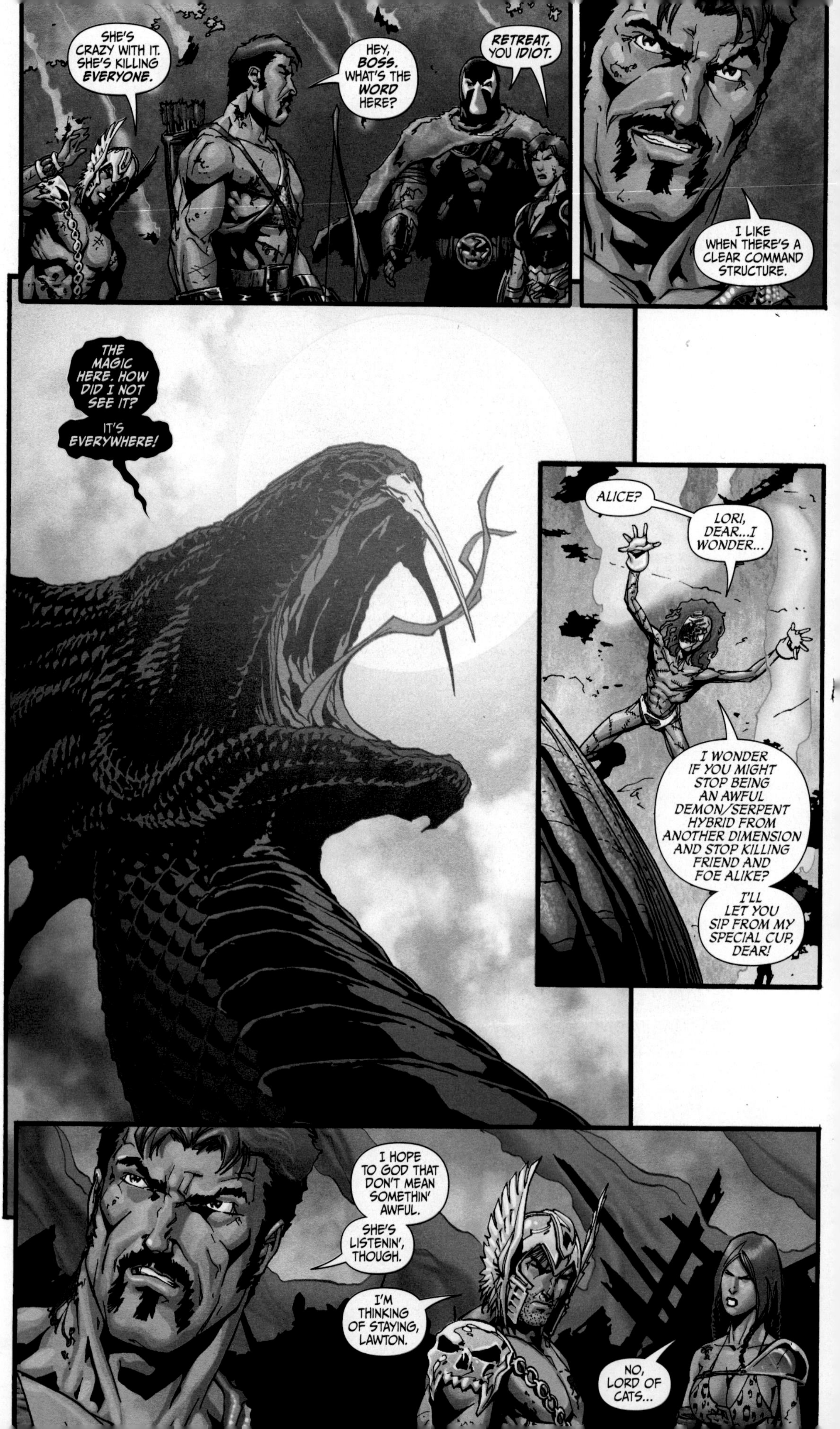
SHE'S CRAZY WITH IT. SHE'S KILLING EVERYONE.
HEY, BOSS. WHAT'S THE WORD HERE?
RETREAT, YOU IDIOT.
I LIKE WHEN THERE'S A CLEAR COMMAND STRUCTURE.
THE MAGIC HERE. HOW DID I NOT SEE IT?
IT'S EVERYWHERE!
ALICE?
LORI, DEAR...I WONDER...
I WONDER IF YOU MIGHT STOP BEING AN AWFUL DEMON/SERPENT HYBRID FROM ANOTHER DIMENSION AND STOP KILLING FRIEND AND FOE ALIKE?
I'LL LET YOU SIP FROM MY SPECIAL CUP, DEAR!
I HOPE TO GOD THAT DON'T MEAN SOMETHIN' AWFUL.
SHE'S LISTENIN', THOUGH.
I'M THINKING OF STAYING, LAWTON.
NO, LORD OF CATS...

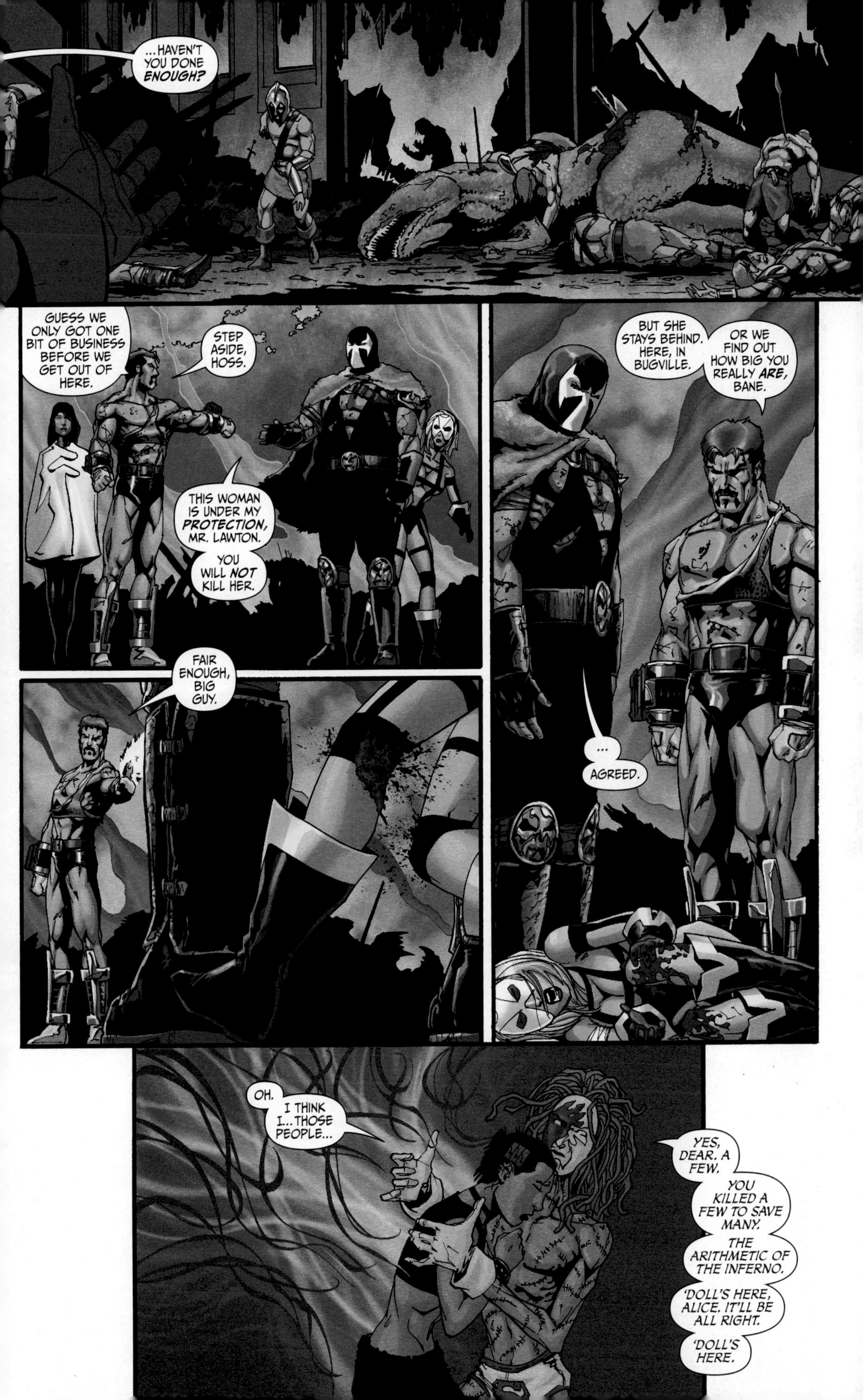
...HAVEN'T YOU DONE ENOUGH?
GUESS WE ONLY GOT ONE BIT OF BUSINESS BEFORE WE GET OUT OF HERE.
STEP ASIDE, HOSS.
THIS WOMAN IS UNDER MY PROTECTION, MR. LAWTON.
YOU WILL NOT KILL HER.
BUT SHE STAYS BEHIND. HERE, IN BUGVILLE.
OR WE FIND OUT HOW BIG YOU REALLY ARE, BANE.
...
AGREED.
FAIR ENOUGH, BIG GUY.
OH. I THINK I...THOSE PEOPLE...
YES, DEAR. A FEW.
YOU KILLED A FEW TO SAVE MANY.
THE ARITHMETIC OF THE INFERNO.
'DOLL'S HERE, ALICE. IT'LL BE ALL RIGHT.
'DOLL'S HERE.

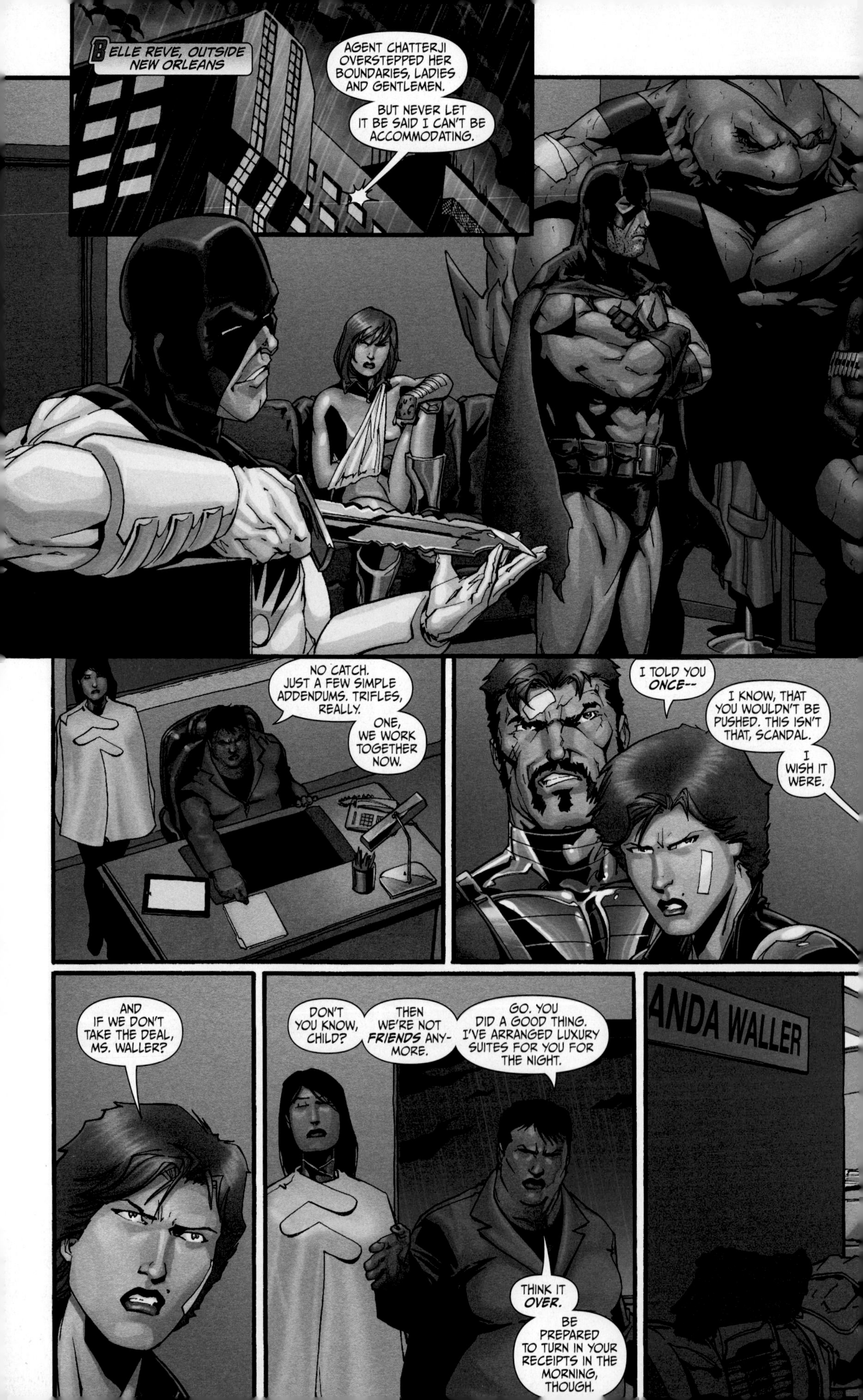

BELLE REVE, OUTSIDE NEW ORLEANS
AGENT CHATTERJI OVERSTEPPED HER BOUNDARIES, LADIES AND GENTLEMEN.
BUT NEVER LET IT BE SAID I CAN'T BE ACCOMMODATING.
NO CATCH. JUST A FEW SIMPLE ADDENDUMS. TRIFLES, REALLY.
ONE, WE WORK TOGETHER NOW.
I TOLD YOU ONCE--
I KNOW, THAT YOU WOULDN'T BE PUSHED. THIS ISN'T THAT, SCANDAL.
I WISH IT WERE.
AND IF WE DON'T TAKE THE DEAL, MS. WALLER?
DON'T YOU KNOW, CHILD?
THEN WE'RE NOT FRIENDS ANYMORE.
GO. YOU DID A GOOD THING. I'VE ARRANGED LUXURY SUITES FOR YOU FOR THE NIGHT.
THINK IT OVER.
BE PREPARED TO TURN IN YOUR RECEIPTS IN THE MORNING, THOUGH.
ANDA WALLER

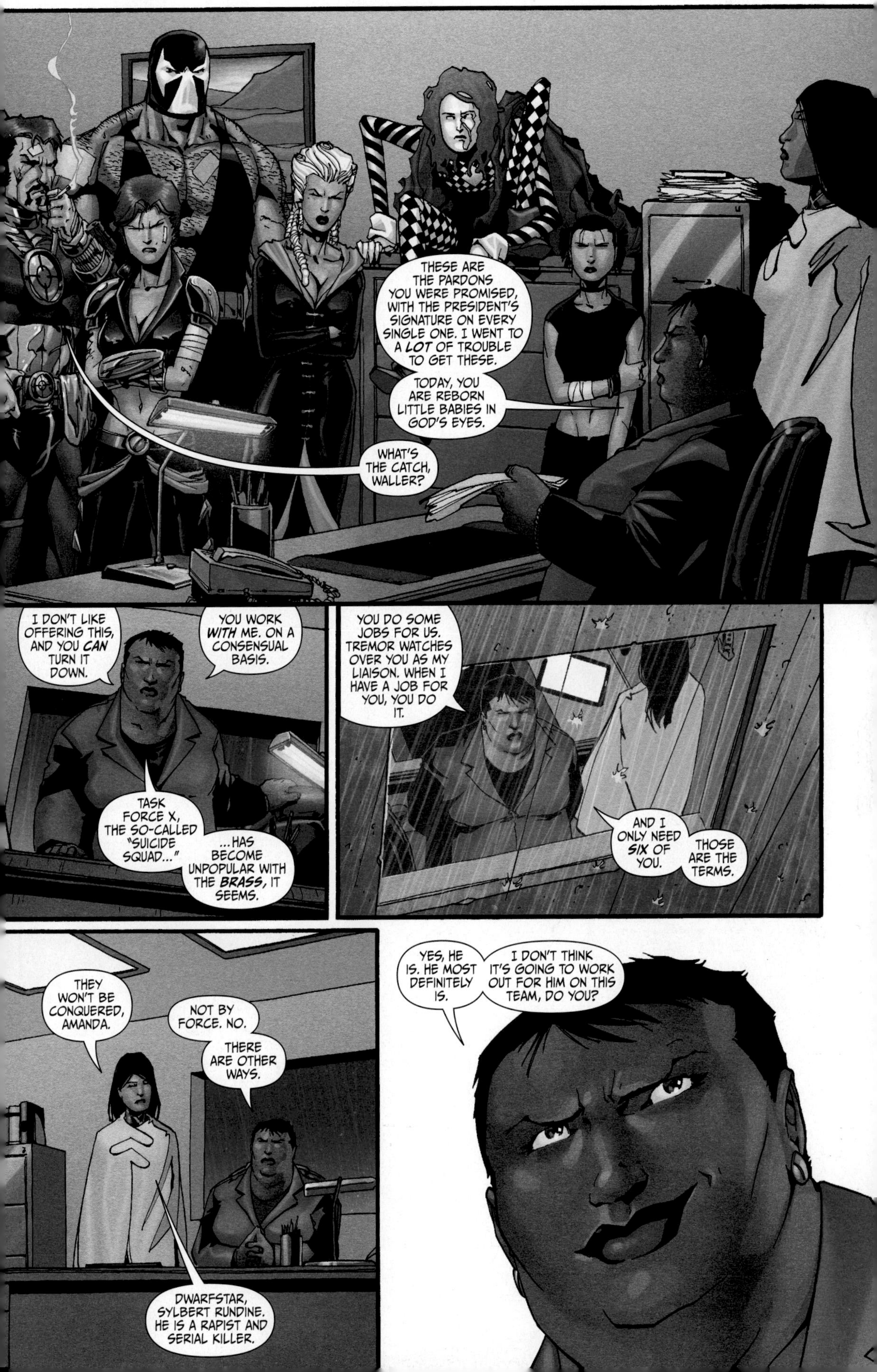
THESE ARE THE PARDONS YOU WERE PROMISED, WITH THE PRESIDENT'S SIGNATURE ON EVERY SINGLE ONE. I WENT TO A *LOT* OF TROUBLE TO GET THESE.
TODAY, YOU ARE REBORN LITTLE BABIES IN GOD'S EYES.
WHAT'S THE CATCH, WALLER?
I DON'T LIKE OFFERING THIS, AND YOU *CAN* TURN IT DOWN.
YOU WORK *WITH* ME. ON A CONSENSUAL BASIS.
TASK FORCE X, THE SO-CALLED "SUICIDE SQUAD..."
...HAS BECOME UNPOPULAR WITH THE *BRASS*, IT SEEMS.
YOU DO SOME JOBS FOR US. TREMOR WATCHES OVER YOU AS MY LIAISON. WHEN I HAVE A JOB FOR YOU, YOU DO IT.
AND I ONLY NEED *SIX* OF YOU.
THOSE ARE THE TERMS.
THEY WON'T BE CONQUERED, AMANDA.
NOT BY FORCE. NO.
THERE ARE OTHER WAYS.
DWARFSTAR, SYLBERT RUNDINE. HE IS A RAPIST AND SERIAL KILLER.
YES, HE IS. HE MOST DEFINITELY IS.
I DON'T THINK IT'S GOING TO WORK OUT FOR HIM ON THIS TEAM, DO YOU?

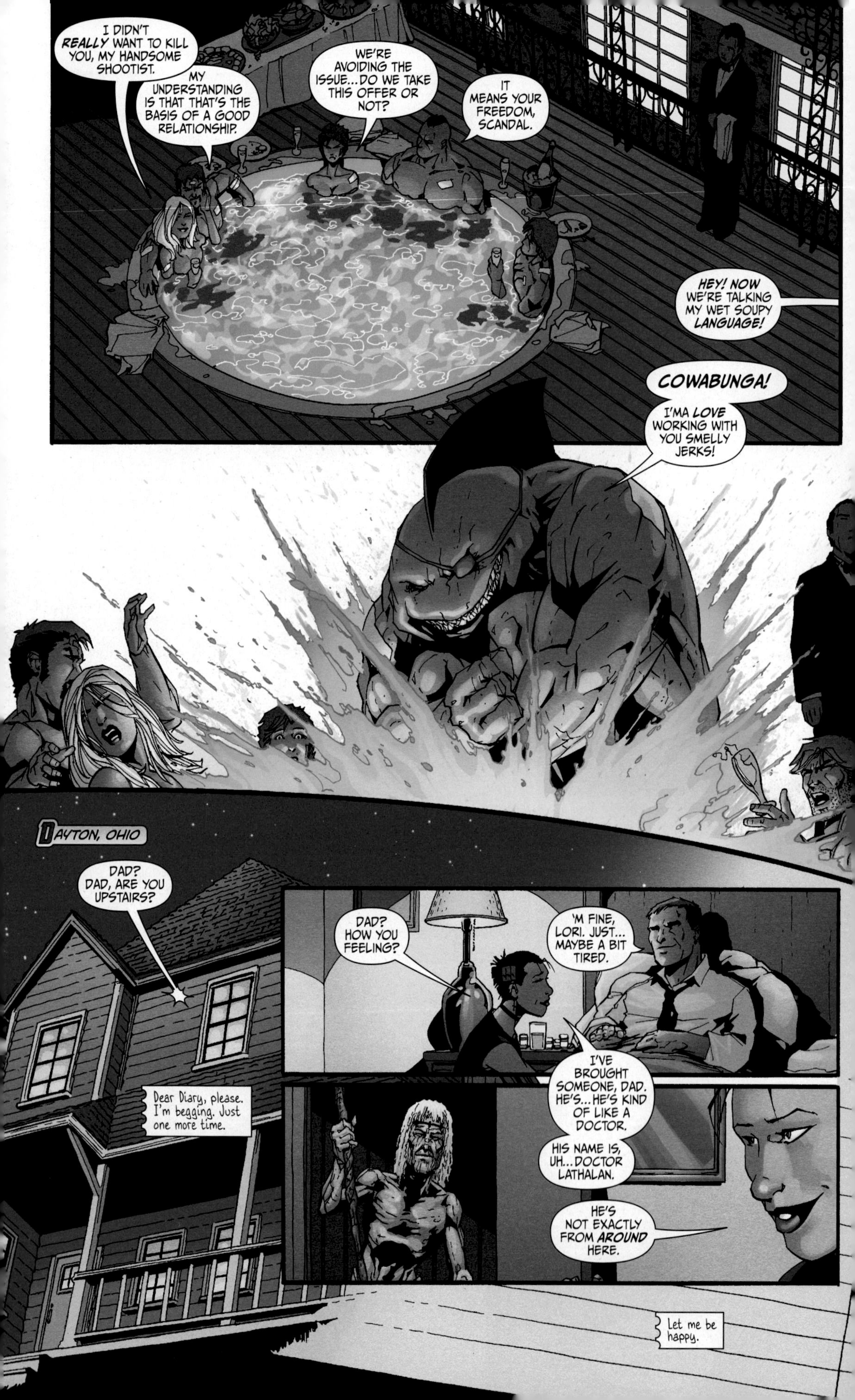
I DIDN'T REALLY WANT TO KILL YOU, MY HANDSOME SHOOTIST.
MY UNDERSTANDING IS THAT THAT'S THE BASIS OF A GOOD RELATIONSHIP.
WE'RE AVOIDING THE ISSUE...DO WE TAKE THIS OFFER OR NOT?
IT MEANS YOUR FREEDOM, SCANDAL.
HEY! NOW WE'RE TALKING MY WET SOUPY LANGUAGE!
COWABUNGA!
I'MA LOVE WORKING WITH YOU SMELLY JERKS!
DAYTON, OHIO
DAD? DAD, ARE YOU UPSTAIRS?
Dear Diary, please. I'm begging. Just one more time.
DAD? HOW YOU FEELING?
'M FINE, LORI. JUST... MAYBE A BIT TIRED.
I'VE BROUGHT SOMEONE, DAD. HE'S...HE'S KIND OF LIKE A DOCTOR.
HIS NAME IS, UH...DOCTOR LATHALAN.
HE'S NOT EXACTLY FROM AROUND HERE.
Let me be happy.

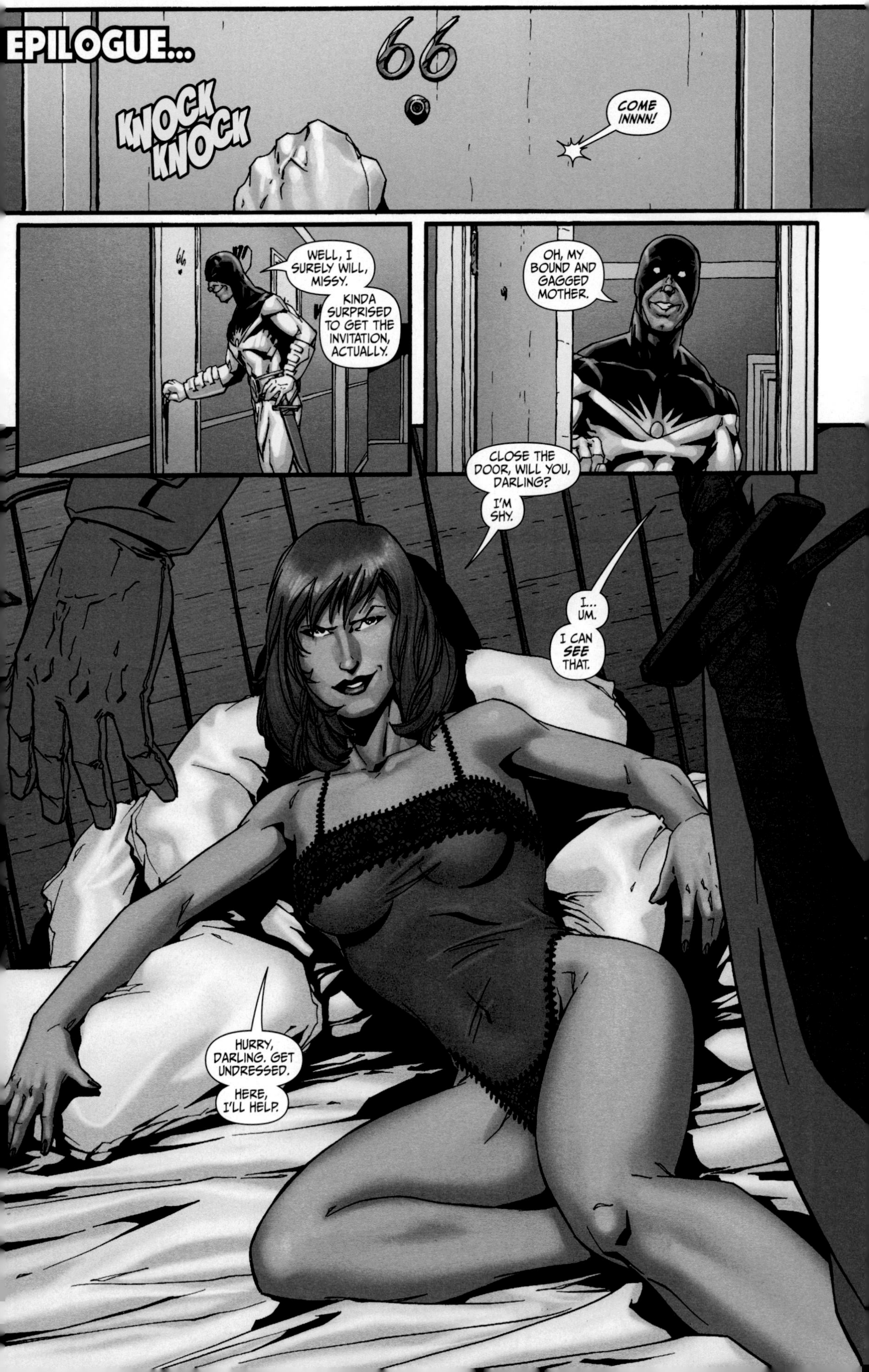
EPILOGUE...
66
KNOCK KNOCK
COME INNNN!
WELL, I SURELY WILL, MISSY.
KINDA SURPRISED TO GET THE INVITATION, ACTUALLY.
OH, MY BOUND AND GAGGED MOTHER.
CLOSE THE DOOR, WILL YOU, DARLING?
I'M SHY.
I... UM.
I CAN SEE THAT.
HURRY, DARLING. GET UNDRESSED.
HERE, I'LL HELP.

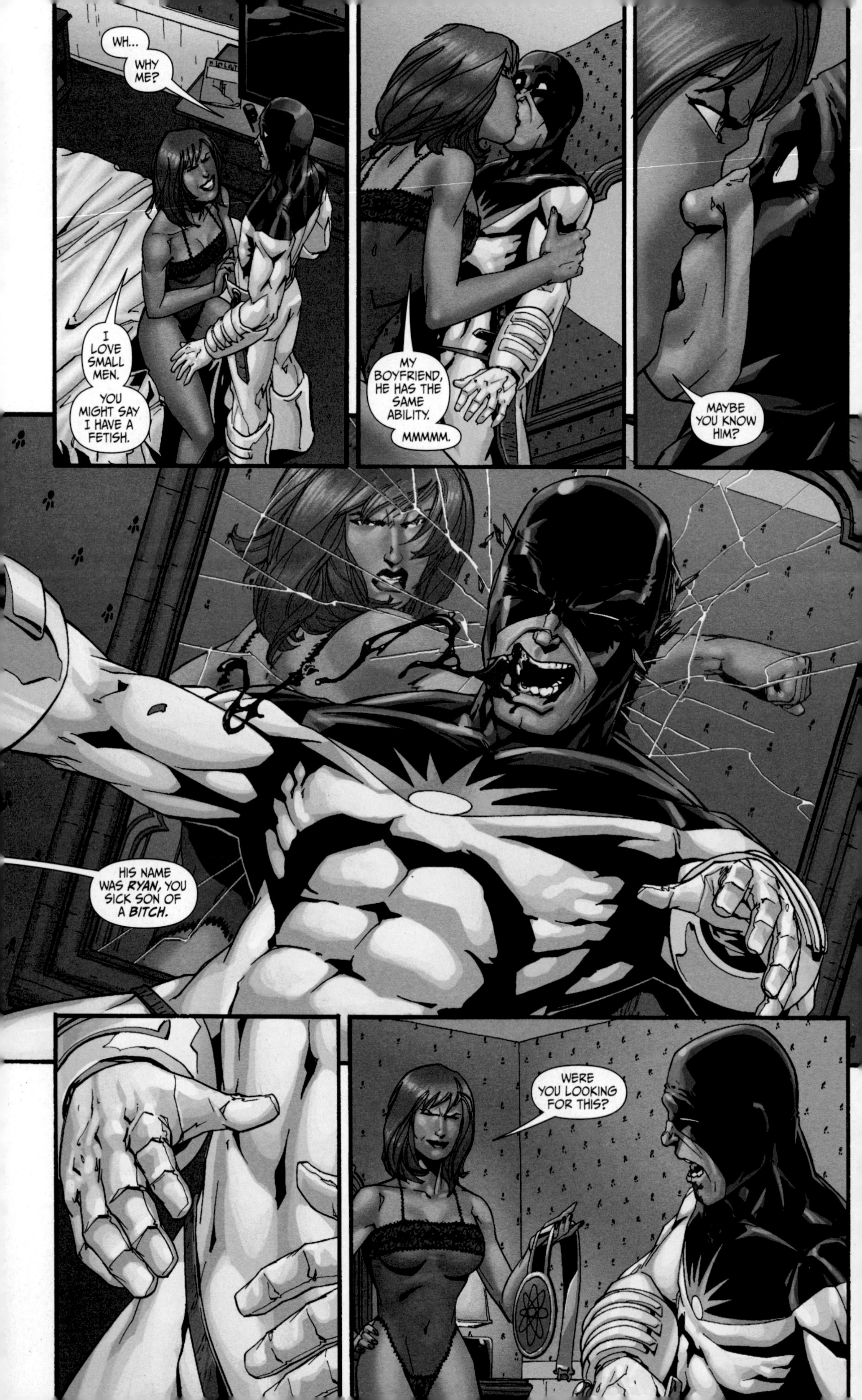
WH... WHY ME?
I LOVE SMALL MEN.
YOU MIGHT SAY I HAVE A FETISH.
MY BOYFRIEND, HE HAS THE SAME ABILITY.
MMMMM.
MAYBE YOU KNOW HIM?
HIS NAME WAS RYAN, YOU SICK SON OF A BITCH.
WERE YOU LOOKING FOR THIS?

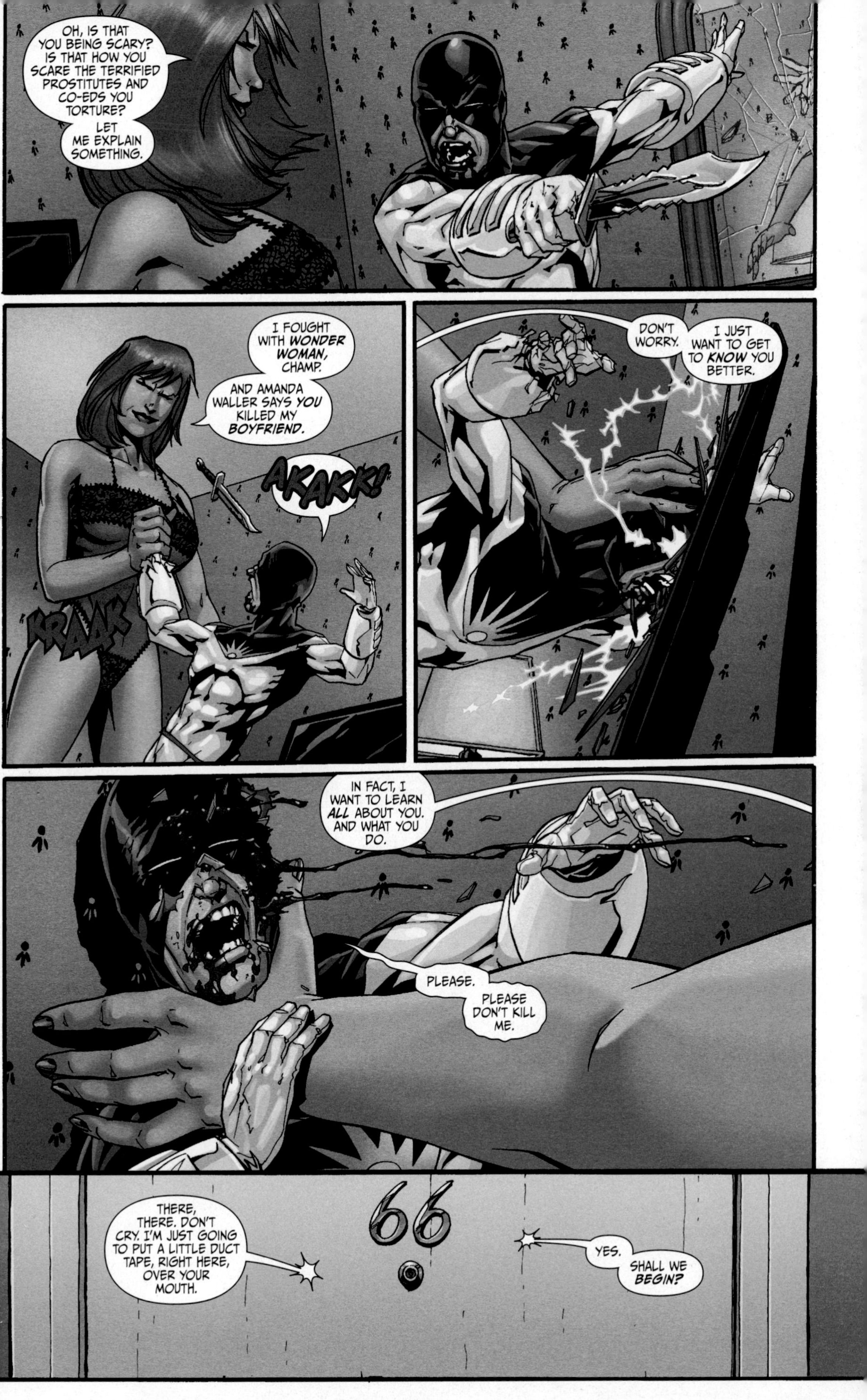
OH, IS THAT YOU BEING SCARY? IS THAT HOW YOU SCARE THE TERRIFIED PROSTITUTES AND CO-EDS YOU TORTURE?
LET ME EXPLAIN SOMETHING.
I FOUGHT WITH WONDER WOMAN, CHAMP.
AND AMANDA WALLER SAYS YOU KILLED MY BOYFRIEND.
AKAKK!
KRAAK
DON'T WORRY.
I JUST WANT TO GET TO KNOW YOU BETTER.
IN FACT, I WANT TO LEARN ALL ABOUT YOU. AND WHAT YOU DO.
PLEASE.
PLEASE DON'T KILL ME.
66
THERE, THERE. DON'T CRY. I'M JUST GOING TO PUT A LITTLE DUCT TAPE, RIGHT HERE, OVER YOUR MOUTH.
YES.
SHALL WE BEGIN?

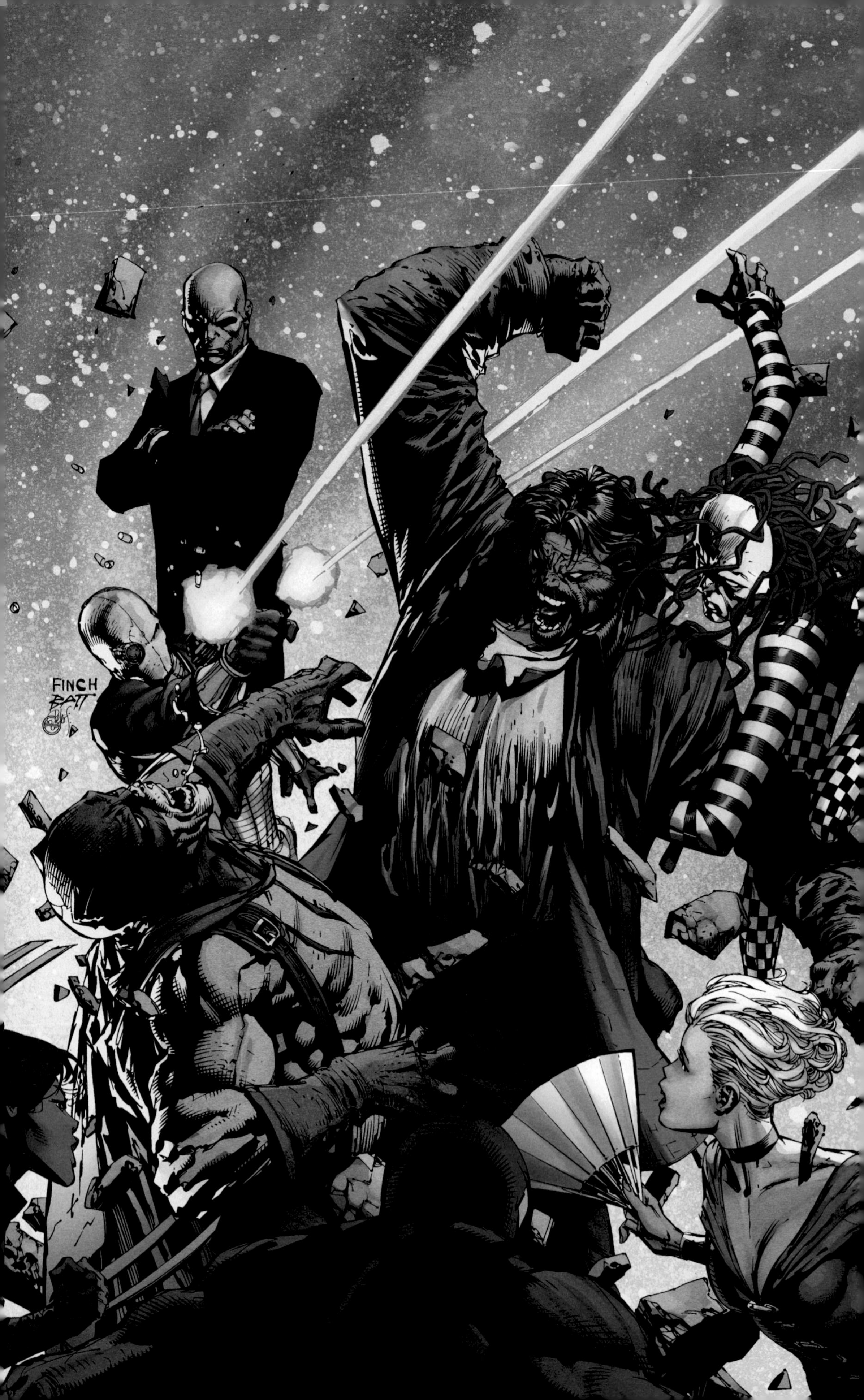
FINCH
BATT

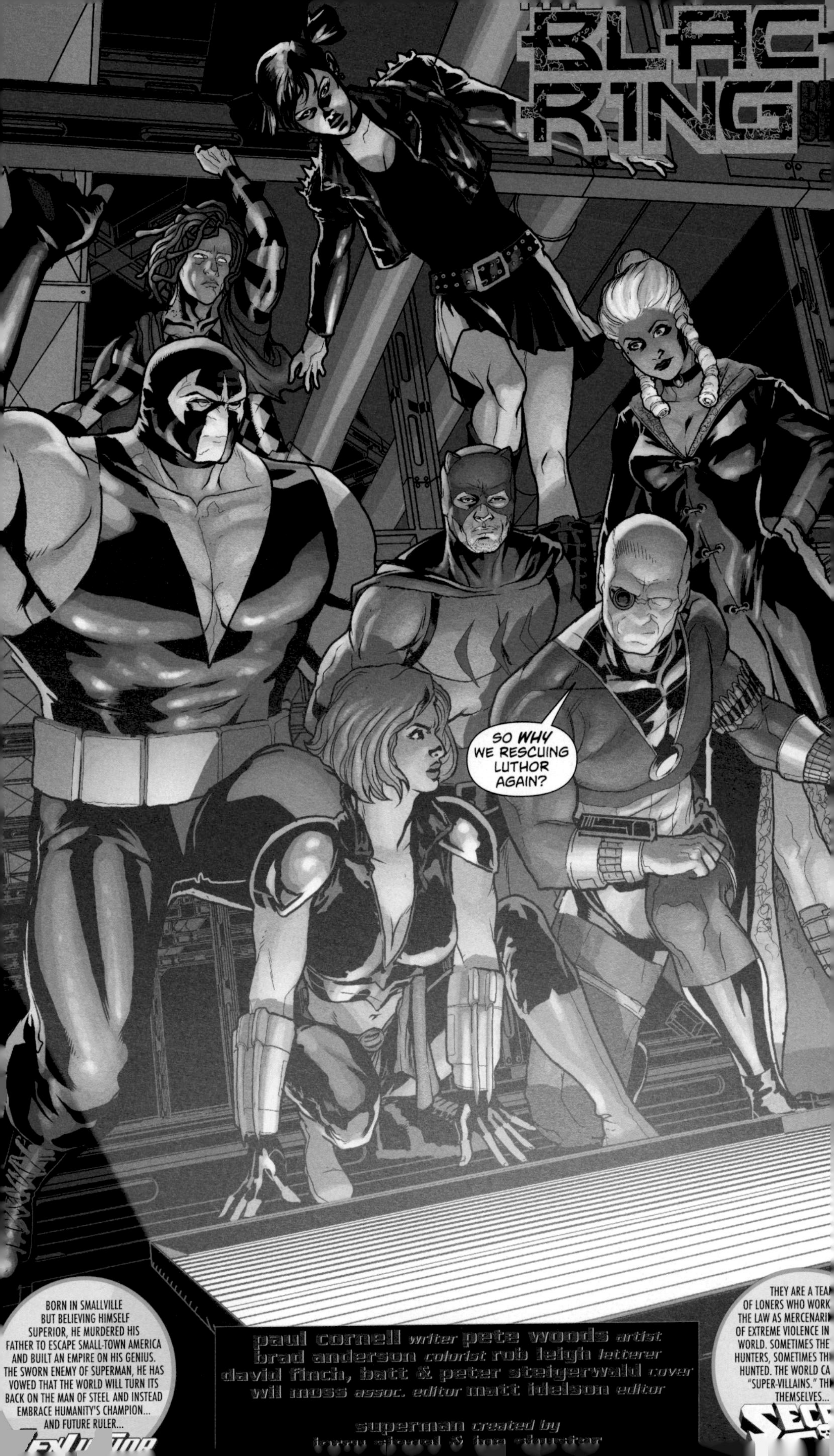

BLAC
RING
SO WHY WE RESCUING LUTHOR AGAIN?
BORN IN SMALLVILLE BUT BELIEVING HIMSELF SUPERIOR, HE MURDERED HIS FATHER TO ESCAPE SMALL-TOWN AMERICA AND BUILT AN EMPIRE ON HIS GENIUS. THE SWORN ENEMY OF SUPERMAN, HE HAS VOWED THAT THE WORLD WILL TURN ITS BACK ON THE MAN OF STEEL AND INSTEAD EMBRACE HUMANITY'S CHAMPION... AND FUTURE RULER...
paul cornell writer pete woods artist
brad anderson colorist rob leigh letterer
david finch, batt & peter steigerwald cover
wil moss assoc. editor matt idelson editor
superman created by

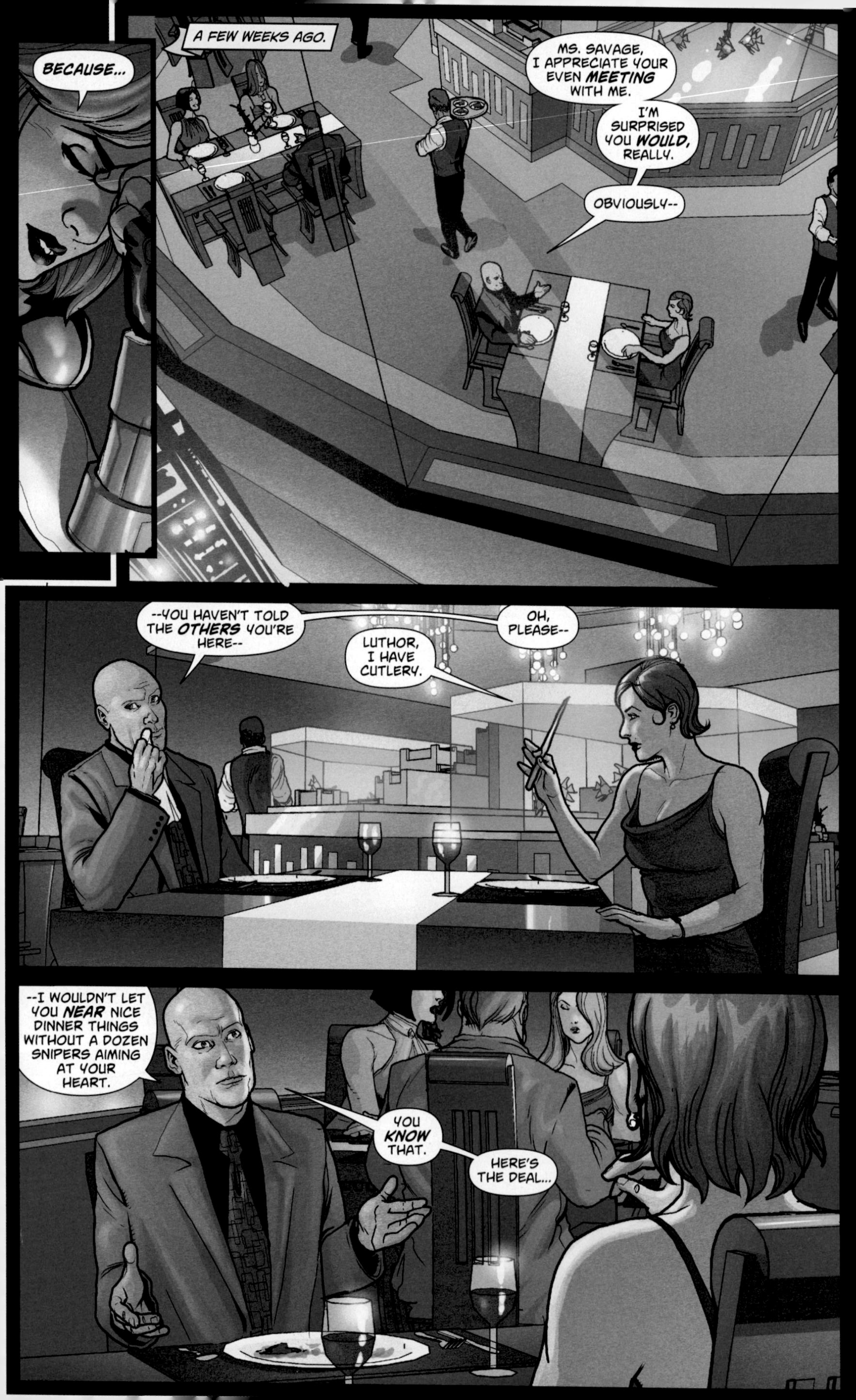
BECAUSE...
A FEW WEEKS AGO.
MS. SAVAGE, I APPRECIATE YOUR EVEN MEETING WITH ME.
I'M SURPRISED YOU WOULD, REALLY.
OBVIOUSLY--
--YOU HAVEN'T TOLD THE OTHERS YOU'RE HERE--
OH, PLEASE--
LUTHOR, I HAVE CUTLERY.
--I WOULDN'T LET YOU NEAR NICE DINNER THINGS WITHOUT A DOZEN SNIPERS AIMING AT YOUR HEART.
YOU KNOW THAT.
HERE'S THE DEAL...

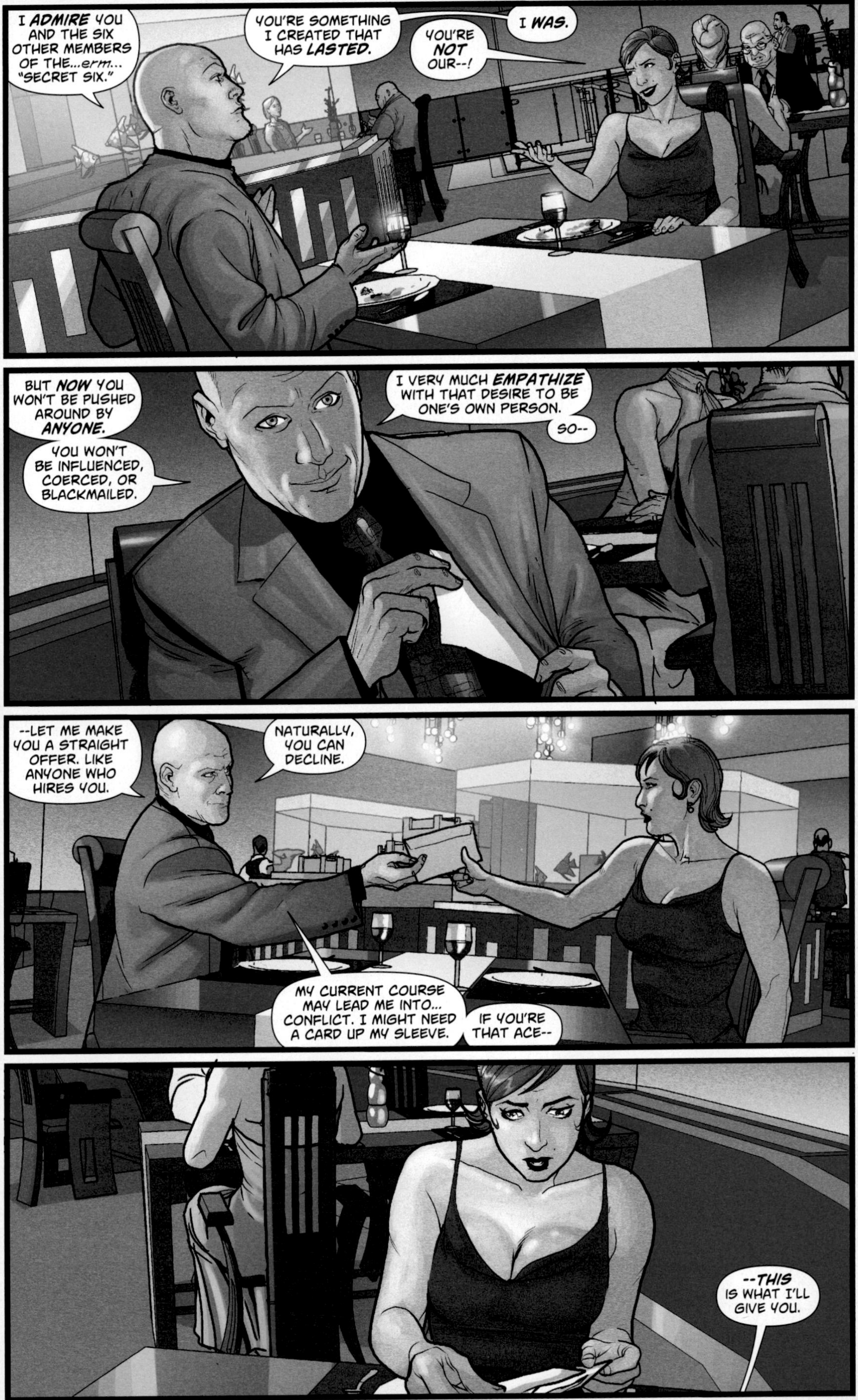
I ADMIRE YOU AND THE SIX OTHER MEMBERS OF THE...erm... "SECRET SIX."
YOU'RE SOMETHING I CREATED THAT HAS LASTED.
I WAS.
YOU'RE NOT OUR--!
BUT NOW YOU WON'T BE PUSHED AROUND BY ANYONE.
YOU WON'T BE INFLUENCED, COERCED, OR BLACKMAILED.
I VERY MUCH EMPATHIZE WITH THAT DESIRE TO BE ONE'S OWN PERSON.
SO--
--LET ME MAKE YOU A STRAIGHT OFFER. LIKE ANYONE WHO HIRES YOU.
NATURALLY, YOU CAN DECLINE.
MY CURRENT COURSE MAY LEAD ME INTO... CONFLICT. I MIGHT NEED A CARD UP MY SLEEVE.
IF YOU'RE THAT ACE--
--THIS IS WHAT I'LL GIVE YOU.

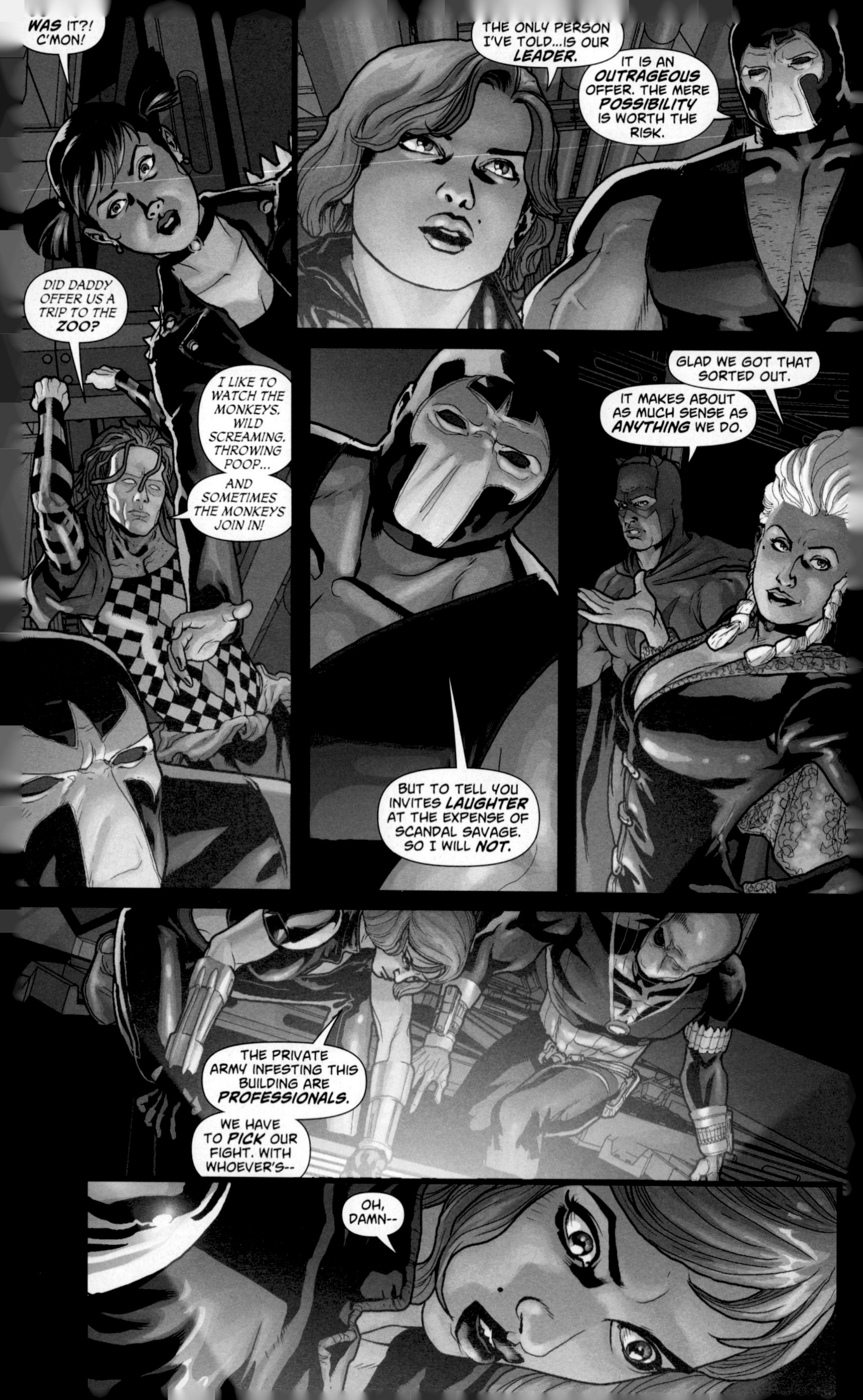
WAS IT?! C'MON!
DID DADDY OFFER US A TRIP TO THE ZOO?
I LIKE TO WATCH THE MONKEYS. WILD SCREAMING. THROWING POOP...
AND SOMETIMES THE MONKEYS JOIN IN!
THE ONLY PERSON I'VE TOLD...IS OUR LEADER.
IT IS AN OUTRAGEOUS OFFER. THE MERE POSSIBILITY IS WORTH THE RISK.
BUT TO TELL YOU INVITES LAUGHTER AT THE EXPENSE OF SCANDAL SAVAGE. SO I WILL NOT.
GLAD WE GOT THAT SORTED OUT.
IT MAKES ABOUT AS MUCH SENSE AS ANYTHING WE DO.
THE PRIVATE ARMY INFESTING THIS BUILDING ARE PROFESSIONALS.
WE HAVE TO PICK OUR FIGHT. WITH WHOEVER'S--
OH, DAMN--

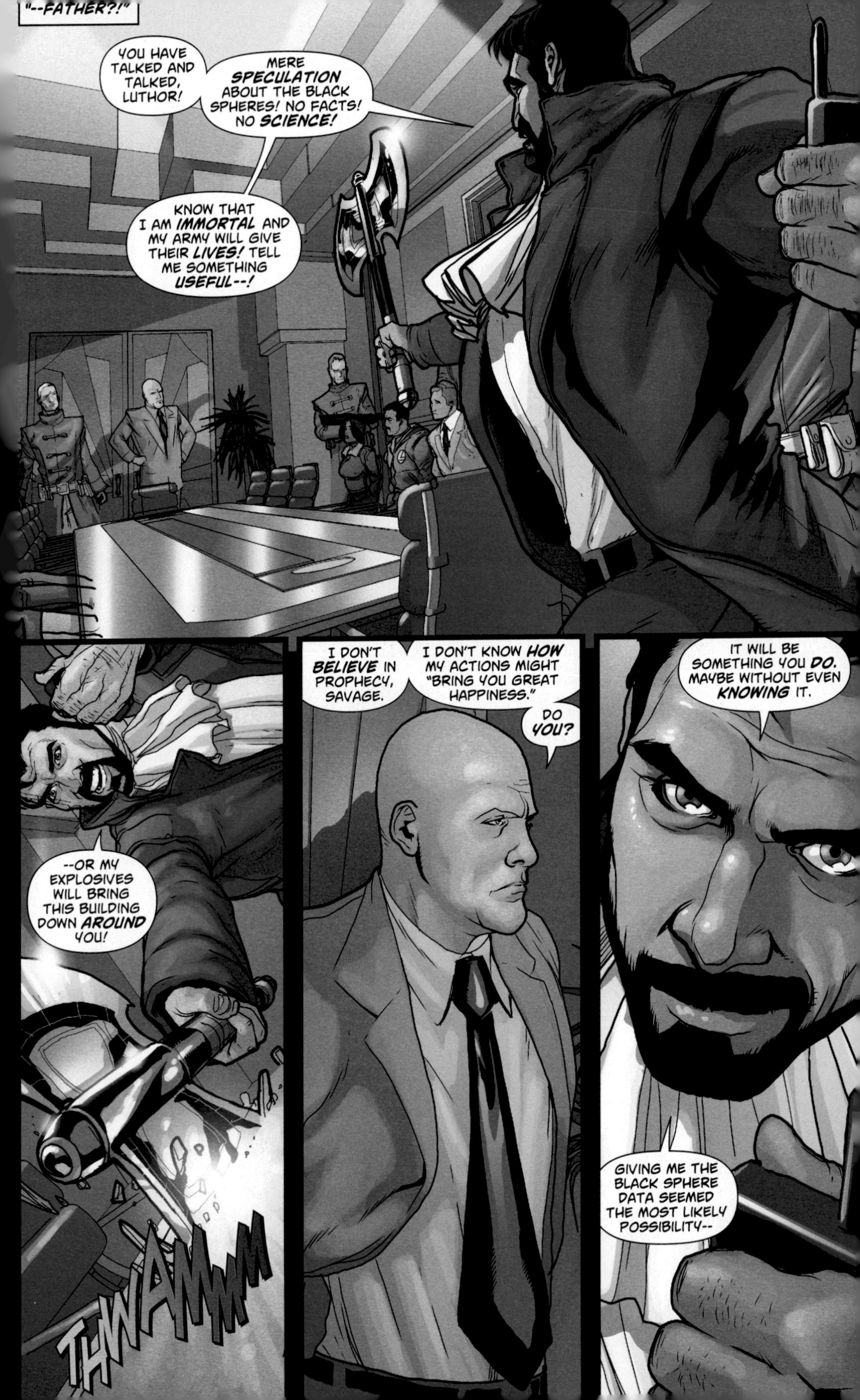
"--FATHER?!"
YOU HAVE TALKED AND TALKED, LUTHOR!
MERE SPECULATION ABOUT THE BLACK SPHERES! NO FACTS! NO SCIENCE!
KNOW THAT I AM IMMORTAL AND MY ARMY WILL GIVE THEIR LIVES! TELL ME SOMETHING USEFUL--!
--OR MY EXPLOSIVES WILL BRING THIS BUILDING DOWN AROUND YOU!
THWAMMM
I DON'T BELIEVE IN PROPHECY, SAVAGE.
I DON'T KNOW HOW MY ACTIONS MIGHT "BRING YOU GREAT HAPPINESS."
DO YOU?
IT WILL BE SOMETHING YOU DO. MAYBE WITHOUT EVEN KNOWING IT.
GIVING ME THE BLACK SPHERE DATA SEEMED THE MOST LIKELY POSSIBILITY--

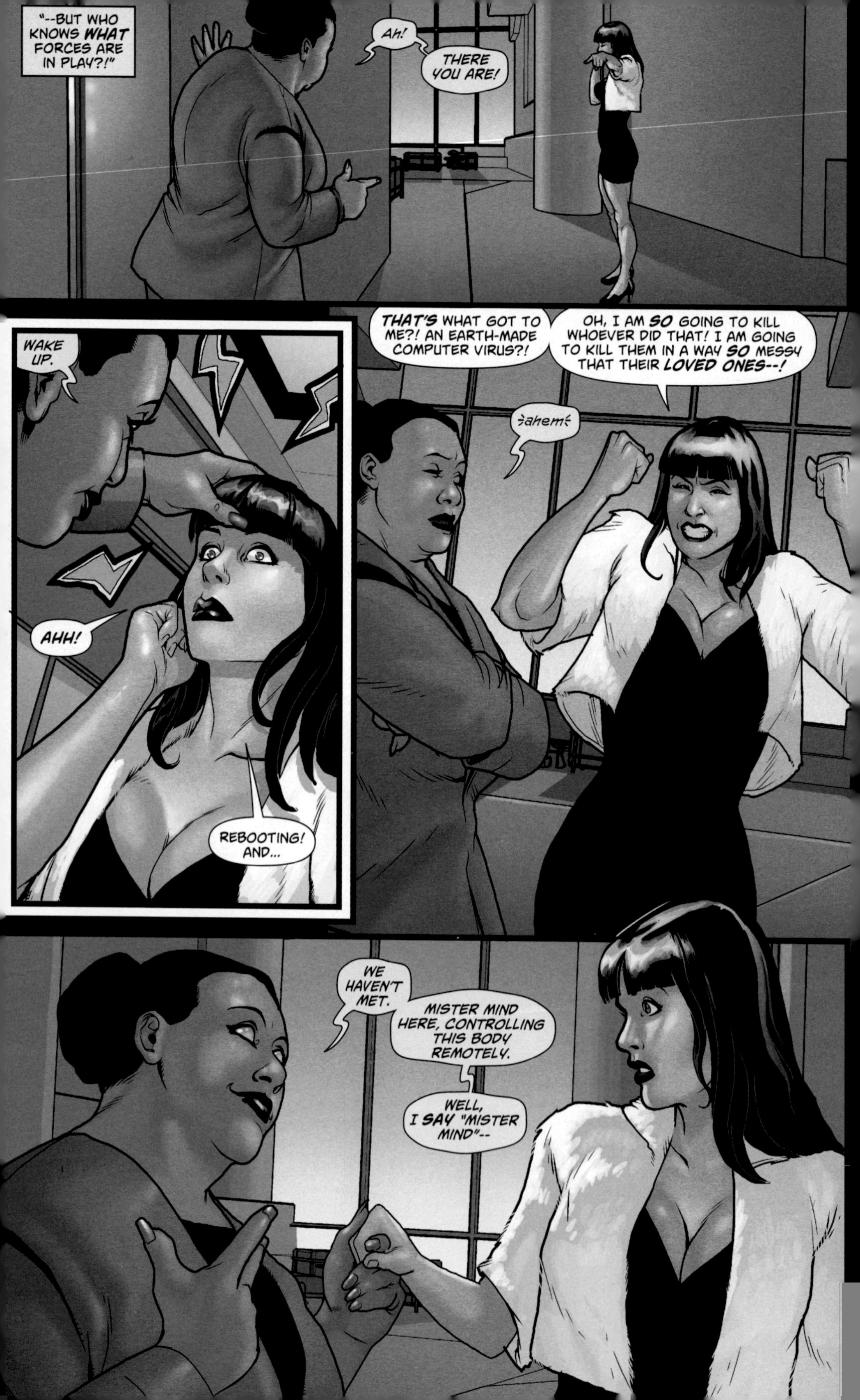
"--BUT WHO KNOWS WHAT FORCES ARE IN PLAY?!"
Ah!
THERE YOU ARE!
WAKE UP.
AHH!
REBOOTING! AND...
THAT'S WHAT GOT TO ME?! AN EARTH-MADE COMPUTER VIRUS?!
OH, I AM SO GOING TO KILL WHOEVER DID THAT! I AM GOING TO KILL THEM IN A WAY SO MESSY THAT THEIR LOVED ONES--!
ahem
WE HAVEN'T MET.
MISTER MIND HERE, CONTROLLING THIS BODY REMOTELY.
WELL, I SAY "MISTER MIND"--

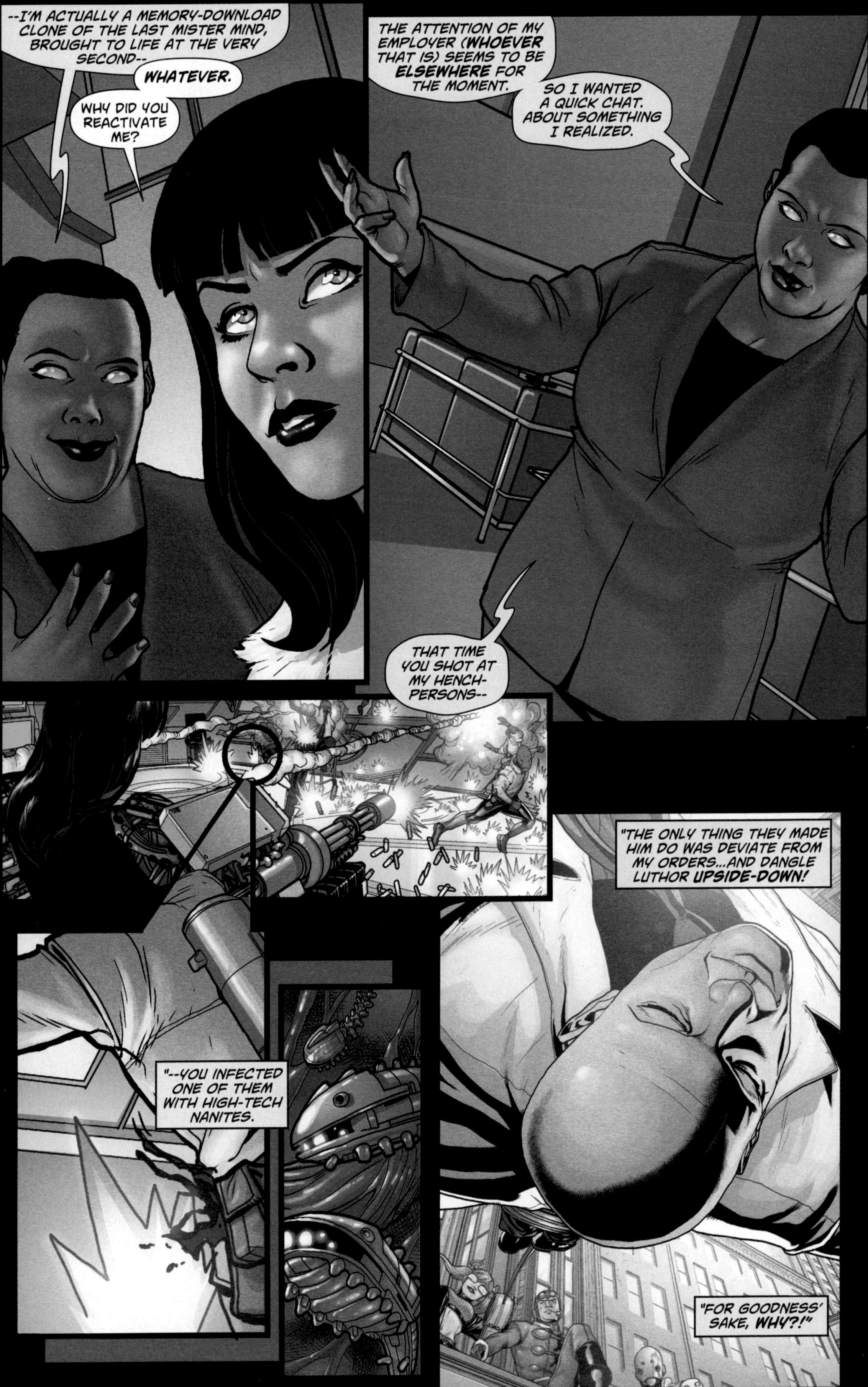
--I'M ACTUALLY A MEMORY-DOWNLOAD CLONE OF THE LAST MISTER MIND, BROUGHT TO LIFE AT THE VERY SECOND--
WHATEVER.
WHY DID YOU REACTIVATE ME?
THE ATTENTION OF MY EMPLOYER (WHOEVER THAT IS) SEEMS TO BE ELSEWHERE FOR THE MOMENT.
SO I WANTED A QUICK CHAT. ABOUT SOMETHING I REALIZED.
THAT TIME YOU SHOT AT MY HENCH-PERSONS--
"--YOU INFECTED ONE OF THEM WITH HIGH-TECH NANITES.
"THE ONLY THING THEY MADE HIM DO WAS DEVIATE FROM MY ORDERS...AND DANGLE LUTHOR UPSIDE-DOWN!
"FOR GOODNESS' SAKE, WHY?!"

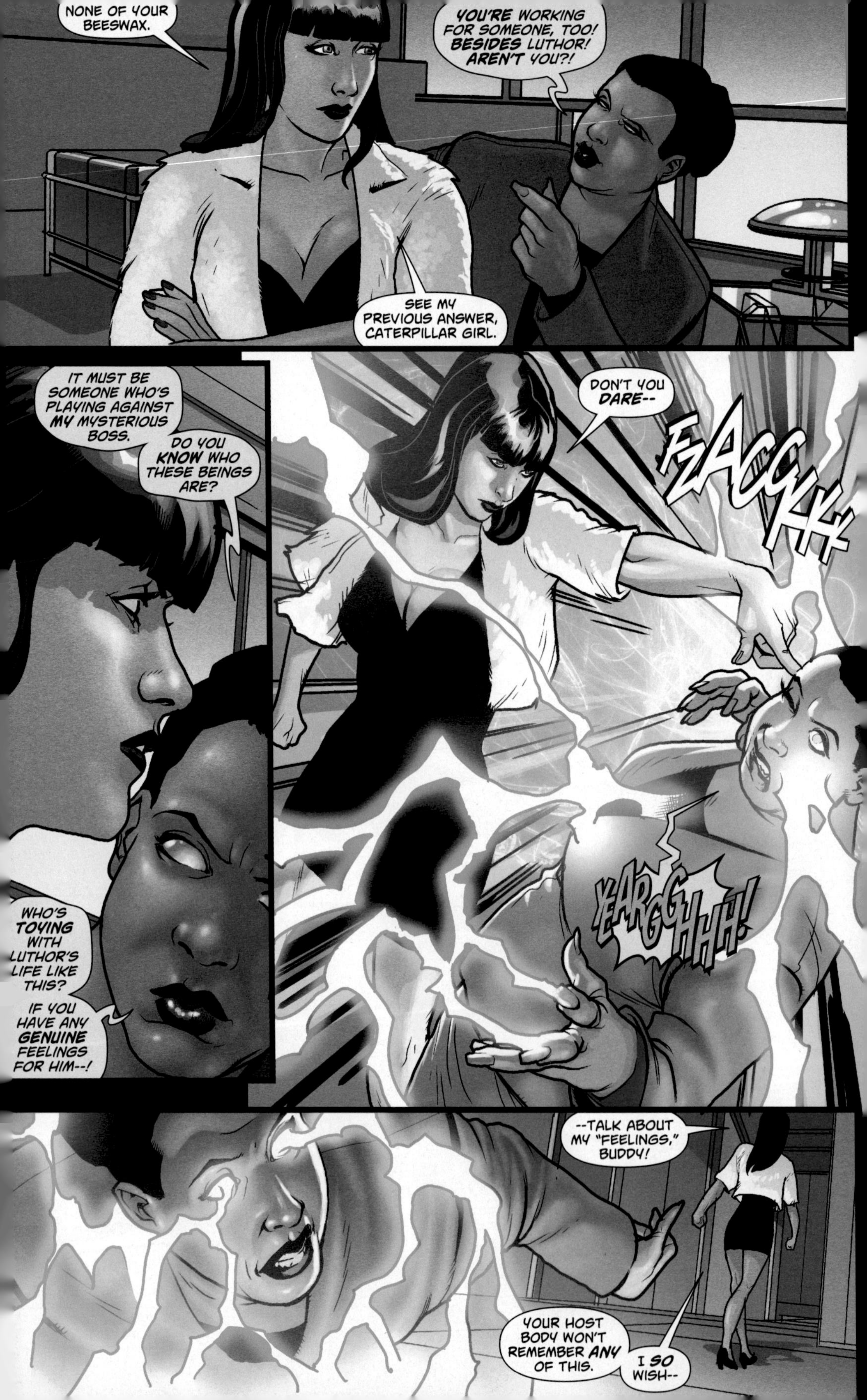
NONE OF YOUR BEESWAX.
YOU'RE WORKING FOR SOMEONE, TOO! BESIDES LUTHOR! AREN'T YOU?!
SEE MY PREVIOUS ANSWER, CATERPILLAR GIRL.
IT MUST BE SOMEONE WHO'S PLAYING AGAINST MY MYSTERIOUS BOSS.
DO YOU KNOW WHO THESE BEINGS ARE?
WHO'S TOYING WITH LUTHOR'S LIFE LIKE THIS?
IF YOU HAVE ANY GENUINE FEELINGS FOR HIM--!
DON'T YOU DARE--
FZACCKKK
YEARGGHHH!
--TALK ABOUT MY "FEELINGS," BUDDY!
YOUR HOST BODY WON'T REMEMBER ANY OF THIS.
I SO WISH--

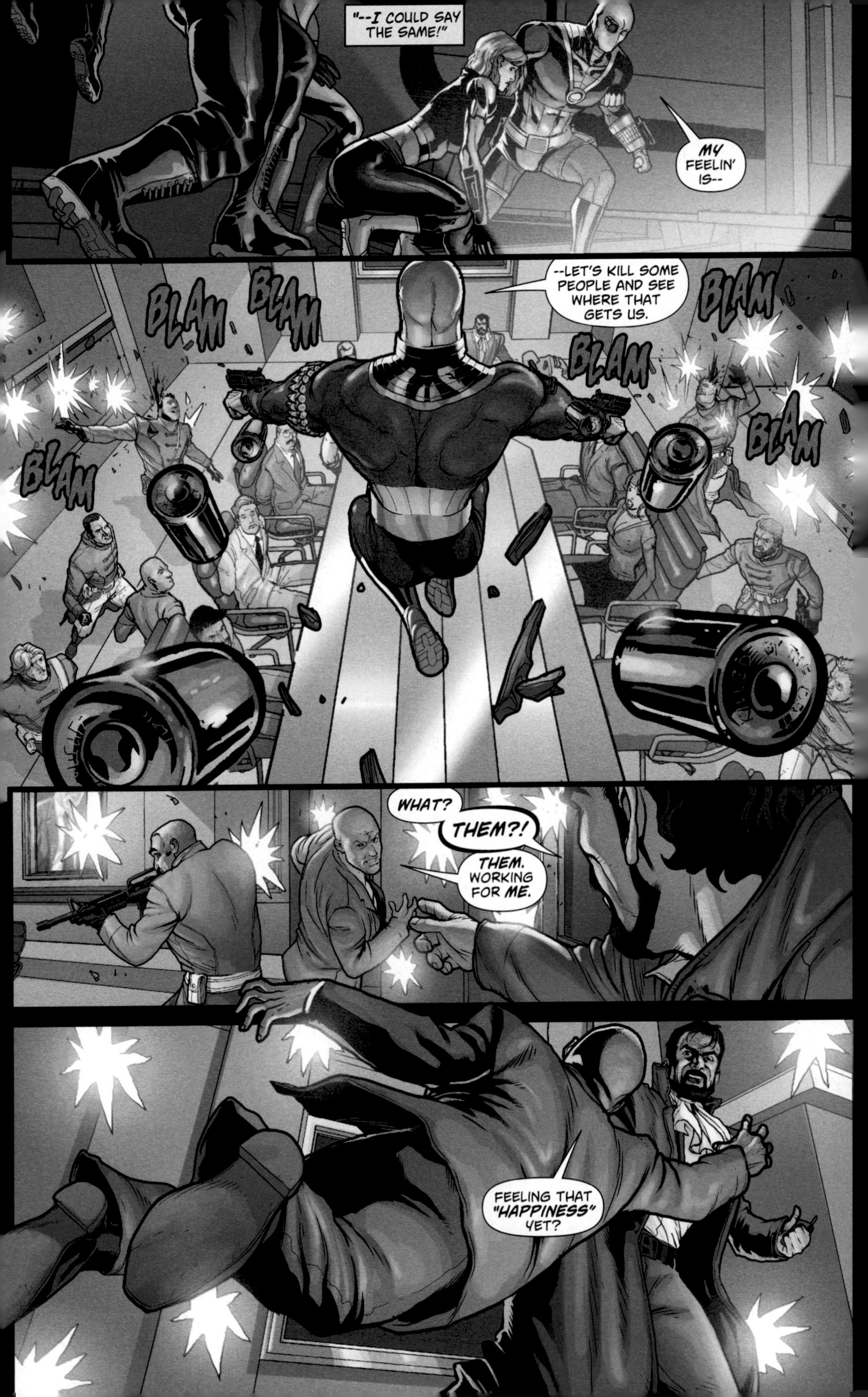
"--I COULD SAY THE SAME!"
MY FEELIN' IS--
--LET'S KILL SOME PEOPLE AND SEE WHERE THAT GETS US.
BLAM
BLAM
BLAM
BLAM
BLAM
BLAM
WHAT?
THEM?!
THEM. WORKING FOR ME.
FEELING THAT "HAPPINESS" YET?

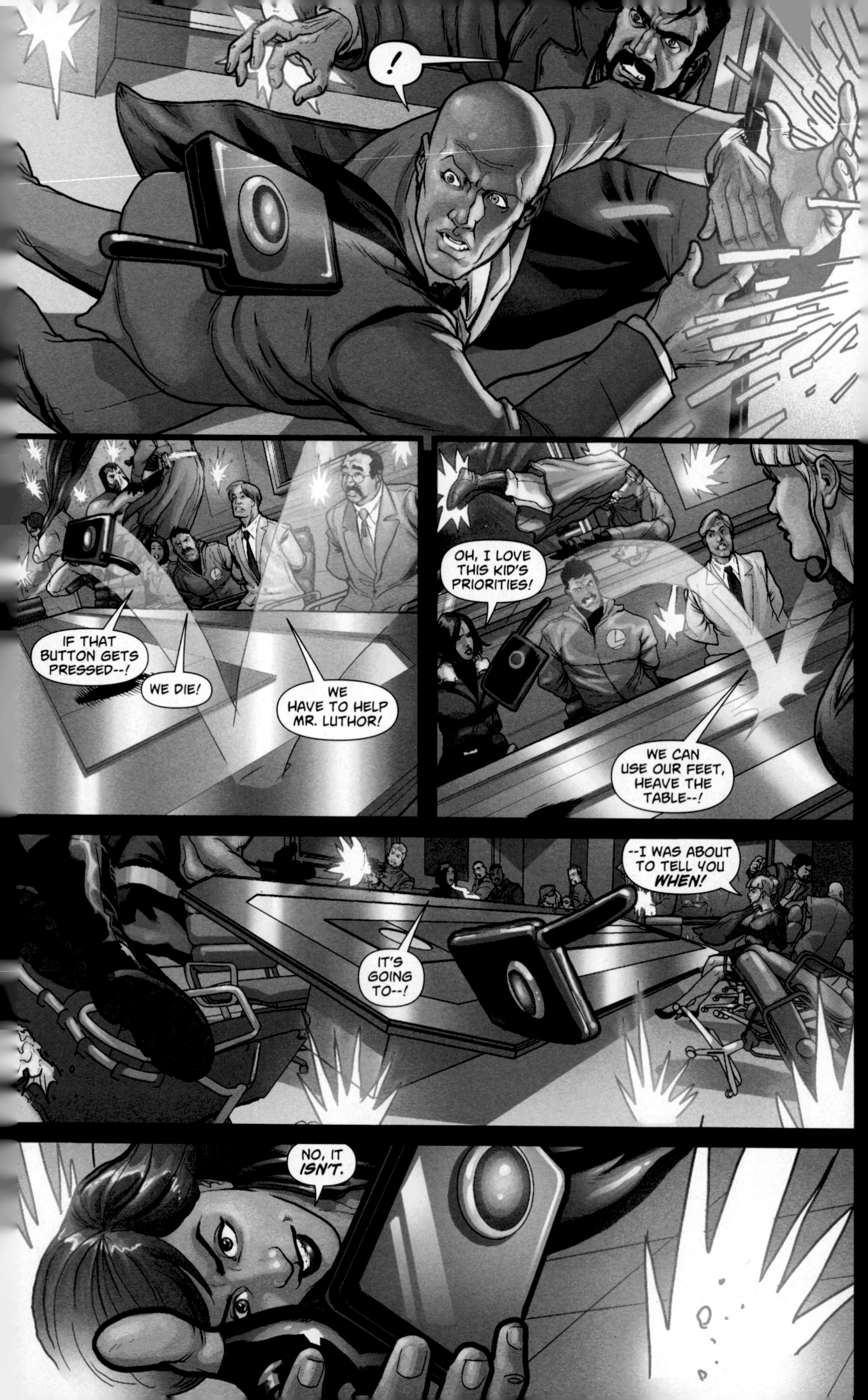
!
IF THAT BUTTON GETS PRESSED--!
WE DIE!
WE HAVE TO HELP MR. LUTHOR!
OH, I LOVE THIS KID'S PRIORITIES!
WE CAN USE OUR FEET, HEAVE THE TABLE--!
--I WAS ABOUT TO TELL YOU *WHEN!*
IT'S GOING TO--!
NO, IT *ISN'T.*

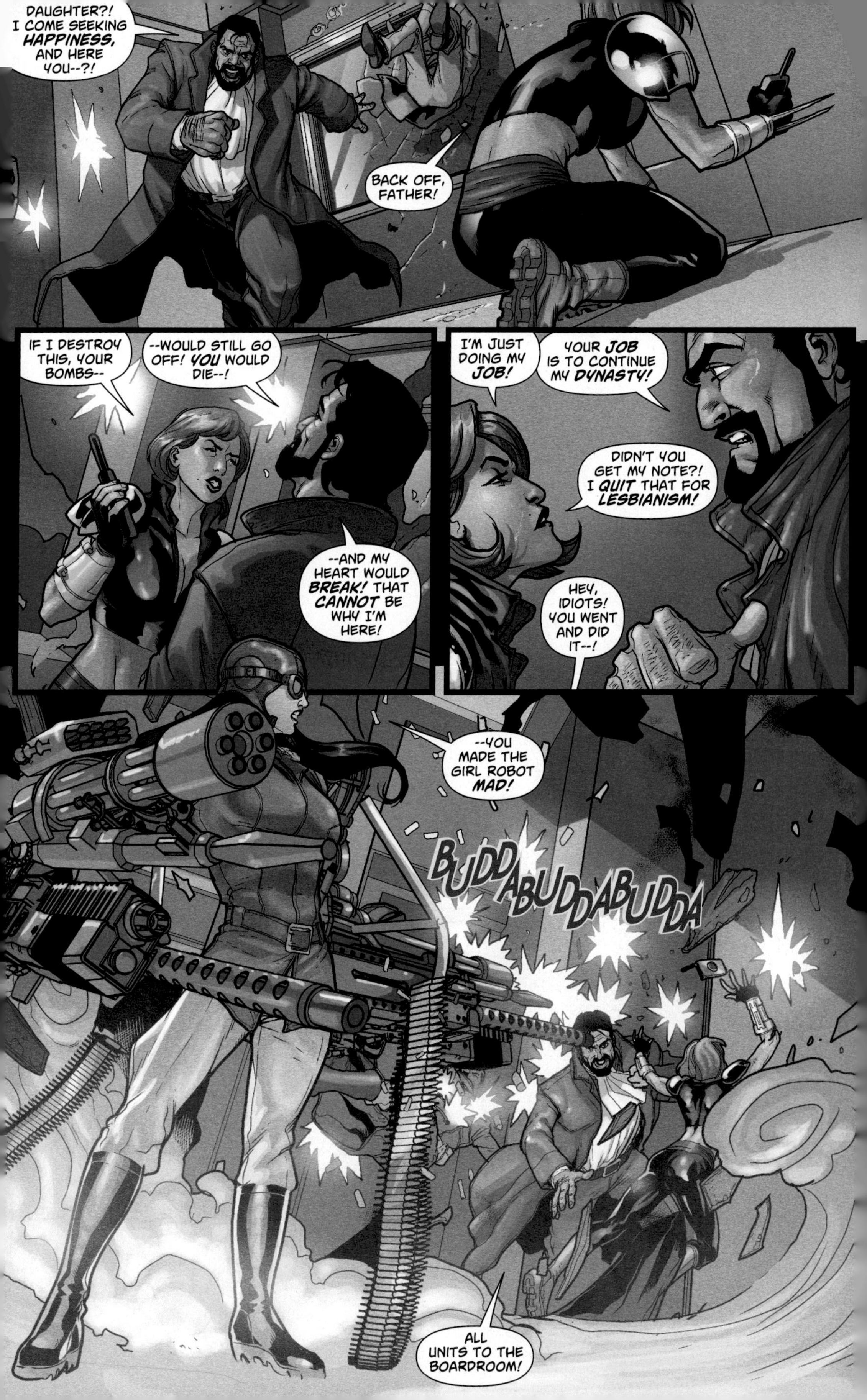
DAUGHTER?! I COME SEEKING HAPPINESS, AND HERE YOU--?!
BACK OFF, FATHER!
IF I DESTROY THIS, YOUR BOMBS--
--WOULD STILL GO OFF! YOU WOULD DIE--!
--AND MY HEART WOULD BREAK! THAT CANNOT BE WHY I'M HERE!
I'M JUST DOING MY JOB!
YOUR JOB IS TO CONTINUE MY DYNASTY!
DIDN'T YOU GET MY NOTE?! I QUIT THAT FOR LESBIANISM!
HEY, IDIOTS! YOU WENT AND DID IT--!
--YOU MADE THE GIRL ROBOT MAD!
BUDDABUDDABUDDA
ALL UNITS TO THE BOARDROOM!

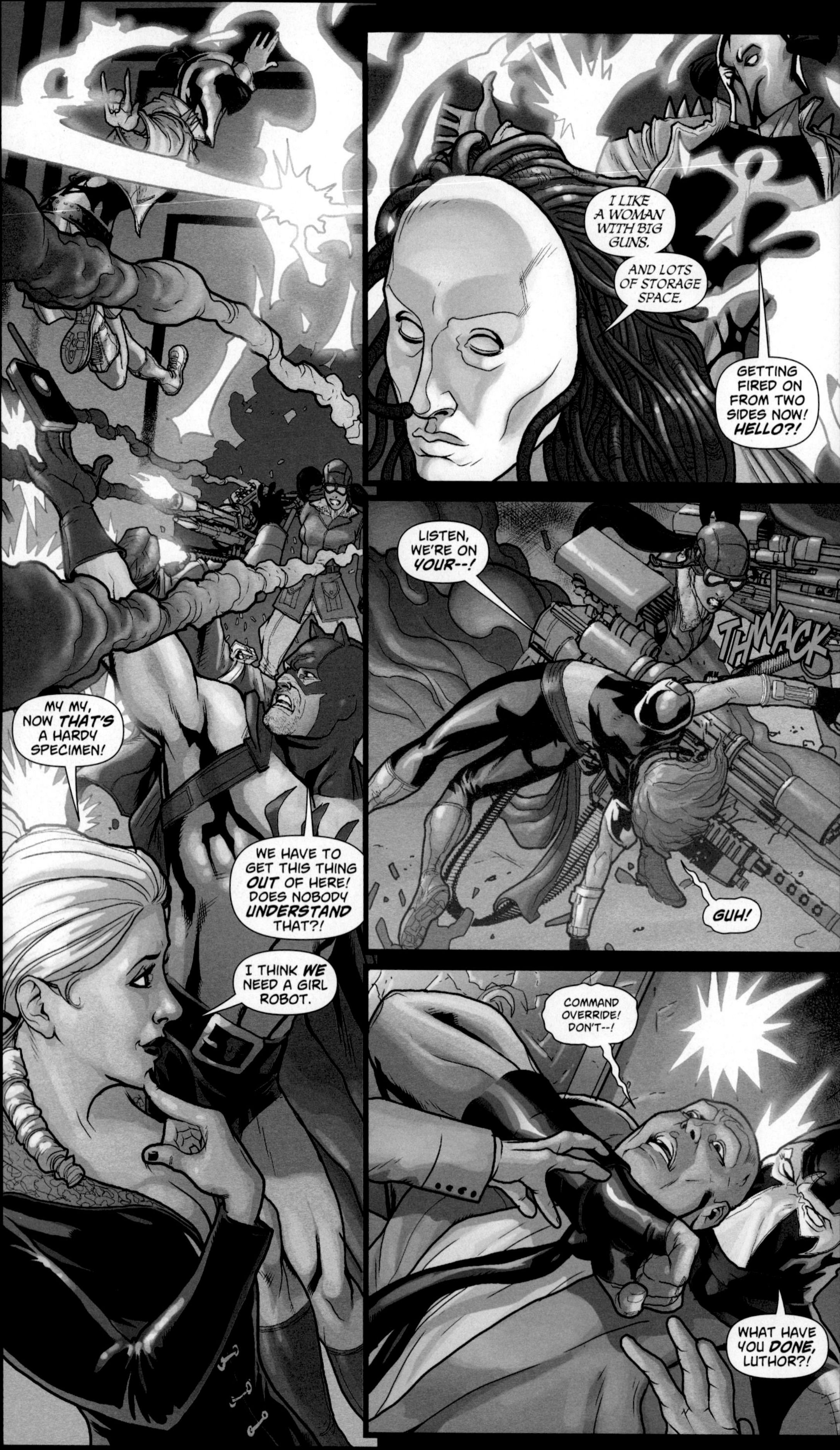
MY MY, NOW THAT'S A HARDY SPECIMEN!
WE HAVE TO GET THIS THING OUT OF HERE! DOES NOBODY UNDERSTAND THAT?!
I THINK WE NEED A GIRL ROBOT.
I LIKE A WOMAN WITH BIG GUNS.
AND LOTS OF STORAGE SPACE.
GETTING FIRED ON FROM TWO SIDES NOW! HELLO?!
LISTEN, WE'RE ON YOUR--!
THWACK
GUH!
COMMAND OVERRIDE! DON'T--!
WHAT HAVE YOU DONE, LUTHOR?!

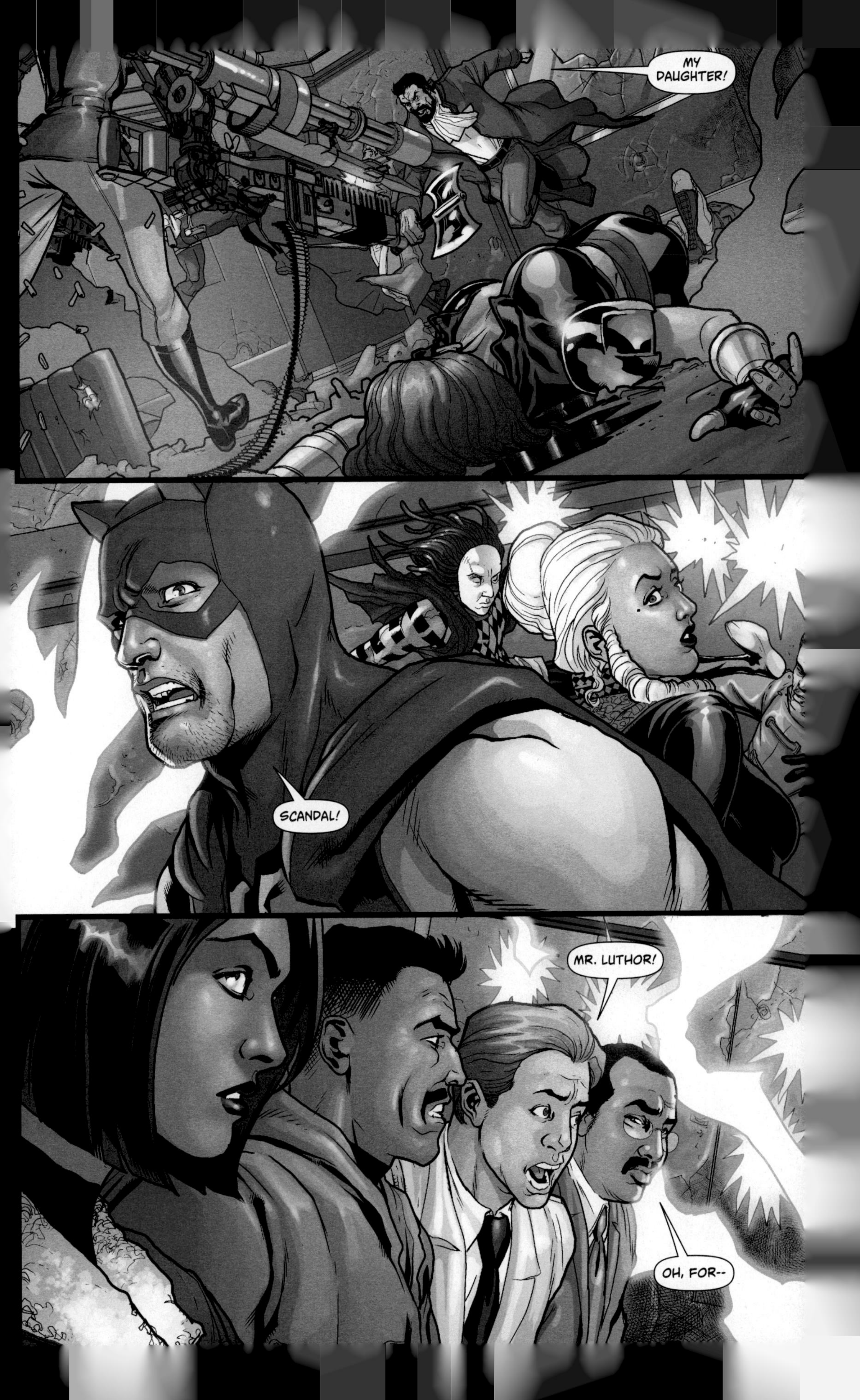
MY DAUGHTER!
SCANDAL!
MR. LUTHOR!
OH, FOR--

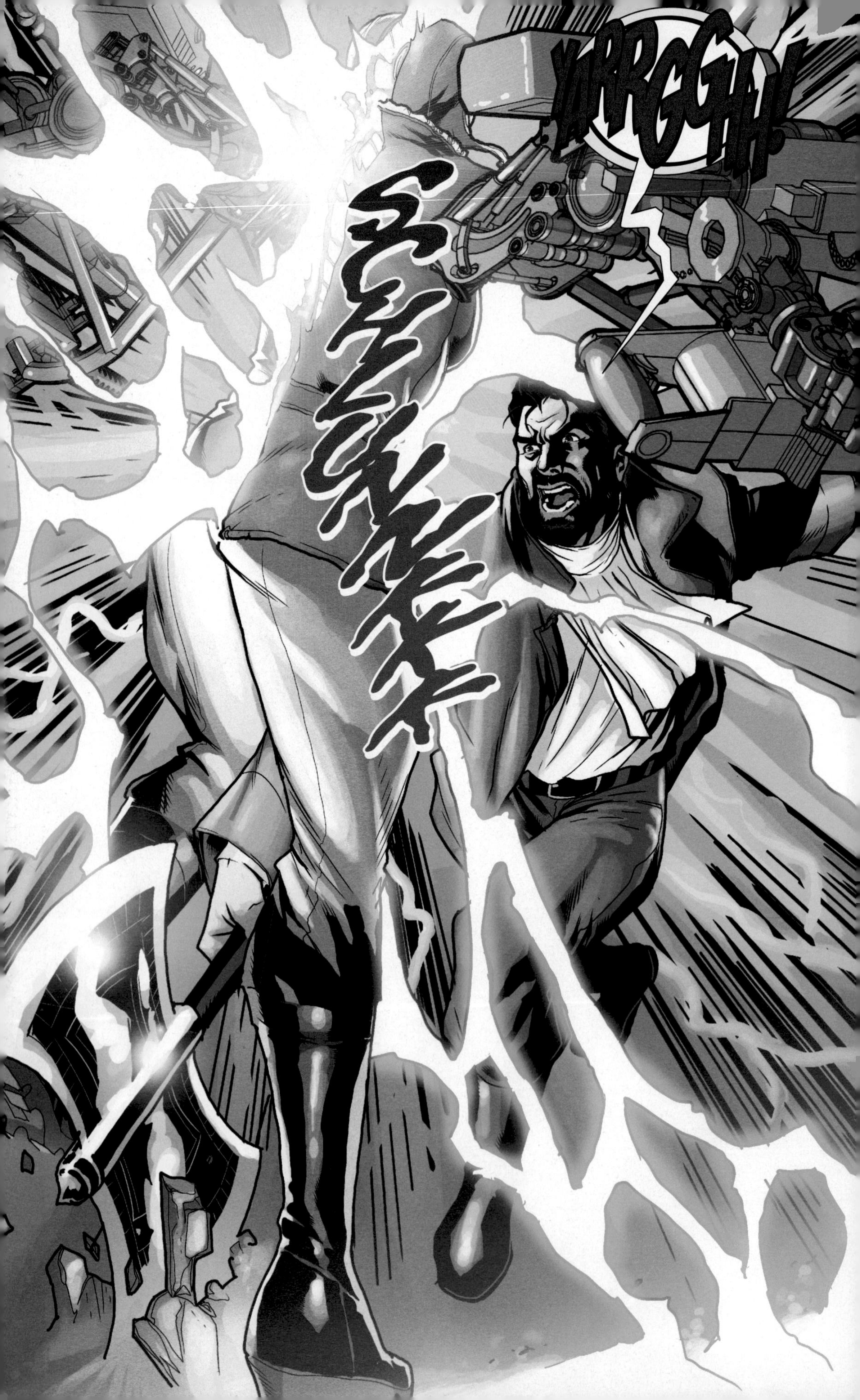
YARRGGHH!
SCHLUNKKK

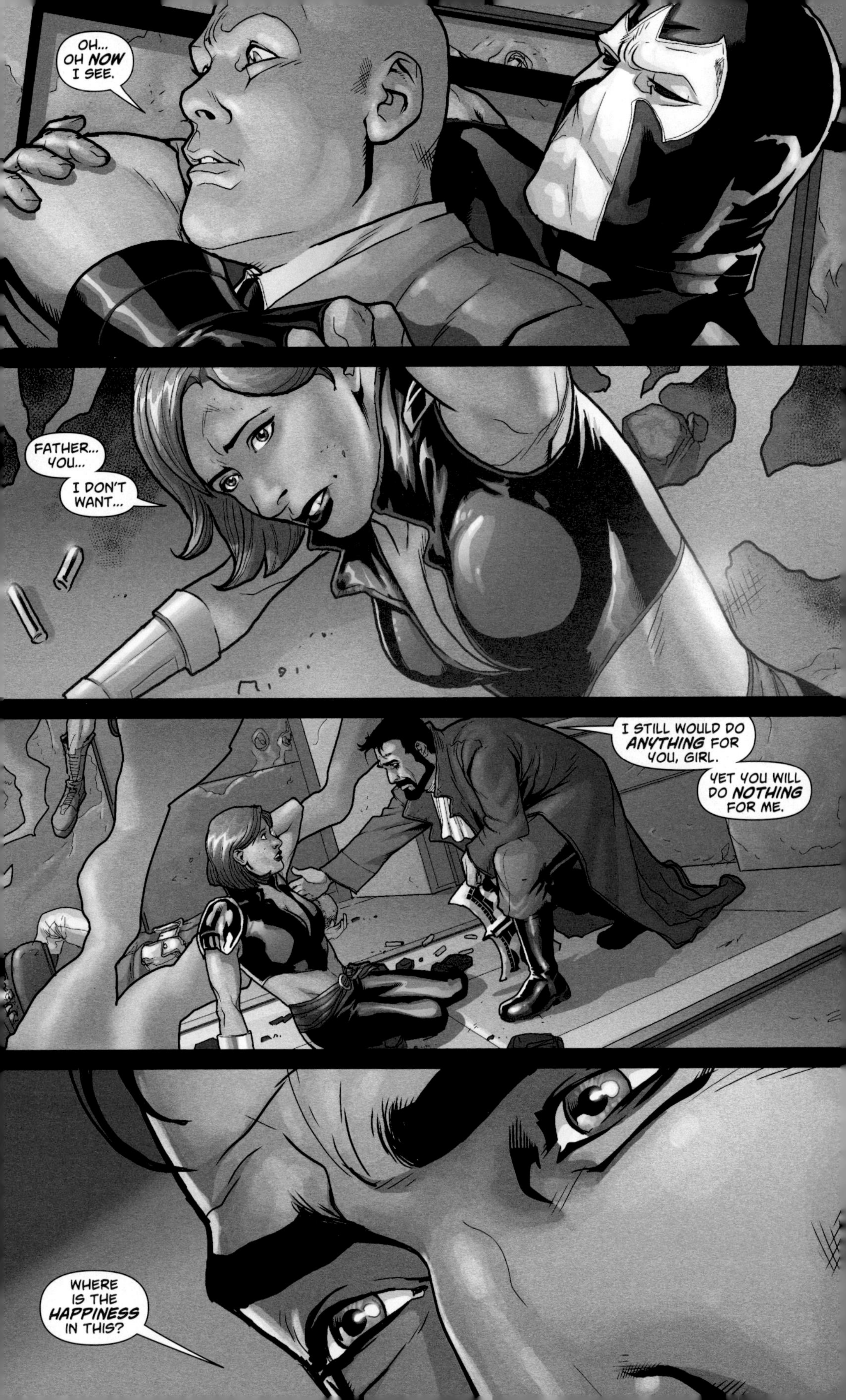
OH... OH NOW I SEE.
FATHER... YOU...
I DON'T WANT...
I STILL WOULD DO ANYTHING FOR YOU, GIRL.
YET YOU WILL DO NOTHING FOR ME.
WHERE IS THE HAPPINESS IN THIS?

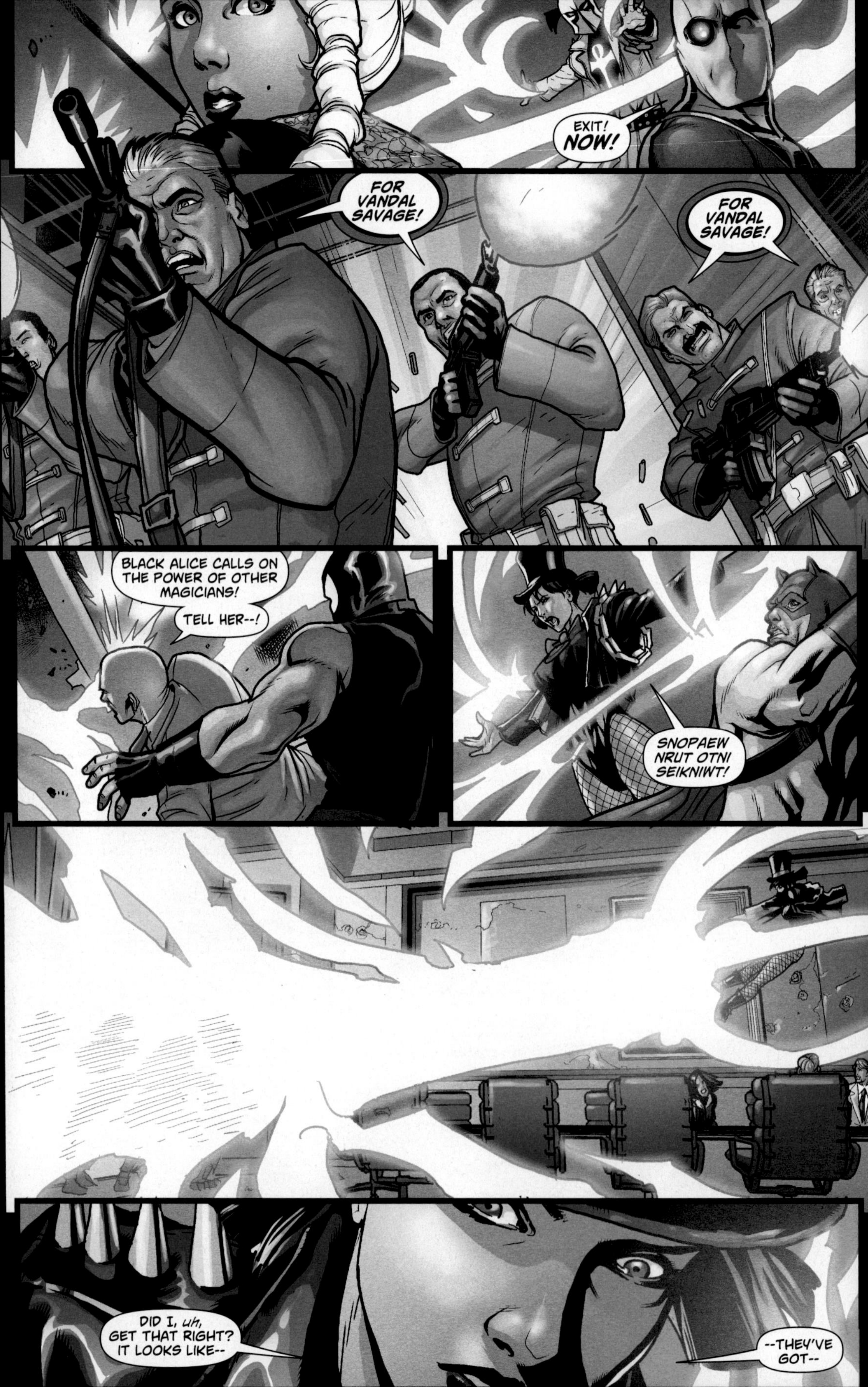
EXIT! NOW!
FOR VANDAL SAVAGE!
FOR VANDAL SAVAGE!
BLACK ALICE CALLS ON THE POWER OF OTHER MAGICIANS!
TELL HER--!
SNOPAEW NRUT OTNI SEIKNIWT!
DID I, *uh,* GET THAT RIGHT? IT LOOKS LIKE--
--THEY'VE GOT--

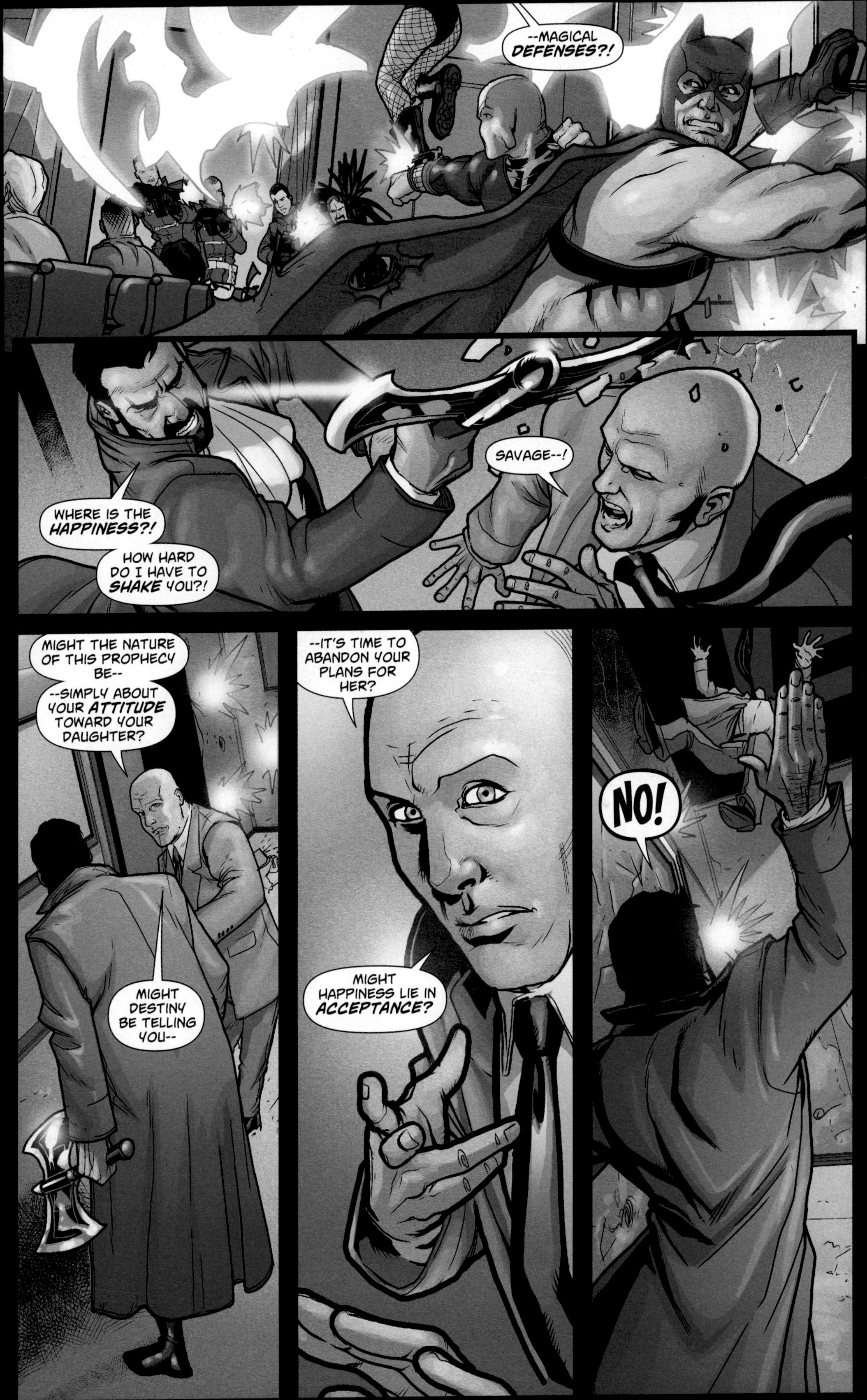

--MAGICAL DEFENSES?!
WHERE IS THE HAPPINESS?!
HOW HARD DO I HAVE TO SHAKE YOU?!
SAVAGE--!
MIGHT THE NATURE OF THIS PROPHECY BE--
--SIMPLY ABOUT YOUR ATTITUDE TOWARD YOUR DAUGHTER?
MIGHT DESTINY BE TELLING YOU--
--IT'S TIME TO ABANDON YOUR PLANS FOR HER?
MIGHT HAPPINESS LIE IN ACCEPTANCE?
NO!

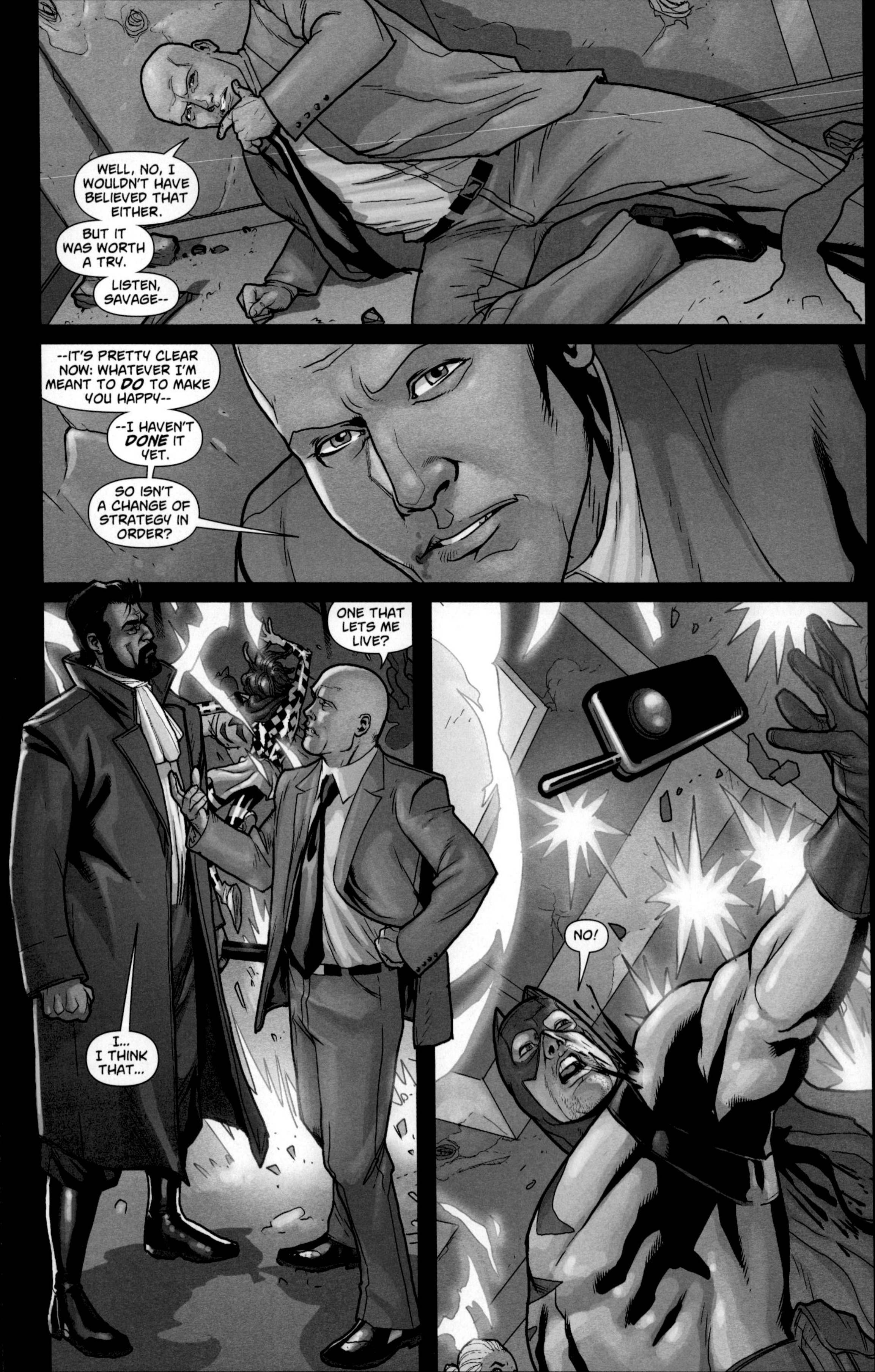
WELL, NO, I WOULDN'T HAVE BELIEVED THAT EITHER.
BUT IT WAS WORTH A TRY.
LISTEN, SAVAGE--
--IT'S PRETTY CLEAR NOW: WHATEVER I'M MEANT TO DO TO MAKE YOU HAPPY--
--I HAVEN'T DONE IT YET.
SO ISN'T A CHANGE OF STRATEGY IN ORDER?
ONE THAT LETS ME LIVE?
I... I THINK THAT...
NO!

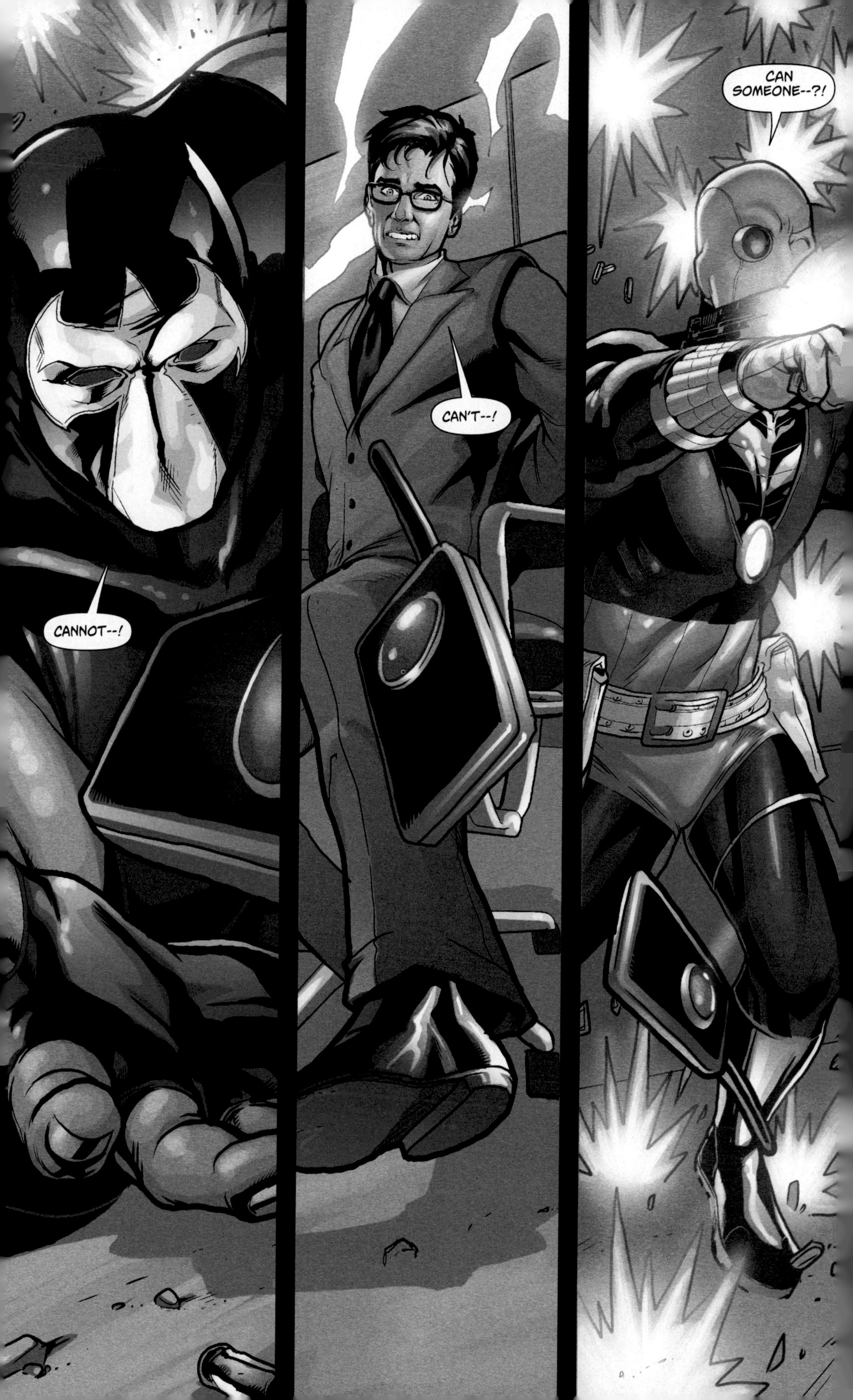
CANNOT--!
CAN'T--!
CAN
SOMEONE--?!

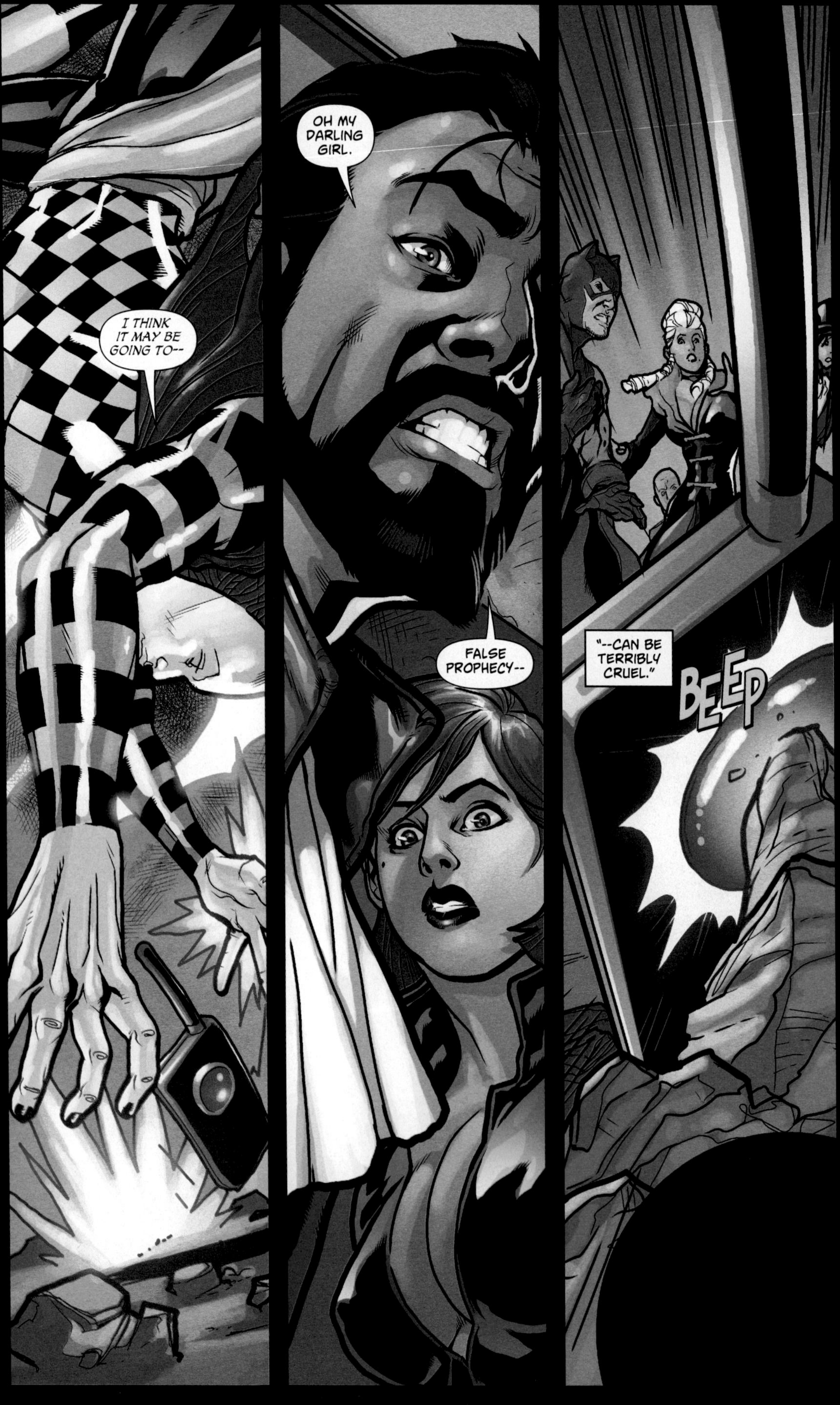

I THINK IT MAY BE GOING TO--
OH MY DARLING GIRL.
FALSE PROPHECY--
"--CAN BE TERRIBLY CRUEL."
BEEP

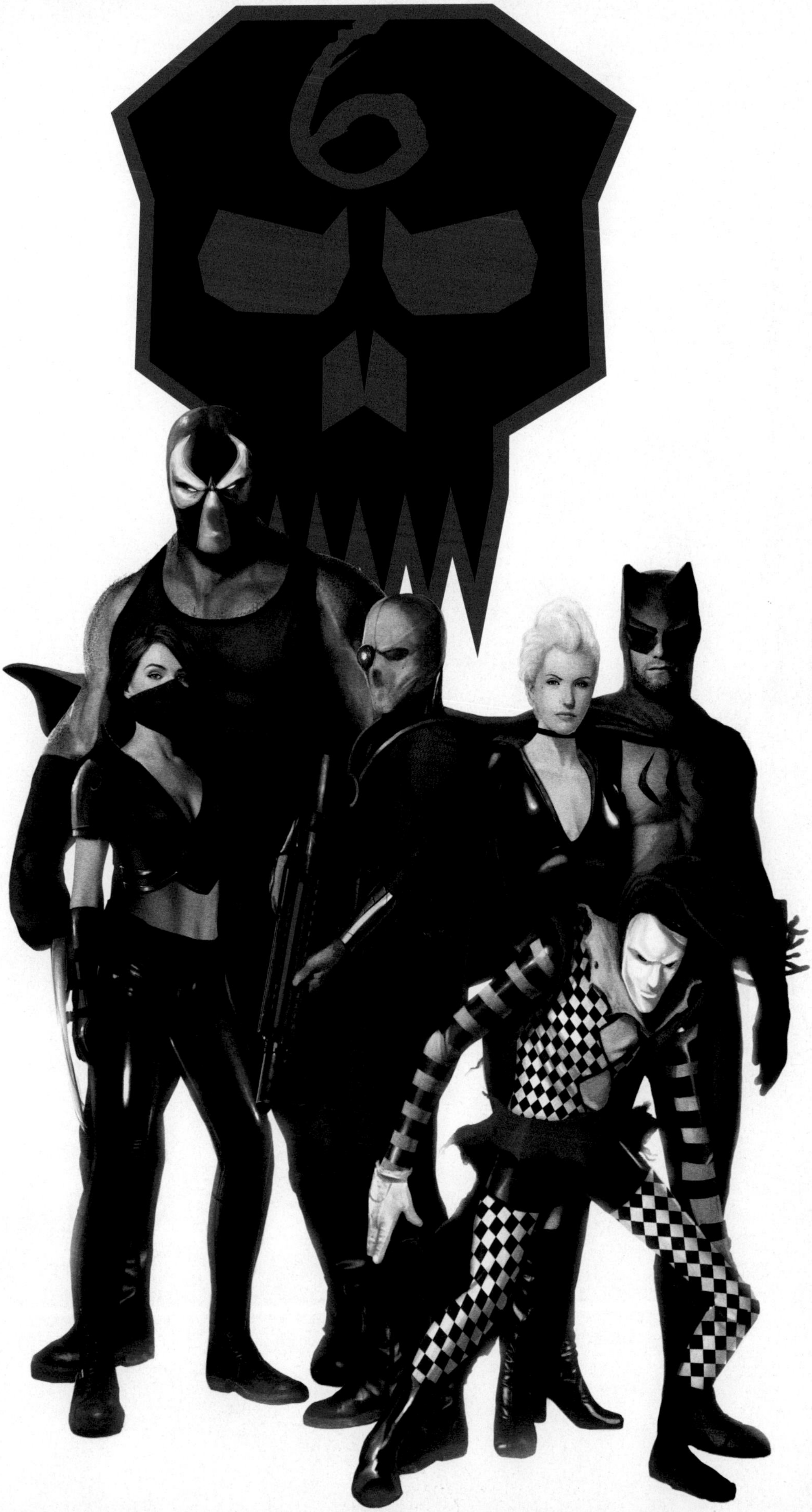

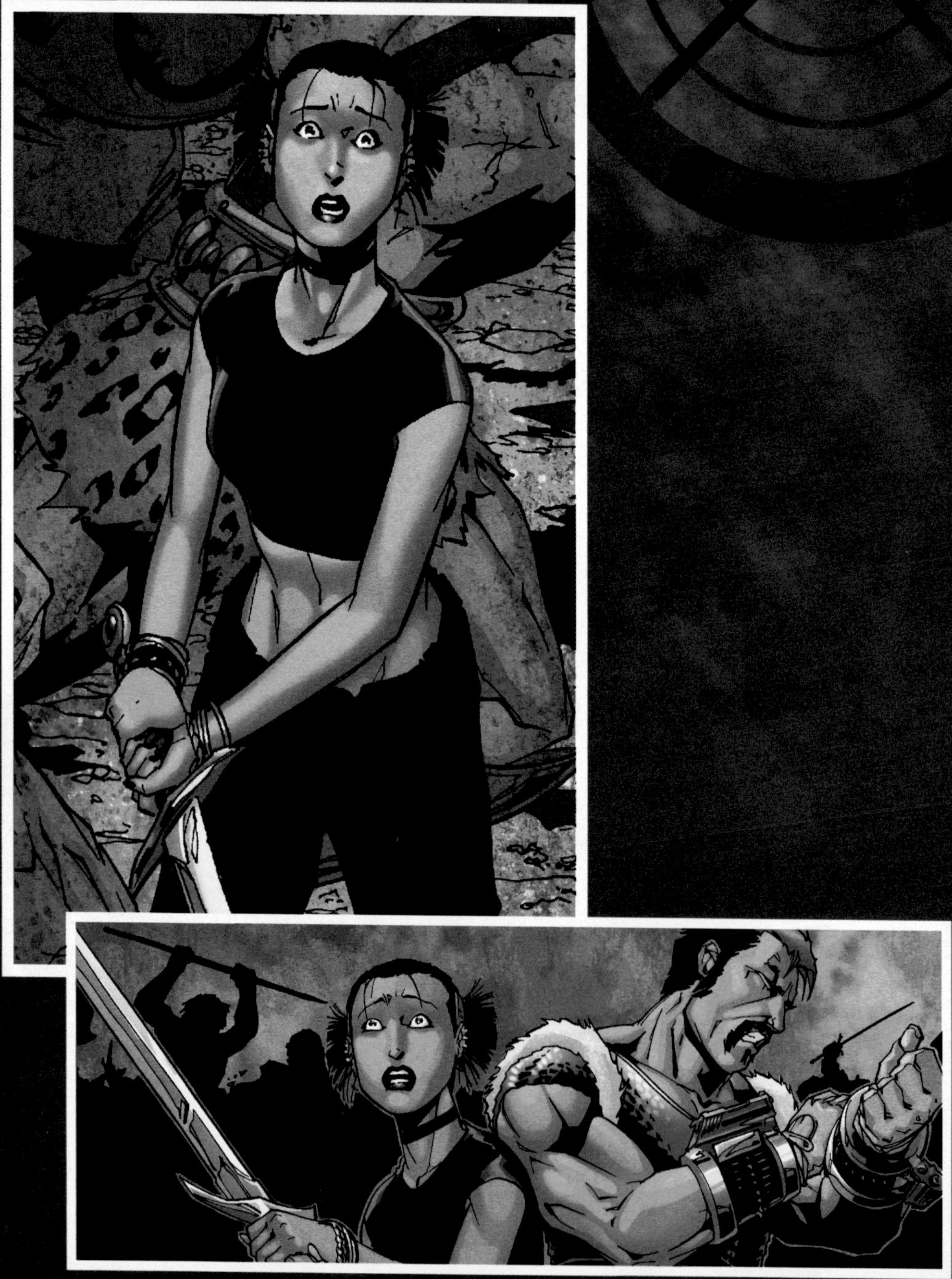

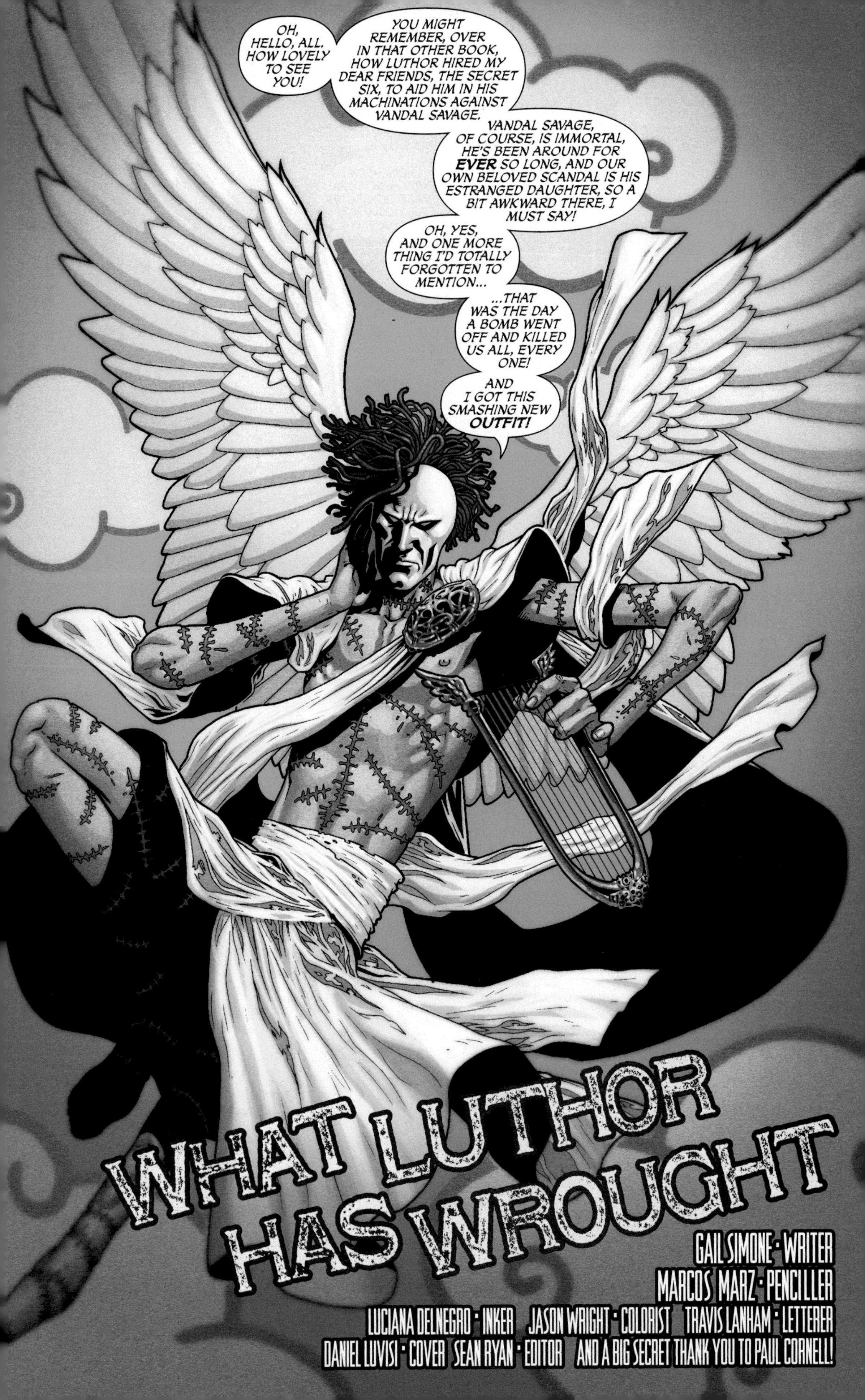
OH, HELLO, ALL. HOW LOVELY TO SEE YOU!
YOU MIGHT REMEMBER, OVER IN THAT OTHER BOOK, HOW LUTHOR HIRED MY DEAR FRIENDS, THE SECRET SIX, TO AID HIM IN HIS MACHINATIONS AGAINST VANDAL SAVAGE.
VANDAL SAVAGE, OF COURSE, IS IMMORTAL, HE'S BEEN AROUND FOR **EVER** SO LONG, AND OUR OWN BELOVED SCANDAL IS HIS ESTRANGED DAUGHTER, SO A BIT AWKWARD THERE, I MUST SAY!
OH, YES, AND ONE MORE THING I'D TOTALLY FORGOTTEN TO MENTION...
...THAT WAS THE DAY A BOMB WENT OFF AND KILLED US ALL, EVERY ONE!
AND I GOT THIS SMASHING NEW **OUTFIT!**
WHAT LUTHOR HAS WROUGHT
GAIL SIMONE • WRITER
MARCOS MARZ • PENCILLER
LUCIANA DELNEGRO • INKER JASON WRIGHT • COLORIST TRAVIS LANHAM • LETTERER
DANIEL LUVISI • COVER SEAN RYAN • EDITOR AND A BIG SECRET THANK YOU TO PAUL CORNELL!

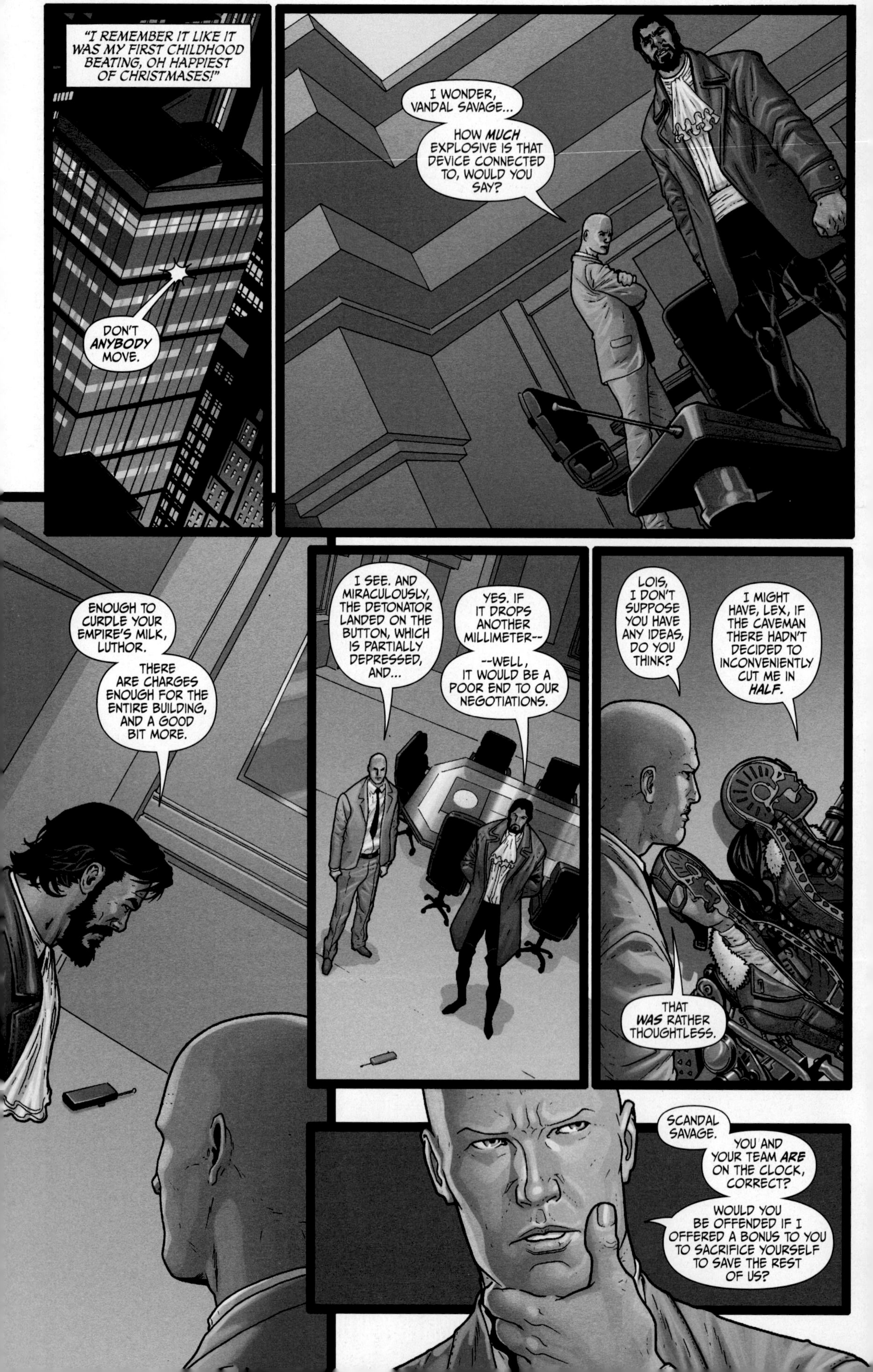
"I REMEMBER IT LIKE IT WAS MY FIRST CHILDHOOD BEATING, OH HAPPIEST OF CHRISTMASES!"
DON'T ANYBODY MOVE.
I WONDER, VANDAL SAVAGE...
HOW MUCH EXPLOSIVE IS THAT DEVICE CONNECTED TO, WOULD YOU SAY?
ENOUGH TO CURDLE YOUR EMPIRE'S MILK, LUTHOR.
THERE ARE CHARGES ENOUGH FOR THE ENTIRE BUILDING, AND A GOOD BIT MORE.
I SEE. AND MIRACULOUSLY, THE DETONATOR LANDED ON THE BUTTON, WHICH IS PARTIALLY DEPRESSED, AND...
YES. IF IT DROPS ANOTHER MILLIMETER--
--WELL, IT WOULD BE A POOR END TO OUR NEGOTIATIONS.
LOIS, I DON'T SUPPOSE YOU HAVE ANY IDEAS, DO YOU THINK?
I MIGHT HAVE, LEX, IF THE CAVEMAN THERE HADN'T DECIDED TO INCONVENIENTLY CUT ME IN HALF.
THAT WAS RATHER THOUGHTLESS.
SCANDAL SAVAGE.
YOU AND YOUR TEAM ARE ON THE CLOCK, CORRECT?
WOULD YOU BE OFFENDED IF I OFFERED A BONUS TO YOU TO SACRIFICE YOURSELF TO SAVE THE REST OF US?

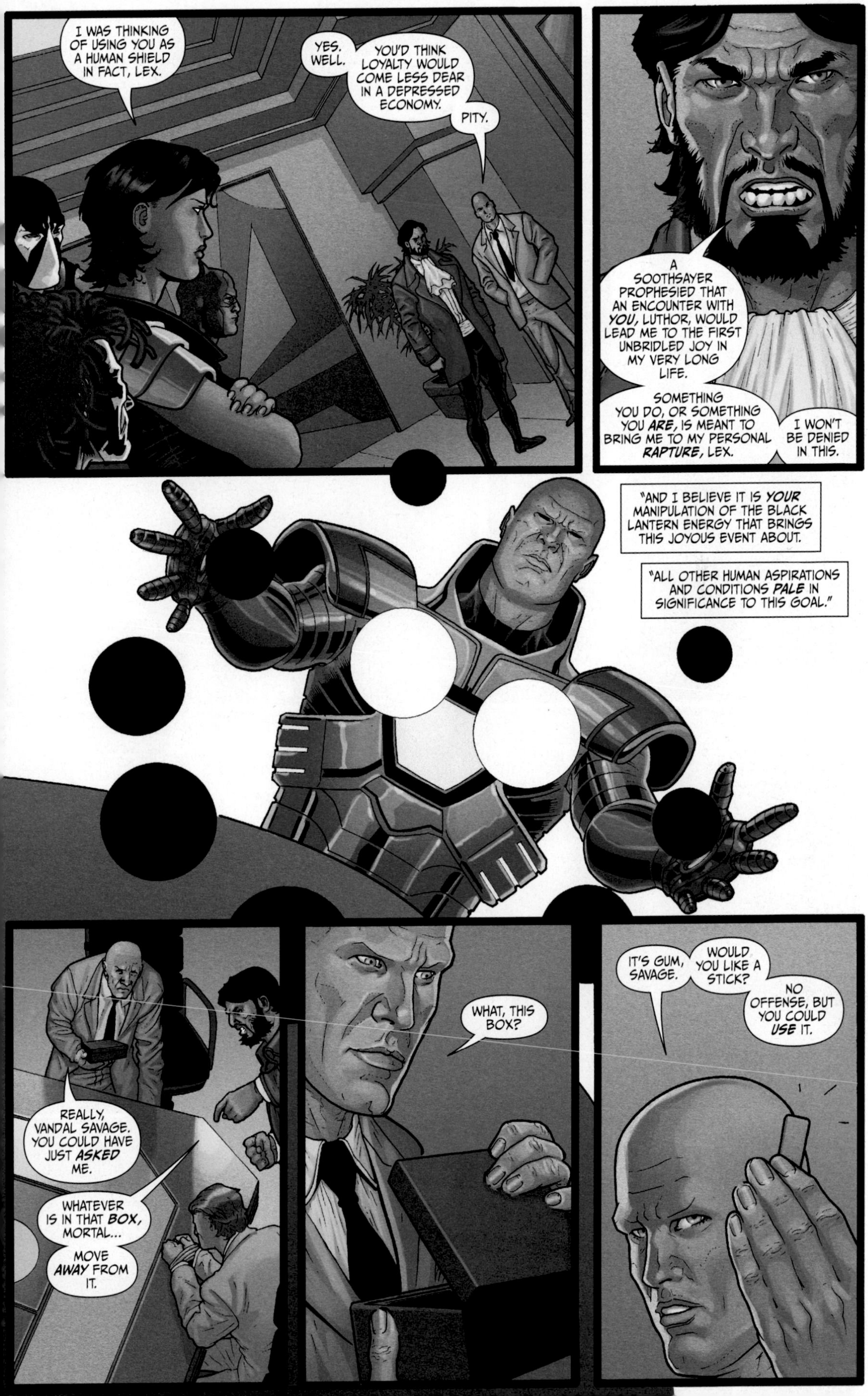
I WAS THINKING OF USING YOU AS A HUMAN SHIELD IN FACT, LEX.
YES. WELL.
YOU'D THINK LOYALTY WOULD COME LESS DEAR IN A DEPRESSED ECONOMY.
PITY.
A SOOTHSAYER PROPHESIED THAT AN ENCOUNTER WITH YOU, LUTHOR, WOULD LEAD ME TO THE FIRST UNBRIDLED JOY IN MY VERY LONG LIFE.
SOMETHING YOU DO, OR SOMETHING YOU ARE, IS MEANT TO BRING ME TO MY PERSONAL RAPTURE, LEX.
I WON'T BE DENIED IN THIS.
"AND I BELIEVE IT IS YOUR MANIPULATION OF THE BLACK LANTERN ENERGY THAT BRINGS THIS JOYOUS EVENT ABOUT.
"ALL OTHER HUMAN ASPIRATIONS AND CONDITIONS PALE IN SIGNIFICANCE TO THIS GOAL."
REALLY, VANDAL SAVAGE. YOU COULD HAVE JUST ASKED ME.
WHATEVER IS IN THAT BOX, MORTAL...
MOVE AWAY FROM IT.
WHAT, THIS BOX?
IT'S GUM, SAVAGE.
WOULD YOU LIKE A STICK?
NO OFFENSE, BUT YOU COULD USE IT.

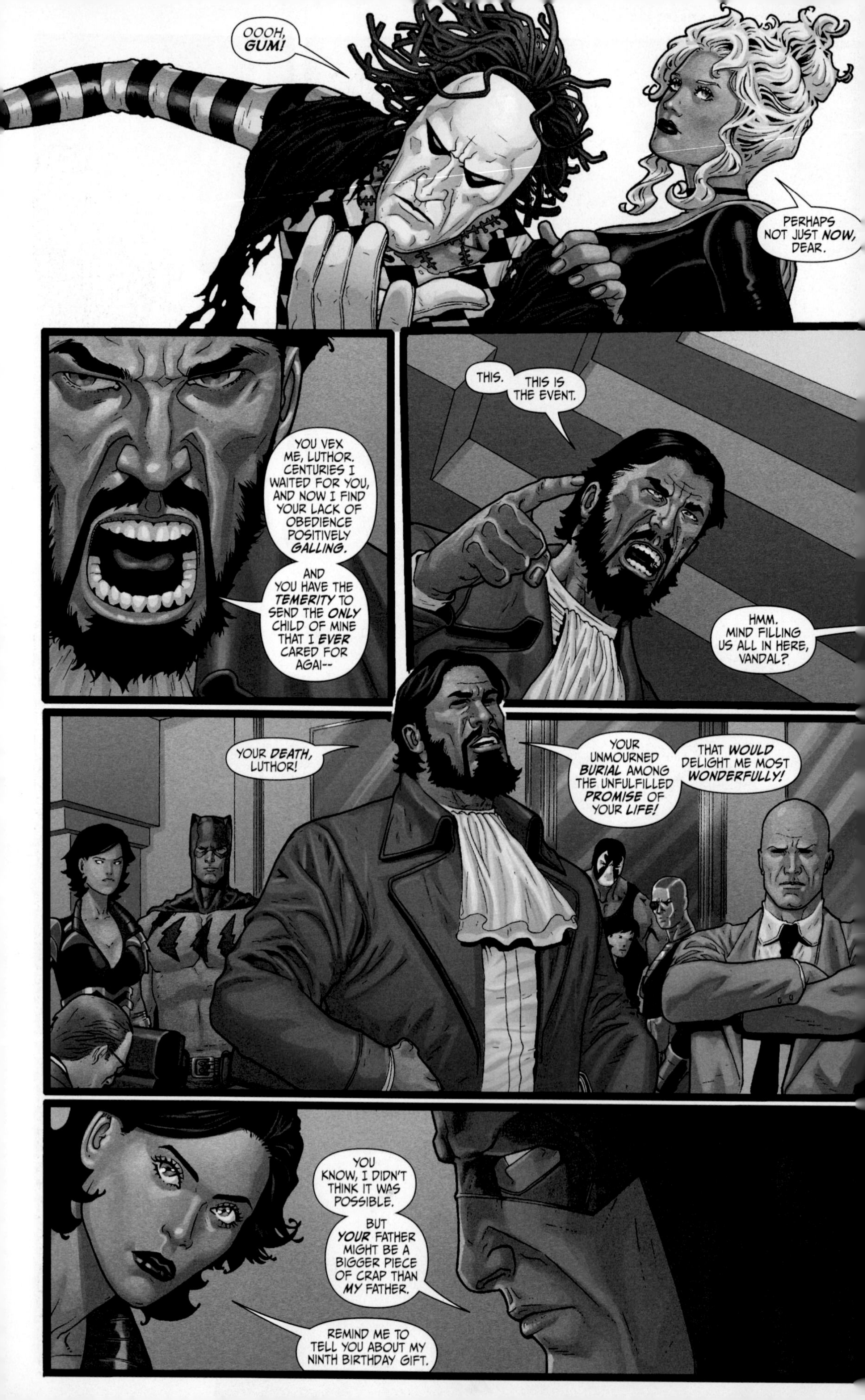
OOOH, GUM!
PERHAPS NOT JUST NOW, DEAR.
YOU VEX ME, LUTHOR. CENTURIES I WAITED FOR YOU, AND NOW I FIND YOUR LACK OF OBEDIENCE POSITIVELY GALLING.
AND YOU HAVE THE TEMERITY TO SEND THE ONLY CHILD OF MINE THAT I EVER CARED FOR AGAI--
THIS.
THIS IS THE EVENT.
HMM. MIND FILLING US ALL IN HERE, VANDAL?
YOUR DEATH, LUTHOR!
YOUR UNMOURNED BURIAL AMONG THE UNFULFILLED PROMISE OF YOUR LIFE!
THAT WOULD DELIGHT ME MOST WONDERFULLY!
YOU KNOW, I DIDN'T THINK IT WAS POSSIBLE.
BUT YOUR FATHER MIGHT BE A BIGGER PIECE OF CRAP THAN MY FATHER.
REMIND ME TO TELL YOU ABOUT MY NINTH BIRTHDAY GIFT.

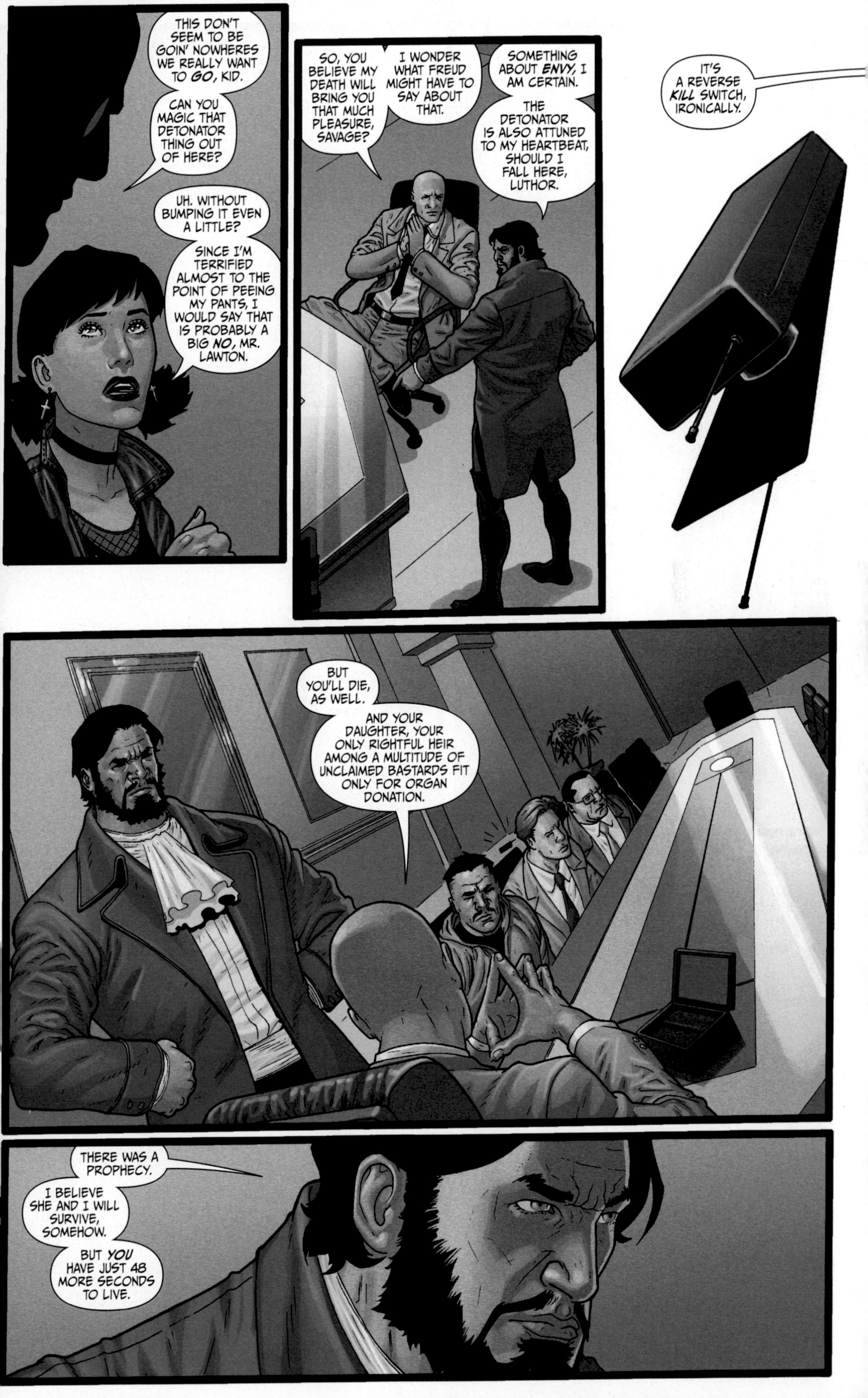
THIS DON'T SEEM TO BE GOIN' NOWHERES WE REALLY WANT TO GO, KID.
CAN YOU MAGIC THAT DETONATOR THING OUT OF HERE?
UH. WITHOUT BUMPING IT EVEN A LITTLE?
SINCE I'M TERRIFIED ALMOST TO THE POINT OF PEEING MY PANTS, I WOULD SAY THAT IS PROBABLY A BIG NO, MR. LAWTON.
SO, YOU BELIEVE MY DEATH WILL BRING YOU THAT MUCH PLEASURE, SAVAGE?
I WONDER WHAT FREUD MIGHT HAVE TO SAY ABOUT THAT.
SOMETHING ABOUT ENVY, I AM CERTAIN.
THE DETONATOR IS ALSO ATTUNED TO MY HEARTBEAT, SHOULD I FALL HERE, LUTHOR.
IT'S A REVERSE KILL SWITCH, IRONICALLY.
BUT YOU'LL DIE, AS WELL.
AND YOUR DAUGHTER, YOUR ONLY RIGHTFUL HEIR AMONG A MULTITUDE OF UNCLAIMED BASTARDS FIT ONLY FOR ORGAN DONATION.
THERE WAS A PROPHECY.
I BELIEVE SHE AND I WILL SURVIVE, SOMEHOW.
BUT YOU HAVE JUST 48 MORE SECONDS TO LIVE.

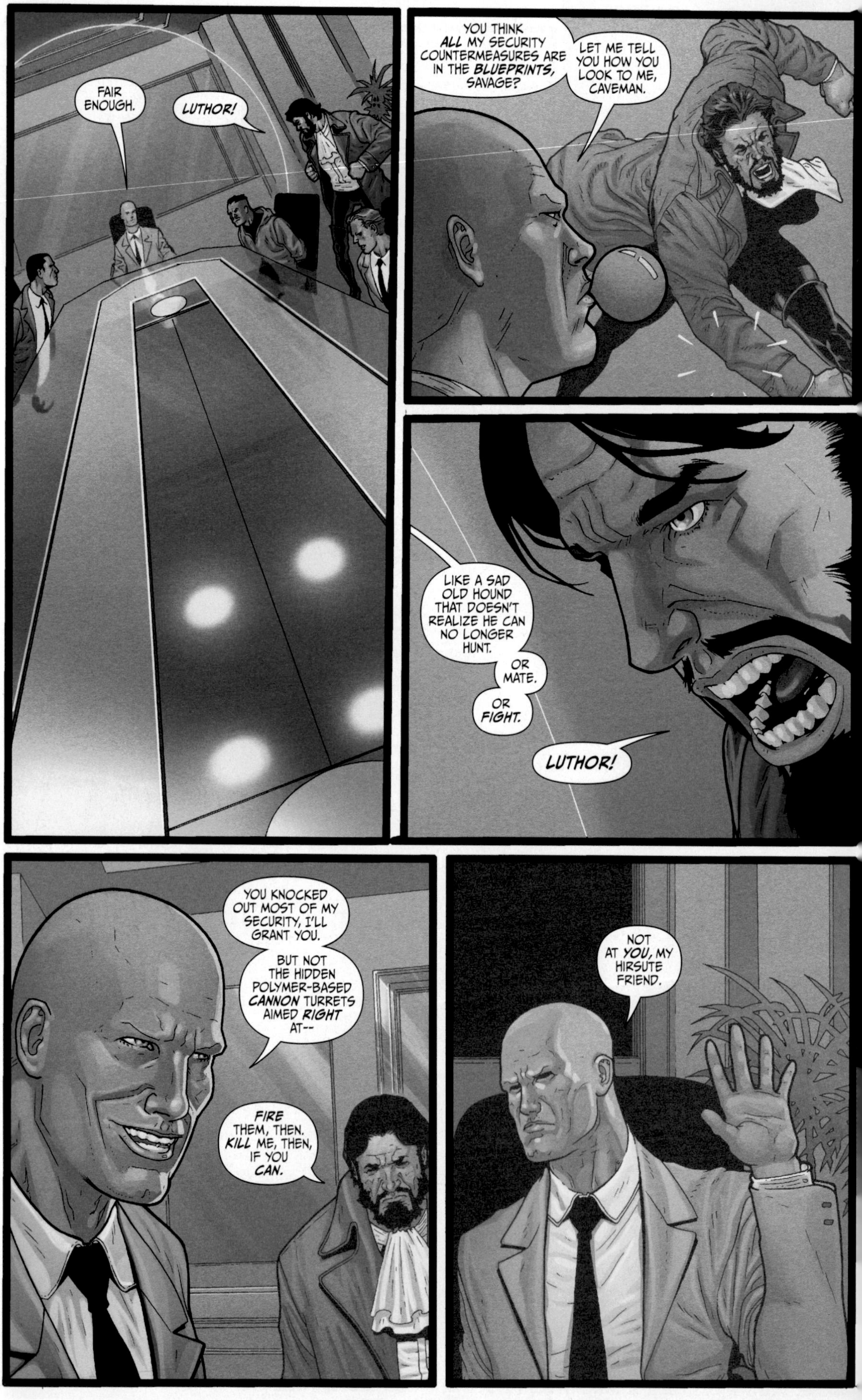
FAIR ENOUGH.
LUTHOR!
YOU THINK ALL MY SECURITY COUNTERMEASURES ARE IN THE BLUEPRINTS, SAVAGE?
LET ME TELL YOU HOW YOU LOOK TO ME, CAVEMAN.
LIKE A SAD OLD HOUND THAT DOESN'T REALIZE HE CAN NO LONGER HUNT.
OR MATE.
OR FIGHT.
LUTHOR!
YOU KNOCKED OUT MOST OF MY SECURITY, I'LL GRANT YOU.
BUT NOT THE HIDDEN POLYMER-BASED CANNON TURRETS AIMED RIGHT AT--
FIRE THEM, THEN. KILL ME, THEN, IF YOU CAN.
NOT AT YOU, MY HIRSUTE FRIEND.

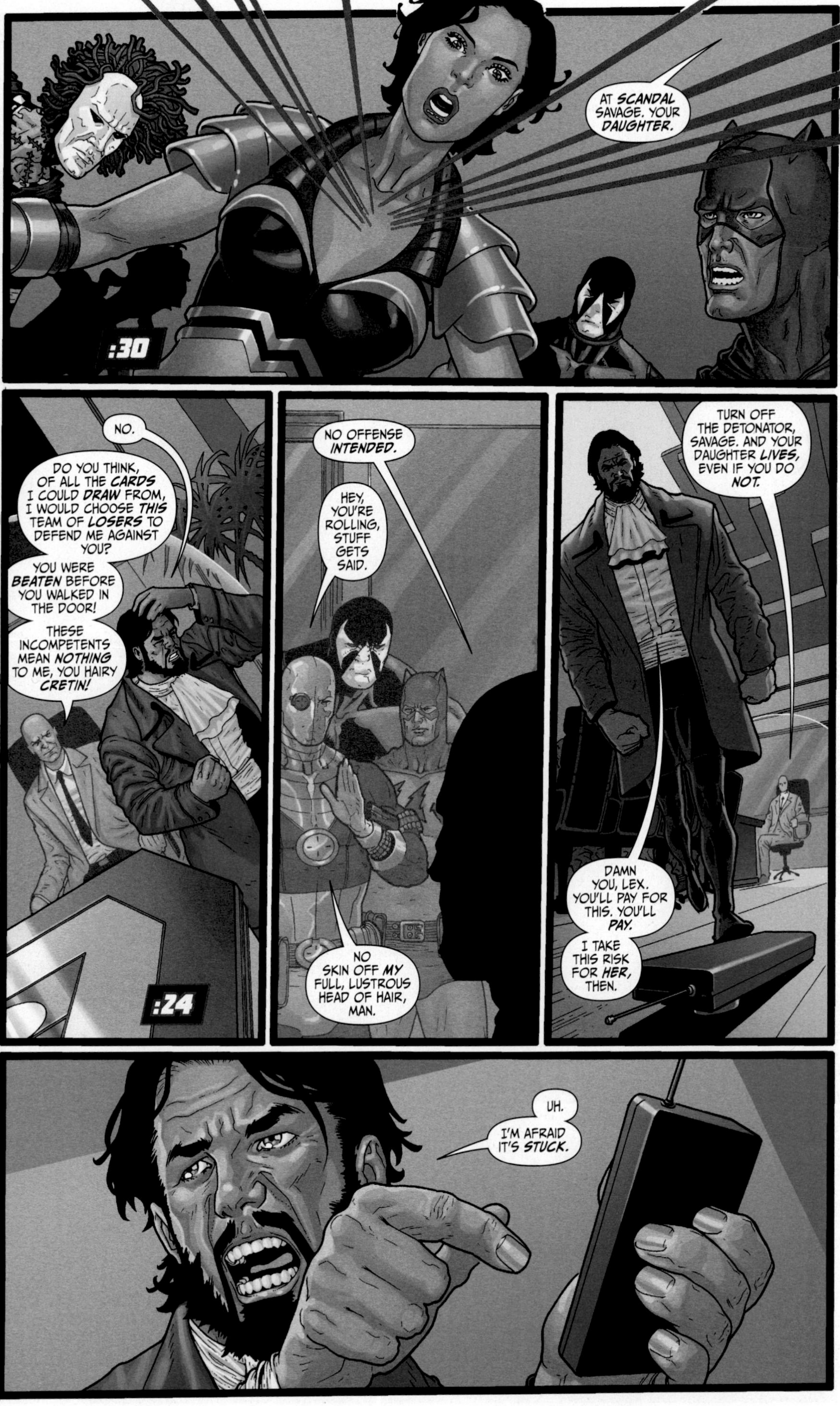
AT SCANDAL SAVAGE. YOUR DAUGHTER.
:30
NO.
DO YOU THINK, OF ALL THE CARDS I COULD DRAW FROM, I WOULD CHOOSE THIS TEAM OF LOSERS TO DEFEND ME AGAINST YOU?
YOU WERE BEATEN BEFORE YOU WALKED IN THE DOOR!
THESE INCOMPETENTS MEAN NOTHING TO ME, YOU HAIRY CRETIN!
:24
NO OFFENSE INTENDED.
HEY, YOU'RE ROLLING, STUFF GETS SAID.
NO SKIN OFF MY FULL, LUSTROUS HEAD OF HAIR, MAN.
TURN OFF THE DETONATOR, SAVAGE. AND YOUR DAUGHTER LIVES, EVEN IF YOU DO NOT.
DAMN YOU, LEX. YOU'LL PAY FOR THIS. YOU'LL PAY.
I TAKE THIS RISK FOR HER, THEN.
UH.
I'M AFRAID IT'S STUCK.

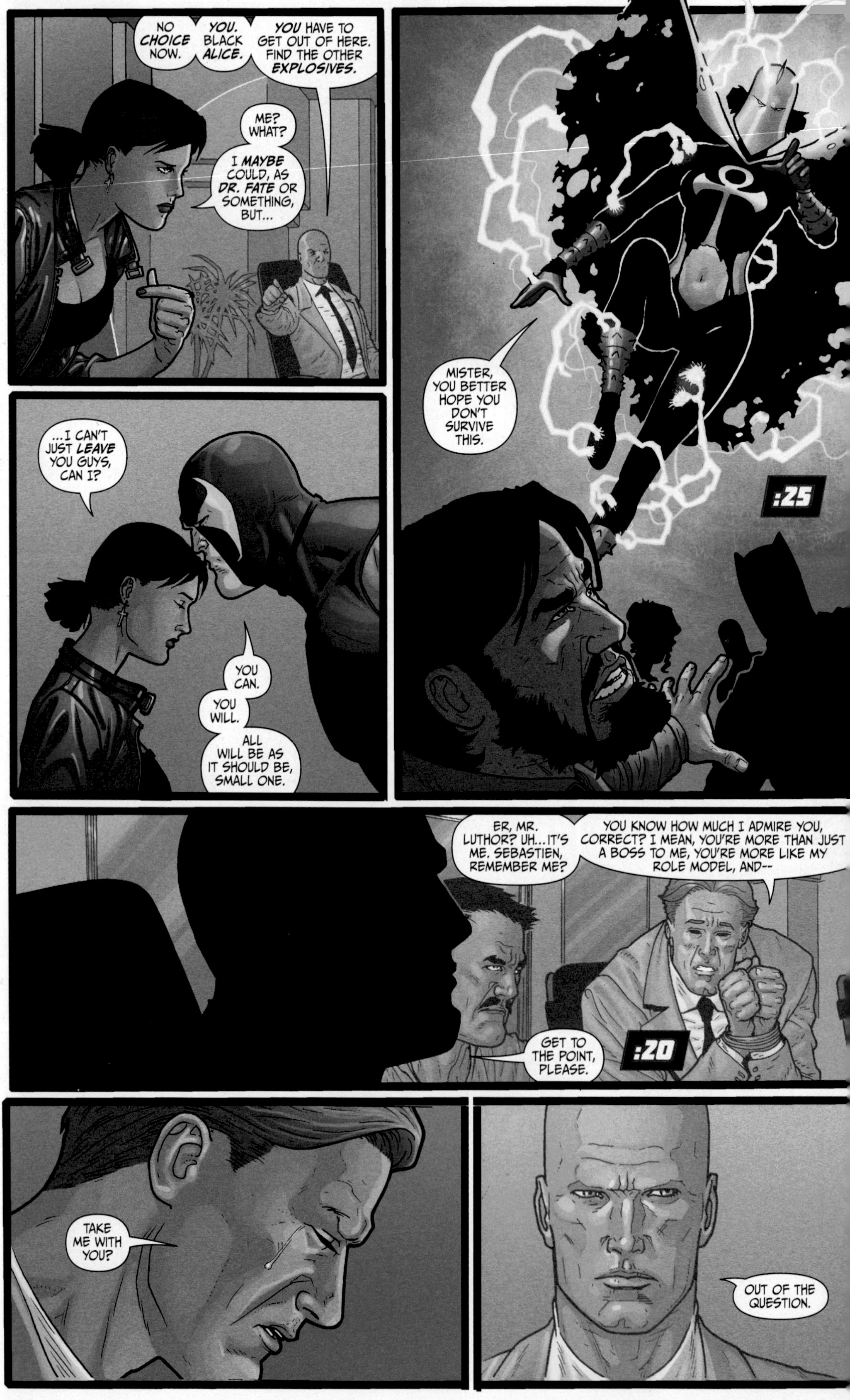
NO CHOICE NOW.
YOU. BLACK ALICE.
YOU HAVE TO GET OUT OF HERE. FIND THE OTHER EXPLOSIVES.
ME? WHAT?
I MAYBE COULD, AS DR. FATE OR SOMETHING, BUT...
...I CAN'T JUST LEAVE YOU GUYS, CAN I?
YOU CAN.
YOU WILL.
ALL WILL BE AS IT SHOULD BE, SMALL ONE.
MISTER, YOU BETTER HOPE YOU DON'T SURVIVE THIS.
:25
ER, MR. LUTHOR? UH...IT'S ME. SEBASTIEN, REMEMBER ME?
YOU KNOW HOW MUCH I ADMIRE YOU, CORRECT? I MEAN, YOU'RE MORE THAN JUST A BOSS TO ME, YOU'RE MORE LIKE MY ROLE MODEL, AND--
GET TO THE POINT, PLEASE.
:20
TAKE ME WITH YOU?
OUT OF THE QUESTION.

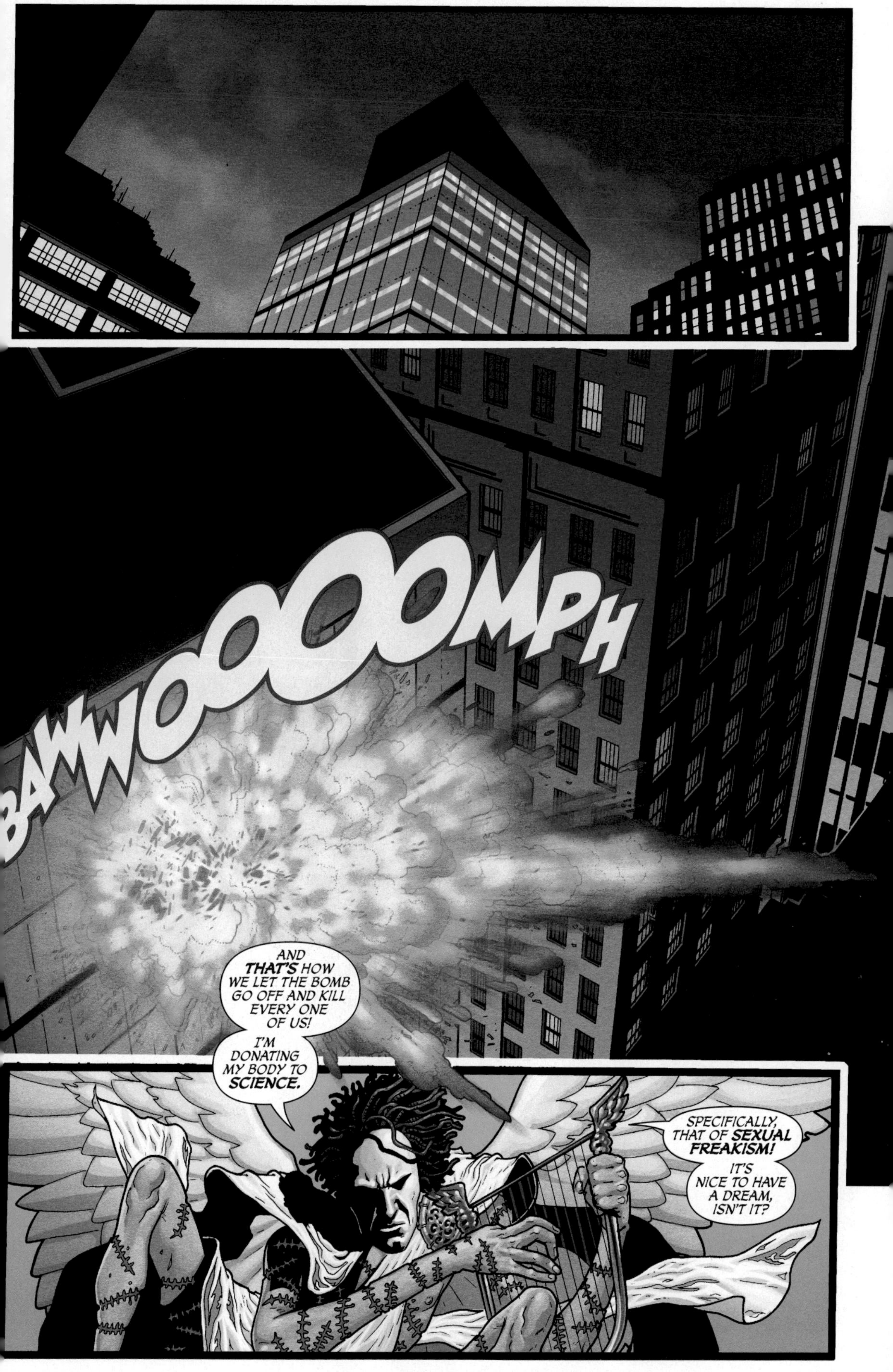
BAWOOOOOMPH
AND THAT'S HOW WE LET THE BOMB GO OFF AND KILL EVERY ONE OF US!
I'M DONATING MY BODY TO SCIENCE.
SPECIFICALLY, THAT OF SEXUAL FREAKISM!
IT'S NICE TO HAVE A DREAM, ISN'T IT?

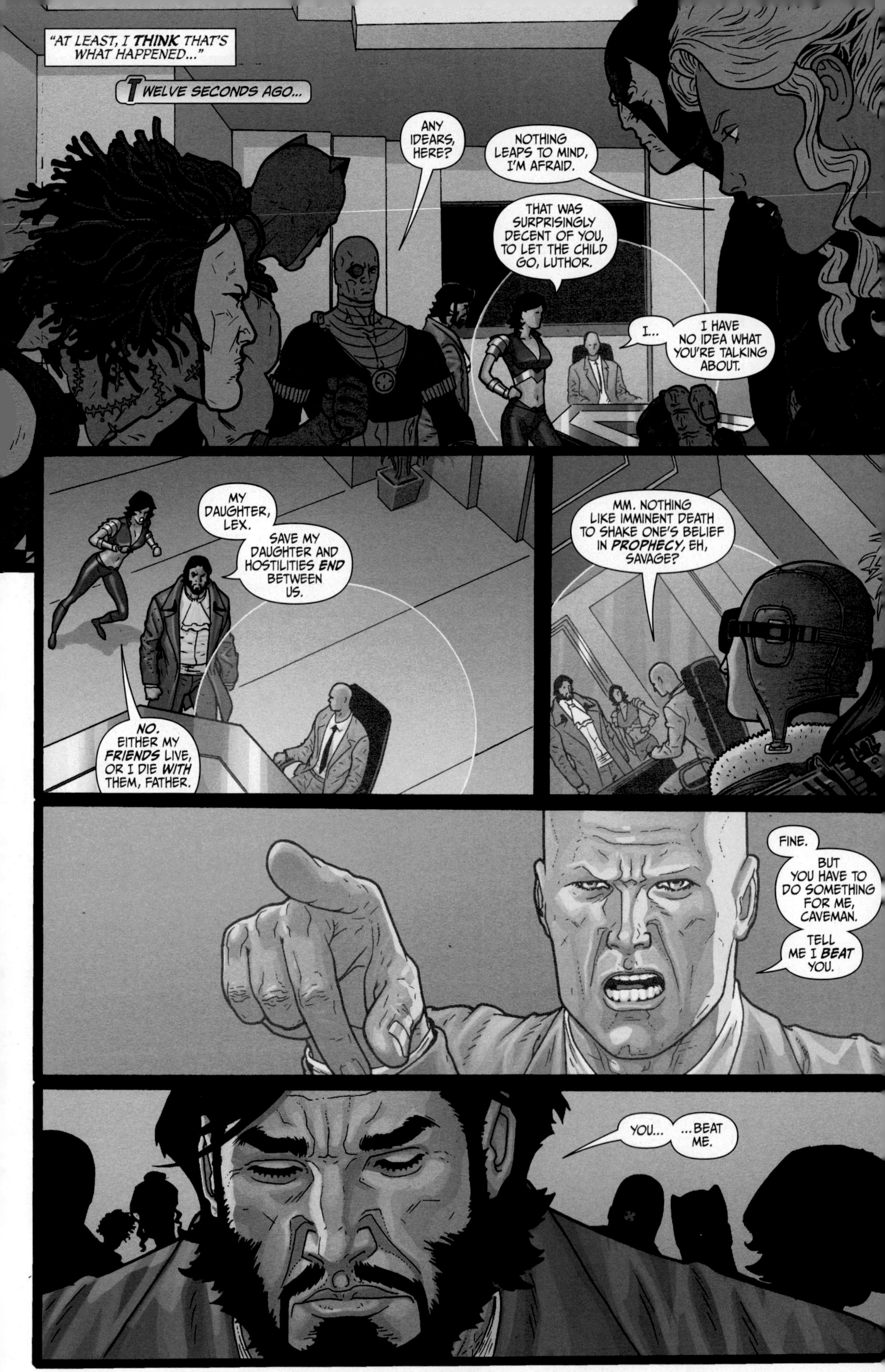
"AT LEAST, I THINK THAT'S WHAT HAPPENED..."
TWELVE SECONDS AGO...
ANY IDEARS, HERE?
NOTHING LEAPS TO MIND, I'M AFRAID.
THAT WAS SURPRISINGLY DECENT OF YOU, TO LET THE CHILD GO, LUTHOR.
I...
I HAVE NO IDEA WHAT YOU'RE TALKING ABOUT.
MY DAUGHTER, LEX.
SAVE MY DAUGHTER AND HOSTILITIES END BETWEEN US.
NO. EITHER MY FRIENDS LIVE, OR I DIE WITH THEM, FATHER.
MM. NOTHING LIKE IMMINENT DEATH TO SHAKE ONE'S BELIEF IN PROPHECY, EH, SAVAGE?
FINE.
BUT YOU HAVE TO DO SOMETHING FOR ME, CAVEMAN.
TELL ME I BEAT YOU.
YOU...
...BEAT ME.

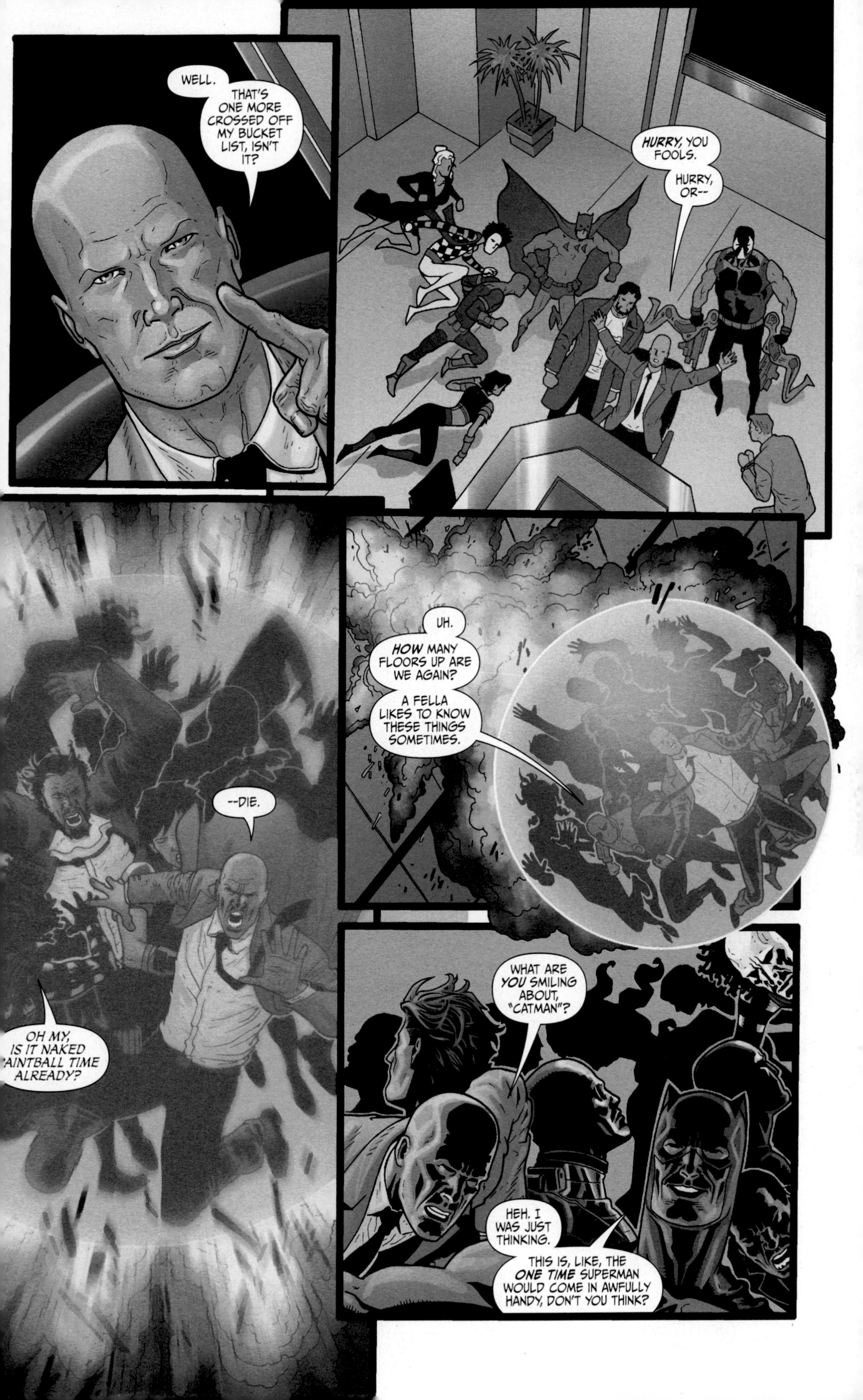
WELL.
THAT'S ONE MORE CROSSED OFF MY BUCKET LIST, ISN'T IT?
HURRY, YOU FOOLS.
HURRY, OR--
--DIE.
OH MY, IS IT NAKED PAINTBALL TIME ALREADY?
UH.
HOW MANY FLOORS UP ARE WE AGAIN?
A FELLA LIKES TO KNOW THESE THINGS SOMETIMES.
WHAT ARE YOU SMILING ABOUT, "CATMAN"?
HEH. I WAS JUST THINKING.
THIS IS, LIKE, THE ONE TIME SUPERMAN WOULD COME IN AWFULLY HANDY, DON'T YOU THINK?

THIS CITY IS TOO BEAUTIFUL TO EXIST.

IT IS ONLY RIGHT THAT WE SHOULD BE GRAFFITI ON ITS WALLS AND FLOORS.

IS THAT...

YEAH, I THINK IT... HUH.

IT'S A...

I GOT YOU GUYS!

...A GIANT GREEN CATCHER'S MITT.

I THINK I'D ALMOST RATHER TAKE THE FALL.

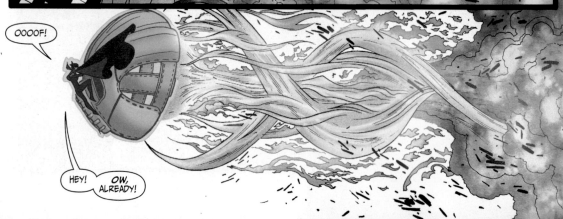

OOOOF!

HEY!

OW, ALREADY!

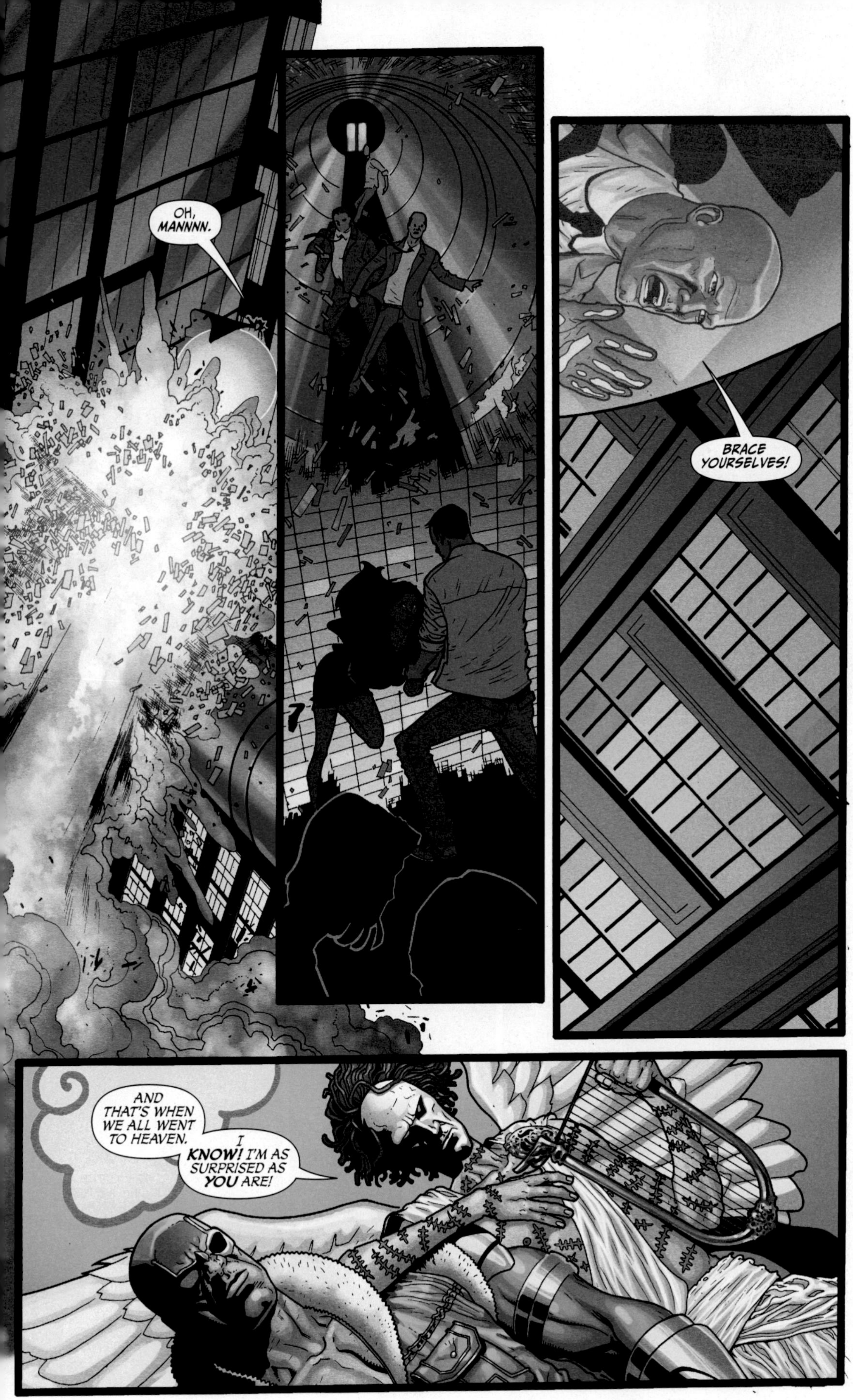
OH, MANNNN.
BRACE YOURSELVES!
AND THAT'S WHEN WE ALL WENT TO HEAVEN.
I KNOW! I'M AS SURPRISED AS YOU ARE!

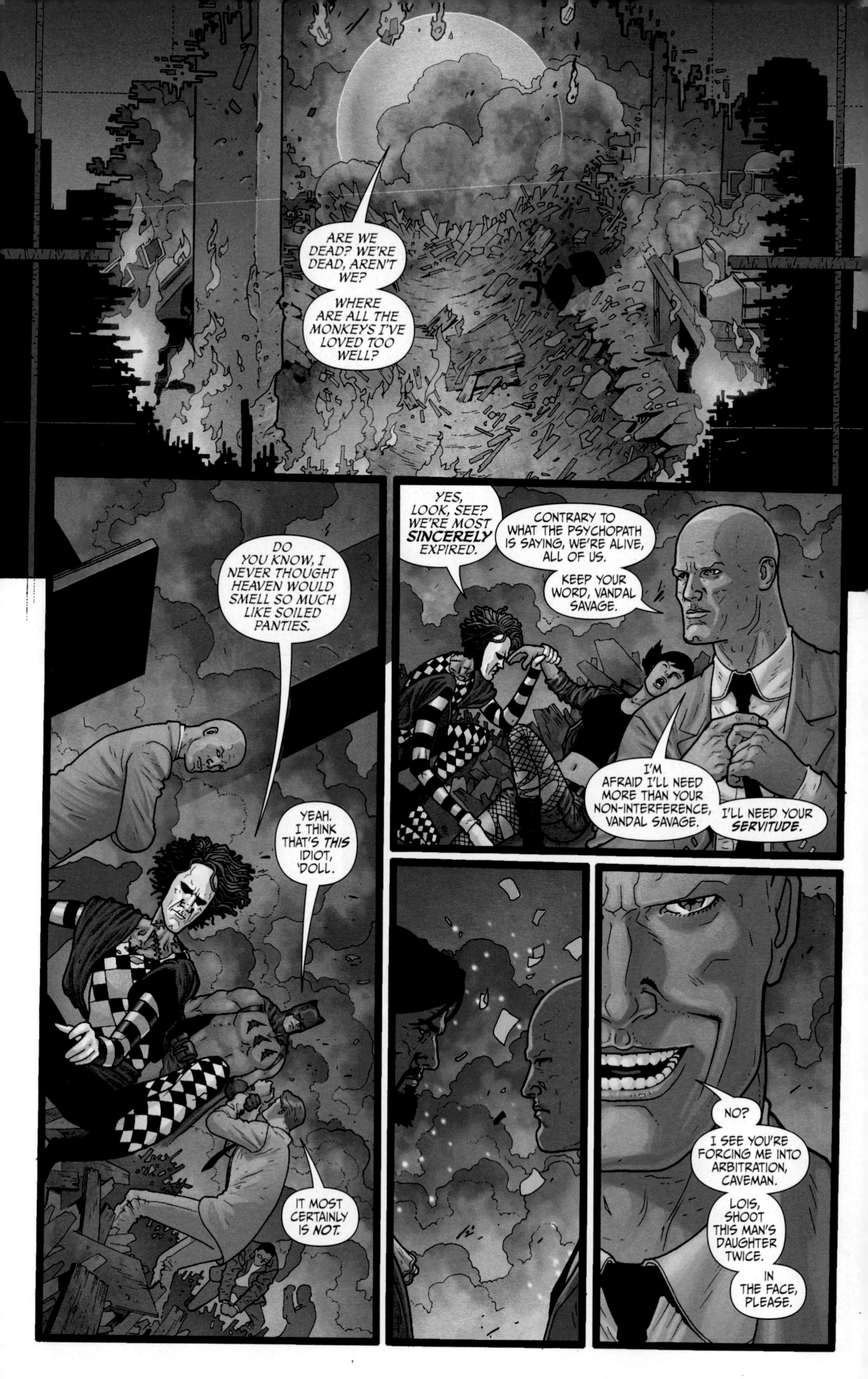
ARE WE DEAD? WE'RE DEAD, AREN'T WE?
WHERE ARE ALL THE MONKEYS I'VE LOVED TOO WELL?
DO YOU KNOW, I NEVER THOUGHT HEAVEN WOULD SMELL SO MUCH LIKE SOILED PANTIES.
YEAH. I THINK THAT'S THIS IDIOT, 'DOLL.
IT MOST CERTAINLY IS NOT.
YES, LOOK, SEE? WE'RE MOST SINCERELY EXPIRED.
CONTRARY TO WHAT THE PSYCHOPATH IS SAYING, WE'RE ALIVE, ALL OF US.
KEEP YOUR WORD, VANDAL SAVAGE.
I'M AFRAID I'LL NEED MORE THAN YOUR NON-INTERFERENCE, VANDAL SAVAGE.
I'LL NEED YOUR SERVITUDE.
NO?
I SEE YOU'RE FORCING ME INTO ARBITRATION, CAVEMAN.
LOIS, SHOOT THIS MAN'S DAUGHTER TWICE.
IN THE FACE, PLEASE.

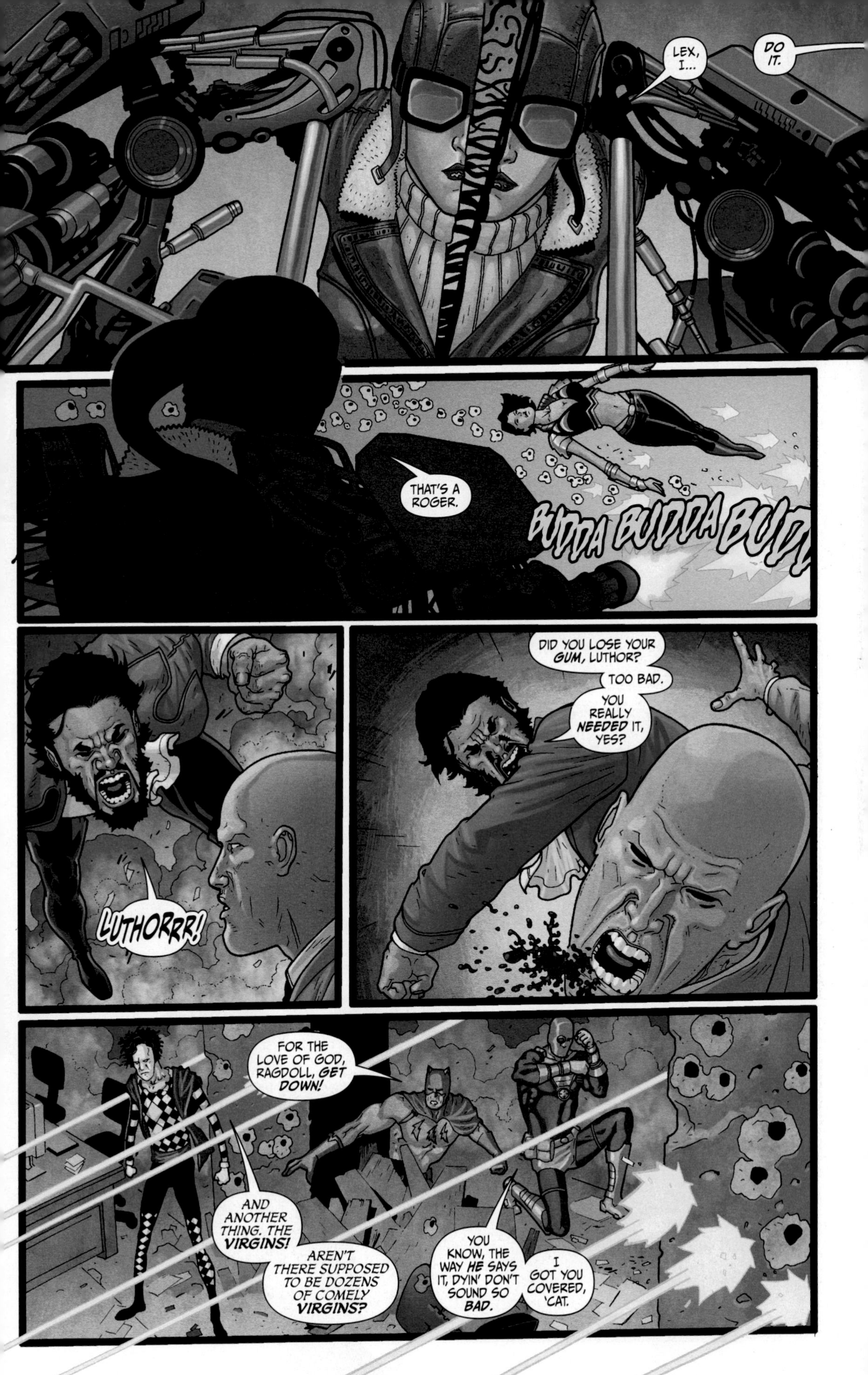
LEX, I...
DO IT.
THAT'S A ROGER.
BUDDA BUDDA BUD
LUTHORRR!
DID YOU LOSE YOUR GUM, LUTHOR?
TOO BAD.
YOU REALLY NEEDED IT, YES?
FOR THE LOVE OF GOD, RAGDOLL, GET DOWN!
AND ANOTHER THING. THE VIRGINS!
AREN'T THERE SUPPOSED TO BE DOZENS OF COMELY VIRGINS?
YOU KNOW, THE WAY HE SAYS IT, DYIN' DON'T SOUND SO BAD.
I GOT YOU COVERED, 'CAT.

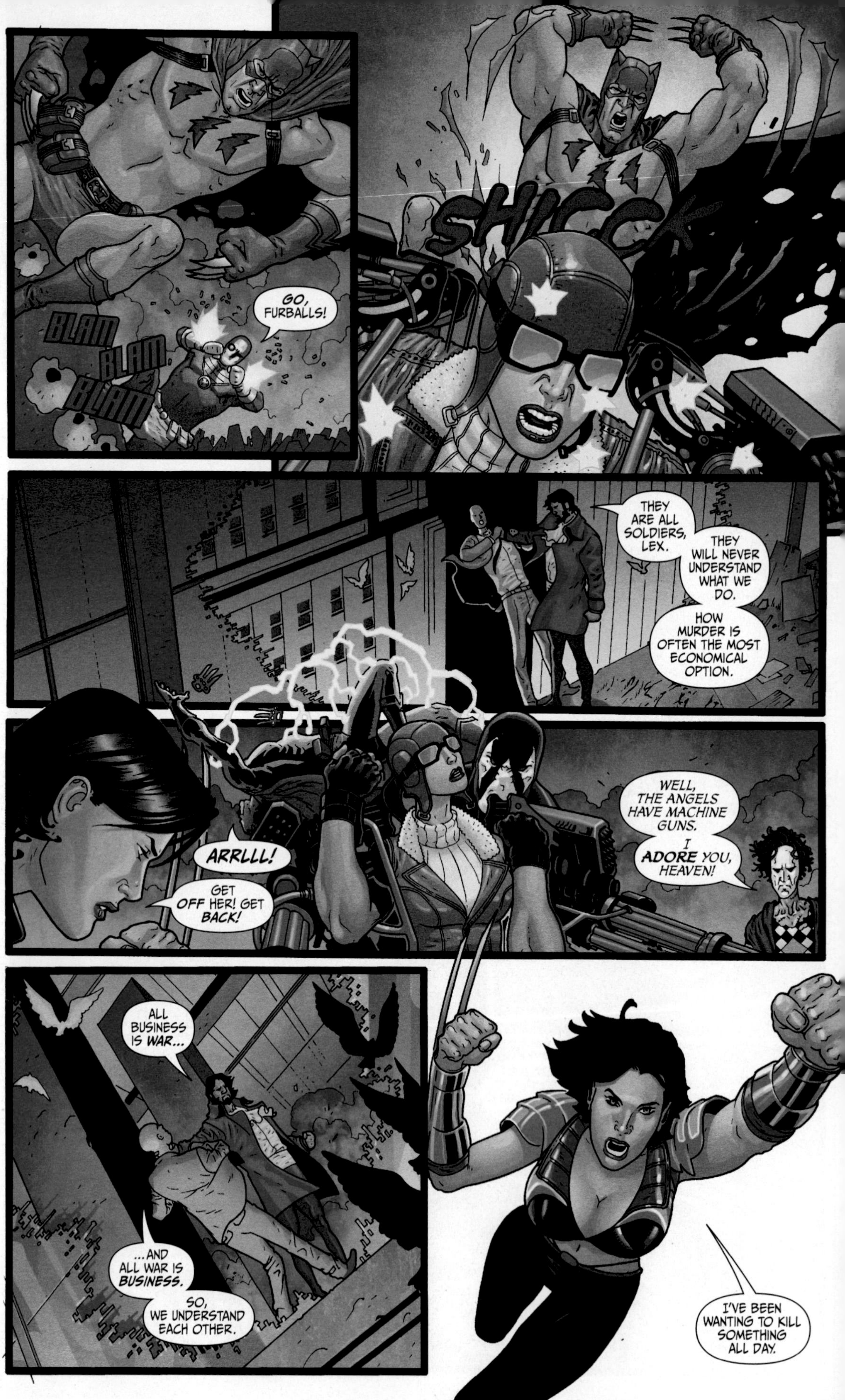
SHICCK
GO, FURBALLS!
BLAM
BLAM
BLAM
THEY ARE ALL SOLDIERS, LEX.
THEY WILL NEVER UNDERSTAND WHAT WE DO.
HOW MURDER IS OFTEN THE MOST ECONOMICAL OPTION.
ARRLLL!
GET OFF HER! GET BACK!
WELL, THE ANGELS HAVE MACHINE GUNS.
I ADORE YOU, HEAVEN!
ALL BUSINESS IS WAR...
...AND ALL WAR IS BUSINESS.
SO, WE UNDERSTAND EACH OTHER.
I'VE BEEN WANTING TO KILL SOMETHING ALL DAY.

WELL, *THIS* IS AWKWARD.

FAMILIES. THEY CAN BE SO *STRESSFUL.*

FATHER. I CAN'T ALLOW YOU TO KILL OUR EMPLOYER. THE SIX HAVING ANOTHER DEAD *EMPLOYER* WOULD *DEMOLISH* OUR REPUTATIONS.

DON'T MAKE ME LIVE OUT MY DREAMS AND SLIT YOUR CAROTID.

FINE. MY DAUGHTER IS SAFE. I'LL KEEP MY VOW.

I'M ASSUMING YOU HAVE A YACHT, LUTHOR?

SEVERAL. ≋KAFF≋

AND THERE'S *RUM* ON THIS VESSEL?

OH, YES.

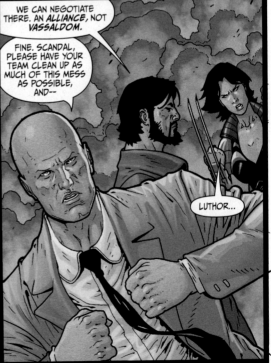

WE CAN NEGOTIATE THERE. AN *ALLIANCE,* NOT *VASSALDOM.*

FINE. SCANDAL, PLEASE HAVE YOUR TEAM CLEAN UP AS MUCH OF THIS MESS AS POSSIBLE, AND--

LUTHOR...

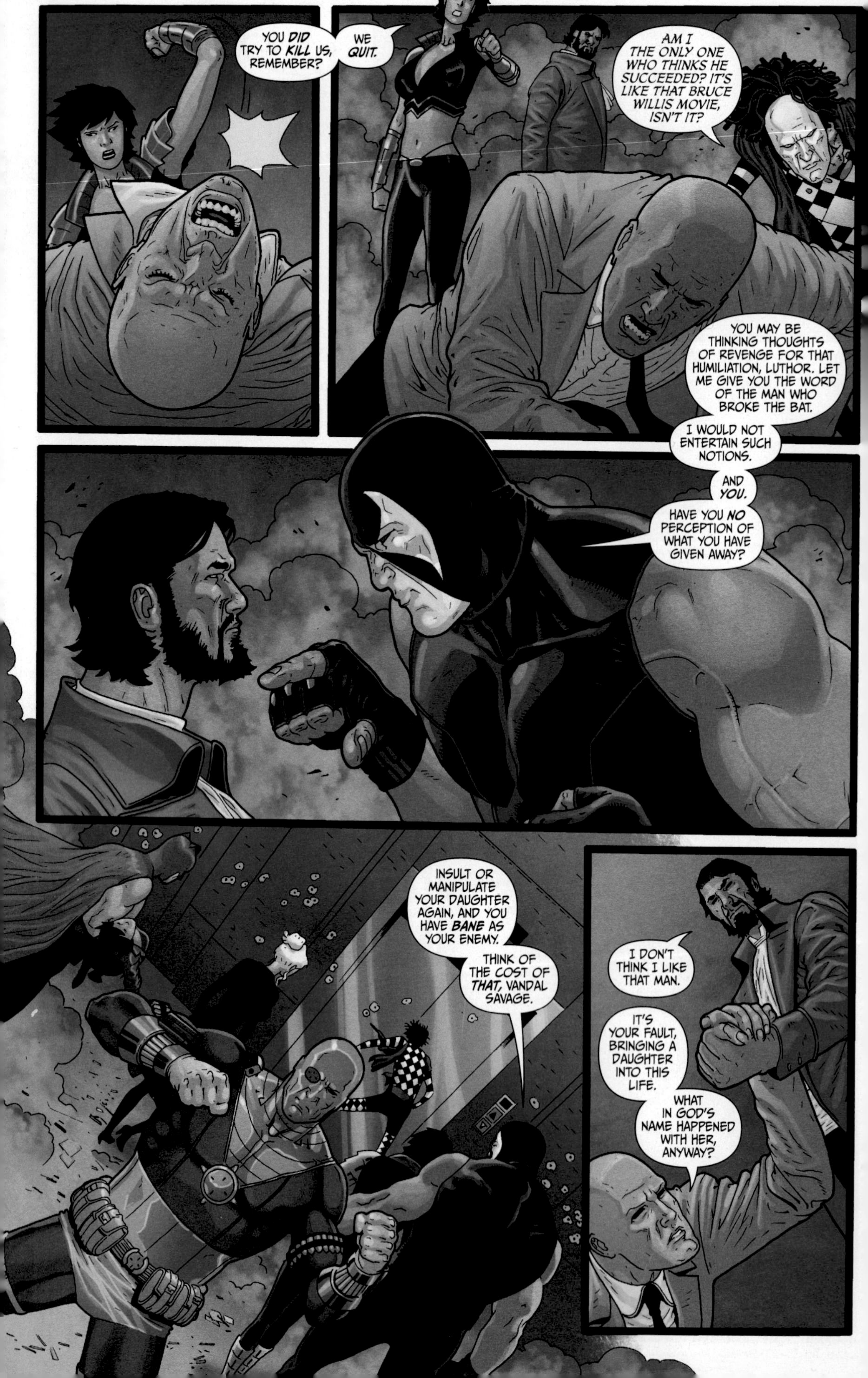
YOU DID TRY TO KILL US, REMEMBER?
WE QUIT.
AM I THE ONLY ONE WHO THINKS HE SUCCEEDED? IT'S LIKE THAT BRUCE WILLIS MOVIE, ISN'T IT?
YOU MAY BE THINKING THOUGHTS OF REVENGE FOR THAT HUMILIATION, LUTHOR. LET ME GIVE YOU THE WORD OF THE MAN WHO BROKE THE BAT.
I WOULD NOT ENTERTAIN SUCH NOTIONS.
AND YOU.
HAVE YOU NO PERCEPTION OF WHAT YOU HAVE GIVEN AWAY?
INSULT OR MANIPULATE YOUR DAUGHTER AGAIN, AND YOU HAVE BANE AS YOUR ENEMY.
THINK OF THE COST OF THAT, VANDAL SAVAGE.
I DON'T THINK I LIKE THAT MAN.
IT'S YOUR FAULT, BRINGING A DAUGHTER INTO THIS LIFE.
WHAT IN GOD'S NAME HAPPENED WITH HER, ANYWAY?

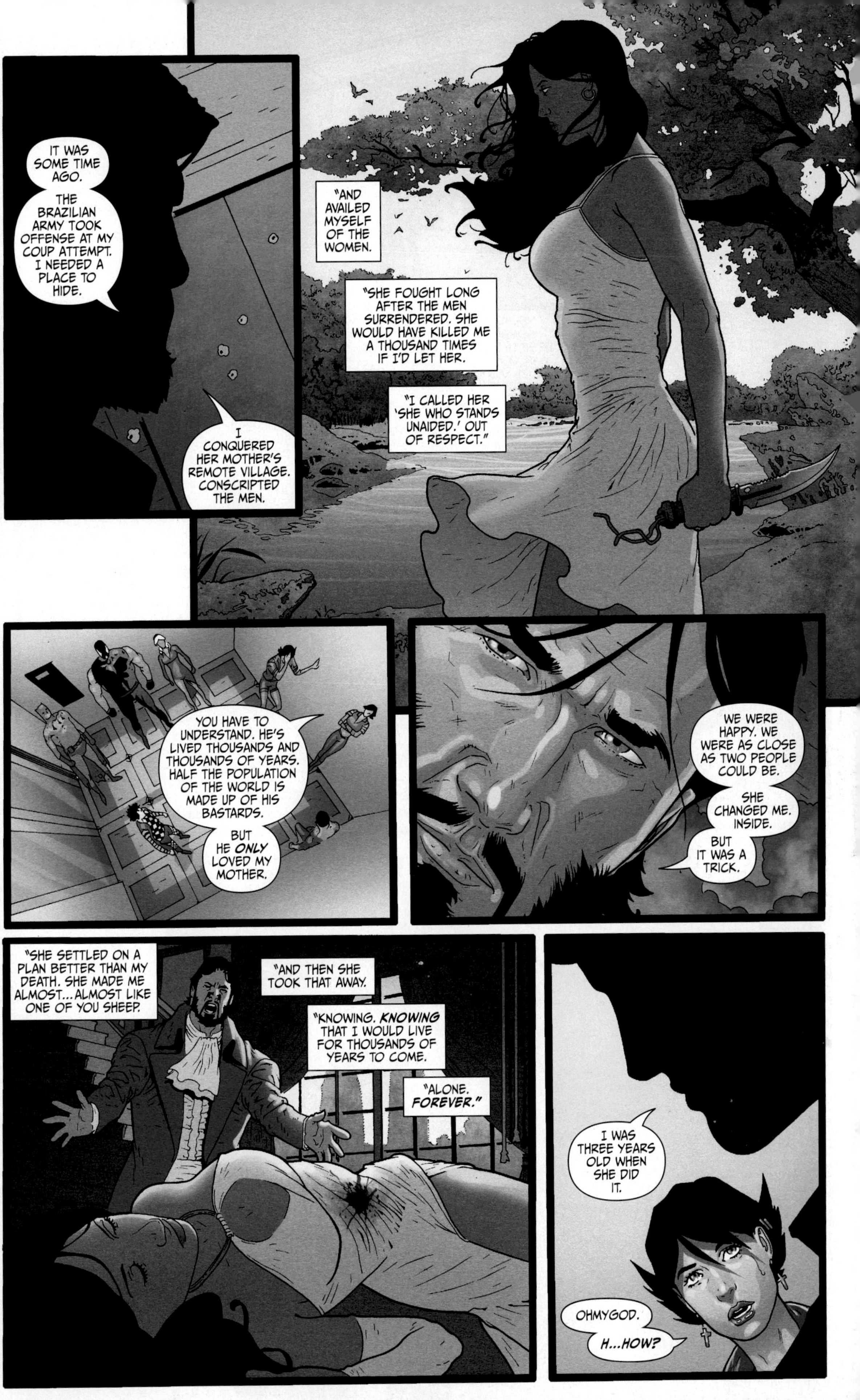
IT WAS SOME TIME AGO.
THE BRAZILIAN ARMY TOOK OFFENSE AT MY COUP ATTEMPT. I NEEDED A PLACE TO HIDE.
I CONQUERED HER MOTHER'S REMOTE VILLAGE. CONSCRIPTED THE MEN.
"AND AVAILED MYSELF OF THE WOMEN.
"SHE FOUGHT LONG AFTER THE MEN SURRENDERED. SHE WOULD HAVE KILLED ME A THOUSAND TIMES IF I'D LET HER.
"I CALLED HER 'SHE WHO STANDS UNAIDED.' OUT OF RESPECT."
YOU HAVE TO UNDERSTAND. HE'S LIVED THOUSANDS AND THOUSANDS OF YEARS. HALF THE POPULATION OF THE WORLD IS MADE UP OF HIS BASTARDS.
BUT HE *ONLY* LOVED MY MOTHER.
WE WERE HAPPY. WE WERE AS CLOSE AS TWO PEOPLE COULD BE.
SHE CHANGED ME. INSIDE.
BUT IT WAS A TRICK.
"SHE SETTLED ON A PLAN BETTER THAN MY DEATH. SHE MADE ME ALMOST...ALMOST LIKE ONE OF YOU SHEEP.
"AND THEN SHE TOOK THAT AWAY.
"KNOWING. ***KNOWING*** THAT I WOULD LIVE FOR THOUSANDS OF YEARS TO COME.
"ALONE. ***FOREVER."***
I WAS THREE YEARS OLD WHEN SHE DID IT.
OHMYGOD.
H...HOW?

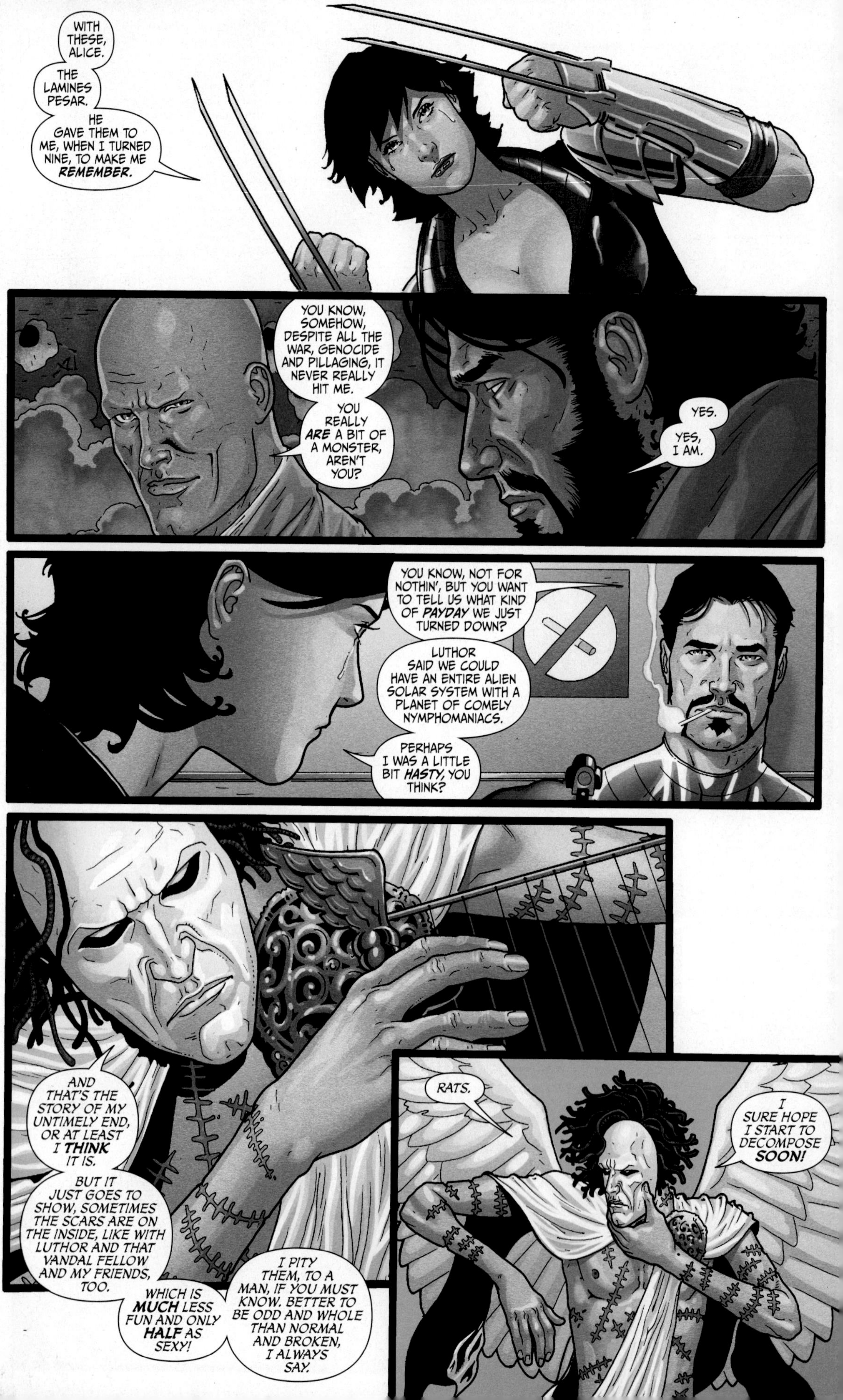

WITH THESE, ALICE.
THE LAMINES PESAR.
HE GAVE THEM TO ME, WHEN I TURNED NINE, TO MAKE ME REMEMBER.
YOU KNOW, SOMEHOW, DESPITE ALL THE WAR, GENOCIDE AND PILLAGING, IT NEVER REALLY HIT ME.
YOU REALLY ARE A BIT OF A MONSTER, AREN'T YOU?
YES.
YES, I AM.
YOU KNOW, NOT FOR NOTHIN', BUT YOU WANT TO TELL US WHAT KIND OF PAYDAY WE JUST TURNED DOWN?
LUTHOR SAID WE COULD HAVE AN ENTIRE ALIEN SOLAR SYSTEM WITH A PLANET OF COMELY NYMPHOMANIACS.
PERHAPS I WAS A LITTLE BIT HASTY, YOU THINK?
AND THAT'S THE STORY OF MY UNTIMELY END, OR AT LEAST I THINK IT IS.
BUT IT JUST GOES TO SHOW, SOMETIMES THE SCARS ARE ON THE INSIDE, LIKE WITH LUTHOR AND THAT VANDAL FELLOW AND MY FRIENDS, TOO.
WHICH IS MUCH LESS FUN AND ONLY HALF AS SEXY!
I PITY THEM, TO A MAN, IF YOU MUST KNOW. BETTER TO BE ODD AND WHOLE THAN NORMAL AND BROKEN, I ALWAYS SAY.
RATS.
I SURE HOPE I START TO DECOMPOSE SOON!

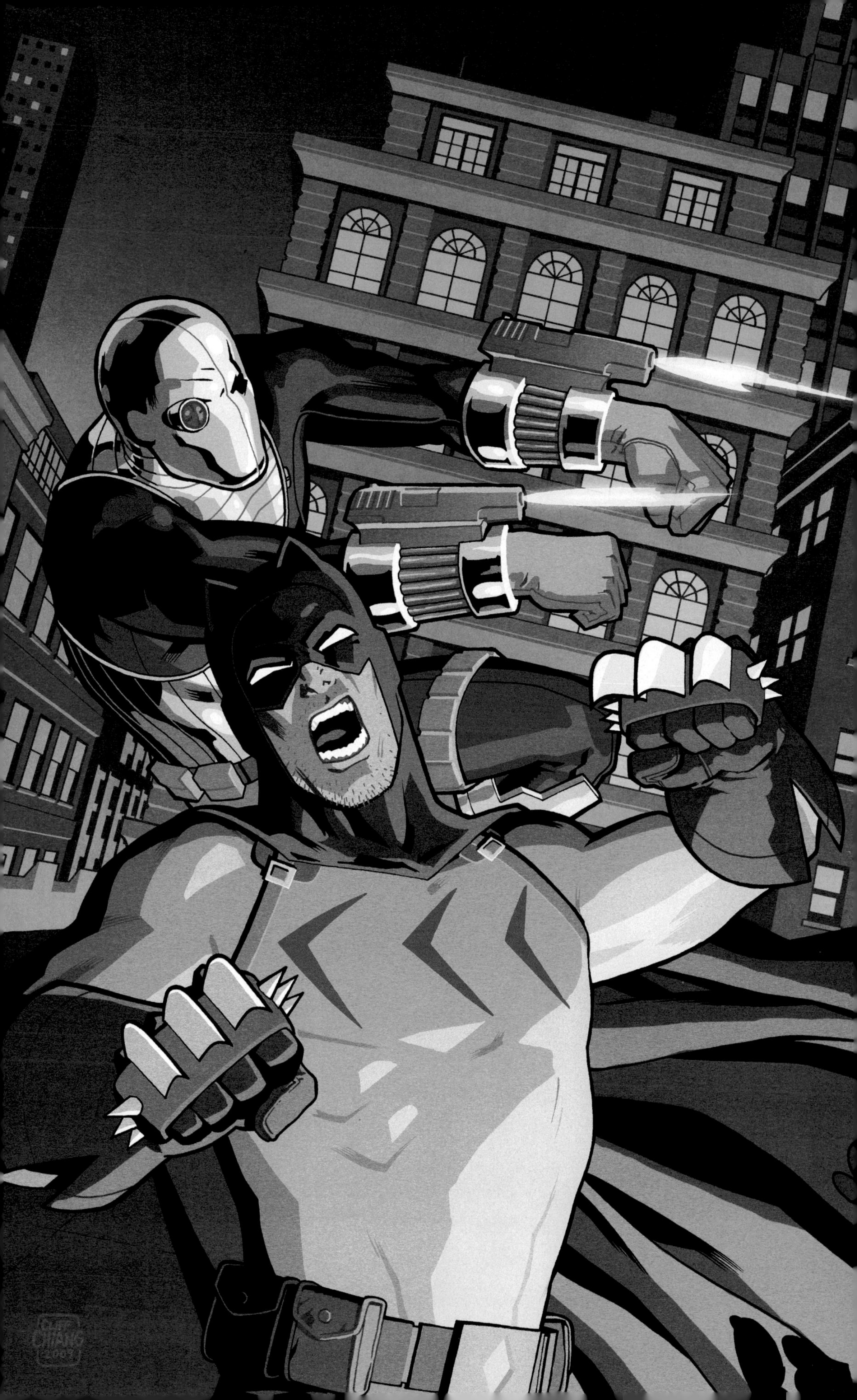
CLIFF
CHIANG
2009

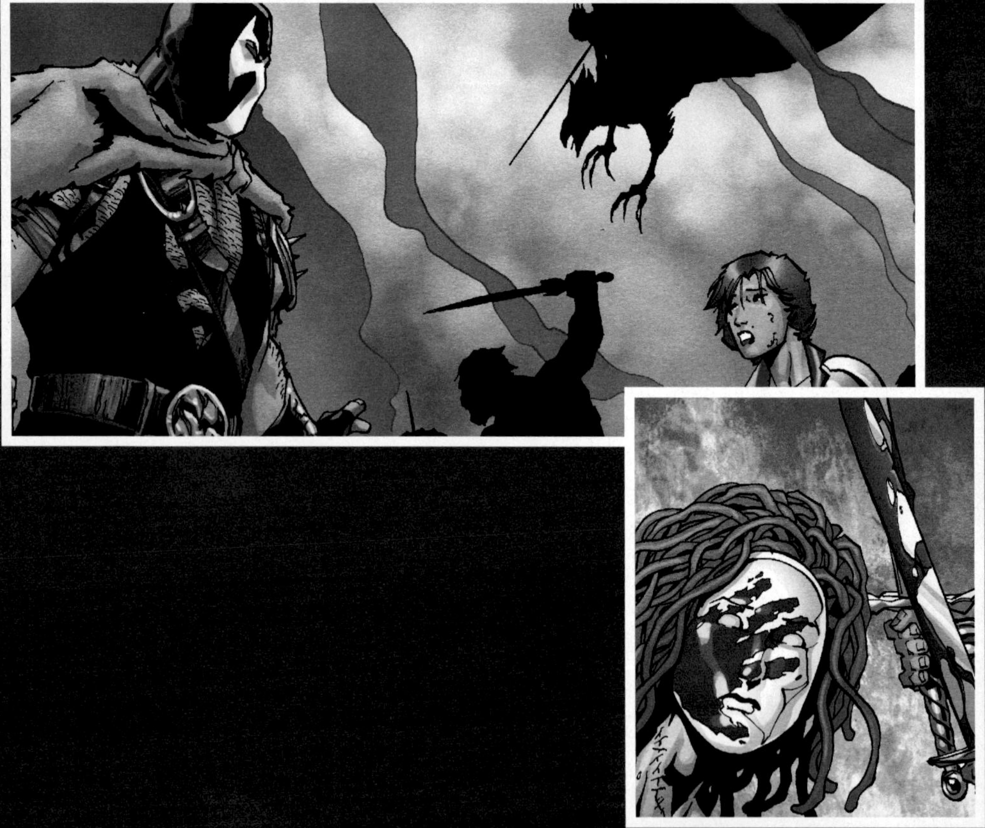

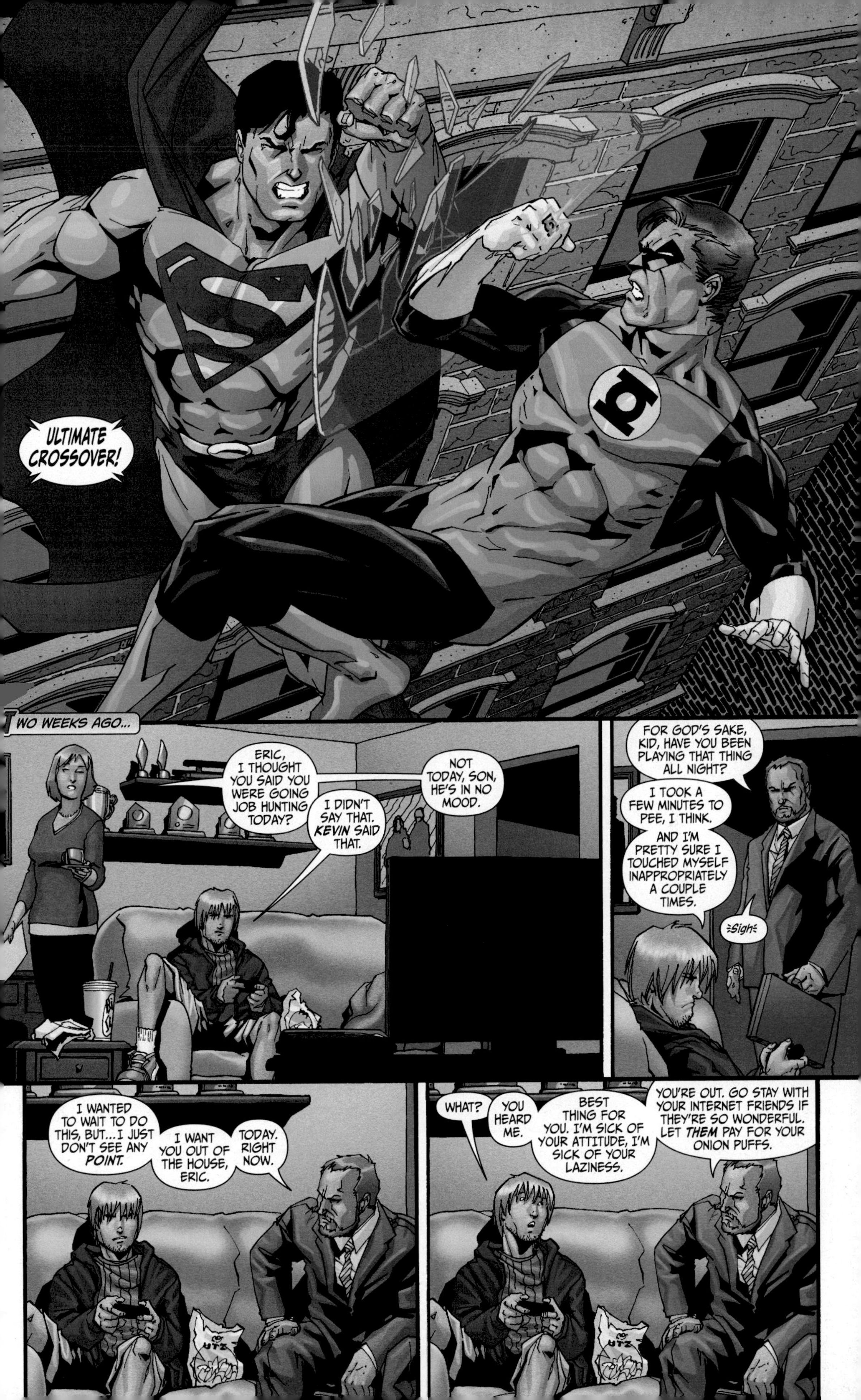
ULTIMATE CROSSOVER!
TWO WEEKS AGO...
ERIC, I THOUGHT YOU SAID YOU WERE GOING JOB HUNTING TODAY?
I DIDN'T SAY THAT. KEVIN SAID THAT.
NOT TODAY, SON, HE'S IN NO MOOD.
FOR GOD'S SAKE, KID, HAVE YOU BEEN PLAYING THAT THING ALL NIGHT?
I TOOK A FEW MINUTES TO PEE, I THINK.
AND I'M PRETTY SURE I TOUCHED MYSELF INAPPROPRIATELY A COUPLE TIMES.
Sigh
I WANTED TO WAIT TO DO THIS, BUT... I JUST DON'T SEE ANY POINT.
I WANT YOU OUT OF THE HOUSE, ERIC.
TODAY. RIGHT NOW.
WHAT?
YOU HEARD ME.
BEST THING FOR YOU. I'M SICK OF YOUR ATTITUDE, I'M SICK OF YOUR LAZINESS.
YOU'RE OUT. GO STAY WITH YOUR INTERNET FRIENDS IF THEY'RE SO WONDERFUL. LET THEM PAY FOR YOUR ONION PUFFS.

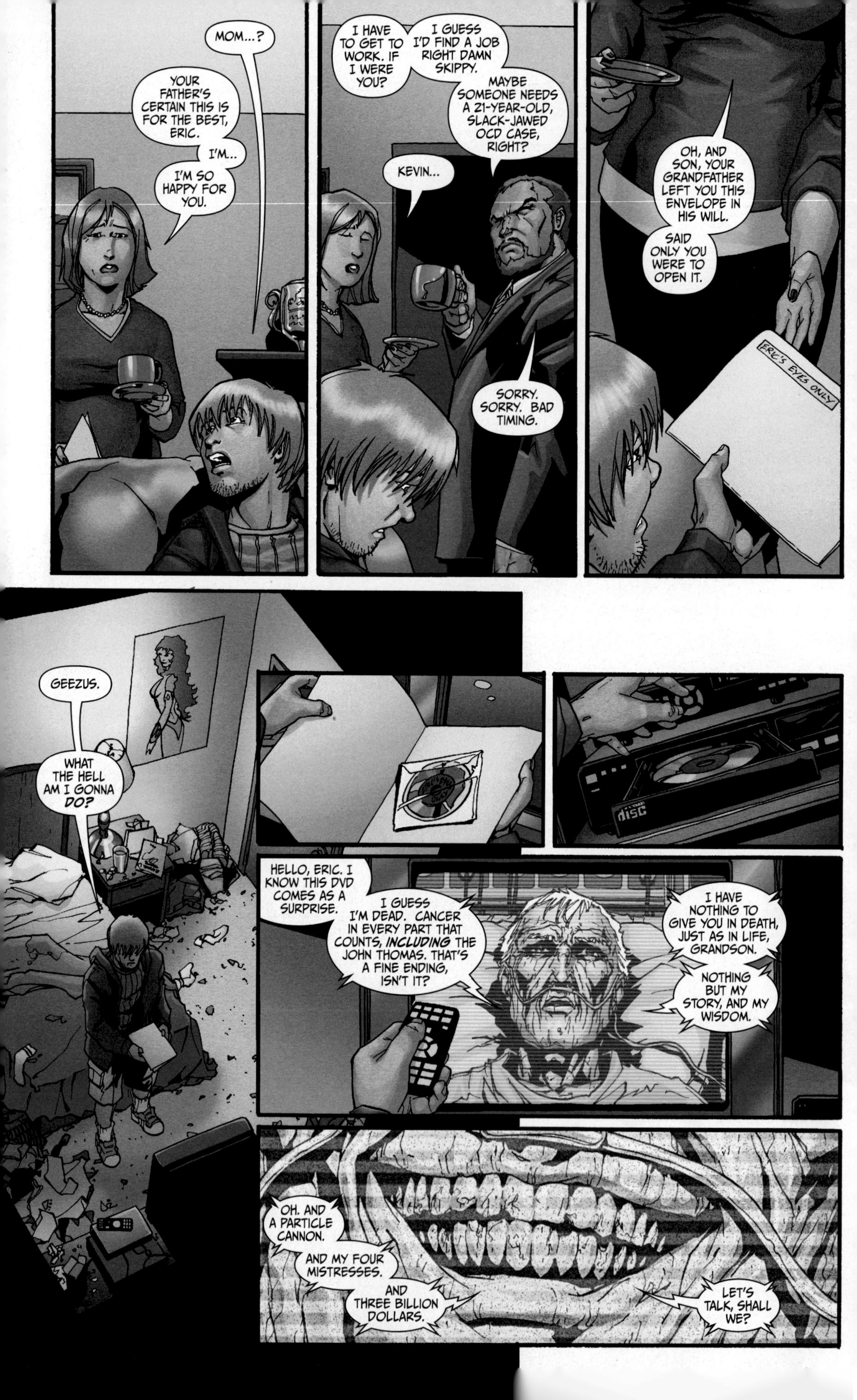
MOM...?
YOUR FATHER'S CERTAIN THIS IS FOR THE BEST, ERIC.
I'M...
I'M SO HAPPY FOR YOU.
I HAVE TO GET TO WORK. IF I WERE YOU?
I GUESS I'D FIND A JOB RIGHT DAMN SKIPPY.
MAYBE SOMEONE NEEDS A 21-YEAR-OLD, SLACK-JAWED OCD CASE, RIGHT?
KEVIN...
SORRY. SORRY. BAD TIMING.
OH, AND SON, YOUR GRANDFATHER LEFT YOU THIS ENVELOPE IN HIS WILL.
SAID ONLY YOU WERE TO OPEN IT.
ERIC'S EYES ONLY
GEEZUS.
WHAT THE HELL AM I GONNA *DO?*
DISC
HELLO, ERIC. I KNOW THIS DVD COMES AS A SURPRISE.
I GUESS I'M DEAD. CANCER IN EVERY PART THAT COUNTS, *INCLUDING* THE JOHN THOMAS. THAT'S A FINE ENDING, ISN'T IT?
I HAVE NOTHING TO GIVE YOU IN DEATH, JUST AS IN LIFE, GRANDSON.
NOTHING BUT MY STORY, AND MY WISDOM.
OH. AND A PARTICLE CANNON.
AND MY FOUR MISTRESSES.
AND THREE BILLION DOLLARS.
LET'S TALK, SHALL WE?

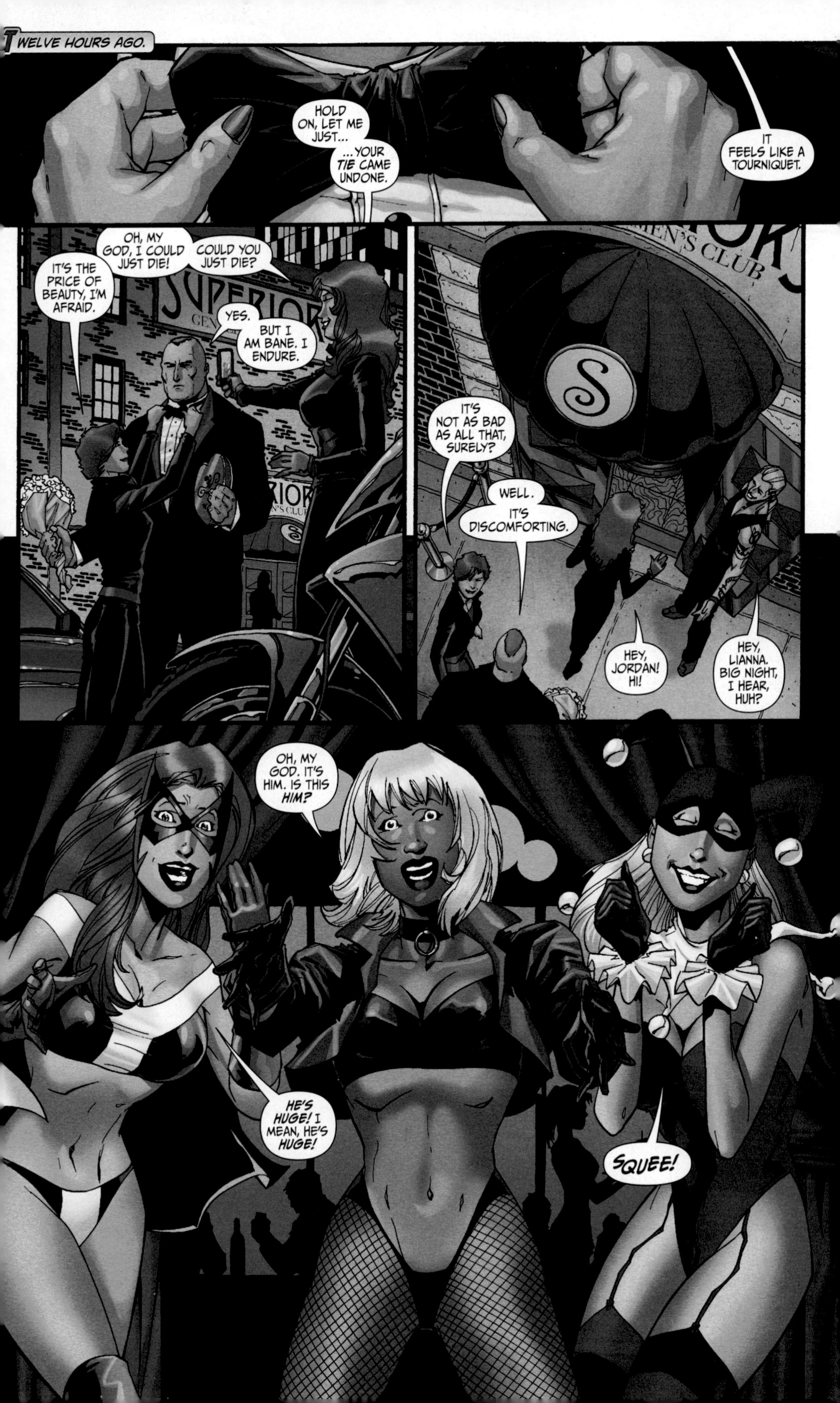
TWELVE HOURS AGO.
HOLD ON, LET ME JUST...
...YOUR TIE CAME UNDONE.
IT FEELS LIKE A TOURNIQUET.
IT'S THE PRICE OF BEAUTY, I'M AFRAID.
OH, MY GOD, I COULD JUST DIE!
COULD YOU JUST DIE?
YES.
BUT I AM BANE. I ENDURE.
SUPERIOR
IT'S NOT AS BAD AS ALL THAT, SURELY?
WELL.
IT'S DISCOMFORTING.
HEY, JORDAN! HI!
HEY, LIANNA. BIG NIGHT, I HEAR, HUH?
OH, MY GOD. IT'S HIM. IS THIS HIM?
HE'S HUGE! I MEAN, HE'S HUGE!
SQUEE!

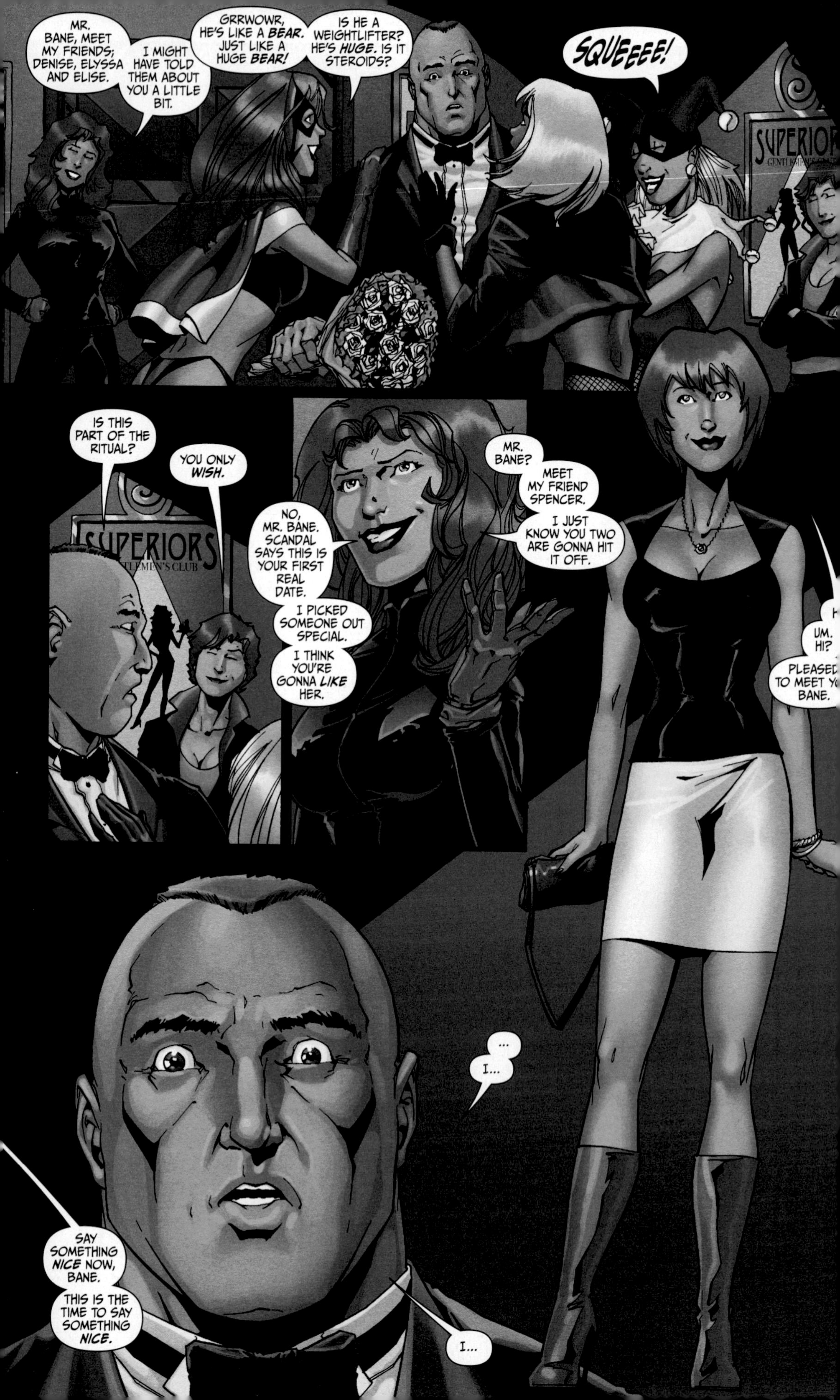
MR. BANE, MEET MY FRIENDS; DENISE, ELYSSA AND ELISE.
I MIGHT HAVE TOLD THEM ABOUT YOU A LITTLE BIT.
GRRWOWR, HE'S LIKE A BEAR. JUST LIKE A HUGE BEAR!
IS HE A WEIGHTLIFTER? HE'S HUGE. IS IT STEROIDS?
SQUEEEE!
SUPERIORS
IS THIS PART OF THE RITUAL?
YOU ONLY WISH.
SUPERIORS GENTLEMEN'S CLUB
NO, MR. BANE. SCANDAL SAYS THIS IS YOUR FIRST REAL DATE.
I PICKED SOMEONE OUT SPECIAL.
I THINK YOU'RE GONNA LIKE HER.
MR. BANE?
MEET MY FRIEND SPENCER.
I JUST KNOW YOU TWO ARE GONNA HIT IT OFF.
UM. HI?
... I...
SAY SOMETHING NICE NOW, BANE.
THIS IS THE TIME TO SAY SOMETHING NICE.
I...

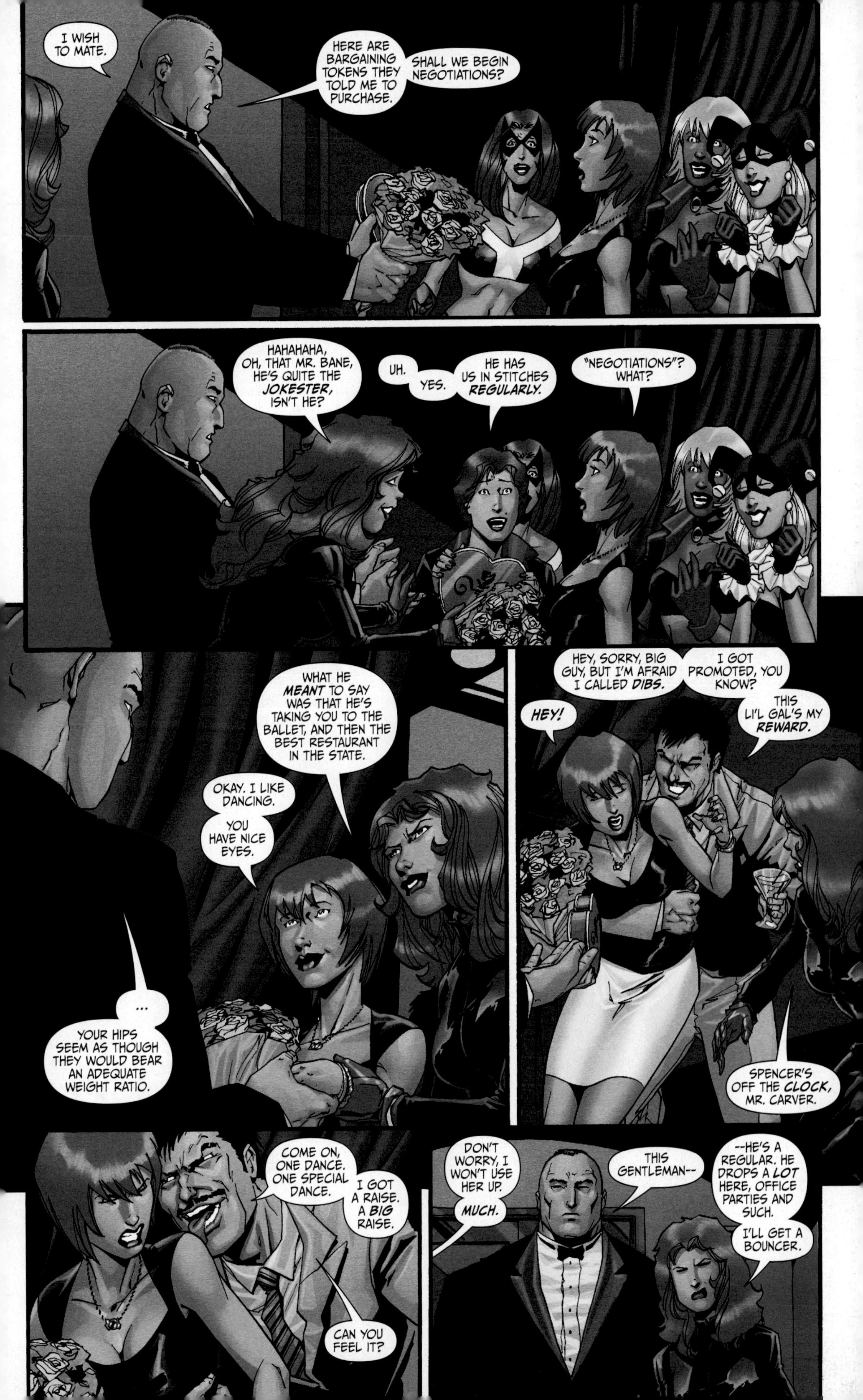
I WISH TO MATE.
HERE ARE BARGAINING TOKENS THEY TOLD ME TO PURCHASE.
SHALL WE BEGIN NEGOTIATIONS?
HAHAHAHA, OH, THAT MR. BANE, HE'S QUITE THE *JOKESTER,* ISN'T HE?
UH.
YES.
HE HAS US IN STITCHES *REGULARLY.*
"NEGOTIATIONS"? WHAT?
WHAT HE *MEANT* TO SAY WAS THAT HE'S TAKING YOU TO THE BALLET, AND THEN THE BEST RESTAURANT IN THE STATE.
OKAY. I LIKE DANCING.
YOU HAVE NICE EYES.
...
YOUR HIPS SEEM AS THOUGH THEY WOULD BEAR AN ADEQUATE WEIGHT RATIO.
HEY, SORRY, BIG GUY, BUT I'M AFRAID I CALLED *DIBS.*
I GOT PROMOTED, YOU KNOW?
THIS LI'L GAL'S MY *REWARD.*
HEY!
SPENCER'S OFF THE *CLOCK,* MR. CARVER.
COME ON, ONE DANCE. ONE SPECIAL DANCE.
I GOT A RAISE. A *BIG* RAISE.
CAN YOU FEEL IT?
DON'T WORRY, I WON'T USE HER UP.
MUCH.
THIS GENTLEMAN--
--HE'S A REGULAR. HE DROPS A *LOT* HERE, OFFICE PARTIES AND SUCH.
I'LL GET A BOUNCER.

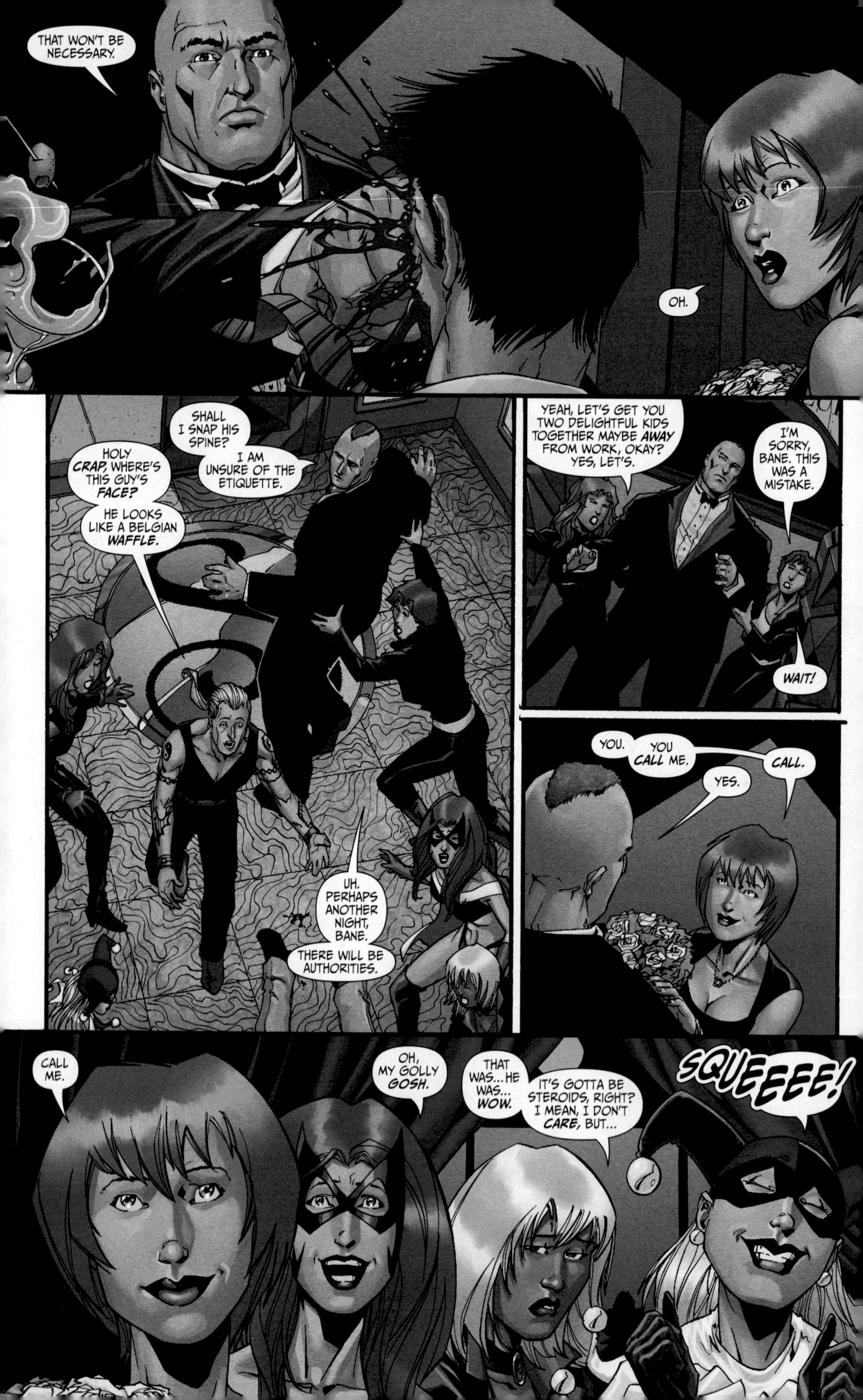
THAT WON'T BE NECESSARY.
OH.
SHALL I SNAP HIS SPINE?
I AM UNSURE OF THE ETIQUETTE.
HOLY CRAP, WHERE'S THIS GUY'S FACE?
HE LOOKS LIKE A BELGIAN WAFFLE.
UH. PERHAPS ANOTHER NIGHT, BANE.
THERE WILL BE AUTHORITIES.
YEAH, LET'S GET YOU TWO DELIGHTFUL KIDS TOGETHER MAYBE AWAY FROM WORK, OKAY? YES, LET'S.
I'M SORRY, BANE. THIS WAS A MISTAKE.
WAIT!
YOU.
YOU CALL ME.
CALL.
YES.
CALL ME.
OH, MY GOLLY GOSH.
THAT WAS... HE WAS... WOW.
IT'S GOTTA BE STEROIDS, RIGHT? I MEAN, I DON'T CARE, BUT...
SQUEEEEE!

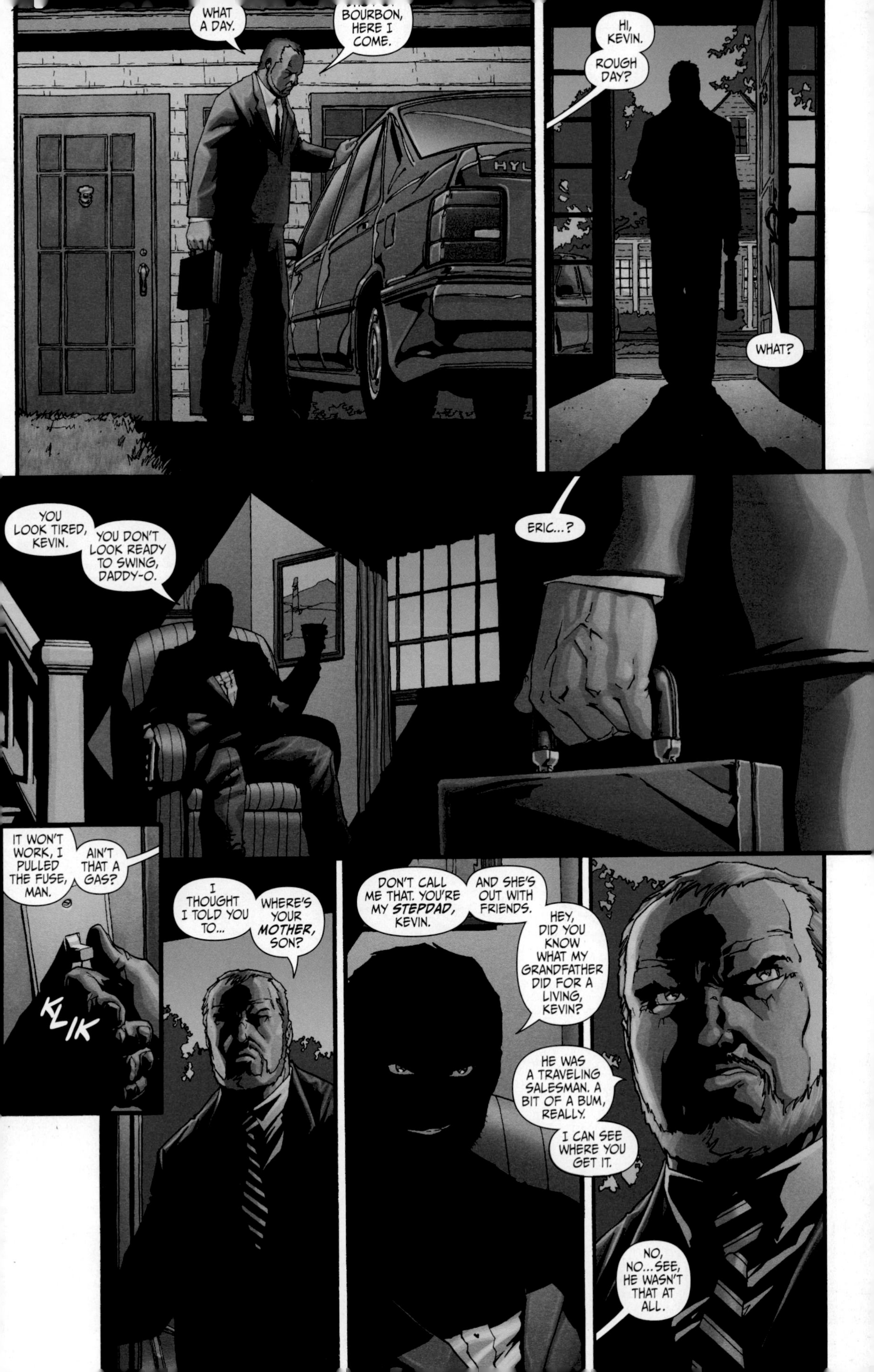
WHAT A DAY.
BOURBON, HERE I COME.
HI, KEVIN.
ROUGH DAY?
WHAT?
YOU LOOK TIRED, KEVIN.
YOU DON'T LOOK READY TO SWING, DADDY-O.
ERIC...?
IT WON'T WORK, I PULLED THE FUSE, MAN.
AIN'T THAT A GAS?
KLIK
I THOUGHT I TOLD YOU TO...
WHERE'S YOUR MOTHER, SON?
DON'T CALL ME THAT. YOU'RE MY STEPDAD, KEVIN.
AND SHE'S OUT WITH FRIENDS.
HEY, DID YOU KNOW WHAT MY GRANDFATHER DID FOR A LIVING, KEVIN?
HE WAS A TRAVELING SALESMAN. A BIT OF A BUM, REALLY.
I CAN SEE WHERE YOU GET IT.
NO, NO... SEE, HE WASN'T THAT AT ALL.

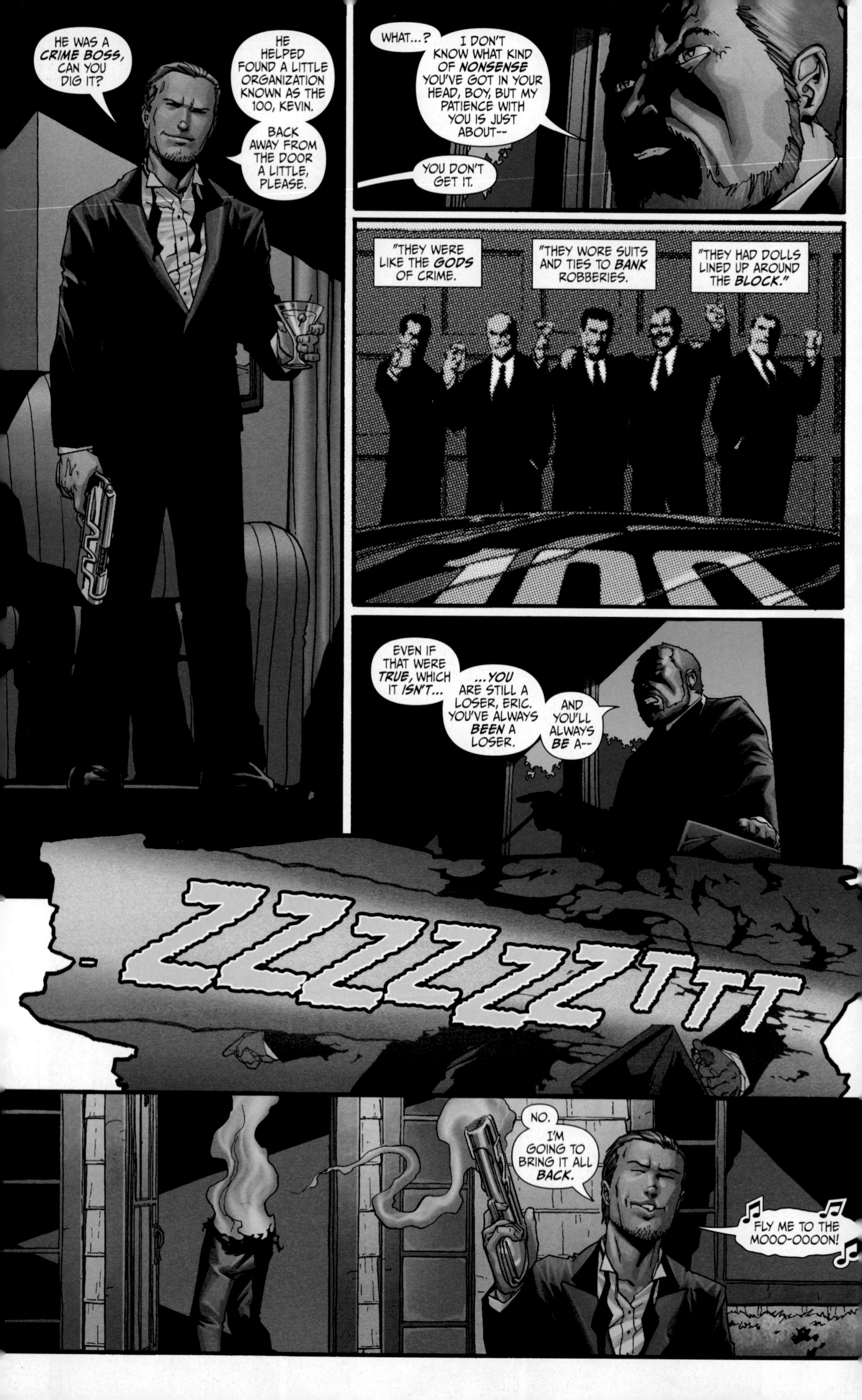
HE WAS A CRIME BOSS, CAN YOU DIG IT?
HE HELPED FOUND A LITTLE ORGANIZATION KNOWN AS THE 100, KEVIN.
BACK AWAY FROM THE DOOR A LITTLE, PLEASE.
WHAT...?
I DON'T KNOW WHAT KIND OF NONSENSE YOU'VE GOT IN YOUR HEAD, BOY, BUT MY PATIENCE WITH YOU IS JUST ABOUT--
YOU DON'T GET IT.
"THEY WERE LIKE THE GODS OF CRIME.
"THEY WORE SUITS AND TIES TO BANK ROBBERIES.
"THEY HAD DOLLS LINED UP AROUND THE BLOCK."
EVEN IF THAT WERE TRUE, WHICH IT ISN'T...
...YOU ARE STILL A LOSER, ERIC. YOU'VE ALWAYS BEEN A LOSER.
AND YOU'LL ALWAYS BE A--
ZZZZZZTTT
NO.
I'M GOING TO BRING IT ALL BACK.
FLY ME TO THE MOOO-OOOON!

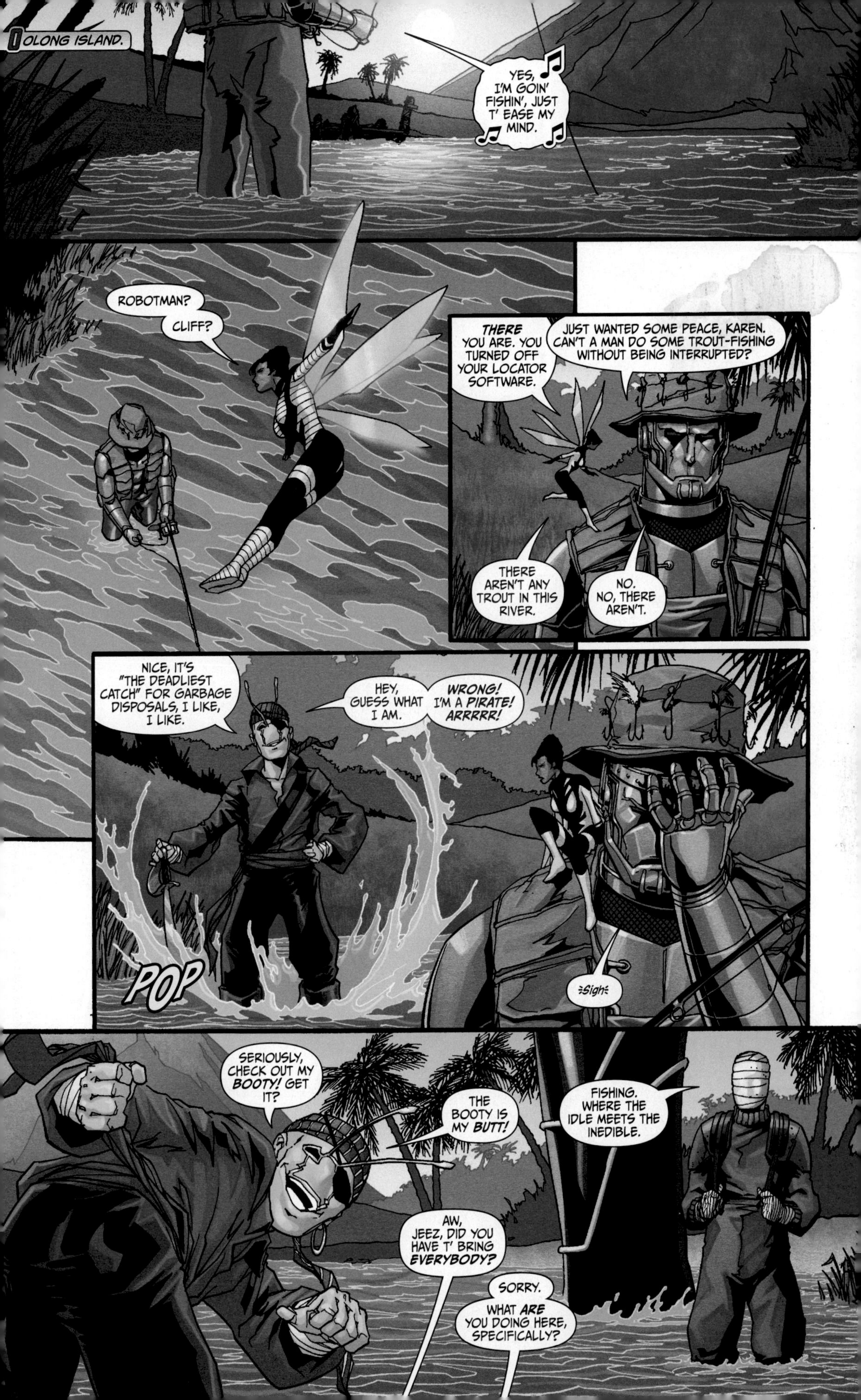
OLONG ISLAND.
YES, I'M GOIN' FISHIN', JUST T' EASE MY MIND.
ROBOTMAN?
CLIFF?
THERE YOU ARE. YOU TURNED OFF YOUR LOCATOR SOFTWARE.
JUST WANTED SOME PEACE, KAREN. CAN'T A MAN DO SOME TROUT-FISHING WITHOUT BEING INTERRUPTED?
THERE AREN'T ANY TROUT IN THIS RIVER.
NO. NO, THERE AREN'T.
NICE, IT'S "THE DEADLIEST CATCH" FOR GARBAGE DISPOSALS, I LIKE, I LIKE.
HEY, GUESS WHAT I AM.
WRONG! I'M A PIRATE! ARRRRR!
POP
Sigh
SERIOUSLY, CHECK OUT MY BOOTY! GET IT?
THE BOOTY IS MY BUTT!
FISHING. WHERE THE IDLE MEETS THE INEDIBLE.
AW, JEEZ, DID YOU HAVE T' BRING EVERYBODY?
SORRY.
WHAT ARE YOU DOING HERE, SPECIFICALLY?

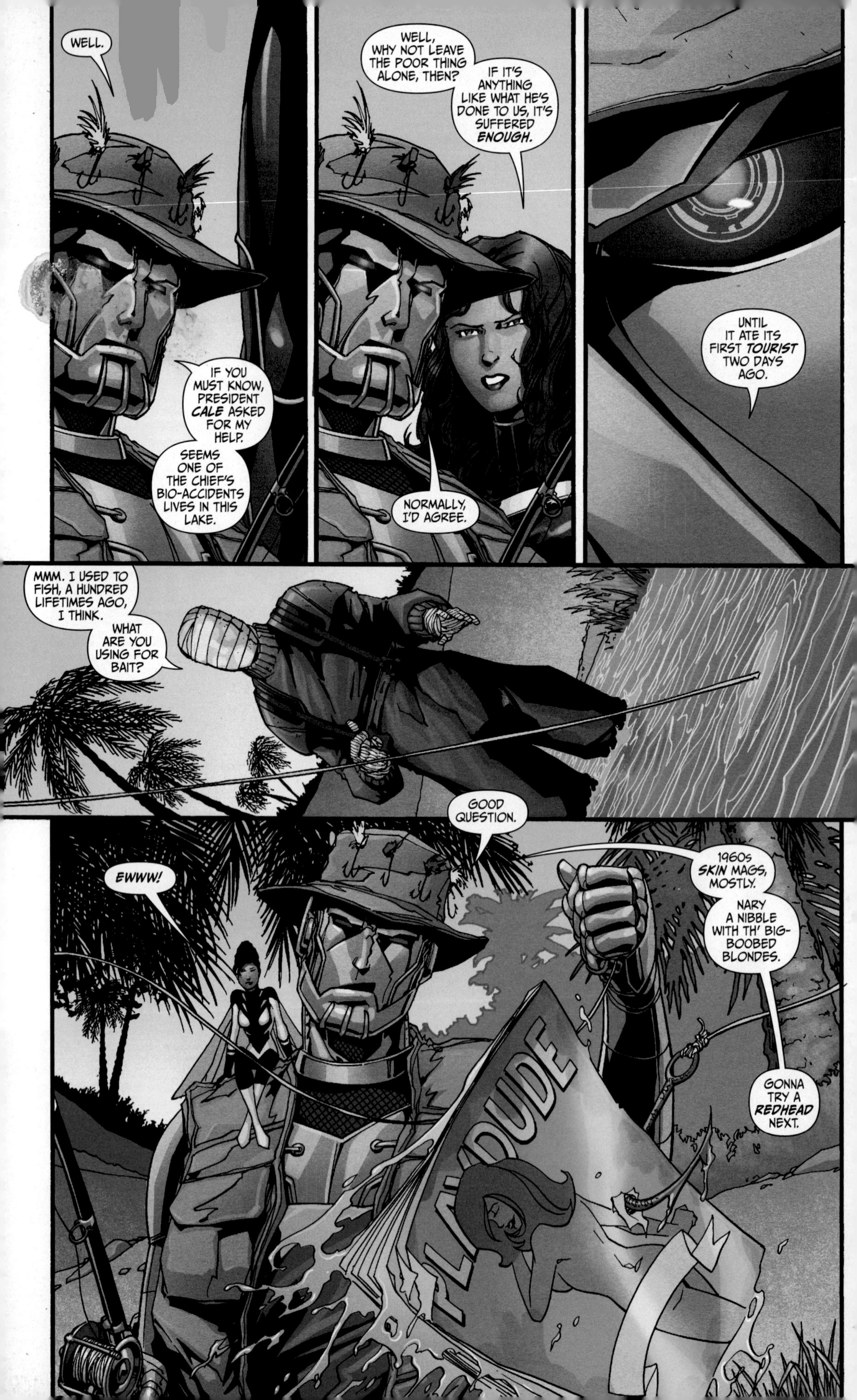
WELL.
IF YOU MUST KNOW, PRESIDENT CALE ASKED FOR MY HELP.
SEEMS ONE OF THE CHIEF'S BIO-ACCIDENTS LIVES IN THIS LAKE.
WELL, WHY NOT LEAVE THE POOR THING ALONE, THEN?
IF IT'S ANYTHING LIKE WHAT HE'S DONE TO US, IT'S SUFFERED ENOUGH.
NORMALLY, I'D AGREE.
UNTIL IT ATE ITS FIRST TOURIST TWO DAYS AGO.
MMM. I USED TO FISH, A HUNDRED LIFETIMES AGO, I THINK.
WHAT ARE YOU USING FOR BAIT?
GOOD QUESTION.
1960s SKIN MAGS, MOSTLY.
NARY A NIBBLE WITH TH' BIG-BOOBED BLONDES.
GONNA TRY A REDHEAD NEXT.
EWWW!
PLAYDUDE

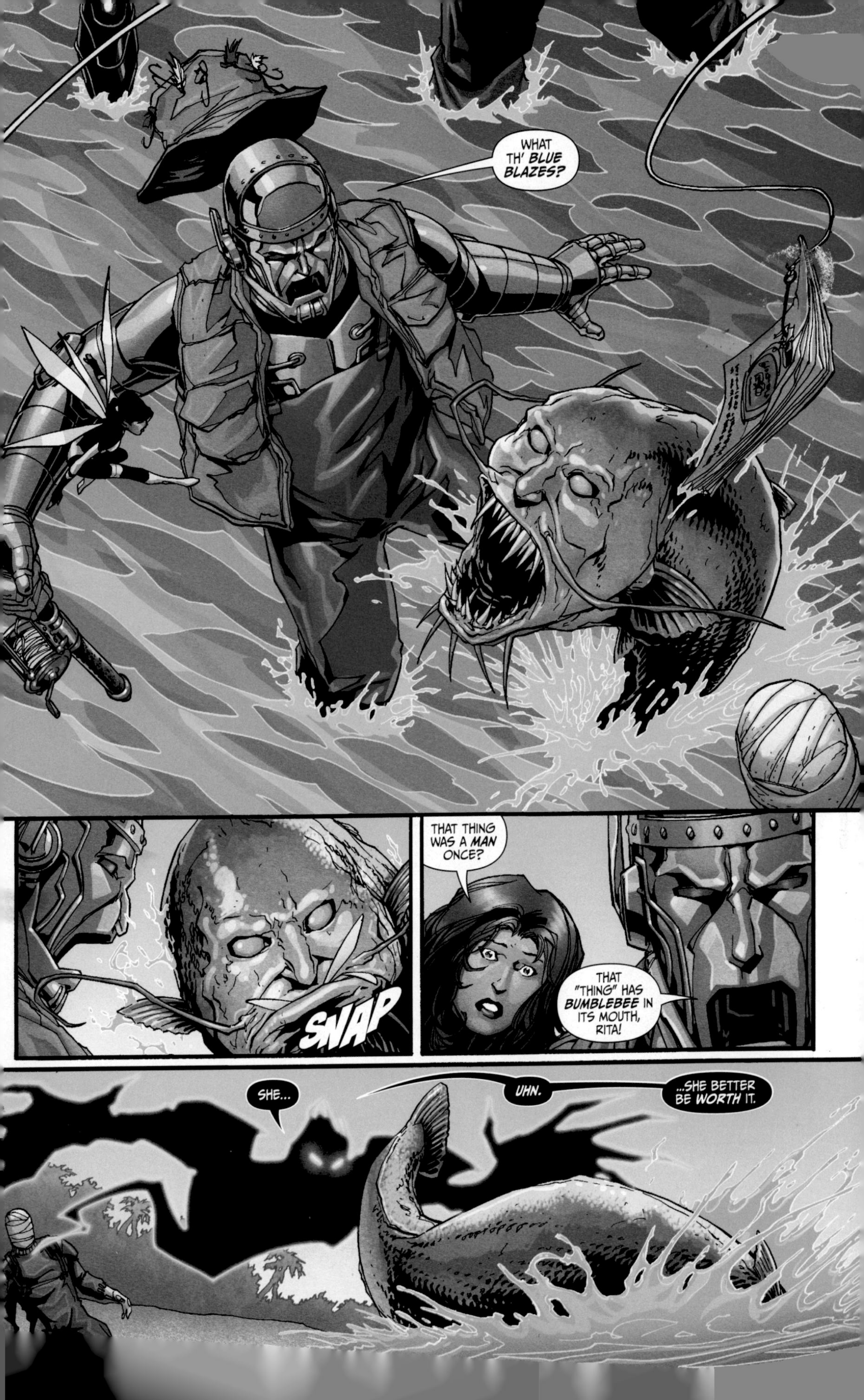
WHAT TH' BLUE BLAZES?
SNAP
THAT THING WAS A MAN ONCE?
THAT "THING" HAS BUMBLEBEE IN ITS MOUTH, RITA!
SHE...
UHN.
...SHE BETTER BE WORTH IT.

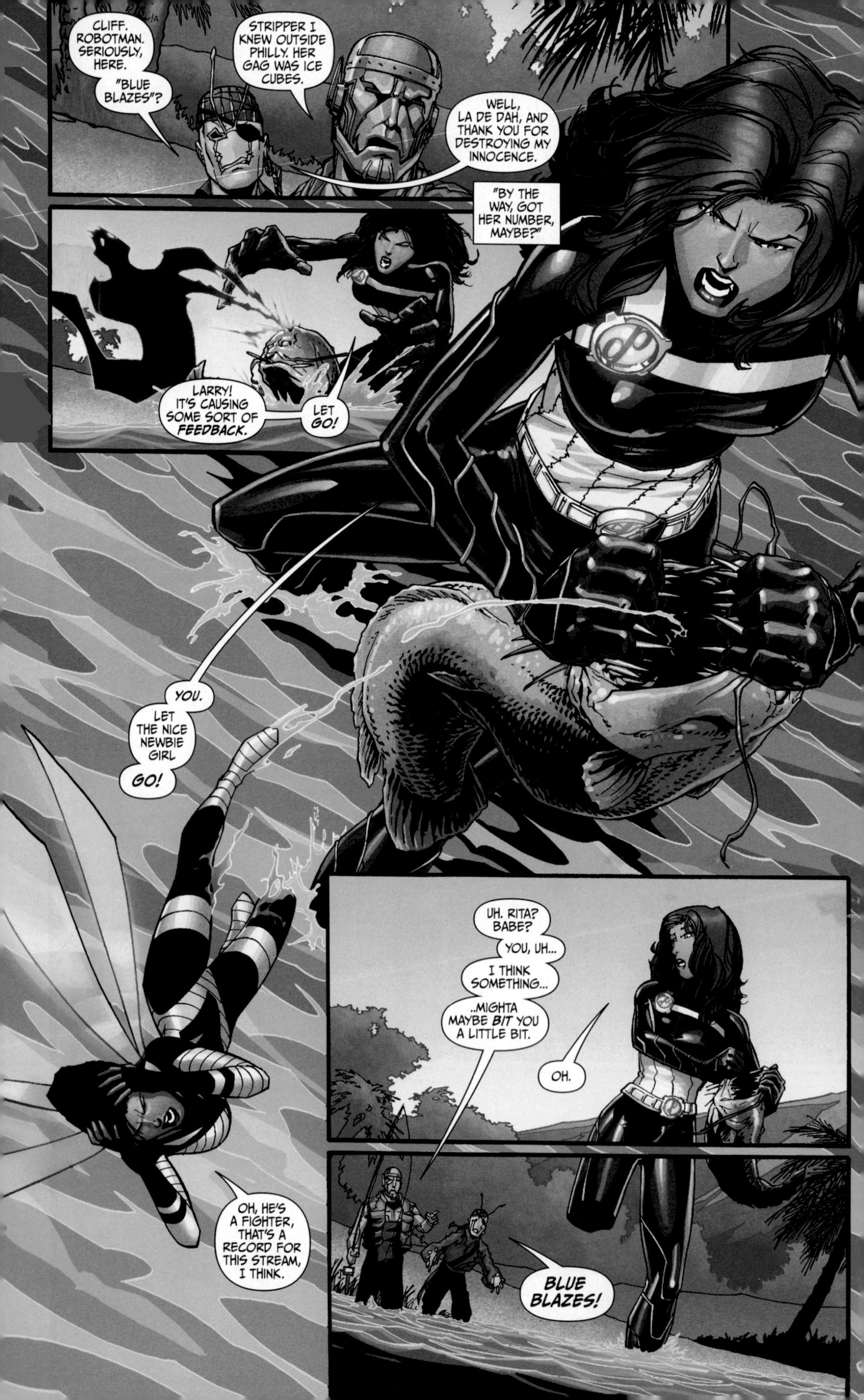
CLIFF. ROBOTMAN. SERIOUSLY, HERE. "BLUE BLAZES"?
STRIPPER I KNEW OUTSIDE PHILLY. HER GAG WAS ICE CUBES.
WELL, LA DE DAH, AND THANK YOU FOR DESTROYING MY INNOCENCE.
"BY THE WAY, GOT HER NUMBER, MAYBE?"
LARRY! IT'S CAUSING SOME SORT OF FEEDBACK.
LET GO!
YOU.
LET THE NICE NEWBIE GIRL
GO!
OH, HE'S A FIGHTER, THAT'S A RECORD FOR THIS STREAM, I THINK.
UH. RITA? BABE?
YOU, UH...
I THINK SOMETHING...
..MIGHTA MAYBE BIT YOU A LITTLE BIT.
OH.
BLUE BLAZES!

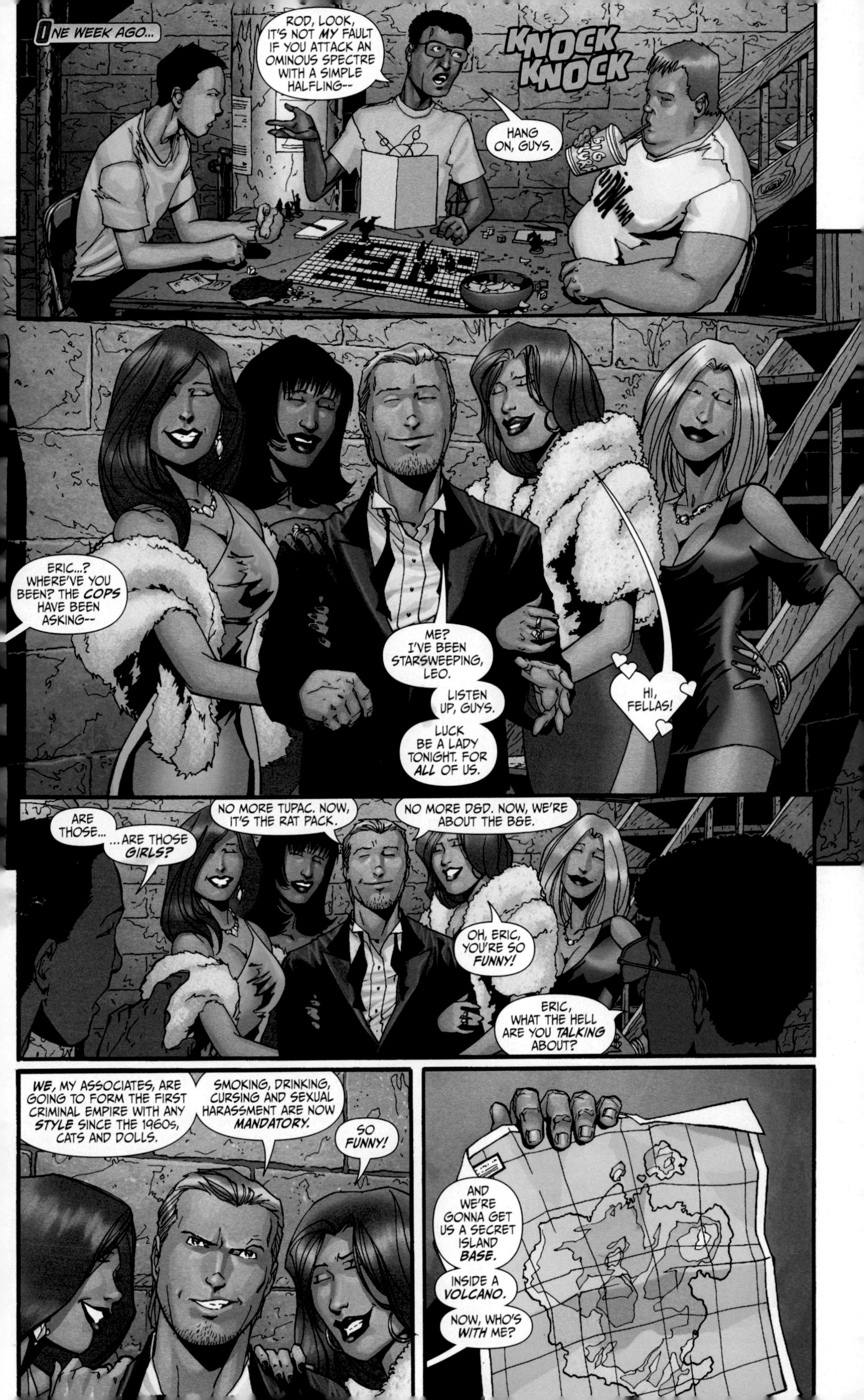
ONE WEEK AGO...
ROD, LOOK, IT'S NOT MY FAULT IF YOU ATTACK AN OMINOUS SPECTRE WITH A SIMPLE HALFLING--
KNOCK KNOCK
HANG ON, GUYS.
ERIC...? WHERE'VE YOU BEEN? THE COPS HAVE BEEN ASKING--
ME? I'VE BEEN STARSWEEPING, LEO.
LISTEN UP, GUYS.
LUCK BE A LADY TONIGHT. FOR ALL OF US.
HI, FELLAS!
ARE THOSE...
...ARE THOSE GIRLS?
NO MORE TUPAC. NOW, IT'S THE RAT PACK.
NO MORE D&D. NOW, WE'RE ABOUT THE B&E.
OH, ERIC, YOU'RE SO FUNNY!
ERIC, WHAT THE HELL ARE YOU TALKING ABOUT?
WE, MY ASSOCIATES, ARE GOING TO FORM THE FIRST CRIMINAL EMPIRE WITH ANY STYLE SINCE THE 1960s, CATS AND DOLLS.
SMOKING, DRINKING, CURSING AND SEXUAL HARASSMENT ARE NOW MANDATORY.
SO FUNNY!
AND WE'RE GONNA GET US A SECRET ISLAND BASE.
INSIDE A VOLCANO.
NOW, WHO'S WITH ME?

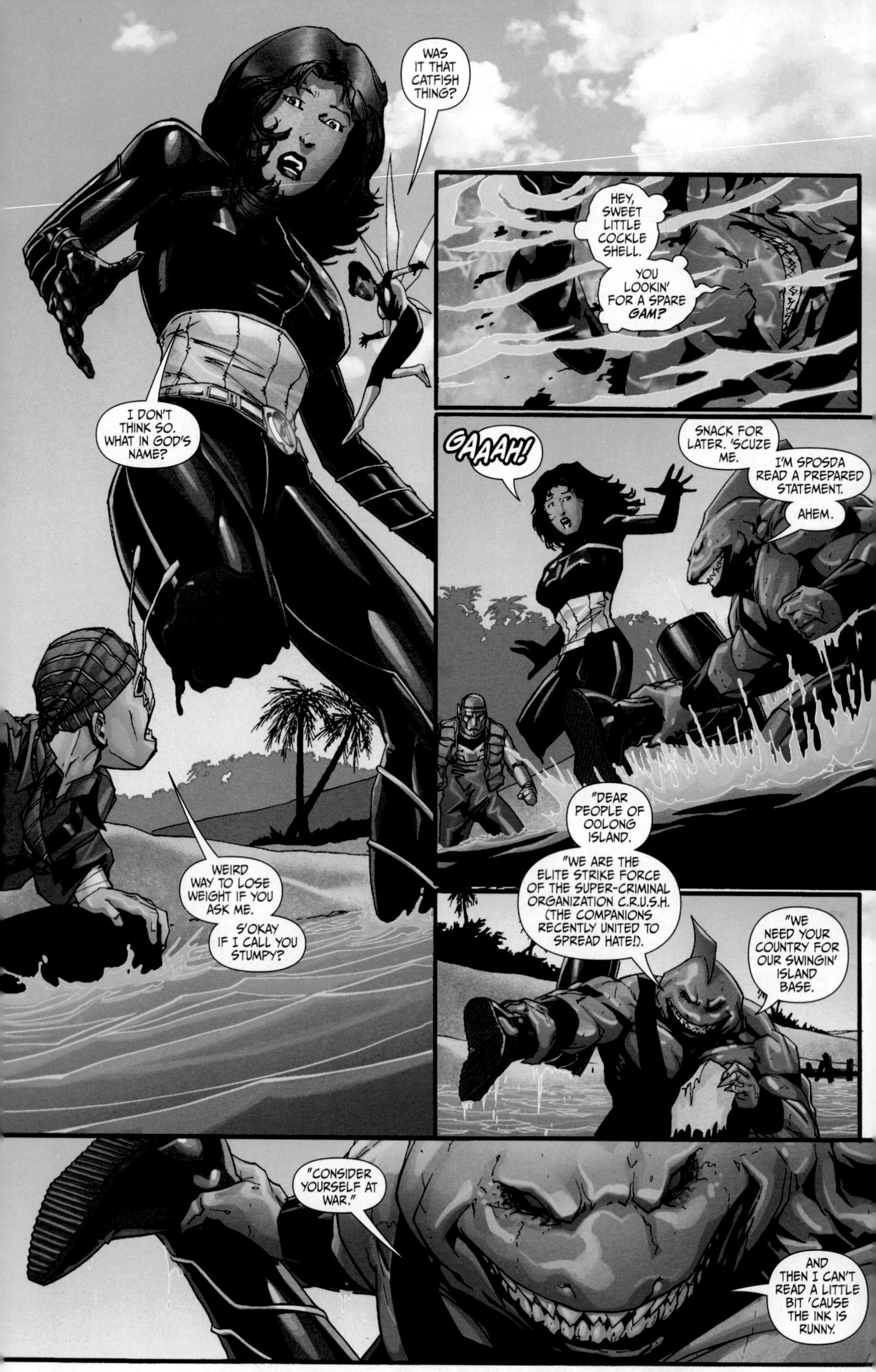

WAS IT THAT CATFISH THING?
I DON'T THINK SO. WHAT IN GOD'S NAME?
WEIRD WAY TO LOSE WEIGHT IF YOU ASK ME.
S'OKAY IF I CALL YOU STUMPY?
HEY, SWEET LITTLE COCKLE SHELL.
YOU LOOKIN' FOR A SPARE GAM?
GAAAH!
SNACK FOR LATER. 'SCUZE ME.
I'M SPOSDA READ A PREPARED STATEMENT.
AHEM.
"DEAR PEOPLE OF OOLONG ISLAND.
"WE ARE THE ELITE STRIKE FORCE OF THE SUPER-CRIMINAL ORGANIZATION C.R.U.S.H. (THE COMPANIONS RECENTLY UNITED TO SPREAD HATE!).
"WE NEED YOUR COUNTRY FOR OUR SWINGIN' ISLAND BASE.
"CONSIDER YOURSELF AT WAR."
AND THEN I CAN'T READ A LITTLE BIT 'CAUSE THE INK IS RUNNY.

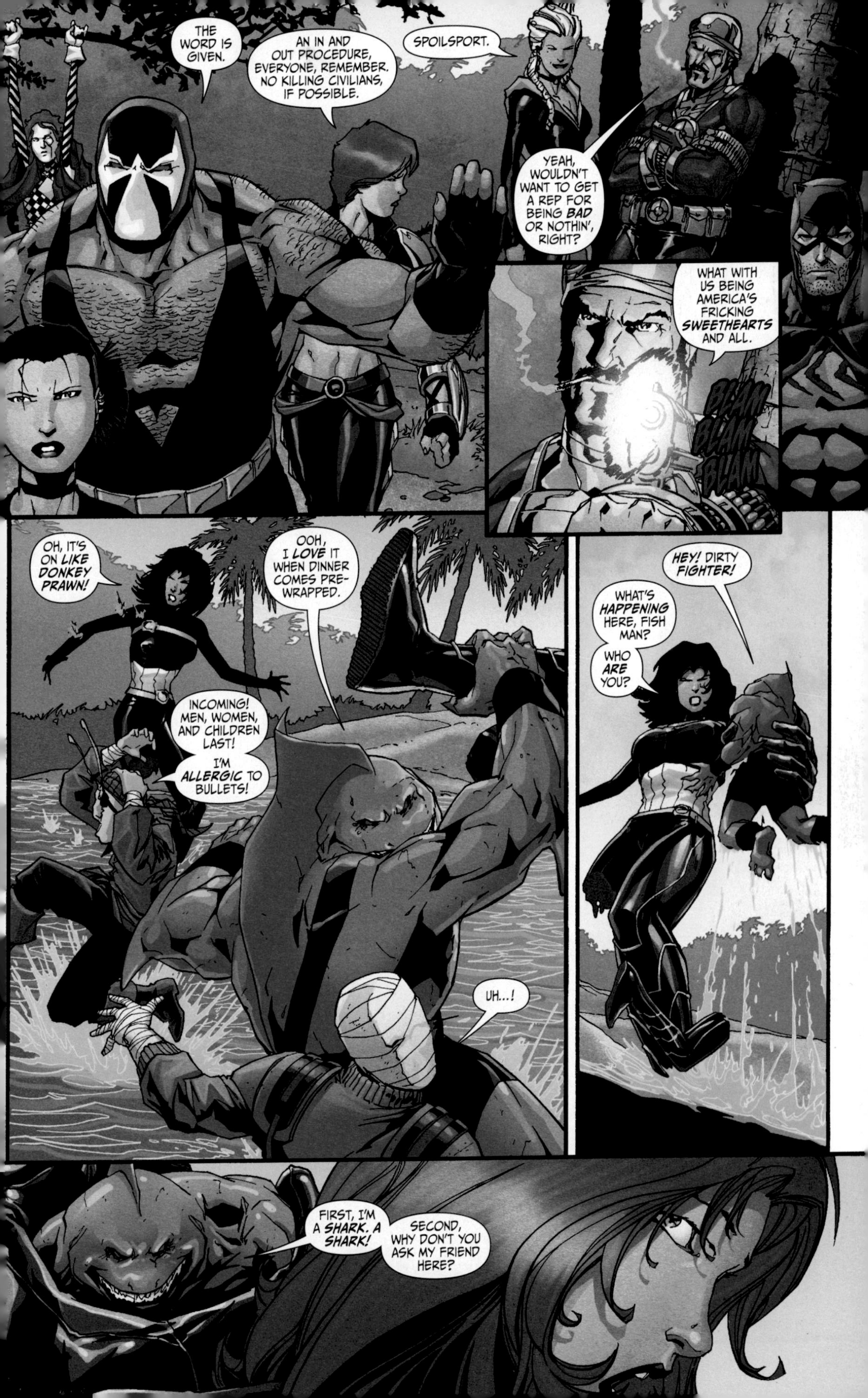
THE WORD IS GIVEN.
AN IN AND OUT PROCEDURE, EVERYONE, REMEMBER. NO KILLING CIVILIANS, IF POSSIBLE.
SPOILSPORT.
YEAH, WOULDN'T WANT TO GET A REP FOR BEING BAD OR NOTHIN', RIGHT?
WHAT WITH US BEING AMERICA'S FRICKING SWEETHEARTS AND ALL.
BLAM BLAM BLAM
OH, IT'S ON LIKE DONKEY PRAWN!
OOH, I LOVE IT WHEN DINNER COMES PRE-WRAPPED.
INCOMING! MEN, WOMEN, AND CHILDREN LAST!
I'M ALLERGIC TO BULLETS!
UH...!
HEY! DIRTY FIGHTER!
WHAT'S HAPPENING HERE, FISH MAN?
WHO ARE YOU?
FIRST, I'M A SHARK. A SHARK!
SECOND, WHY DON'T YOU ASK MY FRIEND HERE?

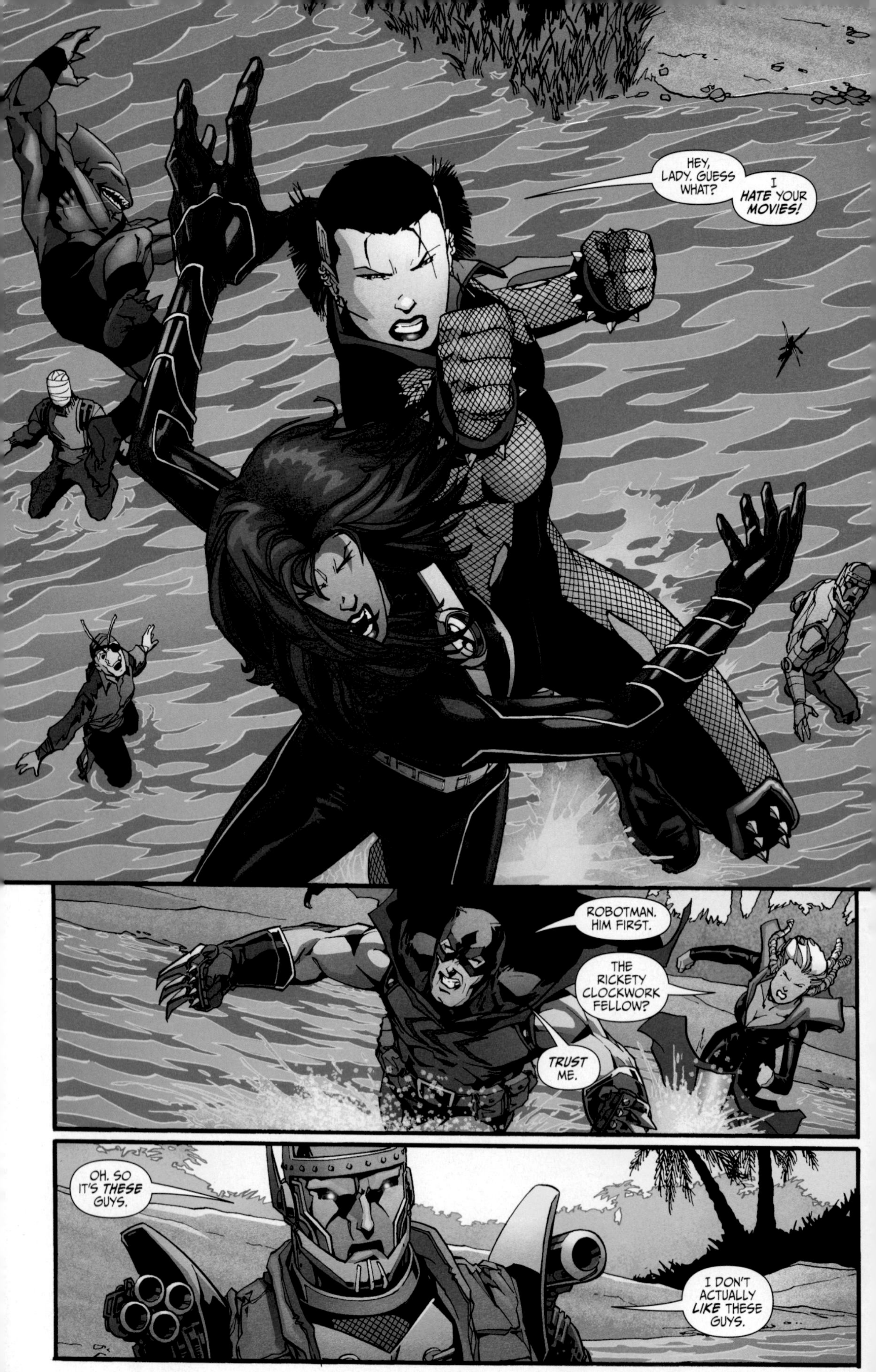
HEY, LADY. GUESS WHAT?
I HATE YOUR MOVIES!
ROBOTMAN. HIM FIRST.
THE RICKETY CLOCKWORK FELLOW?
TRUST ME.
OH. SO IT'S THESE GUYS.
I DON'T ACTUALLY LIKE THESE GUYS.

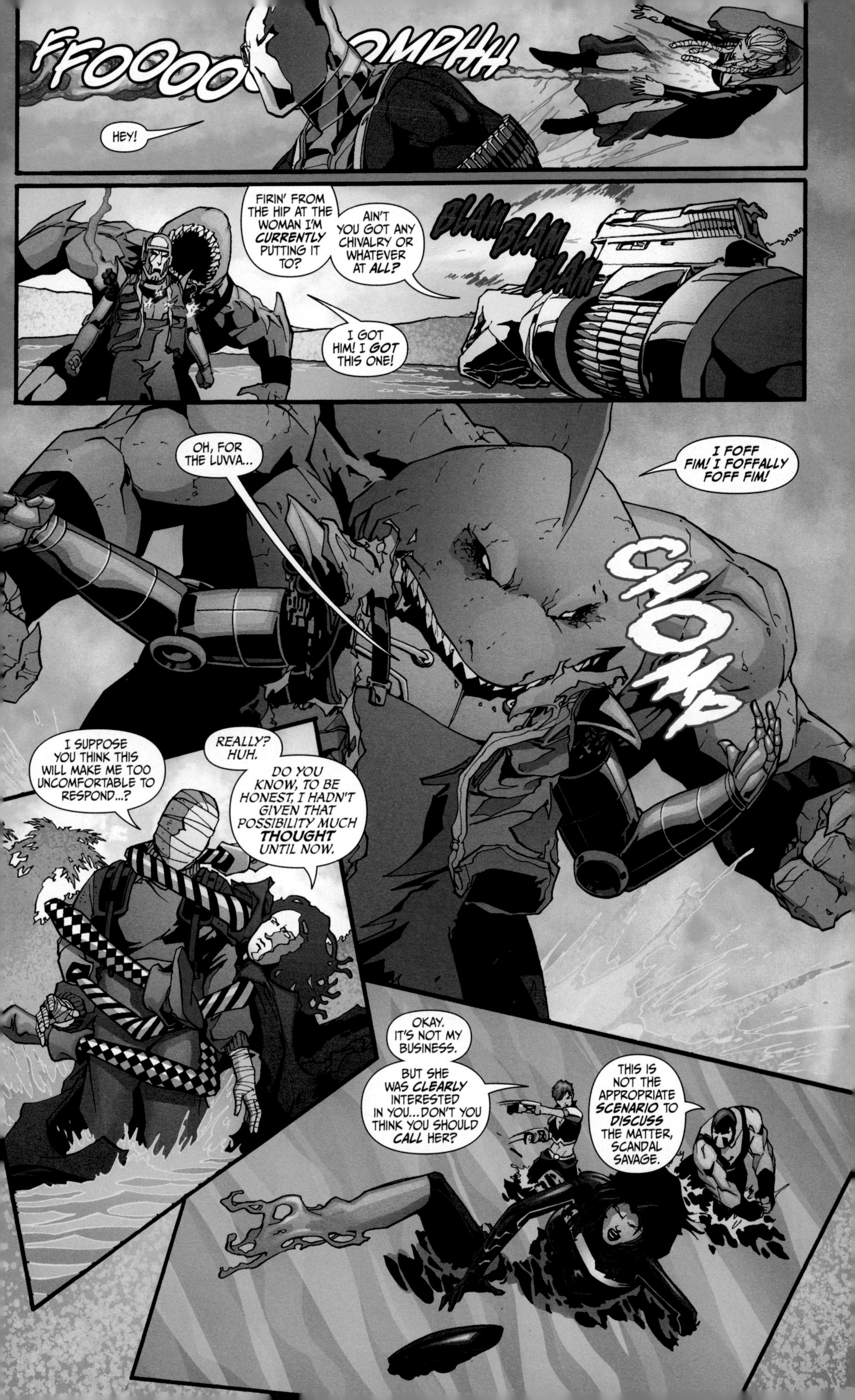
FFOOOOOOMPHH
HEY!
FIRIN' FROM THE HIP AT THE WOMAN I'M CURRENTLY PUTTING IT TO?
AIN'T YOU GOT ANY CHIVALRY OR WHATEVER AT ALL?
BLAM BLAM BLAM
I GOT HIM! I GOT THIS ONE!
OH, FOR THE LUVVA...
I FOFF FIM! I FOFFALLY FOFF FIM!
CHOMP
I SUPPOSE YOU THINK THIS WILL MAKE ME TOO UNCOMFORTABLE TO RESPOND...?
REALLY? HUH.
DO YOU KNOW, TO BE HONEST, I HADN'T GIVEN THAT POSSIBILITY MUCH THOUGHT UNTIL NOW.
OKAY. IT'S NOT MY BUSINESS.
BUT SHE WAS CLEARLY INTERESTED IN YOU...DON'T YOU THINK YOU SHOULD CALL HER?
THIS IS NOT THE APPROPRIATE SCENARIO TO DISCUSS THE MATTER, SCANDAL SAVAGE.

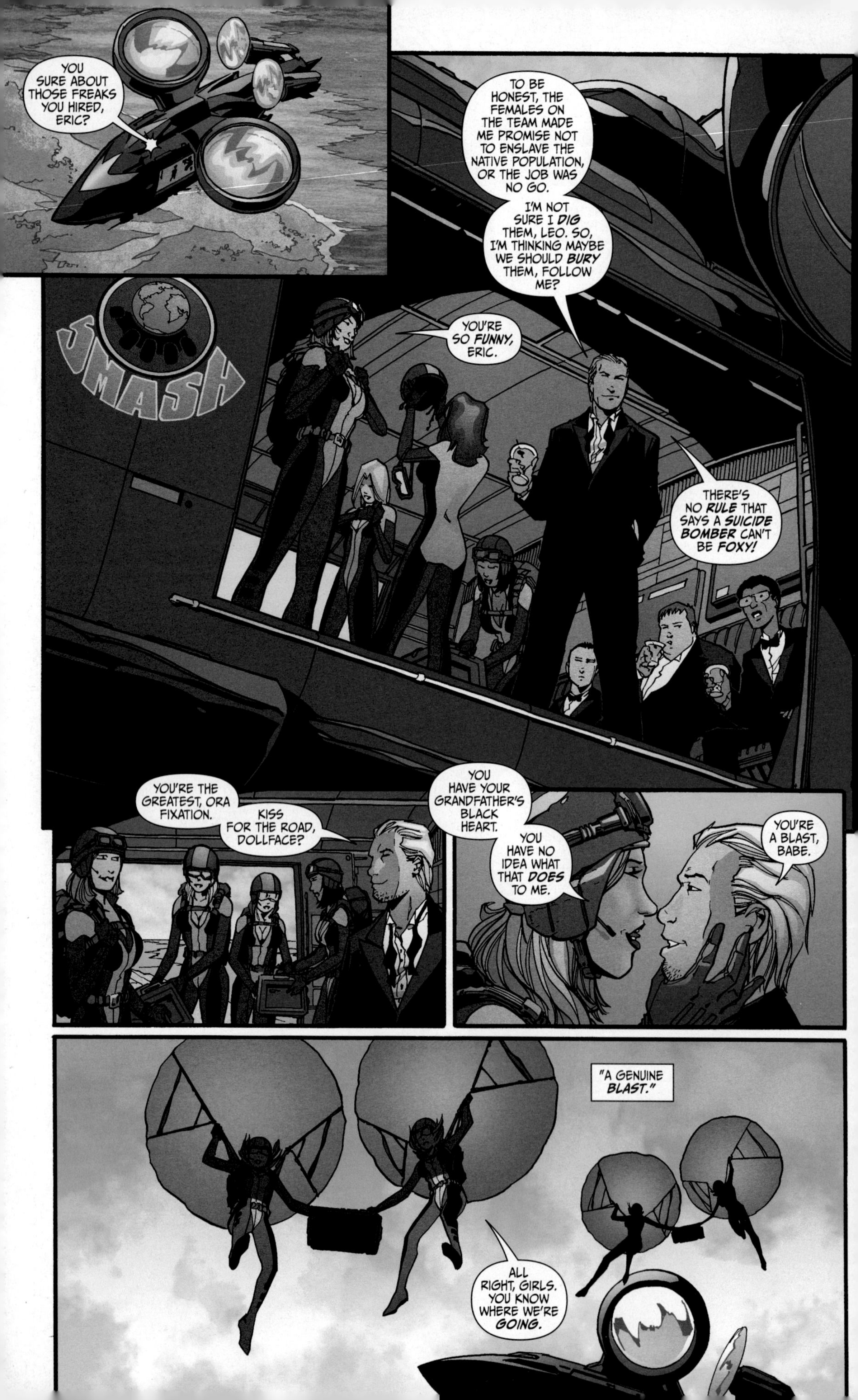
YOU SURE ABOUT THOSE FREAKS YOU HIRED, ERIC?
TO BE HONEST, THE FEMALES ON THE TEAM MADE ME PROMISE NOT TO ENSLAVE THE NATIVE POPULATION, OR THE JOB WAS NO GO.
I'M NOT SURE I DIG THEM, LEO. SO, I'M THINKING MAYBE WE SHOULD BURY THEM, FOLLOW ME?
SMASH
YOU'RE SO FUNNY, ERIC.
THERE'S NO RULE THAT SAYS A SUICIDE BOMBER CAN'T BE FOXY!
YOU'RE THE GREATEST, ORA FIXATION.
KISS FOR THE ROAD, DOLLFACE?
YOU HAVE YOUR GRANDFATHER'S BLACK HEART.
YOU HAVE NO IDEA WHAT THAT DOES TO ME.
YOU'RE A BLAST, BABE.
"A GENUINE BLAST."
ALL RIGHT, GIRLS. YOU KNOW WHERE WE'RE GOING.

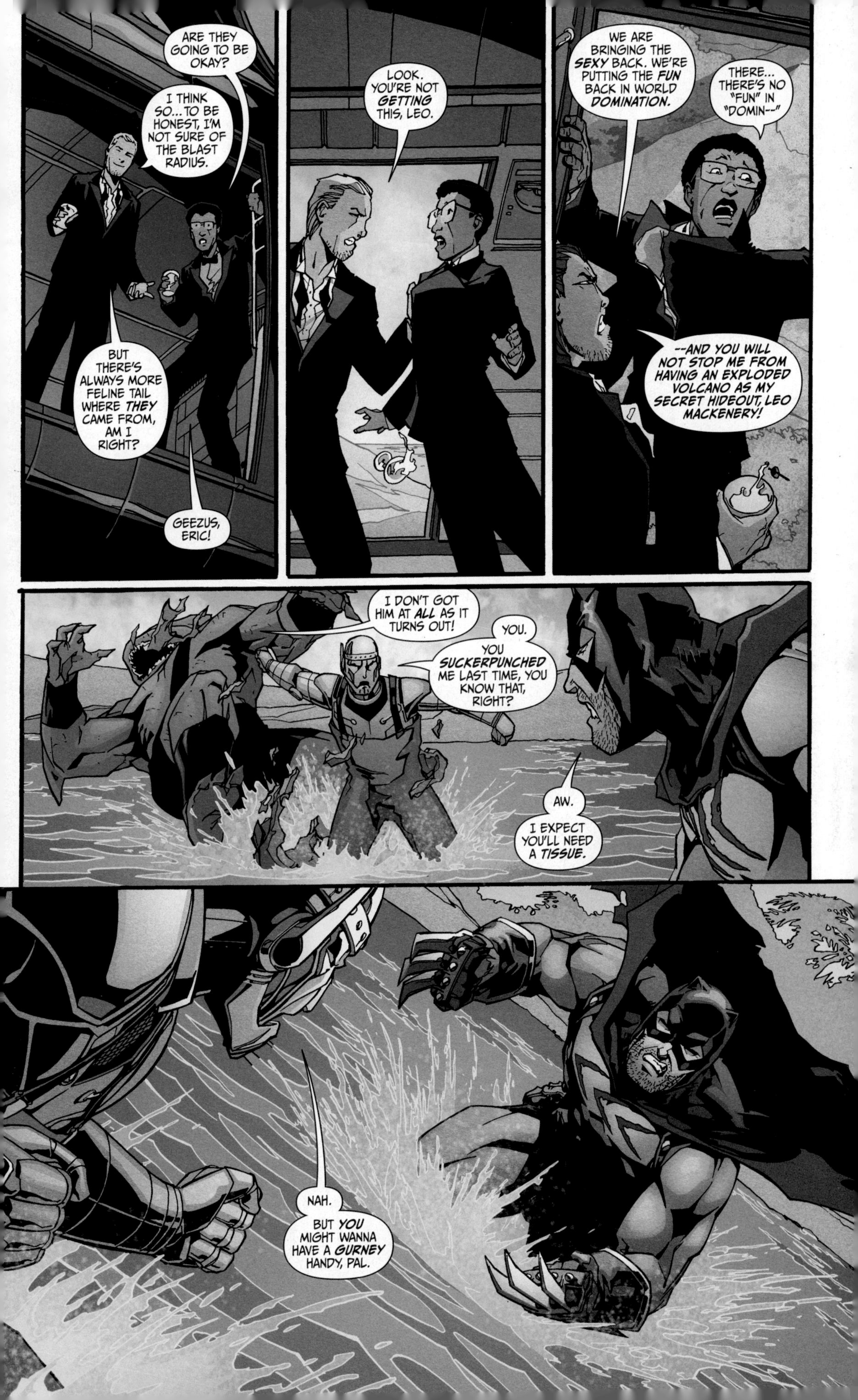

ARE THEY GOING TO BE OKAY?
I THINK SO...TO BE HONEST, I'M NOT SURE OF THE BLAST RADIUS.
BUT THERE'S ALWAYS MORE FELINE TAIL WHERE THEY CAME FROM, AM I RIGHT?
GEEZUS, ERIC!
LOOK. YOU'RE NOT GETTING THIS, LEO.
WE ARE BRINGING THE SEXY BACK. WE'RE PUTTING THE FUN BACK IN WORLD DOMINATION.
THERE... THERE'S NO "FUN" IN "DOMIN--"
--AND YOU WILL NOT STOP ME FROM HAVING AN EXPLODED VOLCANO AS MY SECRET HIDEOUT, LEO MACKENERY!
I DON'T GOT HIM AT ALL AS IT TURNS OUT!
YOU.
YOU SUCKERPUNCHED ME LAST TIME, YOU KNOW THAT, RIGHT?
AW.
I EXPECT YOU'LL NEED A TISSUE.
NAH.
BUT YOU MIGHT WANNA HAVE A GURNEY HANDY, PAL.

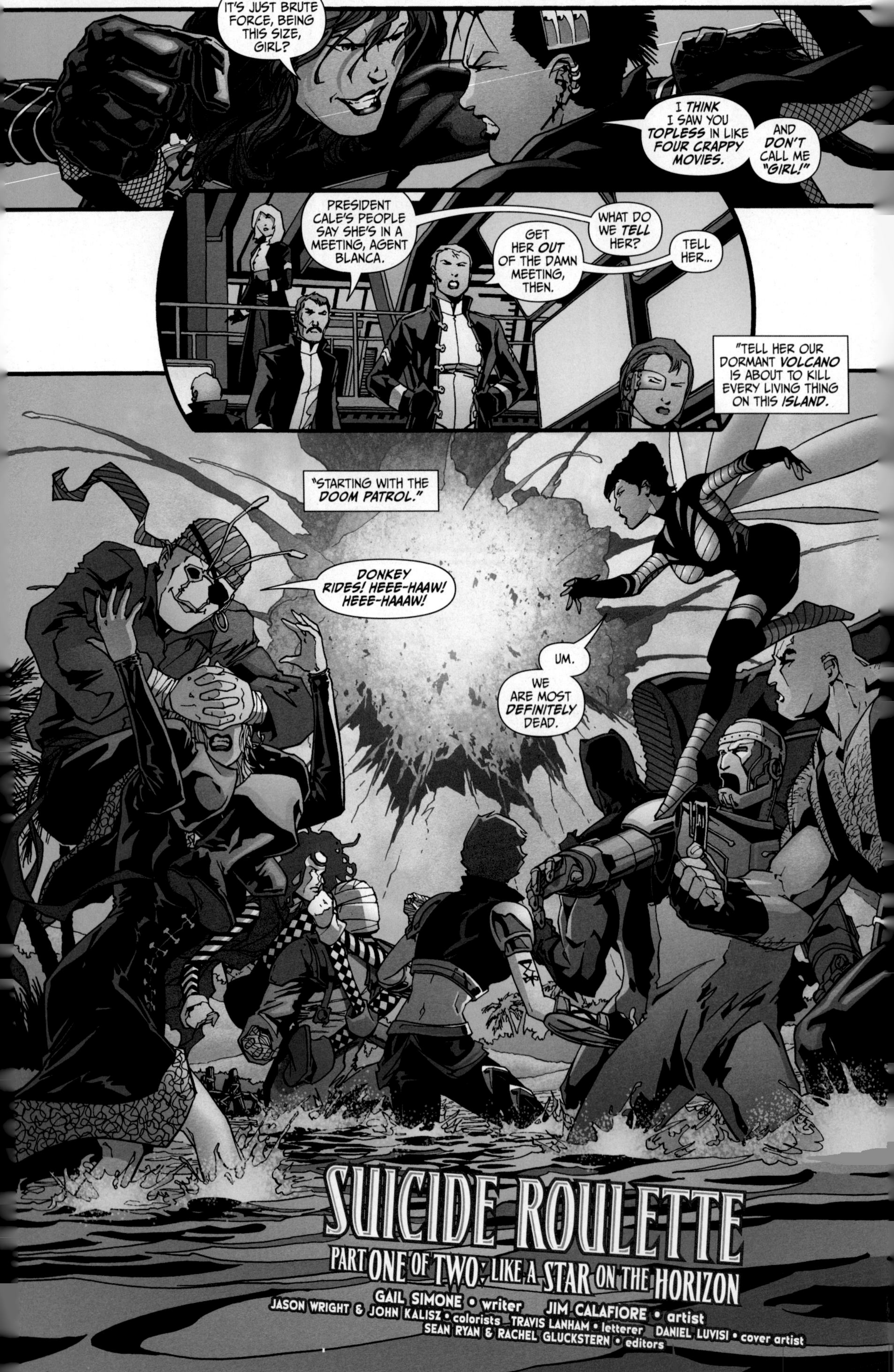
YOU THINK IT'S JUST BRUTE FORCE, BEING THIS SIZE, GIRL?
I THINK I SAW YOU TOPLESS IN LIKE FOUR CRAPPY MOVIES.
AND DON'T CALL ME "GIRL!"
PRESIDENT CALE'S PEOPLE SAY SHE'S IN A MEETING, AGENT BLANCA.
GET HER OUT OF THE DAMN MEETING, THEN.
WHAT DO WE TELL HER?
TELL HER...
"TELL HER OUR DORMANT VOLCANO IS ABOUT TO KILL EVERY LIVING THING ON THIS ISLAND.
"STARTING WITH THE DOOM PATROL."
DONKEY RIDES! HEEE-HAAW! HEEE-HAAAW!
UM.
WE ARE MOST DEFINITELY DEAD.
SUICIDE ROULETTE
PART ONE OF TWO: LIKE A STAR ON THE HORIZON
GAIL SIMONE • writer JIM CALAFIORE • artist
JASON WRIGHT & JOHN KALISZ • colorists TRAVIS LANHAM • letterer DANIEL LUVISI • cover artist
SEAN RYAN & RACHEL GLUCKSTERN • editors

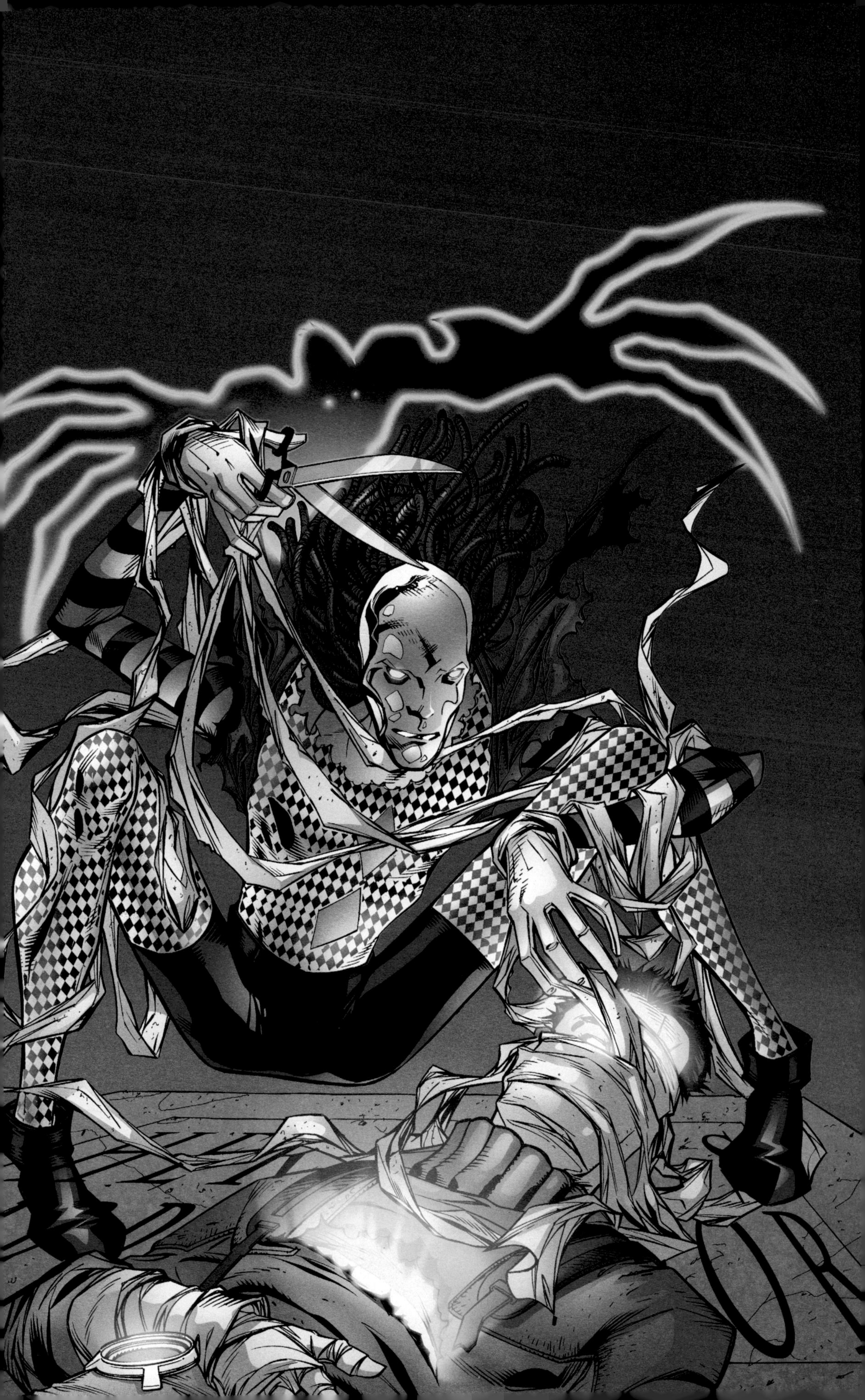

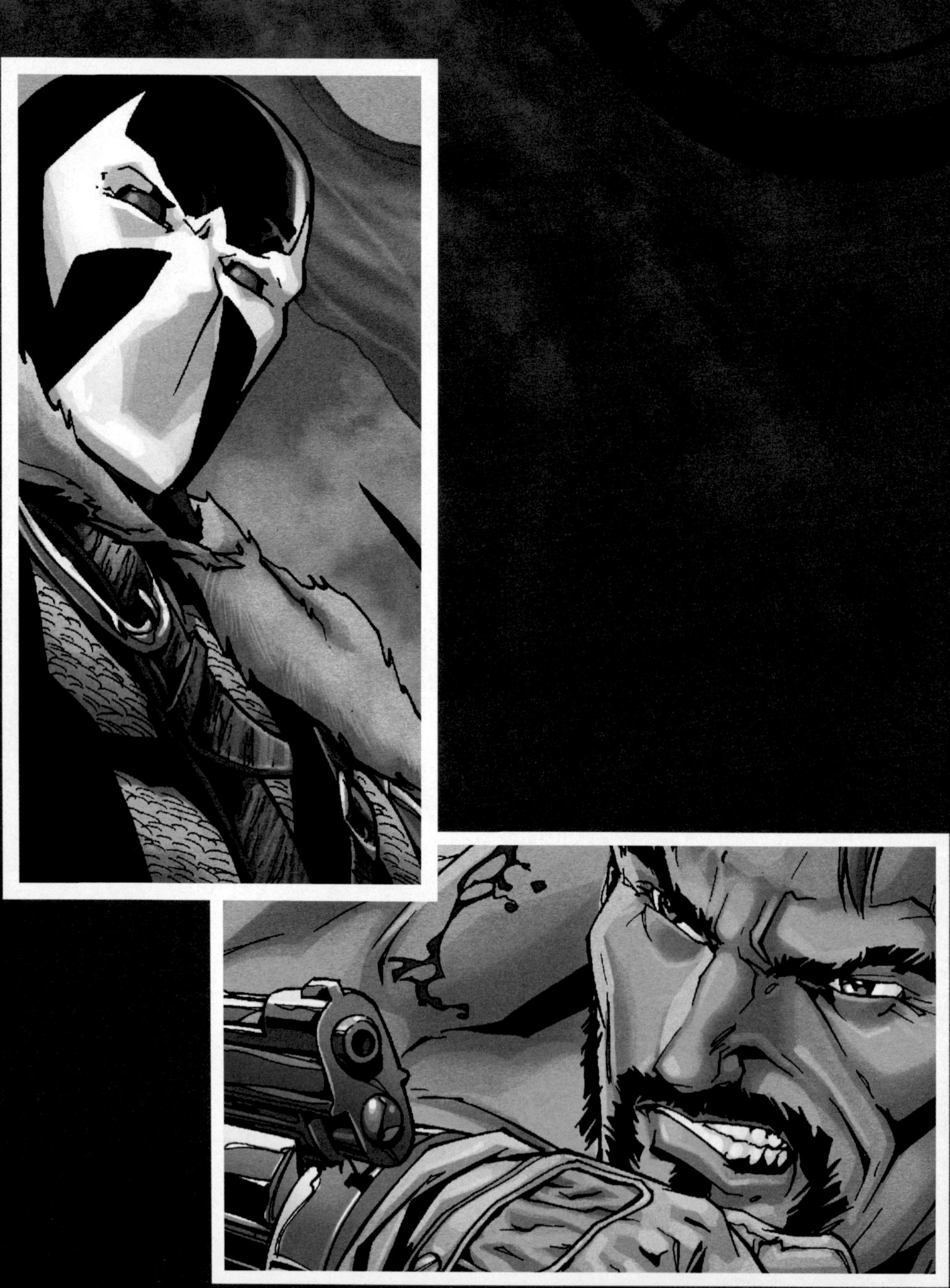

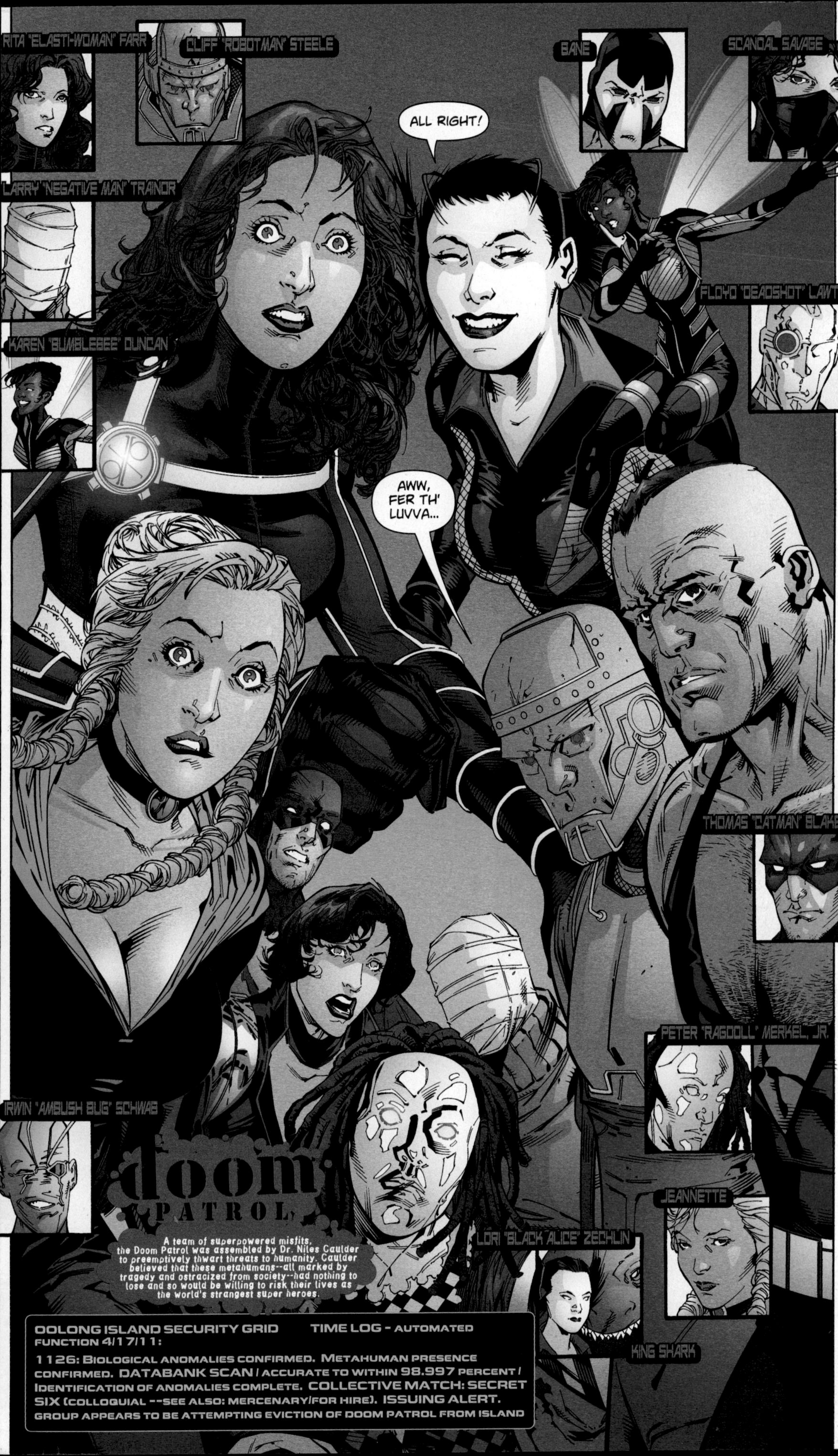
RITA "ELASTI-WOMAN" FARR
CLIFF "ROBOTMAN" STEELE
BANE
SCANDAL SAVAGE
ALL RIGHT!
LARRY "NEGATIVE MAN" TRAINOR
FLOYD "DEADSHOT" LAWTON
KAREN "BUMBLEBEE" DUNCAN
AWW, FER TH' LUVVA...
THOMAS "CATMAN" BLAKE
PETER "RAGDOLL" MERKEL, JR.
IRWIN "AMBUSH BUG" SCHWAB
doom PATROL
JEANNETTE
LORI "BLACK ALICE" ZECHLIN
A team of superpowered misfits, the Doom Patrol was assembled by Dr. Niles Caulder to preemptively thwart threats to humanity. Caulder believed that these metahumans--all marked by tragedy and ostracized from society--had nothing to lose and so would be willing to risk their lives as the world's strangest super heroes.
OOLONG ISLAND SECURITY GRID TIME LOG - AUTOMATED FUNCTION 4/17/11:
1126: BIOLOGICAL ANOMALIES CONFIRMED. METAHUMAN PRESENCE CONFIRMED. DATABANK SCAN / ACCURATE TO WITHIN 98.997 PERCENT / IDENTIFICATION OF ANOMALIES COMPLETE. COLLECTIVE MATCH: SECRET SIX (COLLOQUIAL --SEE ALSO: MERCENARY/FOR HIRE). ISSUING ALERT. GROUP APPEARS TO BE ATTEMPTING EVICTION OF DOOM PATROL FROM ISLAND
KING SHARK

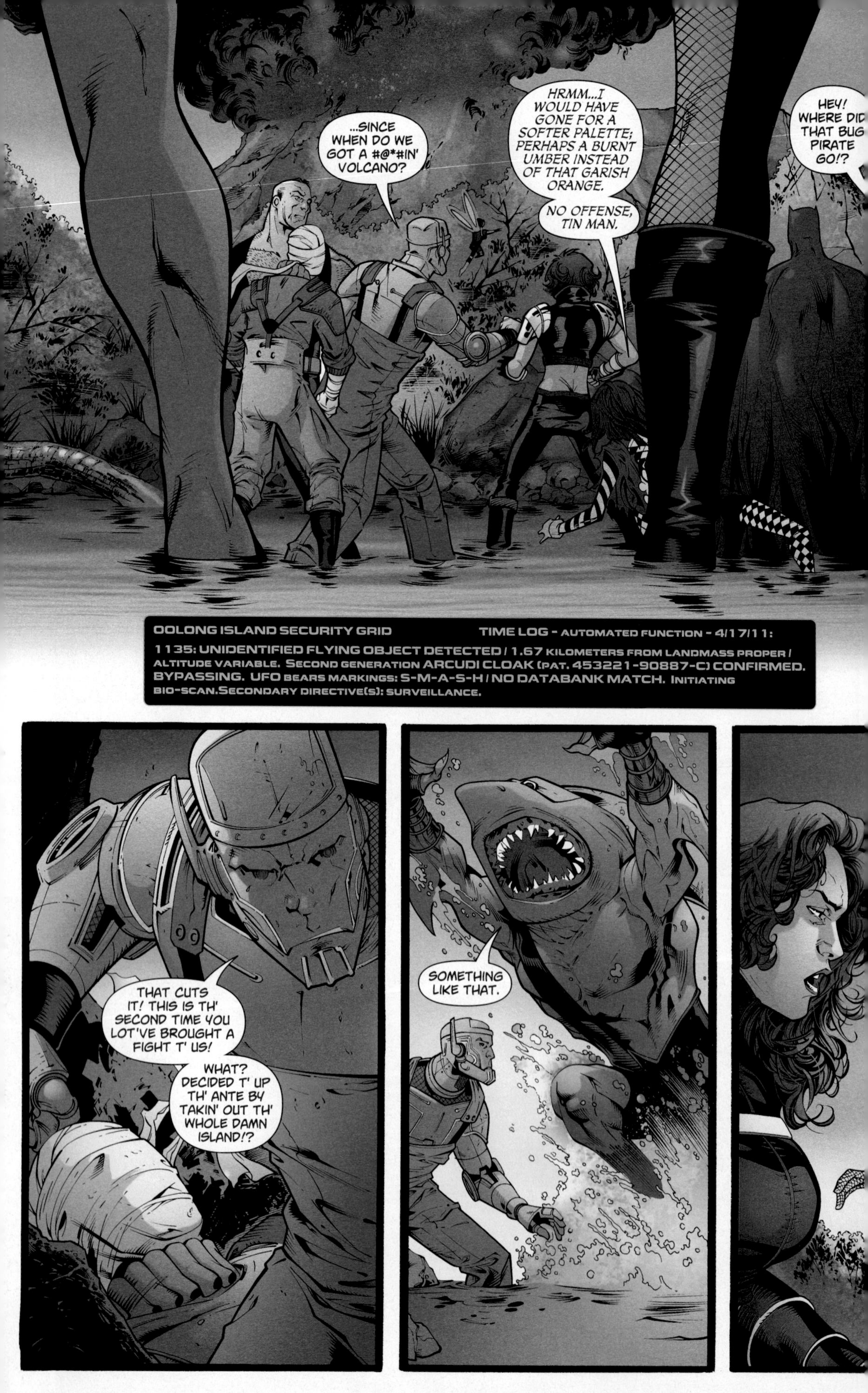
...SINCE WHEN DO WE GOT A #@*#IN' VOLCANO?
HRMM...I WOULD HAVE GONE FOR A SOFTER PALETTE; PERHAPS A BURNT UMBER INSTEAD OF THAT GARISH ORANGE.
NO OFFENSE, TIN MAN.
HEY! WHERE DID THAT BUG PIRATE GO!?
OOLONG ISLAND SECURITY GRID
TIME LOG - AUTOMATED FUNCTION - 4/17/11:
1135: UNIDENTIFIED FLYING OBJECT DETECTED / 1.67 KILOMETERS FROM LANDMASS PROPER / ALTITUDE VARIABLE. SECOND GENERATION ARCUDI CLOAK (PAT. 453221-90887-C) CONFIRMED. BYPASSING. UFO BEARS MARKINGS: S-M-A-S-H / NO DATABANK MATCH. INITIATING BIO-SCAN.SECONDARY DIRECTIVE(S): SURVEILLANCE.
THAT CUTS IT! THIS IS TH' SECOND TIME YOU LOT'VE BROUGHT A FIGHT T' US!
WHAT? DECIDED T' UP TH' ANTE BY TAKIN' OUT TH' WHOLE DAMN ISLAND!?
SOMETHING LIKE THAT.

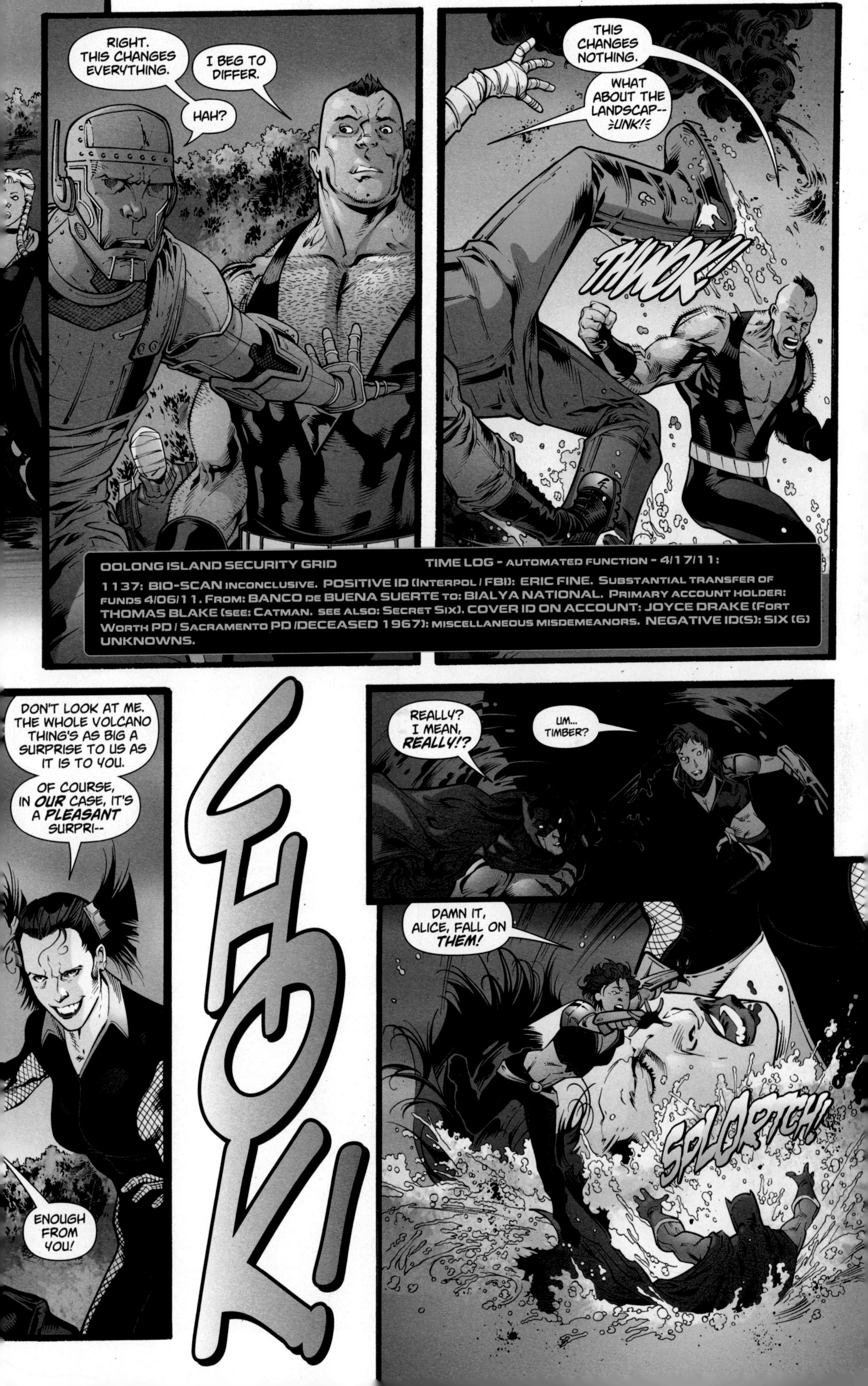
RIGHT. THIS CHANGES EVERYTHING.
I BEG TO DIFFER.
HAH?
THIS CHANGES NOTHING.
WHAT ABOUT THE LANDSCAP-- UNK!
THWOK!
OOLONG ISLAND SECURITY GRID TIME LOG - AUTOMATED FUNCTION - 4/17/11:
1137: BIO-SCAN INCONCLUSIVE. POSITIVE ID (INTERPOL / FBI): ERIC FINE. SUBSTANTIAL TRANSFER OF FUNDS 4/06/11. FROM: BANCO DE BUENA SUERTE TO: BIALYA NATIONAL. PRIMARY ACCOUNT HOLDER: THOMAS BLAKE (SEE: CATMAN. SEE ALSO: SECRET SIX). COVER ID ON ACCOUNT: JOYCE DRAKE (FORT WORTH PD / SACRAMENTO PD /DECEASED 1967): MISCELLANEOUS MISDEMEANORS. NEGATIVE ID(S): SIX (6) UNKNOWNS.
DON'T LOOK AT ME. THE WHOLE VOLCANO THING'S AS BIG A SURPRISE TO US AS IT IS TO YOU.
OF COURSE, IN OUR CASE, IT'S A PLEASANT SURPRI--
CHOK!
ENOUGH FROM YOU!
REALLY? I MEAN, REALLY!?
UM... TIMBER?
DAMN IT, ALICE, FALL ON THEM!
SPLORTCH!

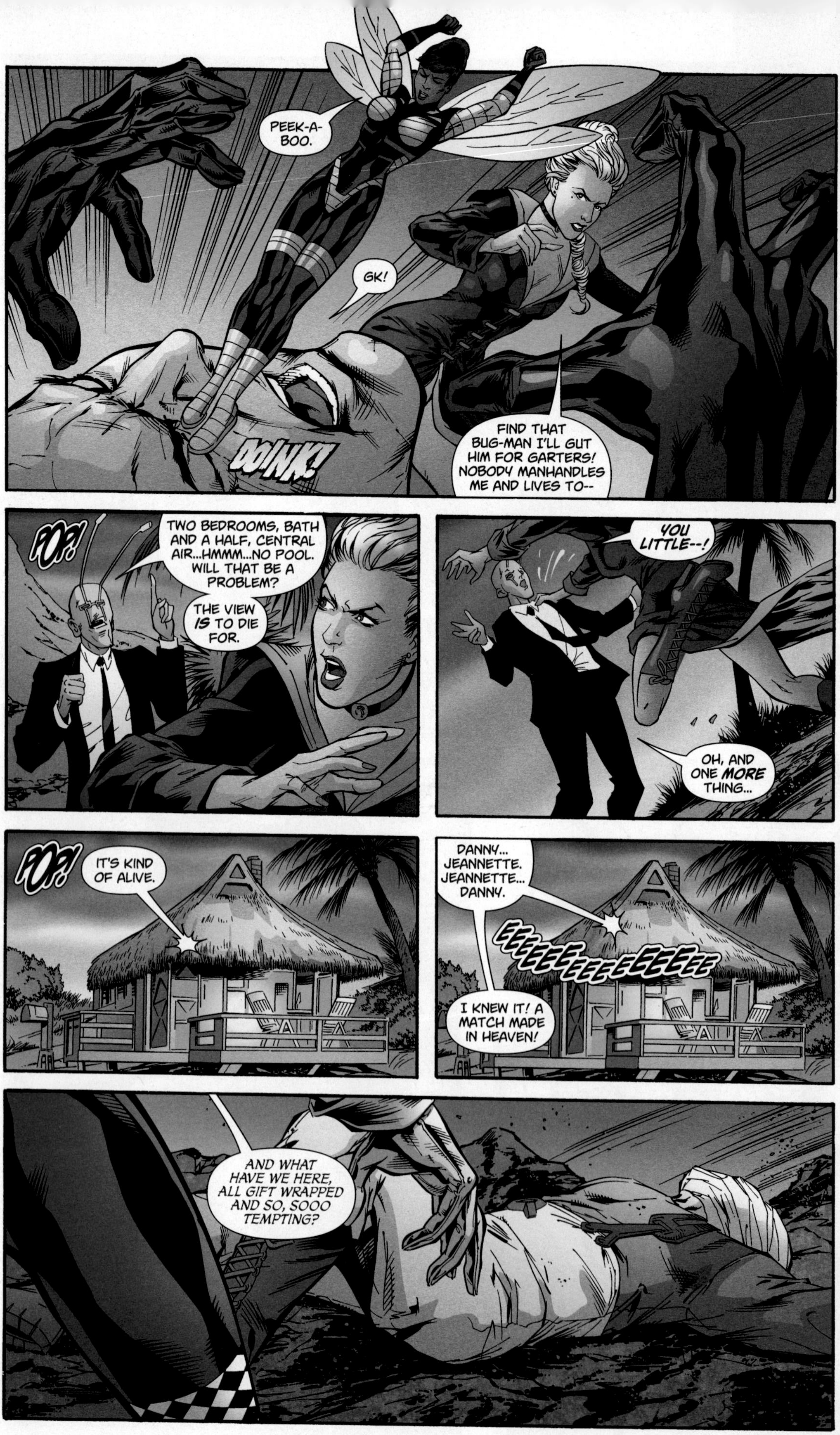
PEEK-A-BOO.
GK!
DOINK!
FIND THAT BUG-MAN I'LL GUT HIM FOR GARTERS! NOBODY MANHANDLES ME AND LIVES TO--
POP!
TWO BEDROOMS, BATH AND A HALF, CENTRAL AIR...HMMM...NO POOL. WILL THAT BE A PROBLEM?
THE VIEW IS TO DIE FOR.
YOU LITTLE--!
OH, AND ONE MORE THING...
POP!
IT'S KIND OF ALIVE.
DANNY... JEANNETTE. JEANNETTE... DANNY.
EEEEEEEEEEEEEEEEEE
I KNEW IT! A MATCH MADE IN HEAVEN!
AND WHAT HAVE WE HERE, ALL GIFT WRAPPED AND SO, SOOO TEMPTING?

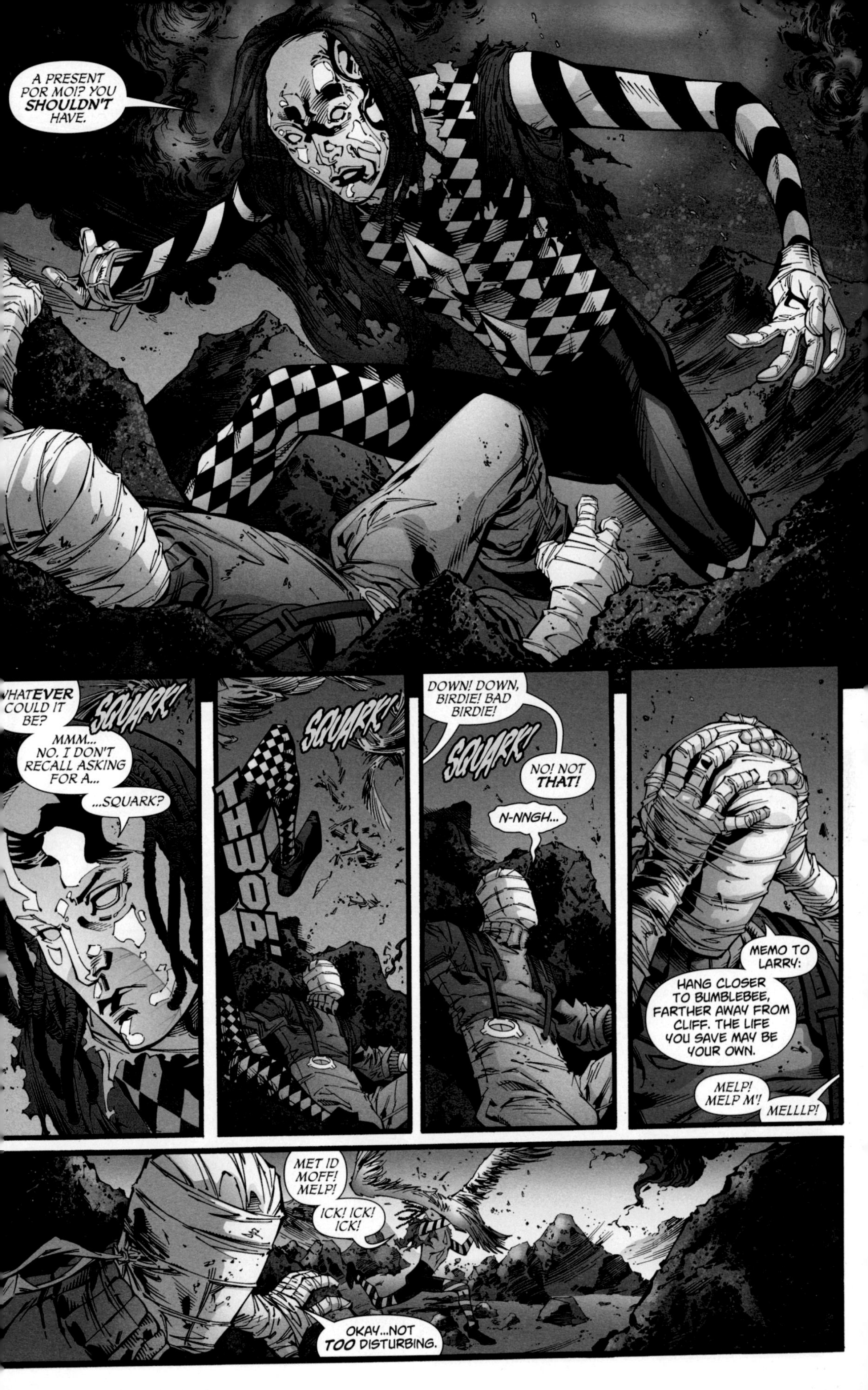
A PRESENT POR MOI? YOU **SHOULDN'T** HAVE.
WHAT**EVER** COULD IT BE?
SQUARK!
MMM... NO. I DON'T RECALL ASKING FOR A...
...SQUARK?
SQUARK!
THWOOP!
DOWN! DOWN, BIRDIE! BAD BIRDIE!
SQUARK!
NO! NOT **THAT!**
N-NNGH...
MEMO TO LARRY:
HANG CLOSER TO BUMBLEBEE, FARTHER AWAY FROM CLIFF. THE LIFE YOU SAVE MAY BE YOUR OWN.
MELP! MELP M'!
MELLLP!
MET ID MOFF! MELP!
ICK! ICK! ICK!
OKAY...NOT **TOO** DISTURBING.

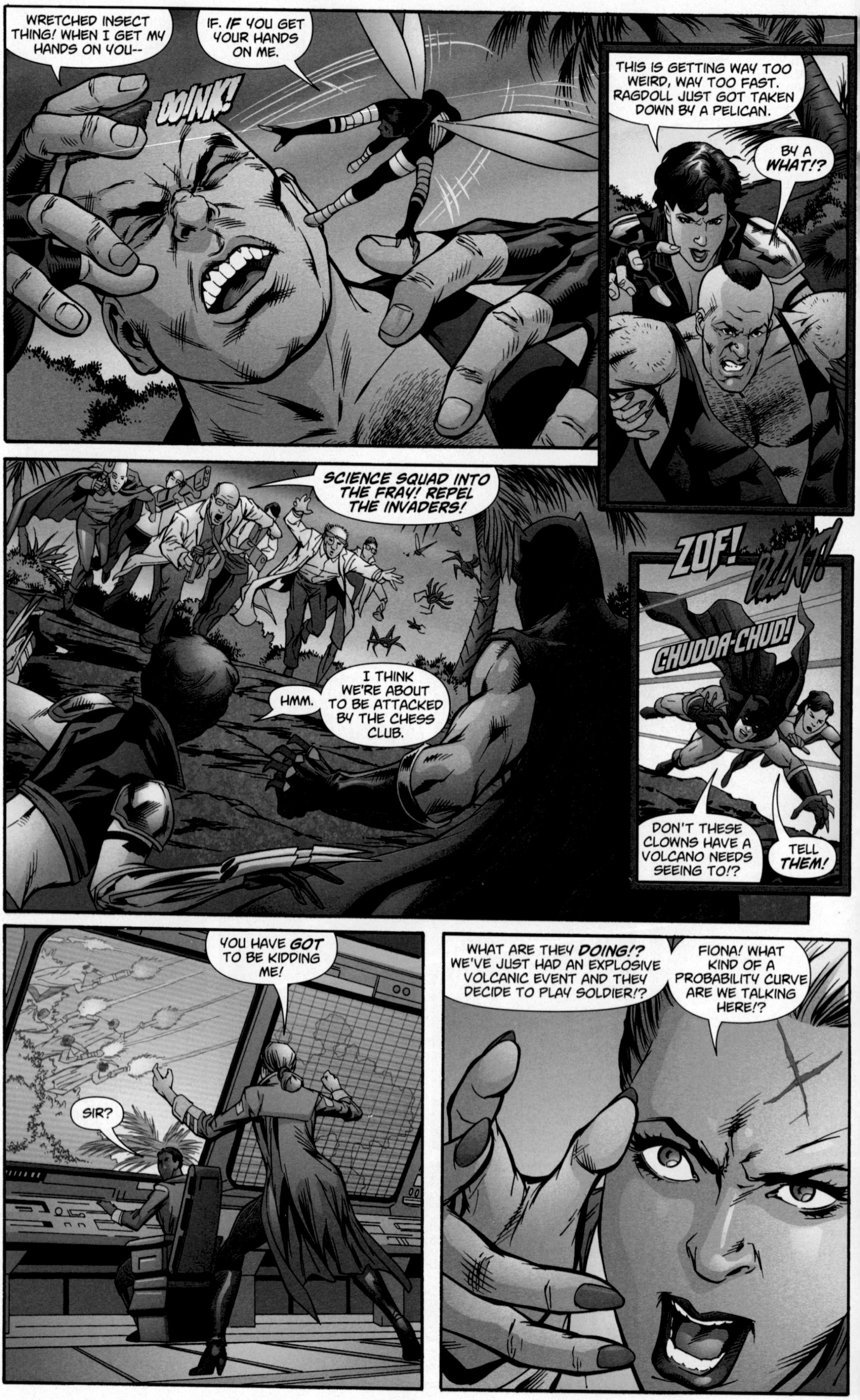

WRETCHED INSECT THING! WHEN I GET MY HANDS ON YOU--
IF. *IF* YOU GET YOUR HANDS ON ME.
DOINK!
THIS IS GETTING WAY TOO WEIRD, WAY TOO FAST. RAGDOLL JUST GOT TAKEN DOWN BY A PELICAN.
BY A *WHAT!?*
SCIENCE SQUAD INTO THE FRAY! REPEL THE INVADERS!
HMM.
I THINK WE'RE ABOUT TO BE ATTACKED BY THE CHESS CLUB.
ZOF!
BLZKT!
CHUDDA-CHUD!
DON'T THESE CLOWNS HAVE A VOLCANO NEEDS SEEING TO!?
TELL *THEM!*
YOU HAVE *GOT* TO BE KIDDING ME!
SIR?
WHAT ARE THEY *DOING!?* WE'VE JUST HAD AN EXPLOSIVE VOLCANIC EVENT AND THEY DECIDE TO PLAY SOLDIER!?
FIONA! WHAT KIND OF A PROBABILITY CURVE ARE WE TALKING HERE!?

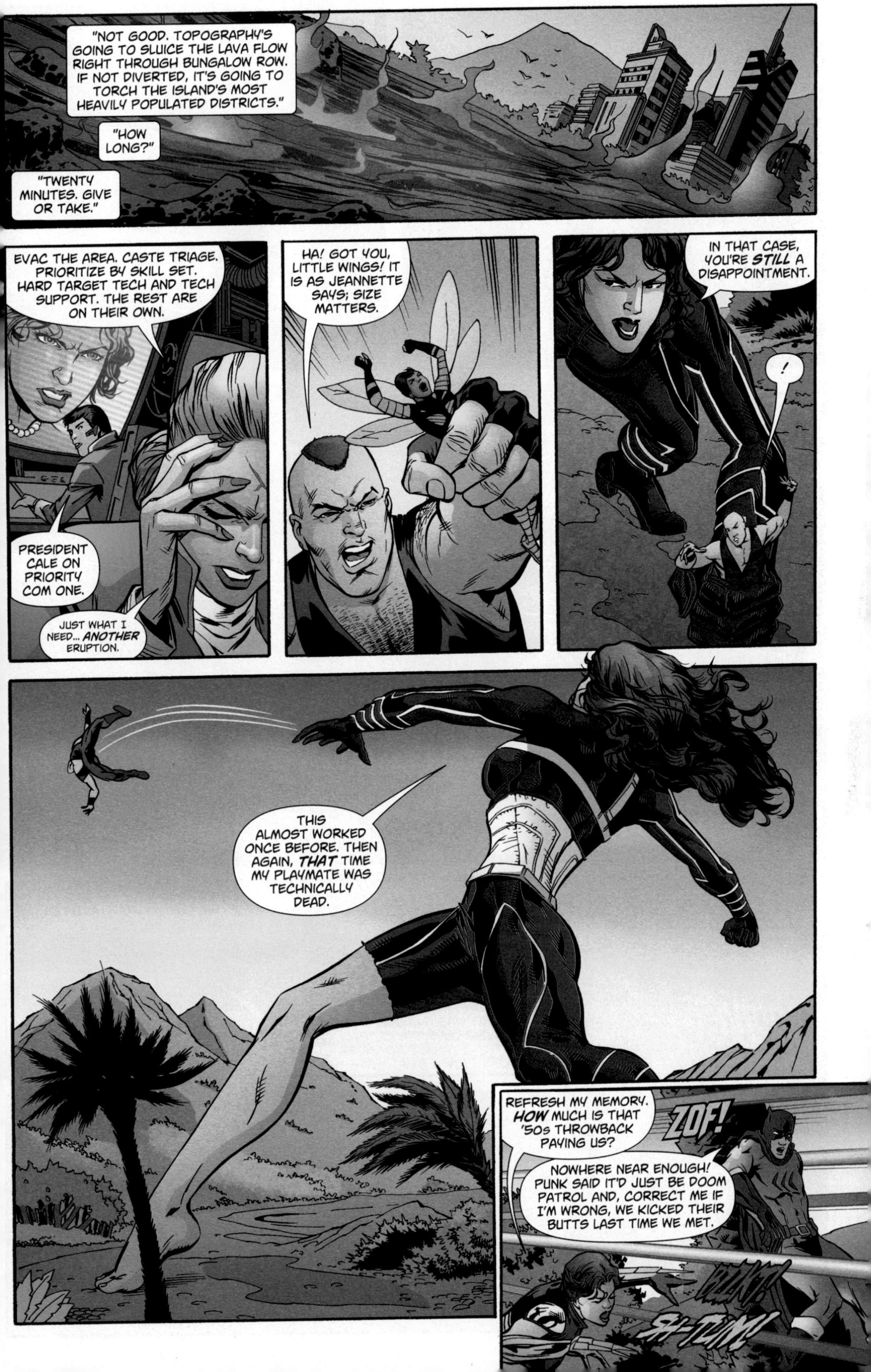
"NOT GOOD. TOPOGRAPHY'S GOING TO SLUICE THE LAVA FLOW RIGHT THROUGH BUNGALOW ROW. IF NOT DIVERTED, IT'S GOING TO TORCH THE ISLAND'S MOST HEAVILY POPULATED DISTRICTS."
"HOW LONG?"
"TWENTY MINUTES. GIVE OR TAKE."
EVAC THE AREA. CASTE TRIAGE. PRIORITIZE BY SKILL SET. HARD TARGET TECH AND TECH SUPPORT. THE REST ARE ON THEIR OWN.
PRESIDENT CALE ON PRIORITY COM ONE.
JUST WHAT I NEED... ANOTHER ERUPTION.
HA! GOT YOU, LITTLE WINGS! IT IS AS JEANNETTE SAYS; SIZE MATTERS.
IN THAT CASE, YOU'RE STILL A DISAPPOINTMENT.
!
THIS ALMOST WORKED ONCE BEFORE. THEN AGAIN, THAT TIME MY PLAYMATE WAS TECHNICALLY DEAD.
REFRESH MY MEMORY. HOW MUCH IS THAT '50s THROWBACK PAYING US?
ZOF!
NOWHERE NEAR ENOUGH! PUNK SAID IT'D JUST BE DOOM PATROL AND, CORRECT ME IF I'M WRONG, WE KICKED THEIR BUTTS LAST TIME WE MET.

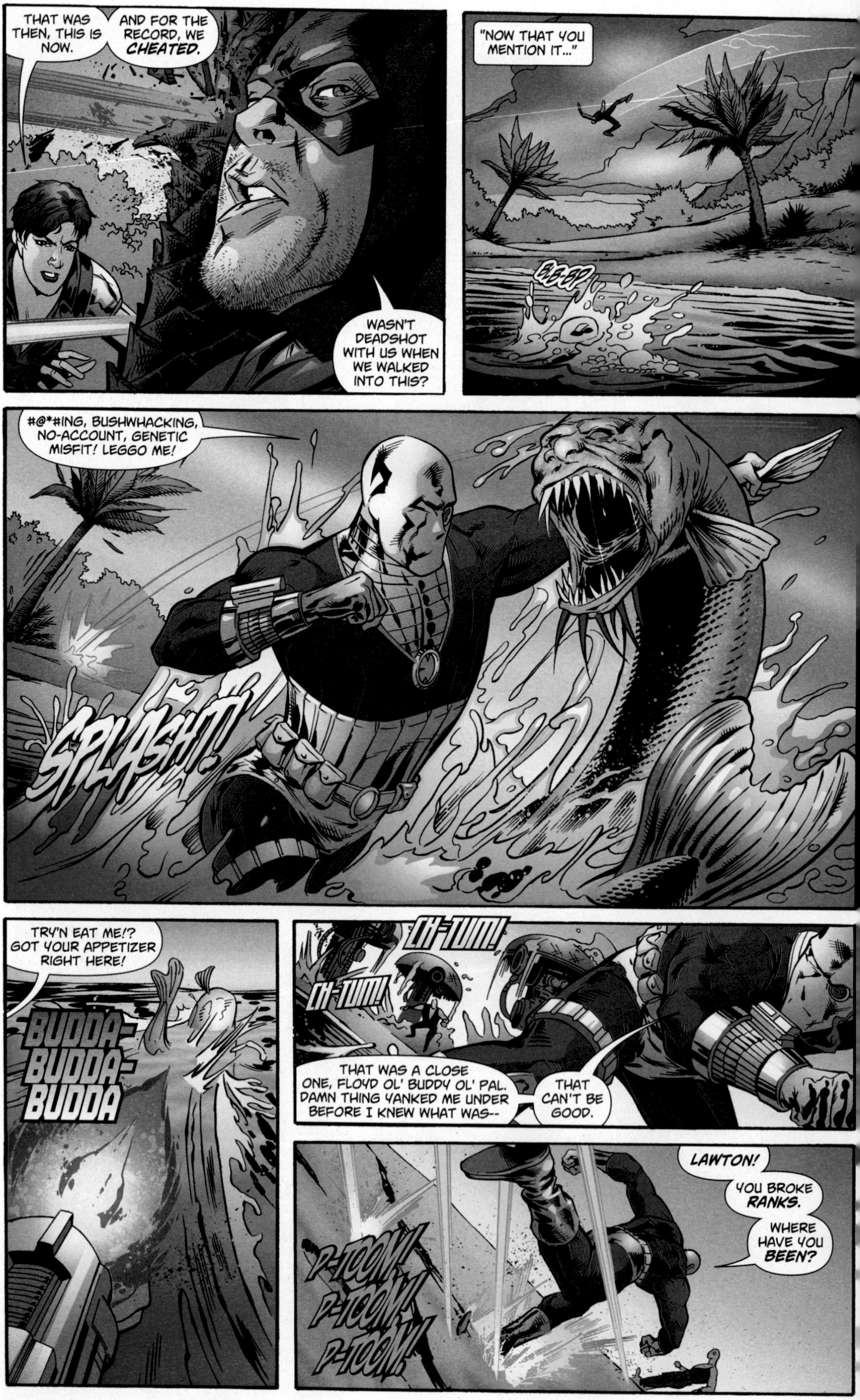
THAT WAS THEN, THIS IS NOW.
AND FOR THE RECORD, WE CHEATED.
WASN'T DEADSHOT WITH US WHEN WE WALKED INTO THIS?
"NOW THAT YOU MENTION IT..."
BLUB-BLP
#@*#ING, BUSHWHACKING, NO-ACCOUNT, GENETIC MISFIT! LEGGO ME!
SPLASH!
TRY'N EAT ME!? GOT YOUR APPETIZER RIGHT HERE!
BUDDA-BUDDA-BUDDA
CH-TUM!
CH-TUM!
THAT WAS A CLOSE ONE, FLOYD OL' BUDDY OL' PAL. DAMN THING YANKED ME UNDER BEFORE I KNEW WHAT WAS--
THAT CAN'T BE GOOD.
LAWTON!
YOU BROKE RANKS.
WHERE HAVE YOU BEEN?
P-TOOM! P-TOOM! P-TOOM!

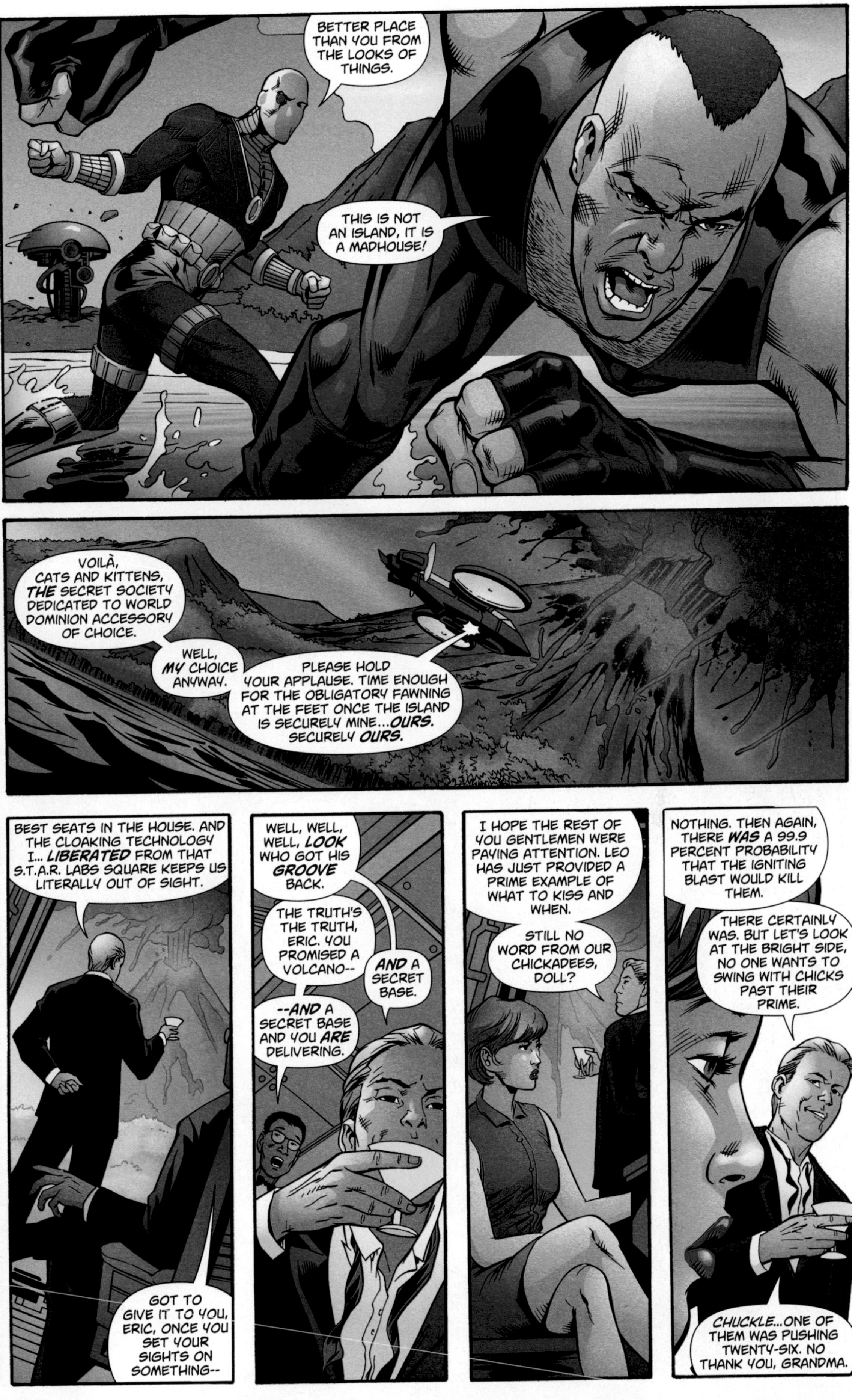
BETTER PLACE THAN YOU FROM THE LOOKS OF THINGS.
THIS IS NOT AN ISLAND, IT IS A MADHOUSE!
VOILÀ, CATS AND KITTENS, THE SECRET SOCIETY DEDICATED TO WORLD DOMINION ACCESSORY OF CHOICE.
WELL, MY CHOICE ANYWAY.
PLEASE HOLD YOUR APPLAUSE. TIME ENOUGH FOR THE OBLIGATORY FAWNING AT THE FEET ONCE THE ISLAND IS SECURELY MINE...OURS. SECURELY OURS.
BEST SEATS IN THE HOUSE. AND THE CLOAKING TECHNOLOGY I... LIBERATED FROM THAT S.T.A.R. LABS SQUARE KEEPS US LITERALLY OUT OF SIGHT.
GOT TO GIVE IT TO YOU, ERIC, ONCE YOU SET YOUR SIGHTS ON SOMETHING--
WELL, WELL, WELL, LOOK WHO GOT HIS GROOVE BACK.
THE TRUTH'S THE TRUTH, ERIC. YOU PROMISED A VOLCANO--
AND A SECRET BASE.
--AND A SECRET BASE AND YOU ARE DELIVERING.
I HOPE THE REST OF YOU GENTLEMEN WERE PAYING ATTENTION. LEO HAS JUST PROVIDED A PRIME EXAMPLE OF WHAT TO KISS AND WHEN.
STILL NO WORD FROM OUR CHICKADEES, DOLL?
NOTHING. THEN AGAIN, THERE WAS A 99.9 PERCENT PROBABILITY THAT THE IGNITING BLAST WOULD KILL THEM.
THERE CERTAINLY WAS. BUT LET'S LOOK AT THE BRIGHT SIDE, NO ONE WANTS TO SWING WITH CHICKS PAST THEIR PRIME.
CHUCKLE...ONE OF THEM WAS PUSHING TWENTY-SIX. NO THANK YOU, GRANDMA.

BLOW IT OUT OF THE SKY!

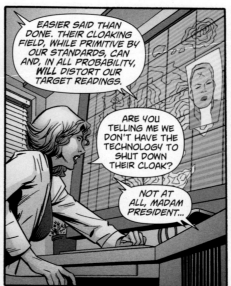

EASIER SAID THAN DONE. THEIR CLOAKING FIELD, WHILE PRIMITIVE BY OUR STANDARDS, CAN AND, IN ALL PROBABILITY, WILL DISTORT OUR TARGET READINGS.

ARE YOU TELLING ME WE DON'T HAVE THE TECHNOLOGY TO SHUT DOWN THEIR CLOAK?

NOT AT ALL, MADAM PRESIDENT...

THEN WHY HAVEN'T WE DONE IT!??

THERE IS THE MATTER OF THE VOLCANO. CRISIS PRIORITIZATION CALLS FOR--

DO I HAVE TO THINK OF EVERYTHING!? PUT THE FARR WOMAN ON IT! AND PATCH ME THROUGH TO THOSE S.M.A.S.H. IMBECILES ASAP!

CLIFF'S COM STILL OPEN?

CLIFF?

THE ROBOT! IS HIS COM OPEN!?

NOT REALLY THINKIN' THIS THROUGH, ARE YA? I MEAN, ME BEIN' METAL 'N' ALL?

I'VE BITTEN THROUGH TOUGHER!

BUT YOU GOT A CHEWY CENTER INSIDE, RIGHT?

SO... EVER SEE ONE'A THESE UP CLOSE?

UK...

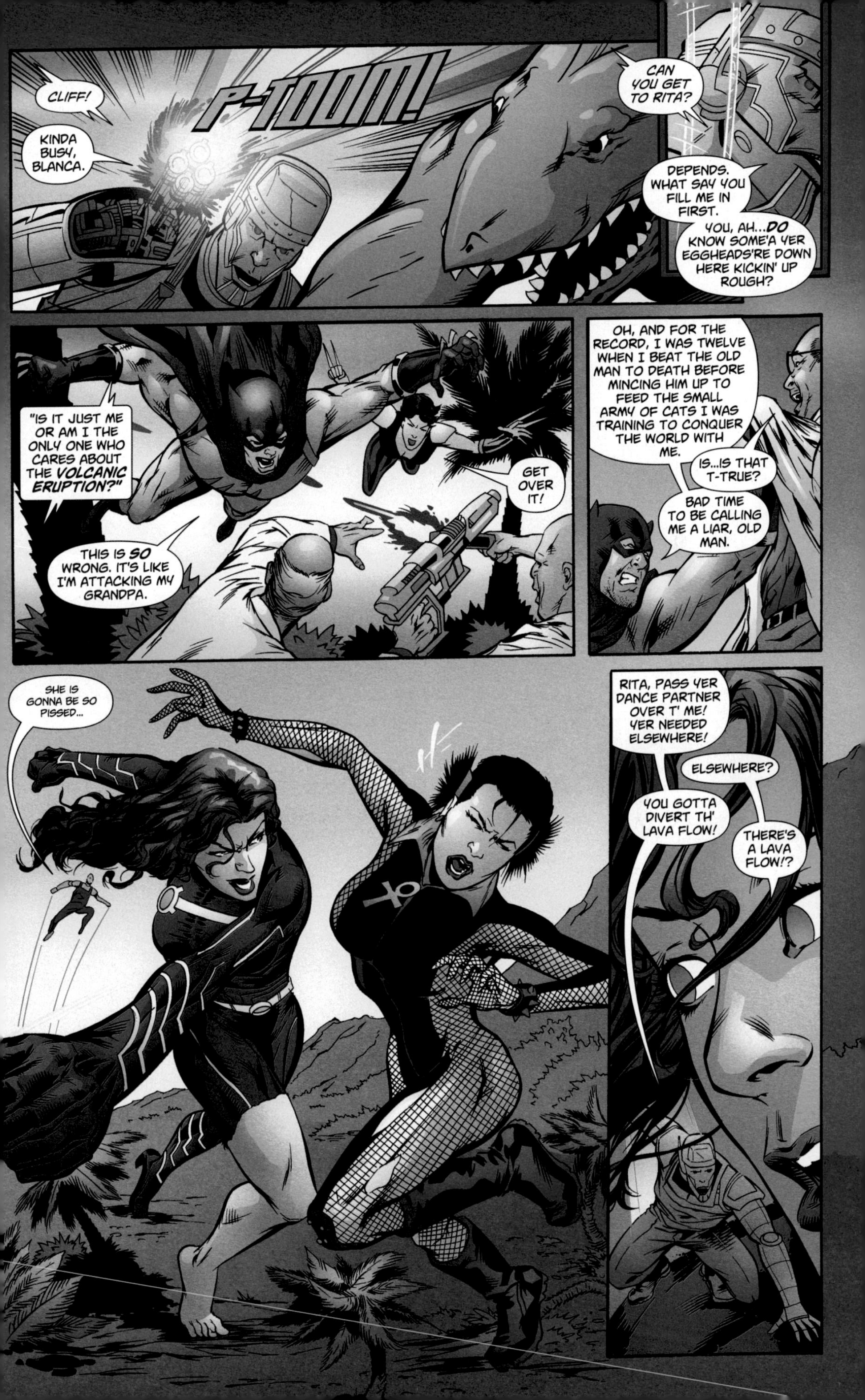
CLIFF!
KINDA BUSY, BLANCA.
P-TOOOM!
CAN YOU GET TO RITA?
DEPENDS. WHAT SAY YOU FILL ME IN FIRST.
YOU, AH...DO KNOW SOME'A YER EGGHEADS'RE DOWN HERE KICKIN' UP ROUGH?
"IS IT JUST ME OR AM I THE ONLY ONE WHO CARES ABOUT THE VOLCANIC ERUPTION?"
GET OVER IT!
THIS IS SO WRONG. IT'S LIKE I'M ATTACKING MY GRANDPA.
OH, AND FOR THE RECORD, I WAS TWELVE WHEN I BEAT THE OLD MAN TO DEATH BEFORE MINCING HIM UP TO FEED THE SMALL ARMY OF CATS I WAS TRAINING TO CONQUER THE WORLD WITH ME.
IS...IS THAT T-TRUE?
BAD TIME TO BE CALLING ME A LIAR, OLD MAN.
SHE IS GONNA BE SO PISSED...
RITA, PASS YER DANCE PARTNER OVER T' ME! YER NEEDED ELSEWHERE!
ELSEWHERE?
YOU GOTTA DIVERT TH' LAVA FLOW!
THERE'S A LAVA FLOW!?

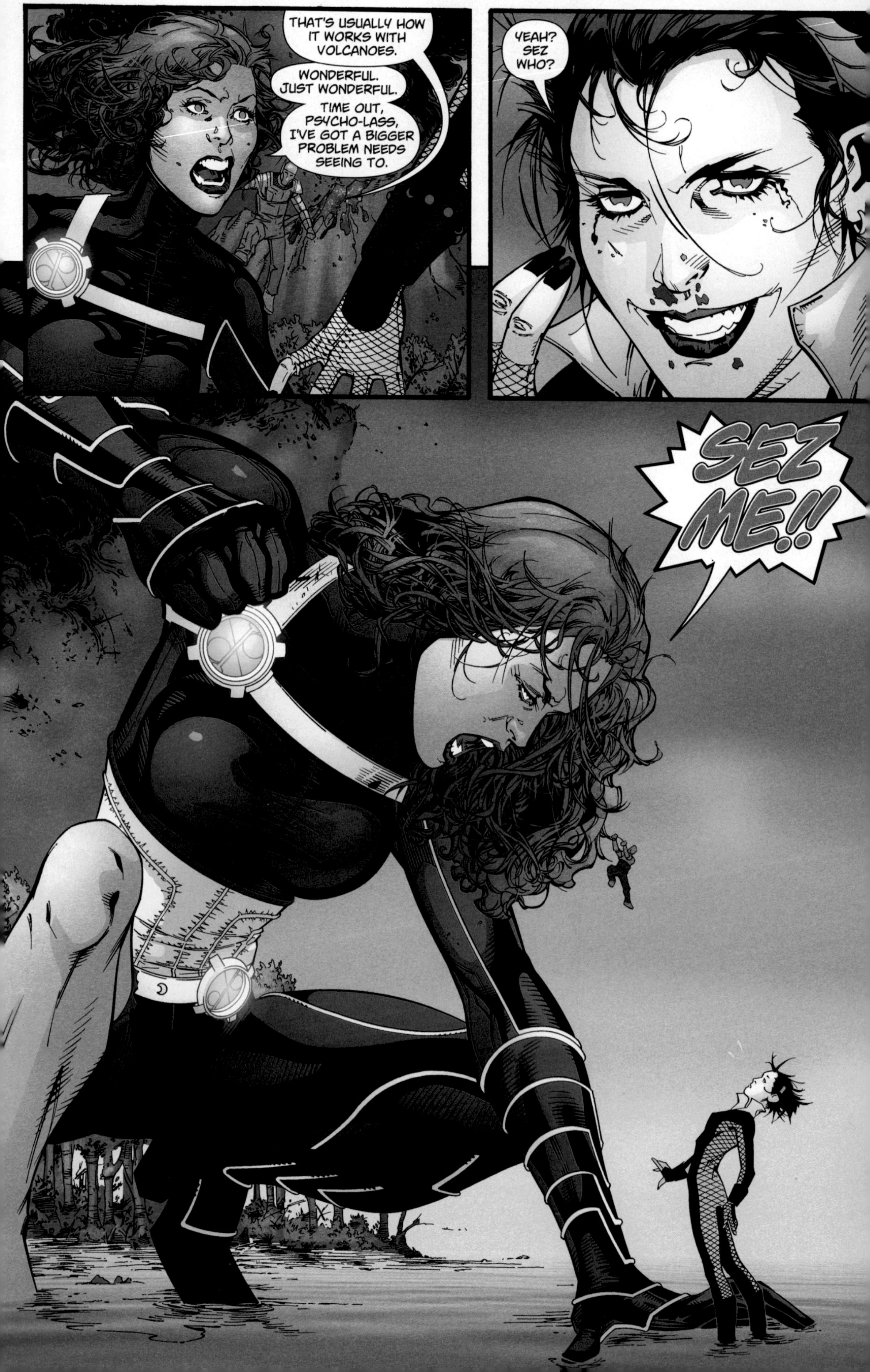
THAT'S USUALLY HOW IT WORKS WITH VOLCANOES.
WONDERFUL. JUST WONDERFUL.
TIME OUT, PSYCHO-LASS, I'VE GOT A BIGGER PROBLEM NEEDS SEEING TO.
YEAH? SEZ WHO?
SEZ ME!!

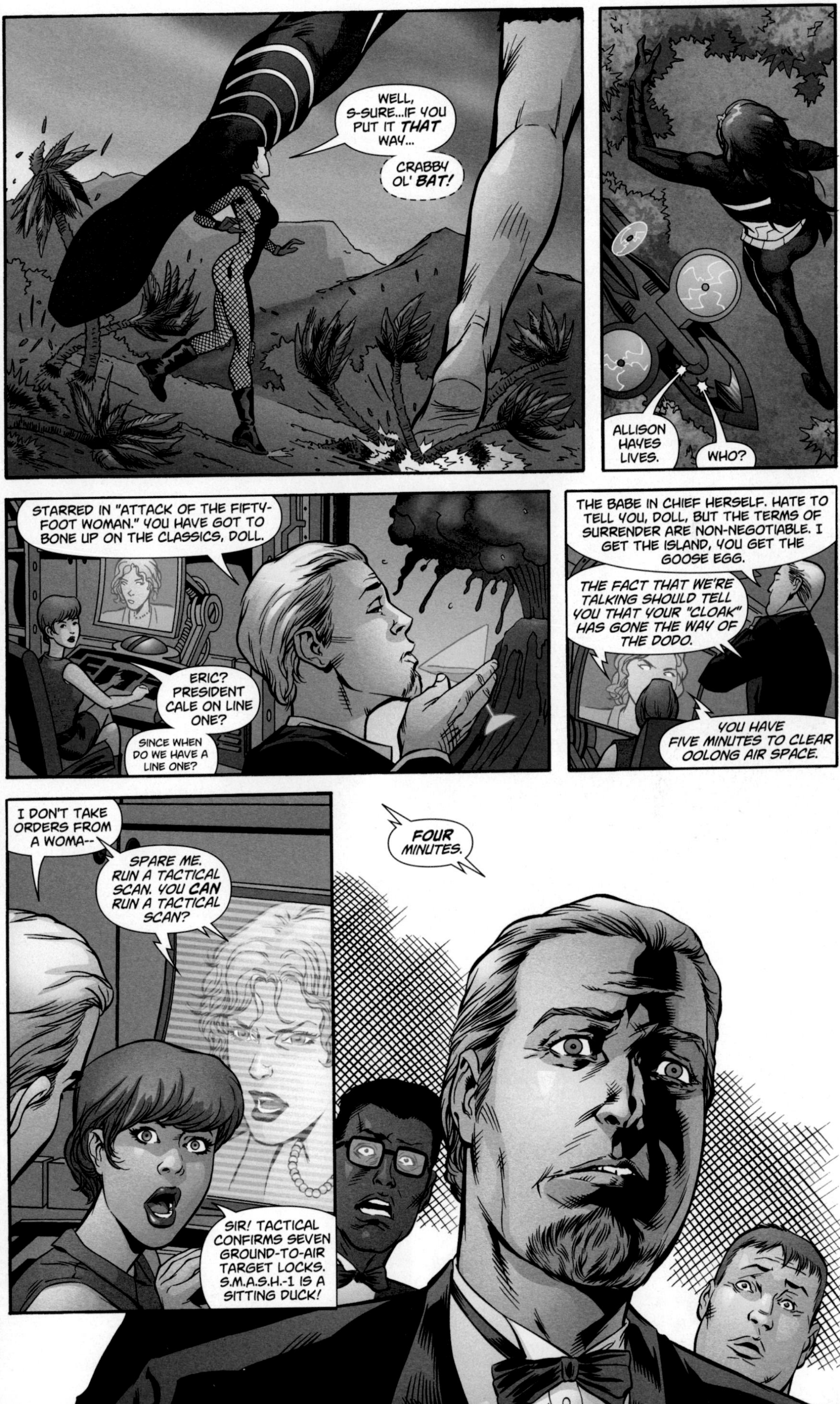
WELL, S-SURE...IF YOU PUT IT THAT WAY...
CRABBY OL' BAT!
ALLISON HAYES LIVES.
WHO?
STARRED IN "ATTACK OF THE FIFTY-FOOT WOMAN." YOU HAVE GOT TO BONE UP ON THE CLASSICS, DOLL.
ERIC? PRESIDENT CALE ON LINE ONE?
SINCE WHEN DO WE HAVE A LINE ONE?
THE BABE IN CHIEF HERSELF. HATE TO TELL YOU, DOLL, BUT THE TERMS OF SURRENDER ARE NON-NEGOTIABLE. I GET THE ISLAND, YOU GET THE GOOSE EGG.
THE FACT THAT WE'RE TALKING SHOULD TELL YOU THAT YOUR "CLOAK" HAS GONE THE WAY OF THE DODO.
YOU HAVE FIVE MINUTES TO CLEAR OOLONG AIR SPACE.
I DON'T TAKE ORDERS FROM A WOMA--
SPARE ME. RUN A TACTICAL SCAN. YOU CAN RUN A TACTICAL SCAN?
FOUR MINUTES.
SIR! TACTICAL CONFIRMS SEVEN GROUND-TO-AIR TARGET LOCKS. S.M.A.S.H.-1 IS A SITTING DUCK!

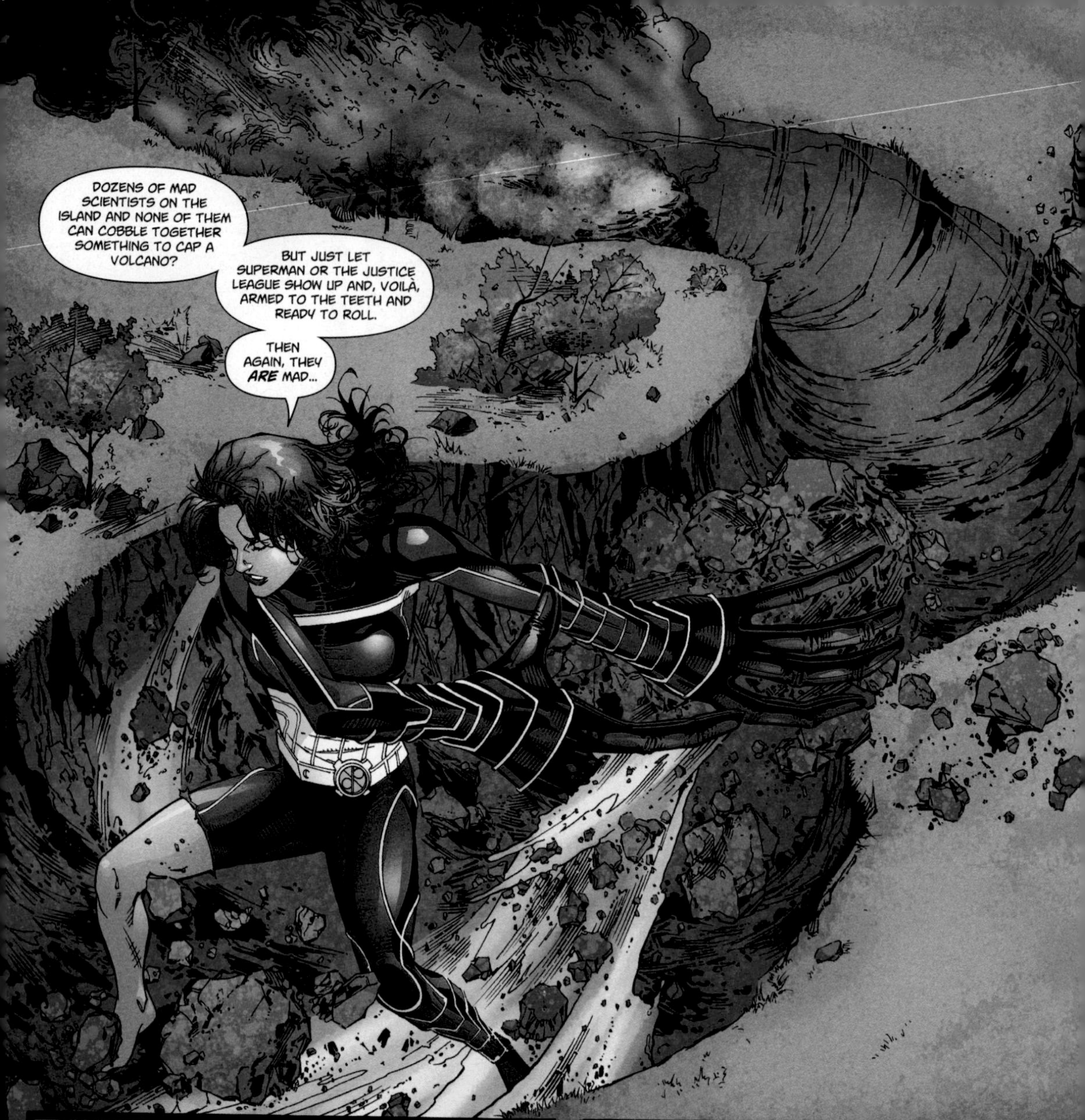
DOZENS OF MAD SCIENTISTS ON THE ISLAND AND NONE OF THEM CAN COBBLE TOGETHER SOMETHING TO CAP A VOLCANO?
BUT JUST LET SUPERMAN OR THE JUSTICE LEAGUE SHOW UP AND, VOILÀ, ARMED TO THE TEETH AND READY TO ROLL.
THEN AGAIN, THEY *ARE* MAD...

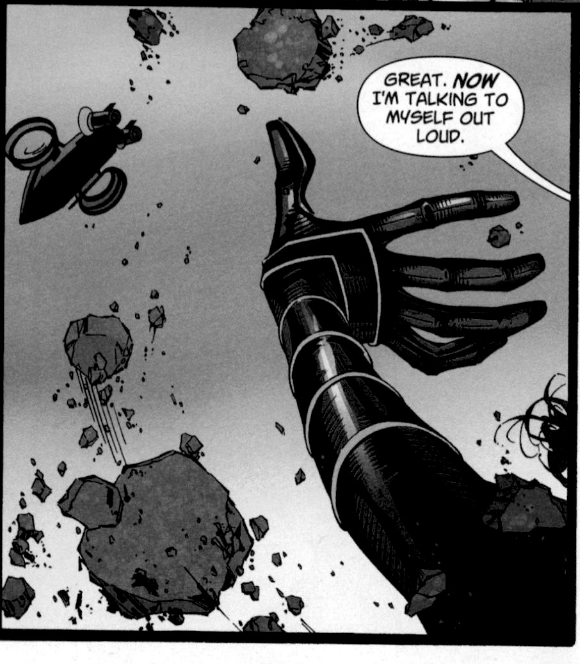
GREAT. *NOW* I'M TALKING TO MYSELF OUT LOUD.

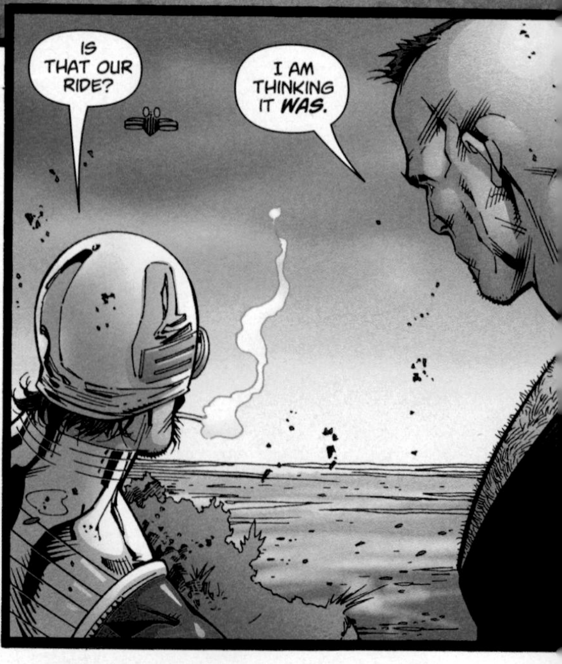
IS THAT OUR RIDE?
I AM THINKING IT *WAS*.

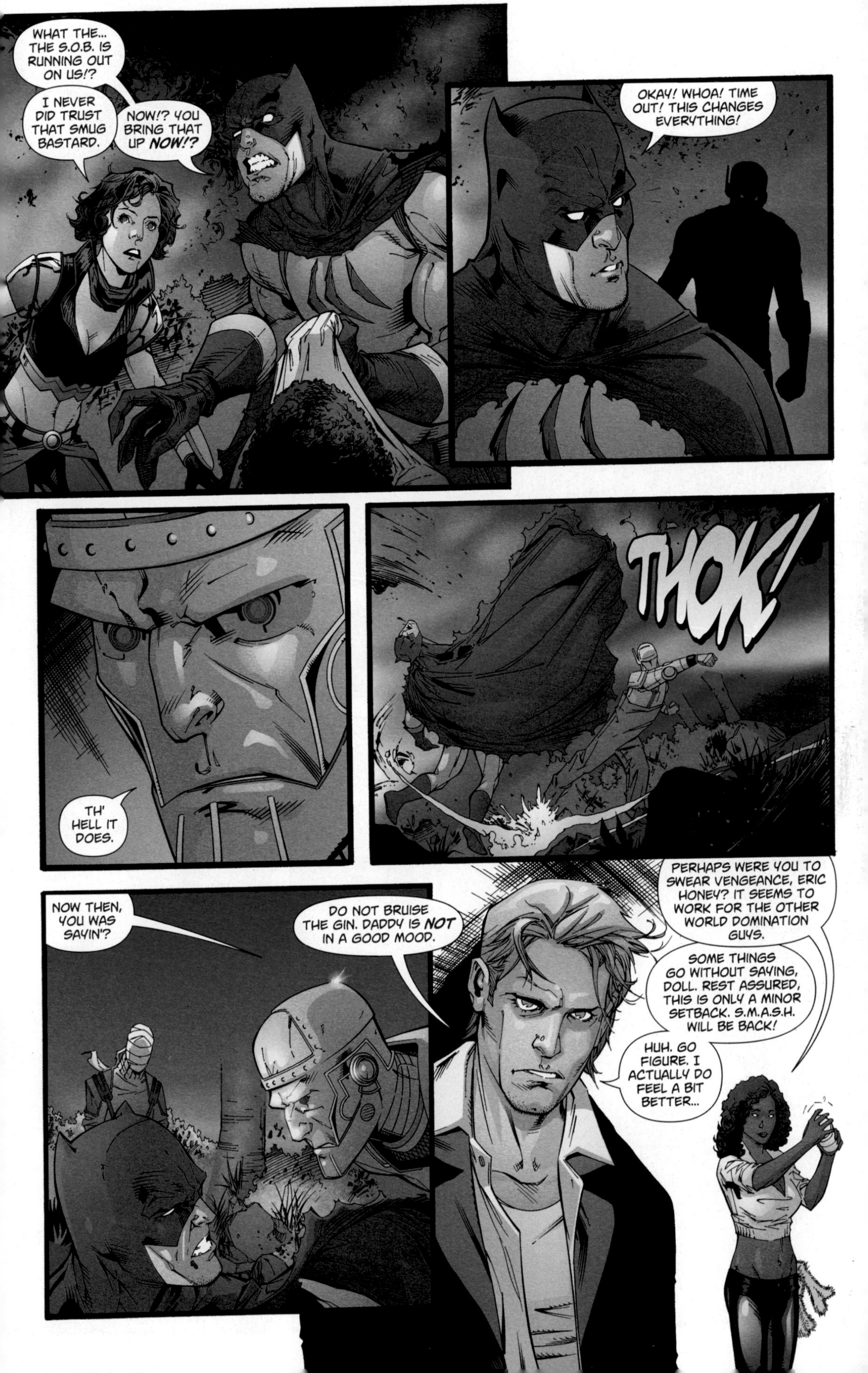

WHAT THE... THE S.O.B. IS RUNNING OUT ON US!?
I NEVER DID TRUST THAT SMUG BASTARD.
NOW!? YOU BRING THAT UP NOW!?
OKAY! WHOA! TIME OUT! THIS CHANGES EVERYTHING!
TH' HELL IT DOES.
THOK!
NOW THEN, YOU WAS SAYIN'?
DO NOT BRUISE THE GIN. DADDY IS NOT IN A GOOD MOOD.
PERHAPS WERE YOU TO SWEAR VENGEANCE, ERIC HONEY? IT SEEMS TO WORK FOR THE OTHER WORLD DOMINATION GUYS.
SOME THINGS GO WITHOUT SAYING, DOLL. REST ASSURED, THIS IS ONLY A MINOR SETBACK. S.M.A.S.H. WILL BE BACK!
HUH. GO FIGURE. I ACTUALLY DO FEEL A BIT BETTER...

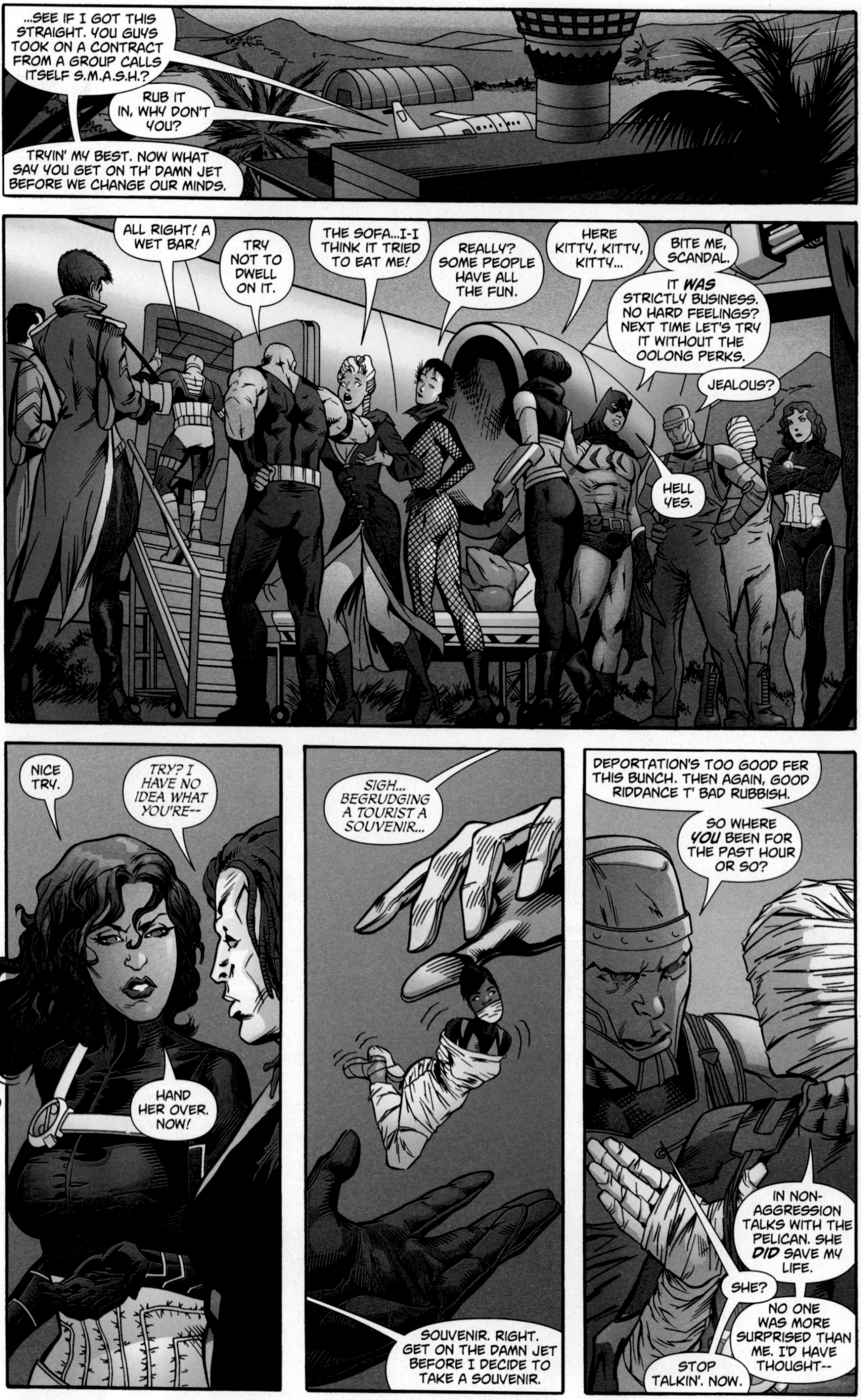
...SEE IF I GOT THIS STRAIGHT. YOU GUYS TOOK ON A CONTRACT FROM A GROUP CALLS ITSELF S.M.A.S.H.?
RUB IT IN, WHY DON'T YOU?
TRYIN' MY BEST. NOW WHAT SAY YOU GET ON TH' DAMN JET BEFORE WE CHANGE OUR MINDS.
ALL RIGHT! A WET BAR!
TRY NOT TO DWELL ON IT.
THE SOFA...I-I THINK IT TRIED TO EAT ME!
REALLY? SOME PEOPLE HAVE ALL THE FUN.
HERE KITTY, KITTY, KITTY...
BITE ME, SCANDAL.
IT WAS STRICTLY BUSINESS. NO HARD FEELINGS? NEXT TIME LET'S TRY IT WITHOUT THE OOLONG PERKS.
JEALOUS?
HELL YES.
NICE TRY.
TRY? I HAVE NO IDEA WHAT YOU'RE--
HAND HER OVER. NOW!
SIGH... BEGRUDGING A TOURIST A SOUVENIR...
SOUVENIR. RIGHT. GET ON THE DAMN JET BEFORE I DECIDE TO TAKE A SOUVENIR.
DEPORTATION'S TOO GOOD FER THIS BUNCH. THEN AGAIN, GOOD RIDDANCE T' BAD RUBBISH.
SO WHERE YOU BEEN FOR THE PAST HOUR OR SO?
IN NON-AGGRESSION TALKS WITH THE PELICAN. SHE DID SAVE MY LIFE.
SHE?
NO ONE WAS MORE SURPRISED THAN ME. I'D HAVE THOUGHT--
STOP TALKIN'. NOW.

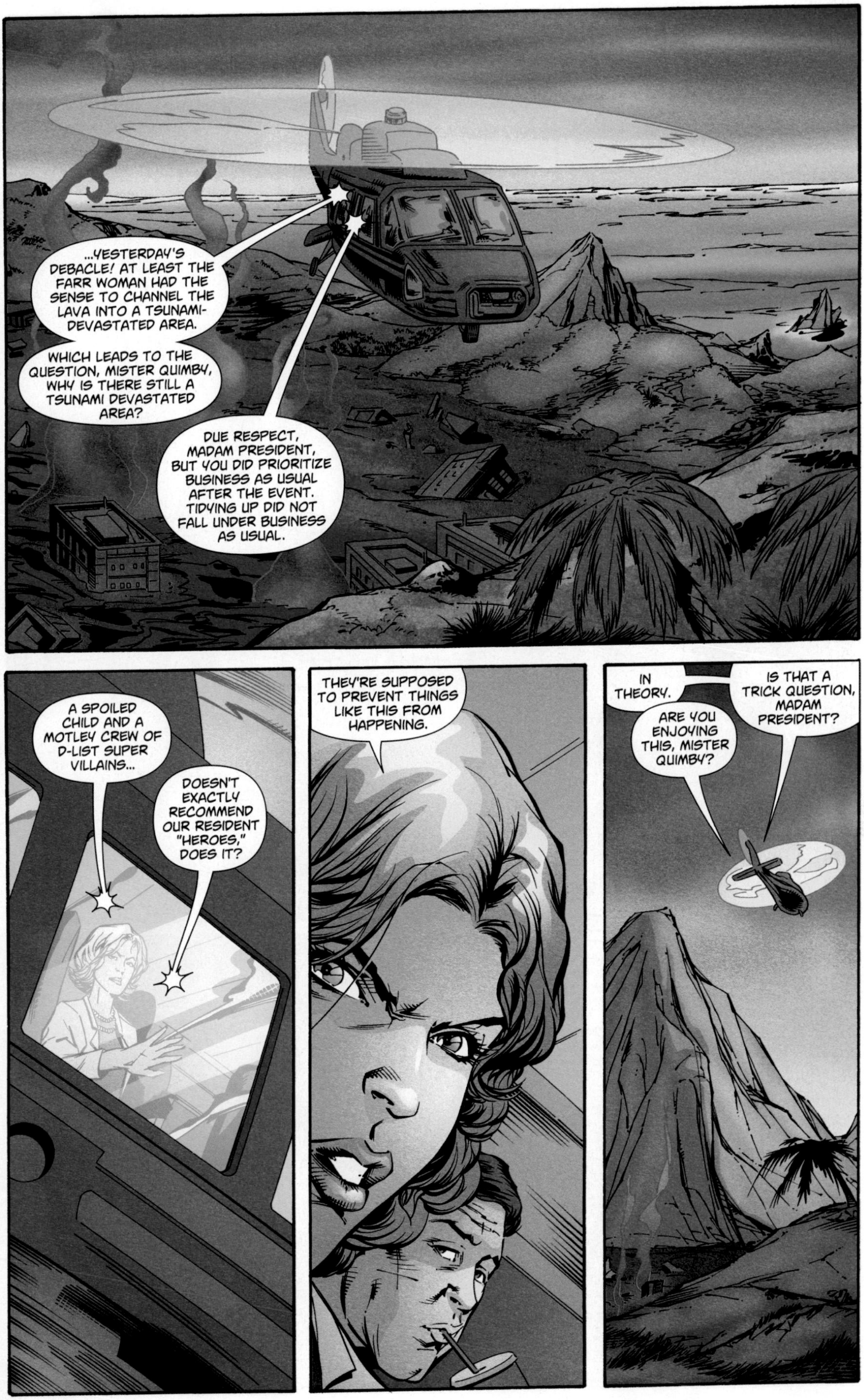
...YESTERDAY'S DEBACLE! AT LEAST THE FARR WOMAN HAD THE SENSE TO CHANNEL THE LAVA INTO A TSUNAMI-DEVASTATED AREA.
WHICH LEADS TO THE QUESTION, MISTER QUIMBY, WHY IS THERE STILL A TSUNAMI DEVASTATED AREA?
DUE RESPECT, MADAM PRESIDENT, BUT YOU DID PRIORITIZE BUSINESS AS USUAL AFTER THE EVENT. TIDYING UP DID NOT FALL UNDER BUSINESS AS USUAL.
A SPOILED CHILD AND A MOTLEY CREW OF D-LIST SUPER VILLAINS...
DOESN'T EXACTLY RECOMMEND OUR RESIDENT "HEROES," DOES IT?
THEY'RE SUPPOSED TO PREVENT THINGS LIKE THIS FROM HAPPENING.
IN THEORY.
ARE YOU ENJOYING THIS, MISTER QUIMBY?
IS THAT A TRICK QUESTION, MADAM PRESIDENT?

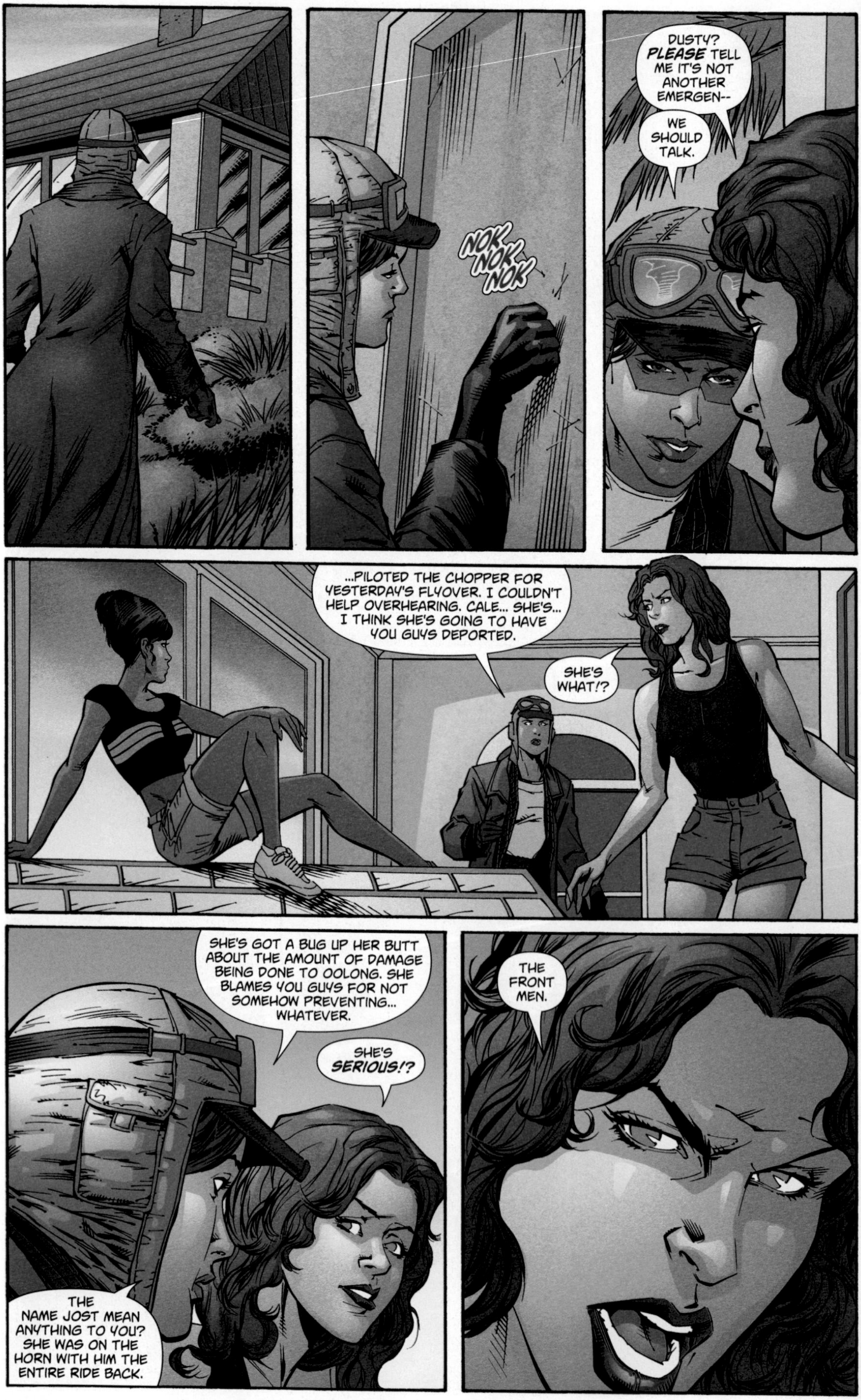
NOK NOK NOK
DUSTY? PLEASE TELL ME IT'S NOT ANOTHER EMERGEN--
WE SHOULD TALK.
...PILOTED THE CHOPPER FOR YESTERDAY'S FLYOVER. I COULDN'T HELP OVERHEARING. CALE... SHE'S... I THINK SHE'S GOING TO HAVE YOU GUYS DEPORTED.
SHE'S WHAT!?
SHE'S GOT A BUG UP HER BUTT ABOUT THE AMOUNT OF DAMAGE BEING DONE TO OOLONG. SHE BLAMES YOU GUYS FOR NOT SOMEHOW PREVENTING... WHATEVER.
SHE'S SERIOUS!?
THE NAME JOST MEAN ANYTHING TO YOU? SHE WAS ON THE HORN WITH HIM THE ENTIRE RIDE BACK.
THE FRONT MEN.

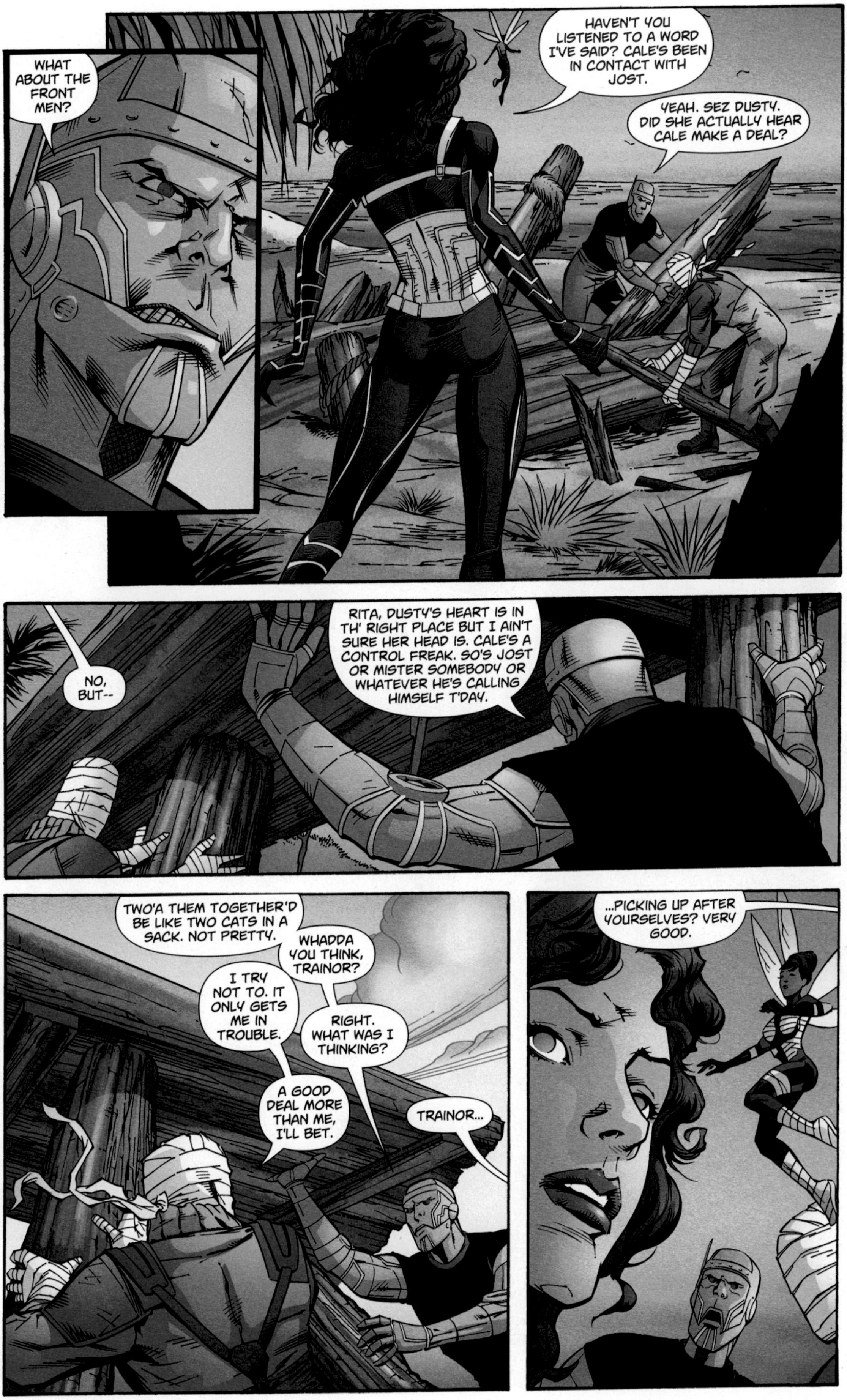
WHAT ABOUT THE FRONT MEN?
HAVEN'T YOU LISTENED TO A WORD I'VE SAID? CALE'S BEEN IN CONTACT WITH JOST.
YEAH. SEZ DUSTY. DID SHE ACTUALLY HEAR CALE MAKE A DEAL?
NO, BUT--
RITA, DUSTY'S HEART IS IN TH' RIGHT PLACE BUT I AIN'T SURE HER HEAD IS. CALE'S A CONTROL FREAK. SO'S JOST OR MISTER SOMEBODY OR WHATEVER HE'S CALLING HIMSELF T'DAY.
TWO'A THEM TOGETHER'D BE LIKE TWO CATS IN A SACK. NOT PRETTY.
WHADDA YOU THINK, TRAINOR?
I TRY NOT TO. IT ONLY GETS ME IN TROUBLE.
RIGHT. WHAT WAS I THINKING?
A GOOD DEAL MORE THAN ME, I'LL BET.
TRAINOR...
...PICKING UP AFTER YOURSELVES? VERY GOOD.

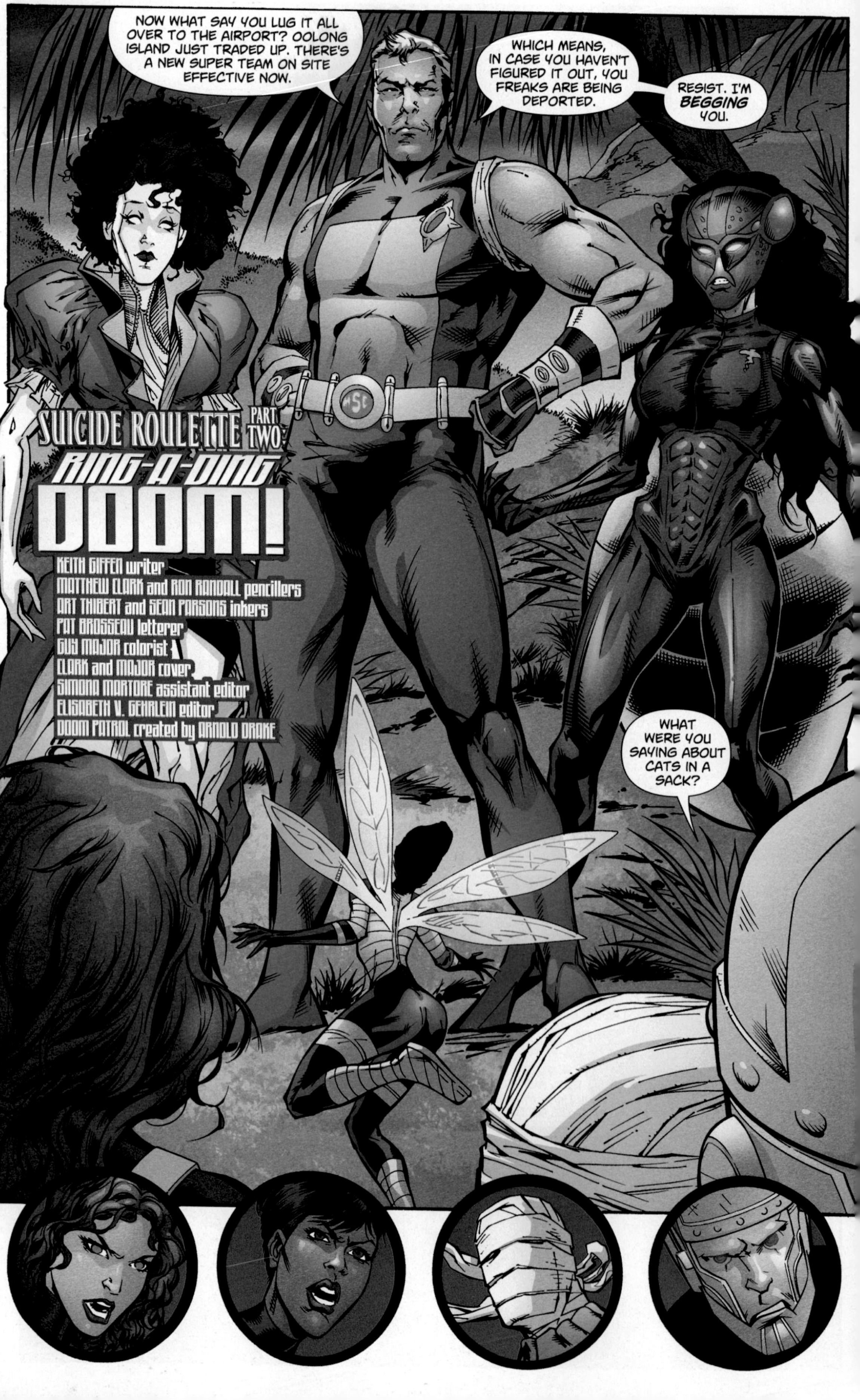
NOW WHAT SAY YOU LUG IT ALL OVER TO THE AIRPORT? OOLONG ISLAND JUST TRADED UP. THERE'S A NEW SUPER TEAM ON SITE EFFECTIVE NOW.
WHICH MEANS, IN CASE YOU HAVEN'T FIGURED IT OUT, YOU FREAKS ARE BEING DEPORTED.
RESIST. I'M BEGGING YOU.
SUICIDE ROULETTE PART TWO:
RING-A-DING DOOM!
KEITH GIFFEN writer
MATTHEW CLARK and RON RANDALL pencillers
ART THIBERT and SEAN PARSONS inkers
PAT BROSSEAU letterer
GUY MAJOR colorist
CLARK and MAJOR cover
SIMONA MARTORE assistant editor
ELISABETH V. GEHRLEIN editor
DOOM PATROL created by ARNOLD DRAKE
WHAT WERE YOU SAYING ABOUT CATS IN A SACK?

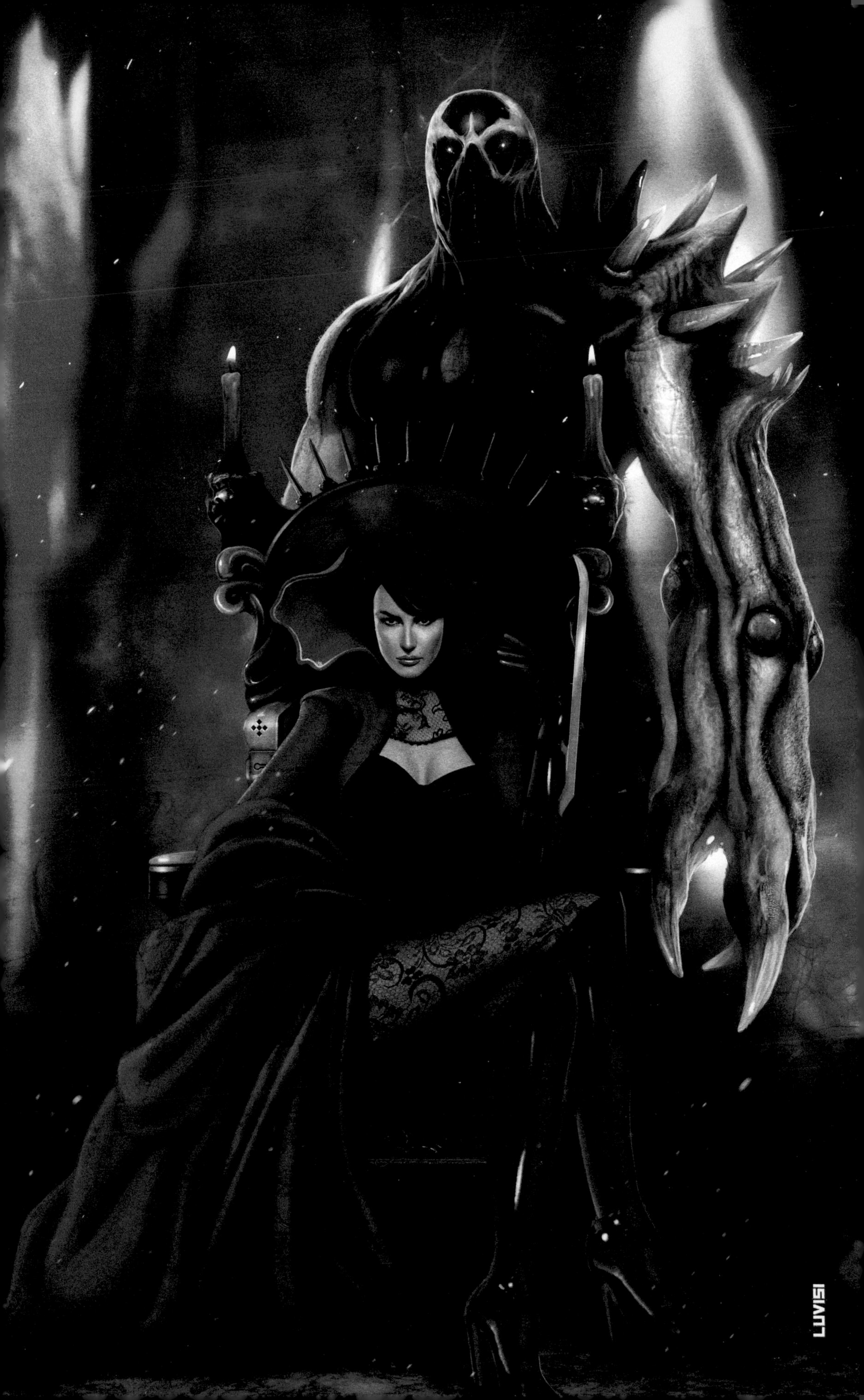
LUVISI

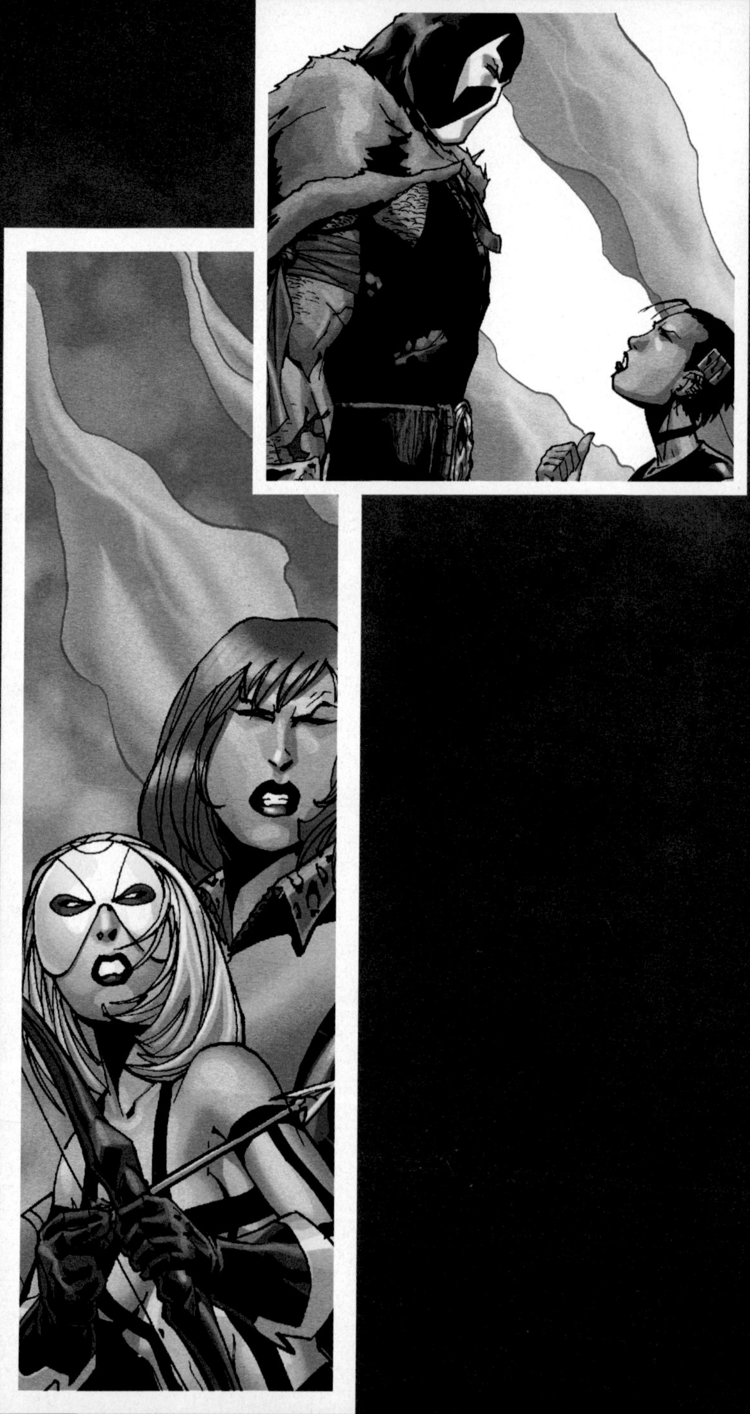

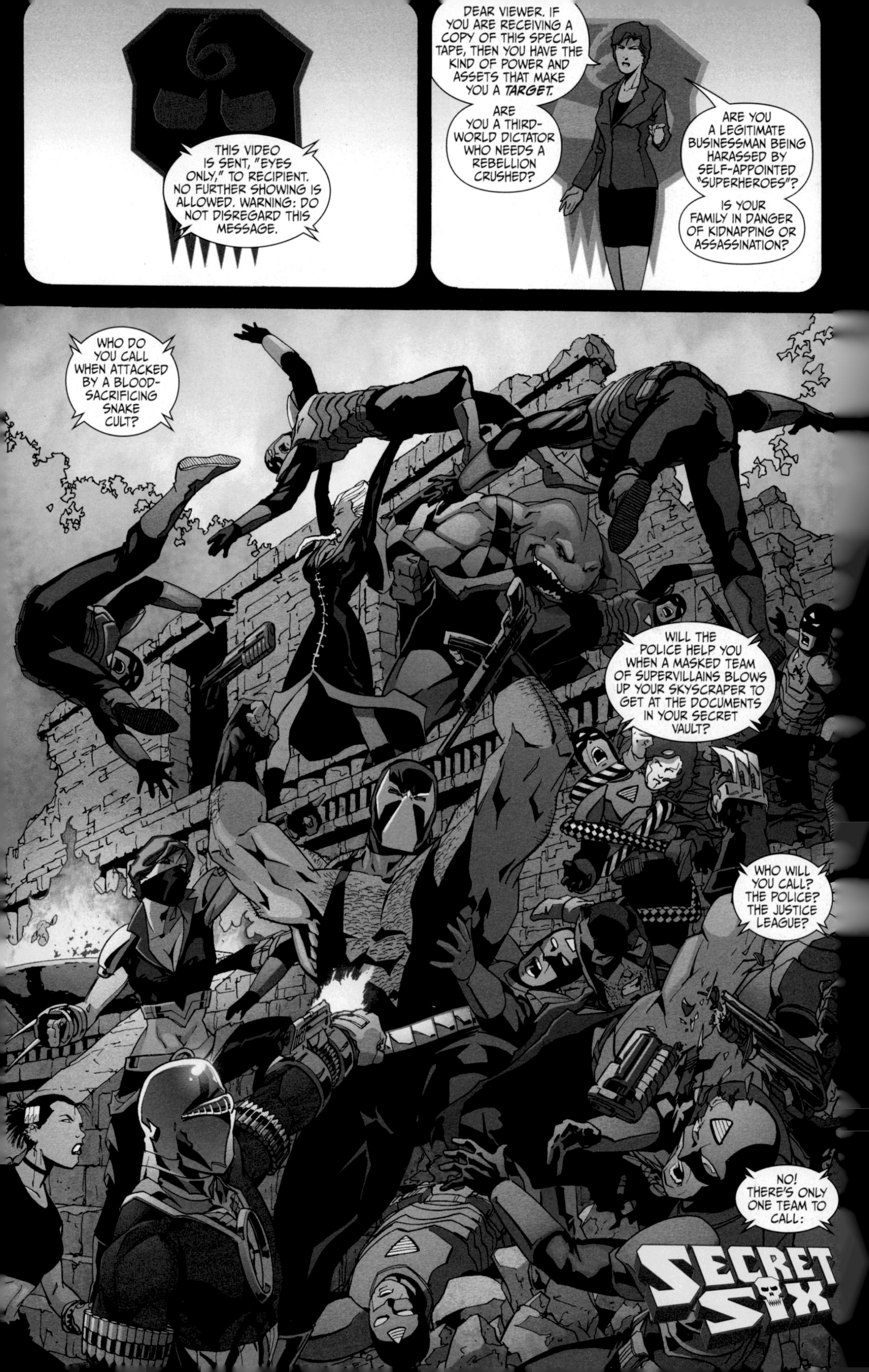
THIS VIDEO IS SENT, "EYES ONLY," TO RECIPIENT. NO FURTHER SHOWING IS ALLOWED. WARNING: DO NOT DISREGARD THIS MESSAGE.
DEAR VIEWER. IF YOU ARE RECEIVING A COPY OF THIS SPECIAL TAPE, THEN YOU HAVE THE KIND OF POWER AND ASSETS THAT MAKE YOU A TARGET.
ARE YOU A THIRD-WORLD DICTATOR WHO NEEDS A REBELLION CRUSHED?
ARE YOU A LEGITIMATE BUSINESSMAN BEING HARASSED BY SELF-APPOINTED "SUPERHEROES"?
IS YOUR FAMILY IN DANGER OF KIDNAPPING OR ASSASSINATION?
WHO DO YOU CALL WHEN ATTACKED BY A BLOOD-SACRIFICING SNAKE CULT?
WILL THE POLICE HELP YOU WHEN A MASKED TEAM OF SUPERVILLAINS BLOWS UP YOUR SKYSCRAPER TO GET AT THE DOCUMENTS IN YOUR SECRET VAULT?
WHO WILL YOU CALL? THE POLICE? THE JUSTICE LEAGUE?
NO! THERE'S ONLY ONE TEAM TO CALL:
SECRET SIX

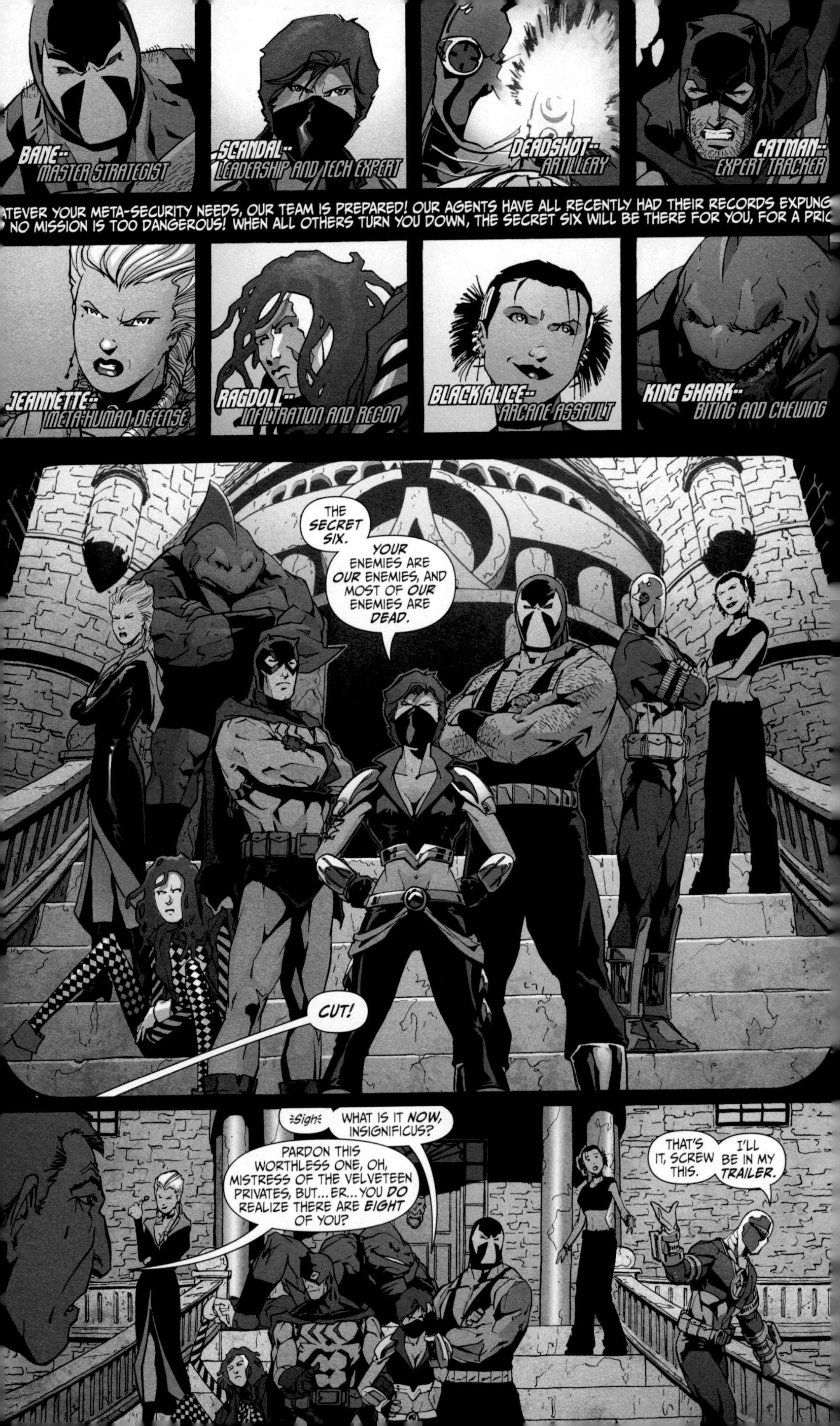
BANE--
MASTER STRATEGIST
SCANDAL--
LEADERSHIP AND TECH EXPERT
DEADSHOT--
ARTILLERY
CATMAN--
EXPERT TRACKER
ATEVER YOUR META-SECURITY NEEDS, OUR TEAM IS PREPARED! OUR AGENTS HAVE ALL RECENTLY HAD THEIR RECORDS EXPUNG
NO MISSION IS TOO DANGEROUS! WHEN ALL OTHERS TURN YOU DOWN, THE SECRET SIX WILL BE THERE FOR YOU, FOR A PRI
JEANNETTE--
META-HUMAN DEFENSE
RAGDOLL--
INFILTRATION AND RECON
BLACK ALICE--
ARCANE ASSAULT
KING SHARK--
BITING AND CHEWING
THE SECRET SIX.
YOUR ENEMIES ARE OUR ENEMIES, AND MOST OF OUR ENEMIES ARE DEAD.
CUT!
Sigh
WHAT IS IT NOW, INSIGNIFICUS?
PARDON THIS WORTHLESS ONE, OH, MISTRESS OF THE VELVETEEN PRIVATES, BUT...ER... YOU DO REALIZE THERE ARE EIGHT OF YOU?
THAT'S IT, SCREW THIS.
I'LL BE IN MY TRAILER.

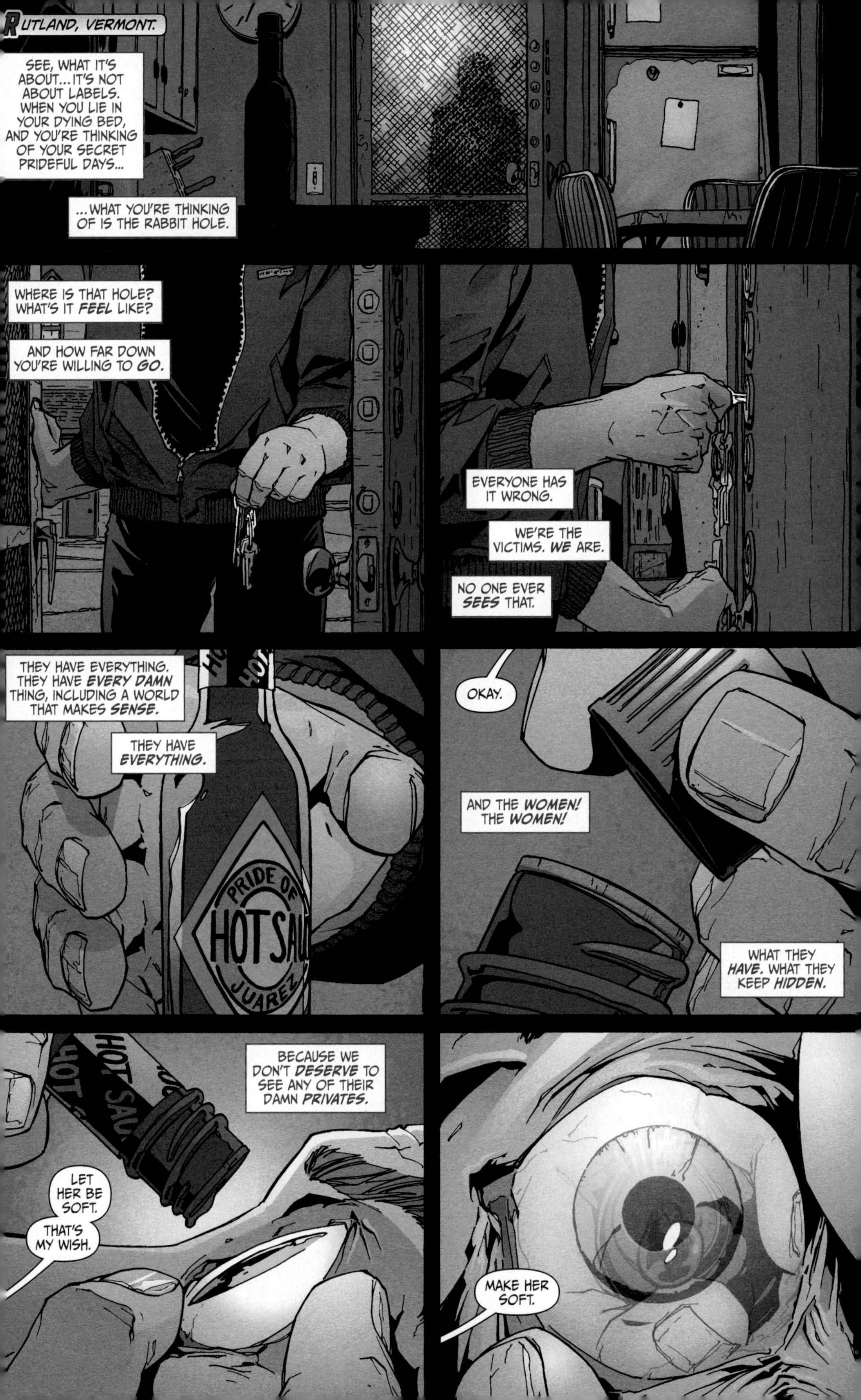
RUTLAND, VERMONT.
SEE, WHAT IT'S ABOUT... IT'S NOT ABOUT LABELS. WHEN YOU LIE IN YOUR DYING BED, AND YOU'RE THINKING OF YOUR SECRET PRIDEFUL DAYS...
...WHAT YOU'RE THINKING OF IS THE RABBIT HOLE.
WHERE IS THAT HOLE? WHAT'S IT FEEL LIKE?
AND HOW FAR DOWN YOU'RE WILLING TO GO.
EVERYONE HAS IT WRONG.
WE'RE THE VICTIMS. WE ARE.
NO ONE EVER SEES THAT.
THEY HAVE EVERYTHING. THEY HAVE EVERY DAMN THING, INCLUDING A WORLD THAT MAKES SENSE.
THEY HAVE EVERYTHING.
PRIDE OF
HOT SAU
JUAREZ
OKAY.
AND THE WOMEN! THE WOMEN!
WHAT THEY HAVE. WHAT THEY KEEP HIDDEN.
BECAUSE WE DON'T DESERVE TO SEE ANY OF THEIR DAMN PRIVATES.
LET HER BE SOFT.
THAT'S MY WISH.
MAKE HER SOFT.

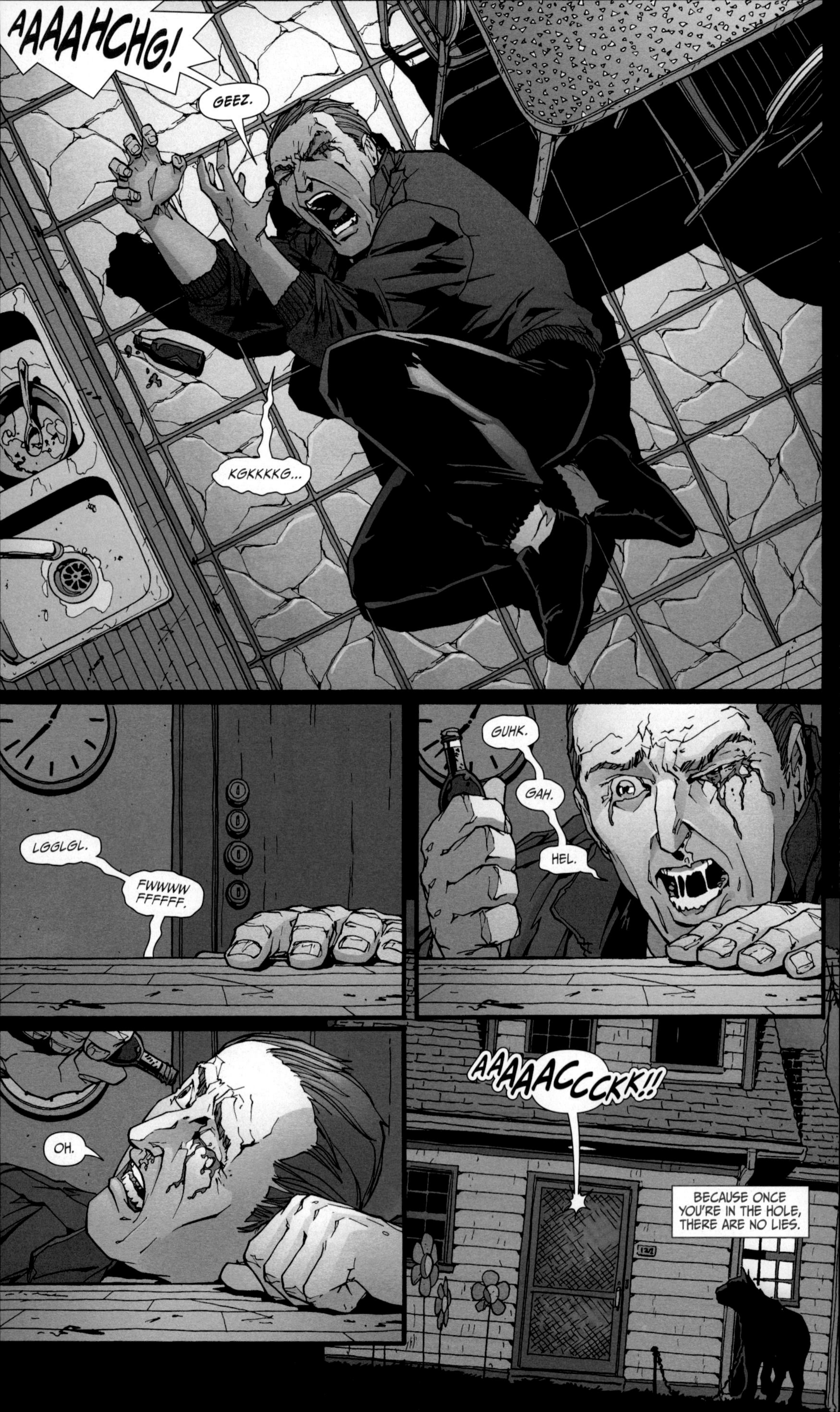
AAAAHCHG!
GEEZ.
KGKKKKG...
LGGLGL.
FWWWW FFFFFF.
GUHK.
GAH.
HEL.
OH.
AAAAACCCCKK!!
BECAUSE ONCE YOU'RE IN THE HOLE, THERE ARE NO LIES.

SUPERIORS GENTLEMEN'S CLUB

...CE YOU'RE IN THE ...LE, THE LABELS DON'T MATTER.

WHEN YOU GO ...IS DEEP, VICTIM ...ND KILLER ARE ...E SAME THING. ...E SAME DIRTY, ...ULGAR THING.

...FORGIVE HER ...N ADVANCE.

FOR EVERYTHING I'M GOING TO DO, I FORGIVE HER.

...GIVE THOSE THINGS A REST OR NO ONE'S GONNA *PAY* TO SEE 'EM, LIANA.

I THINK MY INCOME'S SAFE FOR A WHILE YET.

'NIGHT, SPENCE. GOT A *DATE*.

RAWWRRR!

I'VE PREPARED MYSELF.

THE THINGS I'VE DONE, THE THINGS I'VE PUT INSIDE MYSELF.

ALL FOR HER.

I HOPE TO *HELL* SHE *APPRECIATES* IT.

SCANDAL?

HEY, BABY, YOU MISS ME?

I'VE BEEN THINKING ABOUT YOU ALL *NIGHT*, AND--

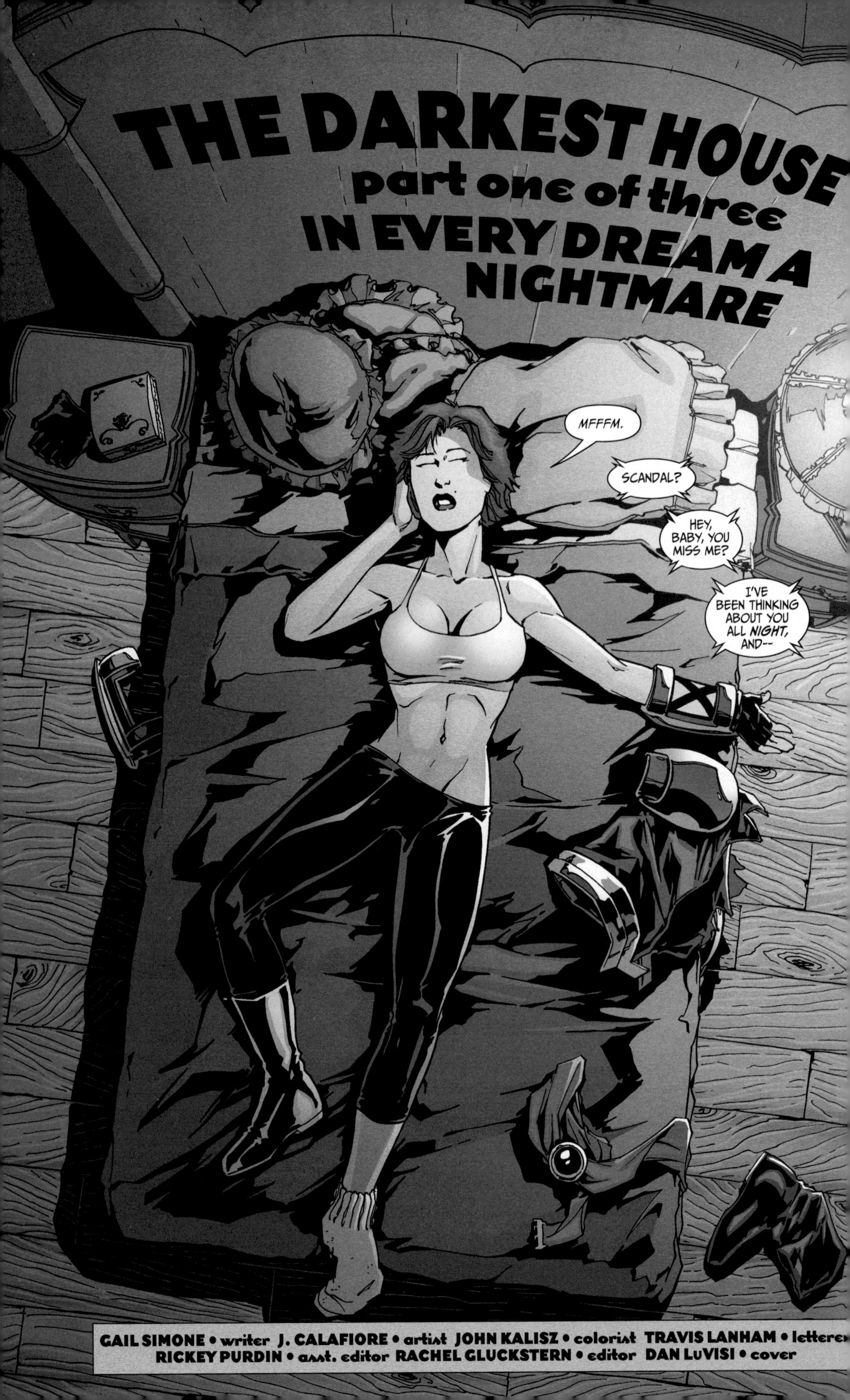
THE DARKEST HOUSE
part one of three
IN EVERY DREAM A NIGHTMARE
MFFFM.
SCANDAL?
HEY, BABY, YOU MISS ME?
I'VE BEEN THINKING ABOUT YOU ALL NIGHT, AND--
GAIL SIMONE • writer J. CALAFIORE • artist JOHN KALISZ • colorist TRAVIS LANHAM • lettere
RICKEY PURDIN • asst. editor RACHEL GLUCKSTERN • editor DAN LuVISI • cover

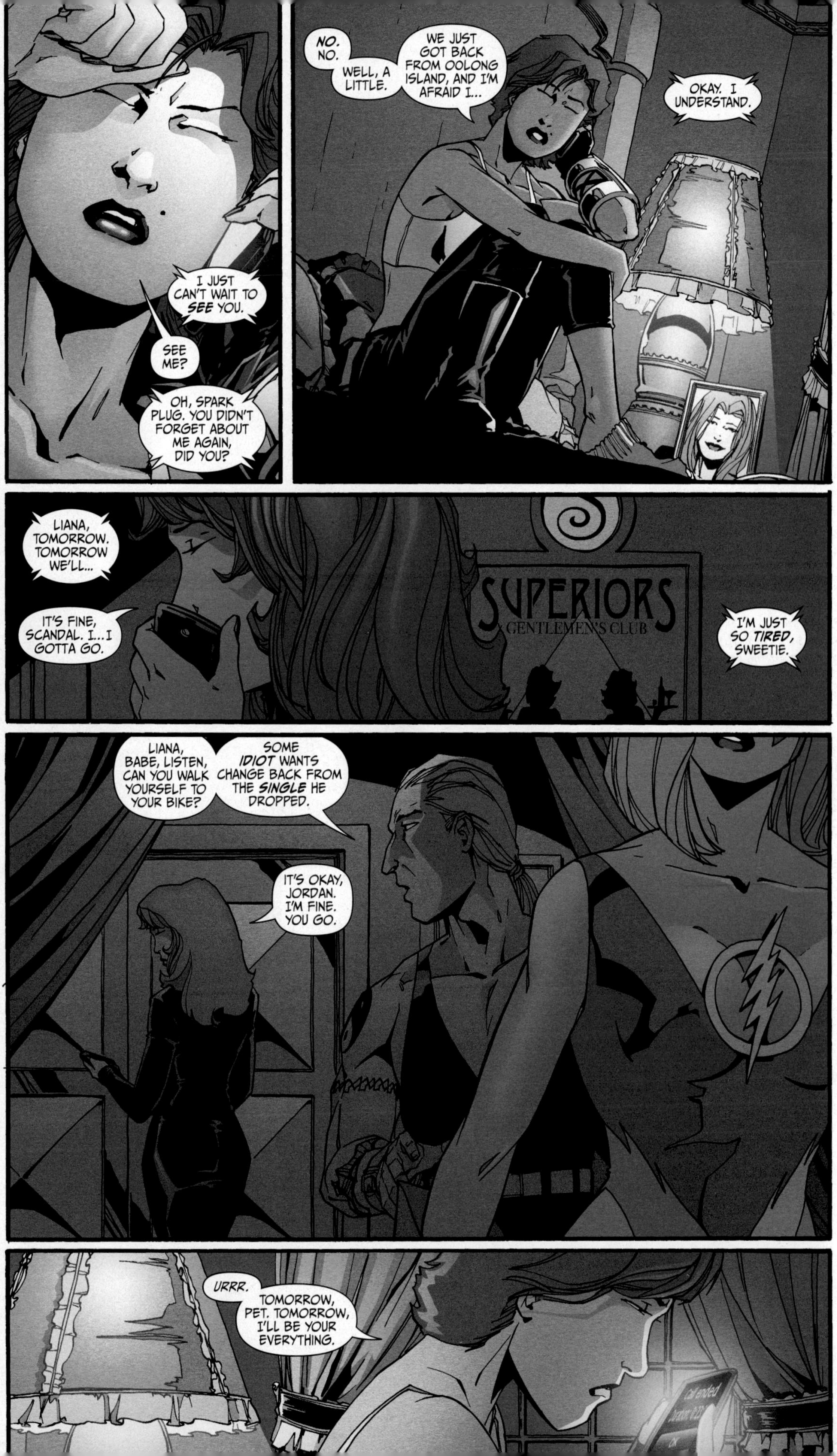
I JUST CAN'T WAIT TO *SEE* YOU.
SEE ME?
OH, SPARK PLUG. YOU DIDN'T FORGET ABOUT ME AGAIN, DID YOU?
NO. NO.
WELL, A LITTLE.
WE JUST GOT BACK FROM OOLONG ISLAND, AND I'M AFRAID I...
OKAY. I UNDERSTAND.
LIANA, TOMORROW. TOMORROW WE'LL...
IT'S FINE, SCANDAL. I...I GOTTA GO.
SUPERIORS
GENTLEMEN'S CLUB
I'M JUST SO *TIRED,* SWEETIE.
LIANA, BABE, LISTEN, CAN YOU WALK YOURSELF TO YOUR BIKE?
SOME *IDIOT* WANTS CHANGE BACK FROM THE *SINGLE* HE DROPPED.
IT'S OKAY, JORDAN. I'M FINE. YOU GO.
URRR.
TOMORROW, PET. TOMORROW, I'LL BE YOUR EVERYTHING.

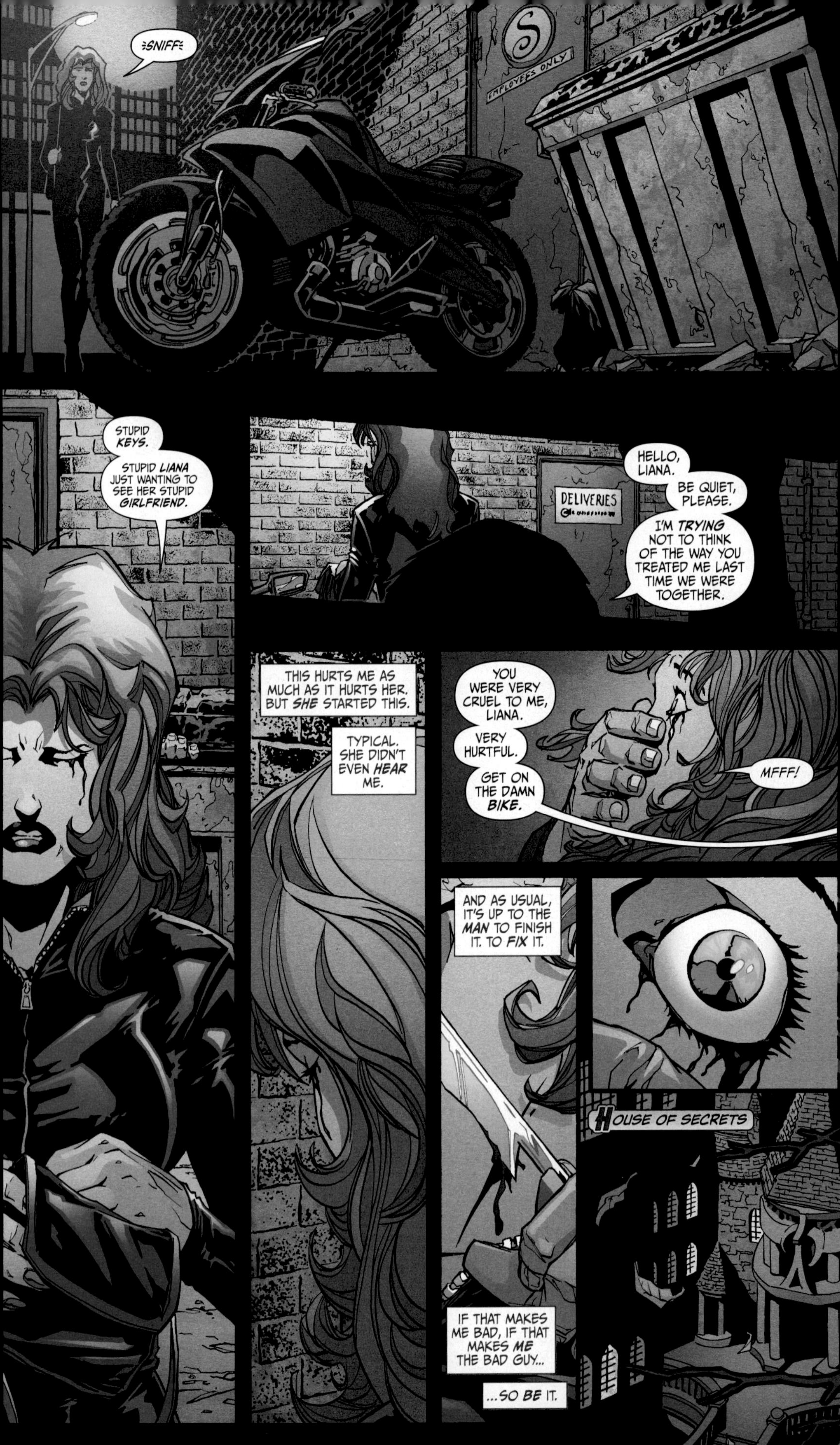
SNIFF
EMPLOYEES ONLY
STUPID KEYS.
STUPID LIANA JUST WANTING TO SEE HER STUPID GIRLFRIEND.
DELIVERIES
HELLO, LIANA.
BE QUIET, PLEASE.
I'M TRYING NOT TO THINK OF THE WAY YOU TREATED ME LAST TIME WE WERE TOGETHER.
THIS HURTS ME AS MUCH AS IT HURTS HER. BUT SHE STARTED THIS.
TYPICAL. SHE DIDN'T EVEN HEAR ME.
YOU WERE VERY CRUEL TO ME, LIANA.
VERY HURTFUL.
GET ON THE DAMN BIKE.
MFFF!
AND AS USUAL, IT'S UP TO THE MAN TO FINISH IT. TO FIX IT.
HOUSE OF SECRETS
IF THAT MAKES ME BAD, IF THAT MAKES ME THE BAD GUY...
...SO BE IT.

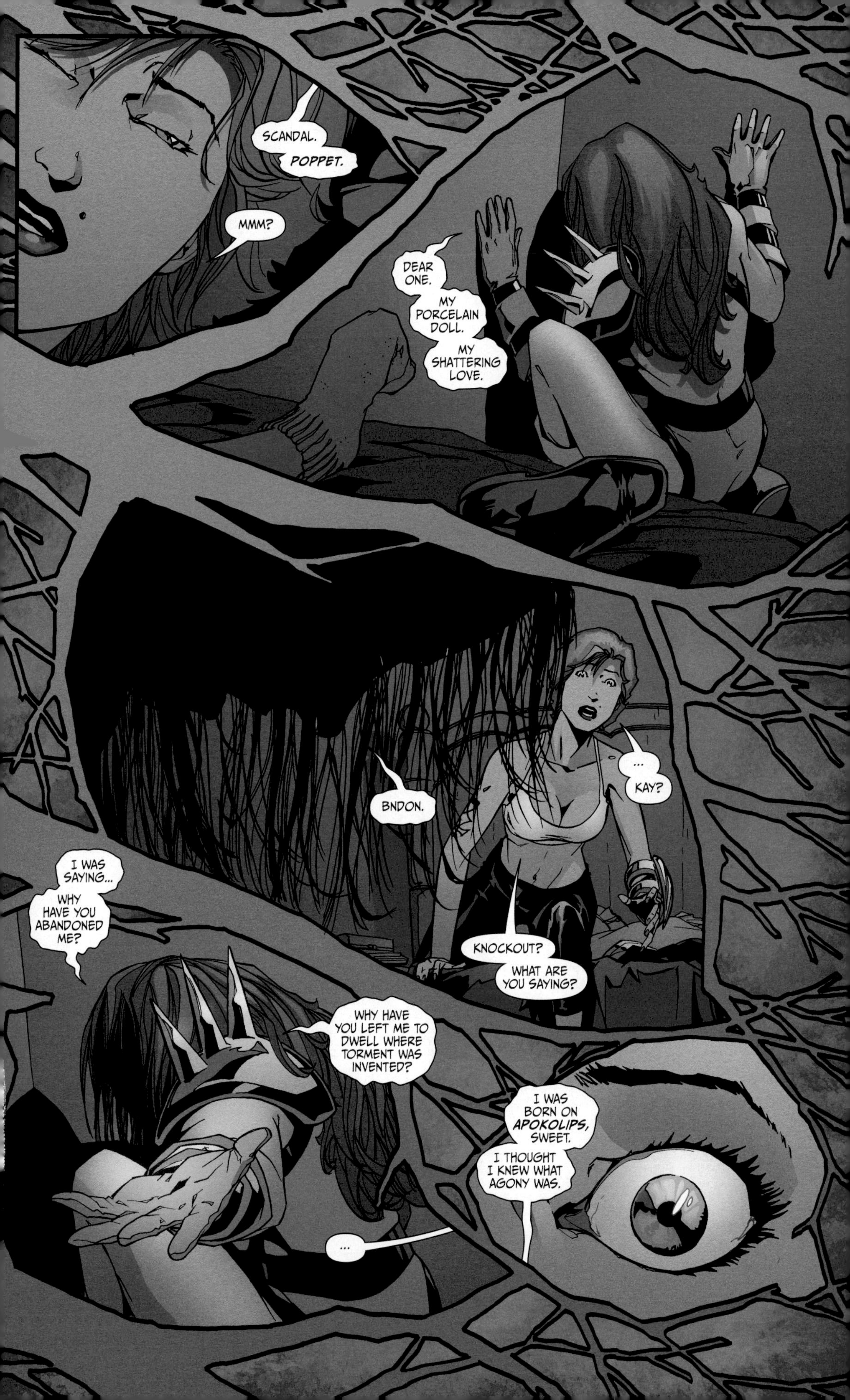
SCANDAL.
POPPET.
MMM?
DEAR ONE.
MY PORCELAIN DOLL.
MY SHATTERING LOVE.
BNDON.
...
KAY?
KNOCKOUT?
WHAT ARE YOU SAYING?
I WAS SAYING...
WHY HAVE YOU ABANDONED ME?
WHY HAVE YOU LEFT ME TO DWELL WHERE TORMENT WAS INVENTED?
I WAS BORN ON APOKOLIPS, SWEET.
I THOUGHT I KNEW WHAT AGONY WAS.
...

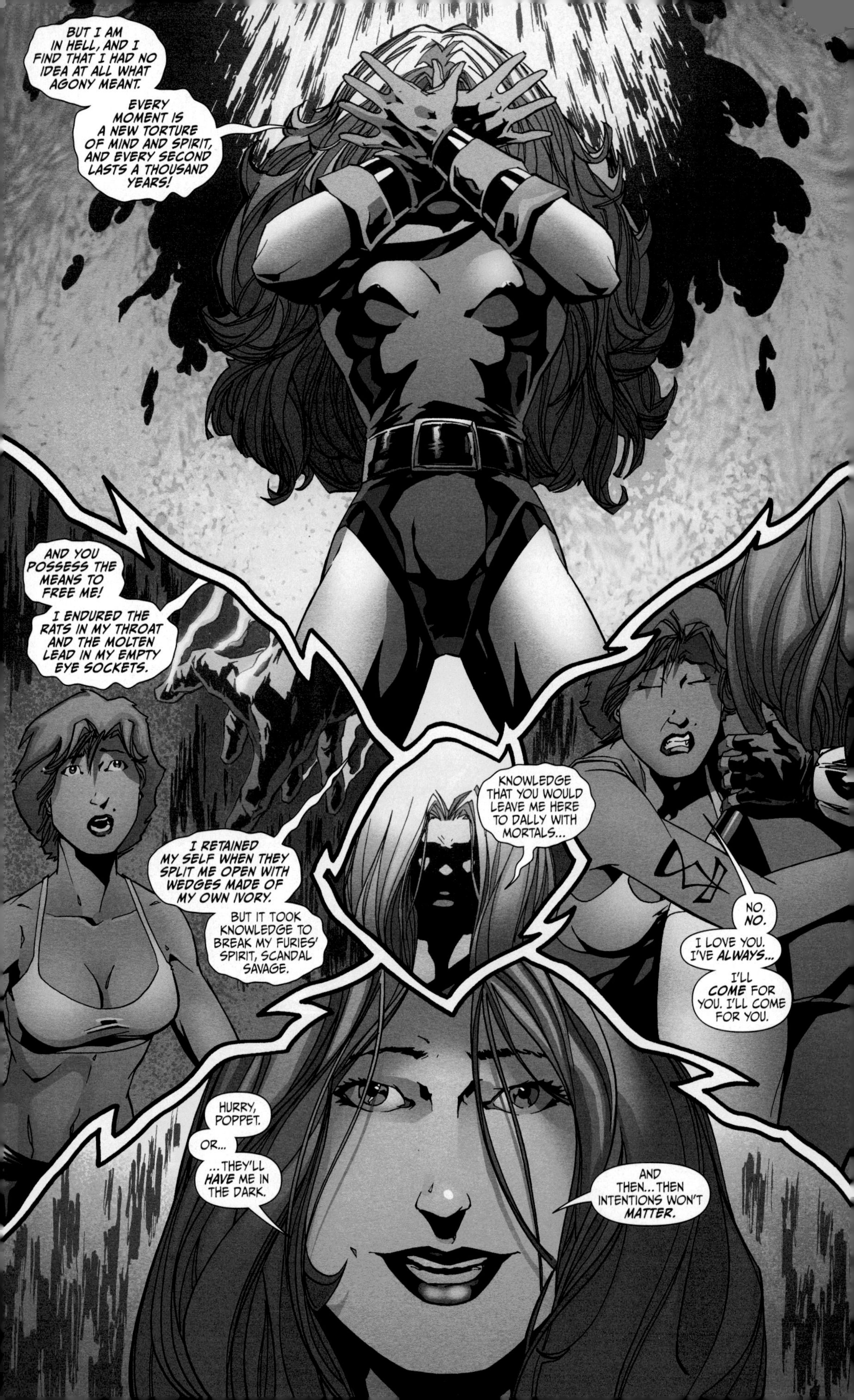
BUT I AM IN HELL, AND I FIND THAT I HAD NO IDEA AT ALL WHAT AGONY MEANT.
EVERY MOMENT IS A NEW TORTURE OF MIND AND SPIRIT, AND EVERY SECOND LASTS A THOUSAND YEARS!
AND YOU POSSESS THE MEANS TO FREE ME!
I ENDURED THE RATS IN MY THROAT AND THE MOLTEN LEAD IN MY EMPTY EYE SOCKETS.
I RETAINED MY SELF WHEN THEY SPLIT ME OPEN WITH WEDGES MADE OF MY OWN IVORY.
BUT IT TOOK KNOWLEDGE TO BREAK MY FURIES' SPIRIT, SCANDAL SAVAGE.
KNOWLEDGE THAT YOU WOULD LEAVE ME HERE TO DALLY WITH MORTALS...
NO. NO.
I LOVE YOU. I'VE ALWAYS...
I'LL COME FOR YOU. I'LL COME FOR YOU.
HURRY, POPPET.
OR...
...THEY'LL HAVE ME IN THE DARK.
AND THEN...THEN INTENTIONS WON'T MATTER.

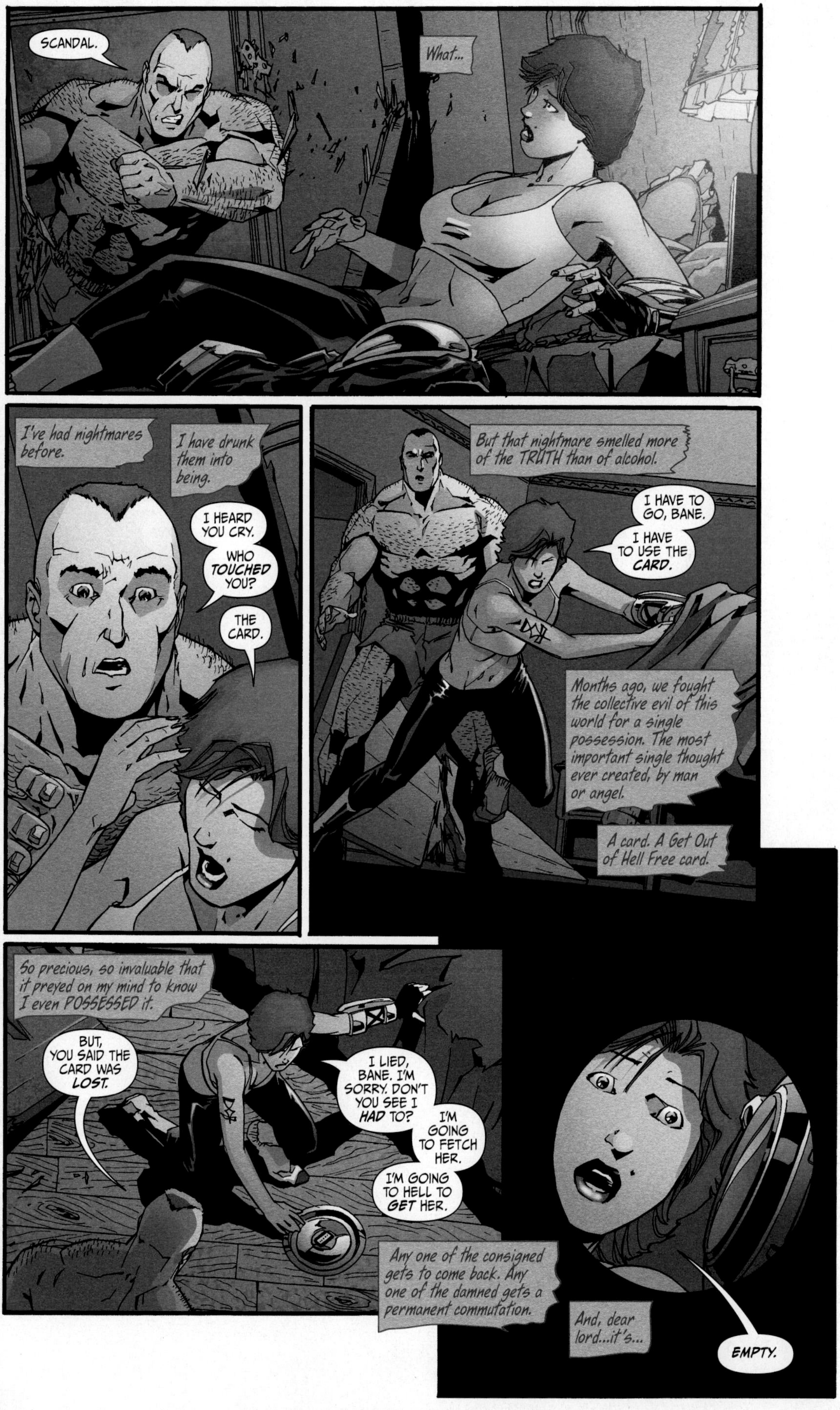

SCANDAL.
What...
I've had nightmares before.
I have drunk them into being.
I HEARD YOU CRY.
WHO *TOUCHED* YOU?
THE CARD.
But that nightmare smelled more of the TRUTH than of alcohol.
I HAVE TO GO, BANE.
I HAVE TO USE THE *CARD.*
Months ago, we fought the collective evil of this world for a single possession. The most important single thought ever created, by man or angel.
A card. A Get Out of Hell Free card.
So precious, so invaluable that it preyed on my mind to know I even POSSESSED it.
BUT, YOU SAID THE CARD WAS *LOST.*
I LIED, BANE. I'M SORRY. DON'T YOU SEE I *HAD* TO?
I'M GOING TO FETCH HER.
I'M GOING TO HELL TO *GET* HER.
Any one of the consigned gets to come back. Any one of the damned gets a permanent commutation.
And, dear lord...it's...
EMPTY.

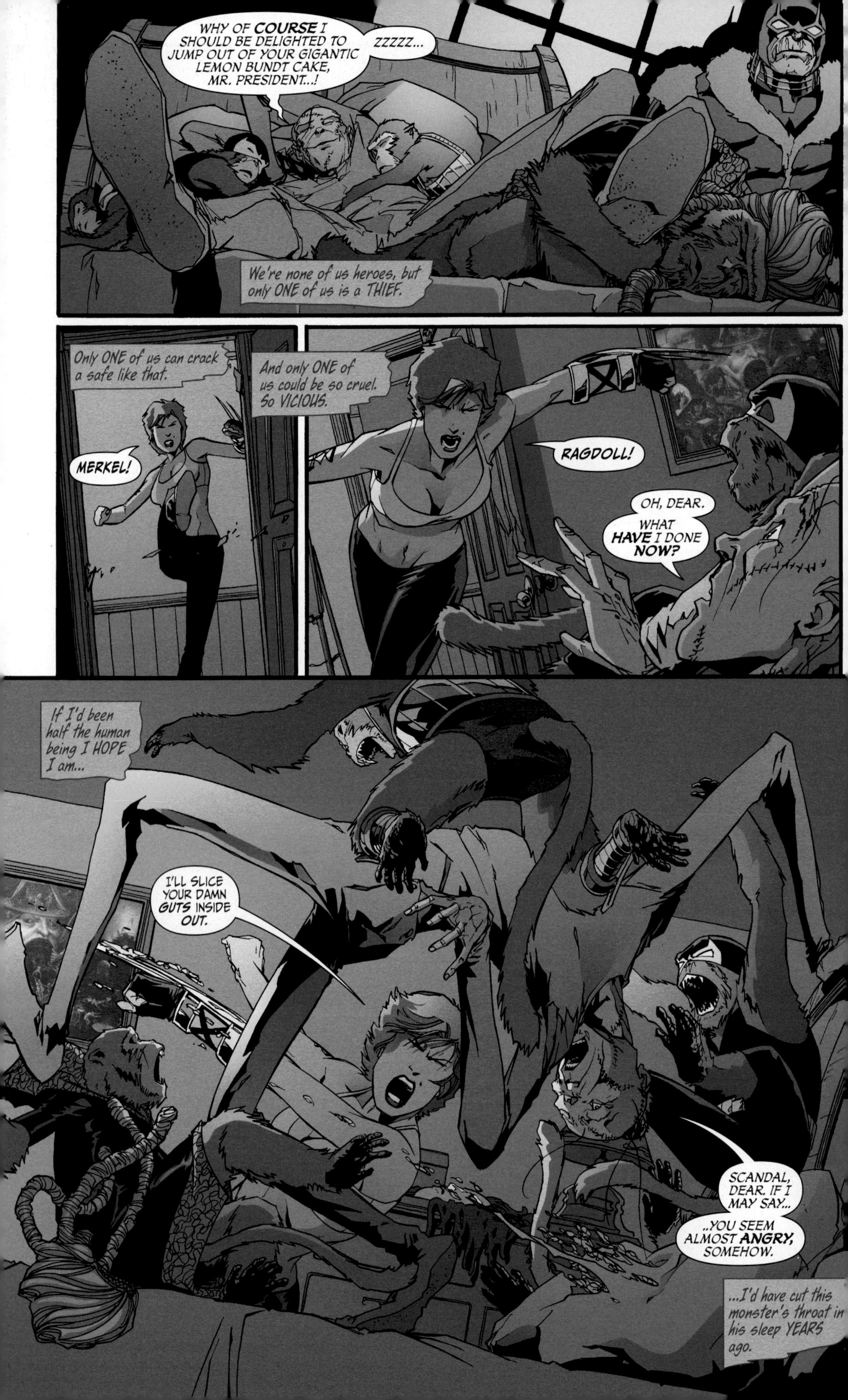
WHY OF COURSE I SHOULD BE DELIGHTED TO JUMP OUT OF YOUR GIGANTIC LEMON BUNDT CAKE, MR. PRESIDENT...!
ZZZZZ...
We're none of us heroes, but only ONE of us is a THIEF.
Only ONE of us can crack a safe like that.
MERKEL!
And only ONE of us could be so cruel. So VICIOUS.
RAGDOLL!
OH, DEAR. WHAT HAVE I DONE NOW?
If I'd been half the human being I HOPE I am...
I'LL SLICE YOUR DAMN GUTS INSIDE OUT.
SCANDAL, DEAR. IF I MAY SAY...
..YOU SEEM ALMOST ANGRY, SOMEHOW.
...I'd have cut this monster's throat in his sleep YEARS ago.

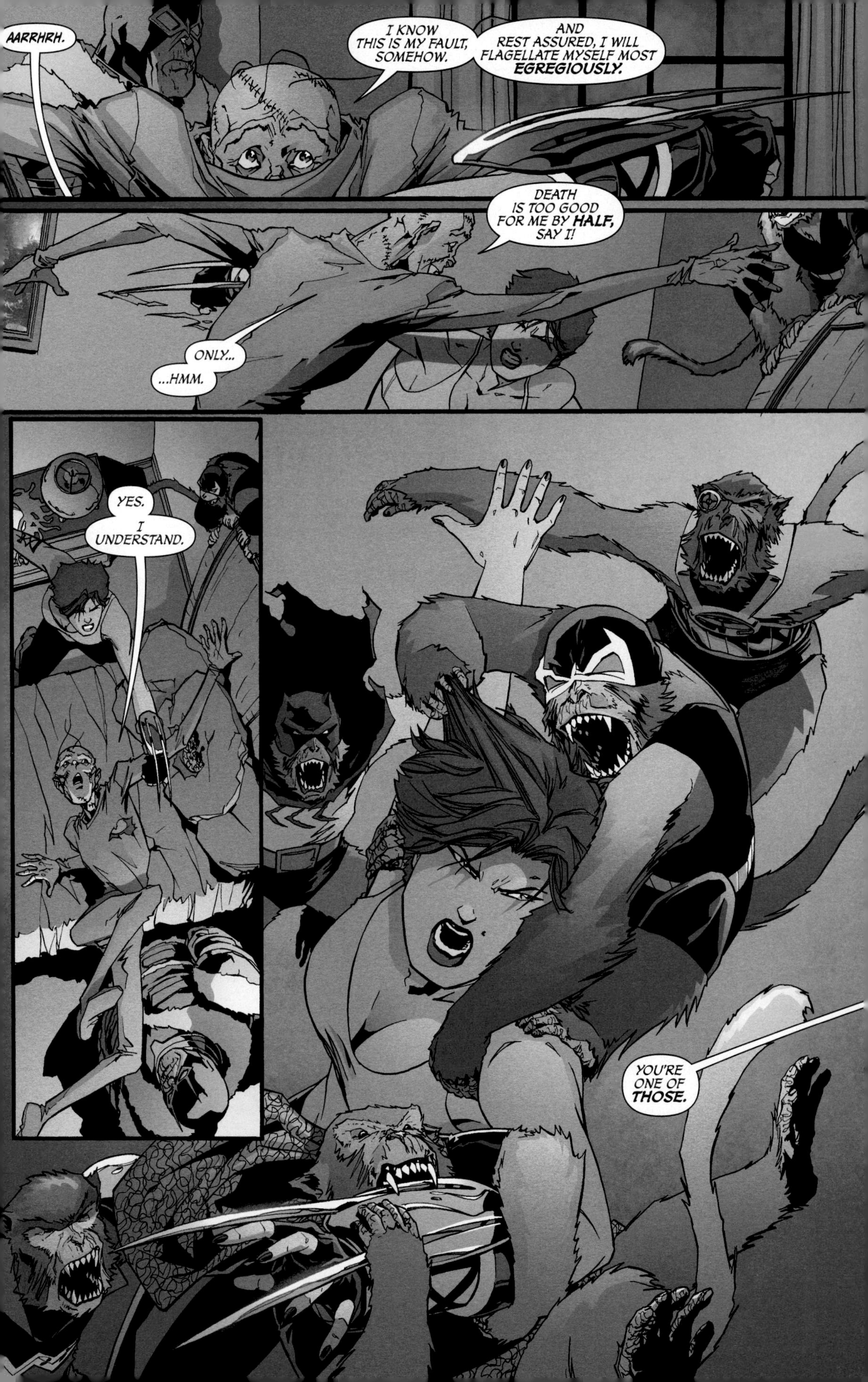
AARRHRH.
I KNOW THIS IS MY FAULT, SOMEHOW.
AND REST ASSURED, I WILL FLAGELLATE MYSELF MOST EGREGIOUSLY.
DEATH IS TOO GOOD FOR ME BY HALF, SAY I!
ONLY...
...HMM.
YES. I UNDERSTAND.
YOU'RE ONE OF THOSE.

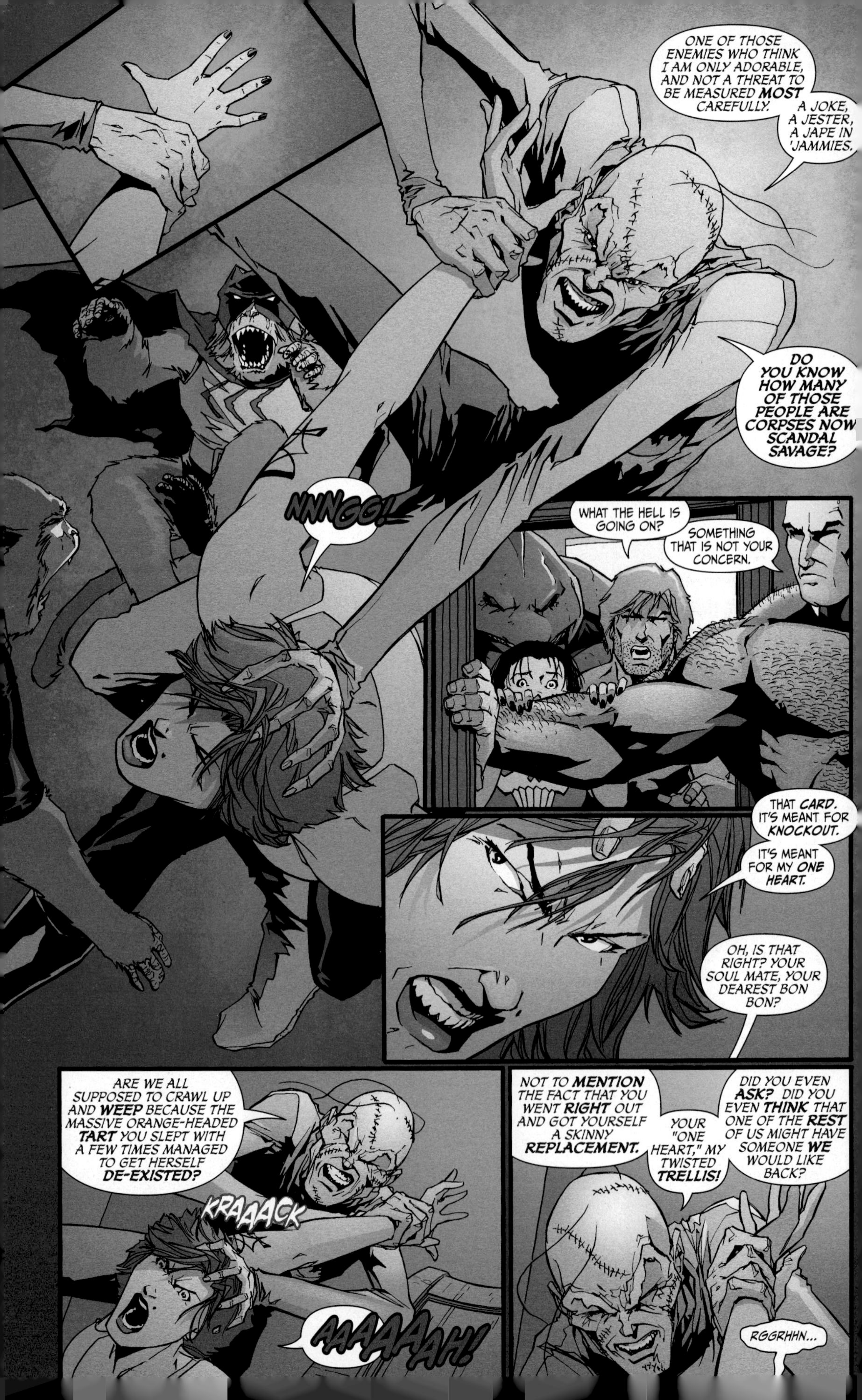
ONE OF THOSE ENEMIES WHO THINK I AM ONLY ADORABLE, AND NOT A THREAT TO BE MEASURED MOST CAREFULLY.
A JOKE, A JESTER, A JAPE IN 'JAMMIES.
DO YOU KNOW HOW MANY OF THOSE PEOPLE ARE CORPSES NOW SCANDAL SAVAGE?
NNNGG!
WHAT THE HELL IS GOING ON?
SOMETHING THAT IS NOT YOUR CONCERN.
THAT CARD. IT'S MEANT FOR KNOCKOUT.
IT'S MEANT FOR MY ONE HEART.
OH, IS THAT RIGHT? YOUR SOUL MATE, YOUR DEAREST BON BON?
ARE WE ALL SUPPOSED TO CRAWL UP AND WEEP BECAUSE THE MASSIVE ORANGE-HEADED TART YOU SLEPT WITH A FEW TIMES MANAGED TO GET HERSELF DE-EXISTED?
KRAAACK
AAAAAAH!
NOT TO MENTION THE FACT THAT YOU WENT RIGHT OUT AND GOT YOURSELF A SKINNY REPLACEMENT.
YOUR "ONE HEART," MY TWISTED TRELLIS!
DID YOU EVEN ASK? DID YOU EVEN THINK THAT ONE OF THE REST OF US MIGHT HAVE SOMEONE WE WOULD LIKE BACK?
RGGRHHN...

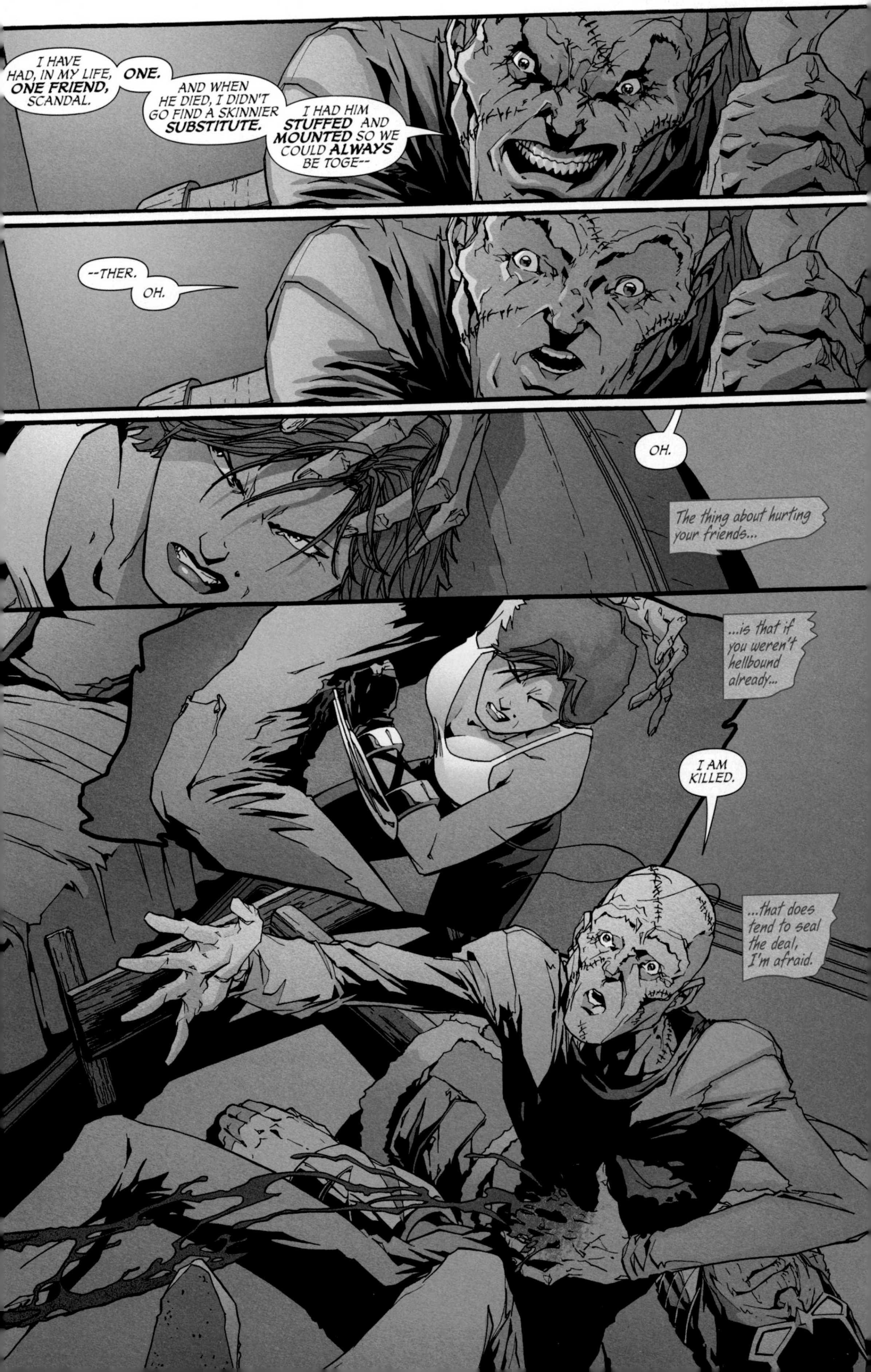

I HAVE HAD, IN MY LIFE, ONE FRIEND, SCANDAL.
ONE.
AND WHEN HE DIED, I DIDN'T GO FIND A SKINNIER SUBSTITUTE.
I HAD HIM STUFFED AND MOUNTED SO WE COULD ALWAYS BE TOGE--
--THER.
OH.
OH.
The thing about hurting your friends...
...is that if you weren't hellbound already...
I AM KILLED.
...that does tend to seal the deal, I'm afraid.

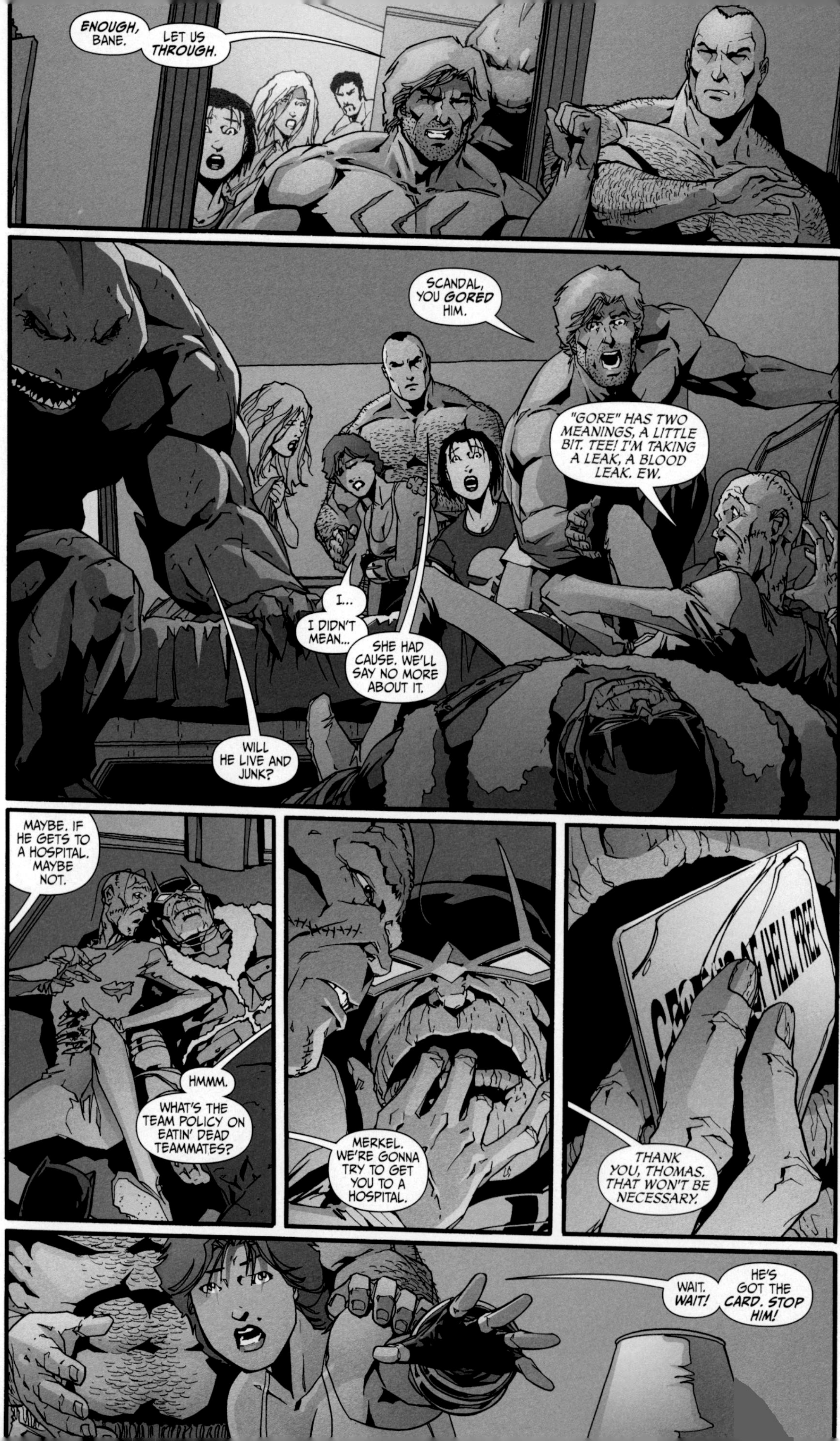
ENOUGH, BANE.
LET US THROUGH.
SCANDAL, YOU GORED HIM.
"GORE" HAS TWO MEANINGS, A LITTLE BIT. TEE! I'M TAKING A LEAK, A BLOOD LEAK. EW.
I...
I DIDN'T MEAN...
SHE HAD CAUSE. WE'LL SAY NO MORE ABOUT IT.
WILL HE LIVE AND JUNK?
MAYBE. IF HE GETS TO A HOSPITAL. MAYBE NOT.
HMMM.
WHAT'S THE TEAM POLICY ON EATIN' DEAD TEAMMATES?
MERKEL. WE'RE GONNA TRY TO GET YOU TO A HOSPITAL.
THANK YOU, THOMAS. THAT WON'T BE NECESSARY.
WAIT. WAIT!
HE'S GOT THE CARD. STOP HIM!

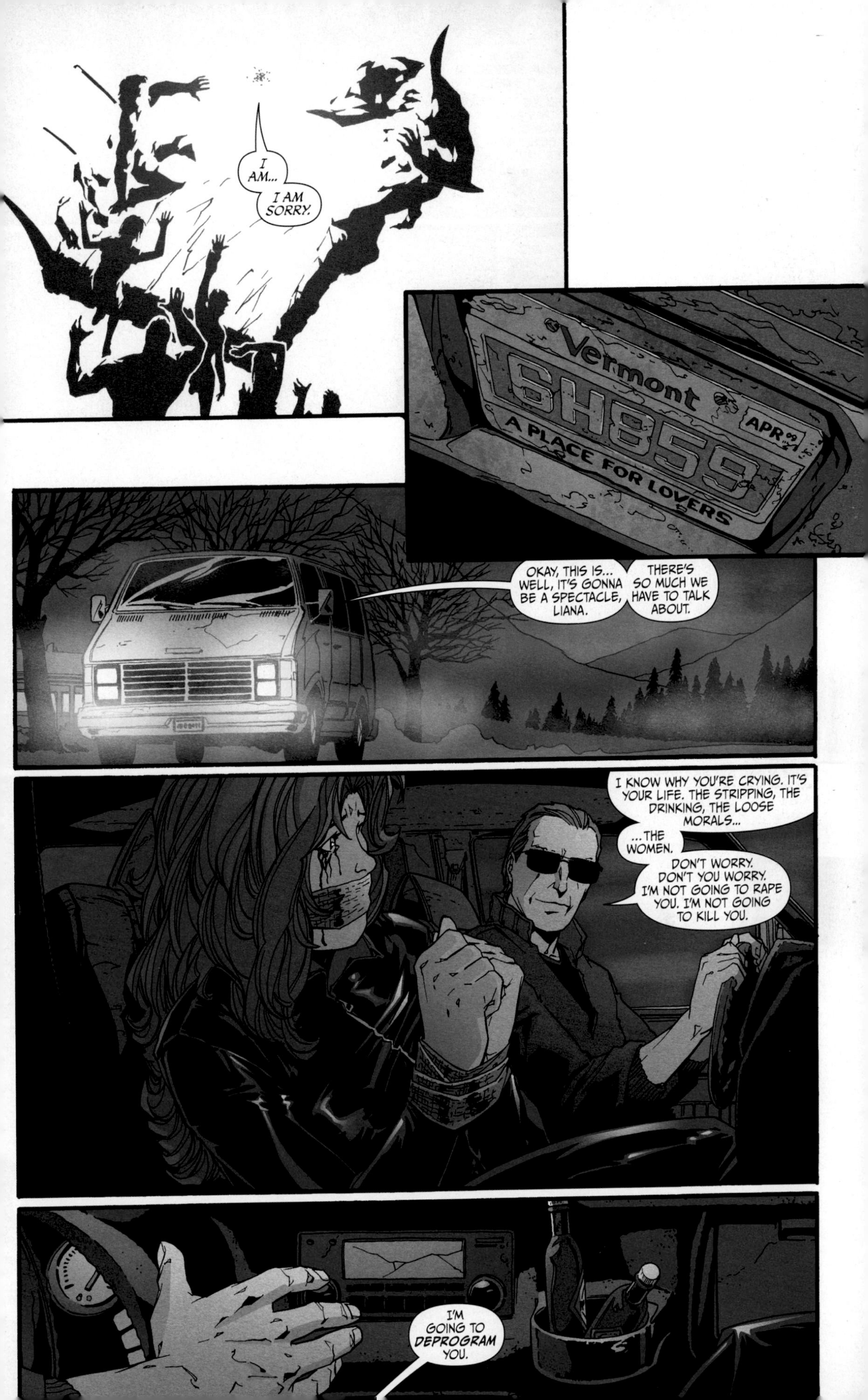

I AM... I AM SORRY.
Vermont
6H859
APR 09
A PLACE FOR LOVERS
OKAY, THIS IS... WELL, IT'S GONNA BE A SPECTACLE, LIANA.
THERE'S SO MUCH WE HAVE TO TALK ABOUT.
I KNOW WHY YOU'RE CRYING. IT'S YOUR LIFE. THE STRIPPING, THE DRINKING, THE LOOSE MORALS...
...THE WOMEN.
DON'T WORRY. DON'T YOU WORRY. I'M NOT GOING TO RAPE YOU. I'M NOT GOING TO KILL YOU.
I'M GOING TO DEPROGRAM YOU.

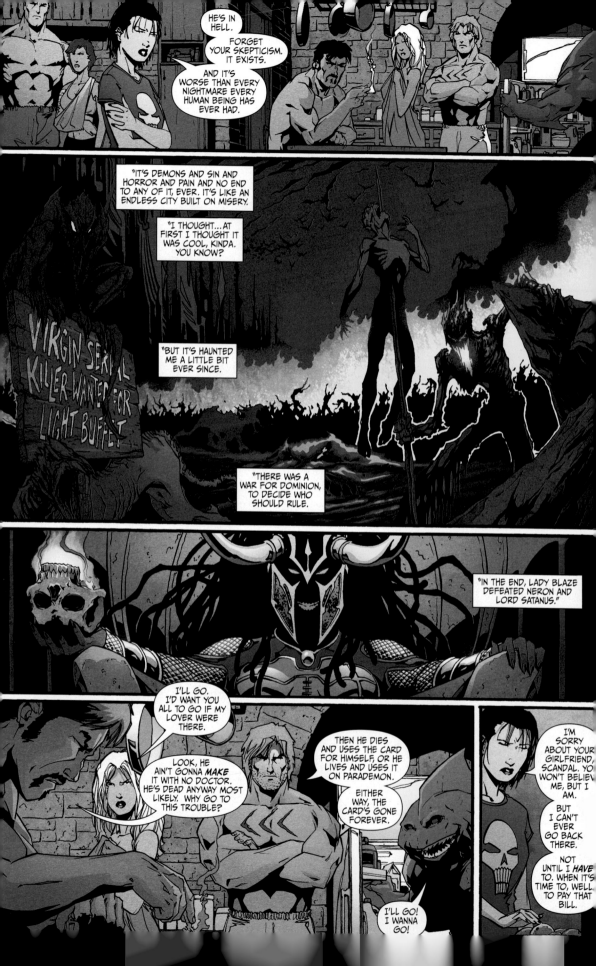

HE'S IN HELL.

FORGET YOUR SKEPTICISM. IT EXISTS.

AND IT'S WORSE THAN EVERY NIGHTMARE EVERY HUMAN BEING HAS EVER HAD.

"IT'S DEMONS AND SIN AND HORROR AND PAIN AND NO END TO ANY OF IT, EVER. IT'S LIKE AN ENDLESS CITY BUILT ON MISERY.

"I THOUGHT...AT FIRST I THOUGHT IT WAS COOL, KINDA. YOU KNOW?

"BUT IT'S HAUNTED ME A LITTLE BIT EVER SINCE.

VIRGIN SERIAL KILLER WANTED FOR LIGHT BUFFET

"THERE WAS A WAR FOR DOMINION, TO DECIDE WHO SHOULD RULE.

"IN THE END, LADY BLAZE DEFEATED NERON AND LORD SATANUS."

I'LL GO. I'D WANT YOU ALL TO GO IF MY LOVER WERE THERE.

LOOK, HE AIN'T GONNA **MAKE** IT WITH NO DOCTOR. HE'S DEAD ANYWAY MOST LIKELY. WHY GO TO THIS TROUBLE?

THEN HE DIES AND USES THE CARD FOR HIMSELF, OR HE LIVES AND USES IT ON PARADEMON.

EITHER WAY, THE CARD'S GONE FOREVER.

I'LL GO! I WANNA GO!

I'M SORRY ABOUT YOUR GIRLFRIEND, SCANDAL. YOU WON'T BELIEVE ME, BUT I AM.

BUT I CAN'T EVER GO BACK THERE.

NOT UNTIL I **HAVE** TO. WHEN IT'S TIME TO, WELL, TO PAY THAT BILL.

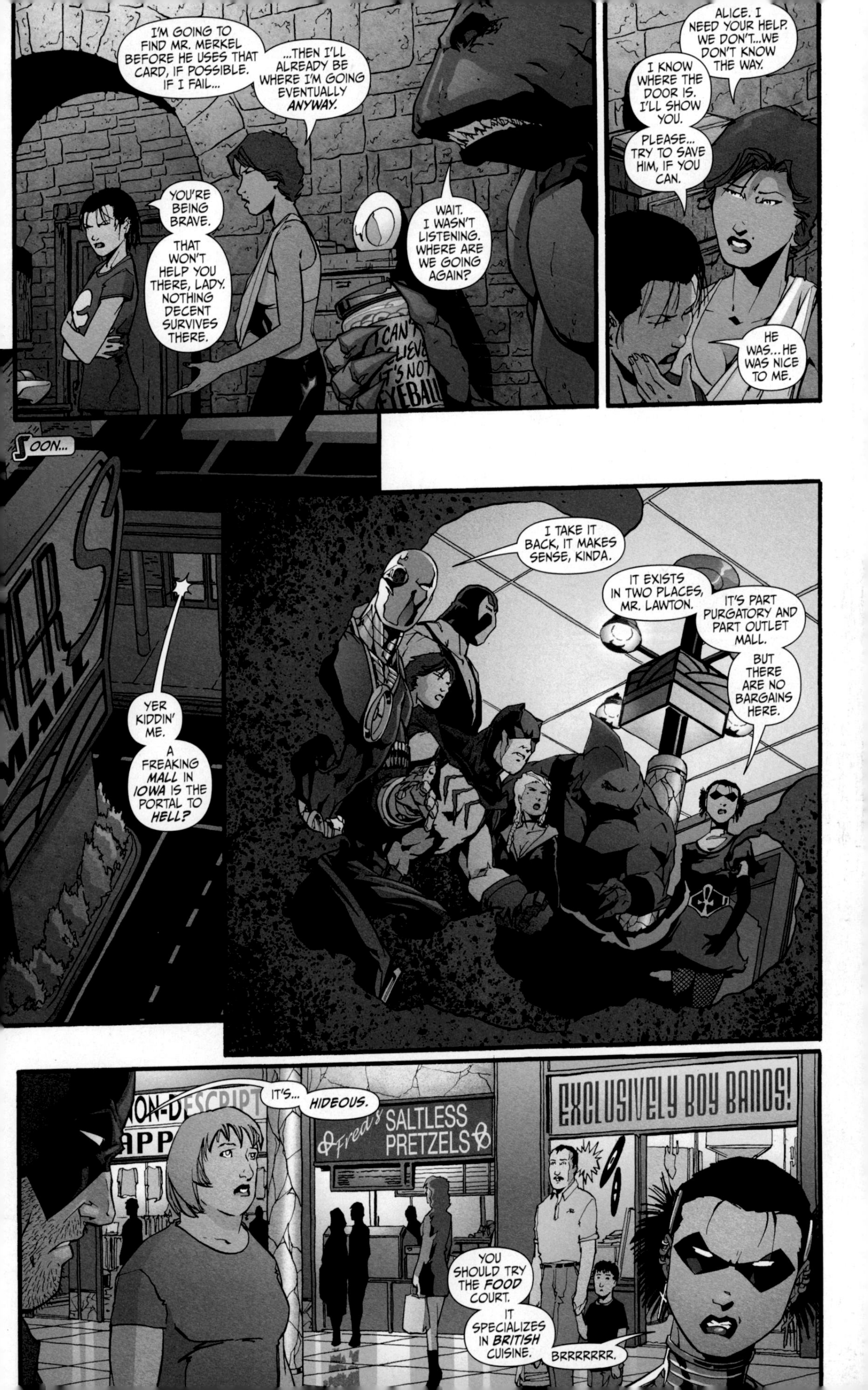
I'M GOING TO FIND MR. MERKEL BEFORE HE USES THAT CARD, IF POSSIBLE. IF I FAIL...
...THEN I'LL ALREADY BE WHERE I'M GOING EVENTUALLY *ANYWAY.*
YOU'RE BEING BRAVE.
THAT WON'T HELP YOU THERE, LADY. NOTHING DECENT SURVIVES THERE.
WAIT. I WASN'T LISTENING. WHERE ARE WE GOING AGAIN?
ALICE. I NEED YOUR HELP. WE DON'T...WE DON'T KNOW THE WAY.
I KNOW WHERE THE DOOR IS. I'LL SHOW YOU.
PLEASE... TRY TO SAVE HIM, IF YOU CAN.
HE WAS...HE WAS NICE TO ME.
SOON...
MALL
YER KIDDIN' ME.
A FREAKING *MALL* IN *IOWA* IS THE PORTAL TO *HELL?*
I TAKE IT BACK, IT MAKES SENSE, KINDA.
IT EXISTS IN TWO PLACES, MR. LAWTON.
IT'S PART PURGATORY AND PART OUTLET MALL.
BUT THERE ARE NO BARGAINS HERE.
NON-DESCRIPT
IT'S... *HIDEOUS.*
Fred's SALTLESS PRETZELS
EXCLUSIVELY BOY BANDS!
YOU SHOULD TRY THE *FOOD* COURT.
IT SPECIALIZES IN *BRITISH* CUISINE.
BRRRRRRR.

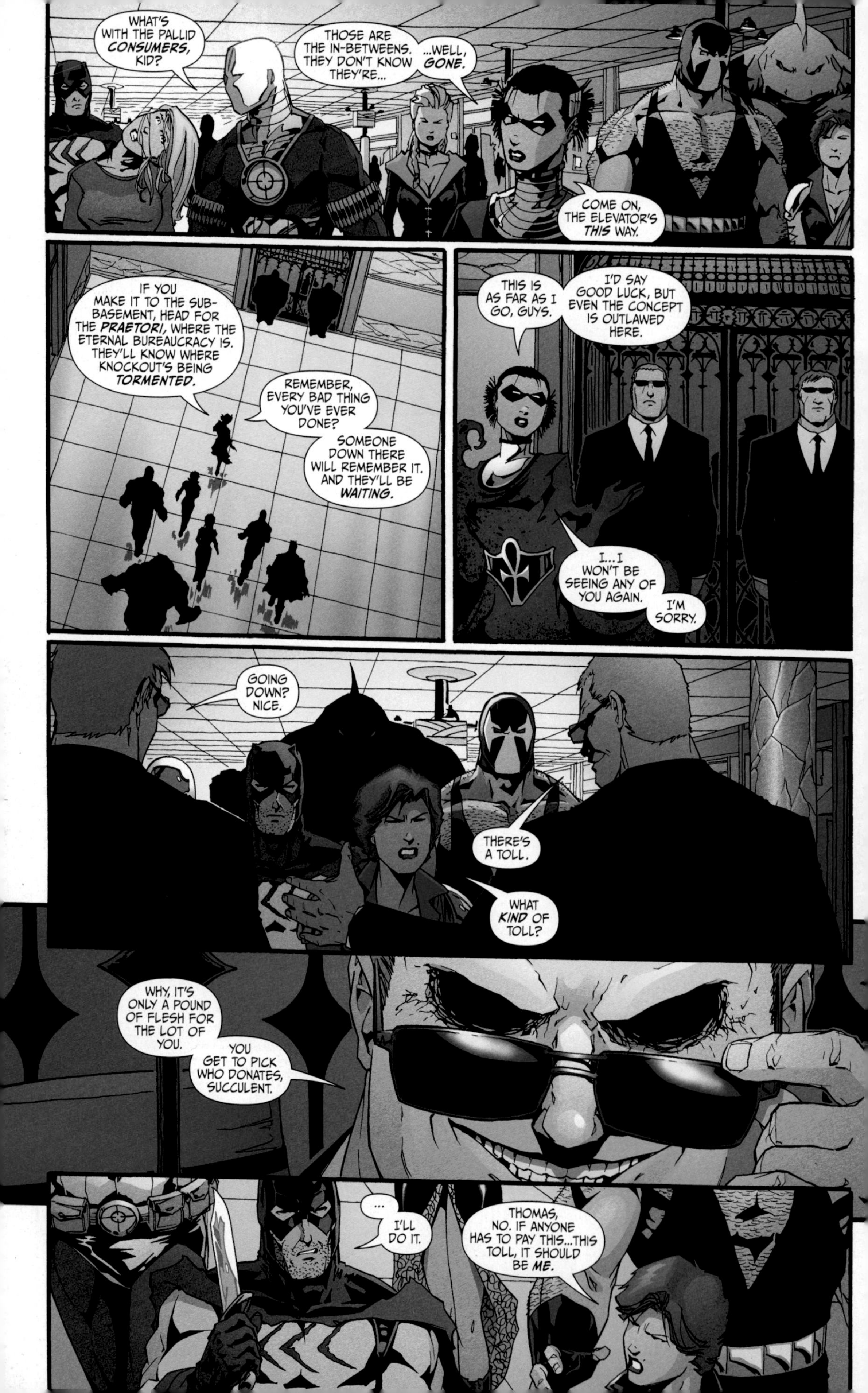
WHAT'S WITH THE PALLID CONSUMERS, KID?
THOSE ARE THE IN-BETWEENS. THEY DON'T KNOW THEY'RE...
...WELL, GONE.
COME ON, THE ELEVATOR'S THIS WAY.
IF YOU MAKE IT TO THE SUB-BASEMENT, HEAD FOR THE PRAETORI, WHERE THE ETERNAL BUREAUCRACY IS. THEY'LL KNOW WHERE KNOCKOUT'S BEING TORMENTED.
REMEMBER, EVERY BAD THING YOU'VE EVER DONE?
SOMEONE DOWN THERE WILL REMEMBER IT. AND THEY'LL BE WAITING.
THIS IS AS FAR AS I GO, GUYS.
I'D SAY GOOD LUCK, BUT EVEN THE CONCEPT IS OUTLAWED HERE.
I...I WON'T BE SEEING ANY OF YOU AGAIN.
I'M SORRY.
GOING DOWN? NICE.
THERE'S A TOLL.
WHAT KIND OF TOLL?
WHY, IT'S ONLY A POUND OF FLESH FOR THE LOT OF YOU.
YOU GET TO PICK WHO DONATES, SUCCULENT.
...
I'LL DO IT.
THOMAS, NO. IF ANYONE HAS TO PAY THIS...THIS TOLL, IT SHOULD BE ME.

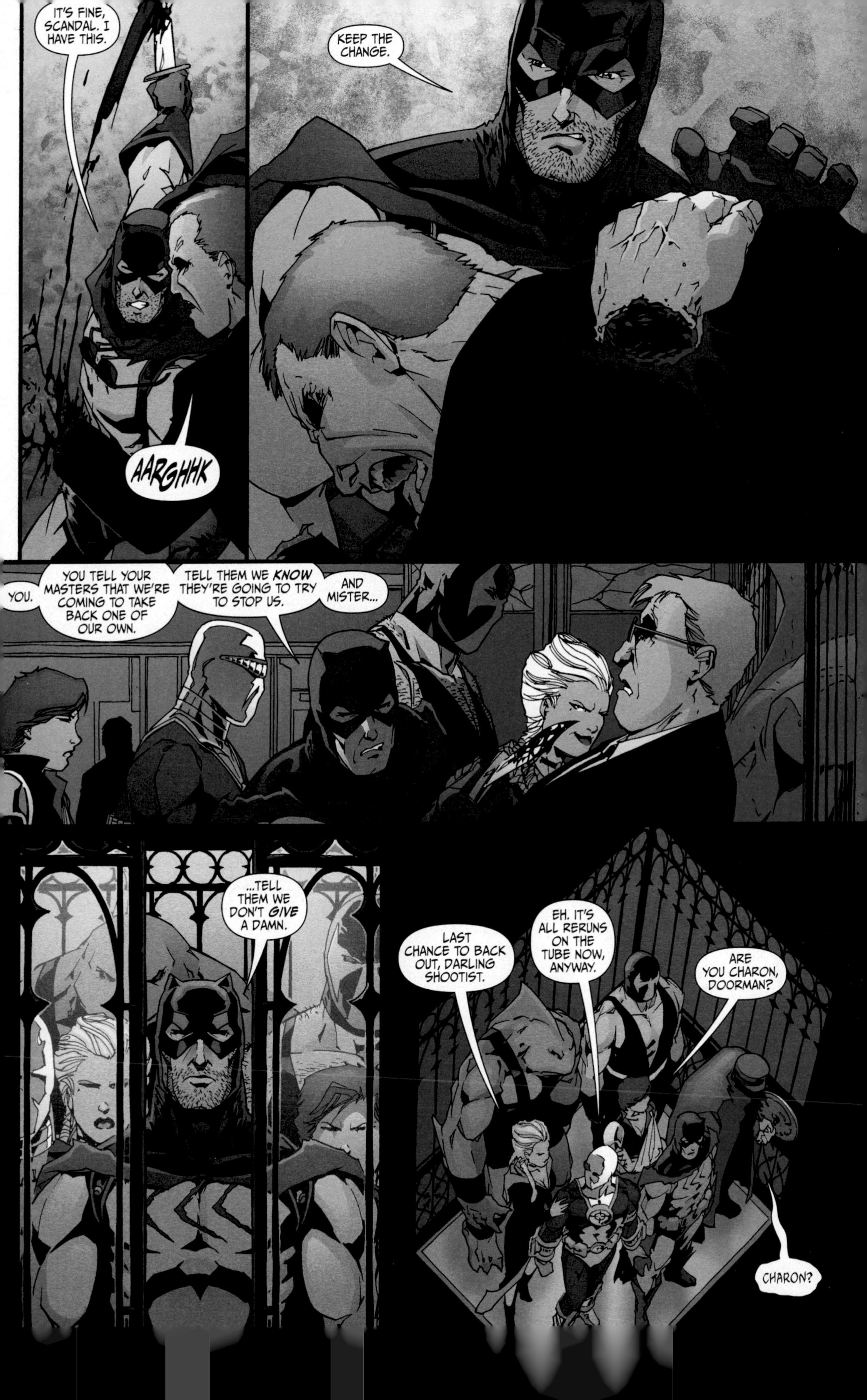
IT'S FINE, SCANDAL. I HAVE THIS.
AARGHHK
KEEP THE CHANGE.
YOU.
YOU TELL YOUR MASTERS THAT WE'RE COMING TO TAKE BACK ONE OF OUR OWN.
TELL THEM WE *KNOW* THEY'RE GOING TO TRY TO STOP US.
AND MISTER...
...TELL THEM WE DON'T *GIVE* A DAMN.
LAST CHANCE TO BACK OUT, DARLING SHOOTIST.
EH. IT'S ALL RERUNS ON THE TUBE NOW, ANYWAY.
ARE YOU CHARON, DOORMAN?
CHARON?

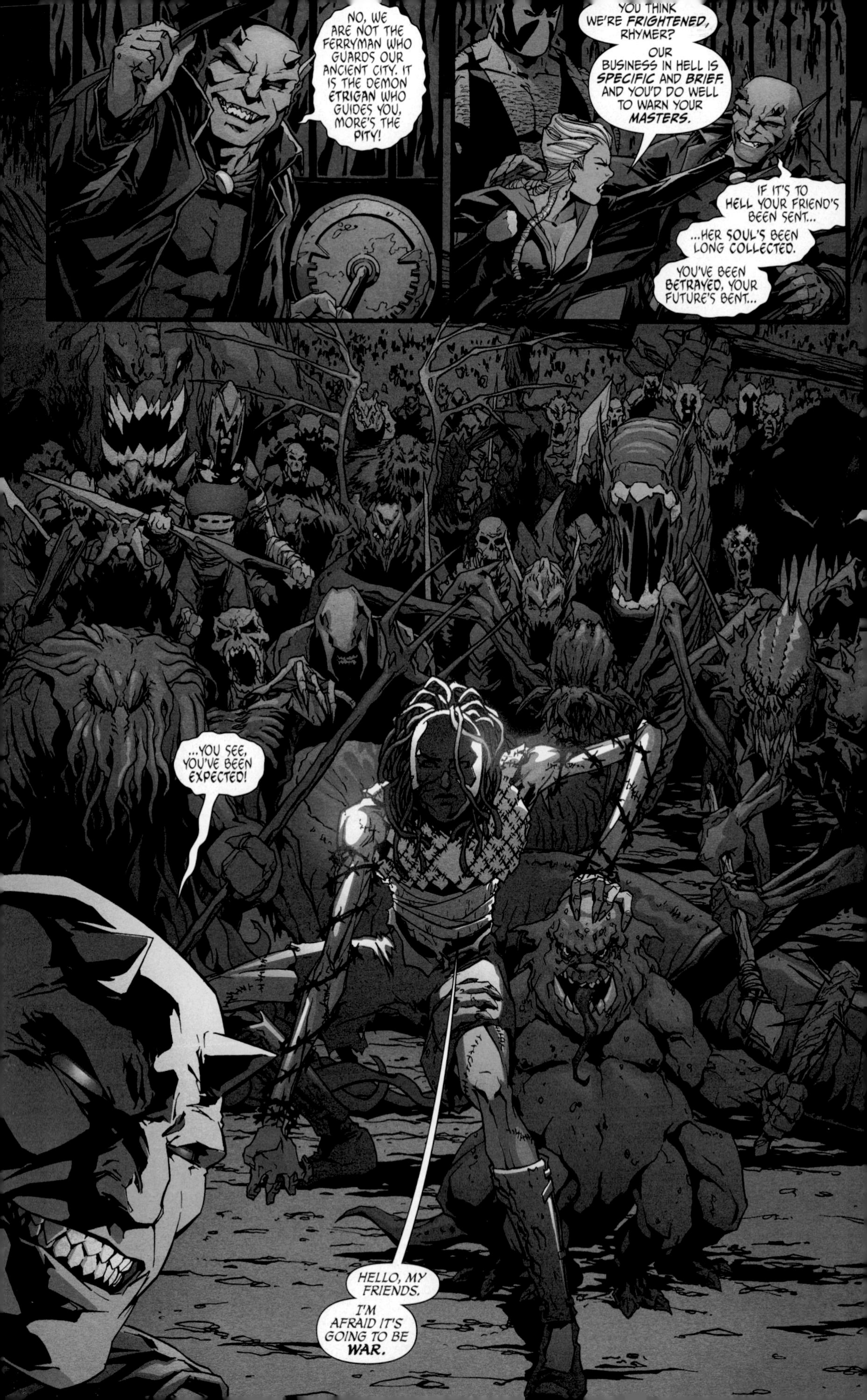
NO, WE ARE NOT THE FERRYMAN WHO GUARDS OUR ANCIENT CITY. IT IS THE DEMON ETRIGAN WHO GUIDES YOU. MORE'S THE PITY!
YOU THINK WE'RE FRIGHTENED, RHYMER?
OUR BUSINESS IN HELL IS SPECIFIC AND BRIEF. AND YOU'D DO WELL TO WARN YOUR MASTERS.
IF IT'S TO HELL YOUR FRIEND'S BEEN SENT...
...HER SOUL'S BEEN LONG COLLECTED.
YOU'VE BEEN BETRAYED, YOUR FUTURE'S BENT...
...YOU SEE, YOU'VE BEEN EXPECTED!
HELLO, MY FRIENDS.
I'M AFRAID IT'S GOING TO BE WAR.

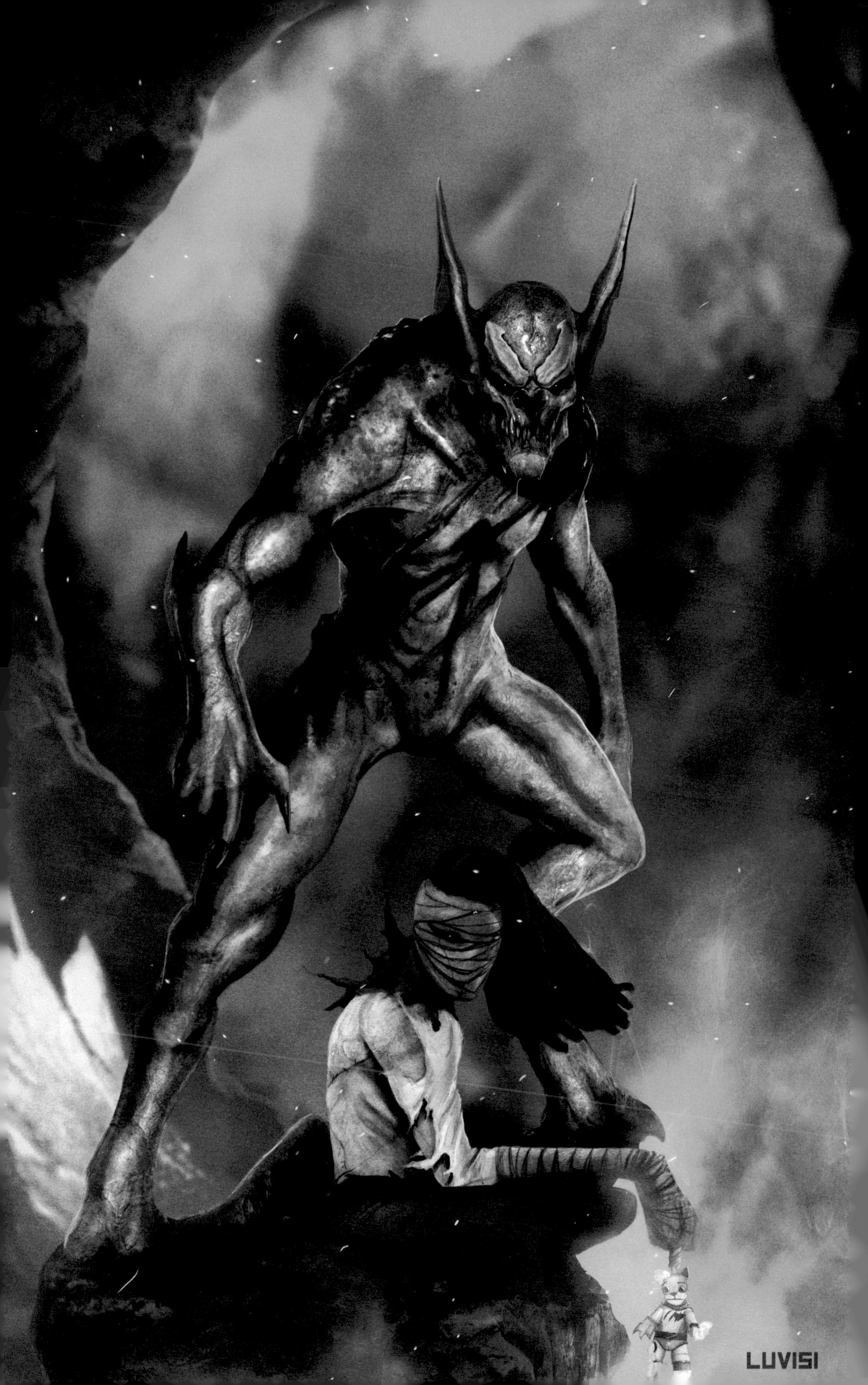
LUVISI

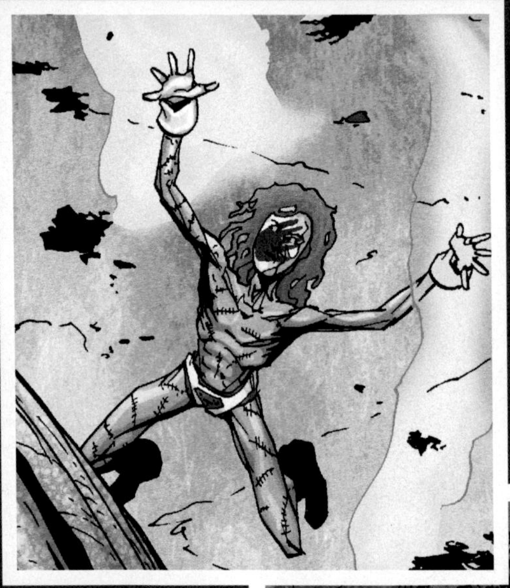

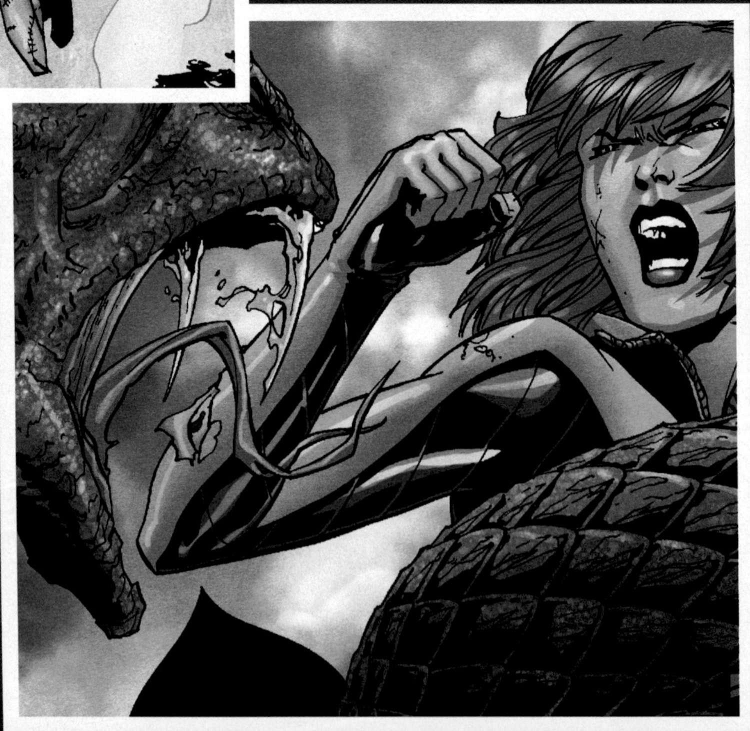

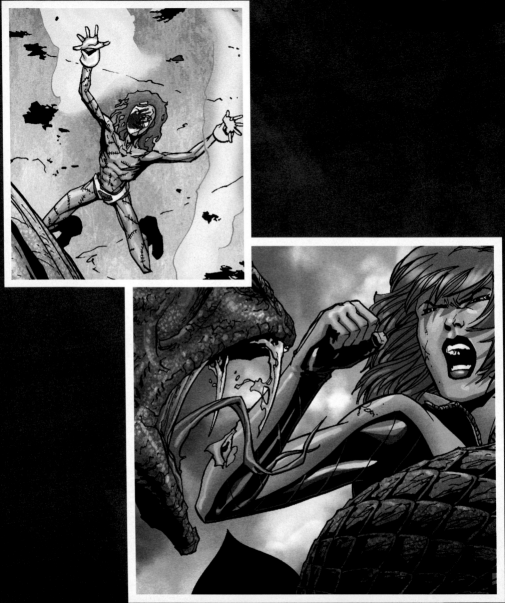

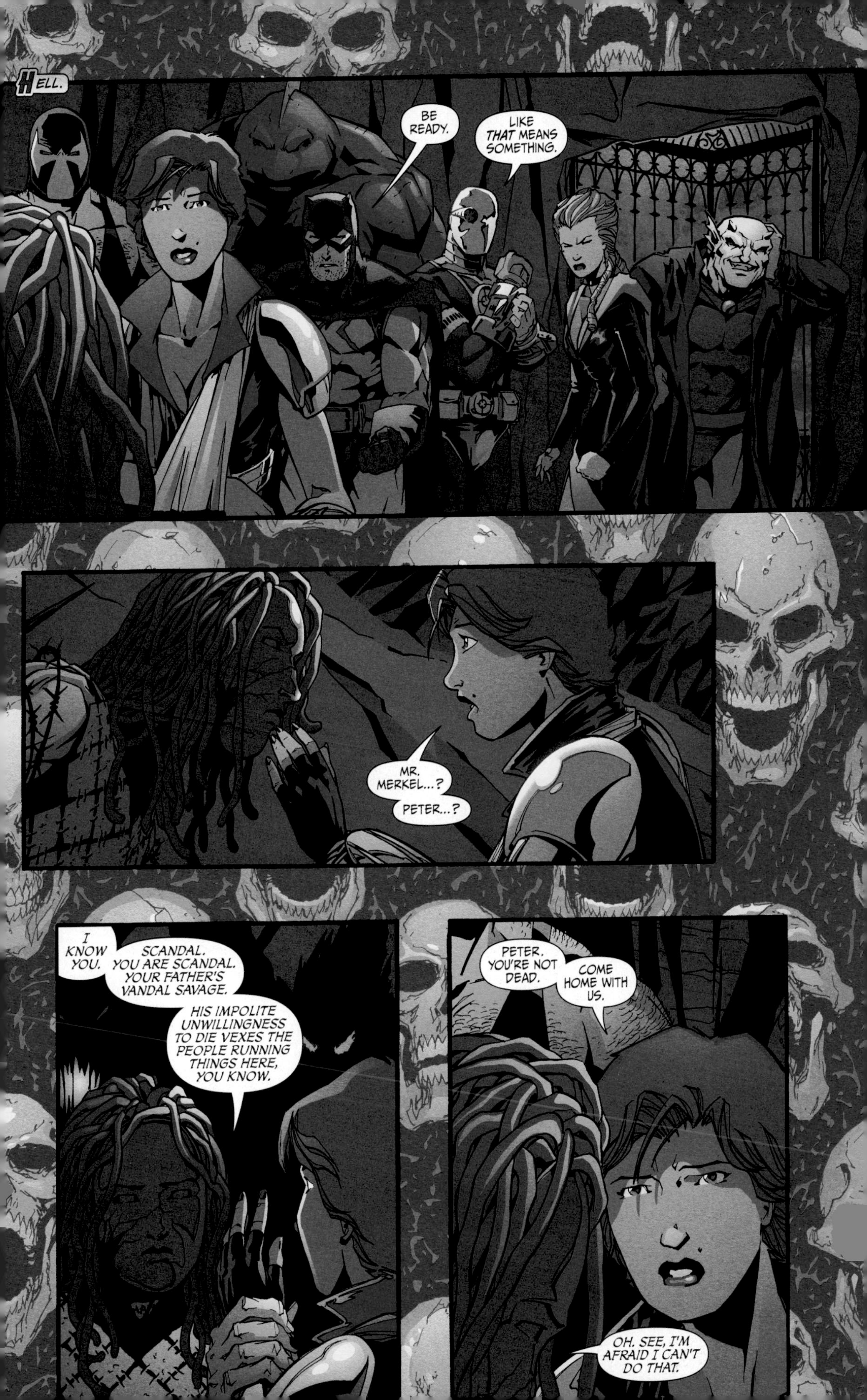
HELL.
BE READY.
LIKE THAT MEANS SOMETHING.
MR. MERKEL...?
PETER...?
I KNOW YOU.
SCANDAL. YOU ARE SCANDAL. YOUR FATHER'S VANDAL SAVAGE.
HIS IMPOLITE UNWILLINGNESS TO DIE VEXES THE PEOPLE RUNNING THINGS HERE, YOU KNOW.
PETER. YOU'RE NOT DEAD.
COME HOME WITH US.
OH. SEE, I'M AFRAID I CAN'T DO THAT.

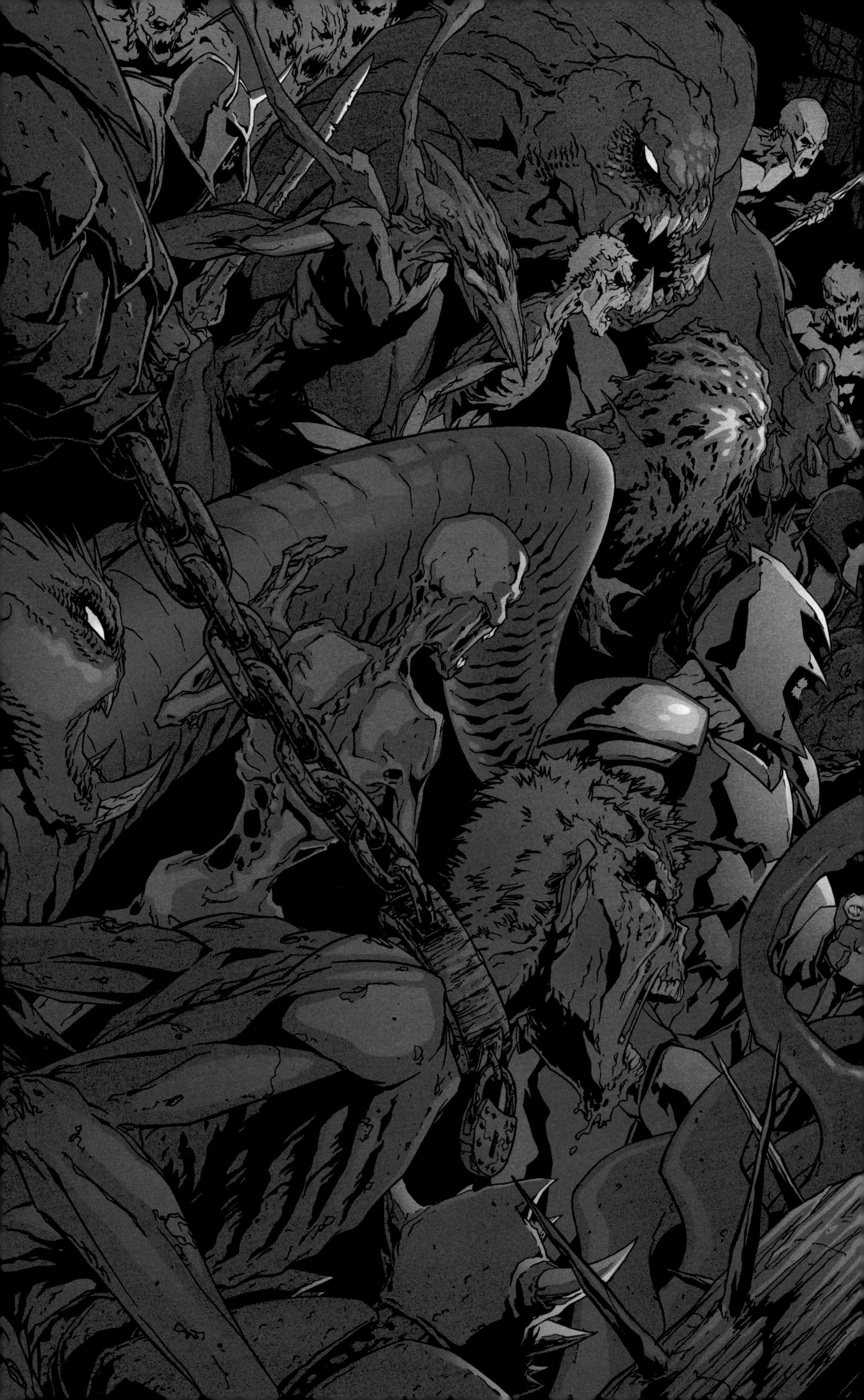

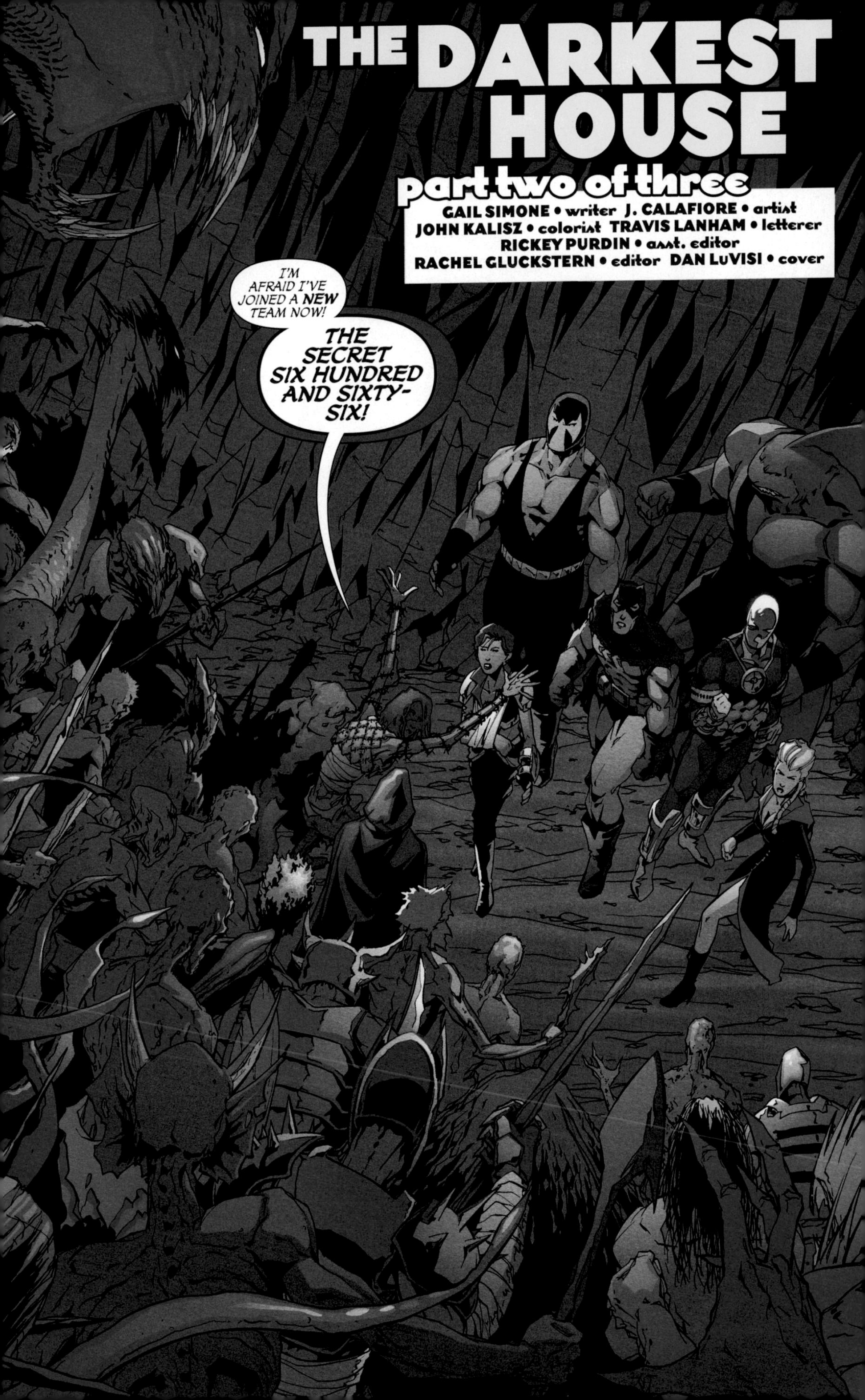
THE DARKEST HOUSE
part two of three
GAIL SIMONE • writer J. CALAFIORE • artist
JOHN KALISZ • colorist TRAVIS LANHAM • letterer
RICKEY PURDIN • asst. editor
RACHEL GLUCKSTERN • editor DAN LuVISI • cover
I'M AFRAID I'VE JOINED A NEW TEAM NOW!
THE SECRET SIX HUNDRED AND SIXTY-SIX!

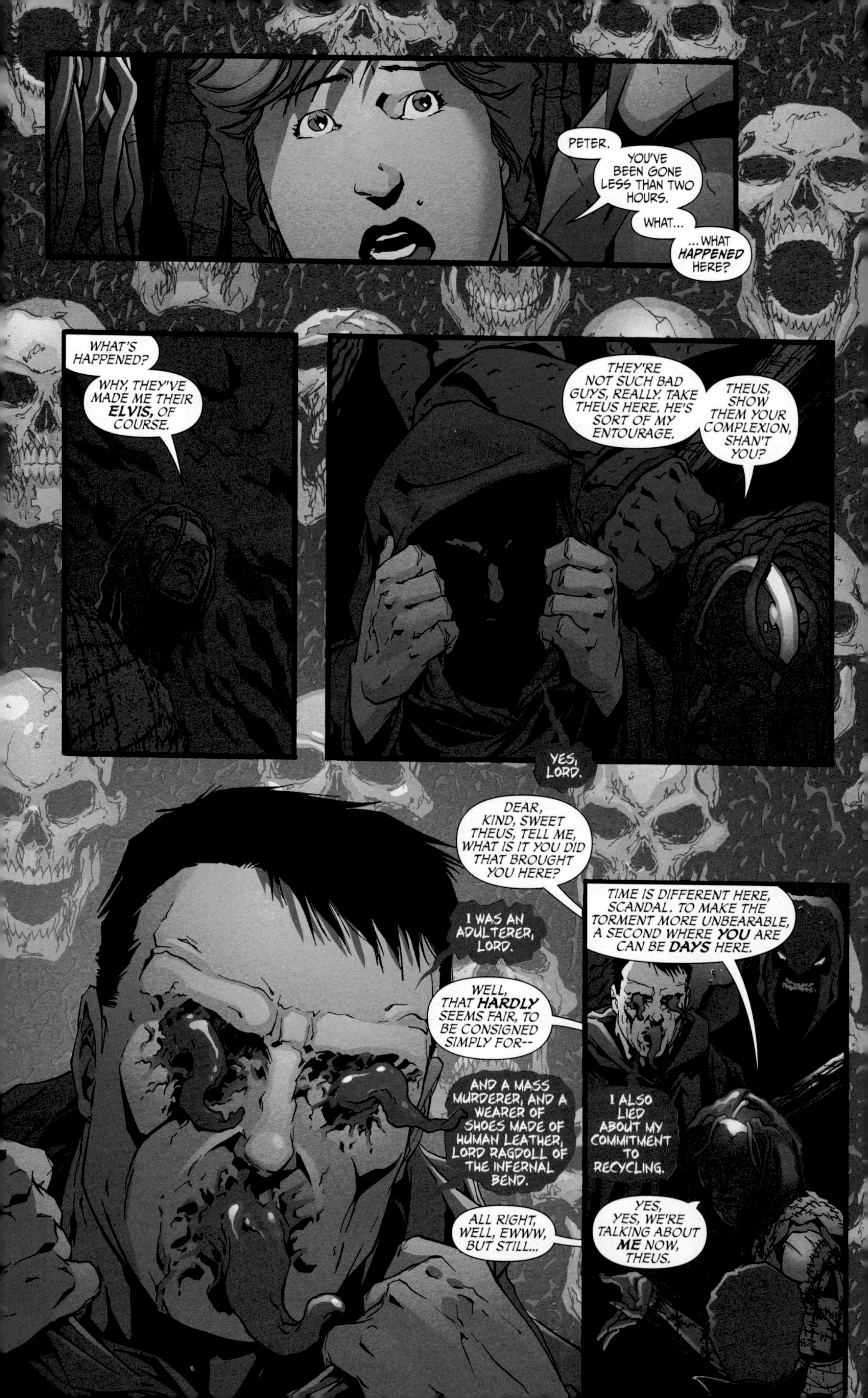
PETER.
YOU'VE BEEN GONE LESS THAN TWO HOURS.
WHAT...
...WHAT HAPPENED HERE?
WHAT'S HAPPENED?
WHY, THEY'VE MADE ME THEIR ELVIS, OF COURSE.
THEY'RE NOT SUCH BAD GUYS, REALLY. TAKE THEUS HERE. HE'S SORT OF MY ENTOURAGE.
THEUS, SHOW THEM YOUR COMPLEXION, SHAN'T YOU?
YES, LORD.
DEAR, KIND, SWEET THEUS, TELL ME, WHAT IS IT YOU DID THAT BROUGHT YOU HERE?
I WAS AN ADULTERER, LORD.
WELL, THAT HARDLY SEEMS FAIR, TO BE CONSIGNED SIMPLY FOR--
AND A MASS MURDERER, AND A WEARER OF SHOES MADE OF HUMAN LEATHER, LORD RAGDOLL OF THE INFERNAL BEND.
ALL RIGHT, WELL, EWWW, BUT STILL...
TIME IS DIFFERENT HERE, SCANDAL. TO MAKE THE TORMENT MORE UNBEARABLE, A SECOND WHERE YOU ARE CAN BE DAYS HERE.
I ALSO LIED ABOUT MY COMMITMENT TO RECYCLING.
YES, YES, WE'RE TALKING ABOUT ME NOW, THEUS.

EAREST
:ANDAL.

"...THAT SETS ONE PERSON FREE FROM HELL FOREVER. YOU SAID IT WAS LOST.

"YOU LIED AND YOU BETRAYED THOSE WHO TRUSTED YOU.

"SO I **TOOK** IT.

"AND I WISHED MYSELF **HERE**, TO THIS PLACE.

"MY **GUTS** WERE FALLING OUT, THANKS TO YOUR PESKY BLADES.

"YOU DIDN'T HAPPEN TO STERILIZE THEM BEFORE YOU STABBED ME, DID YOU?

"DON'T REMEMBER ANYTHING ELSE AFTER A WHILE, I'M AFRAID.

"BUT ALL **MANNER** OF LOATHSOME THINGS MAY HAVE HAD THEIR WAY WITH ME.

"AND I MISSED **ALL** OF IT!

"WHEN I AWOKE, I'D BEEN CLEANED AND SUTURED.

"**LOVELY** STITCHING, REALLY, IT'S SOMETHING TO SEE!

"AND THEY SAID I WAS TO BE THE NEW ROYAL DIGNITARY, ADVISOR TO LADY BLAZE, WHO RULES THIS LAND WITH AN IRON **FIST**.

"THEY'VE EVEN CHOSEN A MATE FOR ME, A MARRIAGE OF STATE TO SOLIDIFY MY **POSITION**.

"PETER MERKEL, JR., PRINCE OF ALL **HELL**."

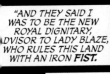

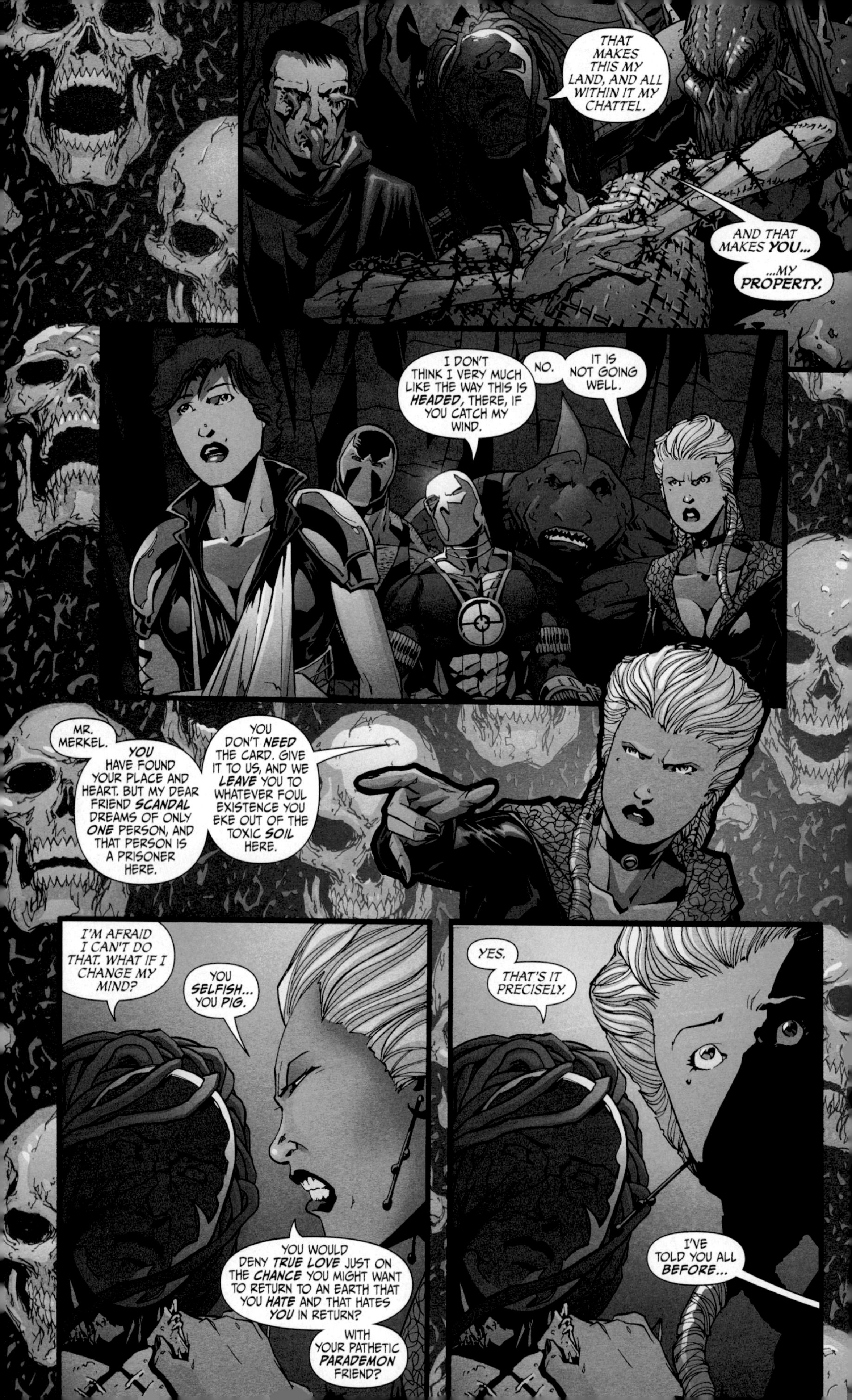
THAT MAKES THIS MY LAND, AND ALL WITHIN IT MY CHATTEL.
AND THAT MAKES YOU...
...MY PROPERTY.
I DON'T THINK I VERY MUCH LIKE THE WAY THIS IS HEADED, THERE, IF YOU CATCH MY WIND.
NO.
IT IS NOT GOING WELL.
MR. MERKEL.
YOU HAVE FOUND YOUR PLACE AND HEART. BUT MY DEAR FRIEND SCANDAL DREAMS OF ONLY ONE PERSON, AND THAT PERSON IS A PRISONER HERE.
YOU DON'T NEED THE CARD. GIVE IT TO US, AND WE LEAVE YOU TO WHATEVER FOUL EXISTENCE YOU EKE OUT OF THE TOXIC SOIL HERE.
I'M AFRAID I CAN'T DO THAT. WHAT IF I CHANGE MY MIND?
YOU SELFISH... YOU PIG.
YOU WOULD DENY TRUE LOVE JUST ON THE CHANCE YOU MIGHT WANT TO RETURN TO AN EARTH THAT YOU HATE AND THAT HATES YOU IN RETURN?
WITH YOUR PATHETIC PARADEMON FRIEND?
YES.
THAT'S IT PRECISELY.
I'VE TOLD YOU ALL BEFORE...

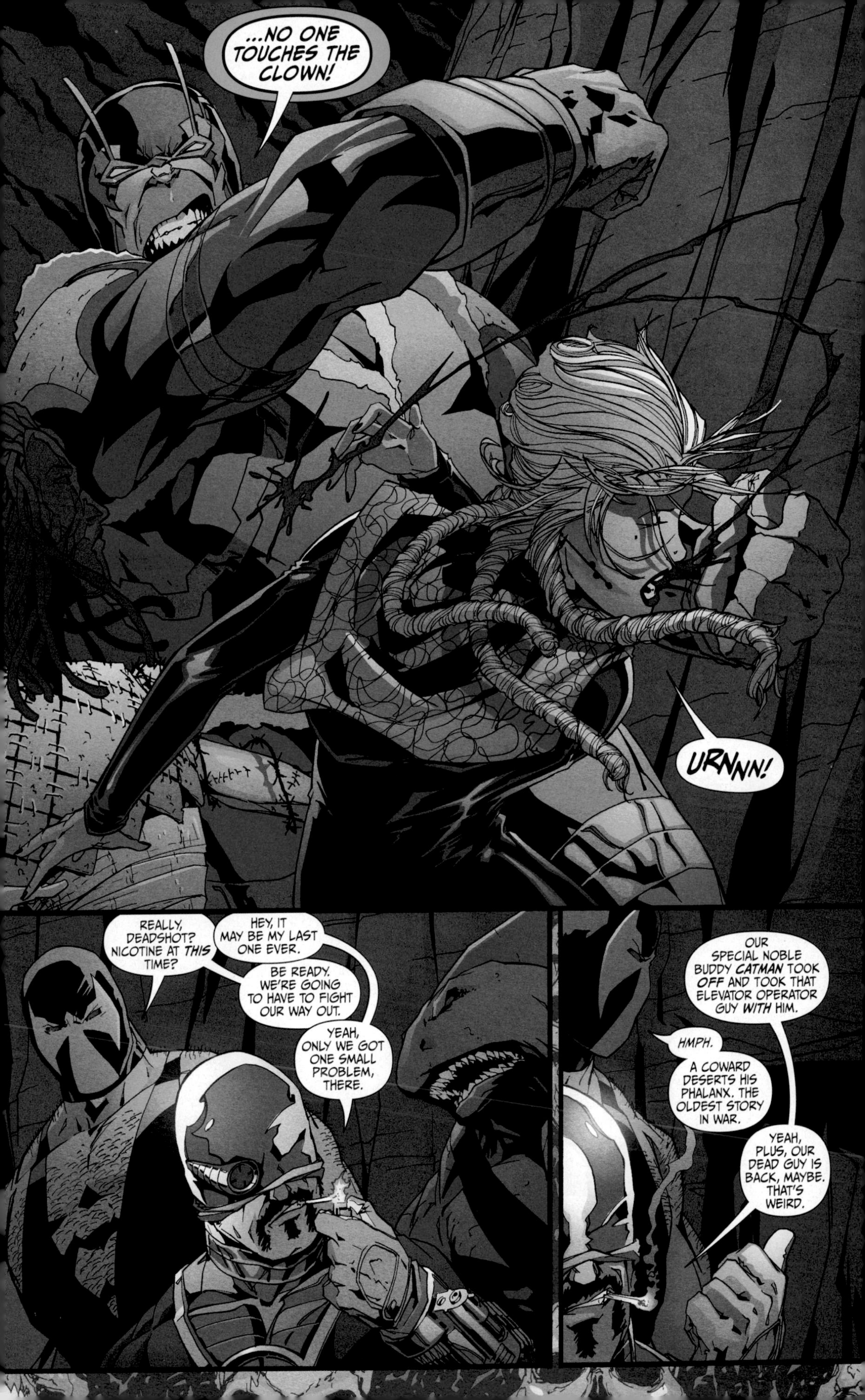
...NO ONE TOUCHES THE CLOWN!
URNNN!
REALLY, DEADSHOT? NICOTINE AT *THIS* TIME?
HEY, IT MAY BE MY LAST ONE EVER.
BE READY. WE'RE GOING TO HAVE TO FIGHT OUR WAY OUT.
YEAH, ONLY WE GOT ONE SMALL PROBLEM, THERE.
OUR SPECIAL NOBLE BUDDY *CATMAN* TOOK *OFF* AND TOOK THAT ELEVATOR OPERATOR GUY *WITH* HIM.
HMPH.
A COWARD DESERTS HIS PHALANX. THE OLDEST STORY IN WAR.
YEAH, PLUS, OUR DEAD GUY IS BACK, MAYBE. THAT'S WEIRD.

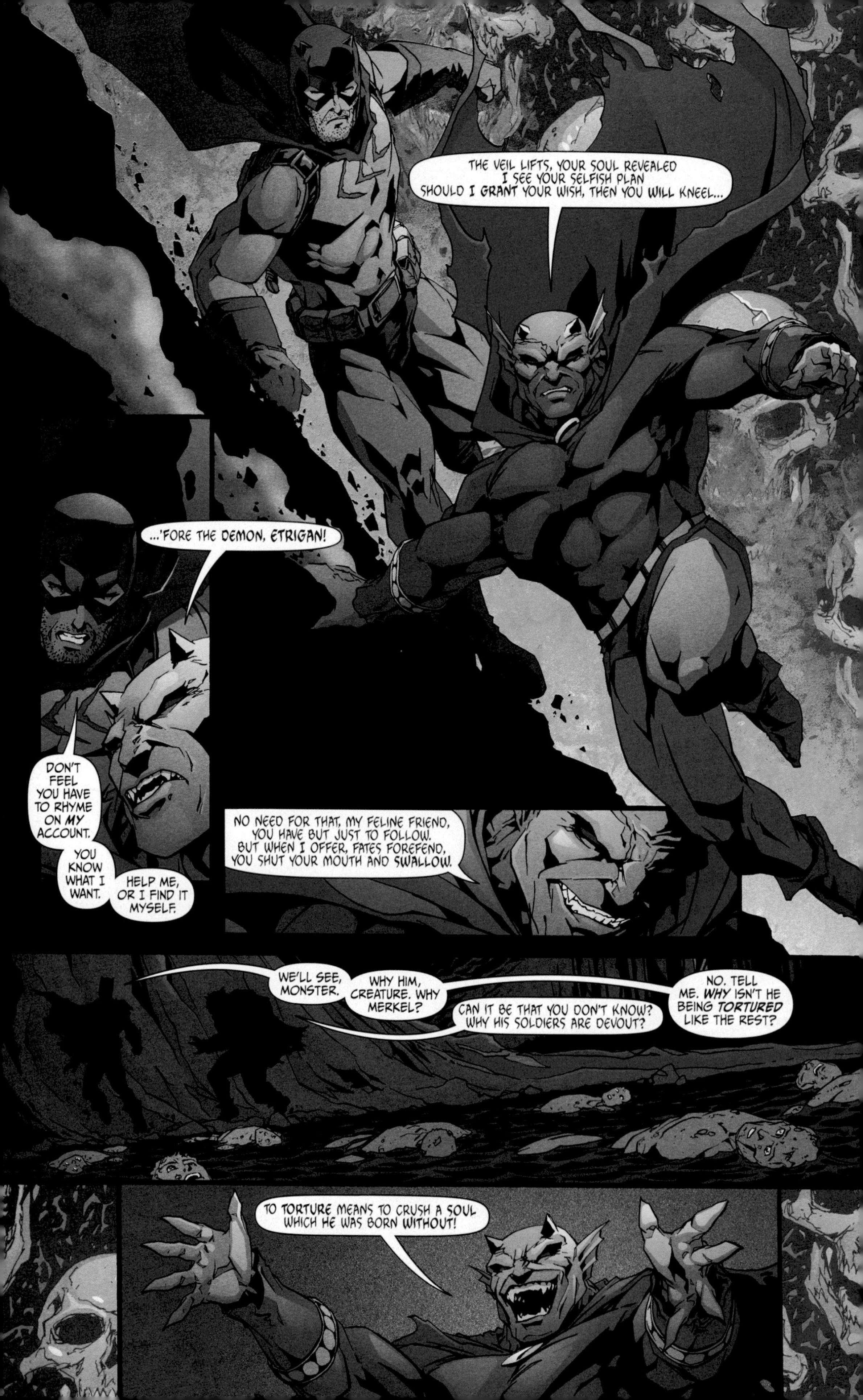
THE VEIL LIFTS, YOUR SOUL REVEALED
I SEE YOUR SELFISH PLAN
SHOULD I GRANT YOUR WISH, THEN YOU WILL KNEEL...
...'FORE THE DEMON, ETRIGAN!
DON'T FEEL YOU HAVE TO RHYME ON MY ACCOUNT.
YOU KNOW WHAT I WANT.
HELP ME, OR I FIND IT MYSELF.
NO NEED FOR THAT, MY FELINE FRIEND, YOU HAVE BUT JUST TO FOLLOW. BUT WHEN I OFFER, FATES FOREFEND, YOU SHUT YOUR MOUTH AND SWALLOW.
WE'LL SEE, MONSTER.
WHY HIM, CREATURE. WHY MERKEL?
NO. TELL ME. WHY ISN'T HE BEING TORTURED LIKE THE REST?
CAN IT BE THAT YOU DON'T KNOW? WHY HIS SOLDIERS ARE DEVOUT?
TO TORTURE MEANS TO CRUSH A SOUL WHICH HE WAS BORN WITHOUT!

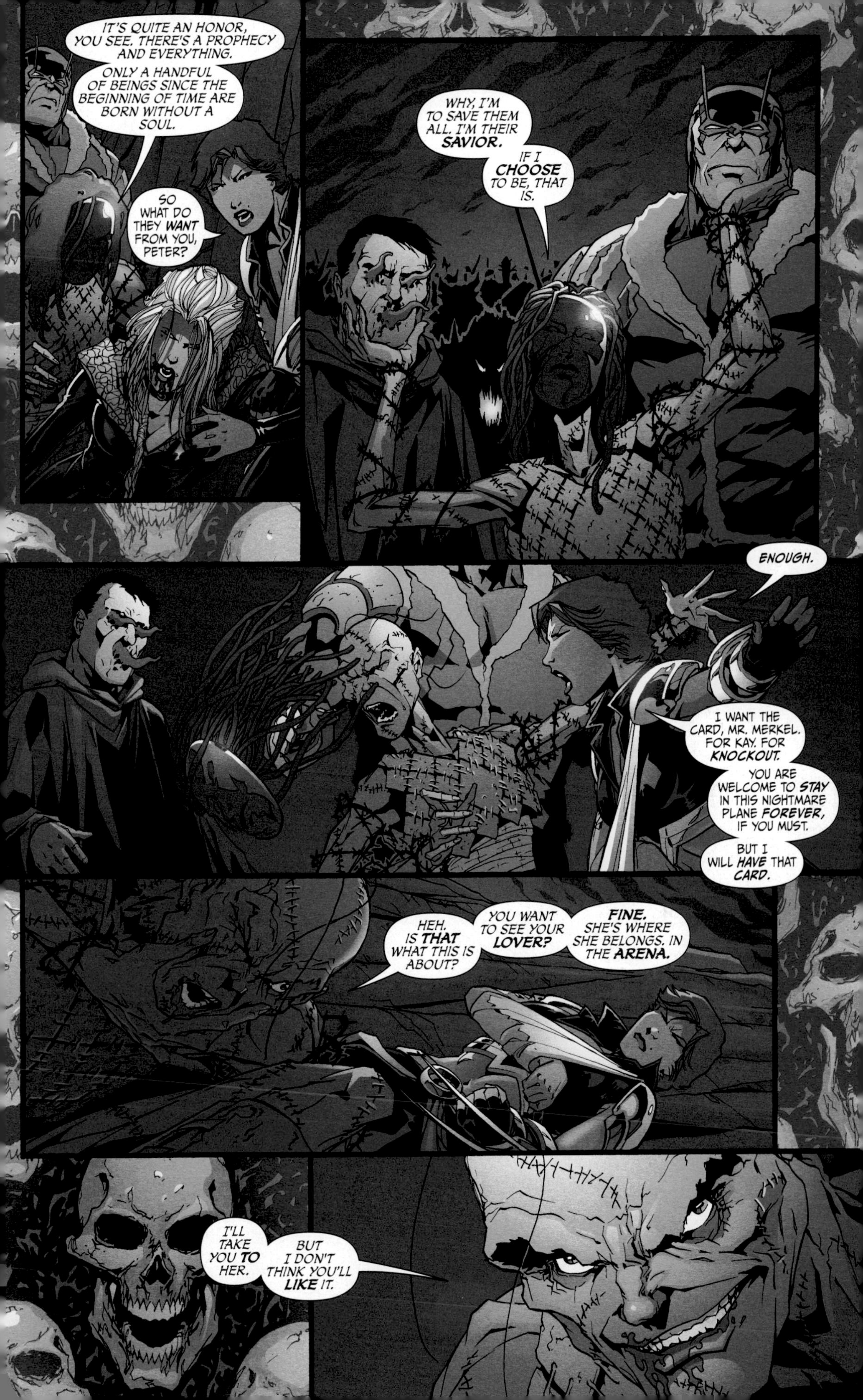
IT'S QUITE AN HONOR, YOU SEE. THERE'S A PROPHECY AND EVERYTHING.
ONLY A HANDFUL OF BEINGS SINCE THE BEGINNING OF TIME ARE BORN WITHOUT A SOUL.
SO WHAT DO THEY WANT FROM YOU, PETER?
WHY, I'M TO SAVE THEM ALL. I'M THEIR SAVIOR.
IF I CHOOSE TO BE, THAT IS.
ENOUGH.
I WANT THE CARD, MR. MERKEL. FOR KAY. FOR KNOCKOUT.
YOU ARE WELCOME TO STAY IN THIS NIGHTMARE PLANE FOREVER, IF YOU MUST.
BUT I WILL HAVE THAT CARD.
HEH. IS THAT WHAT THIS IS ABOUT?
YOU WANT TO SEE YOUR LOVER?
FINE. SHE'S WHERE SHE BELONGS. IN THE ARENA.
I'LL TAKE YOU TO HER.
BUT I DON'T THINK YOU'LL LIKE IT.

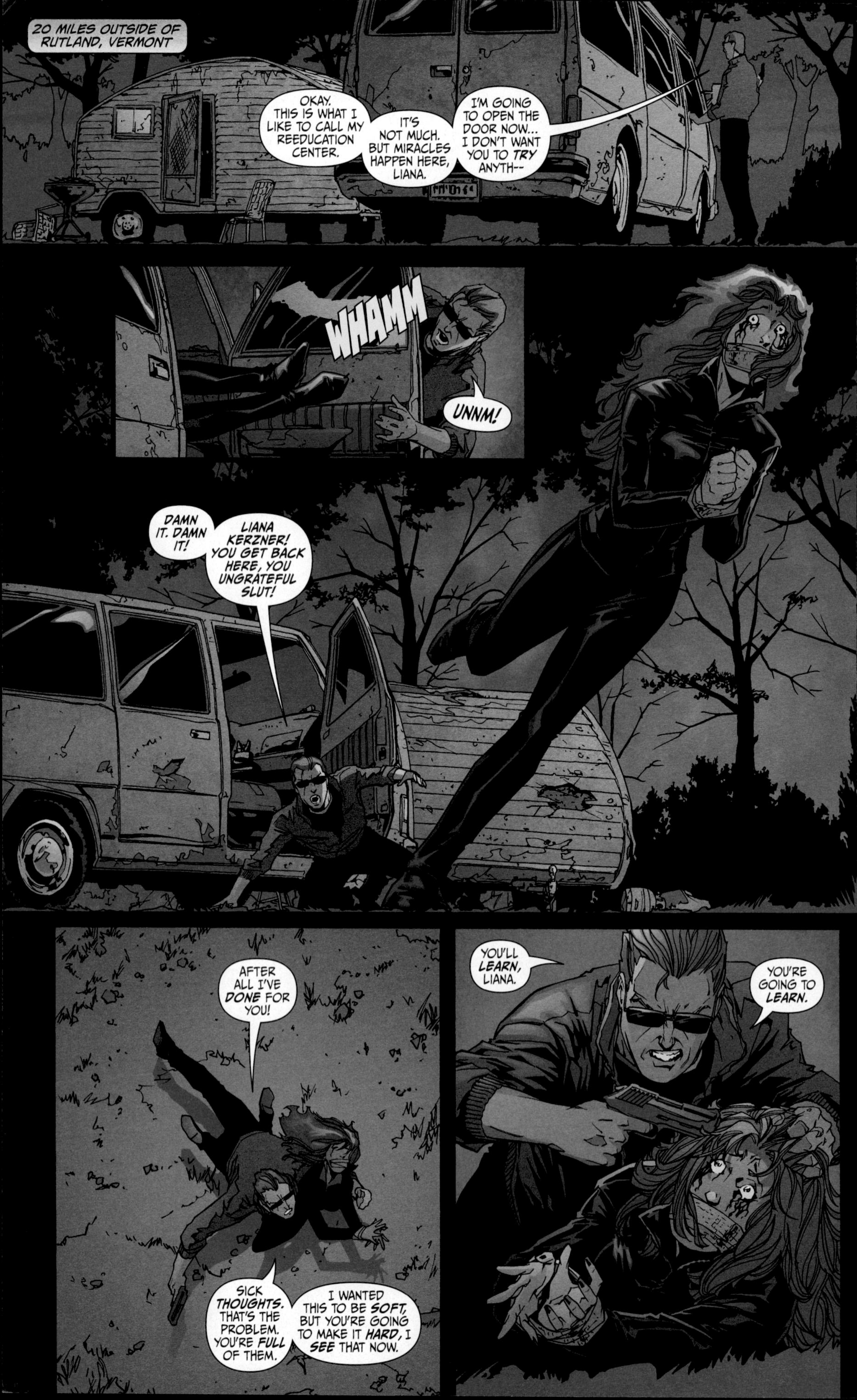

20 MILES OUTSIDE OF RUTLAND, VERMONT
OKAY. THIS IS WHAT I LIKE TO CALL MY REEDUCATION CENTER.
IT'S NOT MUCH. BUT MIRACLES HAPPEN HERE, LIANA.
I'M GOING TO OPEN THE DOOR NOW... I DON'T WANT YOU TO TRY ANYTH--
WHAMM
UNNM!
DAMN IT. DAMN IT!
LIANA KERZNER! YOU GET BACK HERE, YOU UNGRATEFUL SLUT!
AFTER ALL I'VE DONE FOR YOU!
SICK THOUGHTS. THAT'S THE PROBLEM. YOU'RE FULL OF THEM.
I WANTED THIS TO BE SOFT, BUT YOU'RE GOING TO MAKE IT HARD, I SEE THAT NOW.
YOU'LL LEARN, LIANA.
YOU'RE GOING TO LEARN.

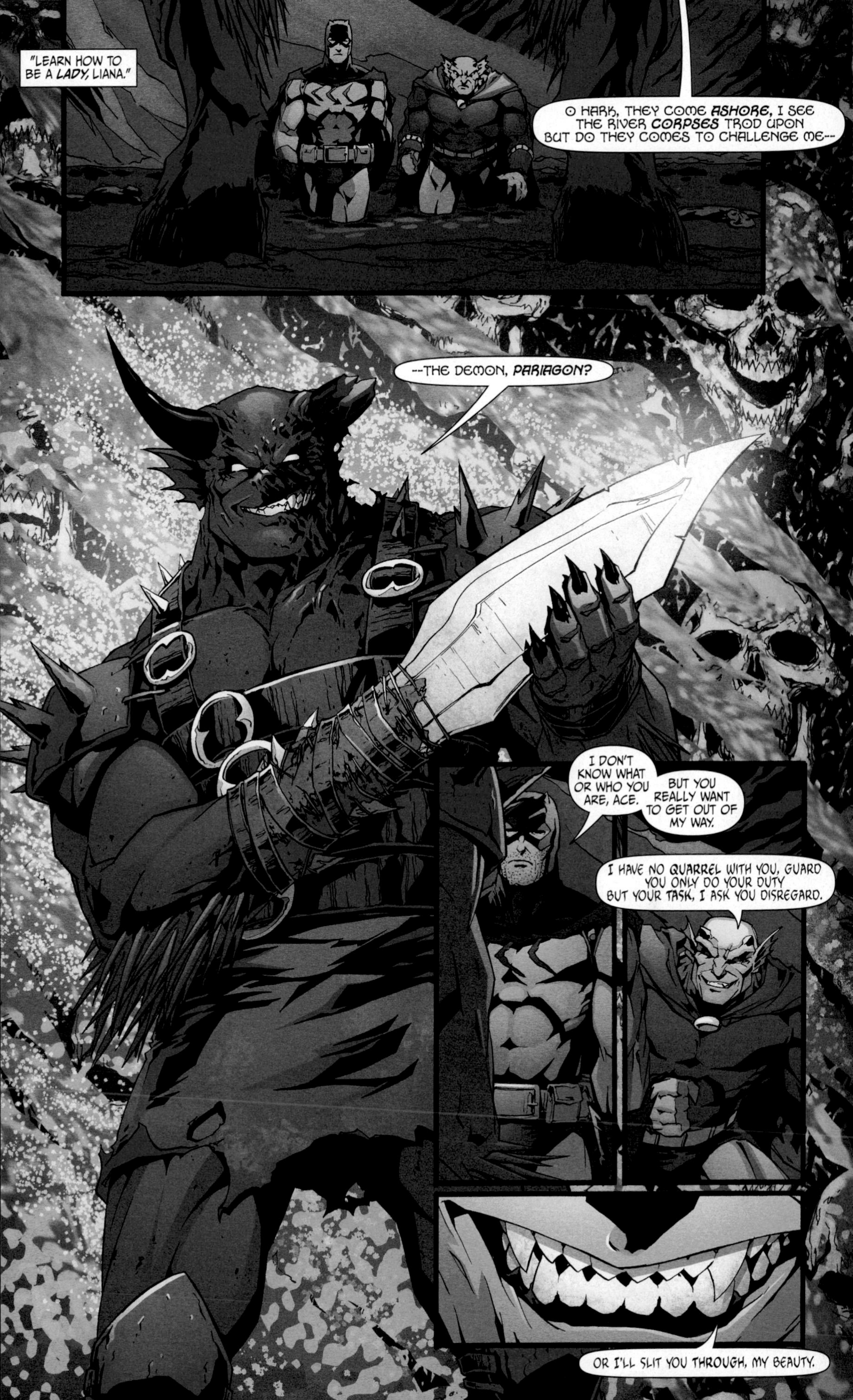
"LEARN HOW TO BE A LADY, LIANA."
O HARK, THEY COME ASHORE, I SEE THE RIVER CORPSES TROD UPON BUT DO THEY COMES TO CHALLENGE ME--
--THE DEMON, PARIAGON?
I DON'T KNOW WHAT OR WHO YOU ARE, ACE.
BUT YOU REALLY WANT TO GET OUT OF MY WAY.
I HAVE NO QUARREL WITH YOU, GUARD YOU ONLY DO YOUR DUTY BUT YOUR TASK, I ASK YOU DISREGARD.
OR I'LL SLIT YOU THROUGH, MY BEAUTY.

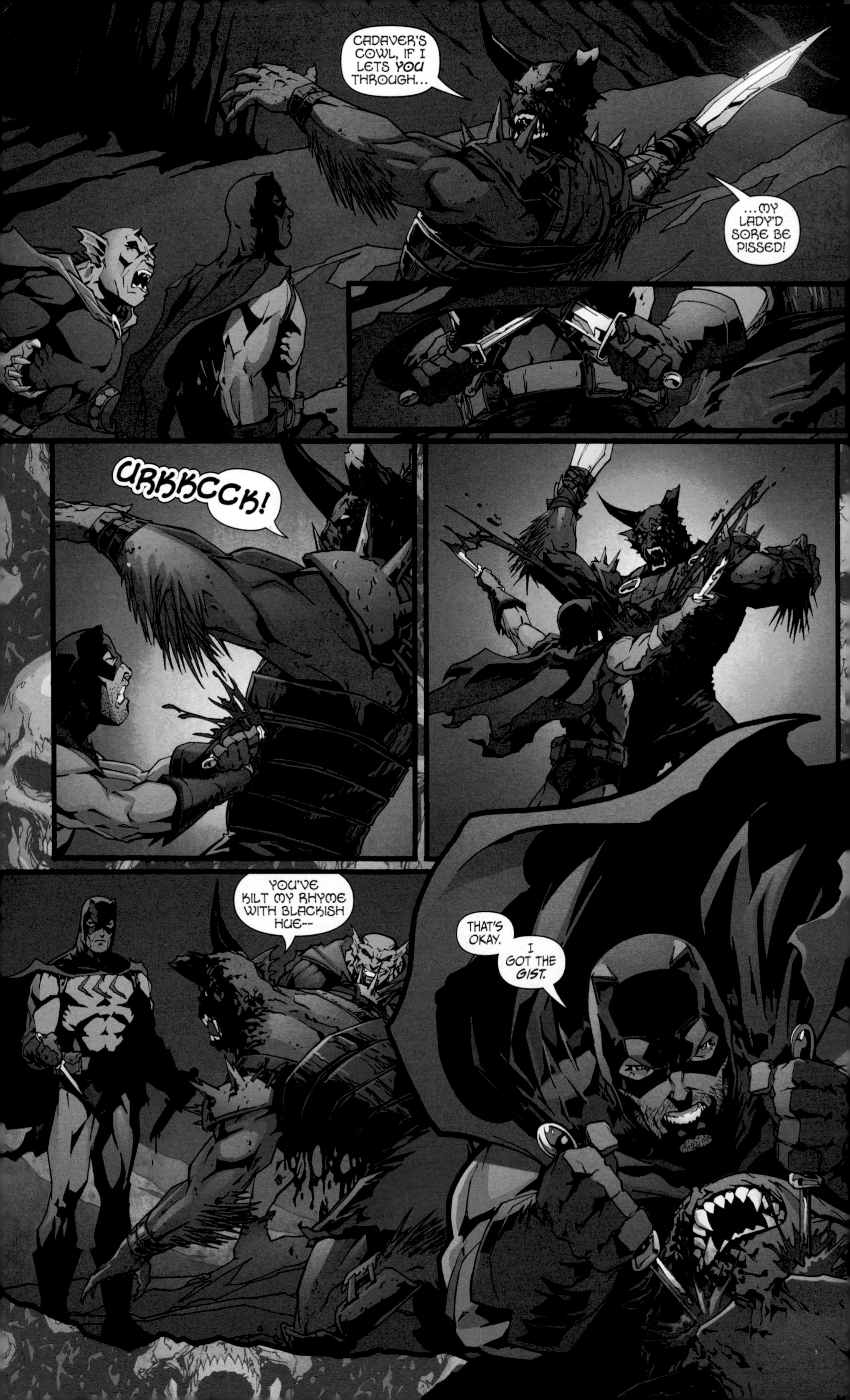
CADAVER'S COWL, IF I LETS YOU THROUGH...
...MY LADY'D SORE BE PISSED!
URKKCCK!
YOU'VE KILT MY RHYME WITH BLACKISH HUE--
THAT'S OKAY.
I GOT THE GIST.

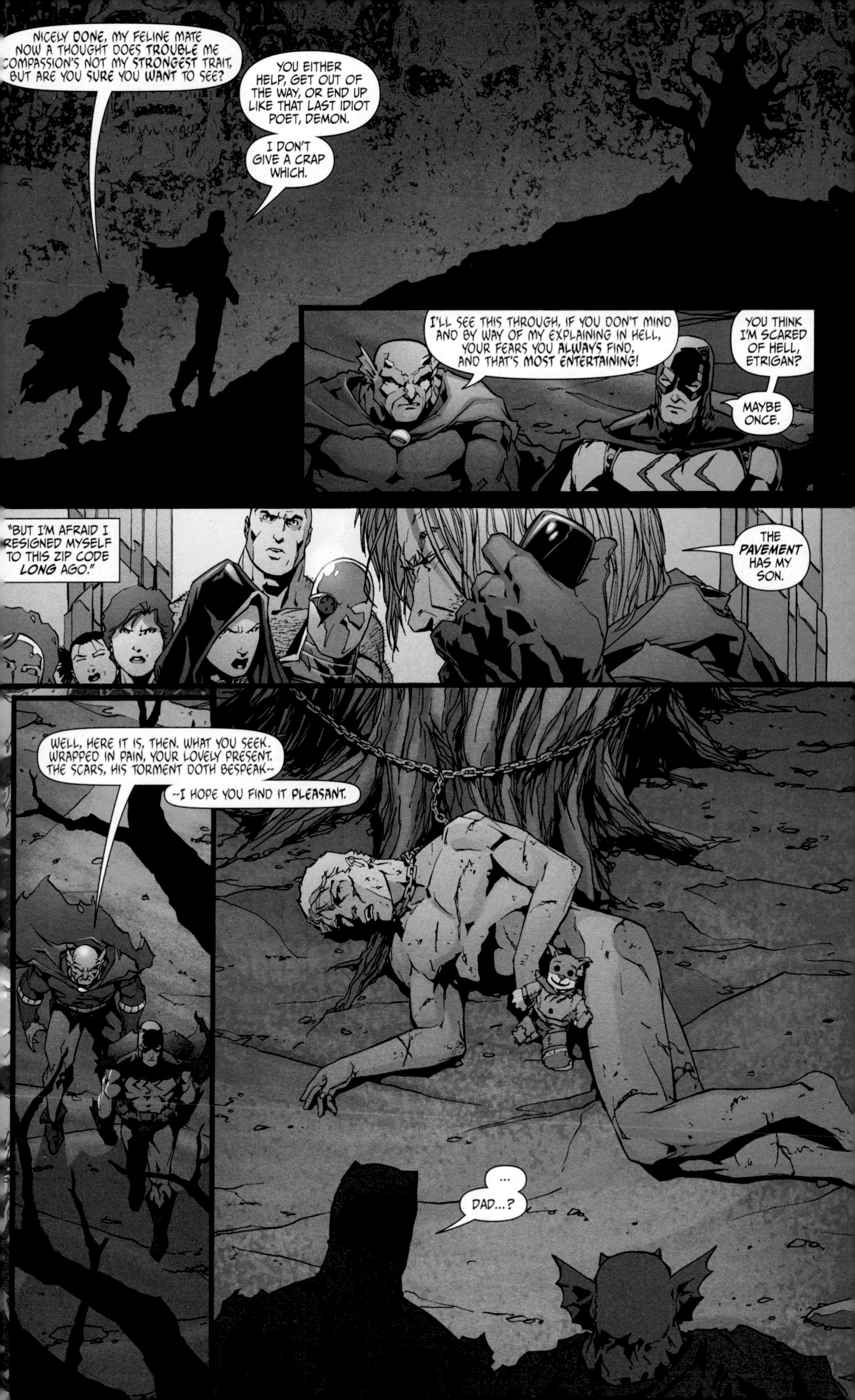
NICELY DONE, MY FELINE MATE
NOW A THOUGHT DOES TROUBLE ME
COMPASSION'S NOT MY STRONGEST TRAIT,
BUT ARE YOU SURE YOU WANT TO SEE?
YOU EITHER HELP, GET OUT OF THE WAY, OR END UP LIKE THAT LAST IDIOT POET, DEMON.
I DON'T GIVE A CRAP WHICH.
I'LL SEE THIS THROUGH, IF YOU DON'T MIND
AND BY WAY OF MY EXPLAINING IN HELL,
YOUR FEARS YOU ALWAYS FIND,
AND THAT'S MOST ENTERTAINING!
YOU THINK I'M SCARED OF HELL, ETRIGAN?
MAYBE ONCE.
"BUT I'M AFRAID I RESIGNED MYSELF TO THIS ZIP CODE LONG AGO."
THE PAVEMENT HAS MY SON.
WELL, HERE IT IS, THEN. WHAT YOU SEEK.
WRAPPED IN PAIN, YOUR LOVELY PRESENT.
THE SCARS, HIS TORMENT DOTH BESPEAK--
--I HOPE YOU FIND IT PLEASANT.
...
DAD...?

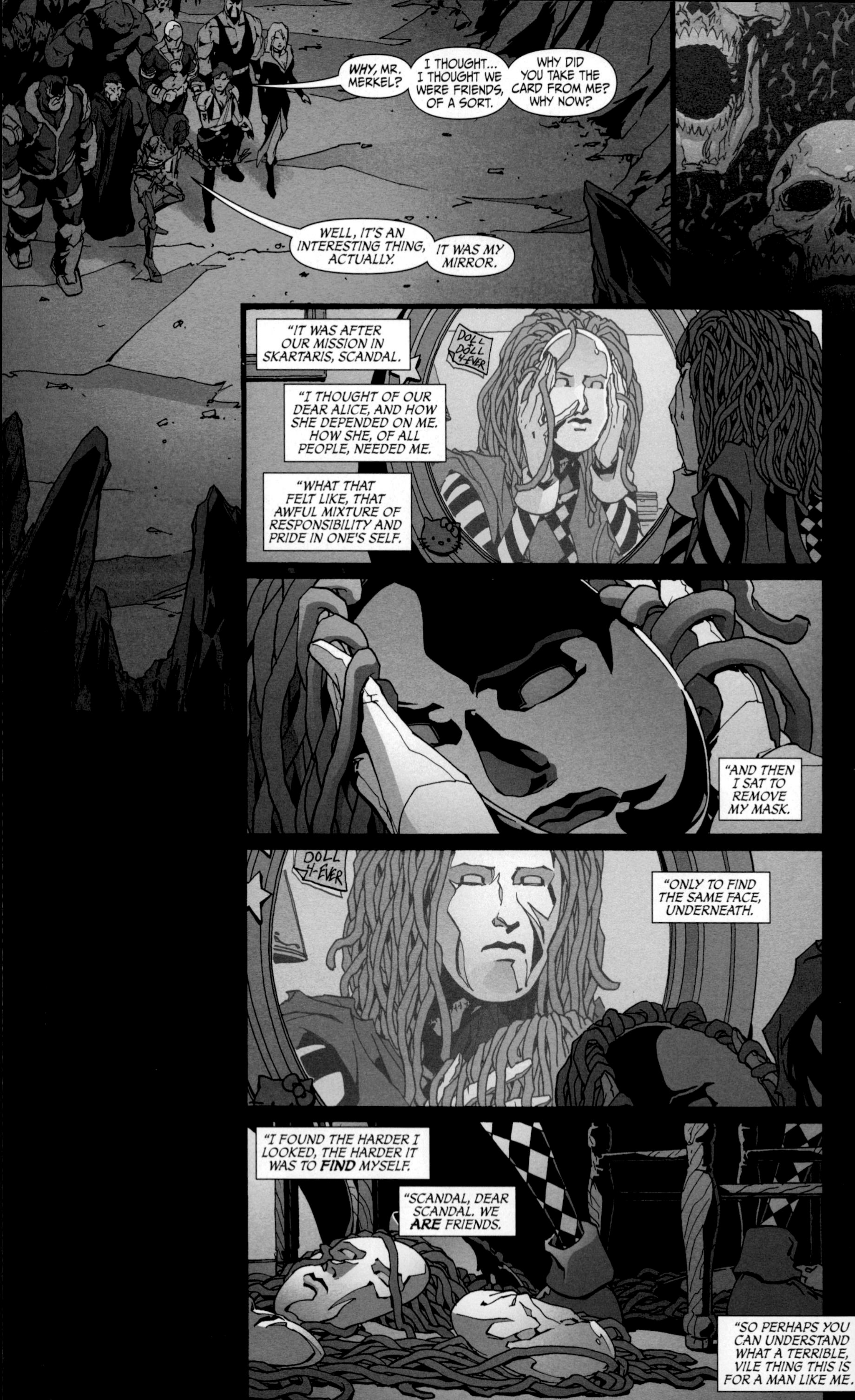
WHY, MR. MERKEL?
I THOUGHT... I THOUGHT WE WERE FRIENDS, OF A SORT.
WHY DID YOU TAKE THE CARD FROM ME? WHY NOW?
WELL, IT'S AN INTERESTING THING, ACTUALLY.
IT WAS MY MIRROR.
"IT WAS AFTER OUR MISSION IN SKARTARIS, SCANDAL.
DOLL DOLL 4-EVER
"I THOUGHT OF OUR DEAR ALICE, AND HOW SHE DEPENDED ON ME. HOW SHE, OF ALL PEOPLE, NEEDED ME.
"WHAT THAT FELT LIKE, THAT AWFUL MIXTURE OF RESPONSIBILITY AND PRIDE IN ONE'S SELF.
"AND THEN I SAT TO REMOVE MY MASK.
DOLL 4-EVER
"ONLY TO FIND THE SAME FACE, UNDERNEATH.
"I FOUND THE HARDER I LOOKED, THE HARDER IT WAS TO FIND MYSELF.
"SCANDAL, DEAR SCANDAL. WE ARE FRIENDS.
"SO PERHAPS YOU CAN UNDERSTAND WHAT A TERRIBLE, VILE THING THIS IS FOR A MAN LIKE ME.

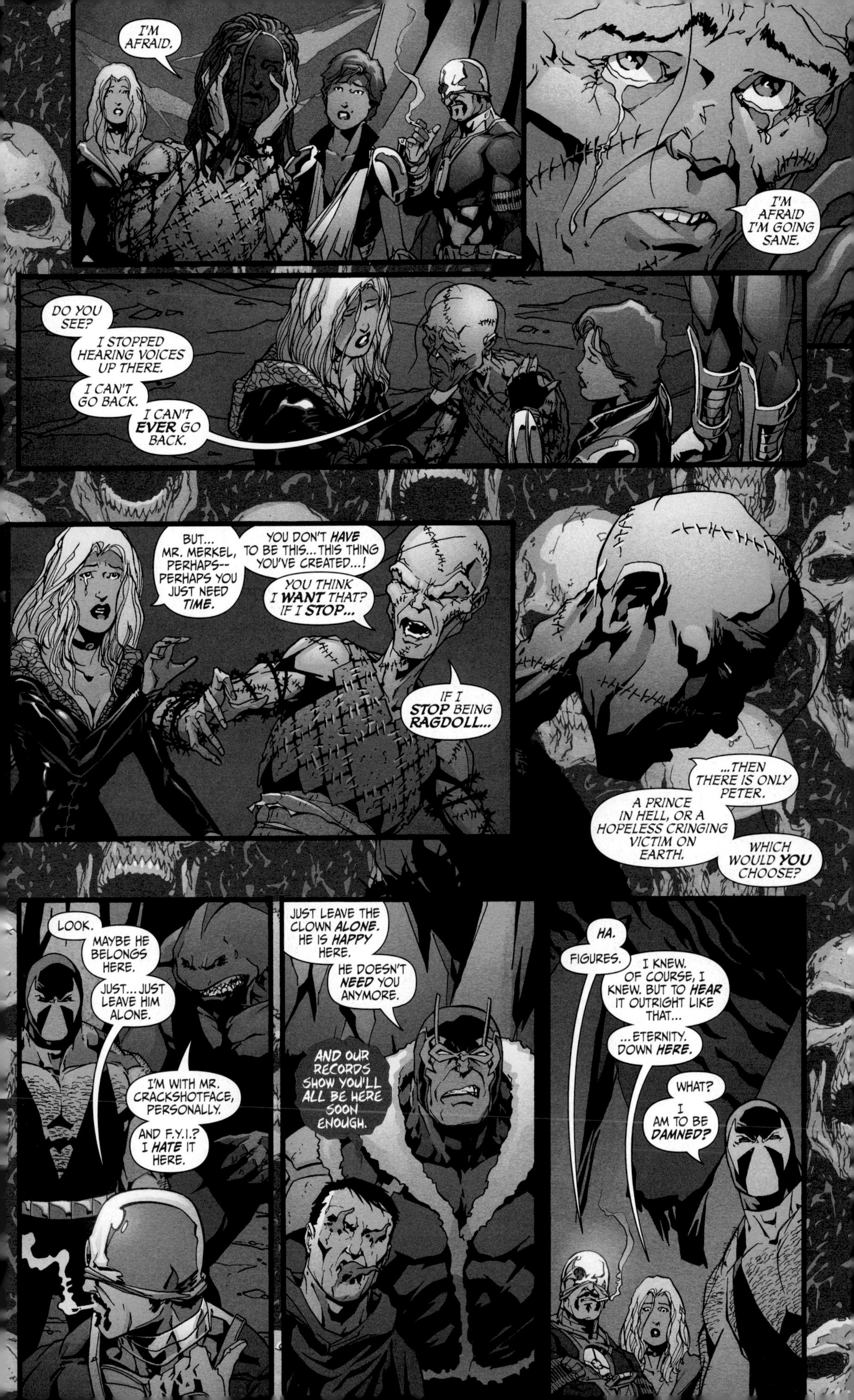
I'M AFRAID.
I'M AFRAID I'M GOING SANE.
DO YOU SEE?
I STOPPED HEARING VOICES UP THERE.
I CAN'T GO BACK.
I CAN'T EVER GO BACK.
BUT... MR. MERKEL, PERHAPS-- PERHAPS YOU JUST NEED TIME.
YOU DON'T HAVE TO BE THIS... THIS THING YOU'VE CREATED...!
YOU THINK I WANT THAT? IF I STOP...
IF I STOP BEING RAGDOLL...
...THEN THERE IS ONLY PETER.
A PRINCE IN HELL, OR A HOPELESS CRINGING VICTIM ON EARTH.
WHICH WOULD YOU CHOOSE?
LOOK.
MAYBE HE BELONGS HERE.
JUST... JUST LEAVE HIM ALONE.
I'M WITH MR. CRACKSHOTFACE, PERSONALLY.
AND F.Y.I.? I HATE IT HERE.
JUST LEAVE THE CLOWN ALONE. HE IS HAPPY HERE.
HE DOESN'T NEED YOU ANYMORE.
AND OUR RECORDS SHOW YOU'LL ALL BE HERE SOON ENOUGH.
HA.
FIGURES.
I KNEW. OF COURSE, I KNEW. BUT TO HEAR IT OUTRIGHT LIKE THAT...
...ETERNITY. DOWN HERE.
WHAT?
I AM TO BE DAMNED?

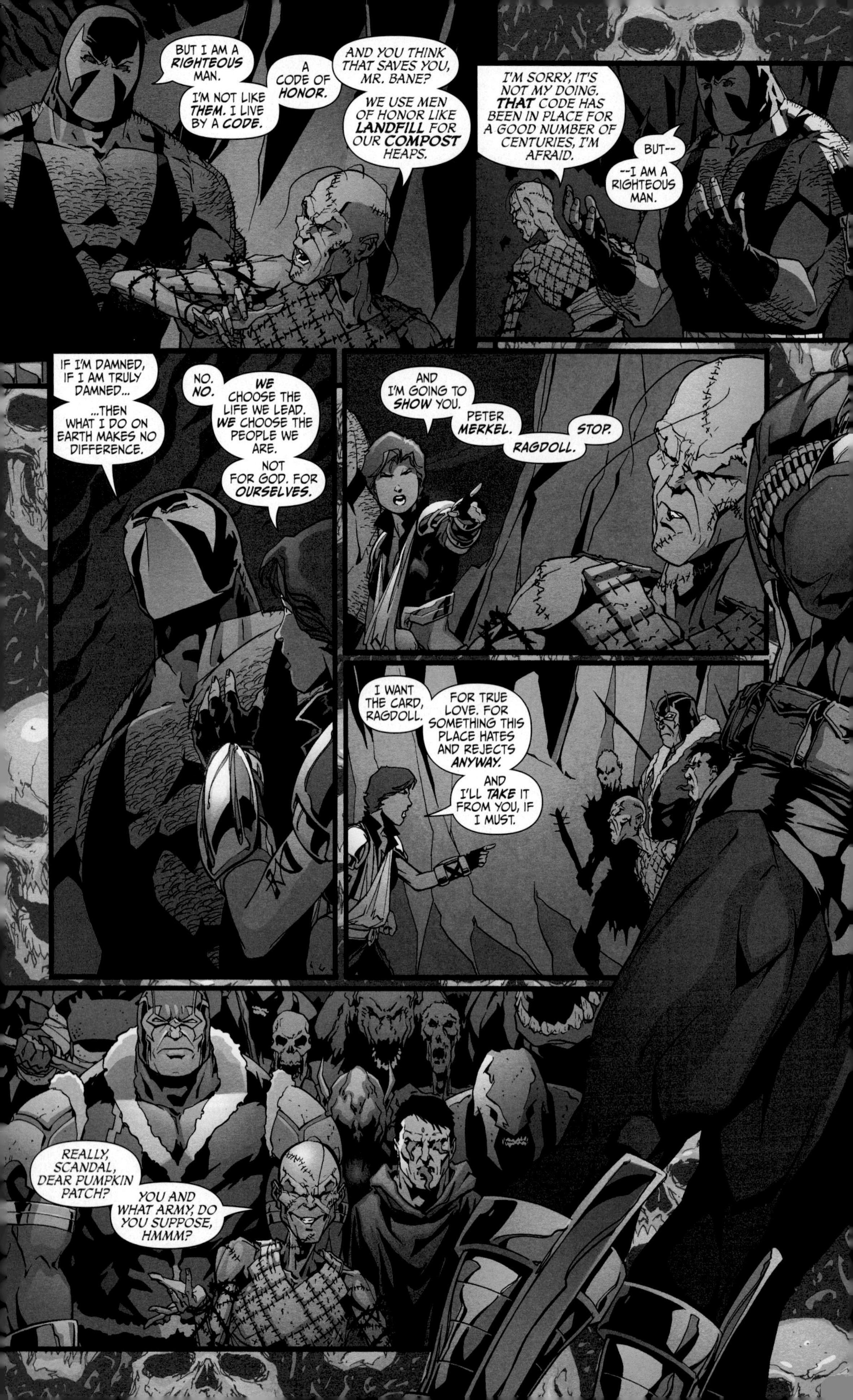
BUT I AM A RIGHTEOUS MAN.
I'M NOT LIKE THEM. I LIVE BY A CODE.
A CODE OF HONOR.
AND YOU THINK THAT SAVES YOU, MR. BANE?
WE USE MEN OF HONOR LIKE LANDFILL FOR OUR COMPOST HEAPS.
I'M SORRY, IT'S NOT MY DOING. THAT CODE HAS BEEN IN PLACE FOR A GOOD NUMBER OF CENTURIES, I'M AFRAID.
BUT--
--I AM A RIGHTEOUS MAN.
IF I'M DAMNED, IF I AM TRULY DAMNED...
...THEN WHAT I DO ON EARTH MAKES NO DIFFERENCE.
NO. NO.
WE CHOOSE THE LIFE WE LEAD. WE CHOOSE THE PEOPLE WE ARE.
NOT FOR GOD. FOR OURSELVES.
AND I'M GOING TO SHOW YOU.
PETER MERKEL.
RAGDOLL.
STOP.
I WANT THE CARD, RAGDOLL.
FOR TRUE LOVE. FOR SOMETHING THIS PLACE HATES AND REJECTS ANYWAY.
AND I'LL TAKE IT FROM YOU, IF I MUST.
REALLY, SCANDAL, DEAR PUMPKIN PATCH?
YOU AND WHAT ARMY, DO YOU SUPPOSE, HMMM?

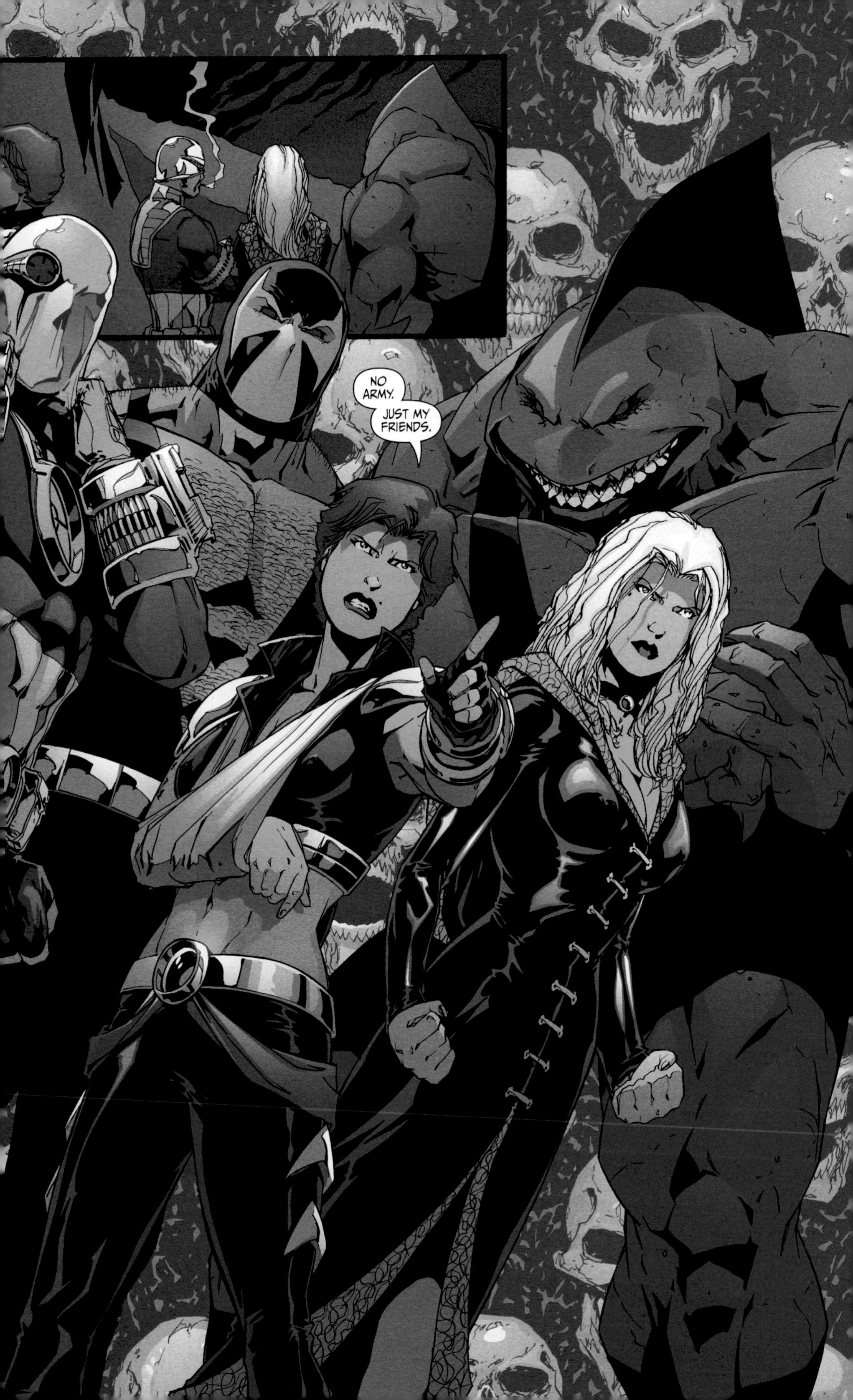
NO ARMY.
JUST MY FRIENDS.

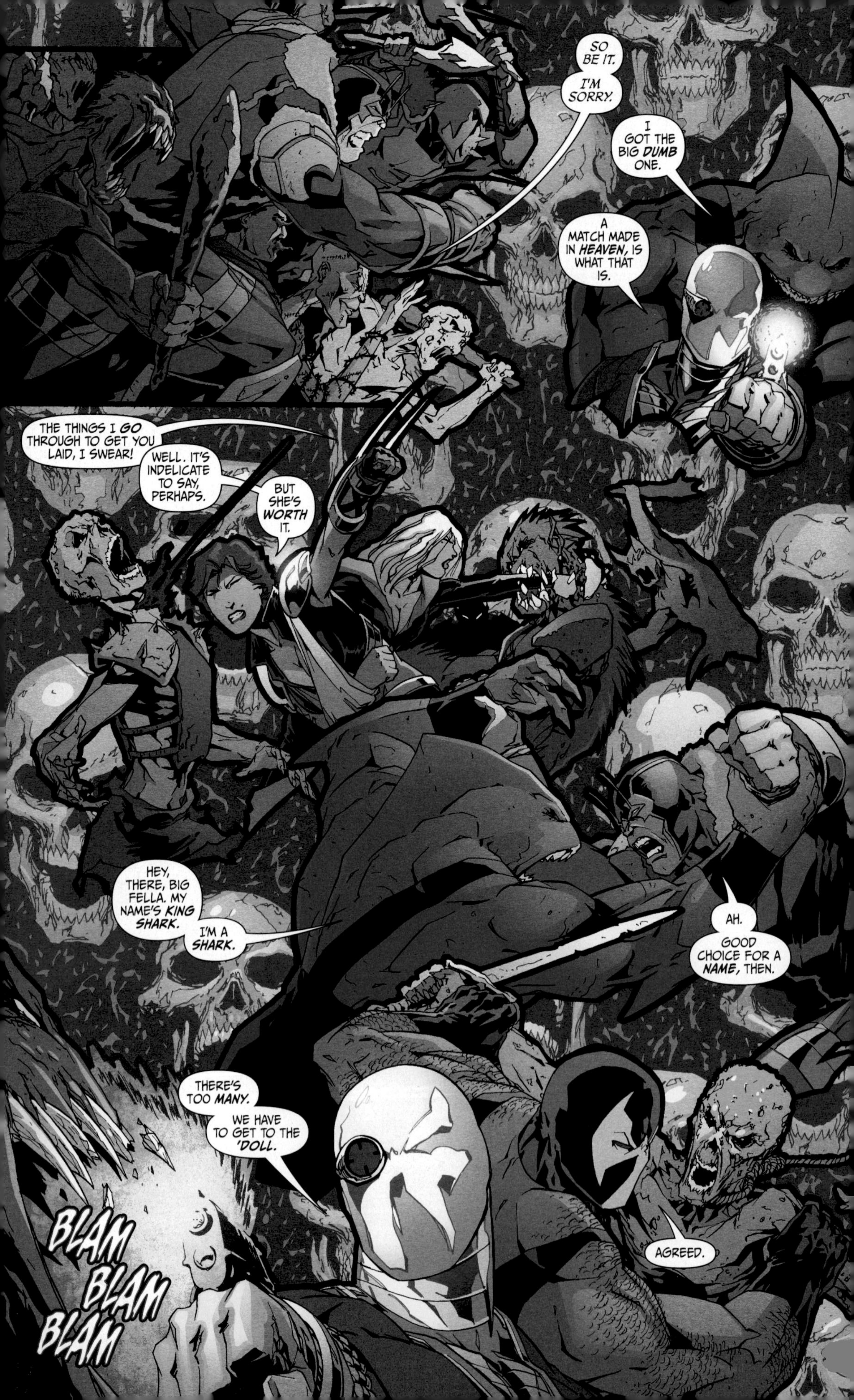
SO BE IT. I'M SORRY.
I GOT THE BIG DUMB ONE.
A MATCH MADE IN HEAVEN, IS WHAT THAT IS.
THE THINGS I GO THROUGH TO GET YOU LAID, I SWEAR!
WELL. IT'S INDELICATE TO SAY, PERHAPS.
BUT SHE'S WORTH IT.
HEY, THERE, BIG FELLA. MY NAME'S KING SHARK.
I'M A SHARK.
AH.
GOOD CHOICE FOR A NAME, THEN.
THERE'S TOO MANY.
WE HAVE TO GET TO THE 'DOLL.
AGREED.
BLAM BLAM BLAM

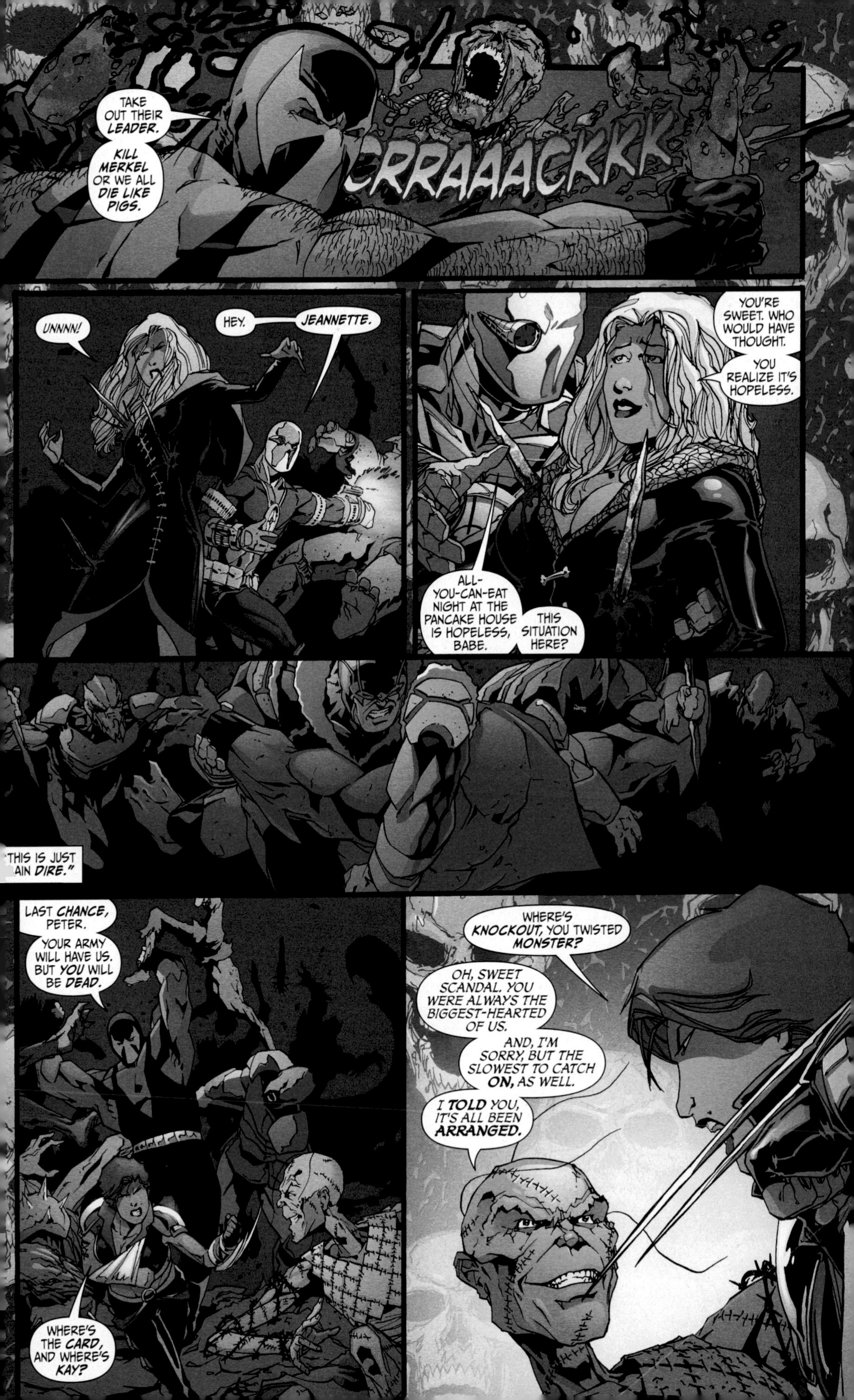

TAKE OUT THEIR LEADER.
KILL MERKEL OR WE ALL DIE LIKE PIGS.
CRRAAACKKK
UNNNN!
HEY.
JEANNETTE.
YOU'RE SWEET. WHO WOULD HAVE THOUGHT.
YOU REALIZE IT'S HOPELESS.
ALL-YOU-CAN-EAT NIGHT AT THE PANCAKE HOUSE IS HOPELESS, BABE.
THIS SITUATION HERE?
THIS IS JUST
AIN DIRE."
LAST CHANCE, PETER.
YOUR ARMY WILL HAVE US. BUT YOU WILL BE DEAD.
WHERE'S THE CARD, AND WHERE'S KAY?
WHERE'S KNOCKOUT, YOU TWISTED MONSTER?
OH, SWEET SCANDAL. YOU WERE ALWAYS THE BIGGEST-HEARTED OF US.
AND, I'M SORRY, BUT THE SLOWEST TO CATCH ON, AS WELL.
I TOLD YOU, IT'S ALL BEEN ARRANGED.

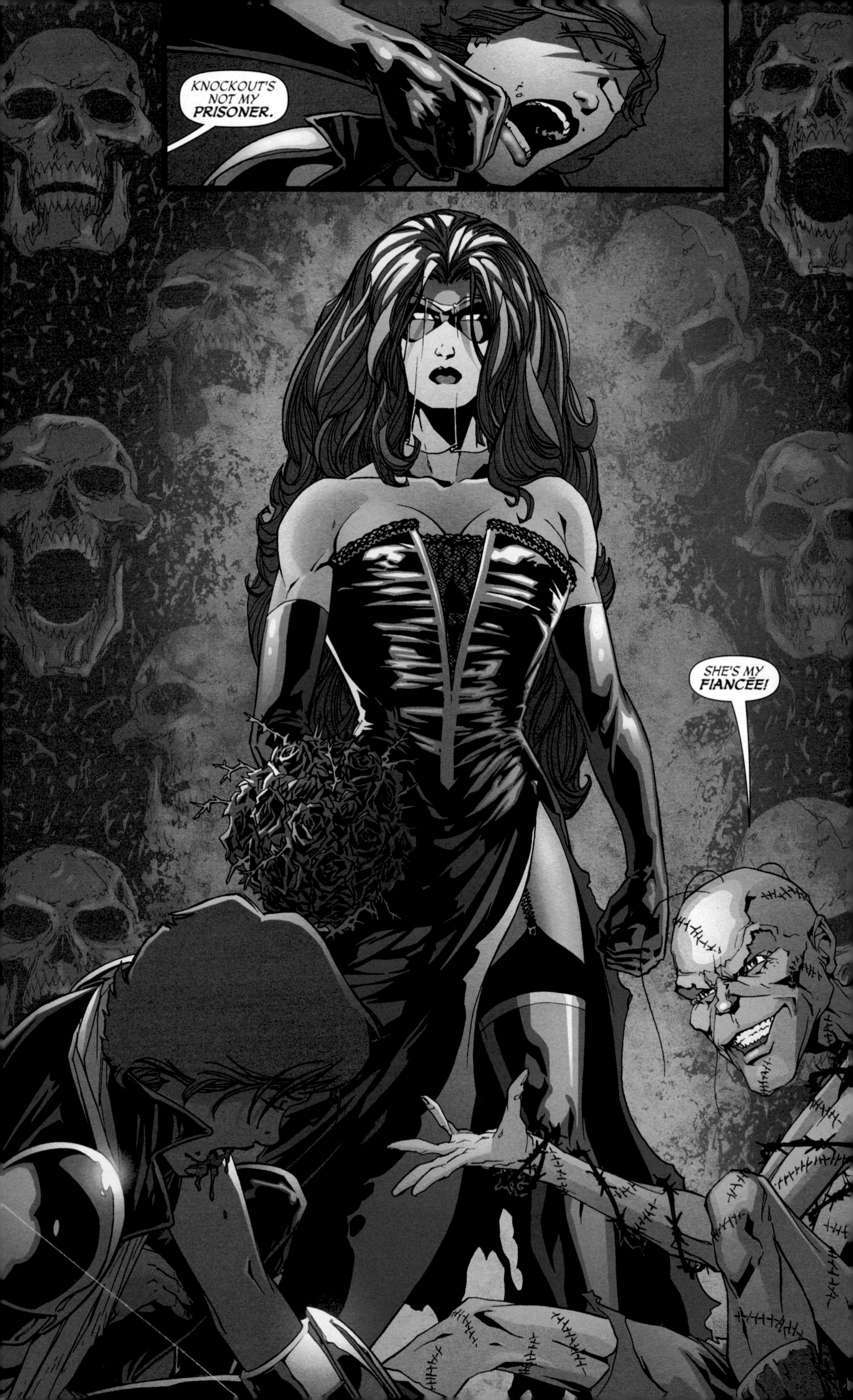
KNOCKOUT'S NOT MY PRISONER.
SHE'S MY FIANCÉE!

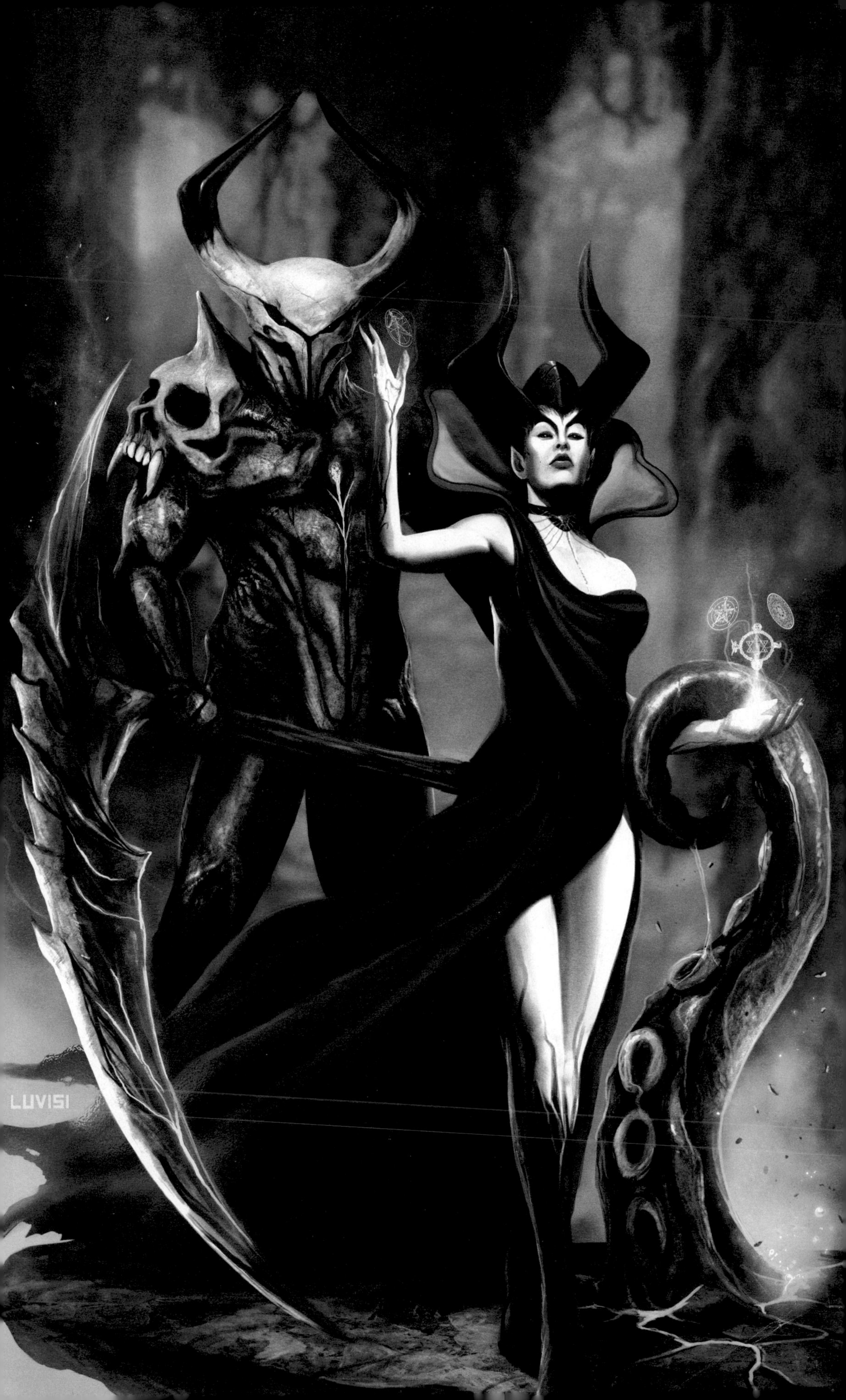
LUVISI

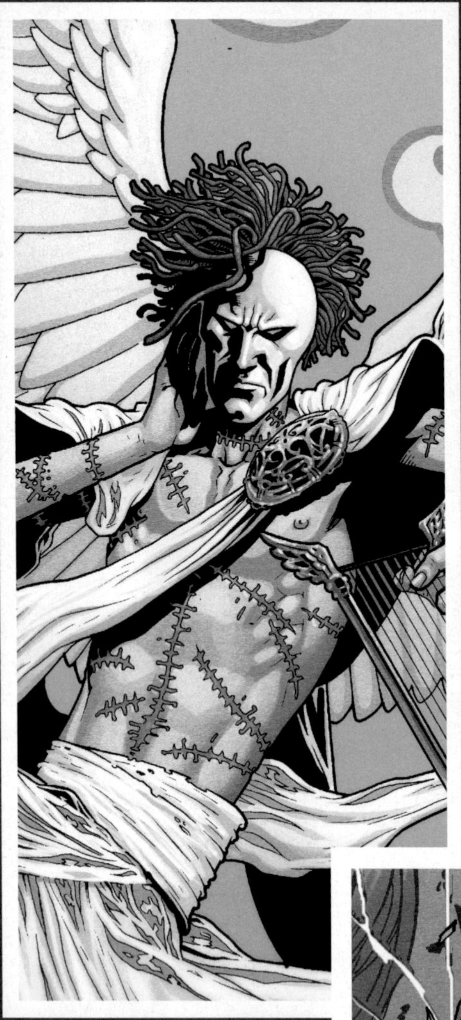
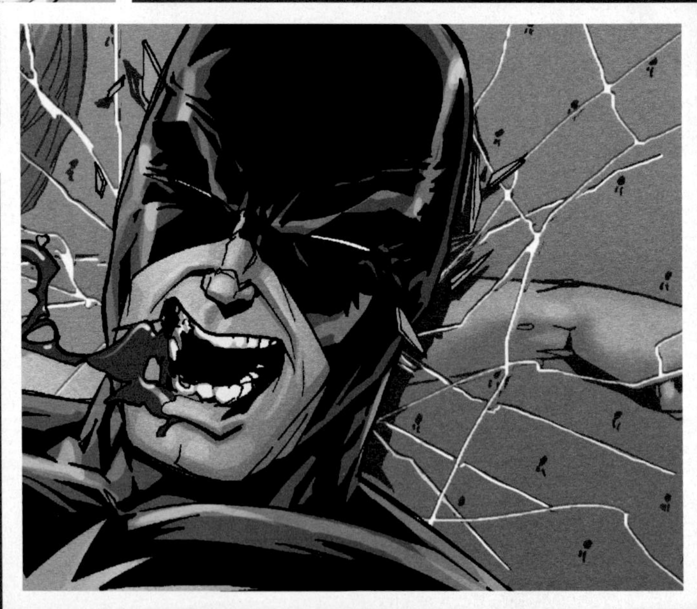

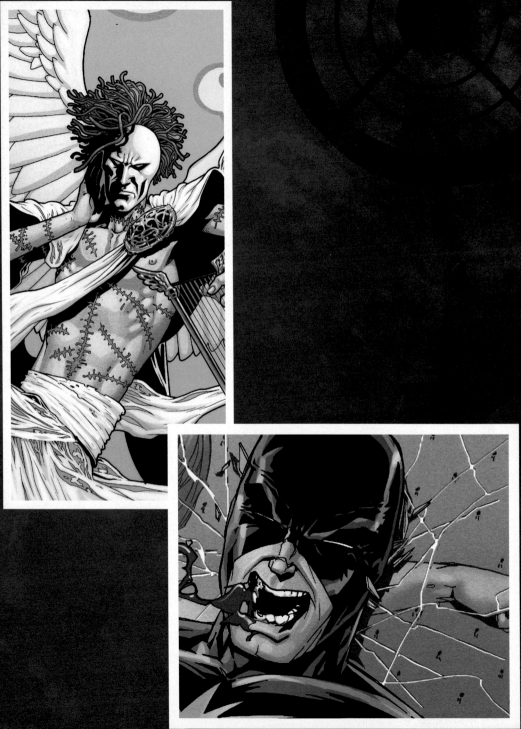

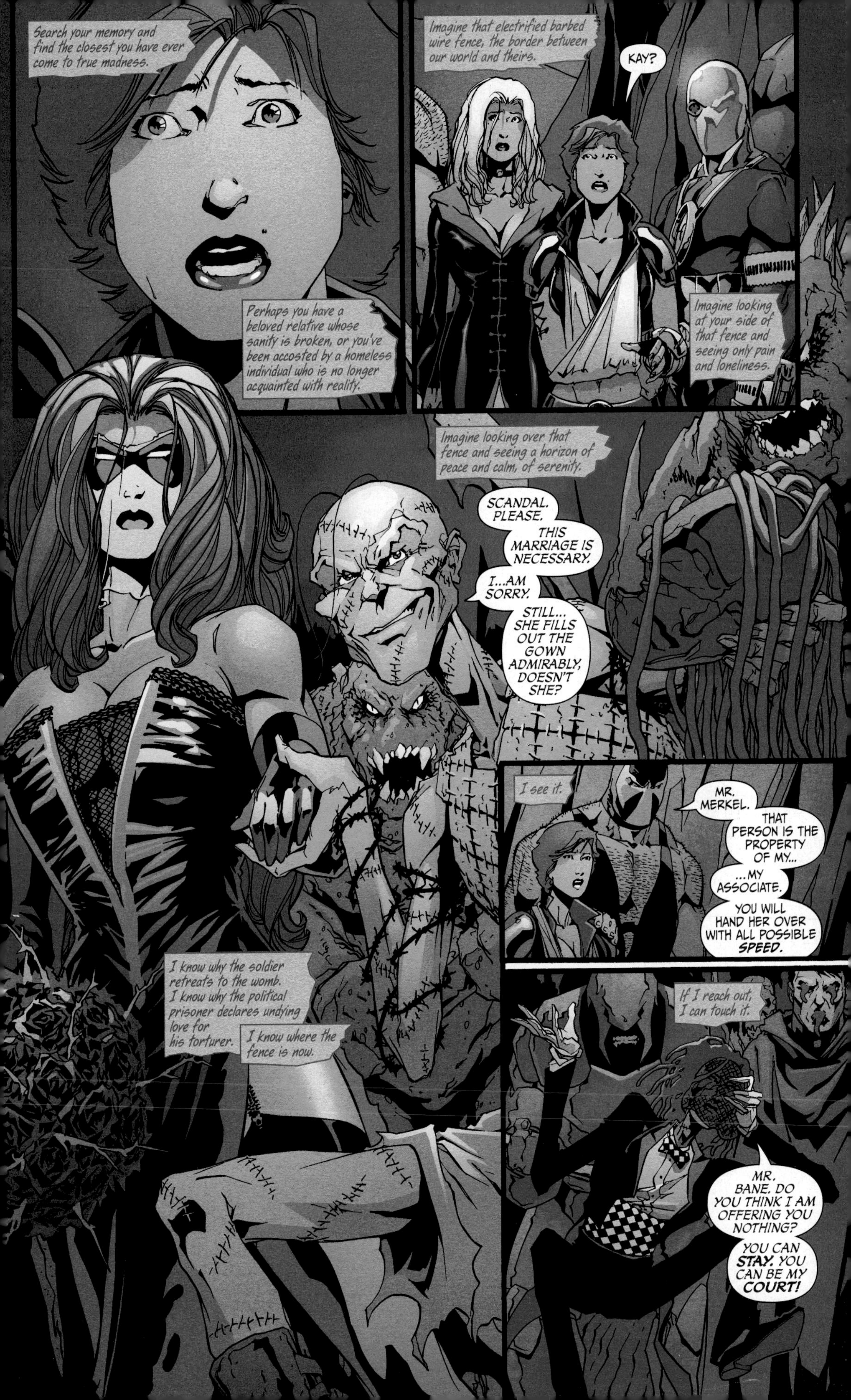

Search your memory and find the closest you have ever come to true madness.
Perhaps you have a beloved relative whose sanity is broken, or you've been accosted by a homeless individual who is no longer acquainted with reality.
Imagine that electrified barbed wire fence, the border between our world and theirs.
KAY?
Imagine looking at your side of that fence and seeing only pain and loneliness.
Imagine looking over that fence and seeing a horizon of peace and calm, of serenity.
SCANDAL. PLEASE.
THIS MARRIAGE IS NECESSARY.
I...AM SORRY.
STILL... SHE FILLS OUT THE GOWN ADMIRABLY, DOESN'T SHE?
I see it.
MR. MERKEL.
THAT PERSON IS THE PROPERTY OF MY...
...MY ASSOCIATE.
YOU WILL HAND HER OVER WITH ALL POSSIBLE SPEED.
I know why the soldier retreats to the womb. I know why the political prisoner declares undying love for his torturer.
I know where the fence is now.
If I reach out, I can touch it.
MR. BANE. DO YOU THINK I AM OFFERING YOU NOTHING?
YOU CAN STAY. YOU CAN BE MY COURT!

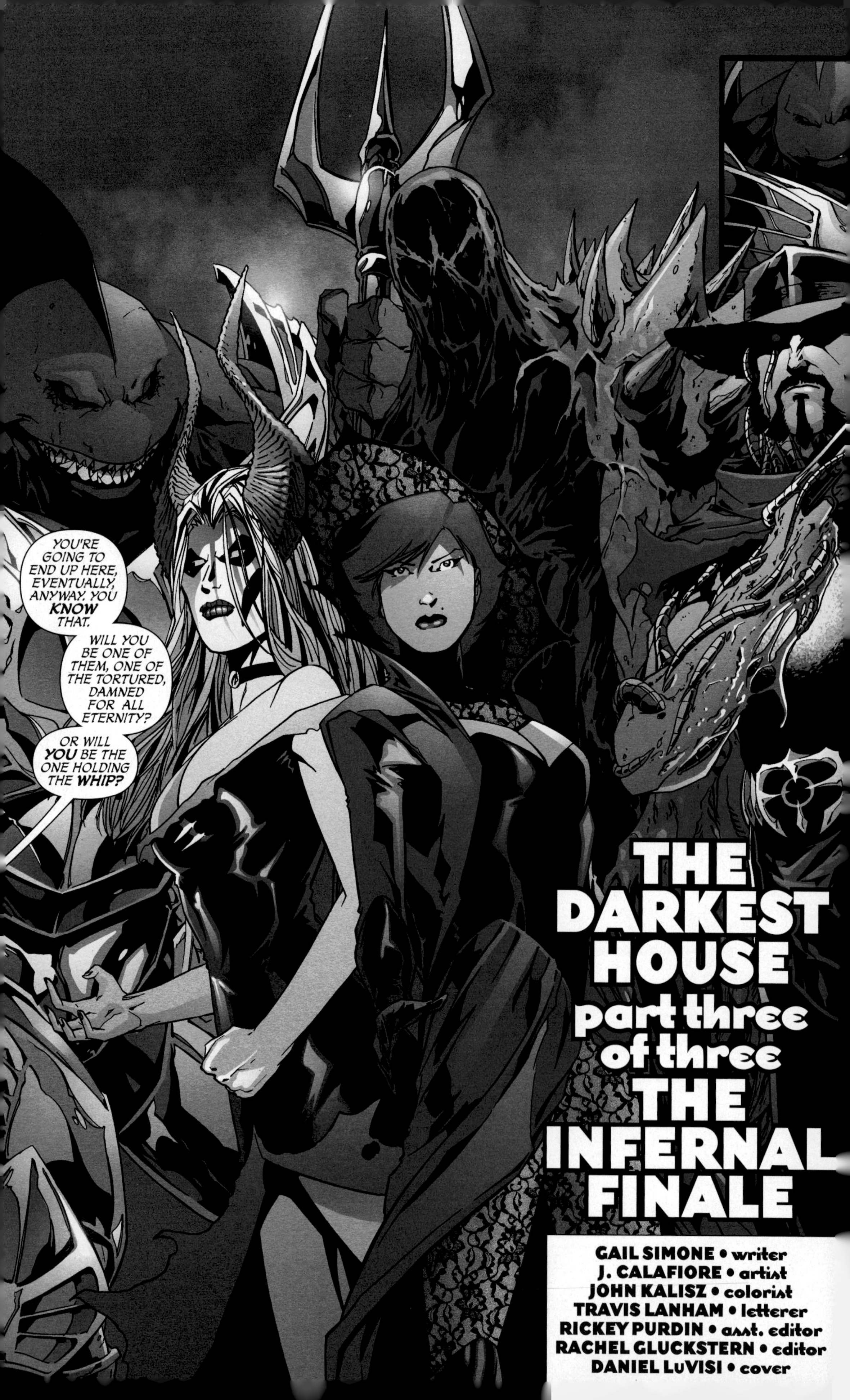
YOU'RE GOING TO END UP HERE, EVENTUALLY, ANYWAY. YOU KNOW THAT.
WILL YOU BE ONE OF THEM, ONE OF THE TORTURED, DAMNED FOR ALL ETERNITY?
OR WILL YOU BE THE ONE HOLDING THE WHIP?
THE DARKEST HOUSE part three of three THE INFERNAL FINALE
GAIL SIMONE • writer
J. CALAFIORE • artist
JOHN KALISZ • colorist
TRAVIS LANHAM • letterer
RICKEY PURDIN • asst. editor
RACHEL GLUCKSTERN • editor
DANIEL LuVISI • cover

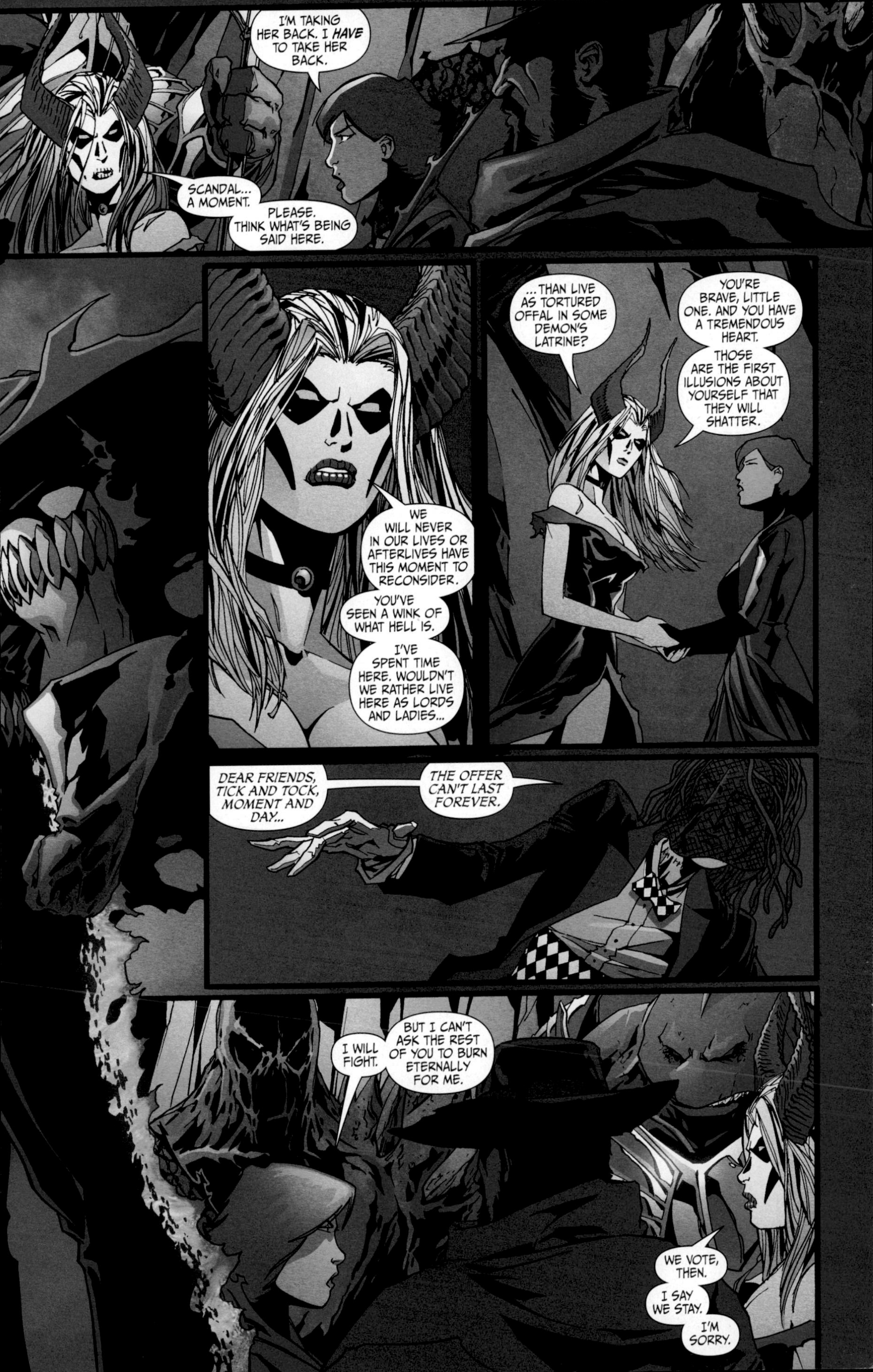
I'M TAKING HER BACK. I *HAVE* TO TAKE HER BACK.
SCANDAL... A MOMENT.
PLEASE. THINK WHAT'S BEING SAID HERE.
WE WILL NEVER IN OUR LIVES OR AFTERLIVES HAVE THIS MOMENT TO RECONSIDER.
YOU'VE SEEN A WINK OF WHAT HELL IS.
I'VE SPENT TIME HERE. WOULDN'T WE RATHER LIVE HERE AS LORDS AND LADIES...
...THAN LIVE AS TORTURED OFFAL IN SOME DEMON'S LATRINE?
YOU'RE BRAVE, LITTLE ONE. AND YOU HAVE A TREMENDOUS HEART.
THOSE ARE THE FIRST ILLUSIONS ABOUT YOURSELF THAT THEY WILL SHATTER.
DEAR FRIENDS, TICK AND TOCK, MOMENT AND DAY...
THE OFFER CAN'T LAST FOREVER.
I WILL FIGHT.
BUT I CAN'T ASK THE REST OF YOU TO BURN ETERNALLY FOR ME.
WE VOTE, THEN.
I SAY WE STAY.
I'M SORRY.

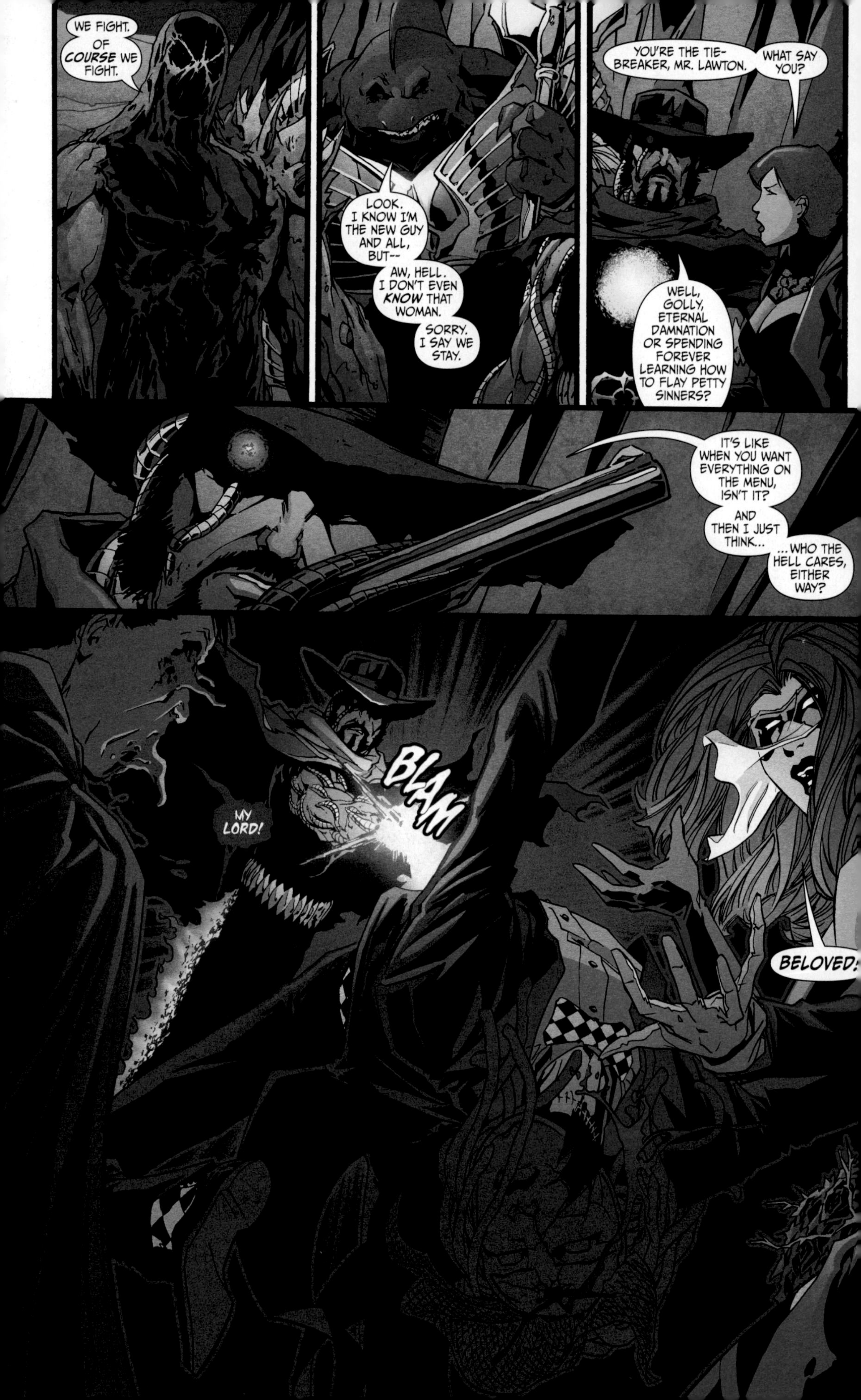
WE FIGHT. OF COURSE WE FIGHT.
LOOK. I KNOW I'M THE NEW GUY AND ALL, BUT--
AW, HELL. I DON'T EVEN KNOW THAT WOMAN.
SORRY. I SAY WE STAY.
YOU'RE THE TIE-BREAKER, MR. LAWTON.
WHAT SAY YOU?
WELL, GOLLY, ETERNAL DAMNATION OR SPENDING FOREVER LEARNING HOW TO FLAY PETTY SINNERS?
IT'S LIKE WHEN YOU WANT EVERYTHING ON THE MENU, ISN'T IT?
AND THEN I JUST THINK...
...WHO THE HELL CARES, EITHER WAY?
BLAM
MY LORD!
BELOVED!

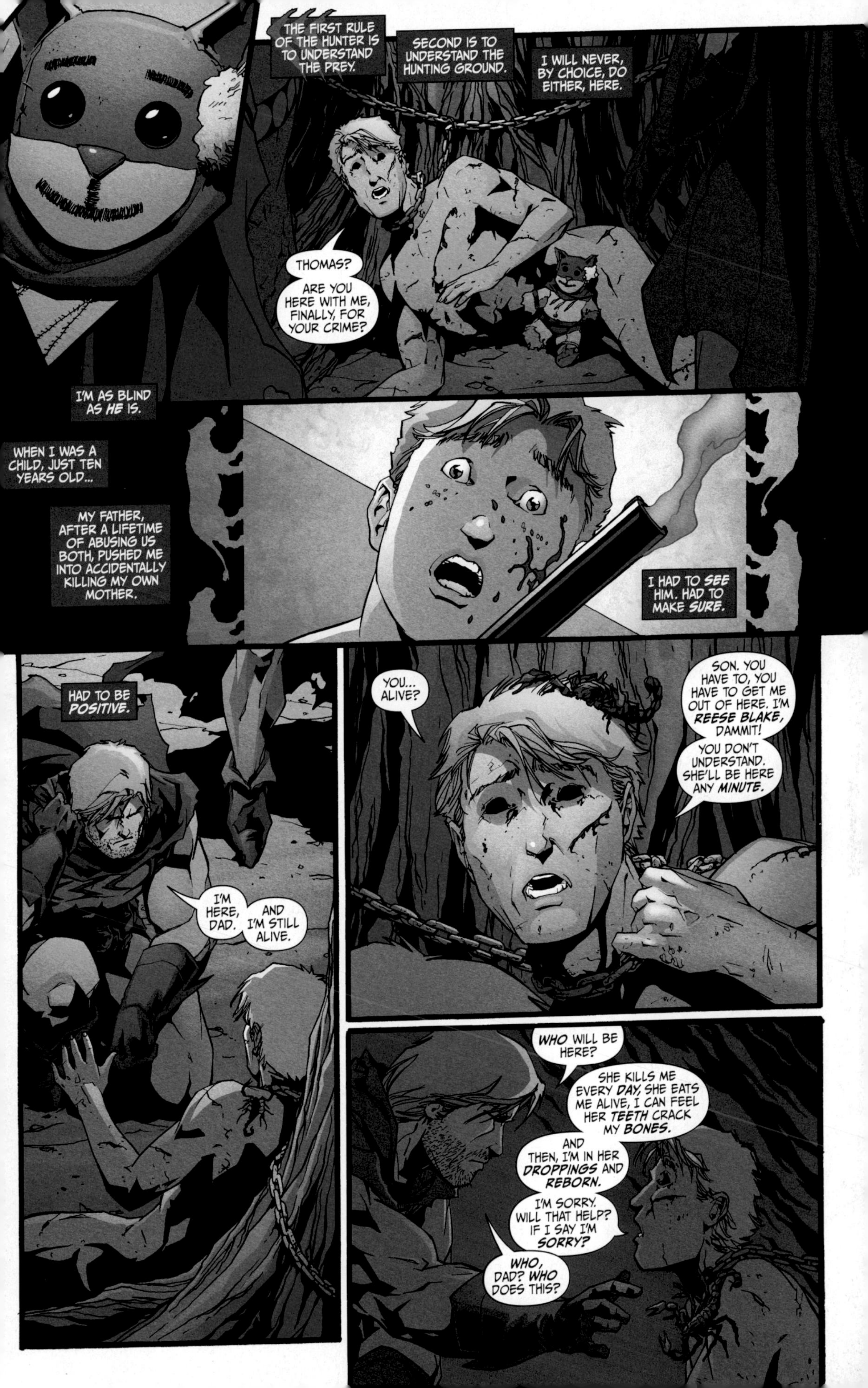
THE FIRST RULE OF THE HUNTER IS TO UNDERSTAND THE PREY.
SECOND IS TO UNDERSTAND THE HUNTING GROUND.
I WILL NEVER, BY CHOICE, DO EITHER, HERE.
THOMAS?
ARE YOU HERE WITH ME, FINALLY, FOR YOUR CRIME?
I'M AS BLIND AS HE IS.
WHEN I WAS A CHILD, JUST TEN YEARS OLD...
MY FATHER, AFTER A LIFETIME OF ABUSING US BOTH, PUSHED ME INTO ACCIDENTALLY KILLING MY OWN MOTHER.
I HAD TO SEE HIM. HAD TO MAKE SURE.
HAD TO BE POSITIVE.
I'M HERE, DAD.
AND I'M STILL ALIVE.
YOU... ALIVE?
SON. YOU HAVE TO, YOU HAVE TO GET ME OUT OF HERE. I'M REESE BLAKE, DAMMIT!
YOU DON'T UNDERSTAND. SHE'LL BE HERE ANY MINUTE.
WHO WILL BE HERE?
SHE KILLS ME EVERY DAY, SHE EATS ME ALIVE, I CAN FEEL HER TEETH CRACK MY BONES.
AND THEN, I'M IN HER DROPPINGS AND REBORN.
I'M SORRY. WILL THAT HELP? IF I SAY I'M SORRY?
WHO, DAD? WHO DOES THIS?

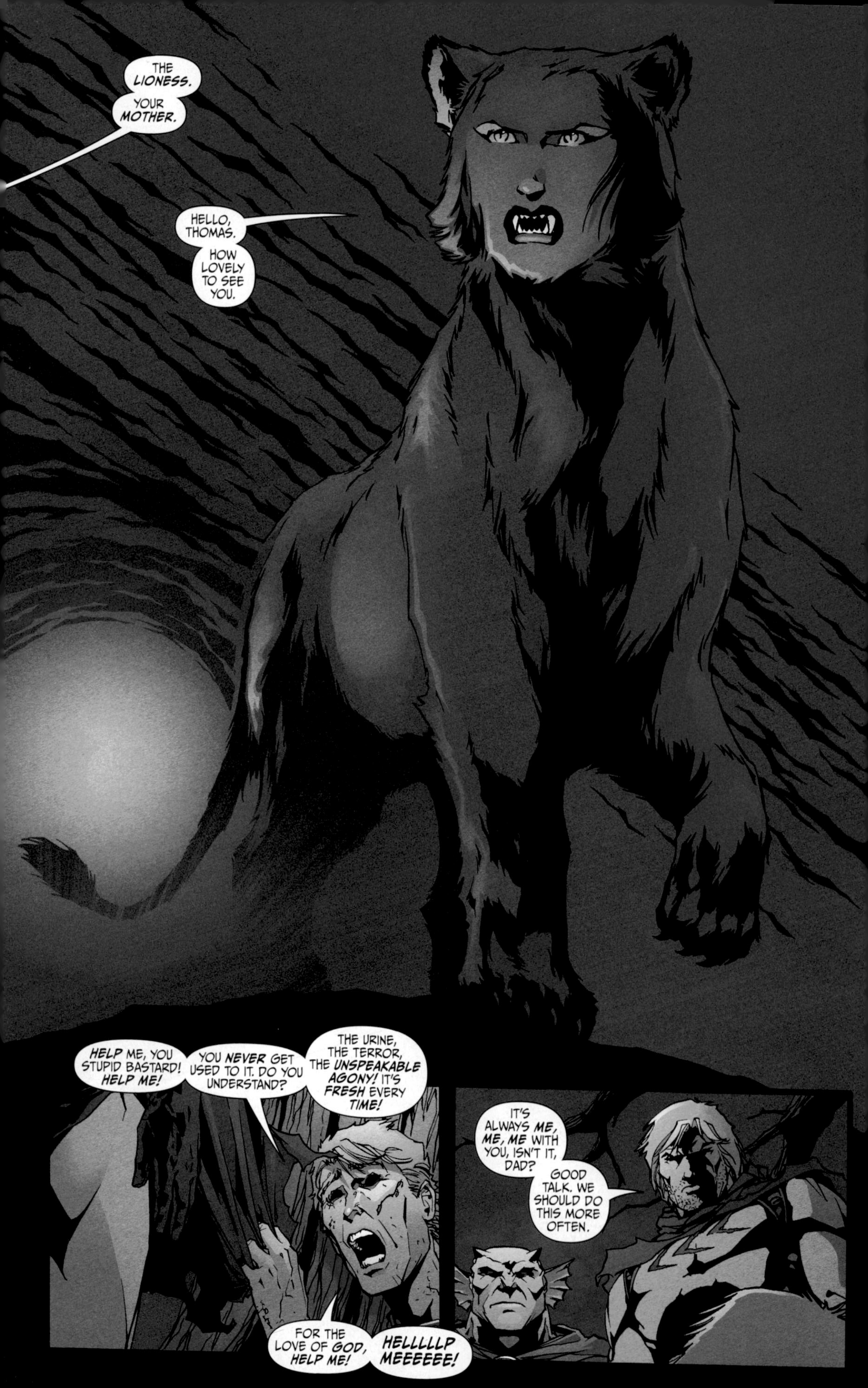
THE **LIONESS.**
YOUR **MOTHER.**
HELLO, THOMAS.
HOW LOVELY TO SEE YOU.
HELP ME, YOU STUPID BASTARD! **HELP ME!**
YOU **NEVER** GET USED TO IT. DO YOU UNDERSTAND?
THE URINE, THE TERROR, THE **UNSPEAKABLE AGONY!** IT'S **FRESH** EVERY **TIME!**
FOR THE LOVE OF **GOD, HELP ME!**
HELLLLLP MEEEEEE!
IT'S ALWAYS **ME, ME, ME** WITH YOU, ISN'T IT, DAD?
GOOD TALK. WE SHOULD DO THIS MORE OFTEN.

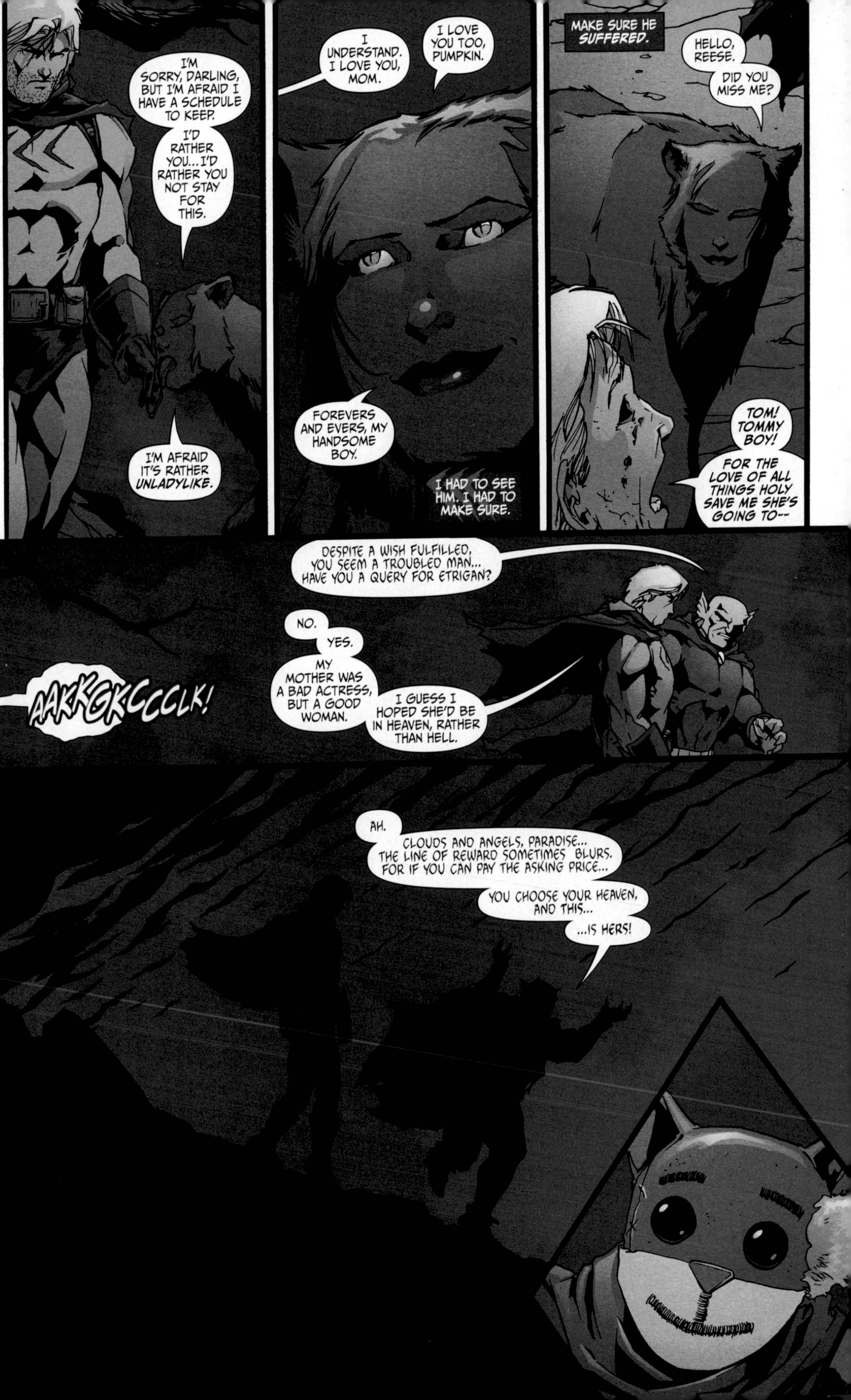
I'M SORRY, DARLING, BUT I'M AFRAID I HAVE A SCHEDULE TO KEEP.
I'D RATHER YOU... I'D RATHER YOU NOT STAY FOR THIS.
I'M AFRAID IT'S RATHER UNLADYLIKE.
I UNDERSTAND. I LOVE YOU, MOM.
I LOVE YOU TOO, PUMPKIN.
FOREVERS AND EVERS, MY HANDSOME BOY.
I HAD TO SEE HIM. I HAD TO MAKE SURE.
MAKE SURE HE SUFFERED.
HELLO, REESE.
DID YOU MISS ME?
TOM! TOMMY BOY!
FOR THE LOVE OF ALL THINGS HOLY SAVE ME SHE'S GOING TO--
AAKKGKCCCLK!
DESPITE A WISH FULFILLED, YOU SEEM A TROUBLED MAN... HAVE YOU A QUERY FOR ETRIGAN?
NO.
YES.
MY MOTHER WAS A BAD ACTRESS, BUT A GOOD WOMAN.
I GUESS I HOPED SHE'D BE IN HEAVEN, RATHER THAN HELL.
AH.
CLOUDS AND ANGELS, PARADISE... THE LINE OF REWARD SOMETIMES BLURS. FOR IF YOU CAN PAY THE ASKING PRICE...
YOU CHOOSE YOUR HEAVEN, AND THIS...
...IS HERS!

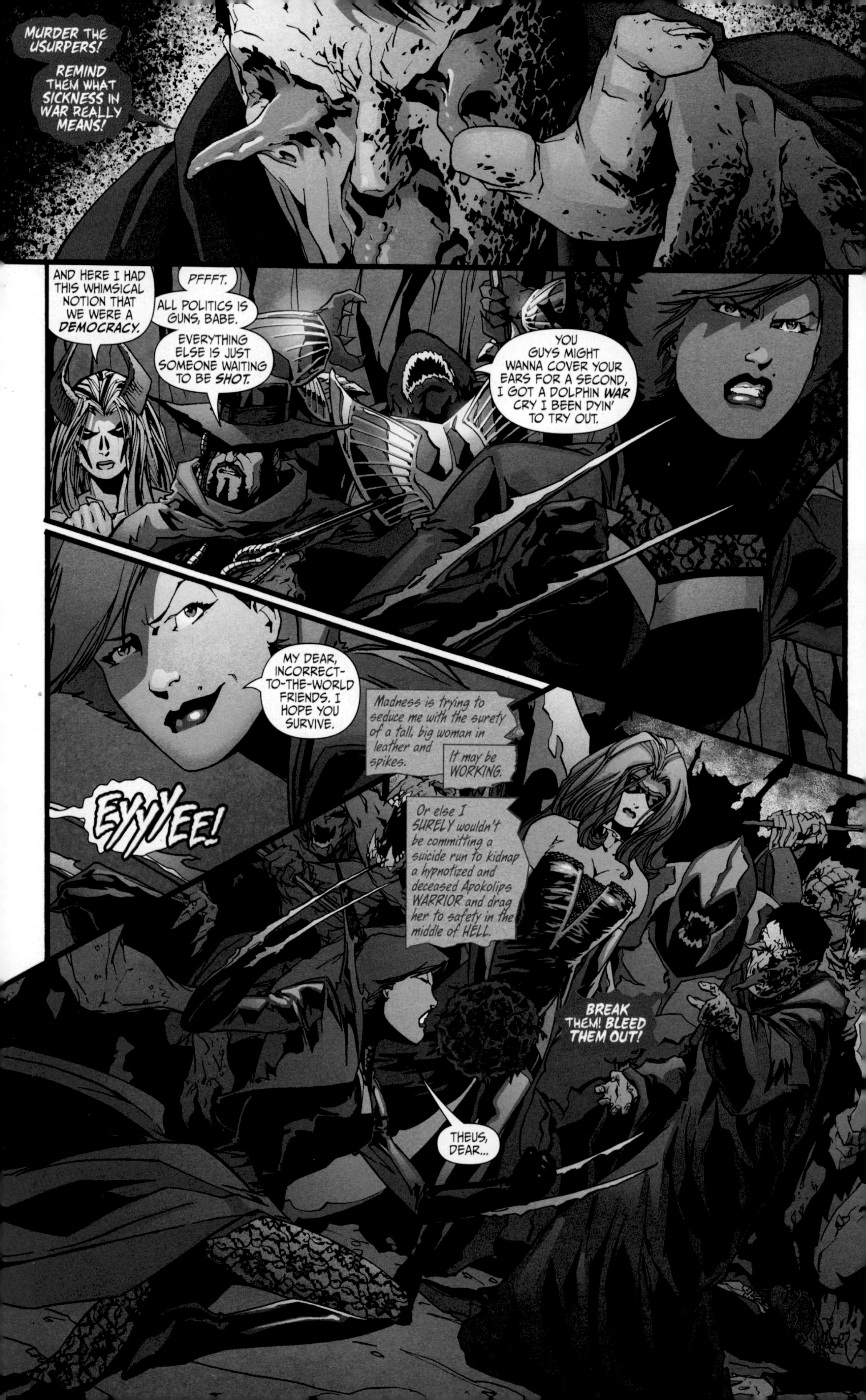
MURDER THE USURPERS!
REMIND THEM WHAT SICKNESS IN WAR REALLY MEANS!
AND HERE I HAD THIS WHIMSICAL NOTION THAT WE WERE A DEMOCRACY.
PFFFT.
ALL POLITICS IS GUNS, BABE.
EVERYTHING ELSE IS JUST SOMEONE WAITING TO BE SHOT.
YOU GUYS MIGHT WANNA COVER YOUR EARS FOR A SECOND, I GOT A DOLPHIN WAR CRY I BEEN DYIN' TO TRY OUT.
MY DEAR, INCORRECT-TO-THE-WORLD FRIENDS. I HOPE YOU SURVIVE.
Madness is trying to seduce me with the surety of a tall, big woman in leather and spikes.
It may be WORKING.
Or else I SURELY wouldn't be committing a suicide run to kidnap a hypnotized and deceased Apokolips WARRIOR and drag her to safety in the middle of HELL.
EYYYEE!
BREAK THEM! BLEED THEM OUT!
THEUS, DEAR...

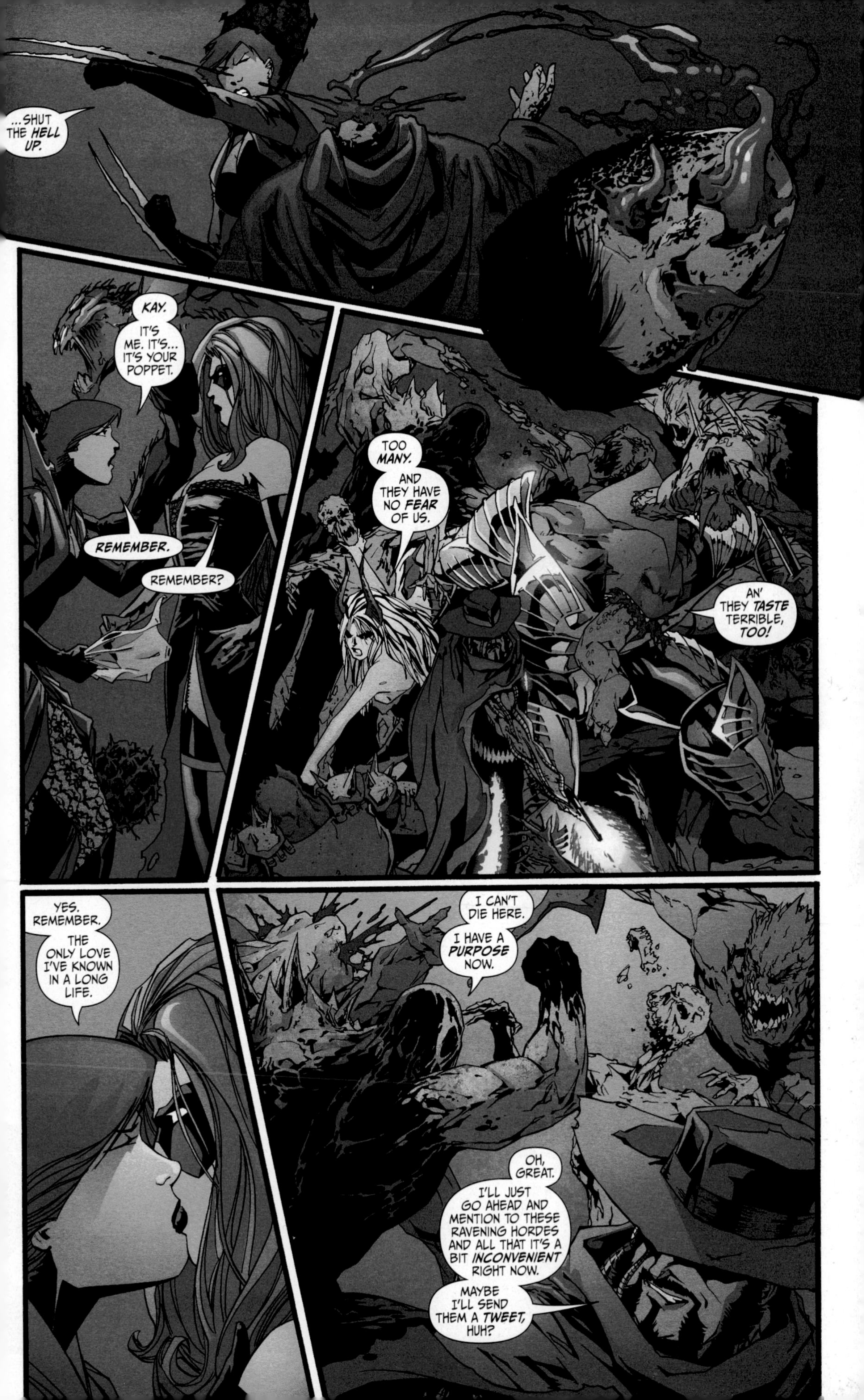

...SHUT THE HELL UP.
KAY.
IT'S ME. IT'S... IT'S YOUR POPPET.
REMEMBER.
REMEMBER?
TOO MANY.
AND THEY HAVE NO FEAR OF US.
AN' THEY TASTE TERRIBLE, TOO!
YES. REMEMBER.
THE ONLY LOVE I'VE KNOWN IN A LONG LIFE.
I CAN'T DIE HERE.
I HAVE A PURPOSE NOW.
OH, GREAT.
I'LL JUST GO AHEAD AND MENTION TO THESE RAVENING HORDES AND ALL THAT IT'S A BIT INCONVENIENT RIGHT NOW.
MAYBE I'LL SEND THEM A TWEET, HUH?

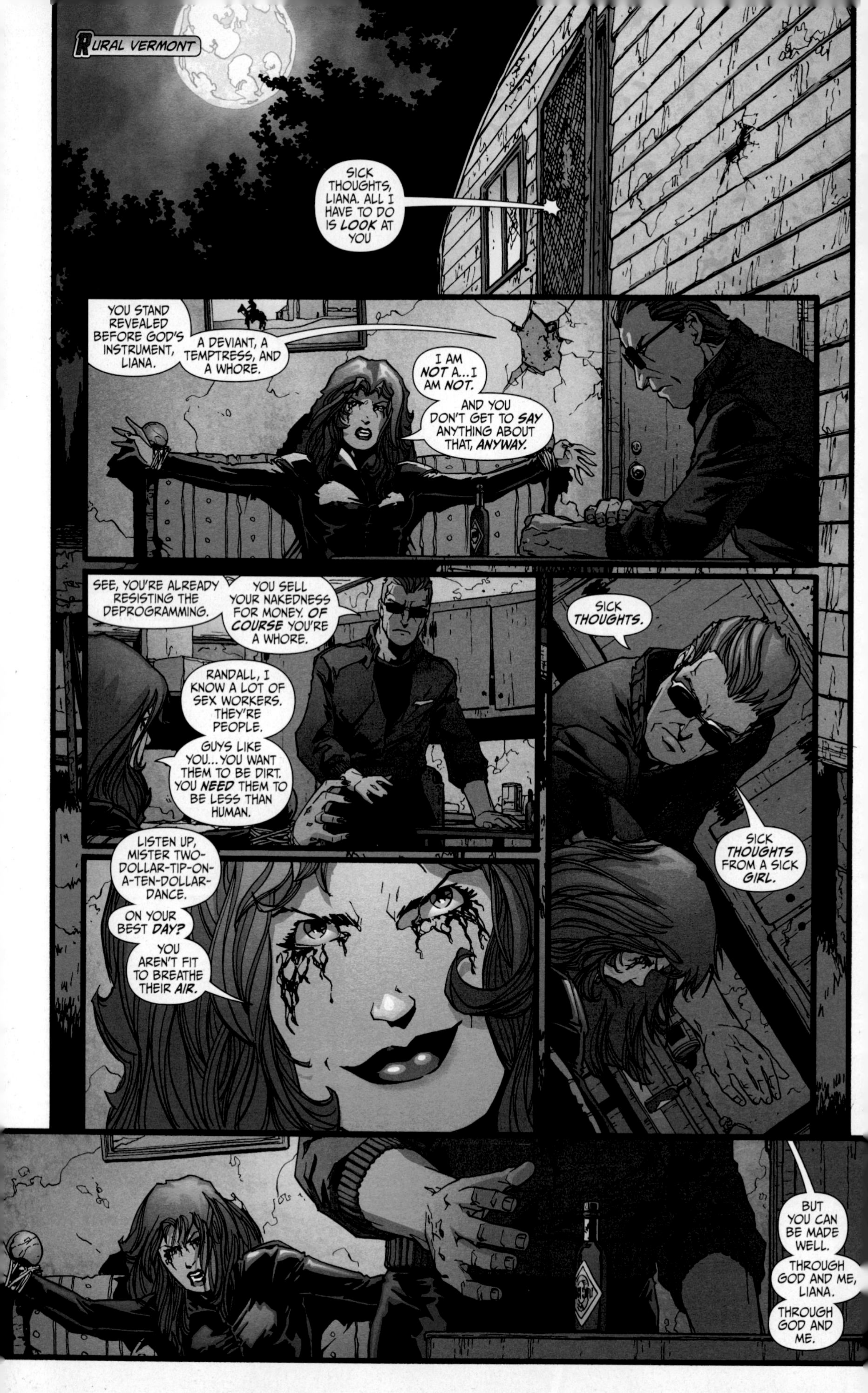
RURAL VERMONT
SICK THOUGHTS, LIANA. ALL I HAVE TO DO IS LOOK AT YOU
YOU STAND REVEALED BEFORE GOD'S INSTRUMENT, LIANA.
A DEVIANT, A TEMPTRESS, AND A WHORE.
I AM NOT A...I AM NOT.
AND YOU DON'T GET TO SAY ANYTHING ABOUT THAT, ANYWAY.
SEE, YOU'RE ALREADY RESISTING THE DEPROGRAMMING.
YOU SELL YOUR NAKEDNESS FOR MONEY. OF COURSE YOU'RE A WHORE.
RANDALL, I KNOW A LOT OF SEX WORKERS. THEY'RE PEOPLE.
GUYS LIKE YOU...YOU WANT THEM TO BE DIRT. YOU NEED THEM TO BE LESS THAN HUMAN.
LISTEN UP, MISTER TWO-DOLLAR-TIP-ON-A-TEN-DOLLAR-DANCE.
ON YOUR BEST DAY?
YOU AREN'T FIT TO BREATHE THEIR AIR.
SICK THOUGHTS.
SICK THOUGHTS FROM A SICK GIRL.
BUT YOU CAN BE MADE WELL.
THROUGH GOD AND ME, LIANA.
THROUGH GOD AND ME.

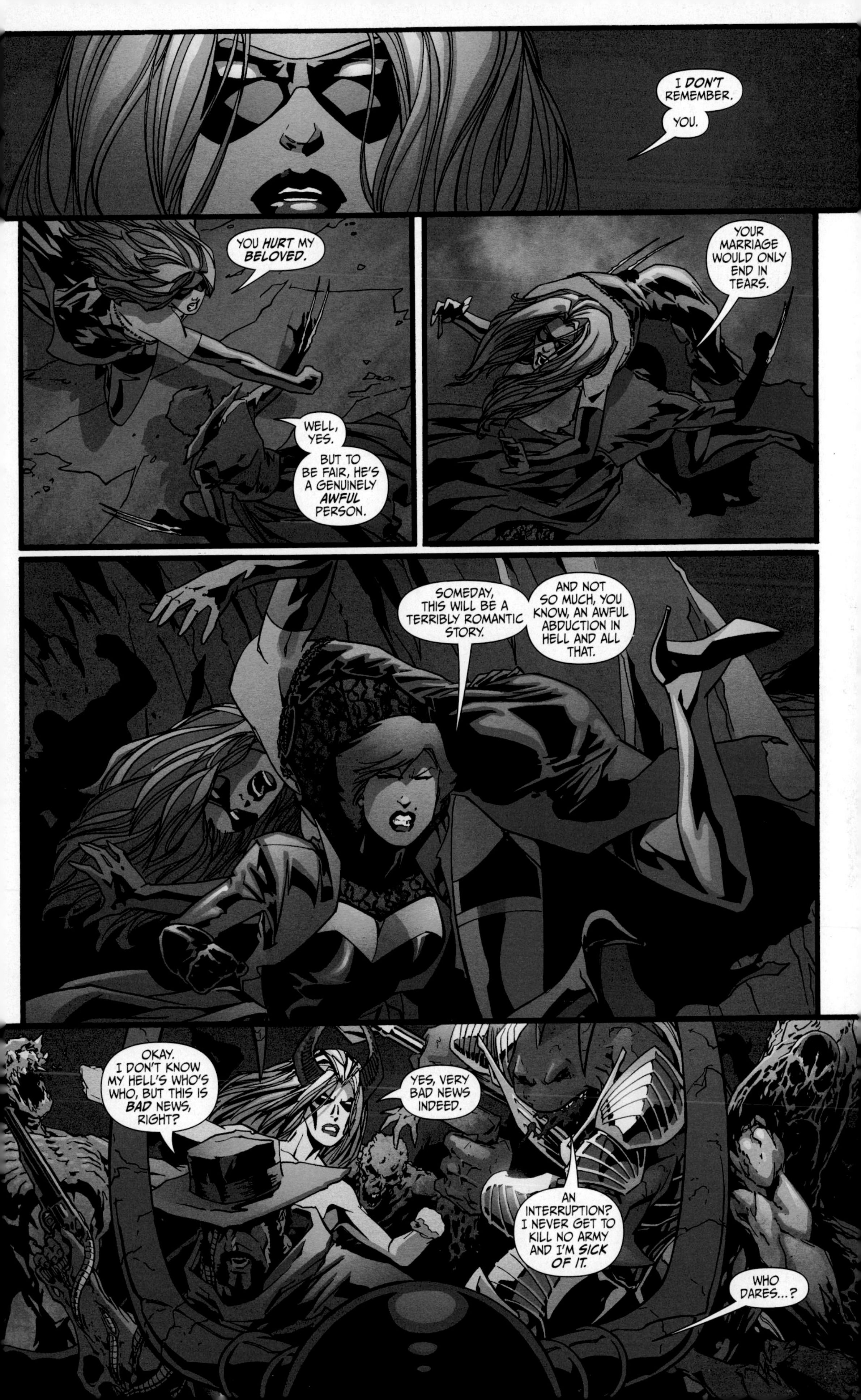
I DON'T REMEMBER.
YOU.
YOU HURT MY BELOVED.
WELL, YES.
BUT TO BE FAIR, HE'S A GENUINELY AWFUL PERSON.
YOUR MARRIAGE WOULD ONLY END IN TEARS.
SOMEDAY, THIS WILL BE A TERRIBLY ROMANTIC STORY.
AND NOT SO MUCH, YOU KNOW, AN AWFUL ABDUCTION IN HELL AND ALL THAT.
OKAY. I DON'T KNOW MY HELL'S WHO'S WHO, BUT THIS IS BAD NEWS, RIGHT?
YES, VERY BAD NEWS INDEED.
AN INTERRUPTION? I NEVER GET TO KILL NO ARMY AND I'M SICK OF IT.
WHO DARES...?

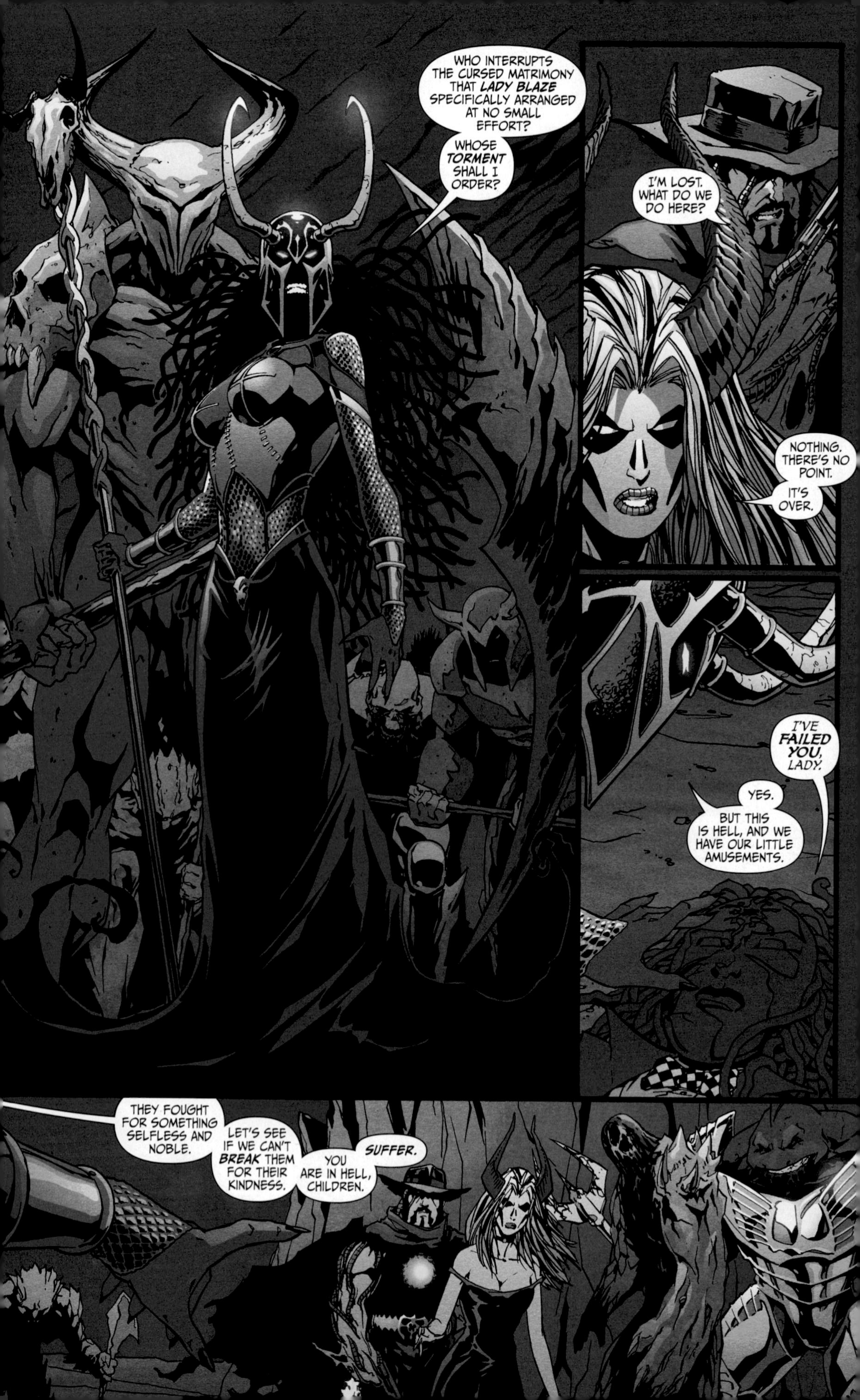
WHO INTERRUPTS THE CURSED MATRIMONY THAT *LADY BLAZE* SPECIFICALLY ARRANGED AT NO SMALL EFFORT?
WHOSE *TORMENT* SHALL I ORDER?
I'M LOST. WHAT DO WE DO HERE?
NOTHING. THERE'S NO POINT.
IT'S OVER.
*I'VE **FAILED YOU,** LADY.*
YES.
BUT THIS IS HELL, AND WE HAVE OUR LITTLE AMUSEMENTS.
THEY FOUGHT FOR SOMETHING SELFLESS AND NOBLE.
LET'S SEE IF WE CAN'T ***BREAK*** THEM FOR THEIR KINDNESS.
YOU ARE IN HELL, CHILDREN.
SUFFER.

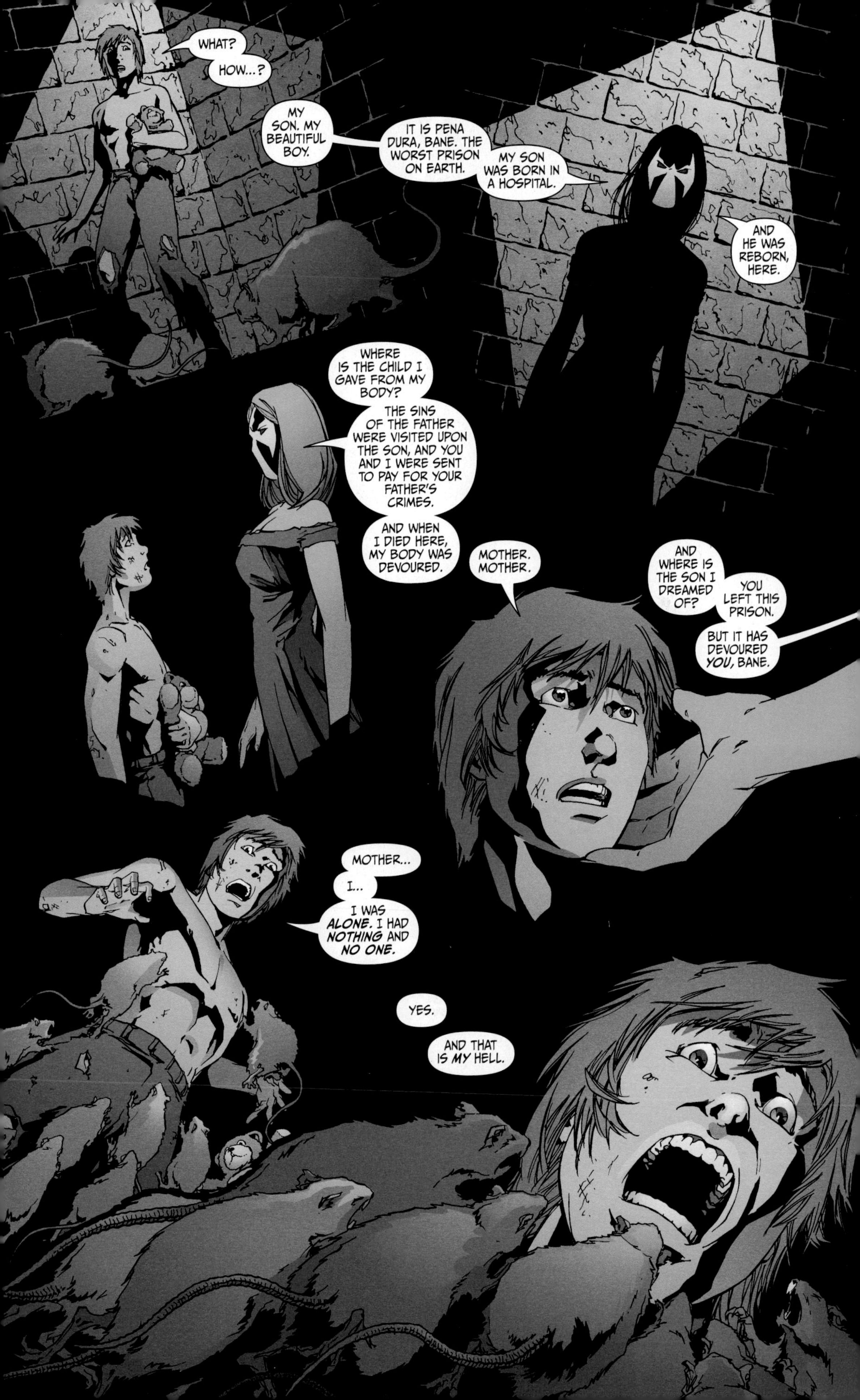
WHAT?
HOW...?
MY SON. MY BEAUTIFUL BOY.
IT IS PENA DURA, BANE. THE WORST PRISON ON EARTH.
MY SON WAS BORN IN A HOSPITAL.
AND HE WAS REBORN, HERE.
WHERE IS THE CHILD I GAVE FROM MY BODY?
THE SINS OF THE FATHER WERE VISITED UPON THE SON, AND YOU AND I WERE SENT TO PAY FOR YOUR FATHER'S CRIMES.
AND WHEN I DIED HERE, MY BODY WAS DEVOURED.
MOTHER. MOTHER.
AND WHERE IS THE SON I DREAMED OF?
YOU LEFT THIS PRISON.
BUT IT HAS DEVOURED *YOU*, BANE.
MOTHER...
I...
I WAS *ALONE*. I HAD *NOTHING* AND *NO ONE*.
YES.
AND THAT IS *MY* HELL.

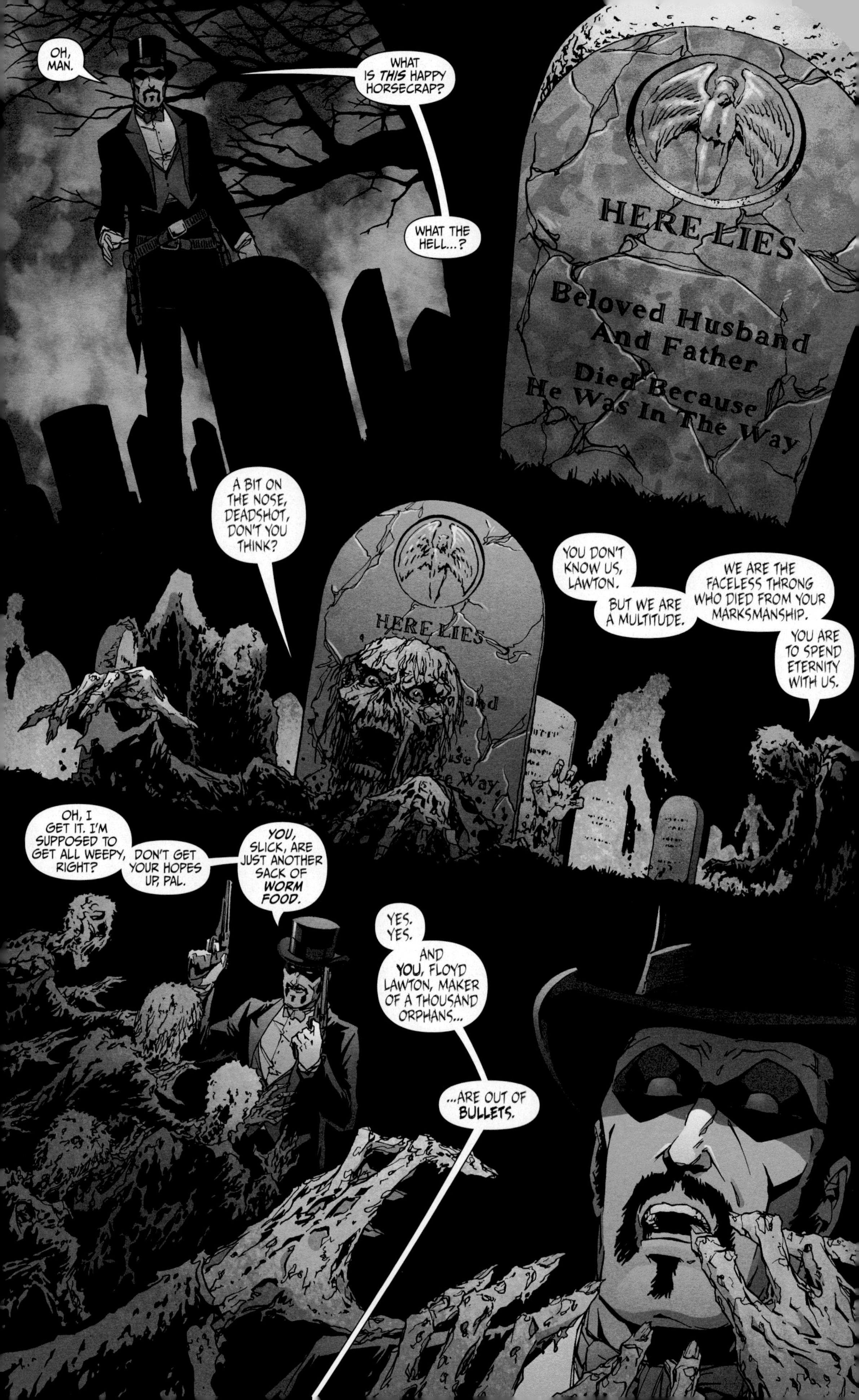
OH, MAN.
WHAT IS THIS HAPPY HORSECRAP?
WHAT THE HELL...?
HERE LIES
Beloved Husband And Father
Died Because He Was In The Way
A BIT ON THE NOSE, DEADSHOT, DON'T YOU THINK?
HERE LIES
YOU DON'T KNOW US, LAWTON.
BUT WE ARE A MULTITUDE.
WE ARE THE FACELESS THRONG WHO DIED FROM YOUR MARKSMANSHIP.
YOU ARE TO SPEND ETERNITY WITH US.
OH, I GET IT. I'M SUPPOSED TO GET ALL WEEPY, RIGHT?
DON'T GET YOUR HOPES UP, PAL.
YOU, SLICK, ARE JUST ANOTHER SACK OF WORM FOOD.
YES. YES.
AND YOU, FLOYD LAWTON, MAKER OF A THOUSAND ORPHANS...
...ARE OUT OF BULLETS.

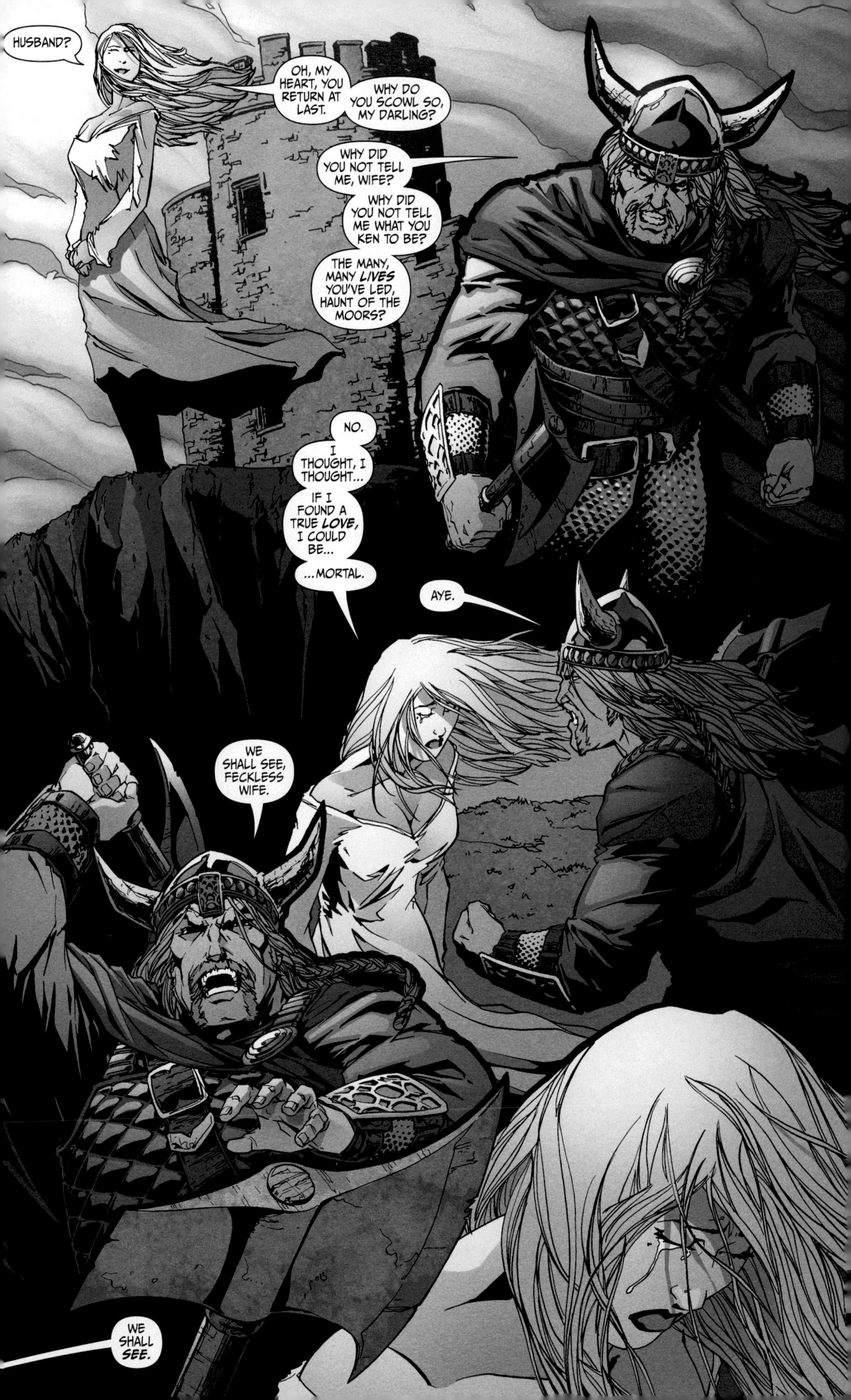
HUSBAND?
OH, MY HEART, YOU RETURN AT LAST.
WHY DO YOU SCOWL SO, MY DARLING?
WHY DID YOU NOT TELL ME, WIFE?
WHY DID YOU NOT TELL ME WHAT YOU KEN TO BE?
THE MANY, MANY LIVES YOU'VE LED, HAUNT OF THE MOORS?
NO.
I THOUGHT, I THOUGHT...
IF I FOUND A TRUE LOVE, I COULD BE...
...MORTAL.
AYE.
WE SHALL SEE, FECKLESS WIFE.
WE SHALL SEE.

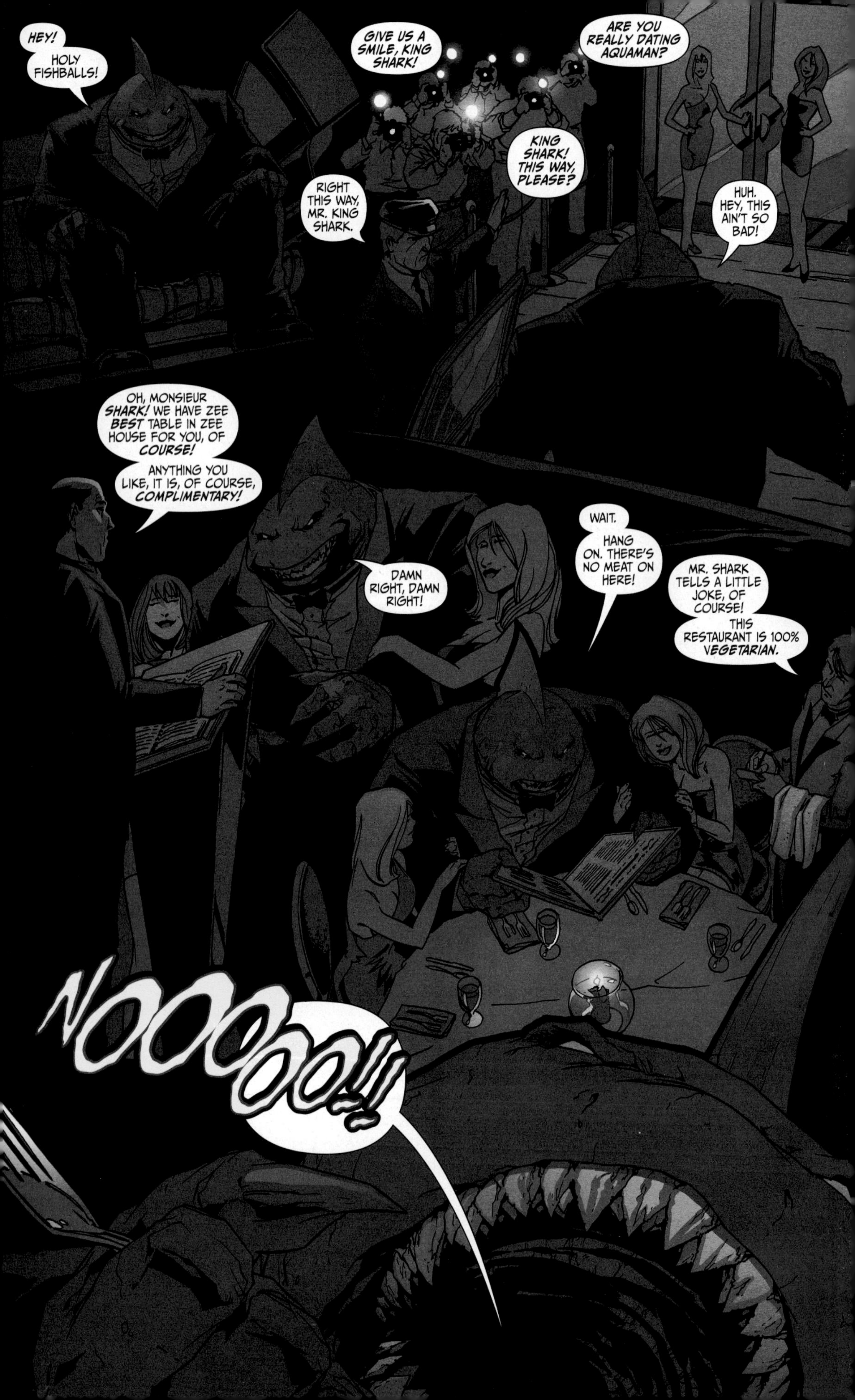
HEY!
HOLY FISHBALLS!
GIVE US A SMILE, KING SHARK!
ARE YOU REALLY DATING AQUAMAN?
KING SHARK! THIS WAY, PLEASE?
RIGHT THIS WAY, MR. KING SHARK.
HUH. HEY, THIS AIN'T SO BAD!
OH, MONSIEUR SHARK! WE HAVE ZEE BEST TABLE IN ZEE HOUSE FOR YOU, OF COURSE!
ANYTHING YOU LIKE, IT IS, OF COURSE, COMPLIMENTARY!
DAMN RIGHT, DAMN RIGHT!
WAIT.
HANG ON. THERE'S NO MEAT ON HERE!
MR. SHARK TELLS A LITTLE JOKE, OF COURSE!
THIS RESTAURANT IS 100% VEGETARIAN.
NOOOOO!!

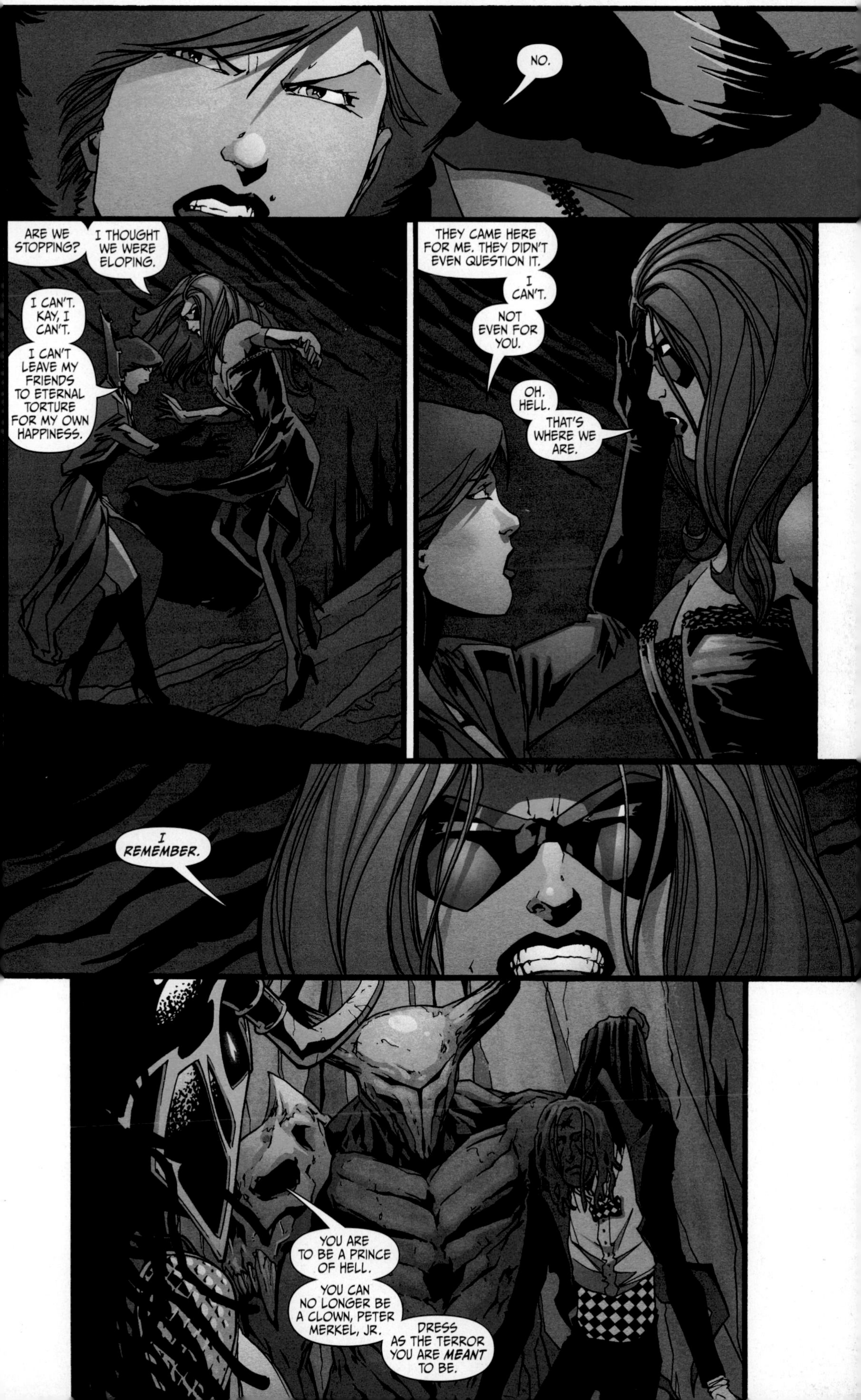
NO.
ARE WE STOPPING?
I THOUGHT WE WERE ELOPING.
I CAN'T. KAY, I CAN'T.
I CAN'T LEAVE MY FRIENDS TO ETERNAL TORTURE FOR MY OWN HAPPINESS.
THEY CAME HERE FOR ME. THEY DIDN'T EVEN QUESTION IT.
I CAN'T.
NOT EVEN FOR YOU.
OH. HELL.
THAT'S WHERE WE ARE.
I *REMEMBER.*
YOU ARE TO BE A PRINCE OF HELL.
YOU CAN NO LONGER BE A CLOWN, PETER MERKEL, JR.
DRESS AS THE TERROR YOU ARE *MEANT* TO BE.

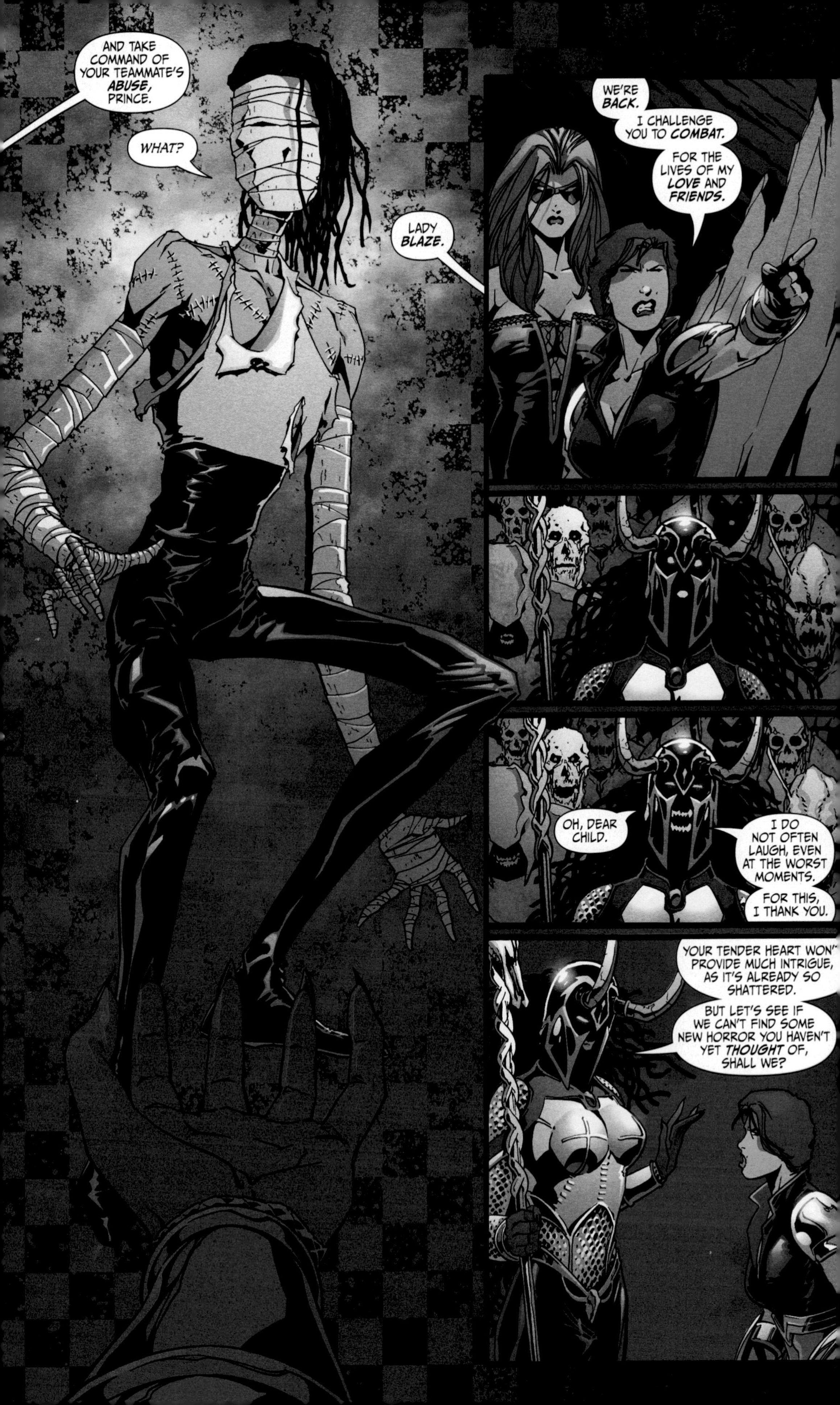
AND TAKE COMMAND OF YOUR TEAMMATE'S ABUSE, PRINCE.
WHAT?
LADY BLAZE.
WE'RE BACK.
I CHALLENGE YOU TO COMBAT.
FOR THE LIVES OF MY LOVE AND FRIENDS.
OH, DEAR CHILD.
I DO NOT OFTEN LAUGH, EVEN AT THE WORST MOMENTS.
FOR THIS, I THANK YOU.
YOUR TENDER HEART WON'T PROVIDE MUCH INTRIGUE, AS IT'S ALREADY SO SHATTERED.
BUT LET'S SEE IF WE CAN'T FIND SOME NEW HORROR YOU HAVEN'T YET THOUGHT OF, SHALL WE?

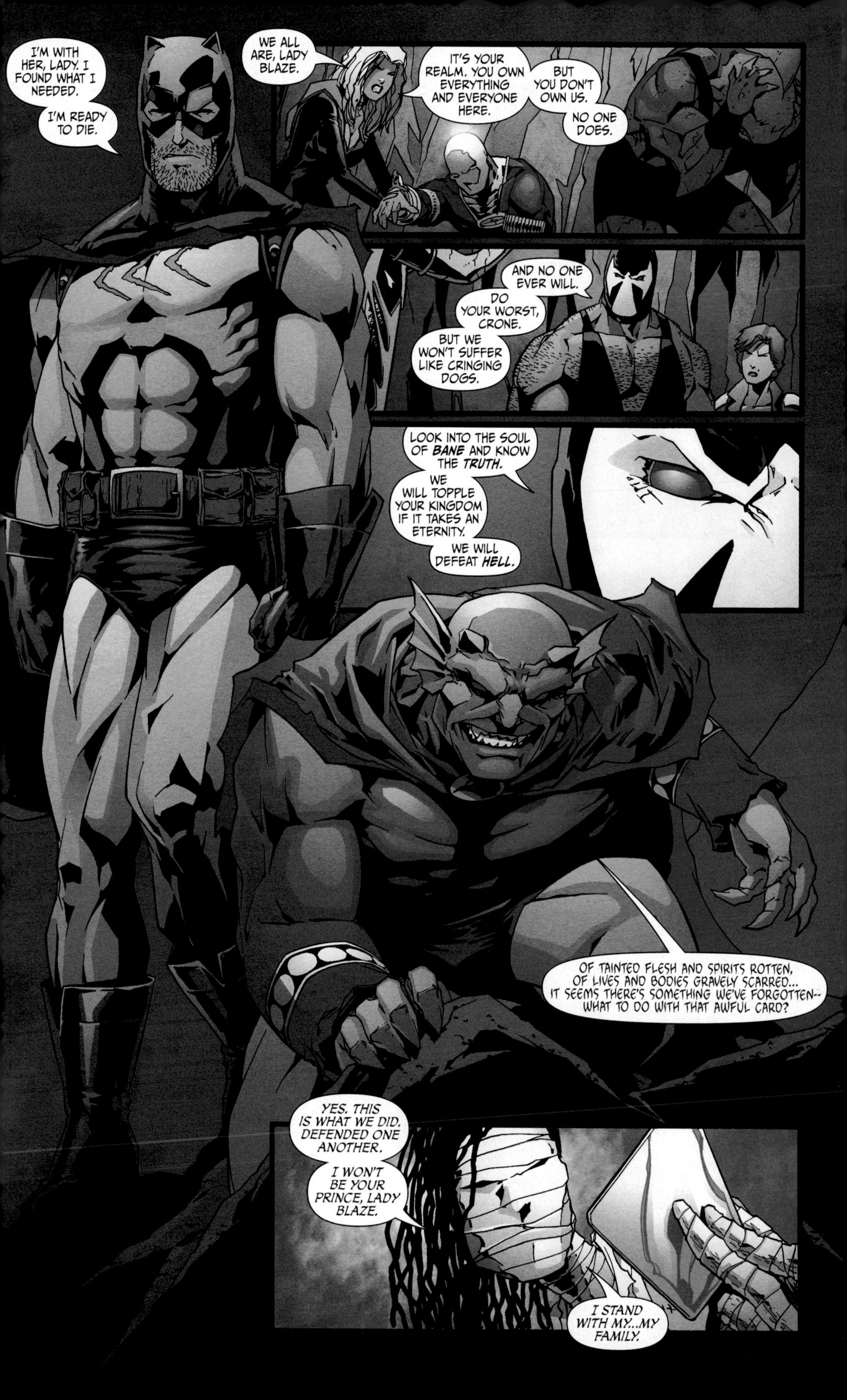

I'M WITH HER, LADY. I FOUND WHAT I NEEDED.
I'M READY TO DIE.
WE ALL ARE, LADY BLAZE.
IT'S YOUR REALM. YOU OWN EVERYTHING AND EVERYONE HERE.
BUT YOU DON'T OWN US.
NO ONE DOES.
AND NO ONE EVER WILL.
DO YOUR WORST, CRONE.
BUT WE WON'T SUFFER LIKE CRINGING DOGS.
LOOK INTO THE SOUL OF BANE AND KNOW THE TRUTH.
WE WILL TOPPLE YOUR KINGDOM IF IT TAKES AN ETERNITY.
WE WILL DEFEAT HELL.
OF TAINTED FLESH AND SPIRITS ROTTEN, OF LIVES AND BODIES GRAVELY SCARRED... IT SEEMS THERE'S SOMETHING WE'VE FORGOTTEN-- WHAT TO DO WITH THAT AWFUL CARD?
YES. THIS IS WHAT WE DID. DEFENDED ONE ANOTHER.
I WON'T BE YOUR PRINCE, LADY BLAZE.
I STAND WITH MY...MY FAMILY.

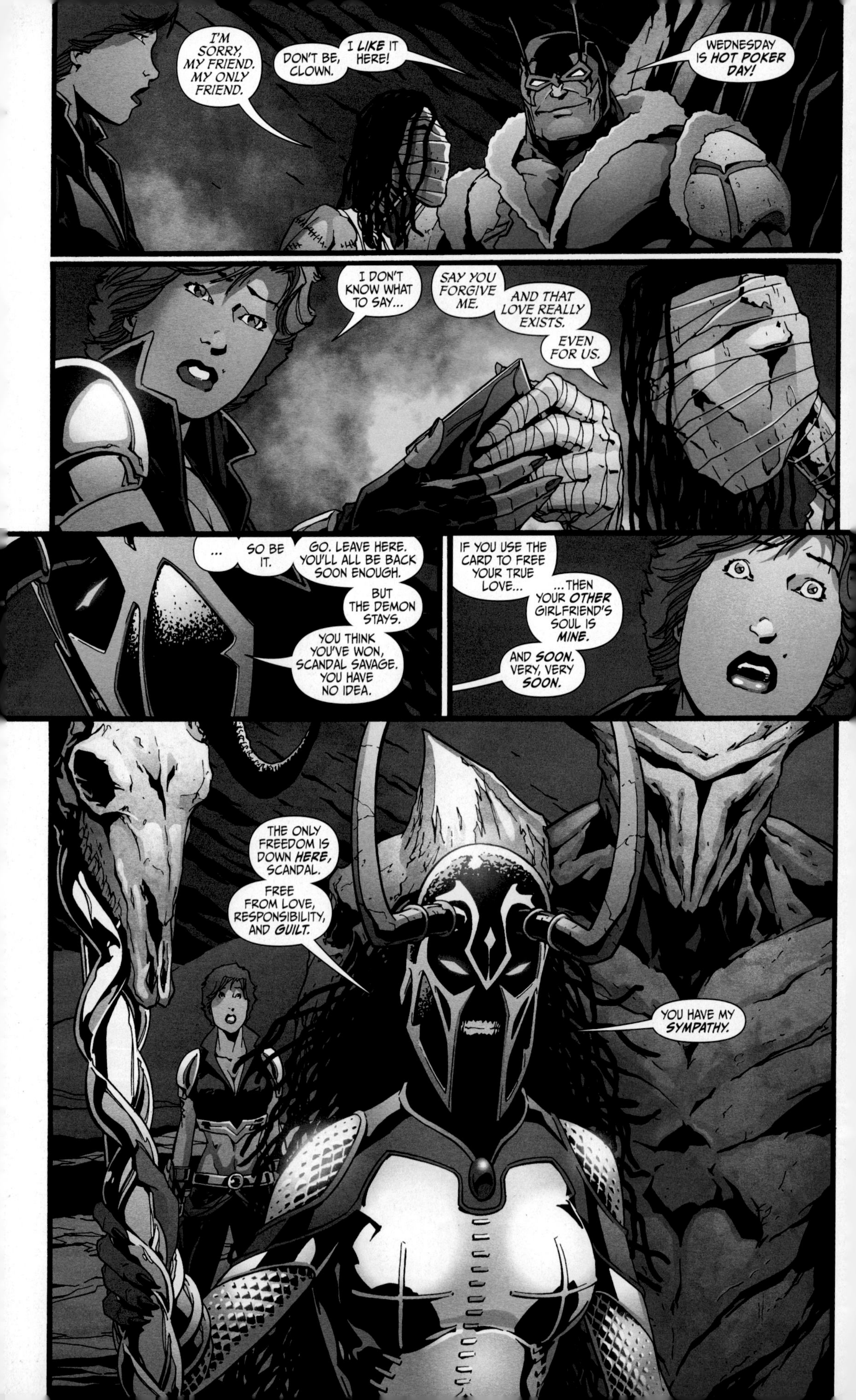
I'M SORRY, MY FRIEND. MY ONLY FRIEND.
DON'T BE, CLOWN.
I LIKE IT HERE!
WEDNESDAY IS HOT POKER DAY!
I DON'T KNOW WHAT TO SAY...
SAY YOU FORGIVE ME.
AND THAT LOVE REALLY EXISTS.
EVEN FOR US.
...
SO BE IT.
GO. LEAVE HERE. YOU'LL ALL BE BACK SOON ENOUGH.
BUT THE DEMON STAYS.
YOU THINK YOU'VE WON, SCANDAL SAVAGE. YOU HAVE NO IDEA.
IF YOU USE THE CARD TO FREE YOUR TRUE LOVE...
...THEN YOUR OTHER GIRLFRIEND'S SOUL IS MINE.
AND SOON. VERY, VERY SOON.
THE ONLY FREEDOM IS DOWN HERE, SCANDAL.
FREE FROM LOVE, RESPONSIBILITY, AND GUILT.
YOU HAVE MY SYMPATHY.

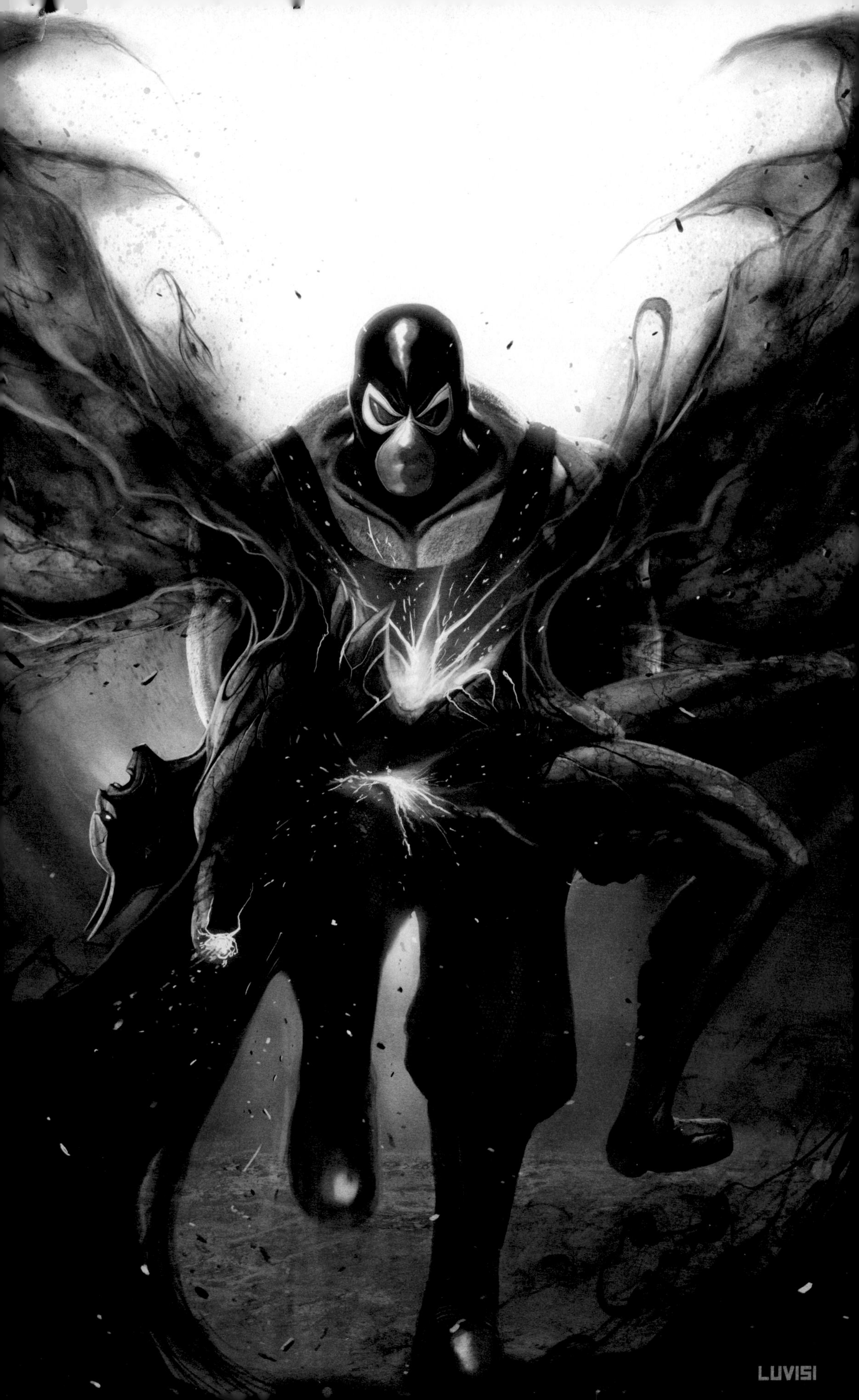
LUVISI

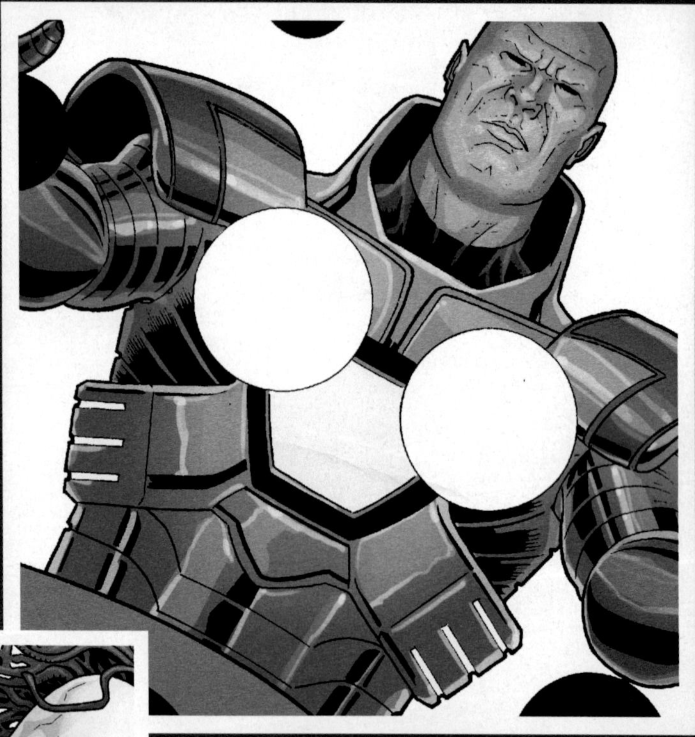
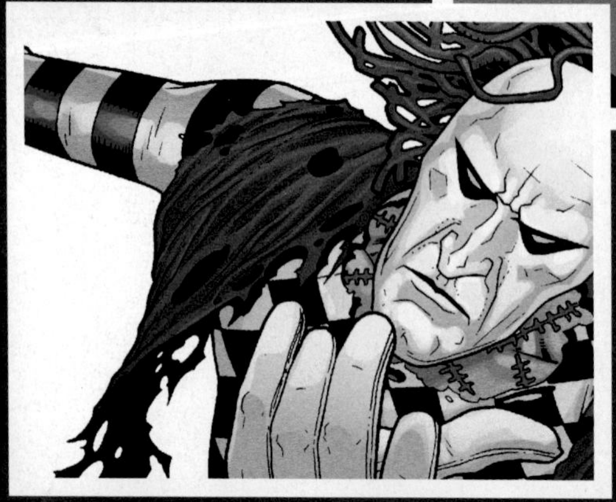

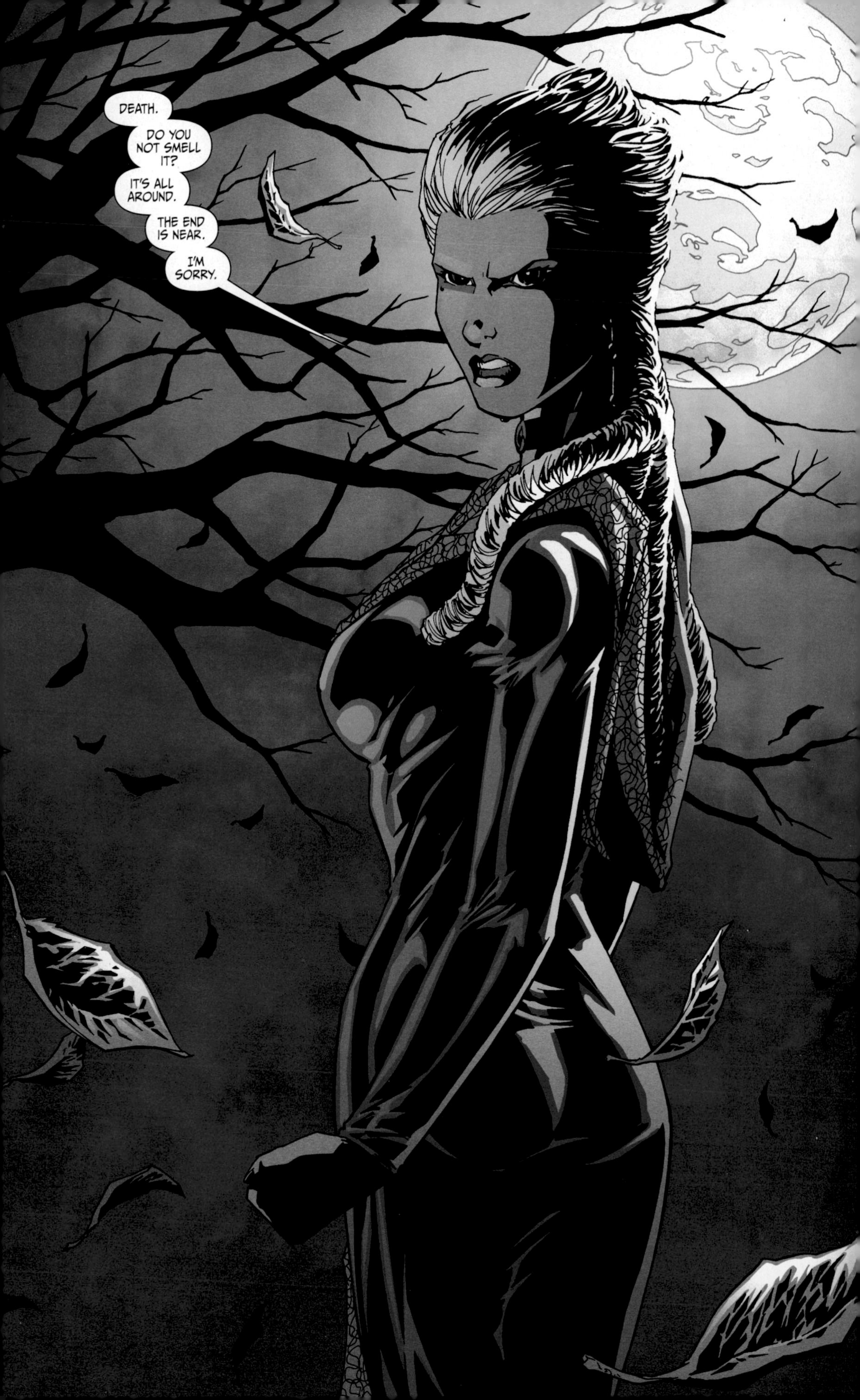
DEATH.
DO YOU NOT SMELL IT?
IT'S ALL AROUND.
THE END IS NEAR.
I'M SORRY.

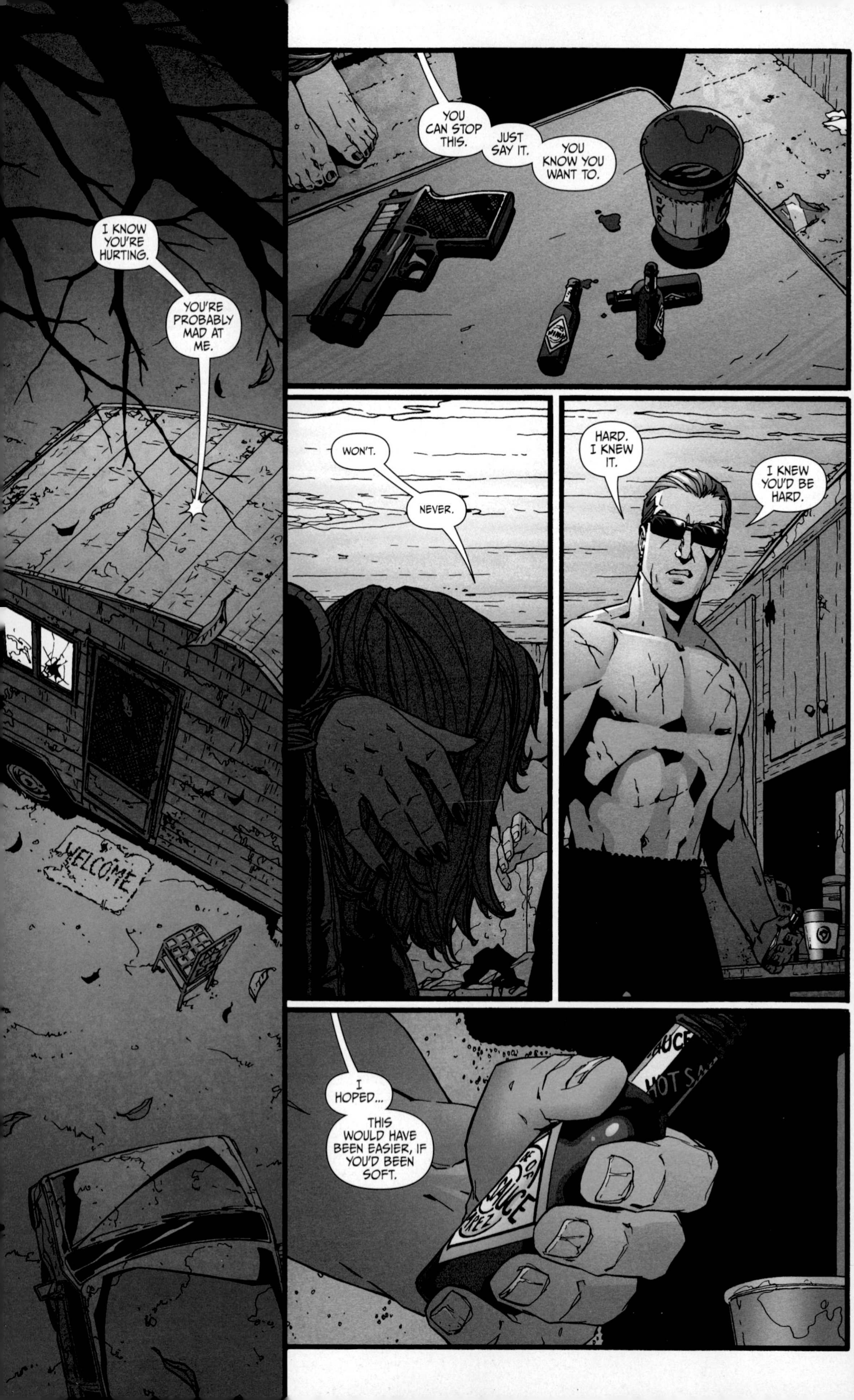
I KNOW YOU'RE HURTING.
YOU'RE PROBABLY MAD AT ME.
WELCOME
YOU CAN STOP THIS.
JUST SAY IT.
YOU KNOW YOU WANT TO.
WON'T.
NEVER.
HARD. I KNEW IT.
I KNEW YOU'D BE HARD.
I HOPED...
THIS WOULD HAVE BEEN EASIER, IF YOU'D BEEN SOFT.

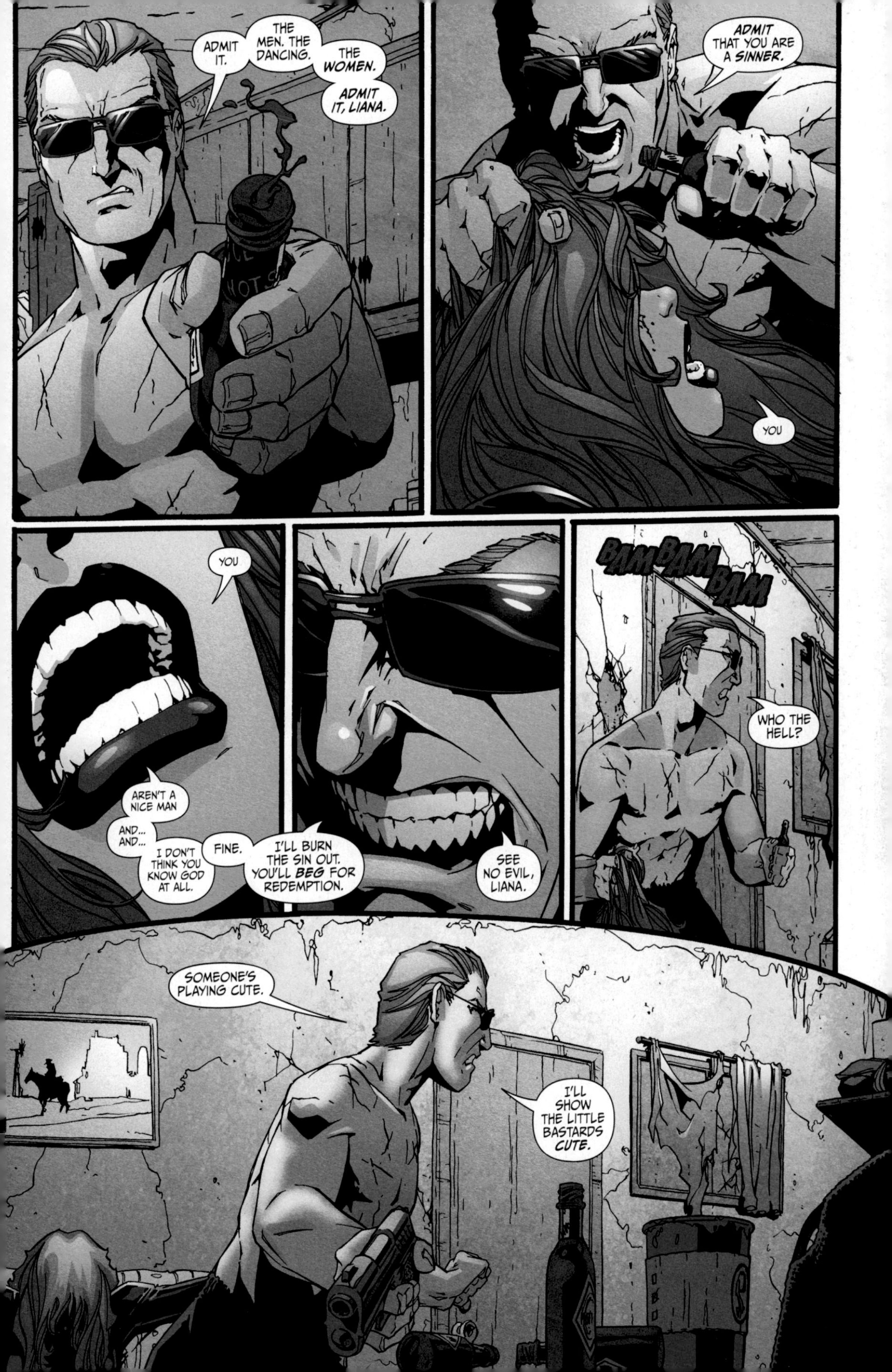

ADMIT IT.
THE MEN. THE DANCING.
THE WOMEN.
ADMIT IT, LIANA.
ADMIT THAT YOU ARE A SINNER.
YOU
YOU
AREN'T A NICE MAN
AND... AND...
I DON'T THINK YOU KNOW GOD AT ALL.
FINE.
I'LL BURN THE SIN OUT. YOU'LL BEG FOR REDEMPTION.
SEE NO EVIL, LIANA.
BAMBAMBAM
WHO THE HELL?
SOMEONE'S PLAYING CUTE.
I'LL SHOW THE LITTLE BASTARDS CUTE.

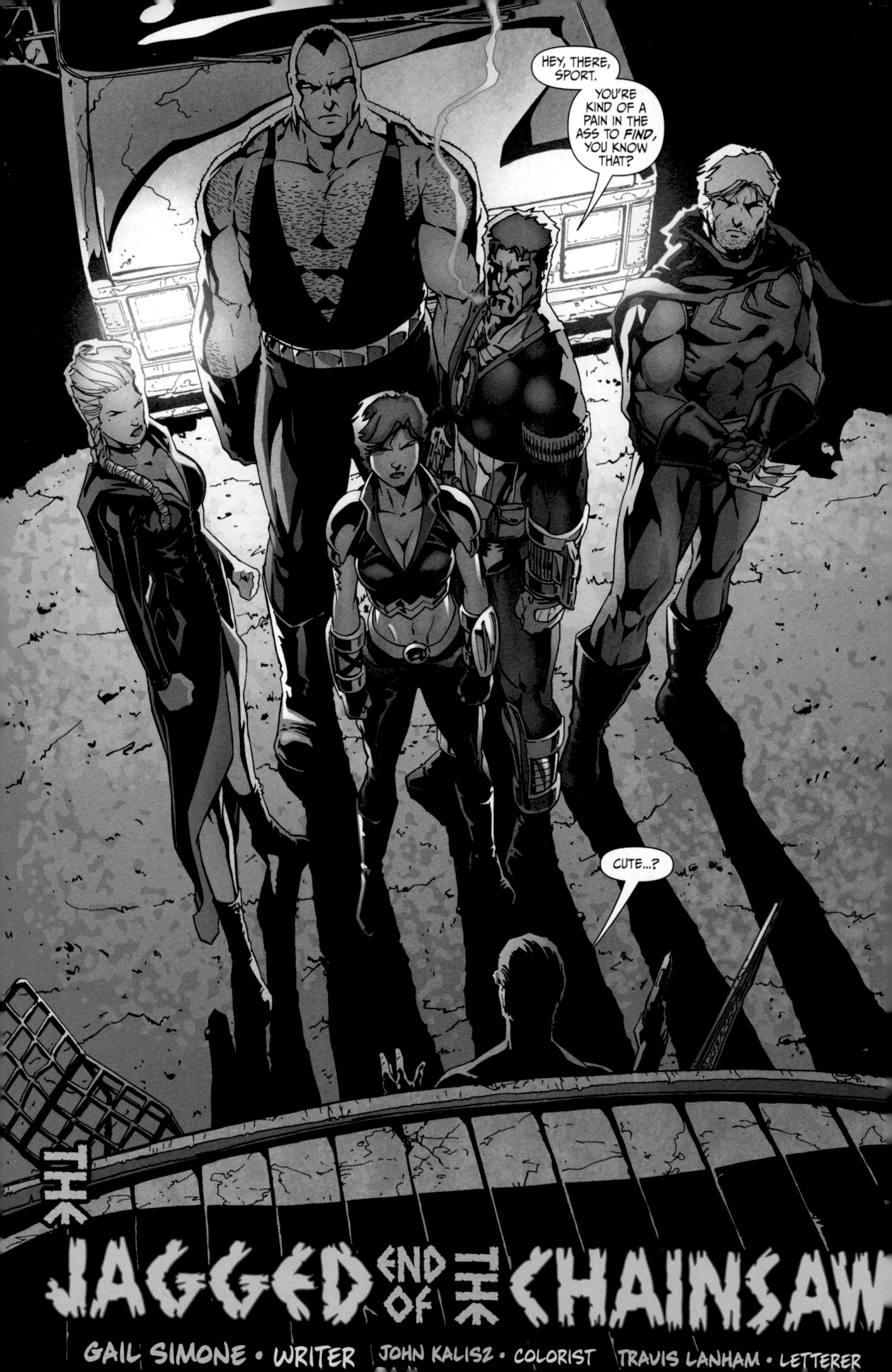
HEY, THERE, SPORT.
YOU'RE KIND OF A PAIN IN THE ASS TO *FIND*, YOU KNOW THAT?
CUTE...?
THE JAGGED END OF THE CHAINSAW
GAIL SIMONE • WRITER JOHN KALISZ • COLORIST TRAVIS LANHAM • LETTERER

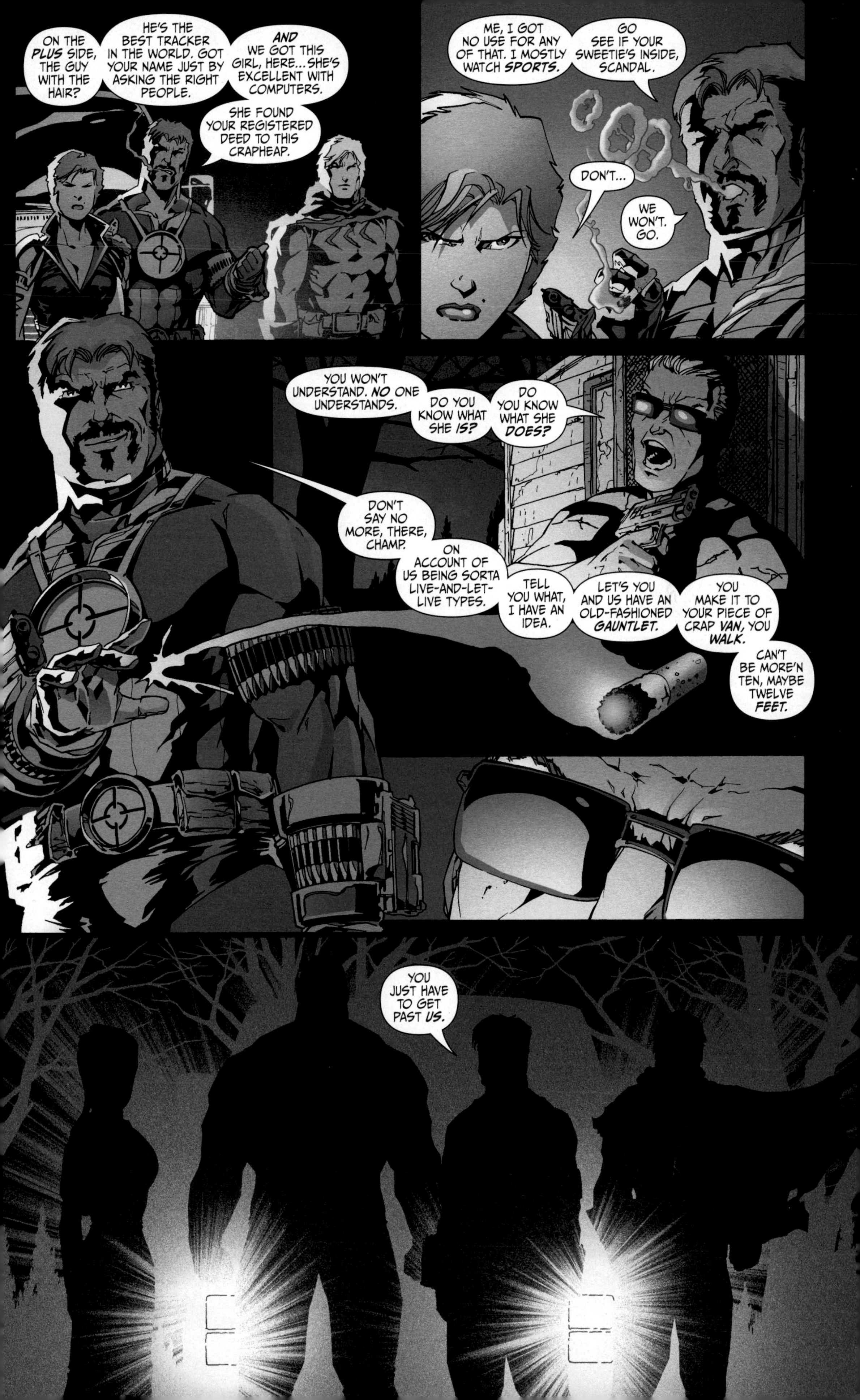
ON THE PLUS SIDE, THE GUY WITH THE HAIR?
HE'S THE BEST TRACKER IN THE WORLD. GOT YOUR NAME JUST BY ASKING THE RIGHT PEOPLE.
AND WE GOT THIS GIRL, HERE... SHE'S EXCELLENT WITH COMPUTERS.
SHE FOUND YOUR REGISTERED DEED TO THIS CRAPHEAP.
ME, I GOT NO USE FOR ANY OF THAT. I MOSTLY WATCH SPORTS.
GO SEE IF YOUR SWEETIE'S INSIDE, SCANDAL.
DON'T...
WE WON'T. GO.
YOU WON'T UNDERSTAND. NO ONE UNDERSTANDS.
DO YOU KNOW WHAT SHE IS?
DO YOU KNOW WHAT SHE DOES?
DON'T SAY NO MORE, THERE, CHAMP.
ON ACCOUNT OF US BEING SORTA LIVE-AND-LET-LIVE TYPES.
TELL YOU WHAT, I HAVE AN IDEA.
LET'S YOU AND US HAVE AN OLD-FASHIONED GAUNTLET.
YOU MAKE IT TO YOUR PIECE OF CRAP VAN, YOU WALK.
CAN'T BE MORE'N TEN, MAYBE TWELVE FEET.
YOU JUST HAVE TO GET PAST US.

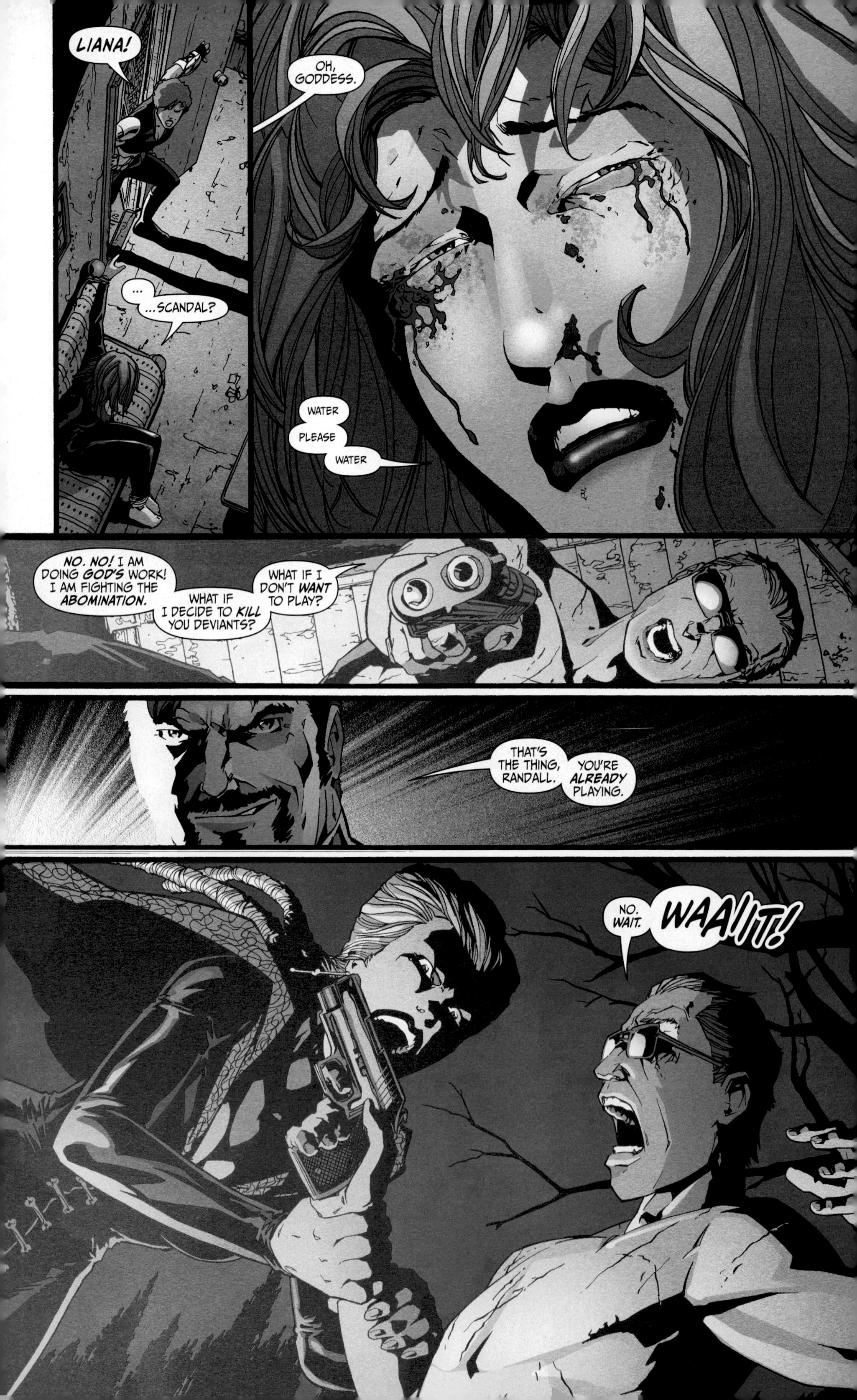
LIANA!
OH, GODDESS.
... ...SCANDAL?
WATER
PLEASE
WATER
NO. NO! I AM DOING GOD'S WORK! I AM FIGHTING THE ABOMINATION.
WHAT IF I DECIDE TO KILL YOU DEVIANTS?
WHAT IF I DON'T WANT TO PLAY?
THAT'S THE THING, RANDALL.
YOU'RE ALREADY PLAYING.
NO. WAIT.
WAAIIT!

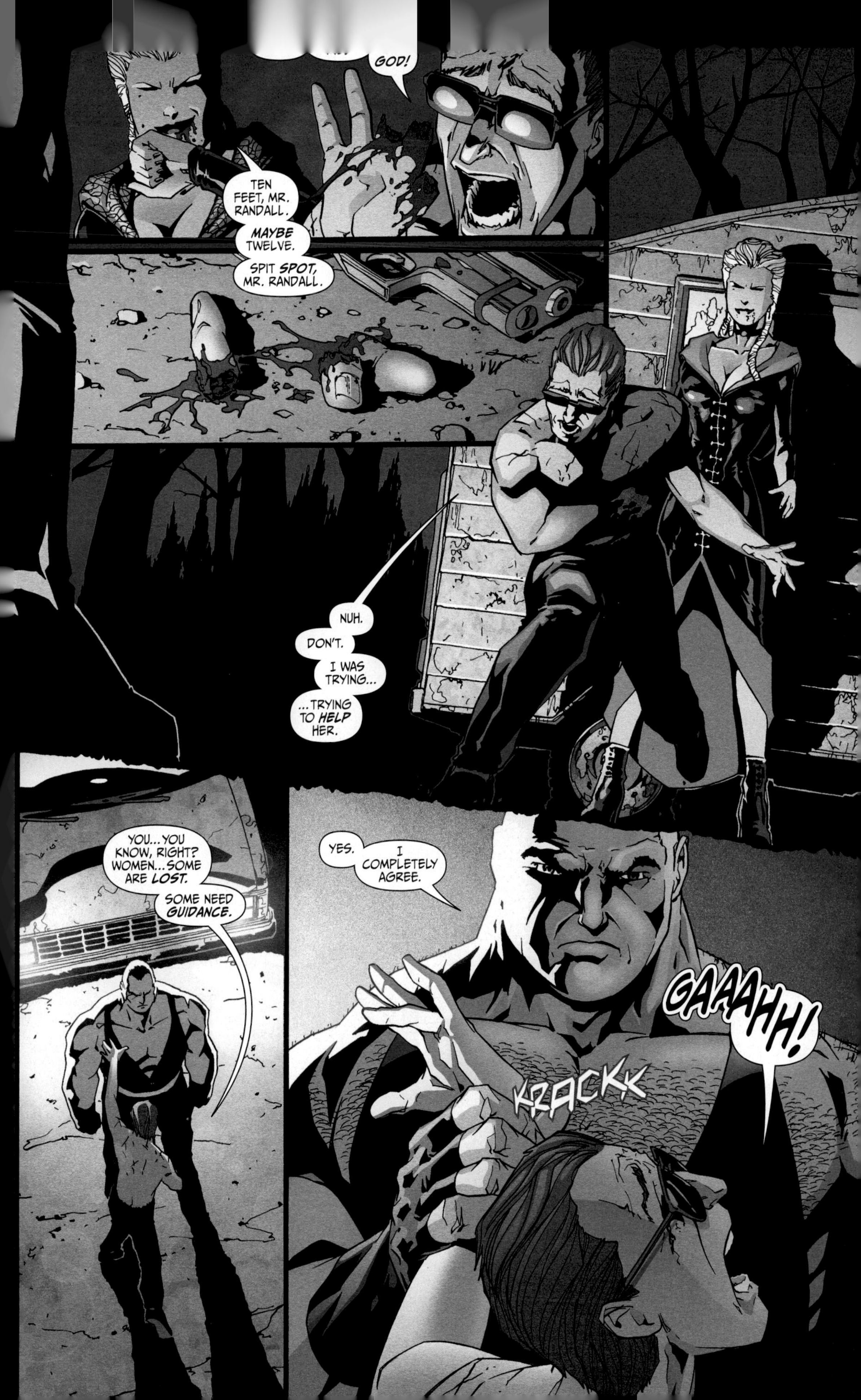
GOD!
TEN FEET, MR. RANDALL.
MAYBE TWELVE.
SPIT SPOT, MR. RANDALL.
NUH.
DON'T.
I WAS TRYING...
...TRYING TO HELP HER.
YOU...YOU KNOW, RIGHT? WOMEN...SOME ARE LOST.
SOME NEED GUIDANCE.
YES.
I COMPLETELY AGREE.
KRACKK
GAAAHH!

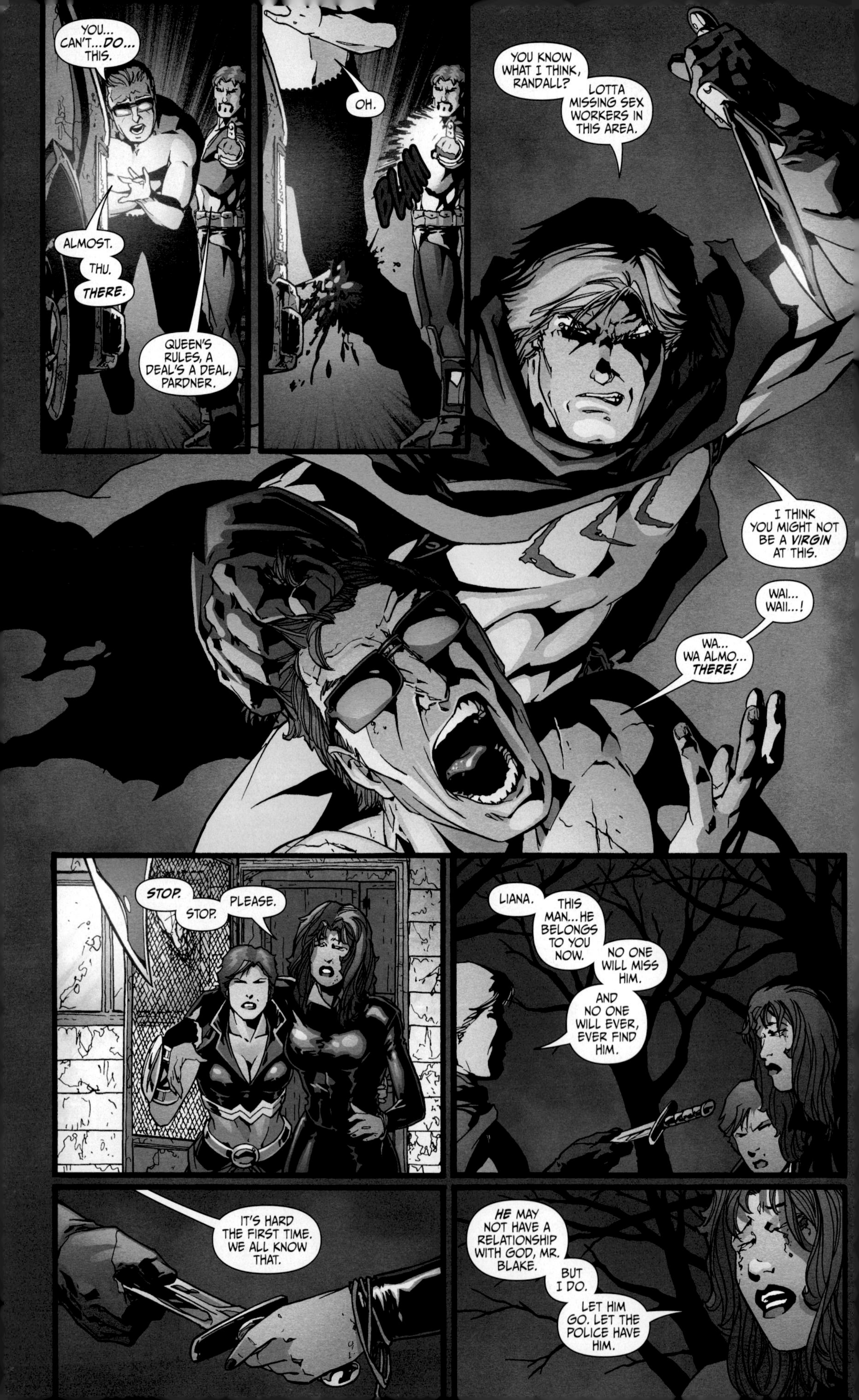

YOU... CAN'T...DO... THIS.
ALMOST.
THU.
THERE.
QUEEN'S RULES, A DEAL'S A DEAL, PARDNER.
OH.
BLAM
YOU KNOW WHAT I THINK, RANDALL?
LOTTA MISSING SEX WORKERS IN THIS AREA.
I THINK YOU MIGHT NOT BE A VIRGIN AT THIS.
WAI... WAII...!
WA... WA ALMO... THERE!
STOP.
STOP.
PLEASE.
LIANA.
THIS MAN...HE BELONGS TO YOU NOW.
NO ONE WILL MISS HIM.
AND NO ONE WILL EVER, EVER FIND HIM.
IT'S HARD THE FIRST TIME. WE ALL KNOW THAT.
HE MAY NOT HAVE A RELATIONSHIP WITH GOD, MR. BLAKE.
BUT I DO.
LET HIM GO. LET THE POLICE HAVE HIM.

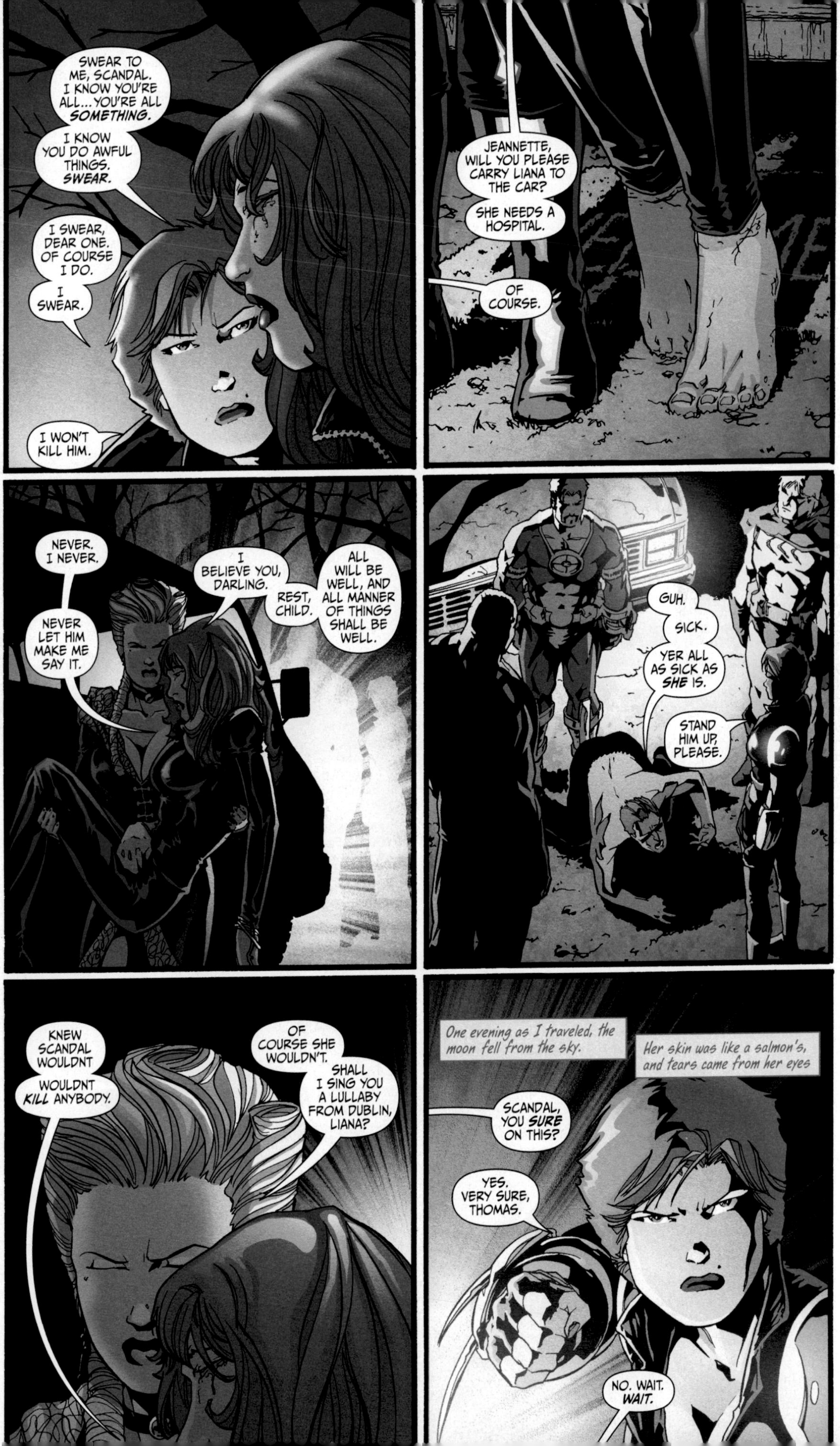
SWEAR TO ME, SCANDAL. I KNOW YOU'RE ALL...YOU'RE ALL SOMETHING.
I KNOW YOU DO AWFUL THINGS. SWEAR.
I SWEAR, DEAR ONE. OF COURSE I DO.
I SWEAR.
I WON'T KILL HIM.
JEANNETTE, WILL YOU PLEASE CARRY LIANA TO THE CAR?
SHE NEEDS A HOSPITAL.
OF COURSE.
NEVER. I NEVER.
NEVER LET HIM MAKE ME SAY IT.
I BELIEVE YOU, DARLING.
REST, CHILD.
ALL WILL BE WELL, AND ALL MANNER OF THINGS SHALL BE WELL.
GUH.
SICK.
YER ALL AS SICK AS SHE IS.
STAND HIM UP, PLEASE.
KNEW SCANDAL WOULDNT
WOULDNT KILL ANYBODY.
OF COURSE SHE WOULDN'T.
SHALL I SING YOU A LULLABY FROM DUBLIN, LIANA?
One evening as I traveled, the moon fell from the sky.
Her skin was like a salmon's, and tears came from her eyes
SCANDAL, YOU SURE ON THIS?
YES. VERY SURE, THOMAS.
NO. WAIT. WAIT.

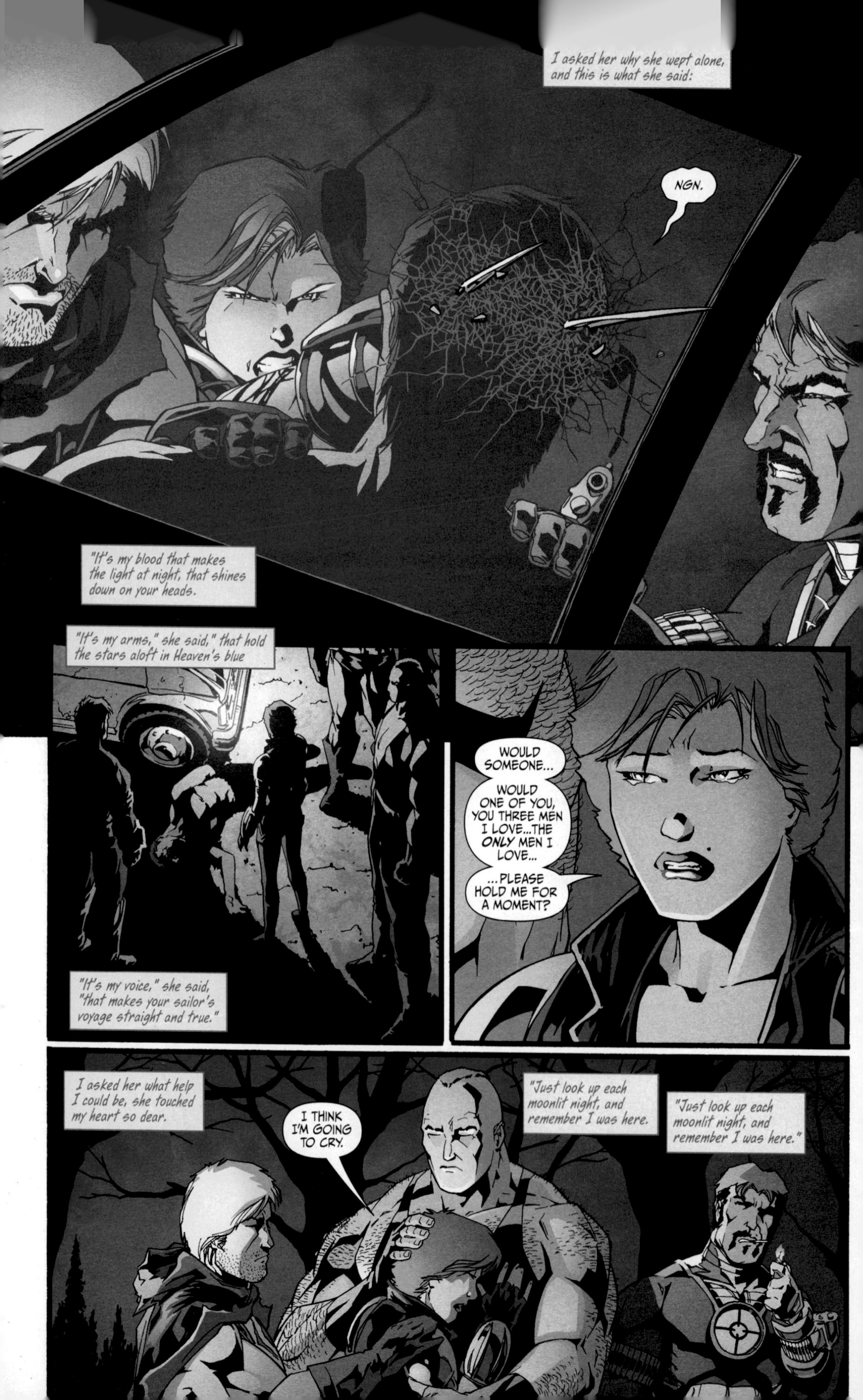

I asked her why she wept alone, and this is what she said:
NGN.
"It's my blood that makes the light at night, that shines down on your heads.
"It's my arms," she said," that hold the stars aloft in Heaven's blue
"It's my voice," she said, "that makes your sailor's voyage straight and true."
WOULD SOMEONE...
WOULD ONE OF YOU, YOU THREE MEN I LOVE...THE ONLY MEN I LOVE...
...PLEASE HOLD ME FOR A MOMENT?
I asked her what help I could be, she touched my heart so dear.
I THINK I'M GOING TO CRY.
"Just look up each moonlit night, and remember I was here.

"Just look up each moonlit night, and remember I was here."

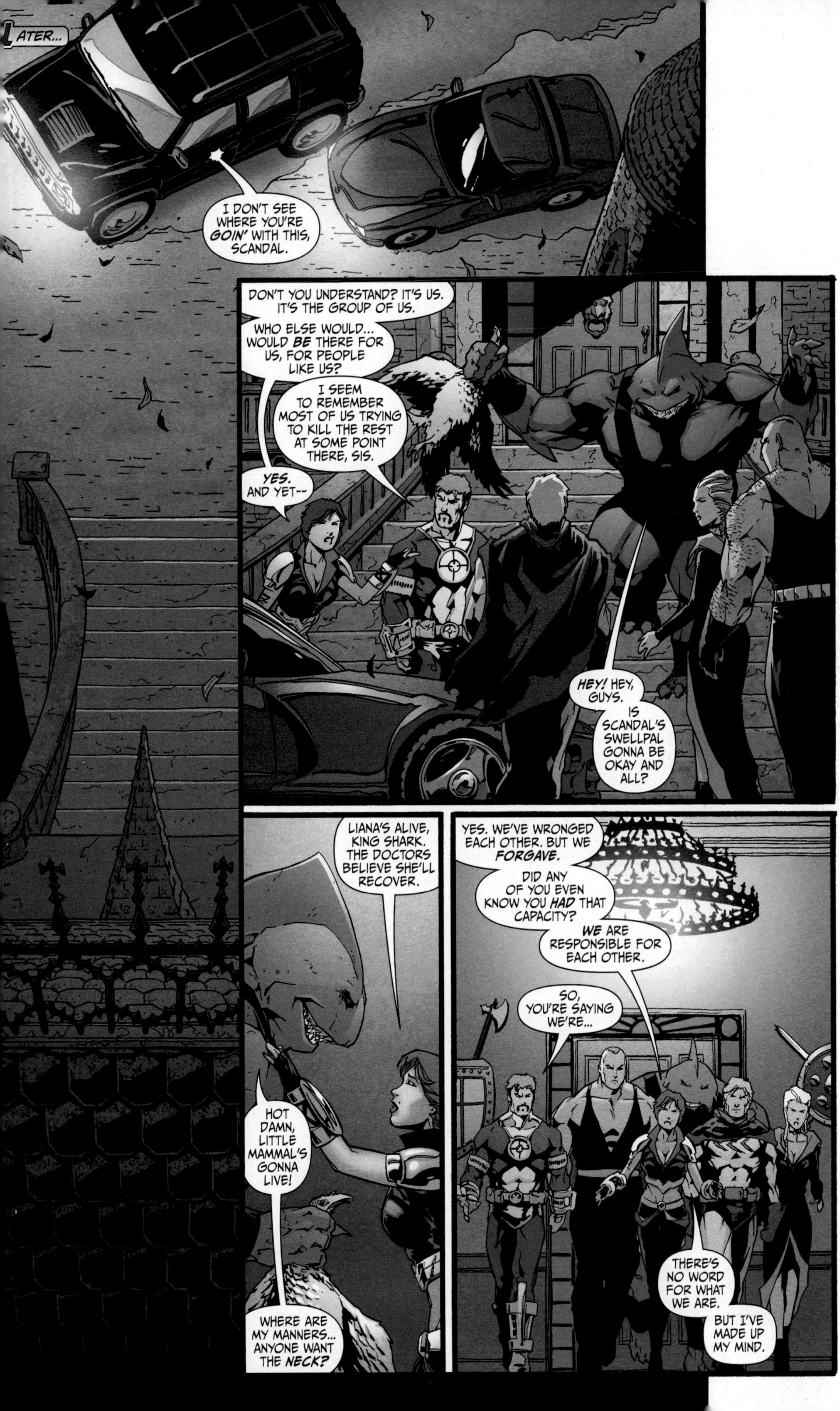
LATER...
I DON'T SEE WHERE YOU'RE GOIN' WITH THIS, SCANDAL.
DON'T YOU UNDERSTAND? IT'S US. IT'S THE GROUP OF US.
WHO ELSE WOULD... WOULD BE THERE FOR US, FOR PEOPLE LIKE US?
I SEEM TO REMEMBER MOST OF US TRYING TO KILL THE REST AT SOME POINT THERE, SIS.
YES. AND YET--
HEY! HEY, GUYS.
IS SCANDAL'S SWELLPAL GONNA BE OKAY AND ALL?
LIANA'S ALIVE, KING SHARK. THE DOCTORS BELIEVE SHE'LL RECOVER.
HOT DAMN, LITTLE MAMMAL'S GONNA LIVE!
WHERE ARE MY MANNERS... ANYONE WANT THE NECK?
YES. WE'VE WRONGED EACH OTHER. BUT WE FORGAVE.
DID ANY OF YOU EVEN KNOW YOU HAD THAT CAPACITY?
WE ARE RESPONSIBLE FOR EACH OTHER.
SO, YOU'RE SAYING WE'RE...
THERE'S NO WORD FOR WHAT WE ARE.
BUT I'VE MADE UP MY MIND.

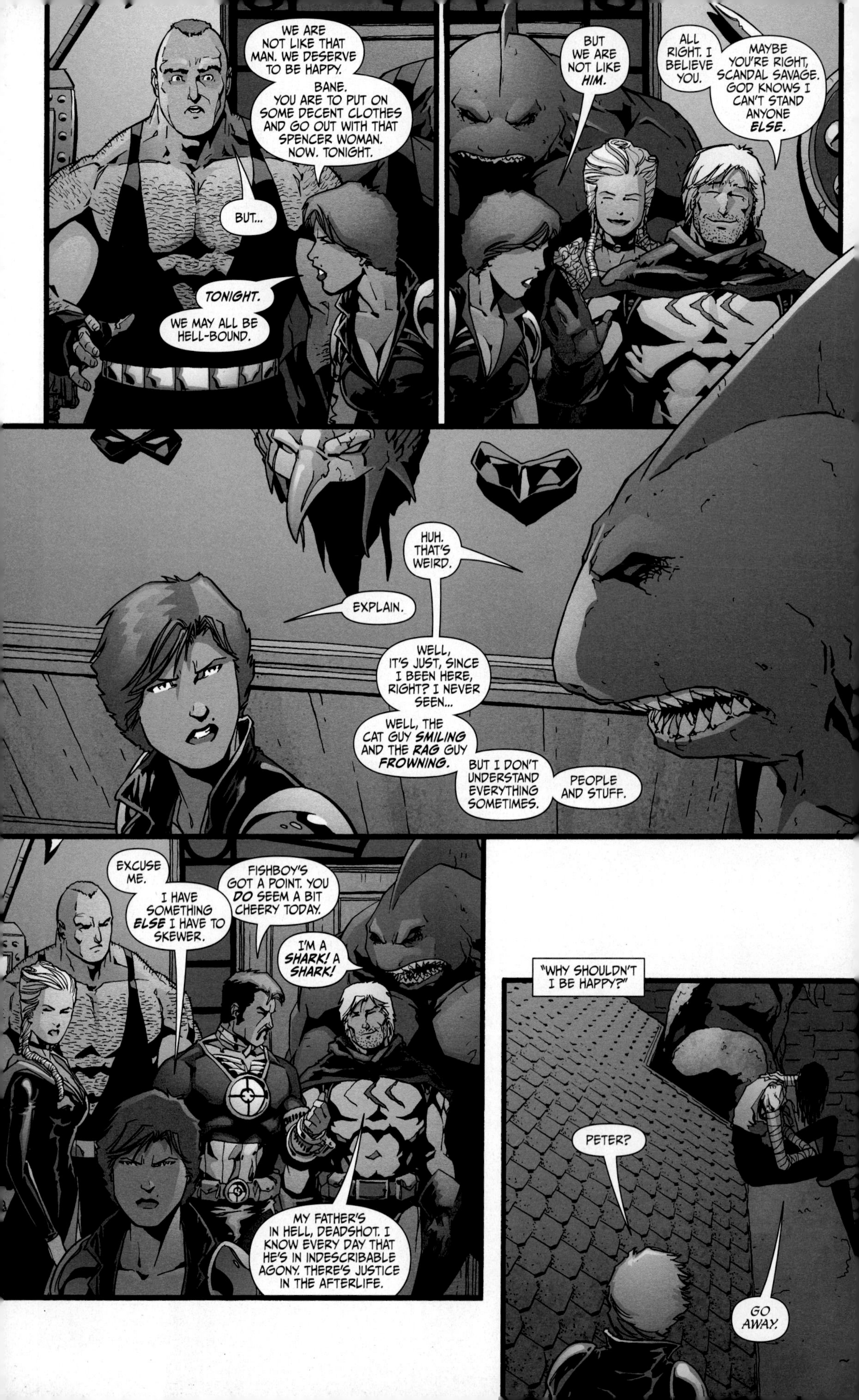
WE ARE NOT LIKE THAT MAN. WE DESERVE TO BE HAPPY.
BANE. YOU ARE TO PUT ON SOME DECENT CLOTHES AND GO OUT WITH THAT SPENCER WOMAN. NOW. TONIGHT.
BUT...
TONIGHT.
WE MAY ALL BE HELL-BOUND.
BUT WE ARE NOT LIKE HIM.
ALL RIGHT. I BELIEVE YOU.
MAYBE YOU'RE RIGHT, SCANDAL SAVAGE. GOD KNOWS I CAN'T STAND ANYONE ELSE.
HUH. THAT'S WEIRD.
EXPLAIN.
WELL, IT'S JUST, SINCE I BEEN HERE, RIGHT? I NEVER SEEN...
WELL, THE CAT GUY SMILING AND THE RAG GUY FROWNING.
BUT I DON'T UNDERSTAND EVERYTHING SOMETIMES.
PEOPLE AND STUFF.
EXCUSE ME.
I HAVE SOMETHING ELSE I HAVE TO SKEWER.
FISHBOY'S GOT A POINT. YOU DO SEEM A BIT CHEERY TODAY.
I'M A SHARK! A SHARK!
MY FATHER'S IN HELL, DEADSHOT. I KNOW EVERY DAY THAT HE'S IN INDESCRIBABLE AGONY. THERE'S JUSTICE IN THE AFTERLIFE.
"WHY SHOULDN'T I BE HAPPY?"
PETER?
GO AWAY.

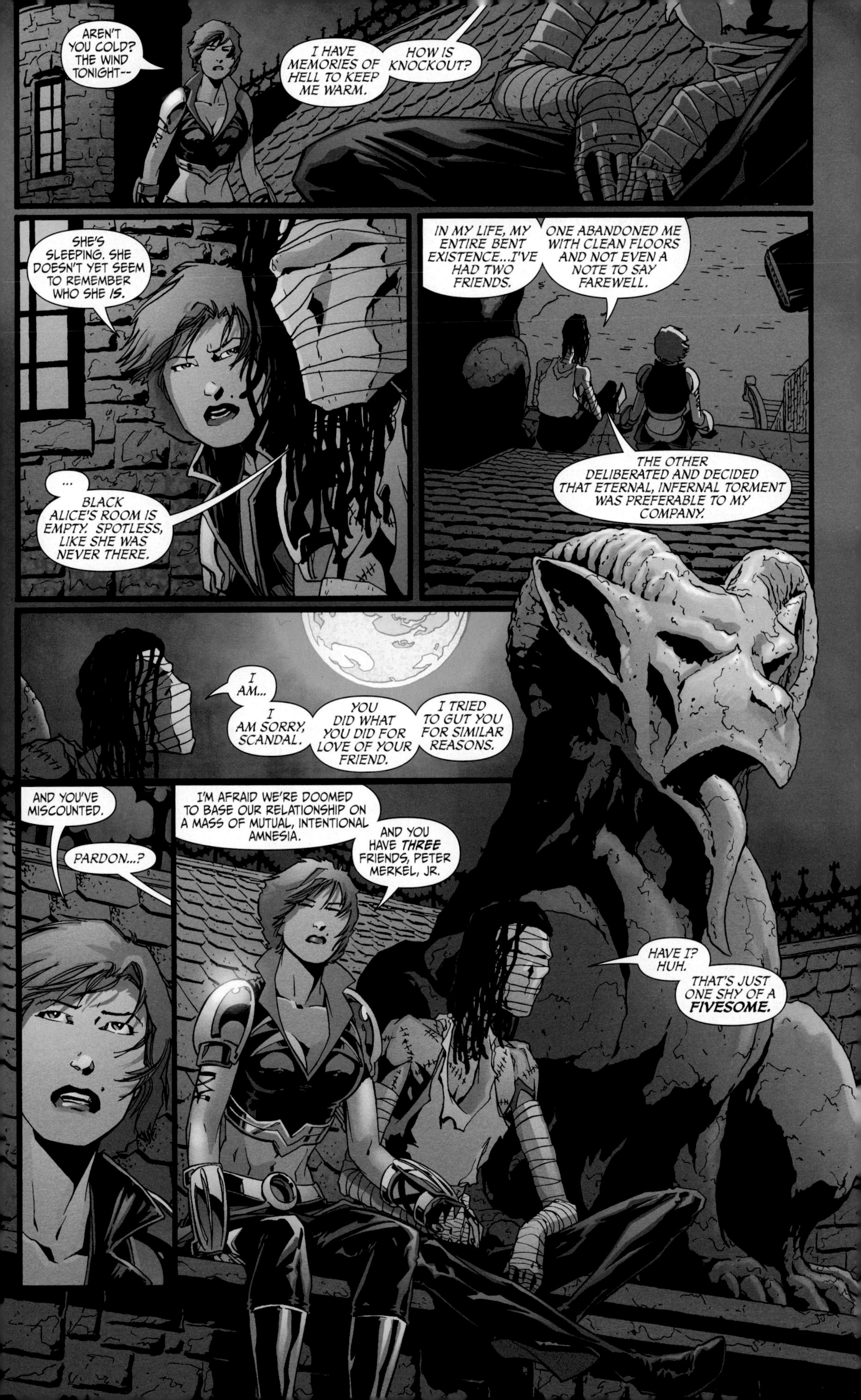

AREN'T YOU COLD? THE WIND TONIGHT--
I HAVE MEMORIES OF HELL TO KEEP ME WARM.
HOW IS KNOCKOUT?
SHE'S SLEEPING. SHE DOESN'T YET SEEM TO REMEMBER WHO SHE IS.
...
BLACK ALICE'S ROOM IS EMPTY. SPOTLESS, LIKE SHE WAS NEVER THERE.
IN MY LIFE, MY ENTIRE BENT EXISTENCE...I'VE HAD TWO FRIENDS.
ONE ABANDONED ME WITH CLEAN FLOORS AND NOT EVEN A NOTE TO SAY FAREWELL.
THE OTHER DELIBERATED AND DECIDED THAT ETERNAL, INFERNAL TORMENT WAS PREFERABLE TO MY COMPANY.
I AM...
I AM SORRY, SCANDAL.
YOU DID WHAT YOU DID FOR LOVE OF YOUR FRIEND.
I TRIED TO GUT YOU FOR SIMILAR REASONS.
AND YOU'VE MISCOUNTED.
PARDON...?
I'M AFRAID WE'RE DOOMED TO BASE OUR RELATIONSHIP ON A MASS OF MUTUAL, INTENTIONAL AMNESIA.
AND YOU HAVE THREE FRIENDS, PETER MERKEL, JR.
HAVE I? HUH.
THAT'S JUST ONE SHY OF A FIVESOME.

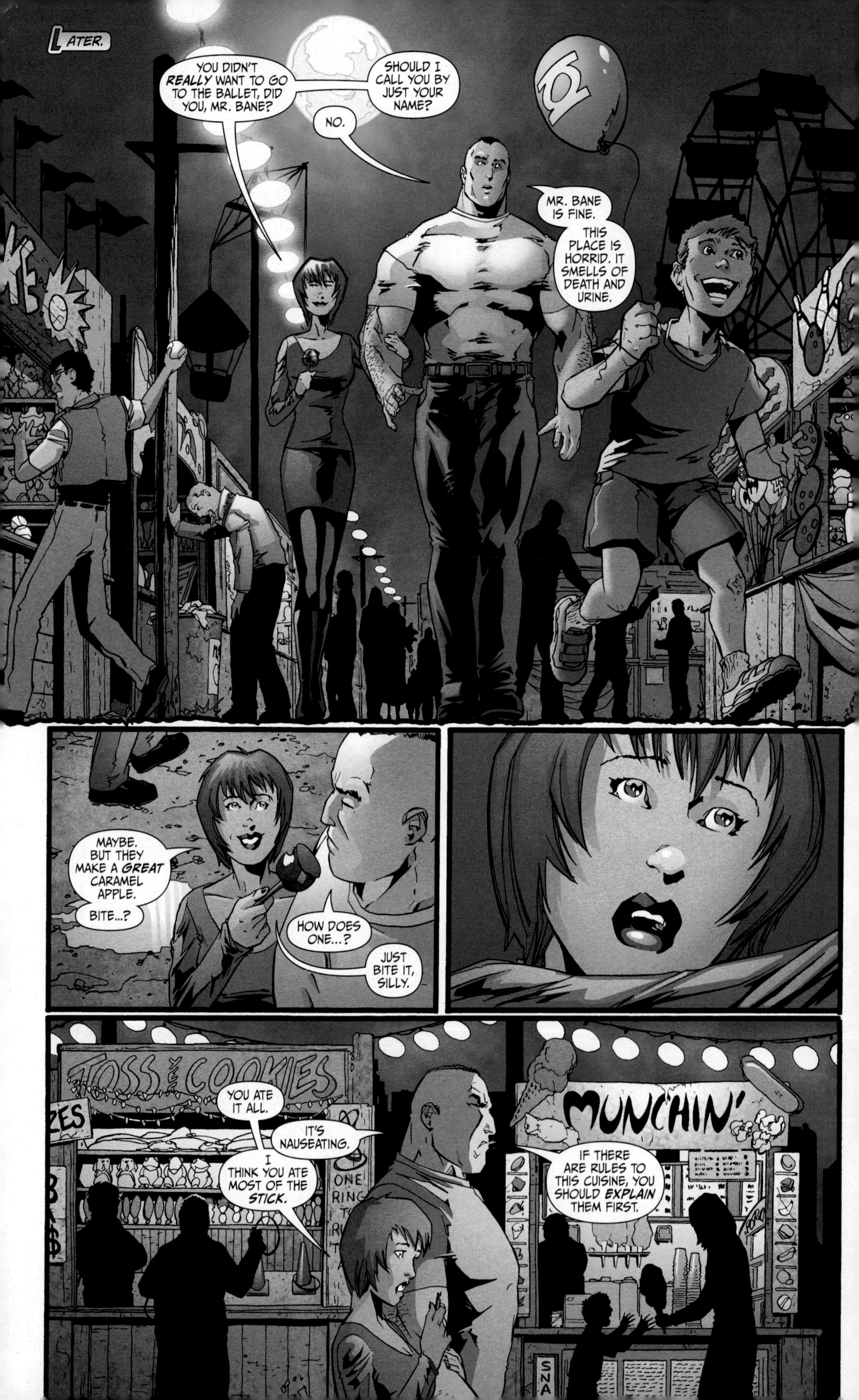
LATER.
YOU DIDN'T REALLY WANT TO GO TO THE BALLET, DID YOU, MR. BANE?
SHOULD I CALL YOU BY JUST YOUR NAME?
NO.
MR. BANE IS FINE.
THIS PLACE IS HORRID. IT SMELLS OF DEATH AND URINE.
MAYBE. BUT THEY MAKE A GREAT CARAMEL APPLE.
BITE...?
HOW DOES ONE...?
JUST BITE IT, SILLY.
TOSS YE COOKIES
MUNCHIN'
YOU ATE IT ALL.
IT'S NAUSEATING.
I THINK YOU ATE MOST OF THE STICK.
IF THERE ARE RULES TO THIS CUISINE, YOU SHOULD EXPLAIN THEM FIRST.

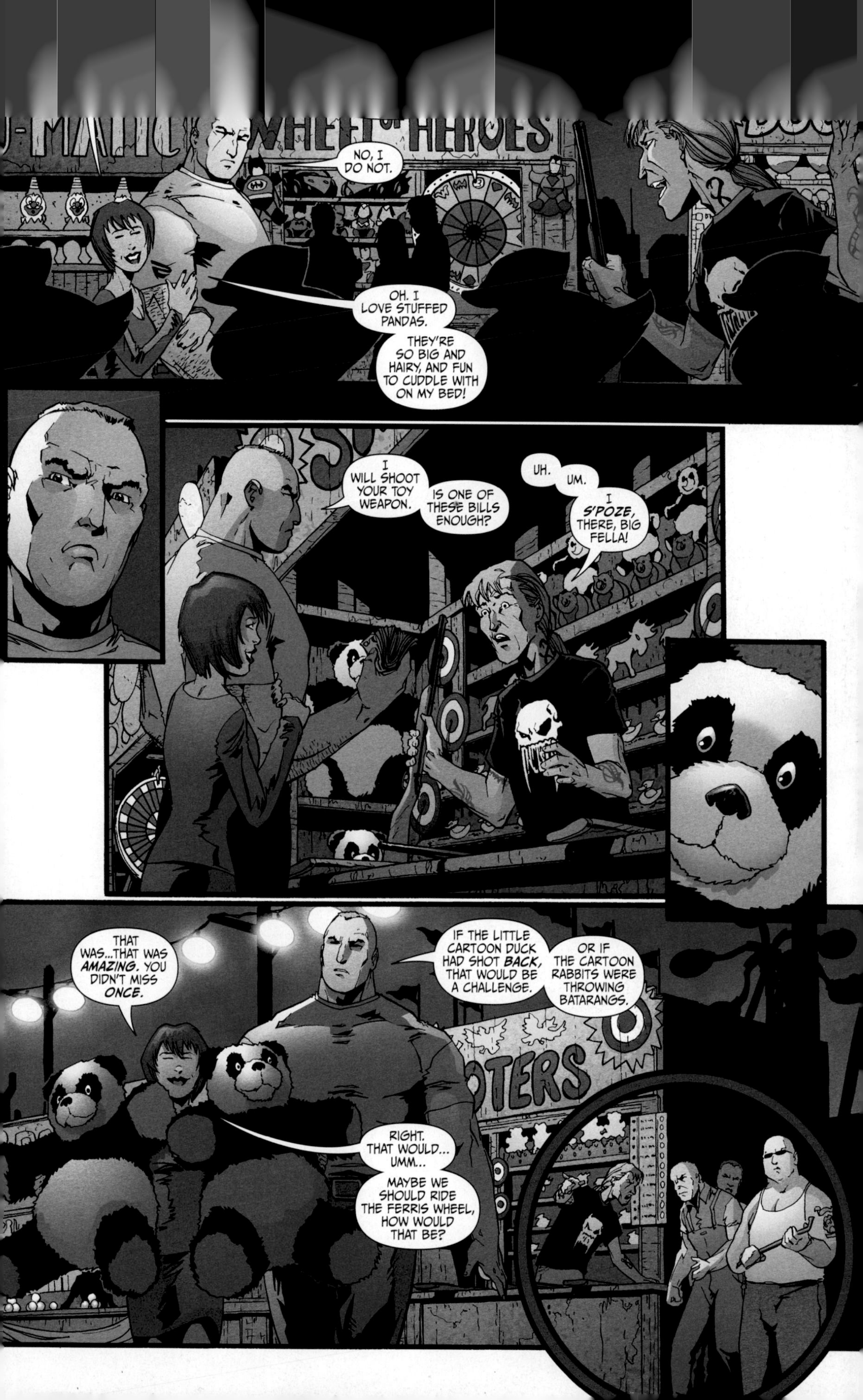

O-MATIC
WHEEL OF HEROES
NO, I DO NOT.
OH. I LOVE STUFFED PANDAS.
THEY'RE SO BIG AND HAIRY, AND FUN TO CUDDLE WITH ON MY BED!
I WILL SHOOT YOUR TOY WEAPON.
IS ONE OF THESE BILLS ENOUGH?
UH.
UM.
I *S'POZE,* THERE, BIG FELLA!
THAT WAS...THAT WAS *AMAZING.* YOU DIDN'T MISS *ONCE.*
IF THE LITTLE CARTOON DUCK HAD SHOT *BACK,* THAT WOULD BE A CHALLENGE.
OR IF THE CARTOON RABBITS WERE THROWING BATARANGS.
RIGHT. THAT WOULD... UMM...
MAYBE WE SHOULD RIDE THE FERRIS WHEEL, HOW WOULD THAT BE?

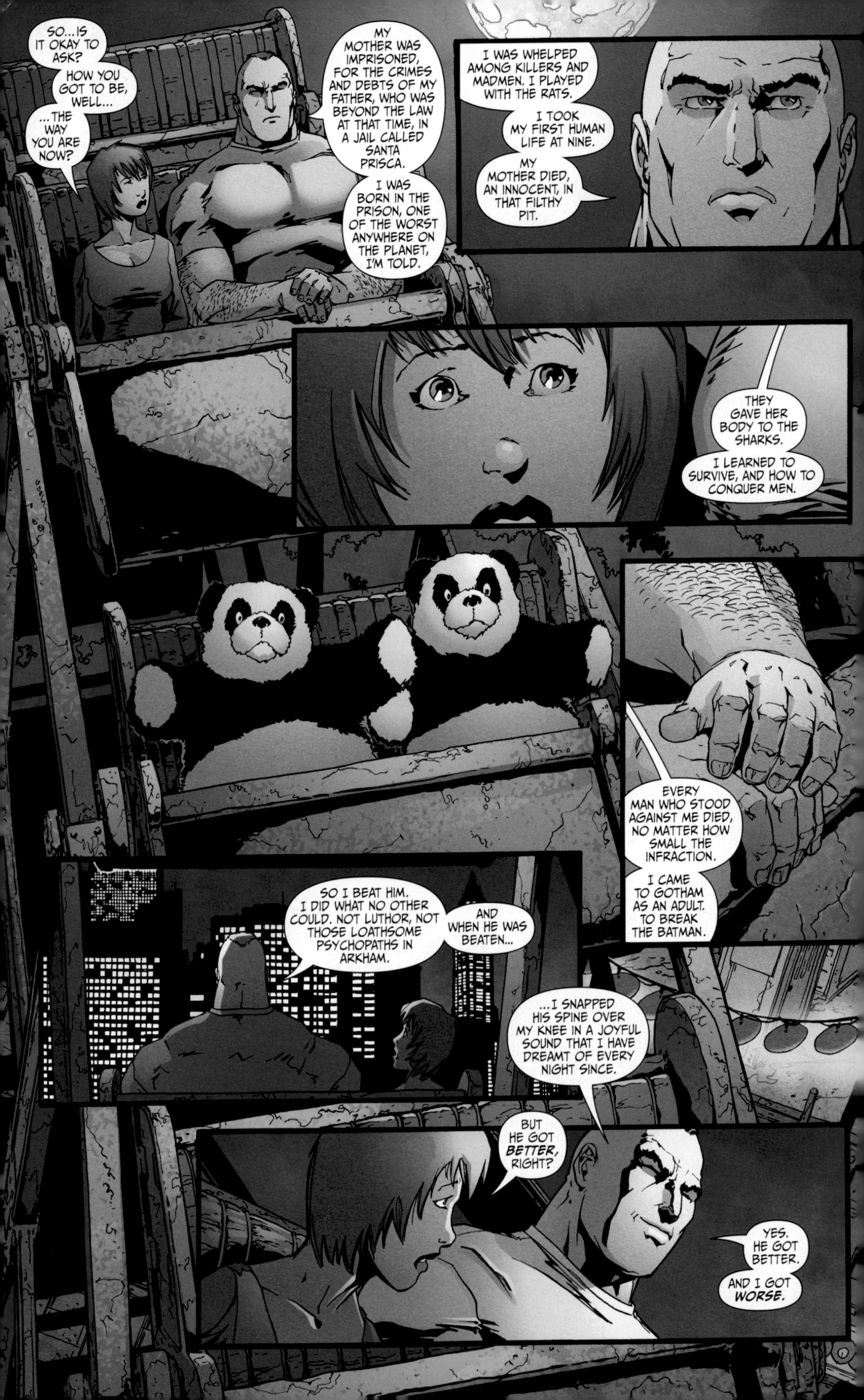
SO...IS IT OKAY TO ASK?
HOW YOU GOT TO BE, WELL...
...THE WAY YOU ARE NOW?
MY MOTHER WAS IMPRISONED, FOR THE CRIMES AND DEBTS OF MY FATHER, WHO WAS BEYOND THE LAW AT THAT TIME, IN A JAIL CALLED SANTA PRISCA.
I WAS BORN IN THE PRISON, ONE OF THE WORST ANYWHERE ON THE PLANET, I'M TOLD.
I WAS WHELPED AMONG KILLERS AND MADMEN. I PLAYED WITH THE RATS.
I TOOK MY FIRST HUMAN LIFE AT NINE.
MY MOTHER DIED, AN INNOCENT, IN THAT FILTHY PIT.
THEY GAVE HER BODY TO THE SHARKS.
I LEARNED TO SURVIVE, AND HOW TO CONQUER MEN.
EVERY MAN WHO STOOD AGAINST ME DIED, NO MATTER HOW SMALL THE INFRACTION.
I CAME TO GOTHAM AS AN ADULT. TO BREAK THE BATMAN.
SO I BEAT HIM. I DID WHAT NO OTHER COULD. NOT LUTHOR, NOT THOSE LOATHSOME PSYCHOPATHS IN ARKHAM.
AND WHEN HE WAS BEATEN...
...I SNAPPED HIS SPINE OVER MY KNEE IN A JOYFUL SOUND THAT I HAVE DREAMT OF EVERY NIGHT SINCE.
BUT HE GOT *BETTER*, RIGHT?
YES. HE GOT BETTER.
AND I GOT ***WORSE.***

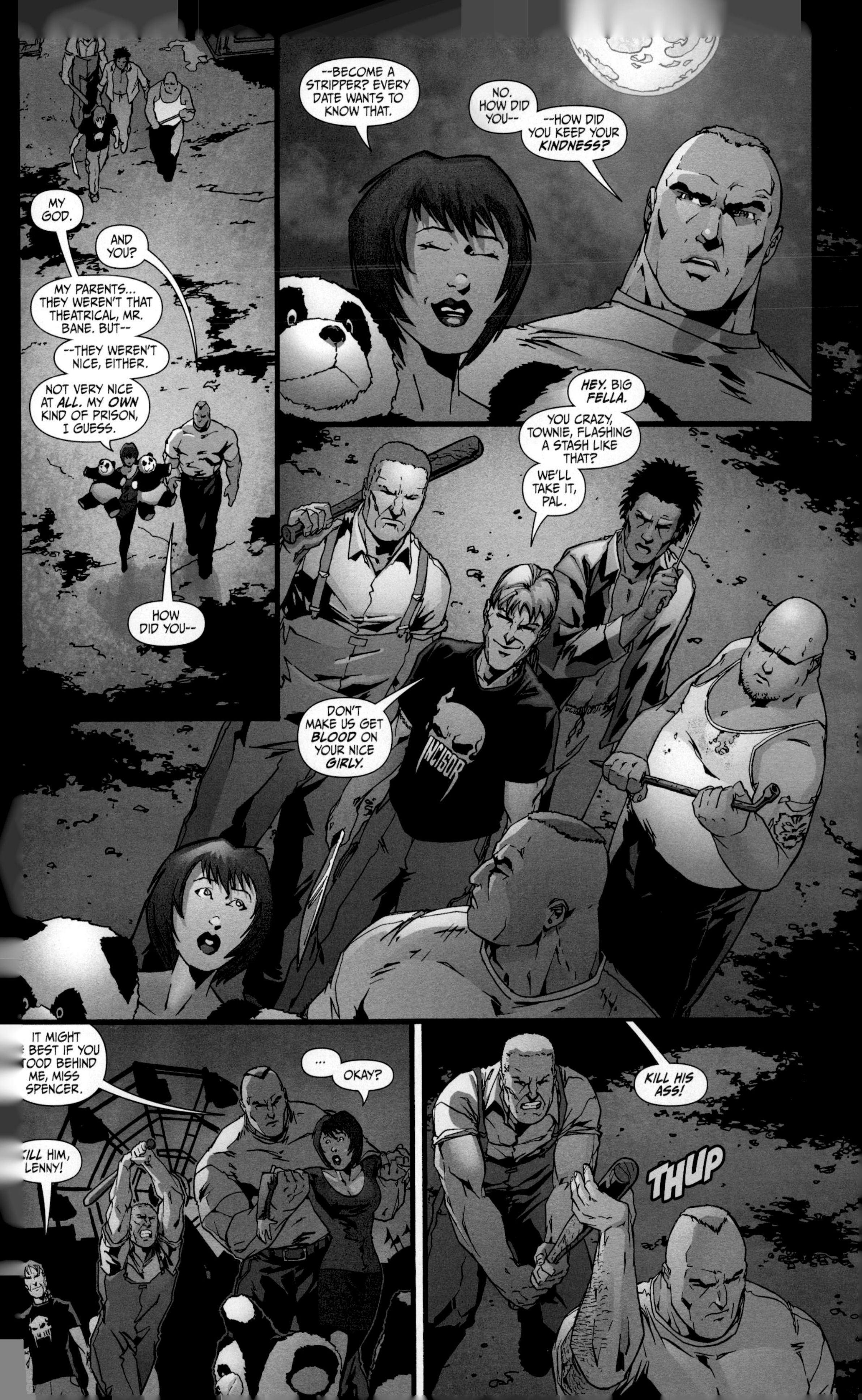
MY GOD.
AND YOU?
MY PARENTS... THEY WEREN'T THAT THEATRICAL, MR. BANE. BUT--
--THEY WEREN'T NICE, EITHER.
NOT VERY NICE AT ALL. MY OWN KIND OF PRISON, I GUESS.
HOW DID YOU--
--BECOME A STRIPPER? EVERY DATE WANTS TO KNOW THAT.
NO. HOW DID YOU--
--HOW DID YOU KEEP YOUR KINDNESS?
HEY. BIG FELLA.
YOU CRAZY, TOWNIE, FLASHING A STASH LIKE THAT?
WE'LL TAKE IT, PAL.
DON'T MAKE US GET BLOOD ON YOUR NICE GIRLY.
INCISOR
IT MIGHT BE BEST IF YOU STOOD BEHIND ME, MISS SPENCER.
... OKAY?
KILL HIM, LENNY!
KILL HIS ASS!
THUP

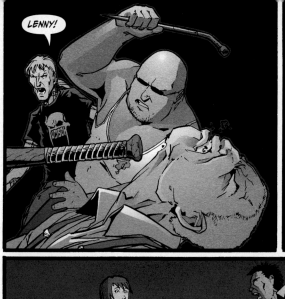

LENNY!

AARRGKK!

HE'S *CRAZY.* KILL THE *CHICK.* GET HIM *OFF* ME!

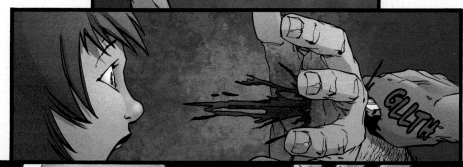

NO!

GLLTH!

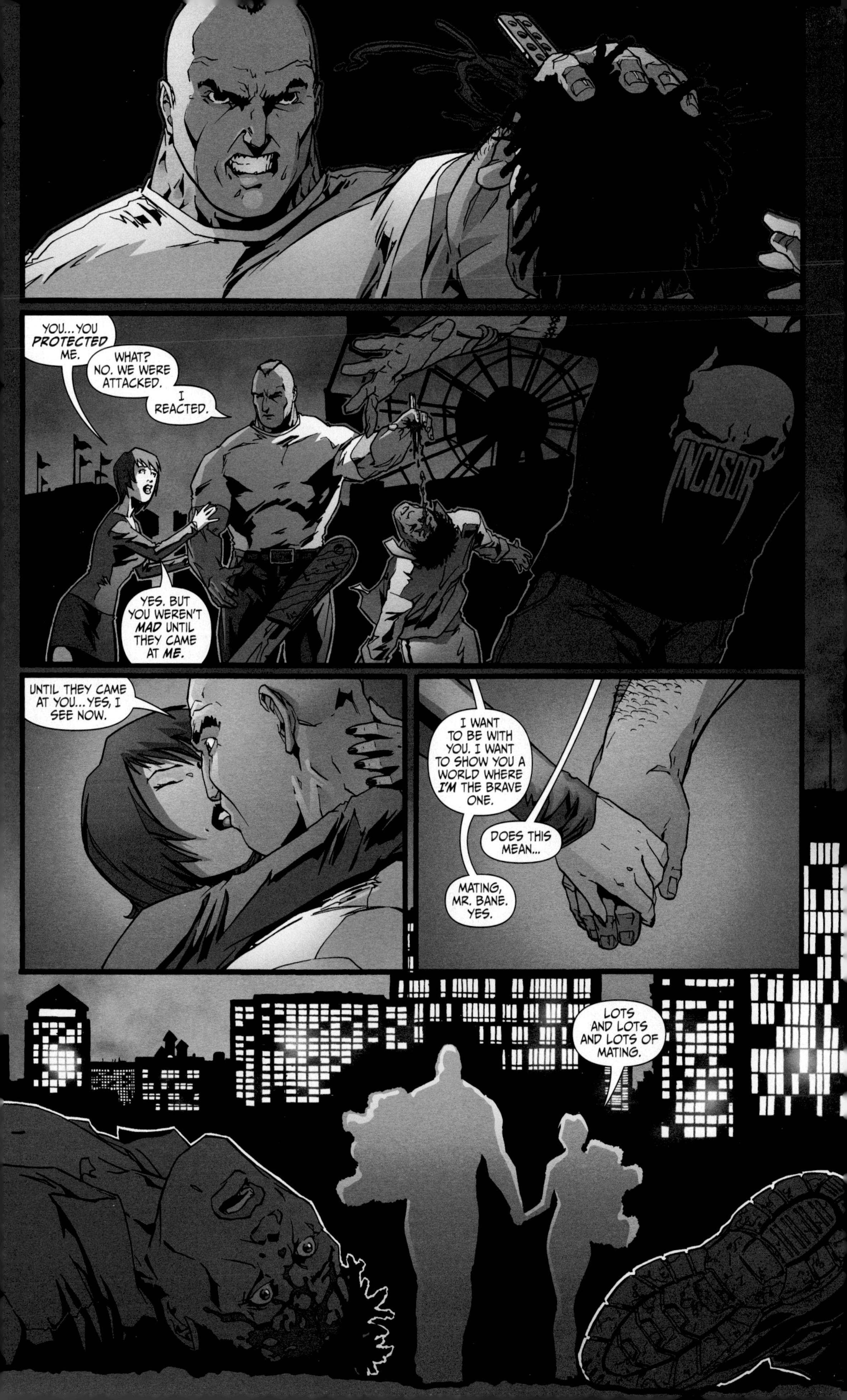
YOU...YOU PROTECTED ME.
WHAT? NO. WE WERE ATTACKED.
I REACTED.
YES. BUT YOU WEREN'T MAD UNTIL THEY CAME AT ME.
INCISOR
UNTIL THEY CAME AT YOU...YES, I SEE NOW.
I WANT TO BE WITH YOU. I WANT TO SHOW YOU A WORLD WHERE I'M THE BRAVE ONE.
DOES THIS MEAN...
MATING, MR. BANE. YES.
LOTS AND LOTS AND LOTS OF MATING.

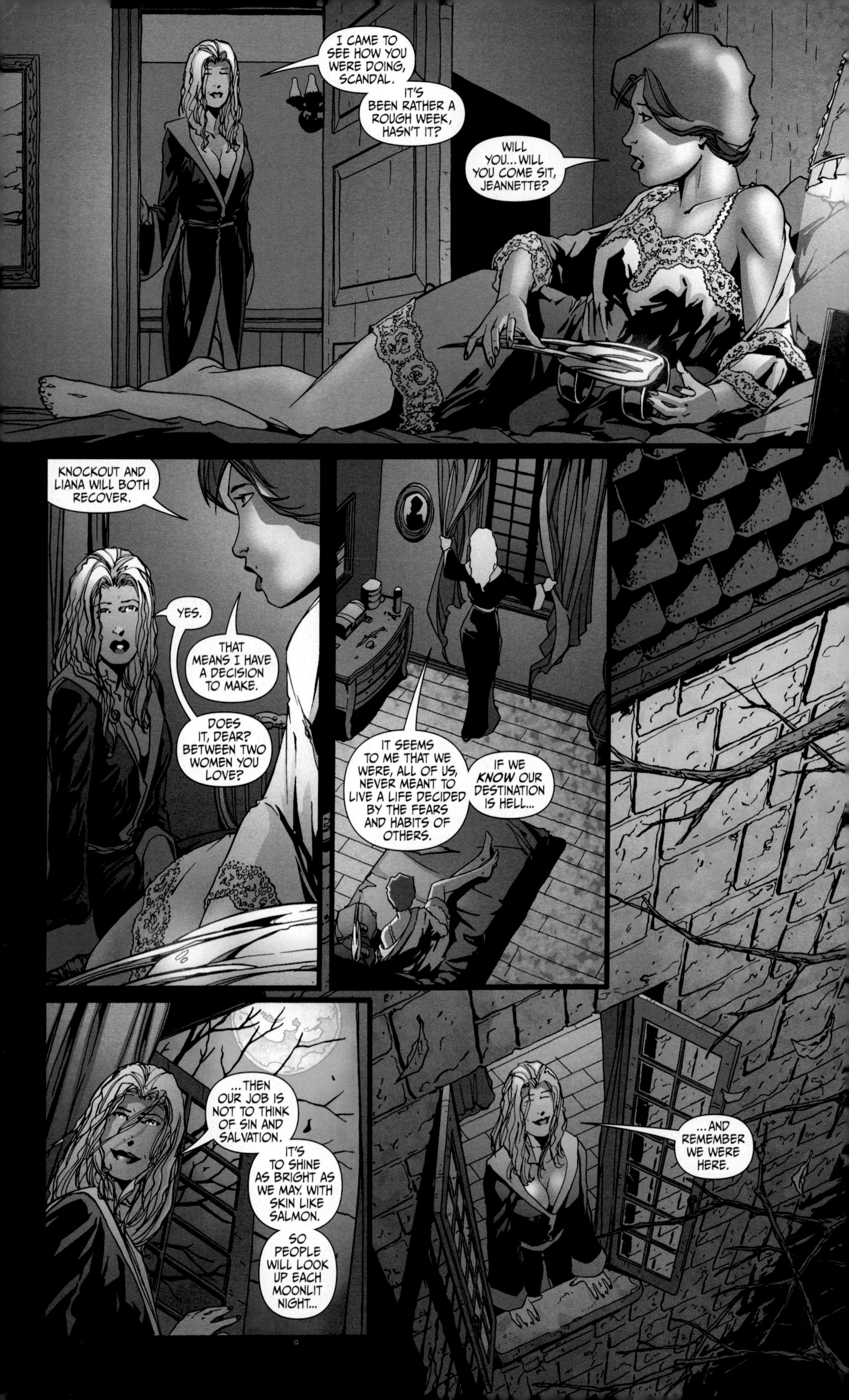
I CAME TO SEE HOW YOU WERE DOING, SCANDAL.
IT'S BEEN RATHER A ROUGH WEEK, HASN'T IT?
WILL YOU... WILL YOU COME SIT, JEANNETTE?
KNOCKOUT AND LIANA WILL BOTH RECOVER.
YES.
THAT MEANS I HAVE A DECISION TO MAKE.
DOES IT, DEAR? BETWEEN TWO WOMEN YOU LOVE?
IT SEEMS TO ME THAT WE WERE, ALL OF US, NEVER MEANT TO LIVE A LIFE DECIDED BY THE FEARS AND HABITS OF OTHERS.
IF WE KNOW OUR DESTINATION IS HELL...
...THEN OUR JOB IS NOT TO THINK OF SIN AND SALVATION.
IT'S TO SHINE AS BRIGHT AS WE MAY. WITH SKIN LIKE SALMON.
SO PEOPLE WILL LOOK UP EACH MOONLIT NIGHT...
...AND REMEMBER WE WERE HERE.

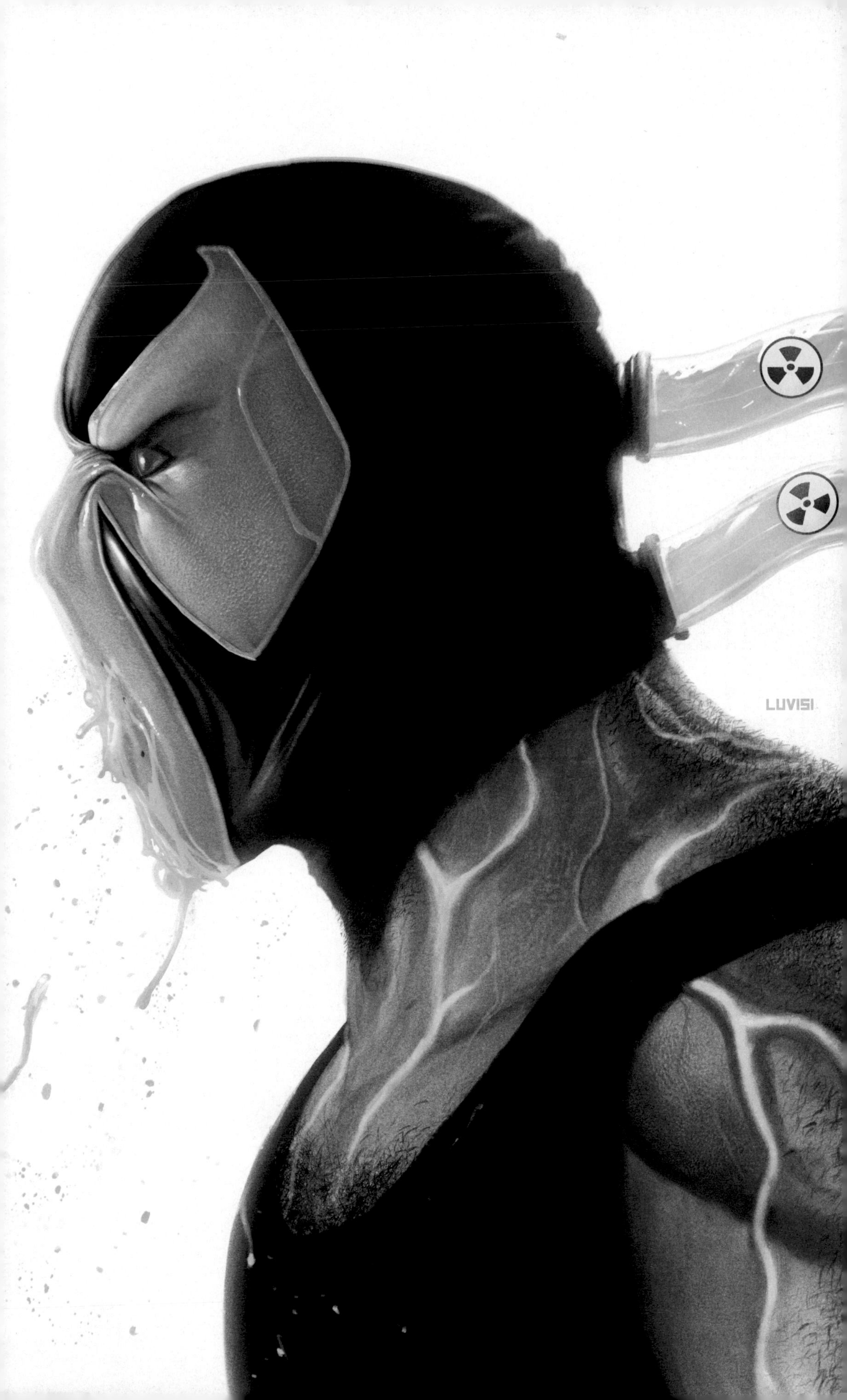
LUVISI

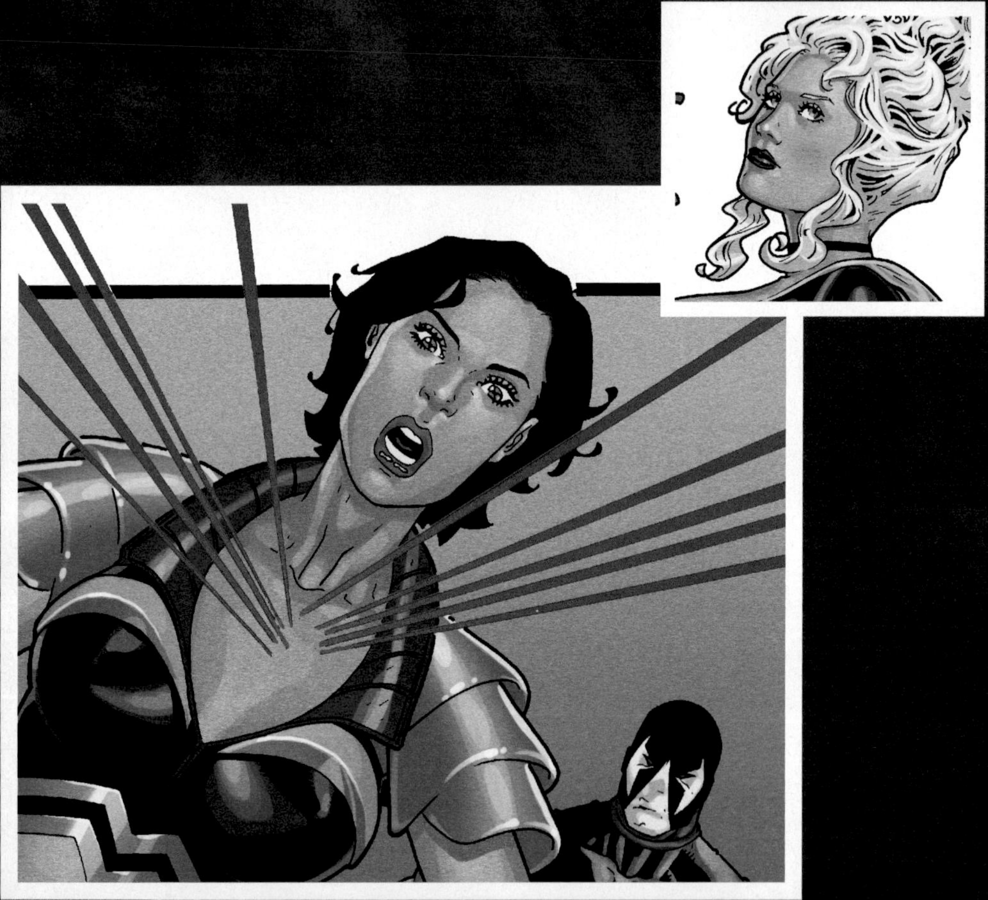

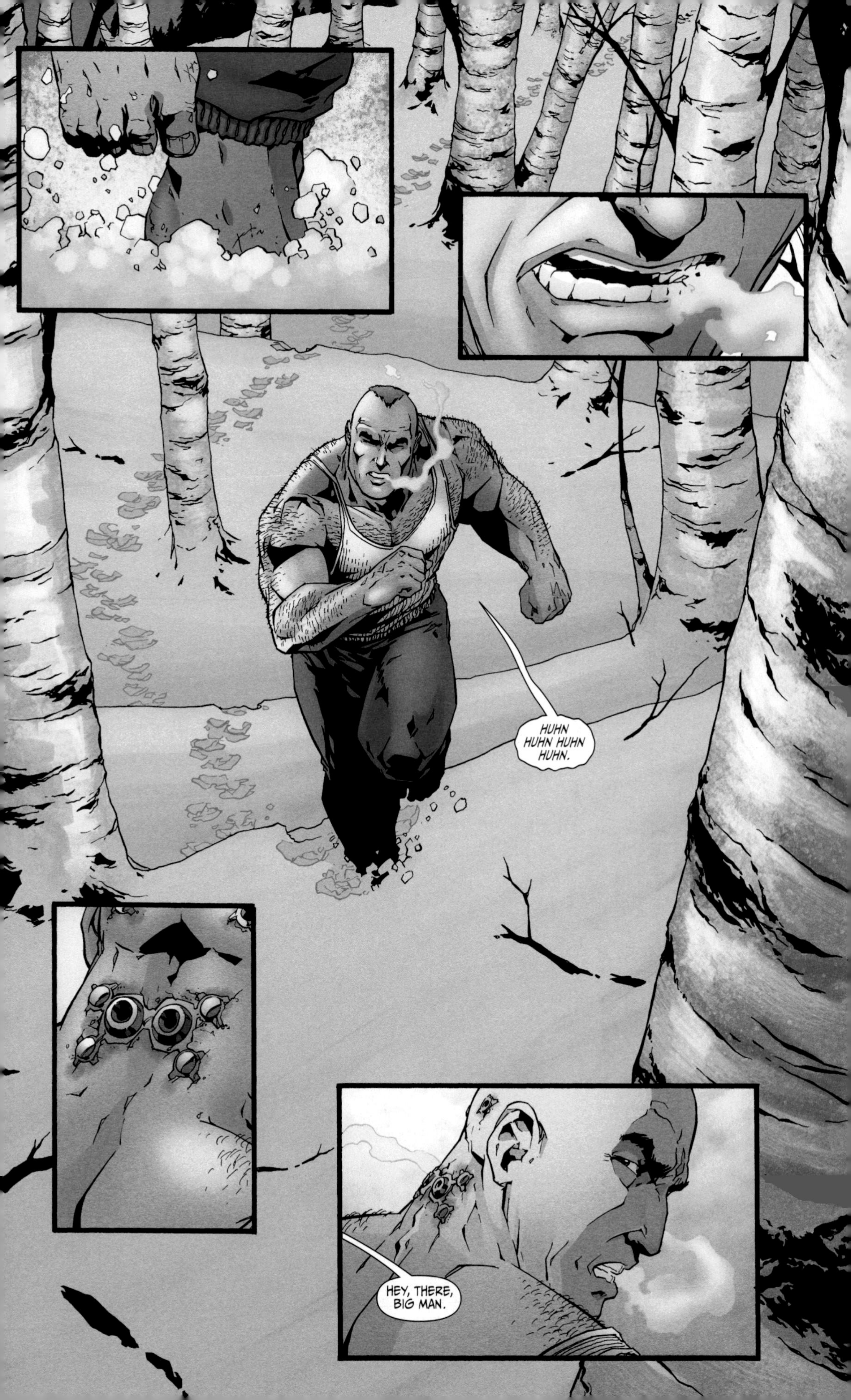
HUHN HUHN HUHN HUHN.
HEY, THERE, BIG MAN.

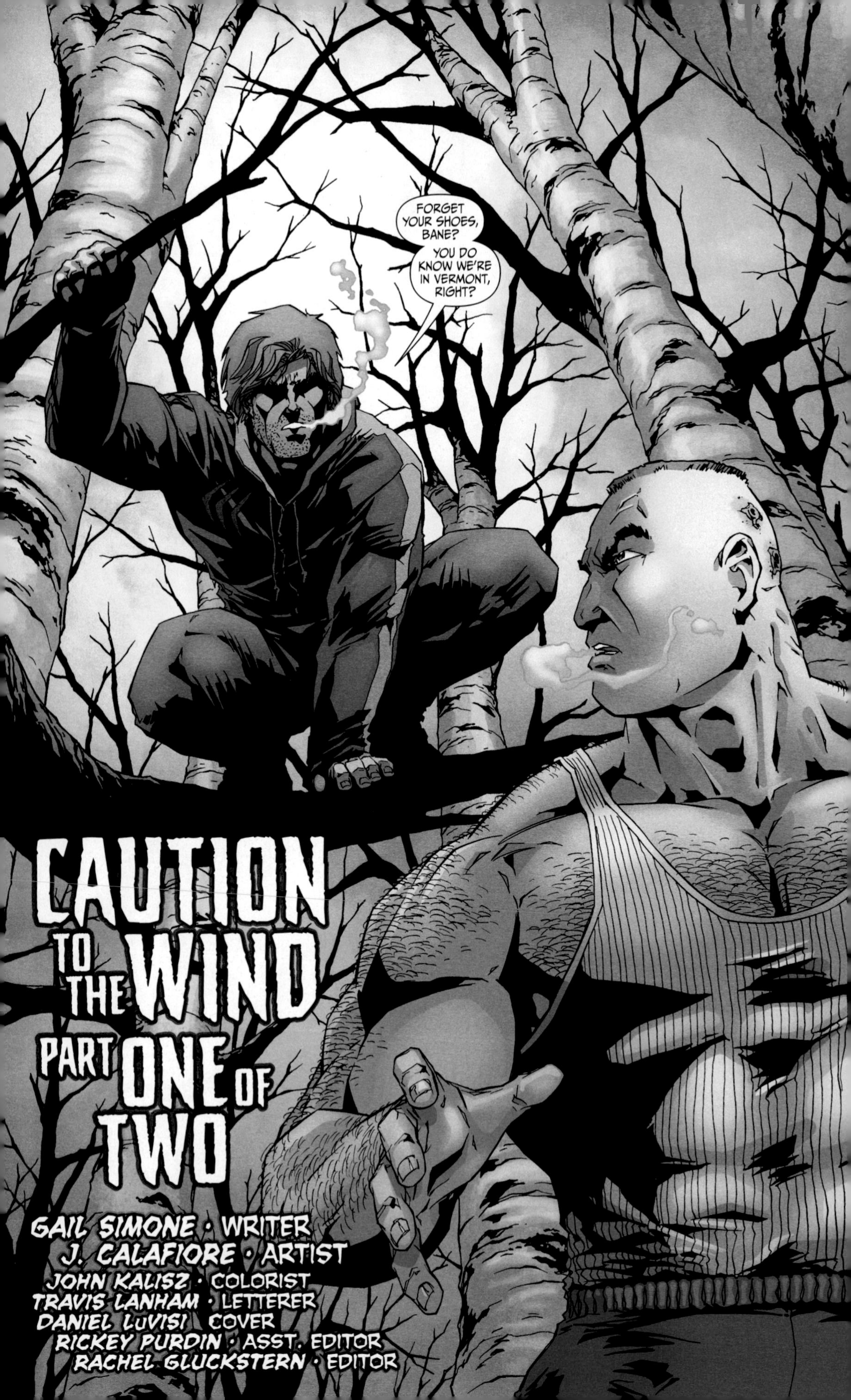
FORGET YOUR SHOES, BANE?
YOU DO KNOW WE'RE IN VERMONT, RIGHT?
CAUTION TO THE WIND
PART ONE OF TWO
GAIL SIMONE · WRITER
J. CALAFIORE · ARTIST
JOHN KALISZ · COLORIST
TRAVIS LANHAM · LETTERER
DANIEL LUVISI COVER
RICKEY PURDIN · ASST. EDITOR
RACHEL GLUCKSTERN · EDITOR

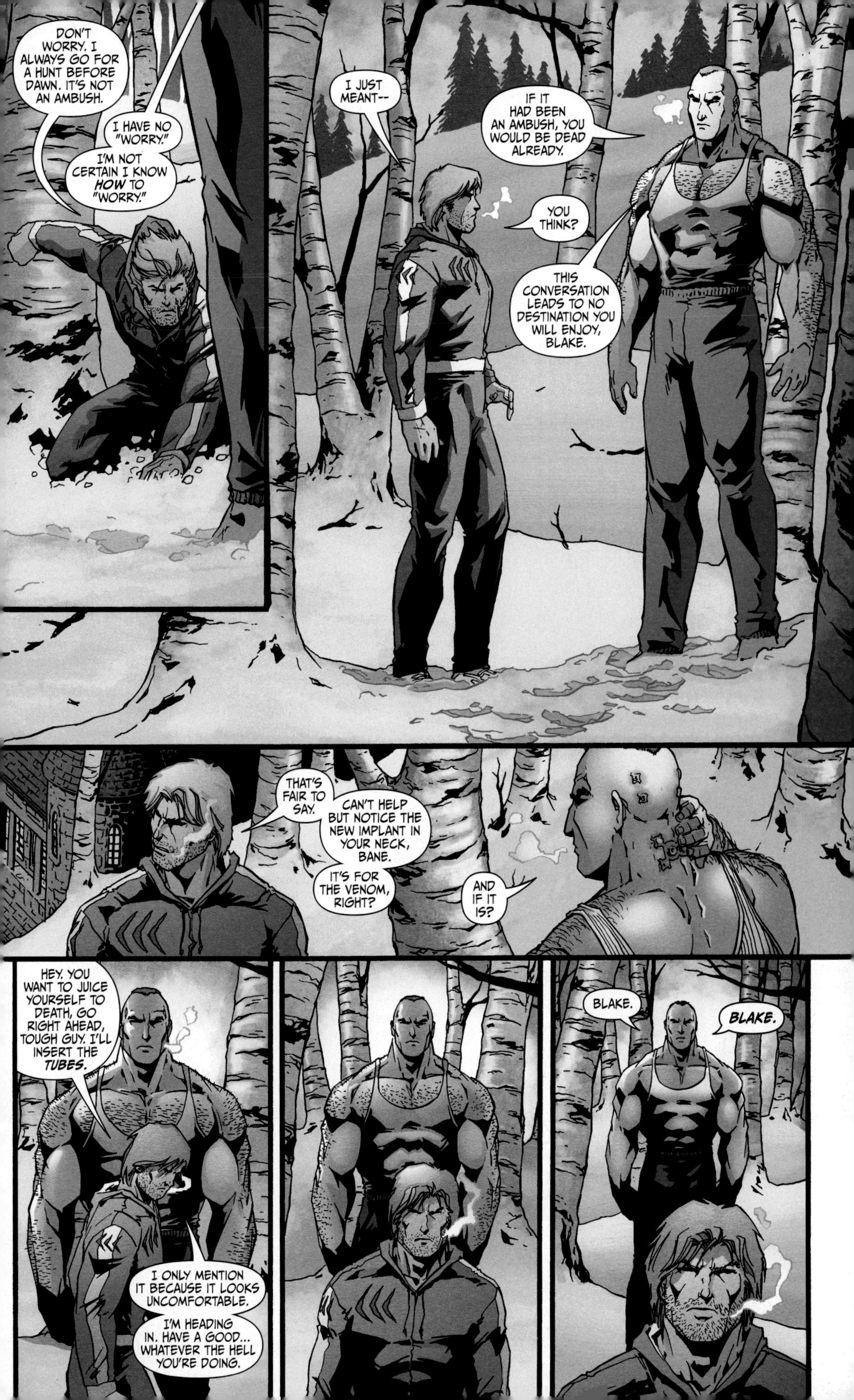
DON'T WORRY. I ALWAYS GO FOR A HUNT BEFORE DAWN. IT'S NOT AN AMBUSH.
I HAVE NO "WORRY."
I'M NOT CERTAIN I KNOW *HOW* TO "WORRY."
I JUST MEANT--
IF IT HAD BEEN AN AMBUSH, YOU WOULD BE DEAD ALREADY.
YOU THINK?
THIS CONVERSATION LEADS TO NO DESTINATION YOU WILL ENJOY, BLAKE.
THAT'S FAIR TO SAY.
CAN'T HELP BUT NOTICE THE NEW IMPLANT IN YOUR NECK, BANE.
IT'S FOR THE VENOM, RIGHT?
AND IF IT IS?
HEY. YOU WANT TO JUICE YOURSELF TO DEATH, GO RIGHT AHEAD, TOUGH GUY. I'LL INSERT THE *TUBES.*
I ONLY MENTION IT BECAUSE IT LOOKS UNCOMFORTABLE.
I'M HEADING IN. HAVE A GOOD... WHATEVER THE HELL YOU'RE DOING.
BLAKE.
BLAKE.

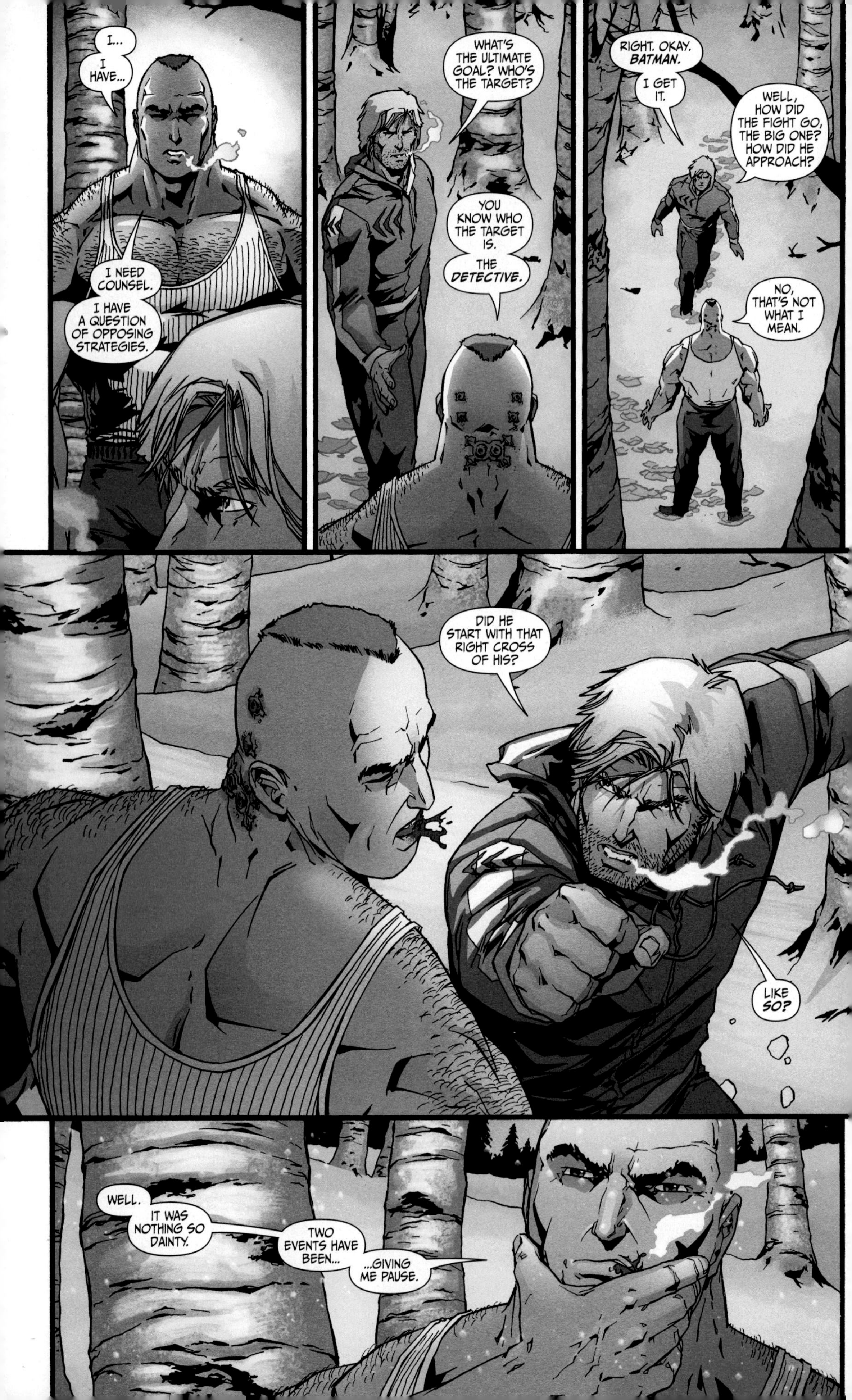
I...
I HAVE...
I NEED COUNSEL.
I HAVE A QUESTION OF OPPOSING STRATEGIES.
WHAT'S THE ULTIMATE GOAL? WHO'S THE TARGET?
YOU KNOW WHO THE TARGET IS.
THE DETECTIVE.
RIGHT. OKAY. BATMAN.
I GET IT.
WELL, HOW DID THE FIGHT GO, THE BIG ONE? HOW DID HE APPROACH?
NO, THAT'S NOT WHAT I MEAN.
DID HE START WITH THAT RIGHT CROSS OF HIS?
LIKE SO?
WELL.
IT WAS NOTHING SO DAINTY.
TWO EVENTS HAVE BEEN...
...GIVING ME PAUSE.

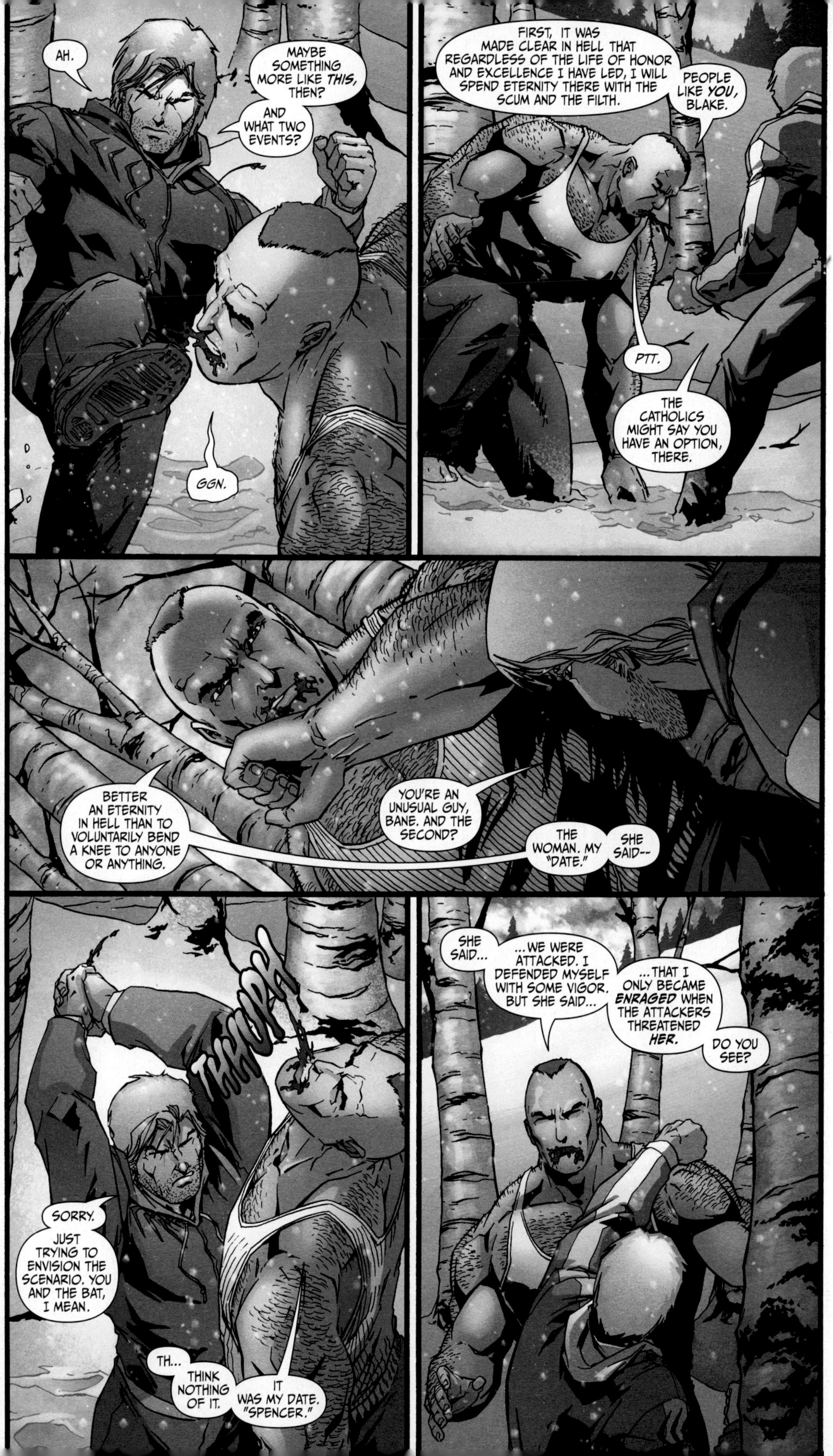
AH.
MAYBE SOMETHING MORE LIKE THIS, THEN?
AND WHAT TWO EVENTS?
GGN.
FIRST, IT WAS MADE CLEAR IN HELL THAT REGARDLESS OF THE LIFE OF HONOR AND EXCELLENCE I HAVE LED, I WILL SPEND ETERNITY THERE WITH THE SCUM AND THE FILTH.
PEOPLE LIKE YOU, BLAKE.
PTT.
THE CATHOLICS MIGHT SAY YOU HAVE AN OPTION, THERE.
BETTER AN ETERNITY IN HELL THAN TO VOLUNTARILY BEND A KNEE TO ANYONE OR ANYTHING.
YOU'RE AN UNUSUAL GUY, BANE. AND THE SECOND?
THE WOMAN. MY "DATE."
SHE SAID--
THROP!
SORRY.
JUST TRYING TO ENVISION THE SCENARIO. YOU AND THE BAT, I MEAN.
TH...
THINK NOTHING OF IT.
IT WAS MY DATE. "SPENCER."
SHE SAID...
...WE WERE ATTACKED. I DEFENDED MYSELF WITH SOME VIGOR. BUT SHE SAID...
...THAT I ONLY BECAME ENRAGED WHEN THE ATTACKERS THREATENED HER.
DO YOU SEE?

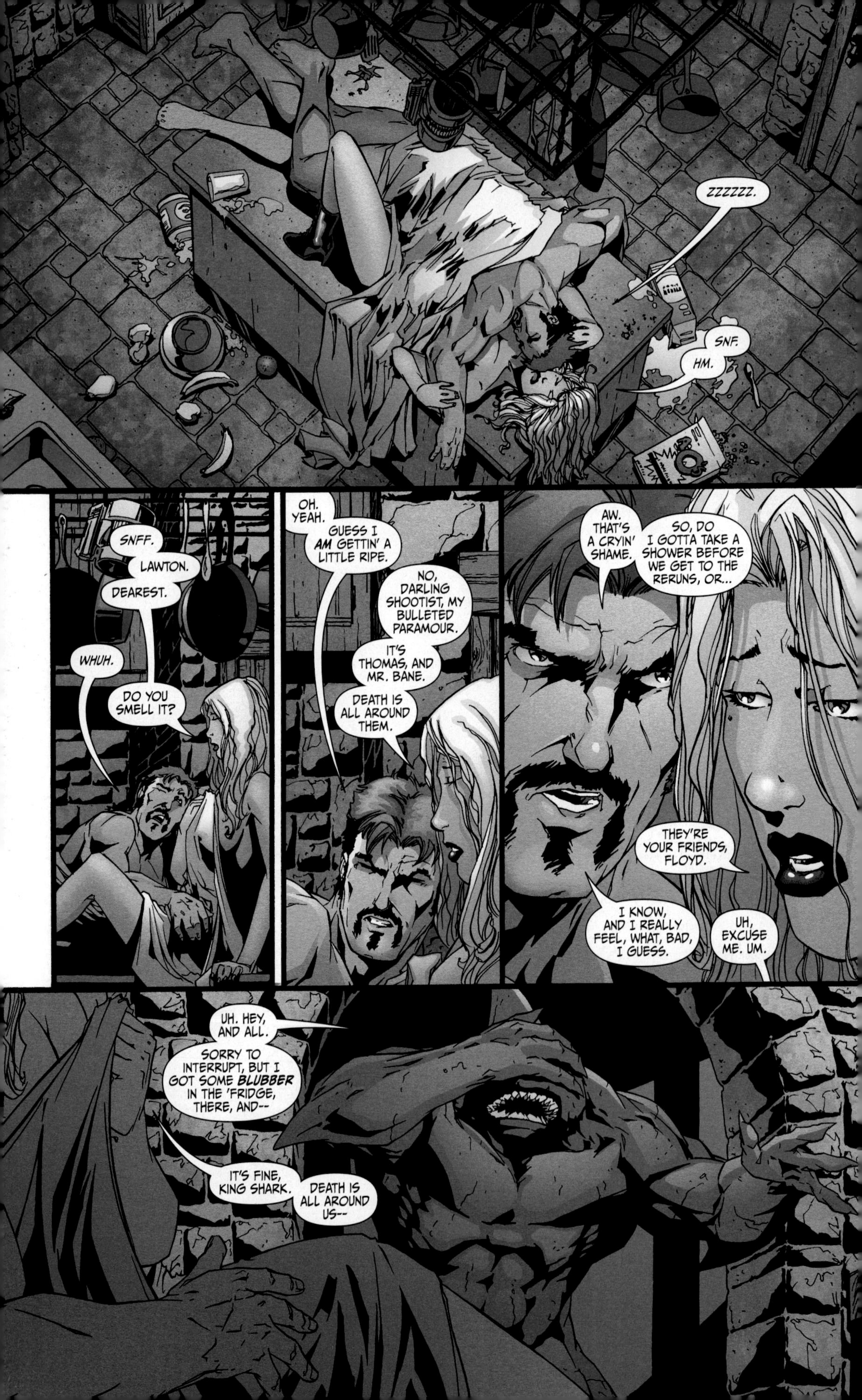
ZZZZZZ.
SNF.
HM.
SNFF.
LAWTON.
DEAREST.
WHUH.
DO YOU SMELL IT?
OH. YEAH.
GUESS I AM GETTIN' A LITTLE RIPE.
NO, DARLING SHOOTIST, MY BULLETED PARAMOUR.
IT'S THOMAS, AND MR. BANE.
DEATH IS ALL AROUND THEM.
AW. THAT'S A CRYIN' SHAME.
SO, DO I GOTTA TAKE A SHOWER BEFORE WE GET TO THE RERUNS, OR...
THEY'RE YOUR FRIENDS, FLOYD.
I KNOW, AND I REALLY FEEL, WHAT, BAD, I GUESS.
UH, EXCUSE ME. UM.
UH. HEY, AND ALL.
SORRY TO INTERRUPT, BUT I GOT SOME BLUBBER IN THE 'FRIDGE, THERE, AND--
IT'S FINE, KING SHARK.
DEATH IS ALL AROUND US--

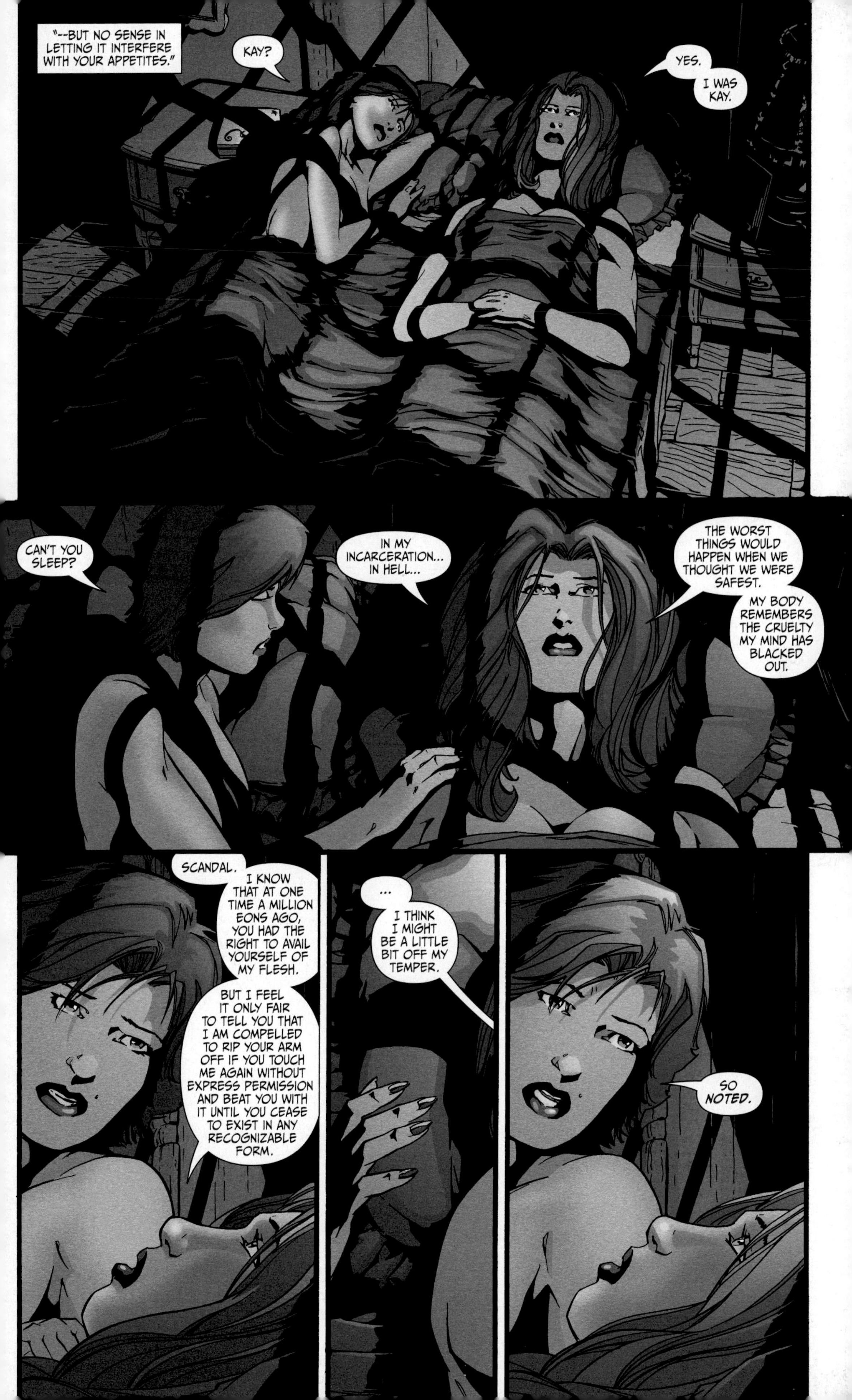
"--BUT NO SENSE IN LETTING IT INTERFERE WITH YOUR APPETITES."
KAY?
YES.
I WAS KAY.
CAN'T YOU SLEEP?
IN MY INCARCERATION... IN HELL...
THE WORST THINGS WOULD HAPPEN WHEN WE THOUGHT WE WERE SAFEST.
MY BODY REMEMBERS THE CRUELTY MY MIND HAS BLACKED OUT.
SCANDAL.
I KNOW THAT AT ONE TIME A MILLION EONS AGO, YOU HAD THE RIGHT TO AVAIL YOURSELF OF MY FLESH.
BUT I FEEL IT ONLY FAIR TO TELL YOU THAT I AM COMPELLED TO RIP YOUR ARM OFF IF YOU TOUCH ME AGAIN WITHOUT EXPRESS PERMISSION AND BEAT YOU WITH IT UNTIL YOU CEASE TO EXIST IN ANY RECOGNIZABLE FORM.
...
I THINK I MIGHT BE A LITTLE BIT OFF MY TEMPER.
SO *NOTED.*

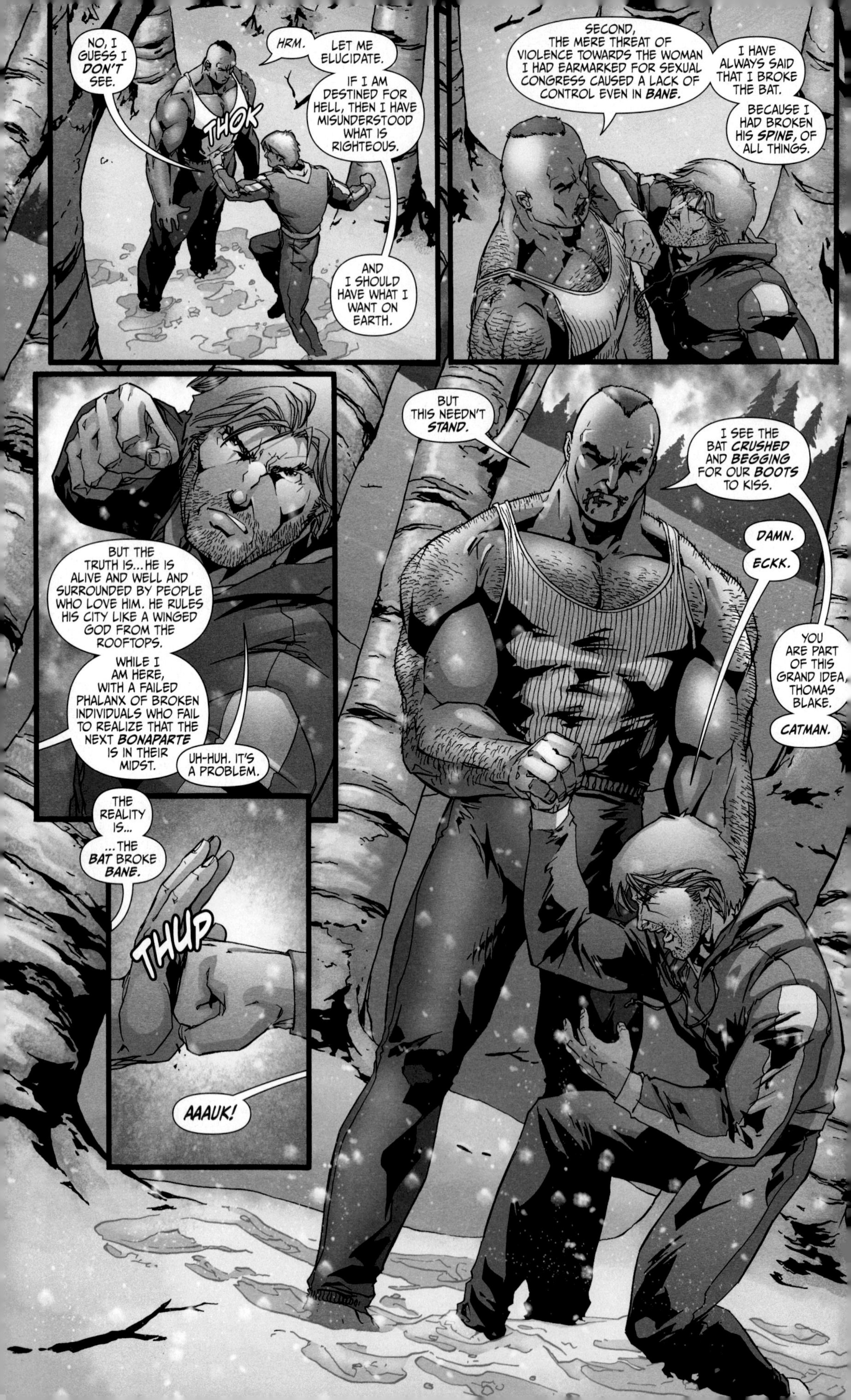
NO, I GUESS I DON'T SEE.
HRM.
LET ME ELUCIDATE.
IF I AM DESTINED FOR HELL, THEN I HAVE MISUNDERSTOOD WHAT IS RIGHTEOUS.
THOK
AND I SHOULD HAVE WHAT I WANT ON EARTH.
SECOND, THE MERE THREAT OF VIOLENCE TOWARDS THE WOMAN I HAD EARMARKED FOR SEXUAL CONGRESS CAUSED A LACK OF CONTROL EVEN IN BANE.
I HAVE ALWAYS SAID THAT I BROKE THE BAT.
BECAUSE I HAD BROKEN HIS SPINE, OF ALL THINGS.
BUT THE TRUTH IS...HE IS ALIVE AND WELL AND SURROUNDED BY PEOPLE WHO LOVE HIM. HE RULES HIS CITY LIKE A WINGED GOD FROM THE ROOFTOPS.
WHILE I AM HERE, WITH A FAILED PHALANX OF BROKEN INDIVIDUALS WHO FAIL TO REALIZE THAT THE NEXT BONAPARTE IS IN THEIR MIDST.
UH-HUH. IT'S A PROBLEM.
THE REALITY IS...
...THE BAT BROKE BANE.
THUP
AAAUK!
BUT THIS NEEDN'T STAND.
I SEE THE BAT CRUSHED AND BEGGING FOR OUR BOOTS TO KISS.
DAMN.
ECKK.
YOU ARE PART OF THIS GRAND IDEA, THOMAS BLAKE.
CATMAN.

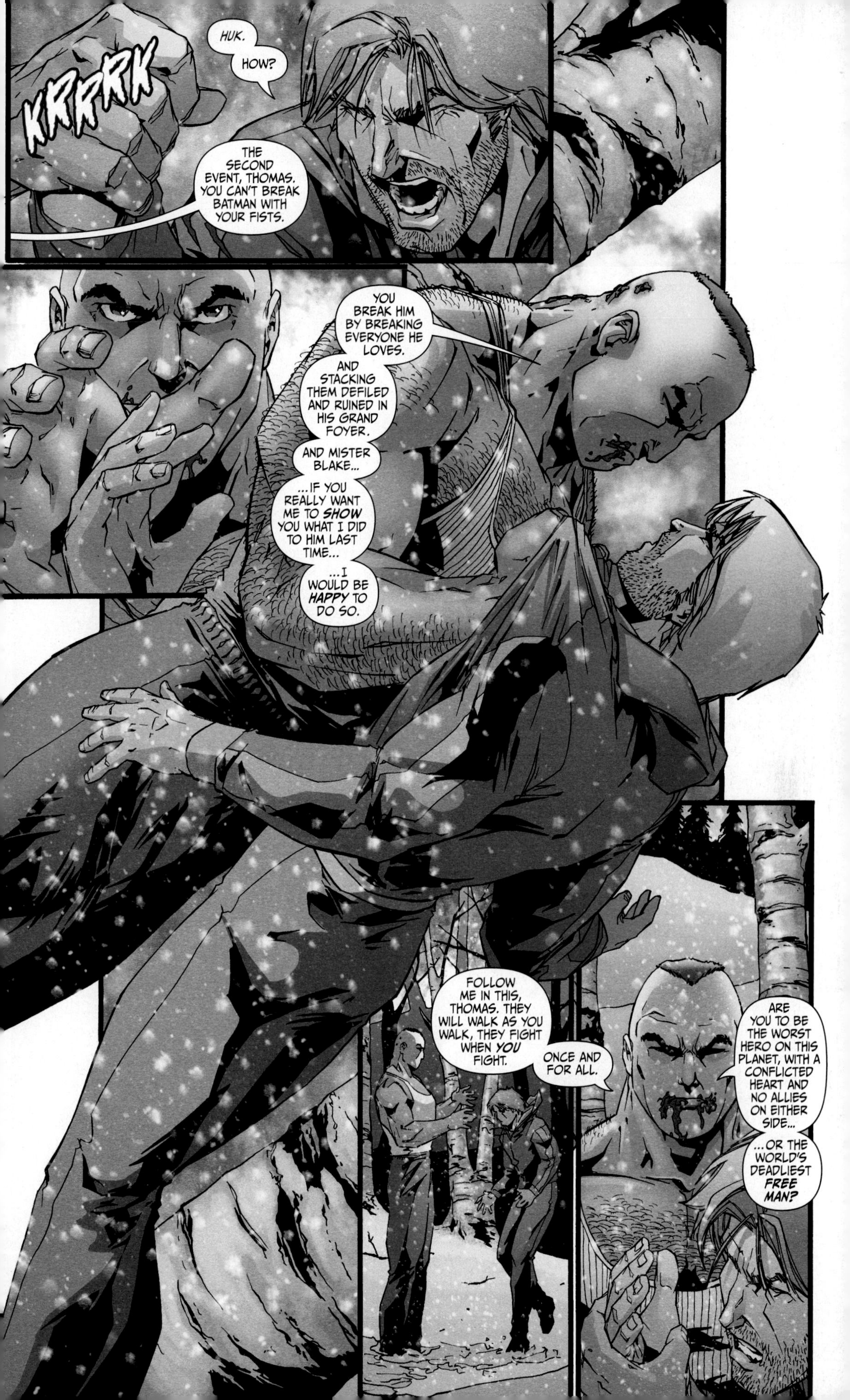
KRRRK
HUK.
HOW?
THE SECOND EVENT, THOMAS. YOU CAN'T BREAK BATMAN WITH YOUR FISTS.
YOU BREAK HIM BY BREAKING EVERYONE HE LOVES.
AND STACKING THEM DEFILED AND RUINED IN HIS GRAND FOYER.
AND MISTER BLAKE...
...IF YOU REALLY WANT ME TO SHOW YOU WHAT I DID TO HIM LAST TIME...
...I WOULD BE HAPPY TO DO SO.
FOLLOW ME IN THIS, THOMAS. THEY WILL WALK AS YOU WALK, THEY FIGHT WHEN YOU FIGHT.
ONCE AND FOR ALL.
ARE YOU TO BE THE WORST HERO ON THIS PLANET, WITH A CONFLICTED HEART AND NO ALLIES ON EITHER SIDE...
...OR THE WORLD'S DEADLIEST FREE MAN?

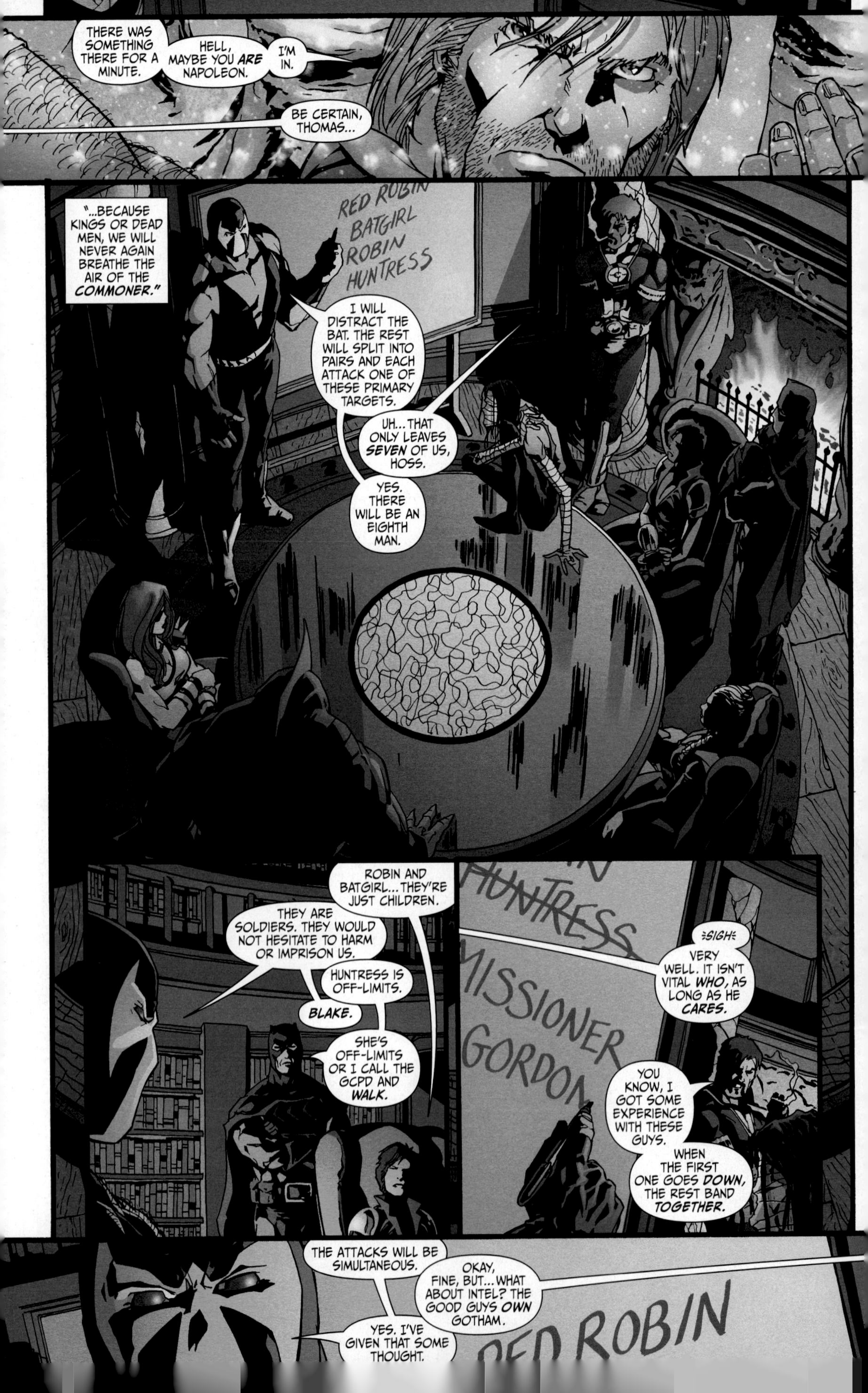
THERE WAS SOMETHING THERE FOR A MINUTE.
HELL, MAYBE YOU *ARE* NAPOLEON.
I'M IN.
BE CERTAIN, THOMAS...
"...BECAUSE KINGS OR DEAD MEN, WE WILL NEVER AGAIN BREATHE THE AIR OF THE *COMMONER.*"
RED ROBIN
BATGIRL
ROBIN
HUNTRESS
I WILL DISTRACT THE BAT. THE REST WILL SPLIT INTO PAIRS AND EACH ATTACK ONE OF THESE PRIMARY TARGETS.
UH...THAT ONLY LEAVES *SEVEN* OF US, HOSS.
YES. THERE WILL BE AN EIGHTH MAN.
ROBIN AND BATGIRL...THEY'RE JUST CHILDREN.
THEY ARE SOLDIERS. THEY WOULD NOT HESITATE TO HARM OR IMPRISON US.
HUNTRESS IS OFF-LIMITS.
BLAKE.
SHE'S OFF-LIMITS OR I CALL THE GCPD AND *WALK.*
HUNTRESS
MISSIONER
GORDON
SIGH
VERY WELL. IT ISN'T VITAL *WHO*, AS LONG AS HE *CARES.*
YOU KNOW, I GOT SOME EXPERIENCE WITH THESE GUYS.
WHEN THE FIRST ONE GOES *DOWN,* THE REST BAND *TOGETHER.*
THE ATTACKS WILL BE SIMULTANEOUS.
OKAY, FINE, BUT...WHAT ABOUT INTEL? THE GOOD GUYS *OWN* GOTHAM.
YES. I'VE GIVEN THAT SOME THOUGHT.

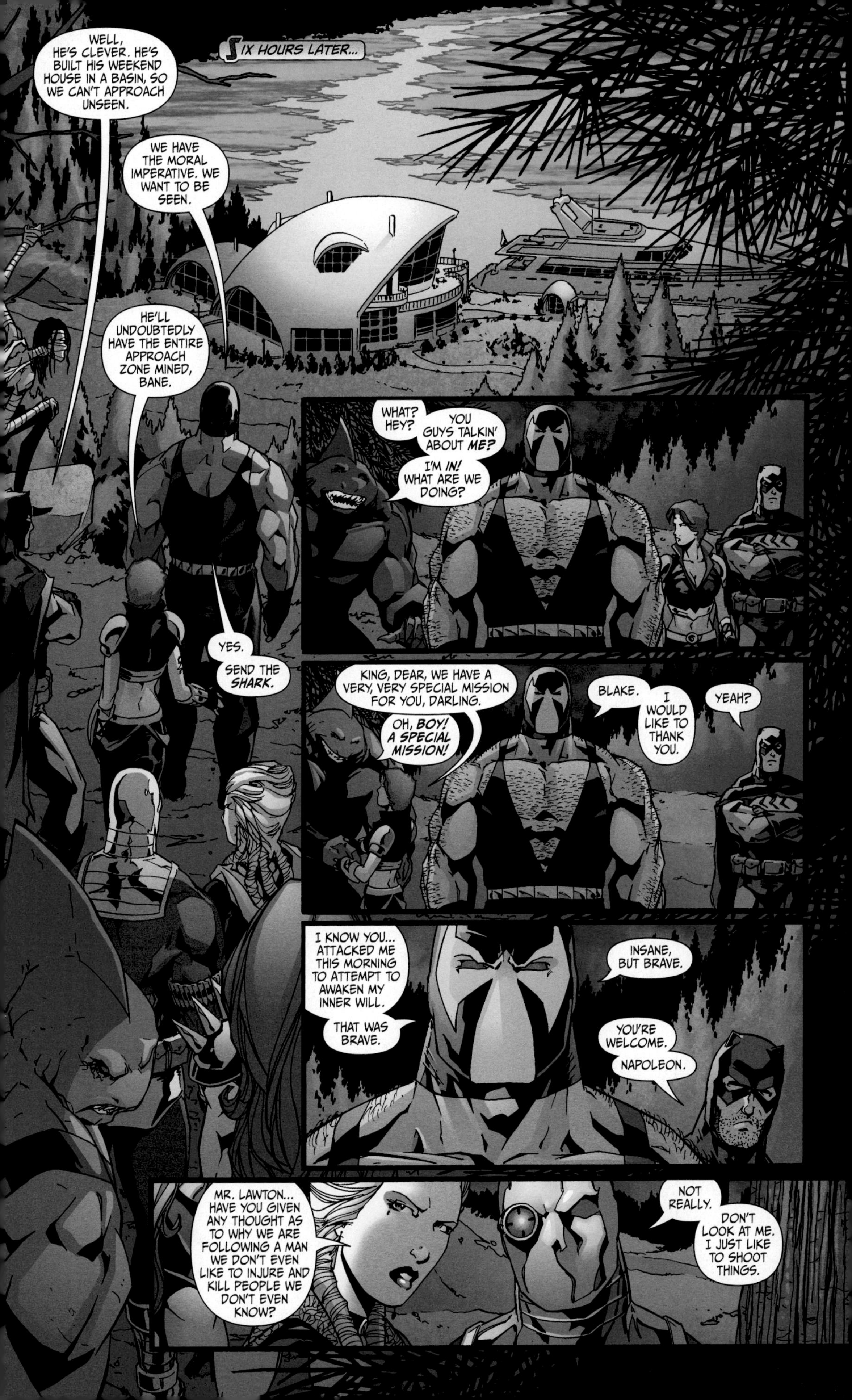
SIX HOURS LATER...
WELL, HE'S CLEVER. HE'S BUILT HIS WEEKEND HOUSE IN A BASIN, SO WE CAN'T APPROACH UNSEEN.
WE HAVE THE MORAL IMPERATIVE. WE WANT TO BE SEEN.
HE'LL UNDOUBTEDLY HAVE THE ENTIRE APPROACH ZONE MINED, BANE.
YES.
SEND THE SHARK.
WHAT? HEY?
YOU GUYS TALKIN' ABOUT ME?
I'M IN! WHAT ARE WE DOING?
KING, DEAR, WE HAVE A VERY, VERY SPECIAL MISSION FOR YOU, DARLING.
OH, BOY! A SPECIAL MISSION!
BLAKE.
I WOULD LIKE TO THANK YOU.
YEAH?
I KNOW YOU... ATTACKED ME THIS MORNING TO ATTEMPT TO AWAKEN MY INNER WILL.
THAT WAS BRAVE.
INSANE, BUT BRAVE.
YOU'RE WELCOME.
NAPOLEON.
MR. LAWTON... HAVE YOU GIVEN ANY THOUGHT AS TO WHY WE ARE FOLLOWING A MAN WE DON'T EVEN LIKE TO INJURE AND KILL PEOPLE WE DON'T EVEN KNOW?
NOT REALLY.
DON'T LOOK AT ME. I JUST LIKE TO SHOOT THINGS.

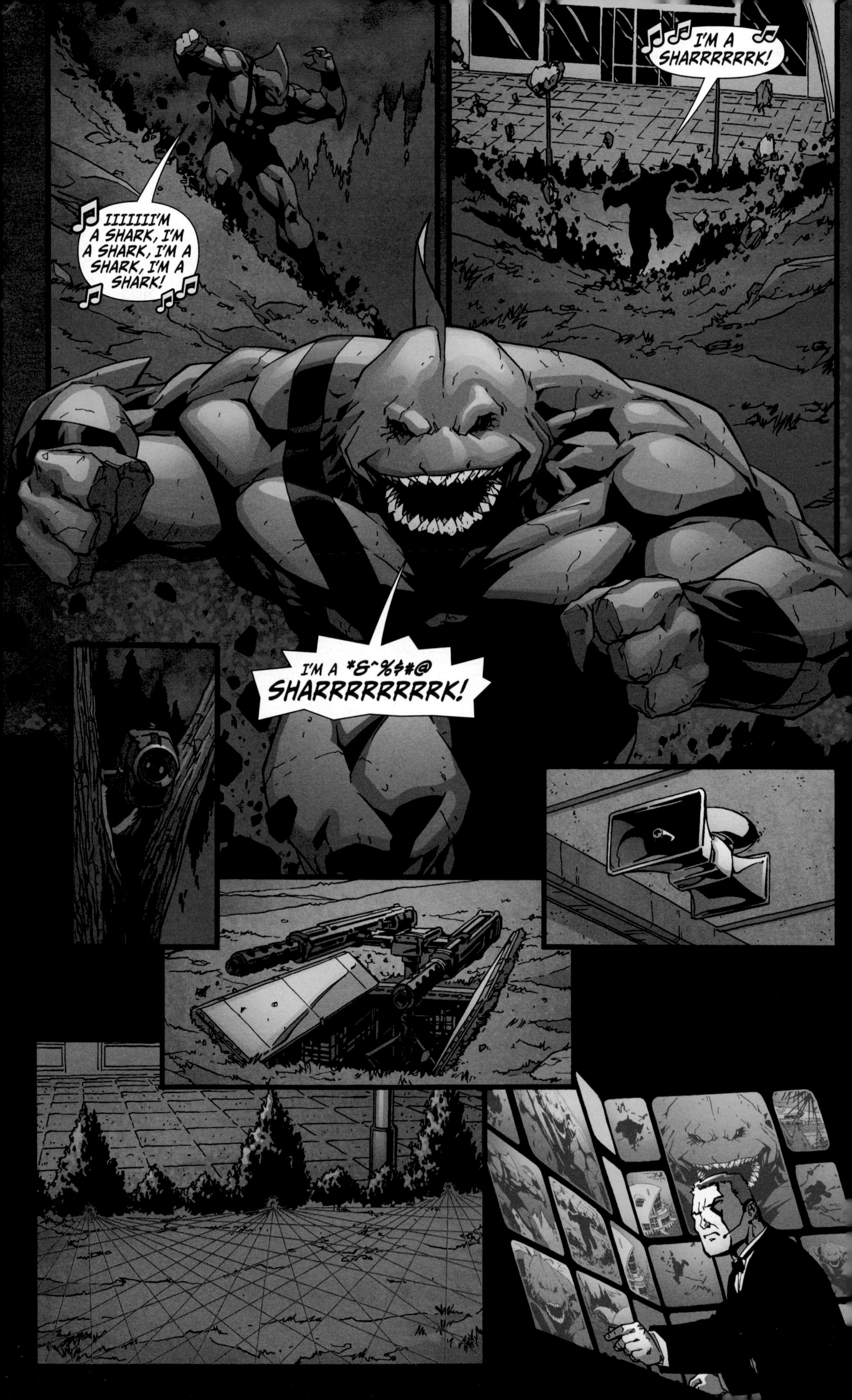
IIIIIII'M A SHARK, I'M A SHARK, I'M A SHARK, I'M A SHARK!
I'M A SHARRRRRRK!
I'M A *&^%$#@ SHARRRRRRRRK!

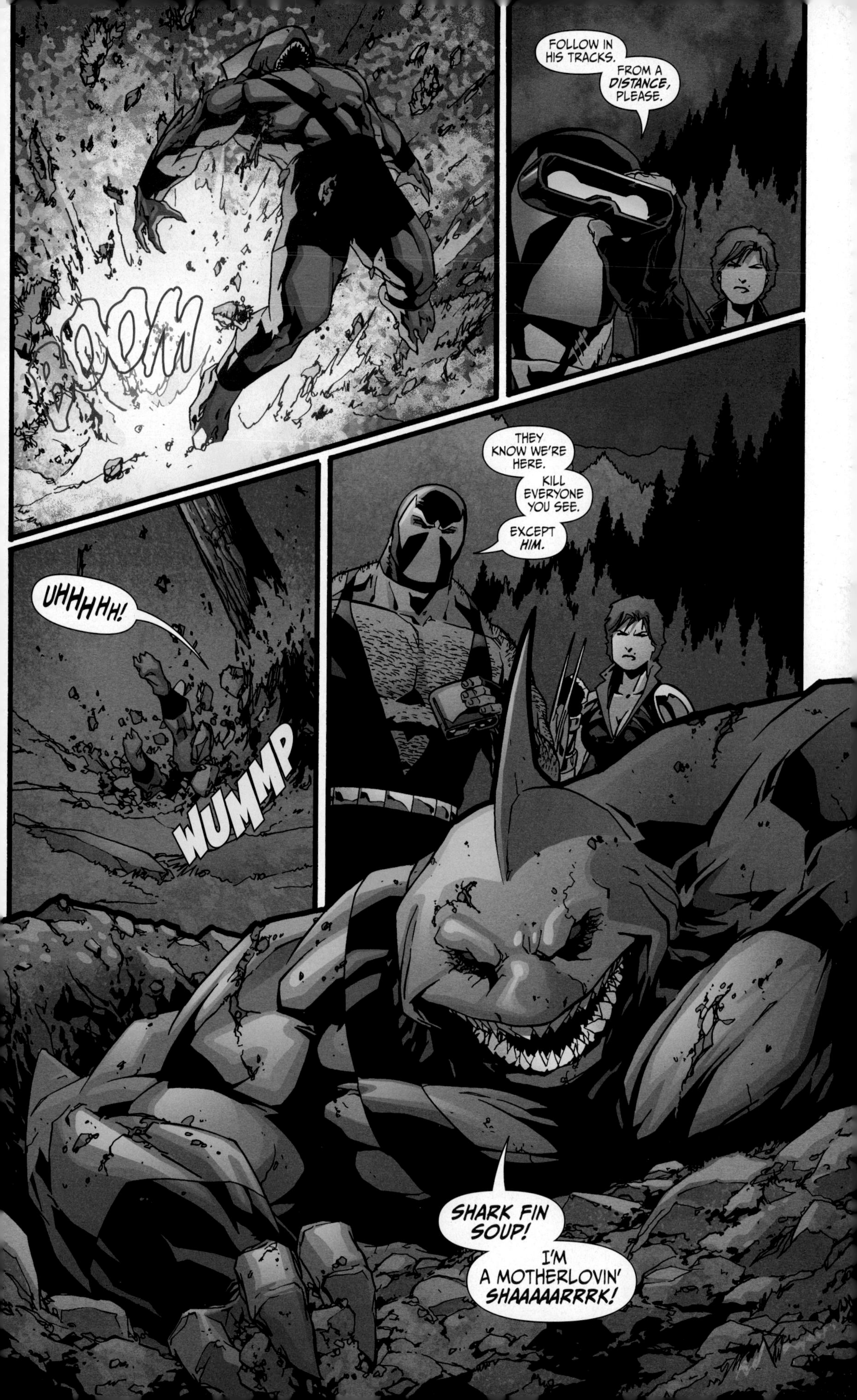
FOOM
FOLLOW IN HIS TRACKS.
FROM A DISTANCE, PLEASE.
THEY KNOW WE'RE HERE.
KILL EVERYONE YOU SEE.
EXCEPT HIM.
UHHHHH!
WUMMP
SHARK FIN SOUP!
I'M A MOTHERLOVIN' SHAAAAARRRK!

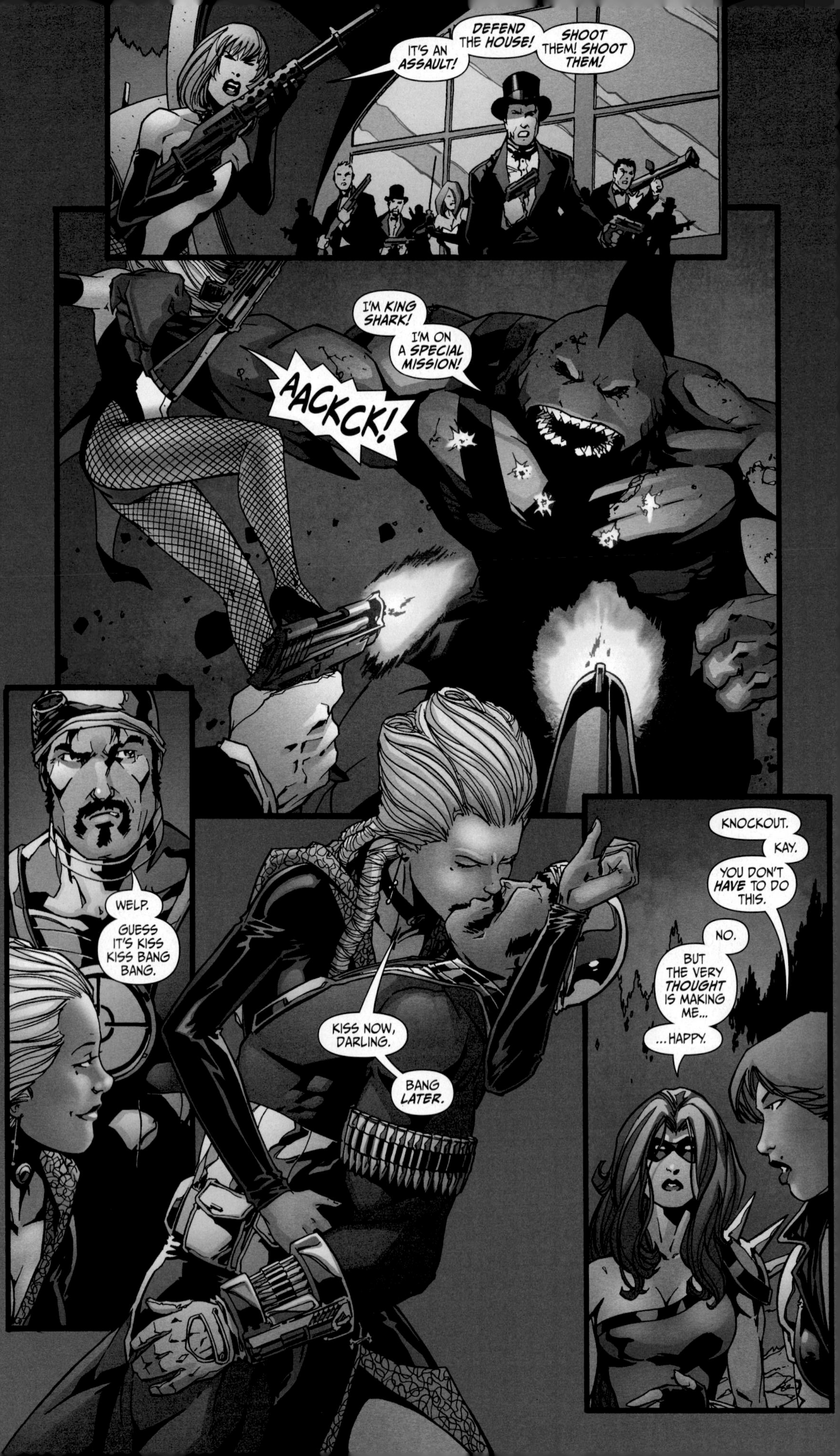
IT'S AN ASSAULT!
DEFEND THE HOUSE!
SHOOT THEM! SHOOT THEM!
I'M KING SHARK!
I'M ON A SPECIAL MISSION!
AACKCK!
WELP.
GUESS IT'S KISS KISS BANG BANG.
KISS NOW, DARLING.
BANG LATER.
KNOCKOUT.
KAY.
YOU DON'T HAVE TO DO THIS.
NO.
BUT THE VERY THOUGHT IS MAKING ME...
...HAPPY.

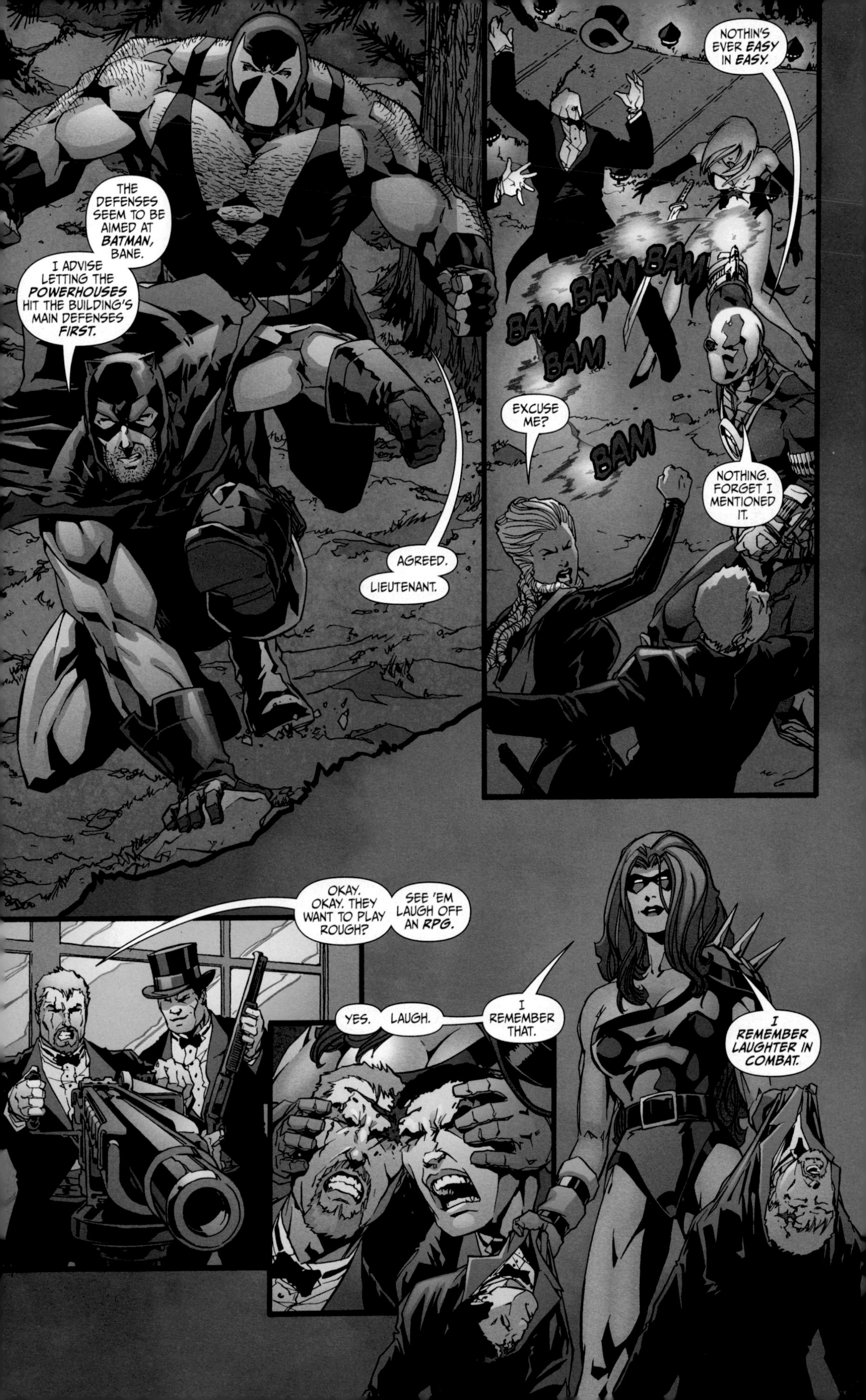
THE DEFENSES SEEM TO BE AIMED AT BATMAN, BANE.
I ADVISE LETTING THE POWERHOUSES HIT THE BUILDING'S MAIN DEFENSES FIRST.
AGREED.
LIEUTENANT.
NOTHIN'S EVER EASY IN EASY.
BAM BAM BAM
BAM
BAM
EXCUSE ME?
NOTHING. FORGET I MENTIONED IT.
OKAY. OKAY. THEY WANT TO PLAY ROUGH?
SEE 'EM LAUGH OFF AN RPG.
YES.
LAUGH.
I REMEMBER THAT.
I REMEMBER LAUGHTER IN COMBAT.

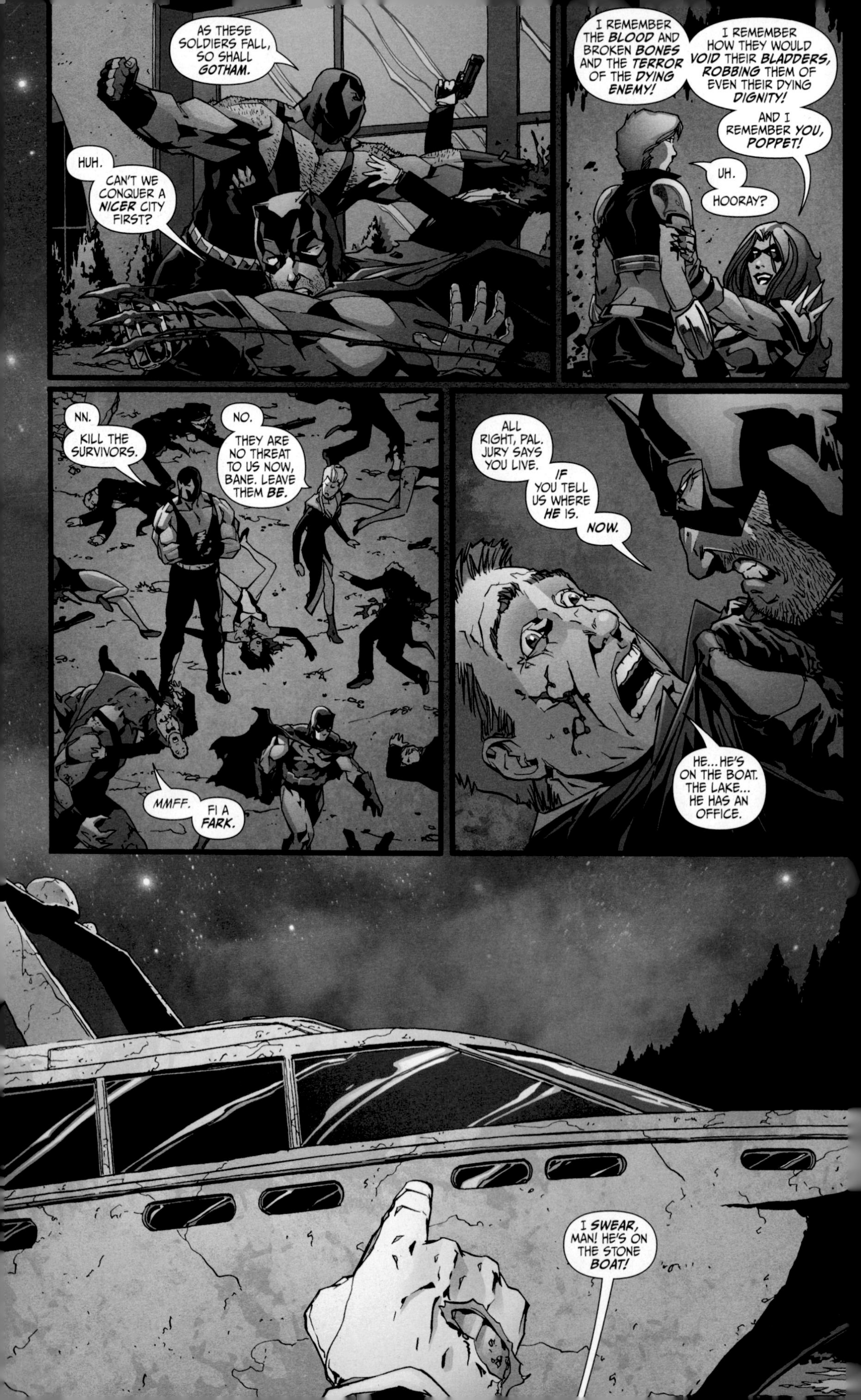
AS THESE SOLDIERS FALL, SO SHALL GOTHAM.
HUH. CAN'T WE CONQUER A NICER CITY FIRST?
I REMEMBER THE BLOOD AND BROKEN BONES AND THE TERROR OF THE DYING ENEMY!
I REMEMBER HOW THEY WOULD VOID THEIR BLADDERS, ROBBING THEM OF EVEN THEIR DYING DIGNITY!
AND I REMEMBER YOU, POPPET!
UH.
HOORAY?
NN. KILL THE SURVIVORS.
NO. THEY ARE NO THREAT TO US NOW, BANE. LEAVE THEM BE.
MMFF. FI A FARK.
ALL RIGHT, PAL. JURY SAYS YOU LIVE.
IF YOU TELL US WHERE HE IS.
NOW.
HE...HE'S ON THE BOAT. THE LAKE... HE HAS AN OFFICE.
I SWEAR, MAN! HE'S ON THE STONE BOAT!

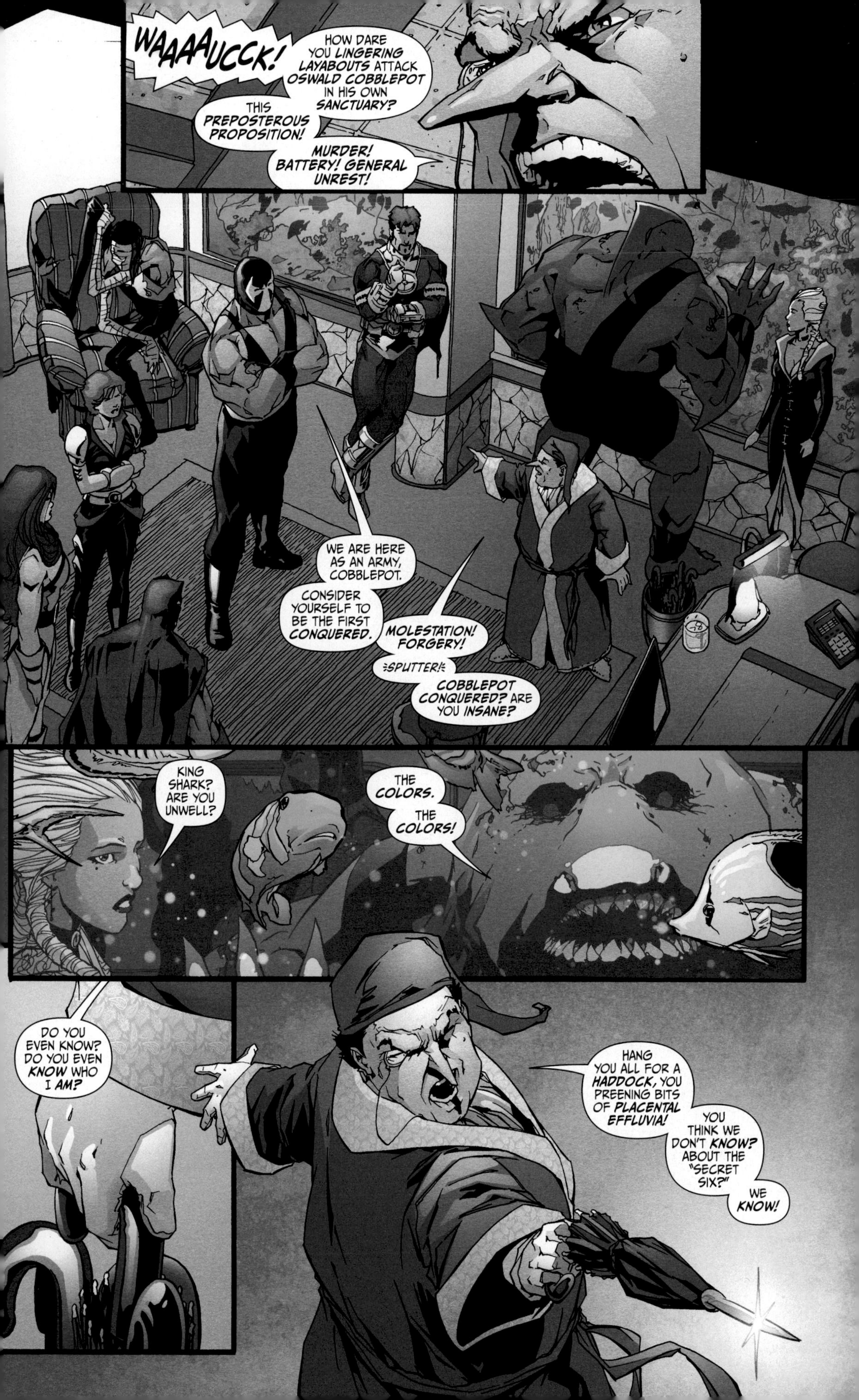

WAAAAUCCK!
HOW DARE YOU LINGERING LAYABOUTS ATTACK OSWALD COBBLEPOT IN HIS OWN SANCTUARY?
THIS PREPOSTEROUS PROPOSITION!
MURDER! BATTERY! GENERAL UNREST!
WE ARE HERE AS AN ARMY, COBBLEPOT.
CONSIDER YOURSELF TO BE THE FIRST CONQUERED.
MOLESTATION! FORGERY!
SPUTTER!
COBBLEPOT CONQUERED? ARE YOU INSANE?
KING SHARK? ARE YOU UNWELL?
THE COLORS.
THE COLORS!
DO YOU EVEN KNOW? DO YOU EVEN KNOW WHO I AM?
HANG YOU ALL FOR A HADDOCK, YOU PREENING BITS OF PLACENTAL EFFLUVIA!
YOU THINK WE DON'T KNOW? ABOUT THE "SECRET SIX?"
WE KNOW!

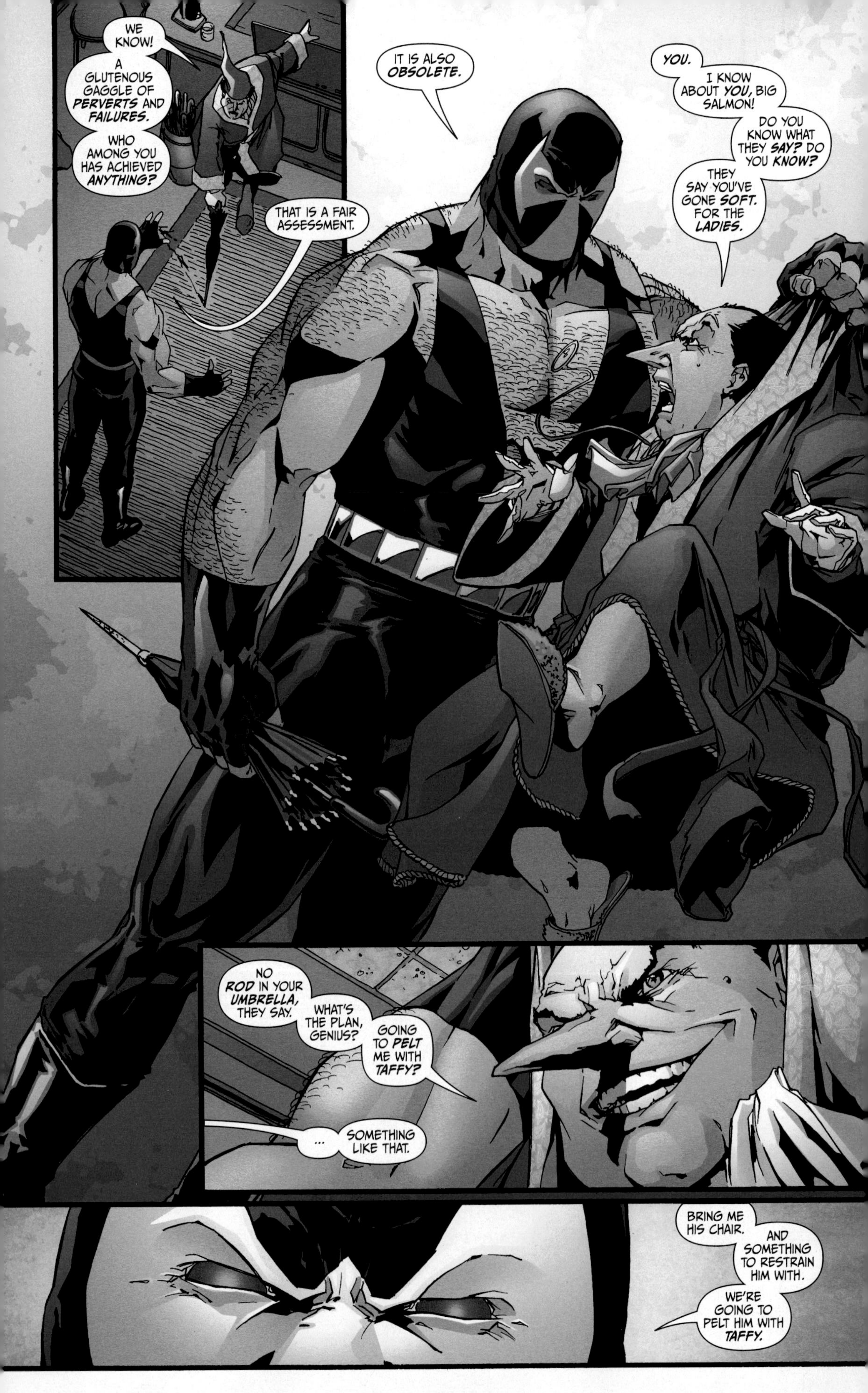
WE KNOW!
A GLUTENOUS GAGGLE OF PERVERTS AND FAILURES.
WHO AMONG YOU HAS ACHIEVED ANYTHING?
THAT IS A FAIR ASSESSMENT.
IT IS ALSO OBSOLETE.
YOU.
I KNOW ABOUT YOU, BIG SALMON!
DO YOU KNOW WHAT THEY SAY? DO YOU KNOW?
THEY SAY YOU'VE GONE SOFT. FOR THE LADIES.
NO ROD IN YOUR UMBRELLA, THEY SAY.
WHAT'S THE PLAN, GENIUS?
GOING TO PELT ME WITH TAFFY?
...
SOMETHING LIKE THAT.
BRING ME HIS CHAIR.
AND SOMETHING TO RESTRAIN HIM WITH.
WE'RE GOING TO PELT HIM WITH TAFFY.

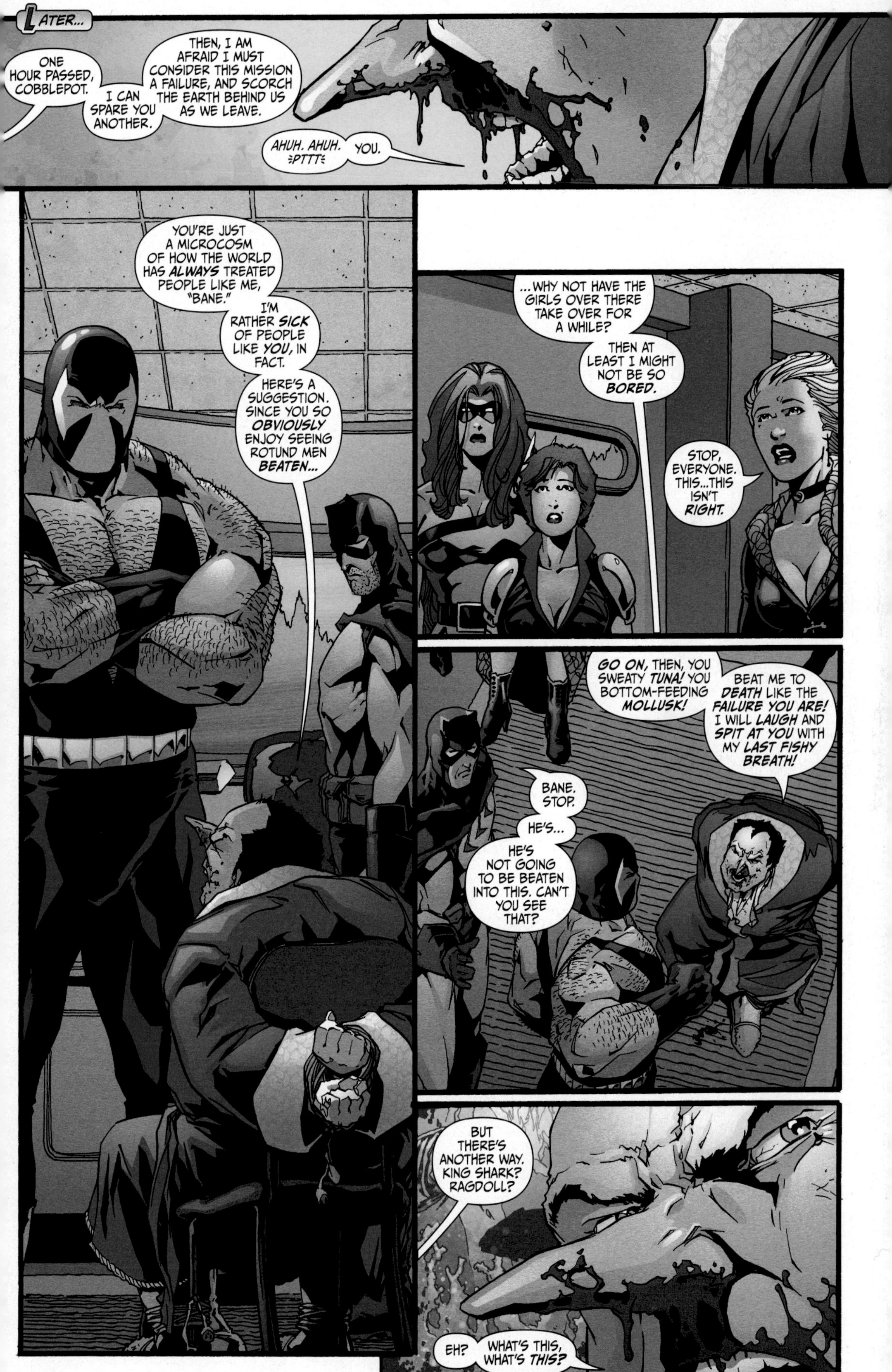
LATER...
ONE HOUR PASSED, COBBLEPOT.
I CAN SPARE YOU ANOTHER.
THEN, I AM AFRAID I MUST CONSIDER THIS MISSION A FAILURE, AND SCORCH THE EARTH BEHIND US AS WE LEAVE.
AHUH. AHUH. PTTT
YOU.
YOU'RE JUST A MICROCOSM OF HOW THE WORLD HAS ALWAYS TREATED PEOPLE LIKE ME, "BANE."
I'M RATHER SICK OF PEOPLE LIKE YOU, IN FACT.
HERE'S A SUGGESTION. SINCE YOU SO OBVIOUSLY ENJOY SEEING ROTUND MEN BEATEN...
...WHY NOT HAVE THE GIRLS OVER THERE TAKE OVER FOR A WHILE?
THEN AT LEAST I MIGHT NOT BE SO BORED.
STOP, EVERYONE. THIS...THIS ISN'T RIGHT.
GO ON, THEN, YOU SWEATY TUNA! YOU BOTTOM-FEEDING MOLLUSK!
BEAT ME TO DEATH LIKE THE FAILURE YOU ARE! I WILL LAUGH AND SPIT AT YOU WITH MY LAST FISHY BREATH!
BANE. STOP.
HE'S...
HE'S NOT GOING TO BE BEATEN INTO THIS. CAN'T YOU SEE THAT?
BUT THERE'S ANOTHER WAY. KING SHARK? RAGDOLL?
EH?
WHAT'S THIS, WHAT'S THIS?

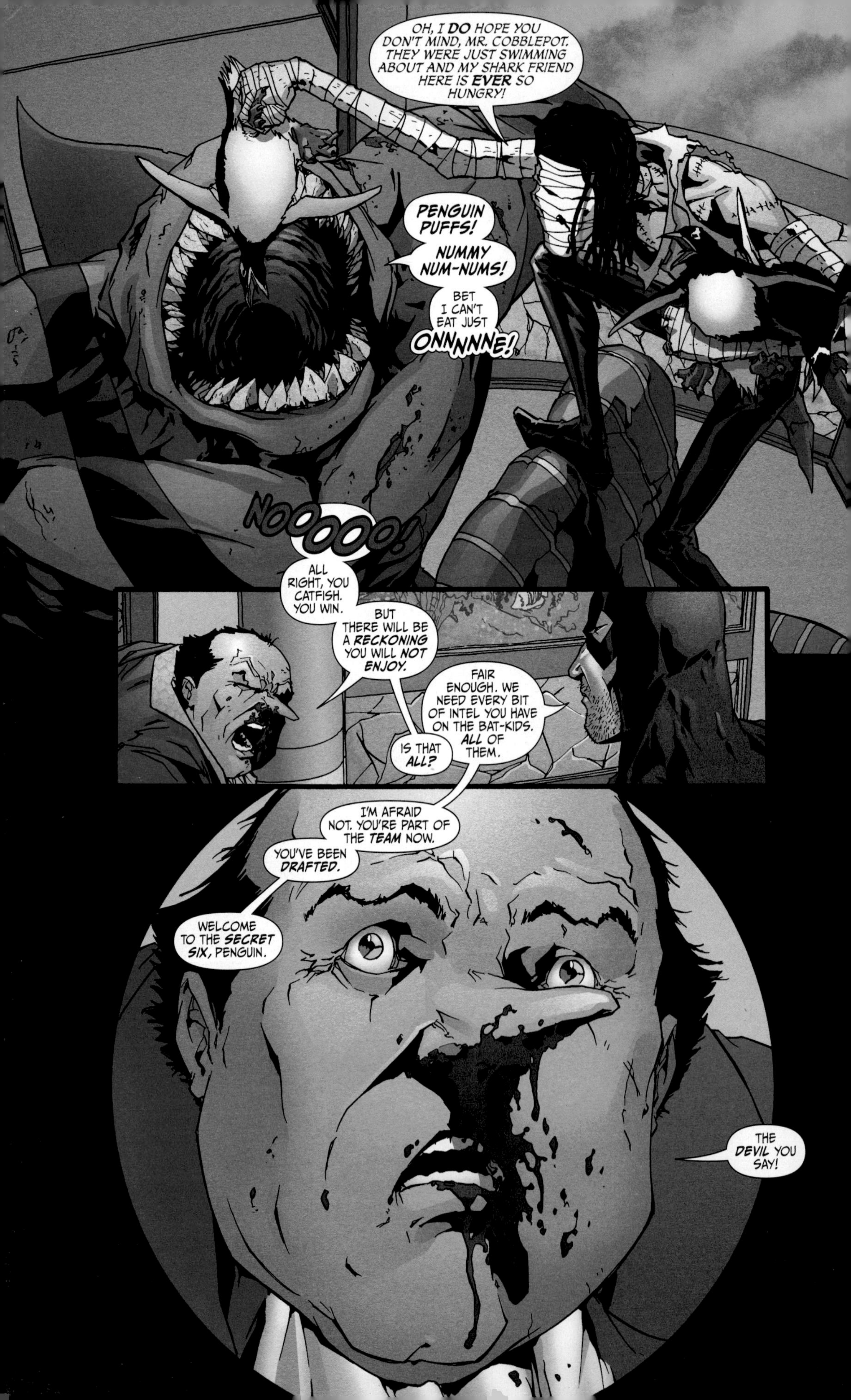

OH, I DO HOPE YOU DON'T MIND, MR. COBBLEPOT. THEY WERE JUST SWIMMING ABOUT AND MY SHARK FRIEND HERE IS EVER SO HUNGRY!
PENGUIN PUFFS!
NUMMY NUM-NUMS!
BET I CAN'T EAT JUST ONNNNNE!
NOOOOOO!
ALL RIGHT, YOU CATFISH. YOU WIN.
BUT THERE WILL BE A RECKONING YOU WILL NOT ENJOY.
FAIR ENOUGH. WE NEED EVERY BIT OF INTEL YOU HAVE ON THE BAT-KIDS. ALL OF THEM.
IS THAT ALL?
I'M AFRAID NOT. YOU'RE PART OF THE TEAM NOW.
YOU'VE BEEN DRAFTED.
WELCOME TO THE SECRET SIX, PENGUIN.
THE DEVIL YOU SAY!

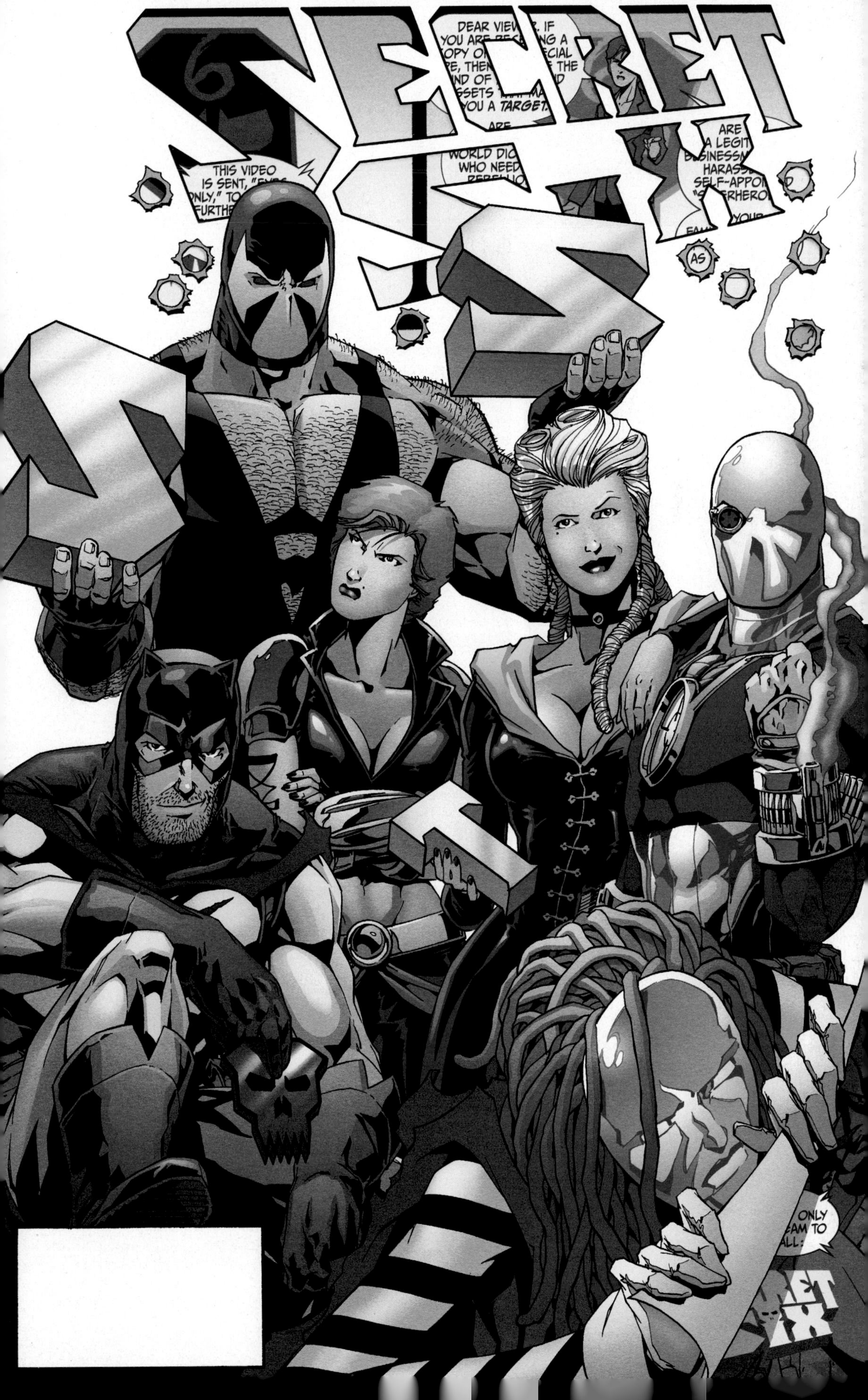
SECRET SIX
DEAR VIEWER, IF
YOU A TARGET.
THIS VIDEO
IS SENT,
SELF-APPO
AS
ONLY

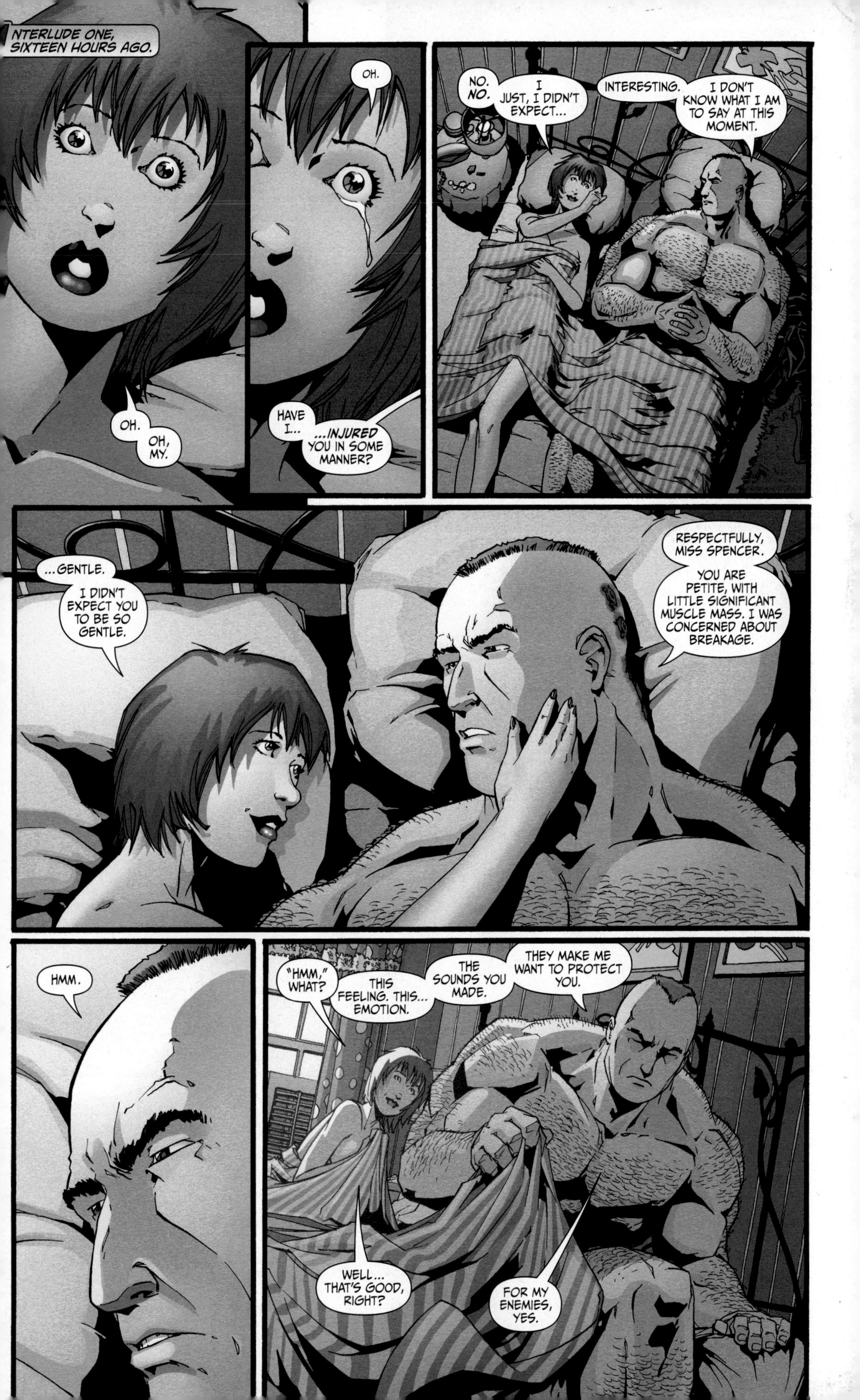
NTERLUDE ONE, SIXTEEN HOURS AGO.
OH.
OH, MY.
OH.
HAVE I...
...INJURED YOU IN SOME MANNER?
NO. NO.
I JUST, I DIDN'T EXPECT...
INTERESTING.
I DON'T KNOW WHAT I AM TO SAY AT THIS MOMENT.
...GENTLE. I DIDN'T EXPECT YOU TO BE SO GENTLE.
RESPECTFULLY, MISS SPENCER.
YOU ARE PETITE, WITH LITTLE SIGNIFICANT MUSCLE MASS. I WAS CONCERNED ABOUT BREAKAGE.
HMM.
"HMM," WHAT?
THIS FEELING. THIS... EMOTION.
THE SOUNDS YOU MADE.
THEY MAKE ME WANT TO PROTECT YOU.
WELL... THAT'S GOOD, RIGHT?
FOR MY ENEMIES, YES.

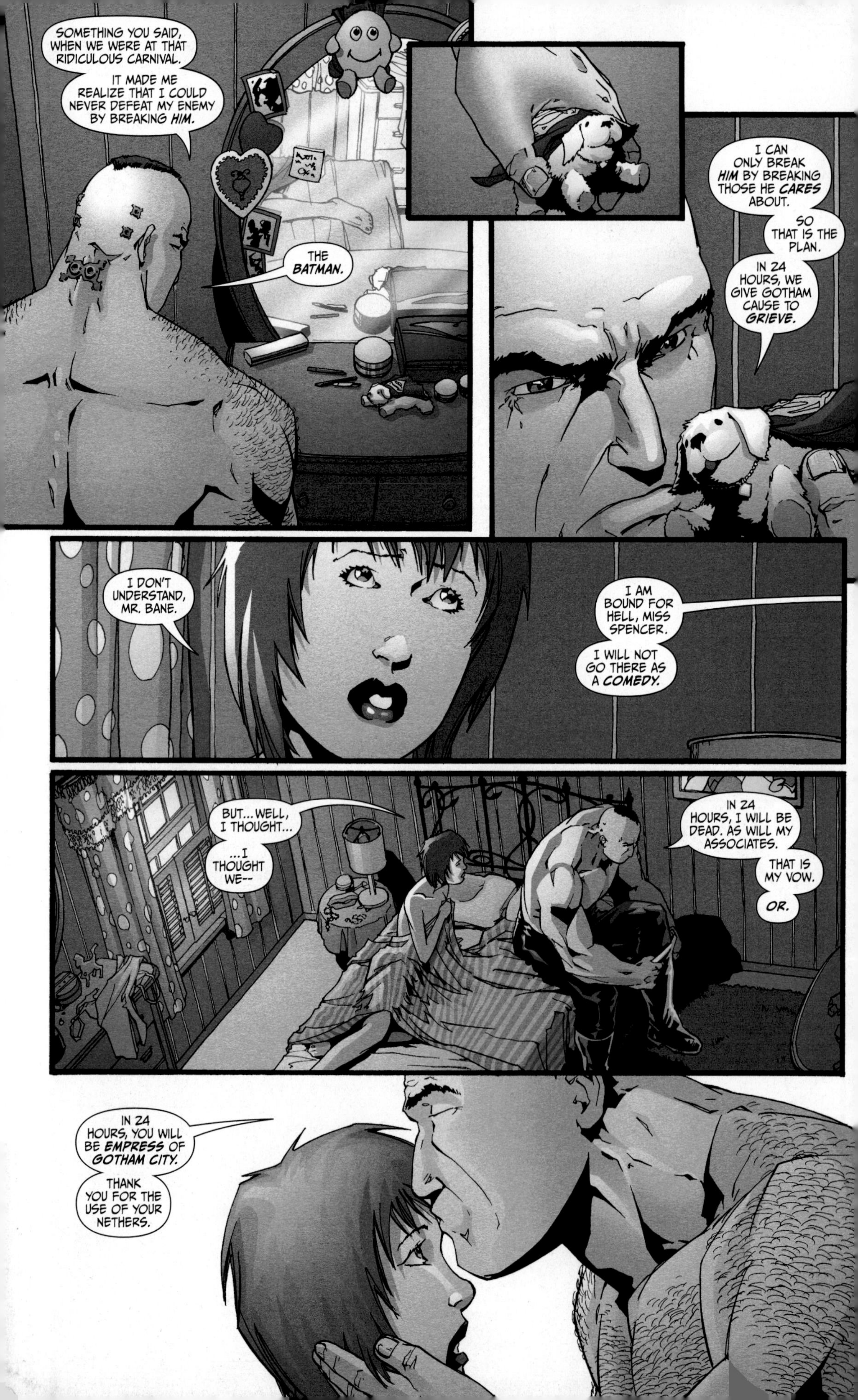
SOMETHING YOU SAID, WHEN WE WERE AT THAT RIDICULOUS CARNIVAL.
IT MADE ME REALIZE THAT I COULD NEVER DEFEAT MY ENEMY BY BREAKING *HIM.*
THE *BATMAN.*
I CAN ONLY BREAK *HIM* BY BREAKING THOSE HE *CARES* ABOUT.
SO THAT IS THE PLAN.
IN 24 HOURS, WE GIVE GOTHAM CAUSE TO *GRIEVE.*
I DON'T UNDERSTAND, MR. BANE.
I AM BOUND FOR HELL, MISS SPENCER.
I WILL NOT GO THERE AS A *COMEDY.*
BUT...WELL, I THOUGHT...
...I THOUGHT WE--
IN 24 HOURS, I WILL BE DEAD. AS WILL MY ASSOCIATES.
THAT IS MY VOW.
OR.
IN 24 HOURS, YOU WILL BE *EMPRESS* OF *GOTHAM CITY.*
THANK YOU FOR THE USE OF YOUR NETHERS.

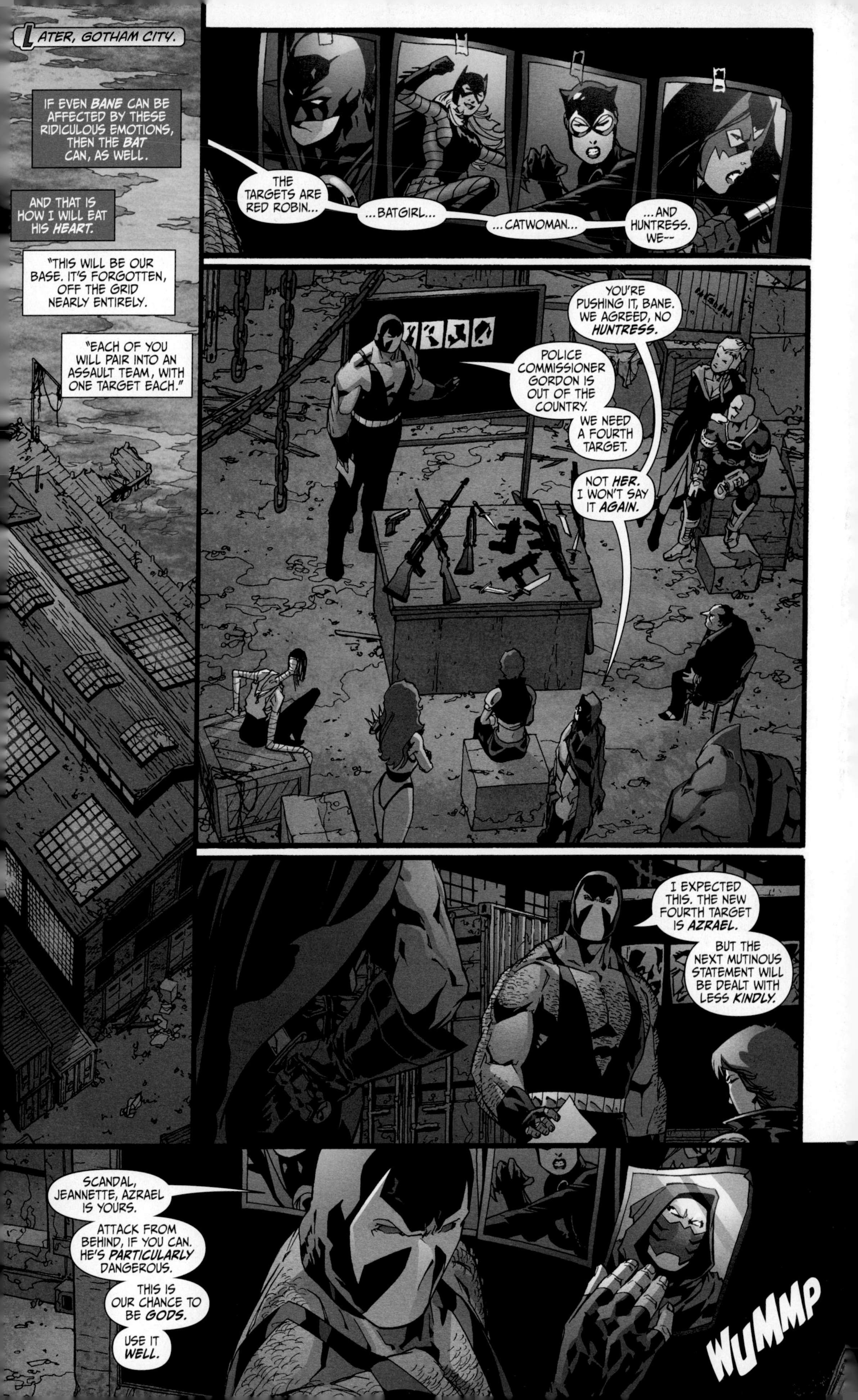
LATER, GOTHAM CITY.
IF EVEN BANE CAN BE AFFECTED BY THESE RIDICULOUS EMOTIONS, THEN THE BAT CAN, AS WELL.
AND THAT IS HOW I WILL EAT HIS HEART.
"THIS WILL BE OUR BASE. IT'S FORGOTTEN, OFF THE GRID NEARLY ENTIRELY.
"EACH OF YOU WILL PAIR INTO AN ASSAULT TEAM, WITH ONE TARGET EACH."
THE TARGETS ARE RED ROBIN...
...BATGIRL...
...CATWOMAN...
...AND HUNTRESS. WE--
YOU'RE PUSHING IT, BANE. WE AGREED, NO HUNTRESS.
POLICE COMMISSIONER GORDON IS OUT OF THE COUNTRY.
WE NEED A FOURTH TARGET.
NOT HER. I WON'T SAY IT AGAIN.
I EXPECTED THIS. THE NEW FOURTH TARGET IS AZRAEL.
BUT THE NEXT MUTINOUS STATEMENT WILL BE DEALT WITH LESS KINDLY.
SCANDAL, JEANNETTE, AZRAEL IS YOURS.
ATTACK FROM BEHIND, IF YOU CAN. HE'S PARTICULARLY DANGEROUS.
THIS IS OUR CHANCE TO BE GODS.
USE IT WELL.
WUMMP

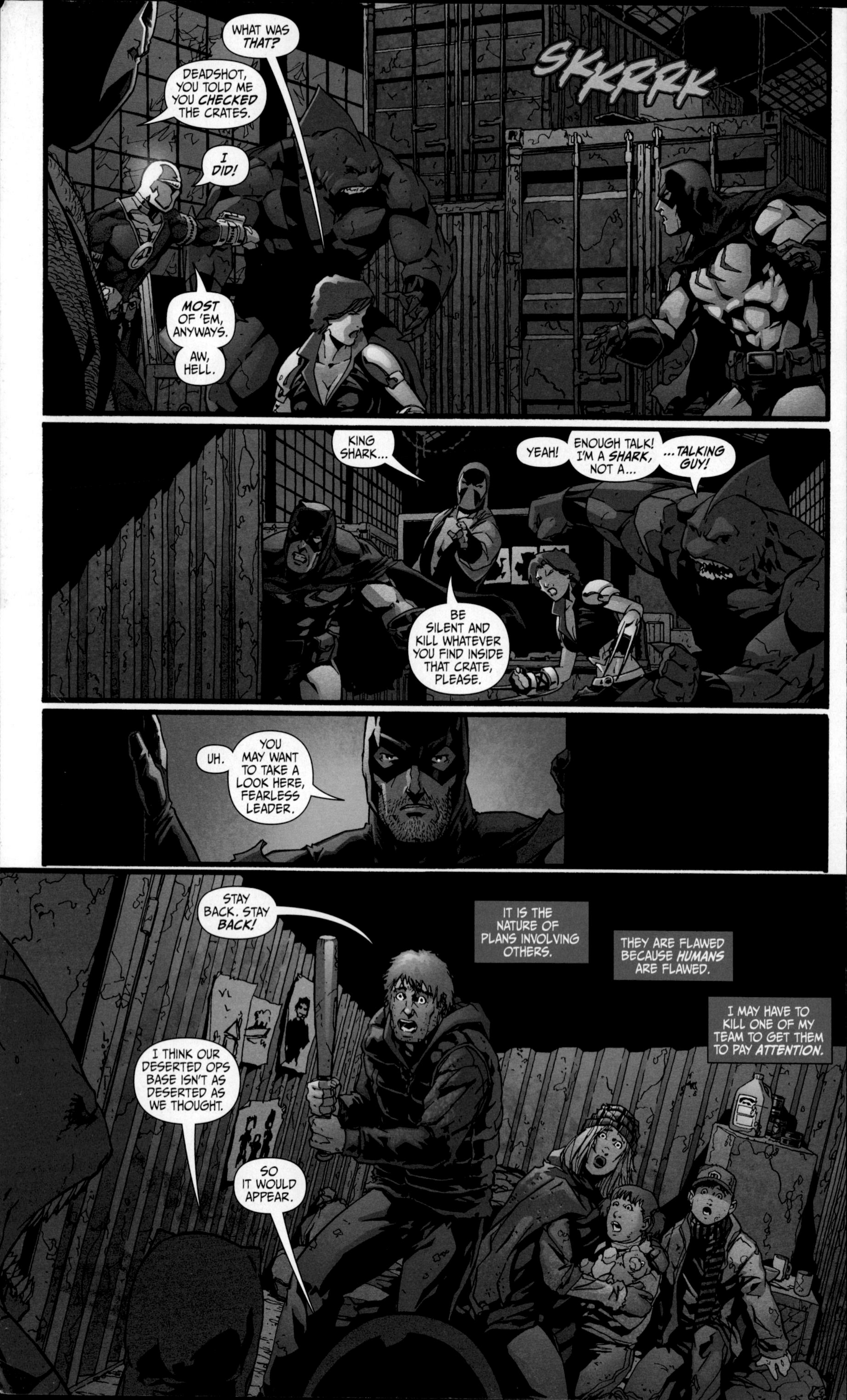
SKKRRK
WHAT WAS THAT?
DEADSHOT, YOU TOLD ME YOU CHECKED THE CRATES.
I DID!
MOST OF 'EM, ANYWAYS.
AW, HELL.
KING SHARK...
BE SILENT AND KILL WHATEVER YOU FIND INSIDE THAT CRATE, PLEASE.
YEAH!
ENOUGH TALK! I'M A SHARK, NOT A...
...TALKING GUY!
UH.
YOU MAY WANT TO TAKE A LOOK HERE, FEARLESS LEADER.
STAY BACK. STAY BACK!
IT IS THE NATURE OF PLANS INVOLVING OTHERS.
THEY ARE FLAWED BECAUSE HUMANS ARE FLAWED.
I MAY HAVE TO KILL ONE OF MY TEAM TO GET THEM TO PAY ATTENTION.
I THINK OUR DESERTED OPS BASE ISN'T AS DESERTED AS WE THOUGHT.
SO IT WOULD APPEAR.

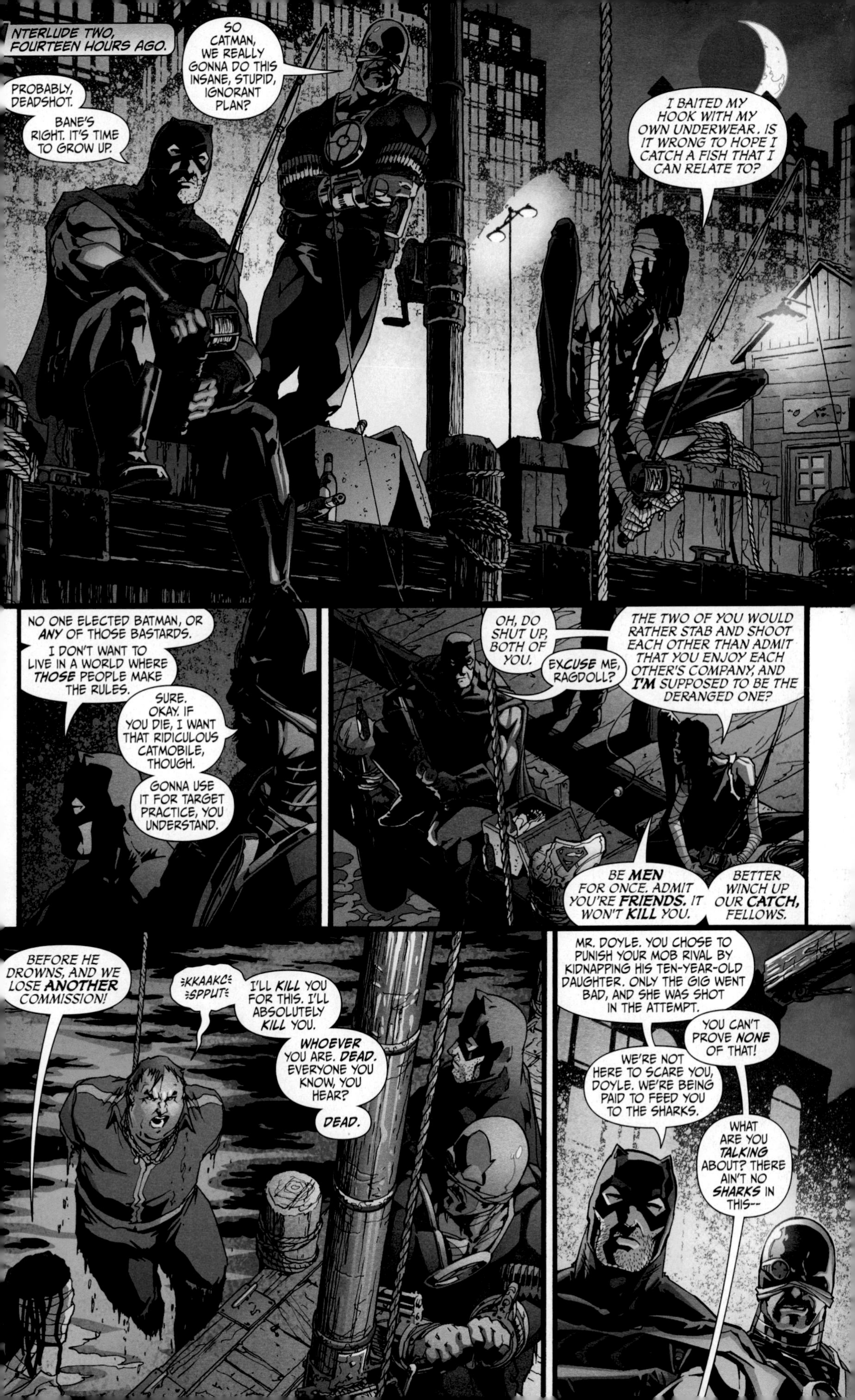

NTERLUDE TWO, FOURTEEN HOURS AGO.
SO CATMAN, WE REALLY GONNA DO THIS INSANE, STUPID, IGNORANT PLAN?
PROBABLY, DEADSHOT.
BANE'S RIGHT. IT'S TIME TO GROW UP.
I BAITED MY HOOK WITH MY OWN UNDERWEAR. IS IT WRONG TO HOPE I CATCH A FISH THAT I CAN RELATE TO?
NO ONE ELECTED BATMAN, OR ANY OF THOSE BASTARDS.
I DON'T WANT TO LIVE IN A WORLD WHERE THOSE PEOPLE MAKE THE RULES.
SURE. OKAY. IF YOU DIE, I WANT THAT RIDICULOUS CATMOBILE, THOUGH.
GONNA USE IT FOR TARGET PRACTICE, YOU UNDERSTAND.
OH, DO SHUT UP, BOTH OF YOU.
EXCUSE ME, RAGDOLL?
THE TWO OF YOU WOULD RATHER STAB AND SHOOT EACH OTHER THAN ADMIT THAT YOU ENJOY EACH OTHER'S COMPANY, AND I'M SUPPOSED TO BE THE DERANGED ONE?
BE MEN FOR ONCE. ADMIT YOU'RE FRIENDS. IT WON'T KILL YOU.
BETTER WINCH UP OUR CATCH, FELLOWS.
BEFORE HE DROWNS, AND WE LOSE ANOTHER COMMISSION!
KKAAKC SPPUT
I'LL KILL YOU FOR THIS. I'LL ABSOLUTELY KILL YOU.
WHOEVER YOU ARE. DEAD. EVERYONE YOU KNOW, YOU HEAR?
DEAD.
MR. DOYLE. YOU CHOSE TO PUNISH YOUR MOB RIVAL BY KIDNAPPING HIS TEN-YEAR-OLD DAUGHTER. ONLY THE GIG WENT BAD, AND SHE WAS SHOT IN THE ATTEMPT.
YOU CAN'T PROVE NONE OF THAT!
WE'RE NOT HERE TO SCARE YOU, DOYLE. WE'RE BEING PAID TO FEED YOU TO THE SHARKS.
WHAT ARE YOU TALKING ABOUT? THERE AIN'T NO SHARKS IN THIS--

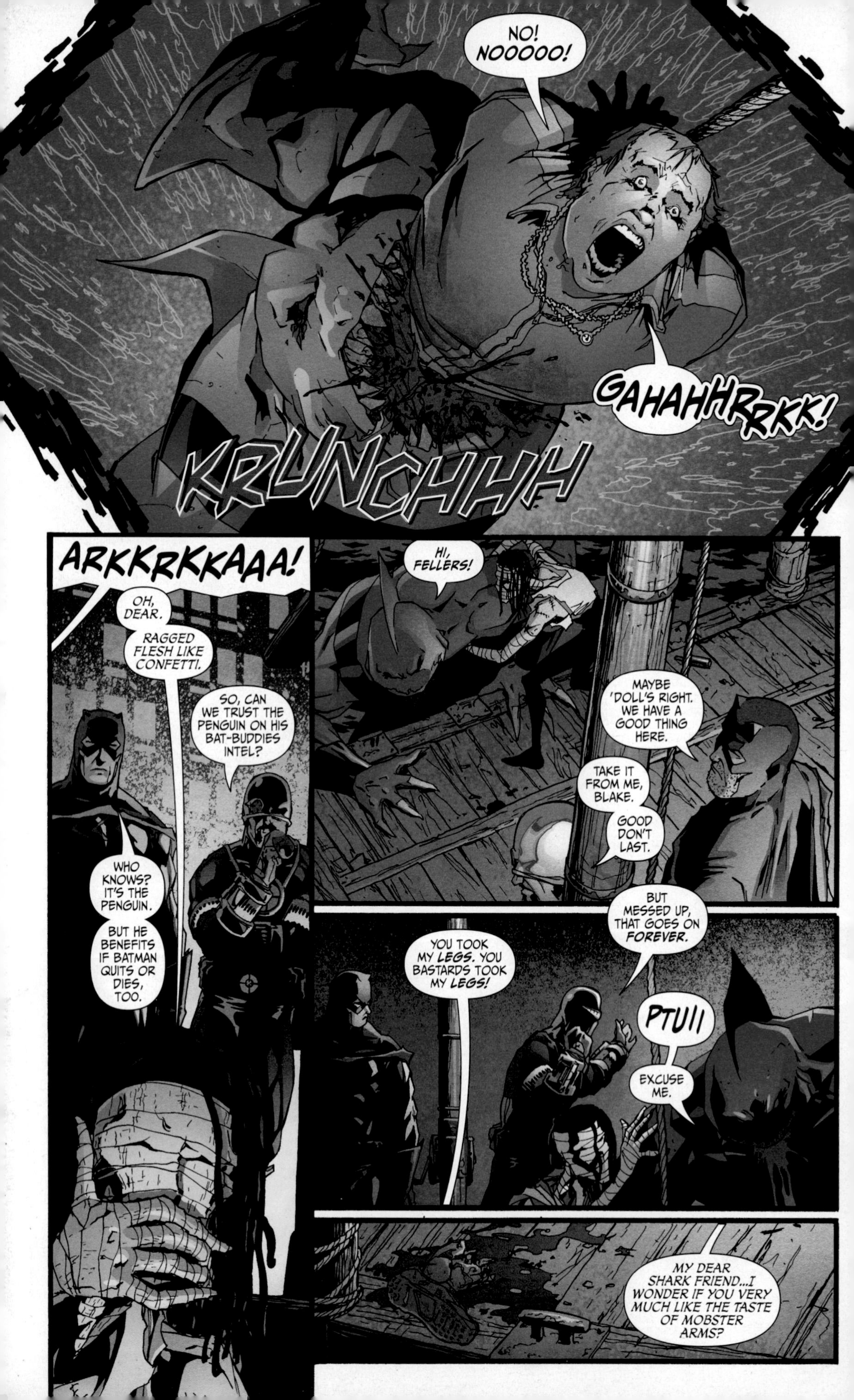

NO! NOOOOO!
GAHAHHRRKK!
KRUNCHHH
ARKKRKKAAA!
OH, DEAR.
RAGGED FLESH LIKE CONFETTI.
SO, CAN WE TRUST THE PENGUIN ON HIS BAT-BUDDIES INTEL?
WHO KNOWS? IT'S THE PENGUIN.
BUT HE BENEFITS IF BATMAN QUITS OR DIES, TOO.
HI, FELLERS!
MAYBE 'DOLL'S RIGHT. WE HAVE A GOOD THING HERE.
TAKE IT FROM ME, BLAKE.
GOOD DON'T LAST.
BUT MESSED UP, THAT GOES ON FOREVER.
YOU TOOK MY LEGS. YOU BASTARDS TOOK MY LEGS!
PTUI!
EXCUSE ME.
MY DEAR SHARK FRIEND...I WONDER IF YOU VERY MUCH LIKE THE TASTE OF MOBSTER ARMS?

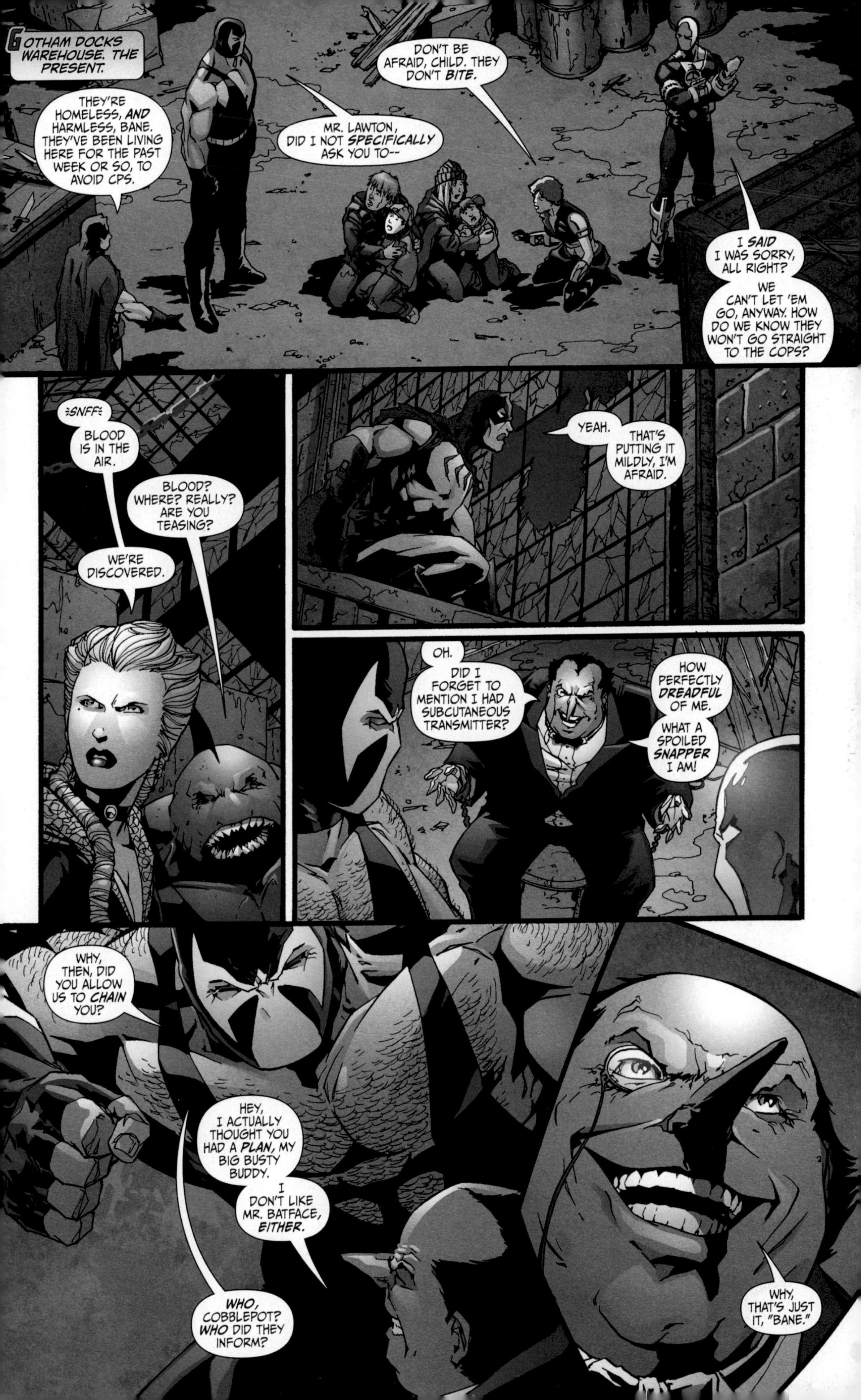
GOTHAM DOCKS WAREHOUSE. THE PRESENT.
THEY'RE HOMELESS, AND HARMLESS, BANE. THEY'VE BEEN LIVING HERE FOR THE PAST WEEK OR SO, TO AVOID CPS.
MR. LAWTON, DID I NOT SPECIFICALLY ASK YOU TO--
DON'T BE AFRAID, CHILD. THEY DON'T BITE.
I SAID I WAS SORRY, ALL RIGHT?
WE CAN'T LET 'EM GO, ANYWAY. HOW DO WE KNOW THEY WON'T GO STRAIGHT TO THE COPS?
SNFF
BLOOD IS IN THE AIR.
BLOOD? WHERE? REALLY? ARE YOU TEASING?
WE'RE DISCOVERED.
YEAH.
THAT'S PUTTING IT MILDLY, I'M AFRAID.
OH.
DID I FORGET TO MENTION I HAD A SUBCUTANEOUS TRANSMITTER?
HOW PERFECTLY DREADFUL OF ME.
WHAT A SPOILED SNAPPER I AM!
WHY, THEN, DID YOU ALLOW US TO CHAIN YOU?
HEY, I ACTUALLY THOUGHT YOU HAD A PLAN, MY BIG BUSTY BUDDY.
I DON'T LIKE MR. BATFACE, EITHER.
WHO, COBBLEPOT? WHO DID THEY INFORM?
WHY, THAT'S JUST IT, "BANE."

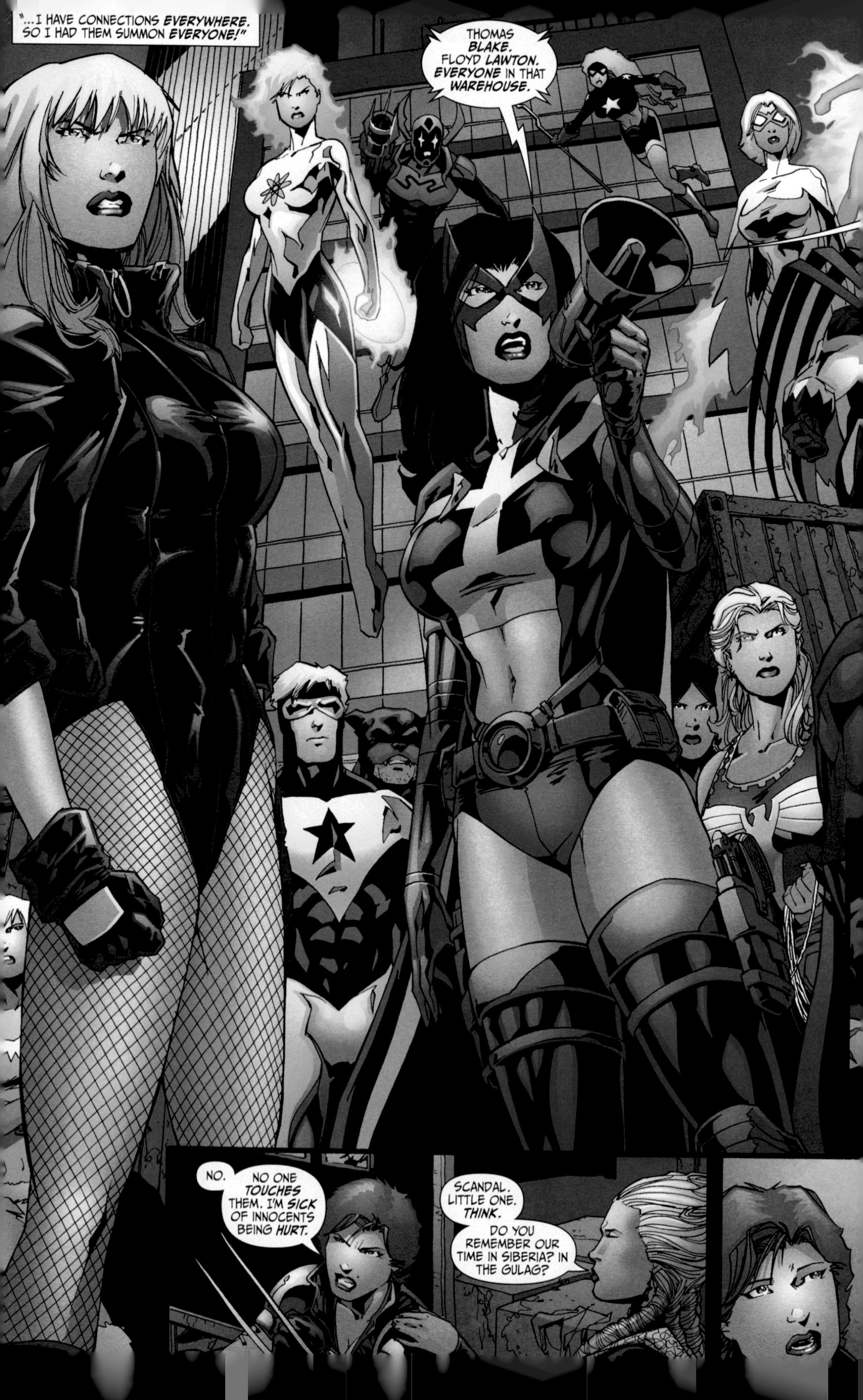
"...I HAVE CONNECTIONS EVERYWHERE. SO I HAD THEM SUMMON EVERYONE!"
THOMAS BLAKE. FLOYD LAWTON. EVERYONE IN THAT WAREHOUSE.
NO.
NO ONE TOUCHES THEM. I'M SICK OF INNOCENTS BEING HURT.
SCANDAL. LITTLE ONE. THINK.
DO YOU REMEMBER OUR TIME IN SIBERIA? IN THE GULAG?

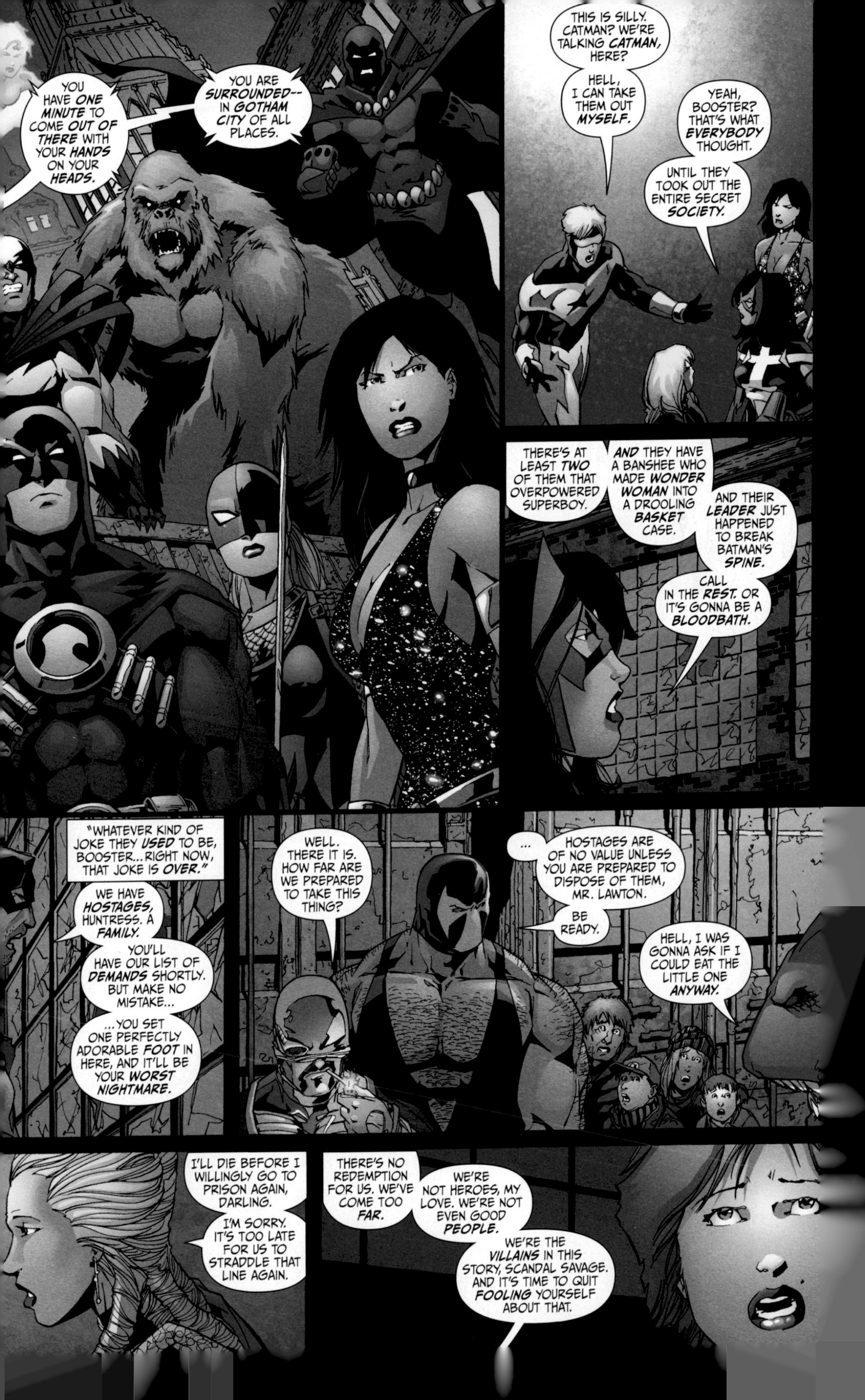
YOU HAVE ONE MINUTE TO COME OUT OF THERE WITH YOUR HANDS ON YOUR HEADS.
YOU ARE SURROUNDED-- IN GOTHAM CITY OF ALL PLACES.
THIS IS SILLY. CATMAN? WE'RE TALKING CATMAN, HERE?
HELL, I CAN TAKE THEM OUT MYSELF.
YEAH, BOOSTER? THAT'S WHAT EVERYBODY THOUGHT.
UNTIL THEY TOOK OUT THE ENTIRE SECRET SOCIETY.
THERE'S AT LEAST TWO OF THEM THAT OVERPOWERED SUPERBOY.
AND THEY HAVE A BANSHEE WHO MADE WONDER WOMAN INTO A DROOLING BASKET CASE.
AND THEIR LEADER JUST HAPPENED TO BREAK BATMAN'S SPINE.
CALL IN THE REST. OR IT'S GONNA BE A BLOODBATH.
"WHATEVER KIND OF JOKE THEY USED TO BE, BOOSTER... RIGHT NOW, THAT JOKE IS OVER."
WE HAVE HOSTAGES, HUNTRESS. A FAMILY.
YOU'LL HAVE OUR LIST OF DEMANDS SHORTLY. BUT MAKE NO MISTAKE...
...YOU SET ONE PERFECTLY ADORABLE FOOT IN HERE, AND IT'LL BE YOUR WORST NIGHTMARE.
WELL. THERE IT IS. HOW FAR ARE WE PREPARED TO TAKE THIS THING?
...
HOSTAGES ARE OF NO VALUE UNLESS YOU ARE PREPARED TO DISPOSE OF THEM, MR. LAWTON.
BE READY.
HELL, I WAS GONNA ASK IF I COULD EAT THE LITTLE ONE ANYWAY.
I'LL DIE BEFORE I WILLINGLY GO TO PRISON AGAIN, DARLING.
I'M SORRY. IT'S TOO LATE FOR US TO STRADDLE THAT LINE AGAIN.
THERE'S NO REDEMPTION FOR US. WE'VE COME TOO FAR.
WE'RE NOT HEROES, MY LOVE. WE'RE NOT EVEN GOOD PEOPLE.
WE'RE THE VILLAINS IN THIS STORY, SCANDAL SAVAGE. AND IT'S TIME TO QUIT FOOLING YOURSELF ABOUT THAT.

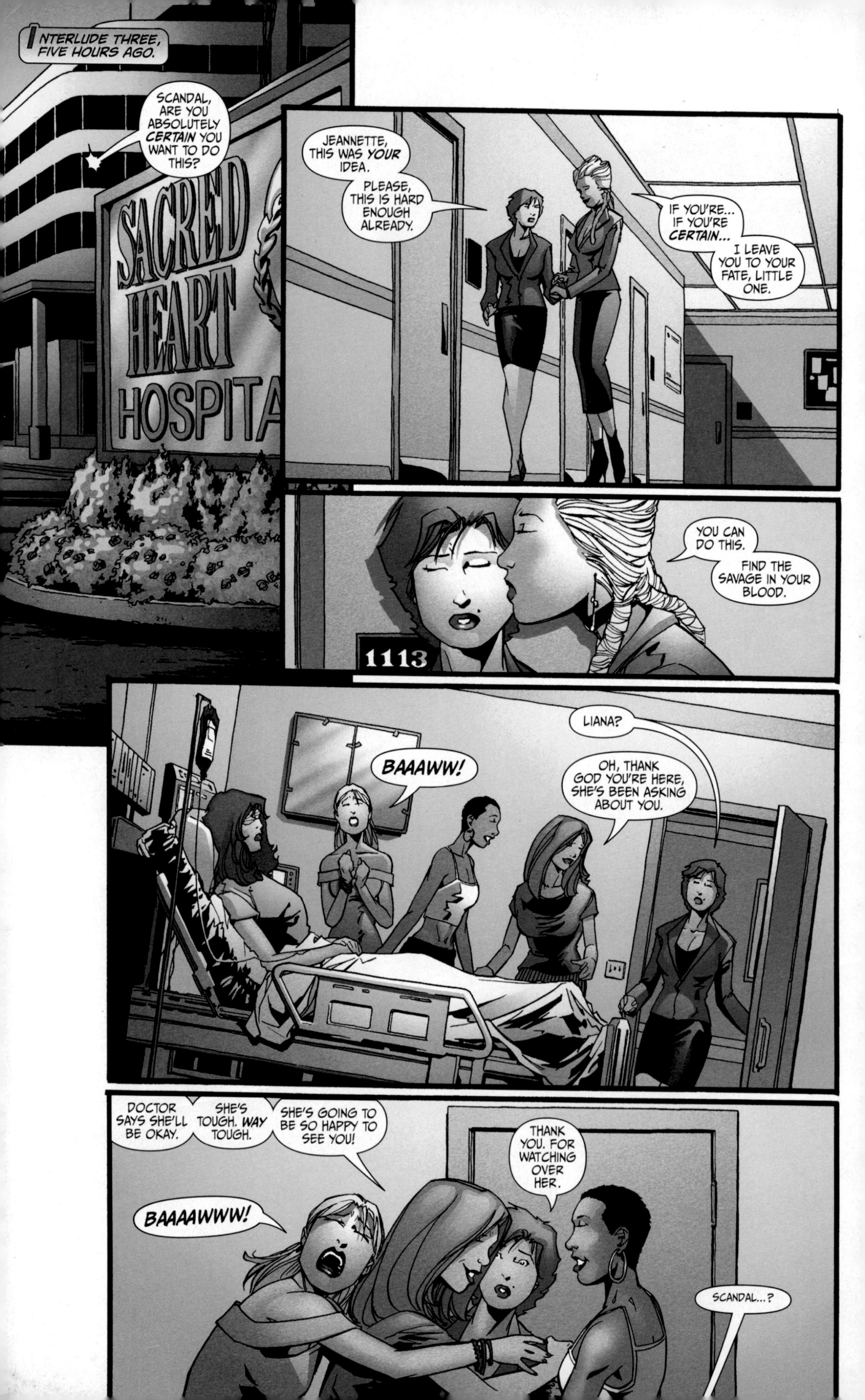
INTERLUDE THREE, FIVE HOURS AGO.
SCANDAL, ARE YOU ABSOLUTELY CERTAIN YOU WANT TO DO THIS?
SACRED HEART HOSPITA
JEANNETTE, THIS WAS YOUR IDEA.
PLEASE, THIS IS HARD ENOUGH ALREADY.
IF YOU'RE... IF YOU'RE CERTAIN...
I LEAVE YOU TO YOUR FATE, LITTLE ONE.
YOU CAN DO THIS.
FIND THE SAVAGE IN YOUR BLOOD.
1113
LIANA?
BAAAWW!
OH, THANK GOD YOU'RE HERE, SHE'S BEEN ASKING ABOUT YOU.
DOCTOR SAYS SHE'LL BE OKAY.
SHE'S TOUGH. WAY TOUGH.
SHE'S GOING TO BE SO HAPPY TO SEE YOU!
THANK YOU. FOR WATCHING OVER HER.
BAAAAWWW!
SCANDAL...?

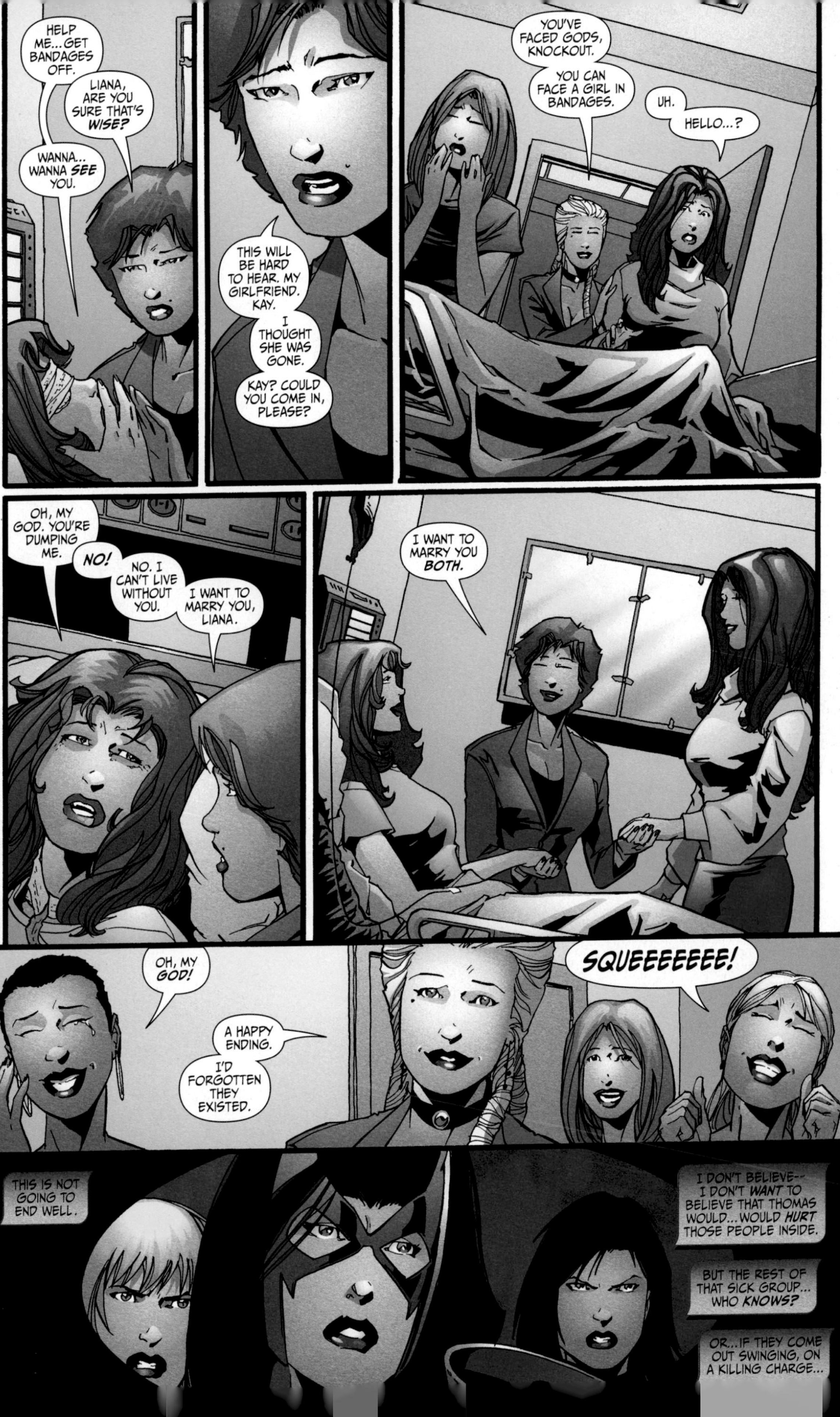
HELP ME...GET BANDAGES OFF.
LIANA, ARE YOU SURE THAT'S WISE?
WANNA... WANNA SEE YOU.
THIS WILL BE HARD TO HEAR. MY GIRLFRIEND. KAY.
I THOUGHT SHE WAS GONE.
KAY? COULD YOU COME IN, PLEASE?
YOU'VE FACED GODS, KNOCKOUT.
YOU CAN FACE A GIRL IN BANDAGES.
UH.
HELLO...?
OH, MY GOD. YOU'RE DUMPING ME.
NO!
NO. I CAN'T LIVE WITHOUT YOU.
I WANT TO MARRY YOU, LIANA.
I WANT TO MARRY YOU BOTH.
OH, MY GOD!
A HAPPY ENDING.
I'D FORGOTTEN THEY EXISTED.
SQUEEEEEEEE!
THIS IS NOT GOING TO END WELL.
I DON'T BELIEVE-- I DON'T WANT TO BELIEVE THAT THOMAS WOULD...WOULD HURT THOSE PEOPLE INSIDE.
BUT THE REST OF THAT SICK GROUP... WHO KNOWS?
OR...IF THEY COME OUT SWINGING, ON A KILLING CHARGE...

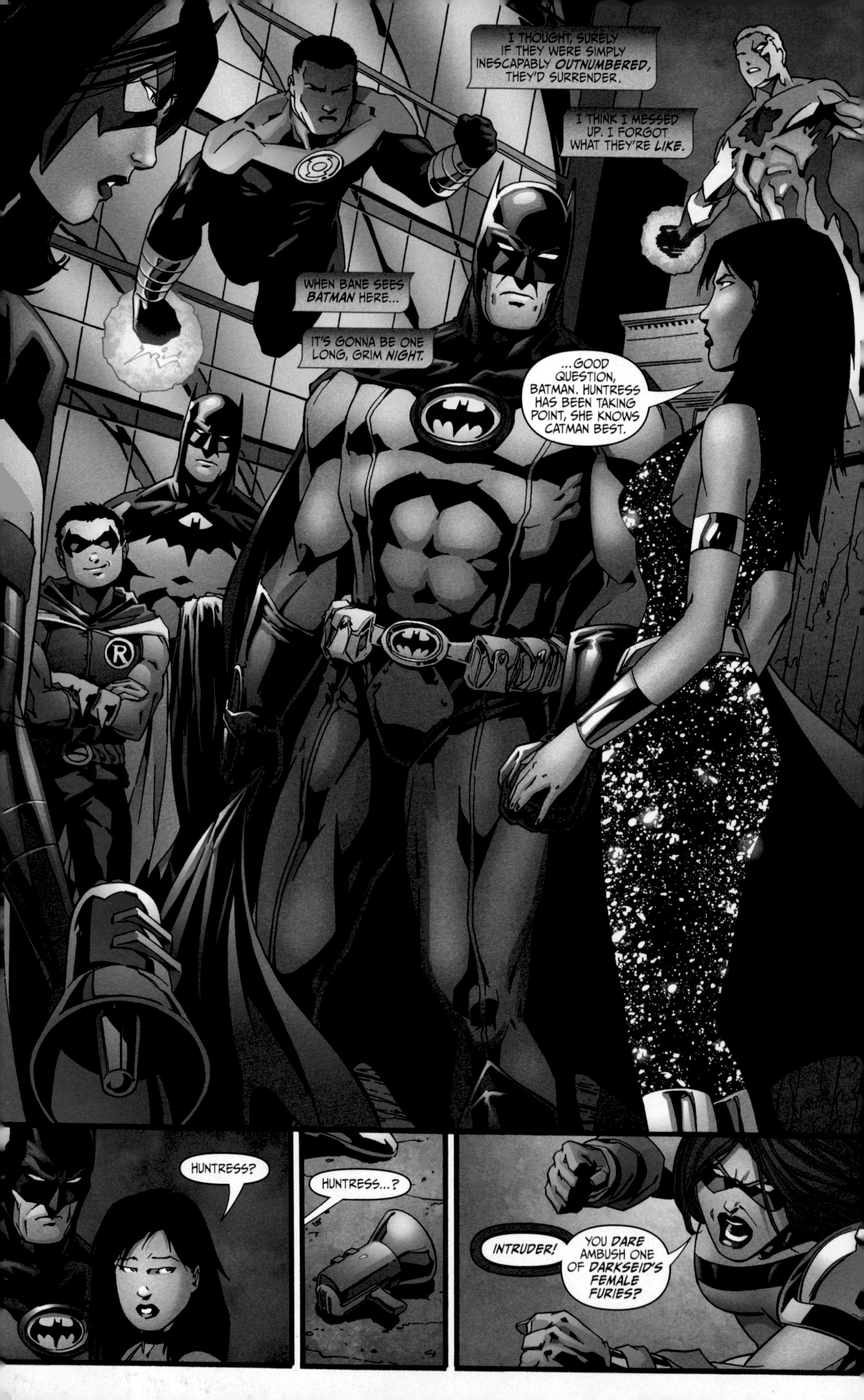
I THOUGHT, SURELY IF THEY WERE SIMPLY INESCAPABLY OUTNUMBERED, THEY'D SURRENDER.
I THINK I MESSED UP. I FORGOT WHAT THEY'RE LIKE.
WHEN BANE SEES BATMAN HERE...
IT'S GONNA BE ONE LONG, GRIM NIGHT.
...GOOD QUESTION, BATMAN. HUNTRESS HAS BEEN TAKING POINT, SHE KNOWS CATMAN BEST.
HUNTRESS?
HUNTRESS...?
INTRUDER!
YOU DARE AMBUSH ONE OF DARKSEID'S FEMALE FURIES?

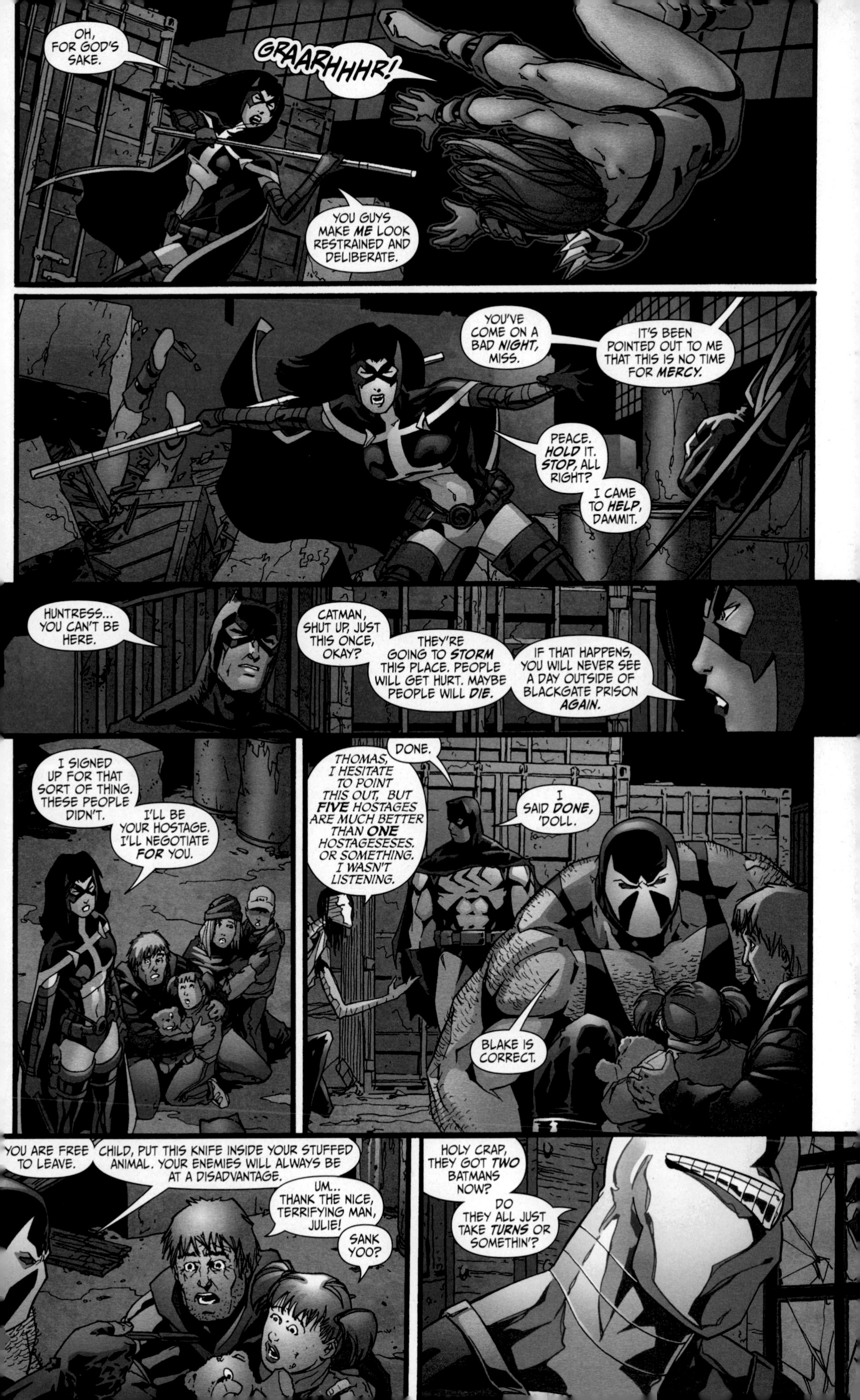
OH, FOR GOD'S SAKE.
GRAARHHHR!
YOU GUYS MAKE ME LOOK RESTRAINED AND DELIBERATE.
YOU'VE COME ON A BAD NIGHT, MISS.
IT'S BEEN POINTED OUT TO ME THAT THIS IS NO TIME FOR MERCY.
PEACE. HOLD IT. STOP, ALL RIGHT?
I CAME TO HELP, DAMMIT.
HUNTRESS... YOU CAN'T BE HERE.
CATMAN, SHUT UP, JUST THIS ONCE, OKAY?
THEY'RE GOING TO STORM THIS PLACE. PEOPLE WILL GET HURT. MAYBE PEOPLE WILL DIE.
IF THAT HAPPENS, YOU WILL NEVER SEE A DAY OUTSIDE OF BLACKGATE PRISON AGAIN.
I SIGNED UP FOR THAT SORT OF THING. THESE PEOPLE DIDN'T.
I'LL BE YOUR HOSTAGE. I'LL NEGOTIATE FOR YOU.
DONE.
THOMAS, I HESITATE TO POINT THIS OUT, BUT FIVE HOSTAGES ARE MUCH BETTER THAN ONE HOSTAGESESES. OR SOMETHING. I WASN'T LISTENING.
I SAID DONE, 'DOLL.
BLAKE IS CORRECT.
YOU ARE FREE TO LEAVE.
CHILD, PUT THIS KNIFE INSIDE YOUR STUFFED ANIMAL. YOUR ENEMIES WILL ALWAYS BE AT A DISADVANTAGE.
UM... THANK THE NICE, TERRIFYING MAN, JULIE!
SANK YOO?
HOLY CRAP, THEY GOT TWO BATMANS NOW?
DO THEY ALL JUST TAKE TURNS OR SOMETHIN'?

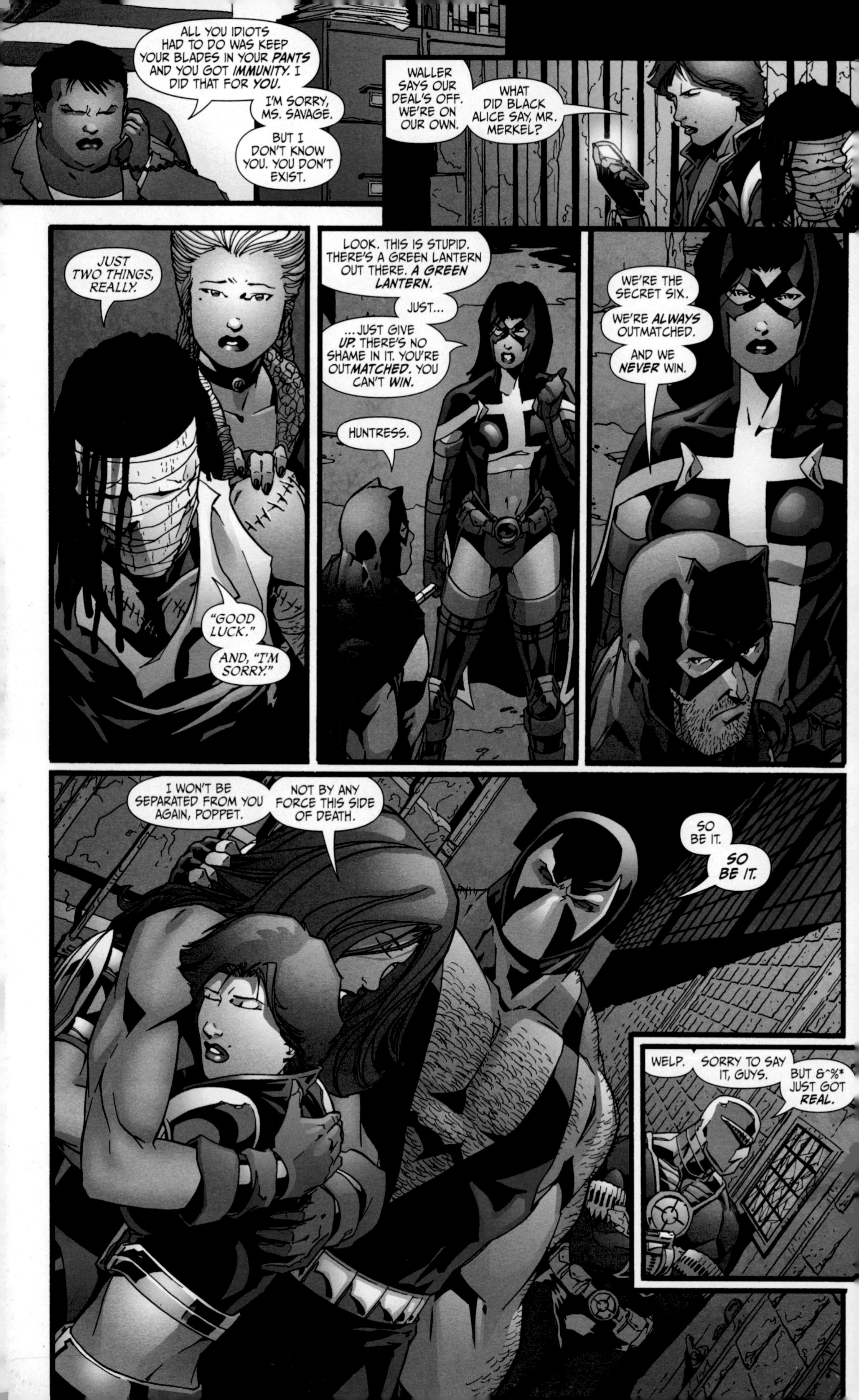

ALL YOU IDIOTS HAD TO DO WAS KEEP YOUR BLADES IN YOUR PANTS AND YOU GOT IMMUNITY. I DID THAT FOR YOU.
I'M SORRY, MS. SAVAGE.
BUT I DON'T KNOW YOU. YOU DON'T EXIST.
WALLER SAYS OUR DEAL'S OFF. WE'RE ON OUR OWN.
WHAT DID BLACK ALICE SAY, MR. MERKEL?
JUST TWO THINGS, REALLY.
"GOOD LUCK."
AND, "I'M SORRY."
LOOK. THIS IS STUPID. THERE'S A GREEN LANTERN OUT THERE. A GREEN LANTERN.
JUST...
...JUST GIVE UP. THERE'S NO SHAME IN IT. YOU'RE OUTMATCHED. YOU CAN'T WIN.
HUNTRESS.
WE'RE THE SECRET SIX.
WE'RE ALWAYS OUTMATCHED.
AND WE NEVER WIN.
I WON'T BE SEPARATED FROM YOU AGAIN, POPPET.
NOT BY ANY FORCE THIS SIDE OF DEATH.
SO BE IT.
SO BE IT.
WELP.
SORRY TO SAY IT, GUYS.
BUT &^%* JUST GOT REAL.

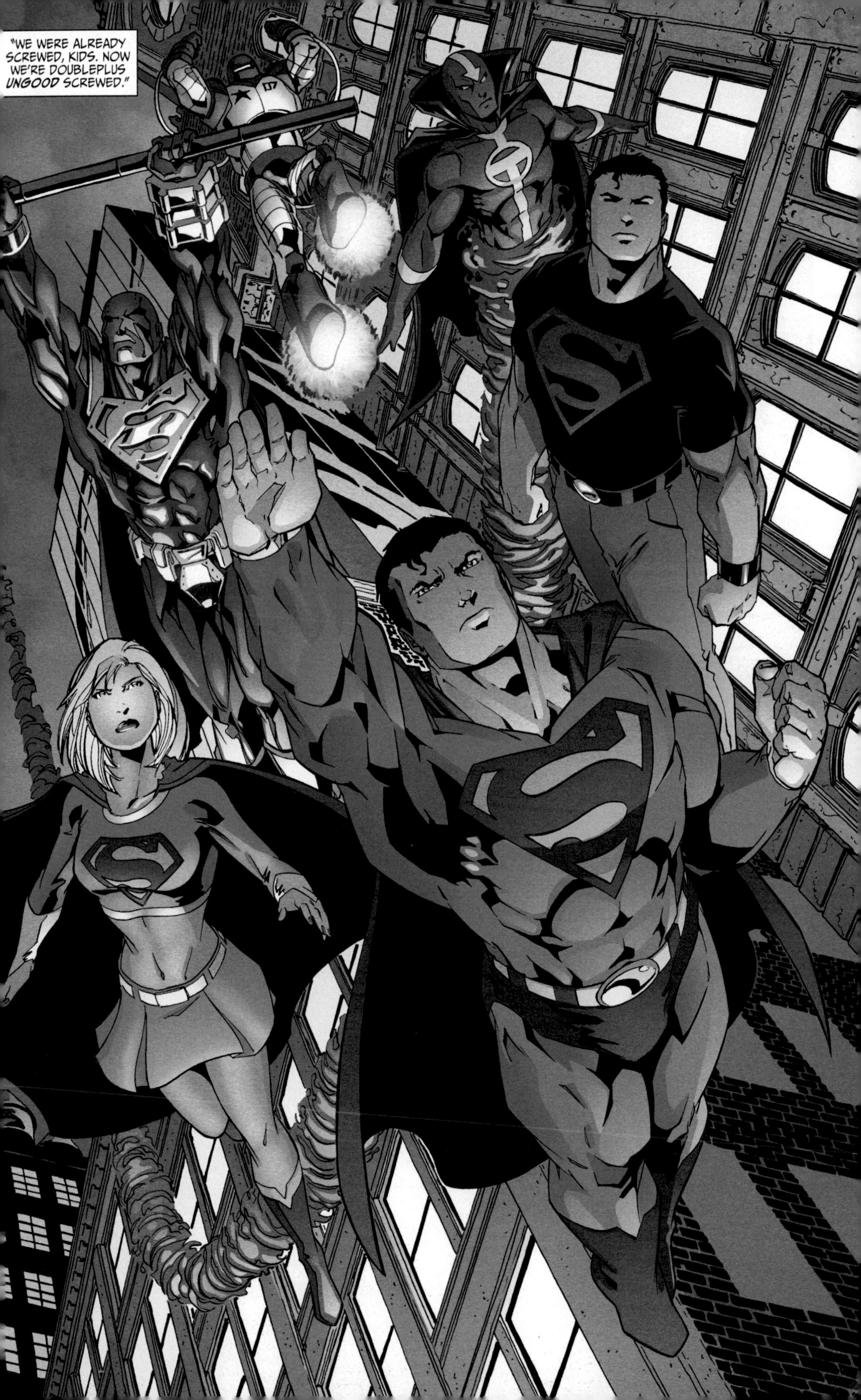
"WE WERE ALREADY SCREWED, KIDS. NOW WE'RE DOUBLEPLUS *UNGOOD* SCREWED."

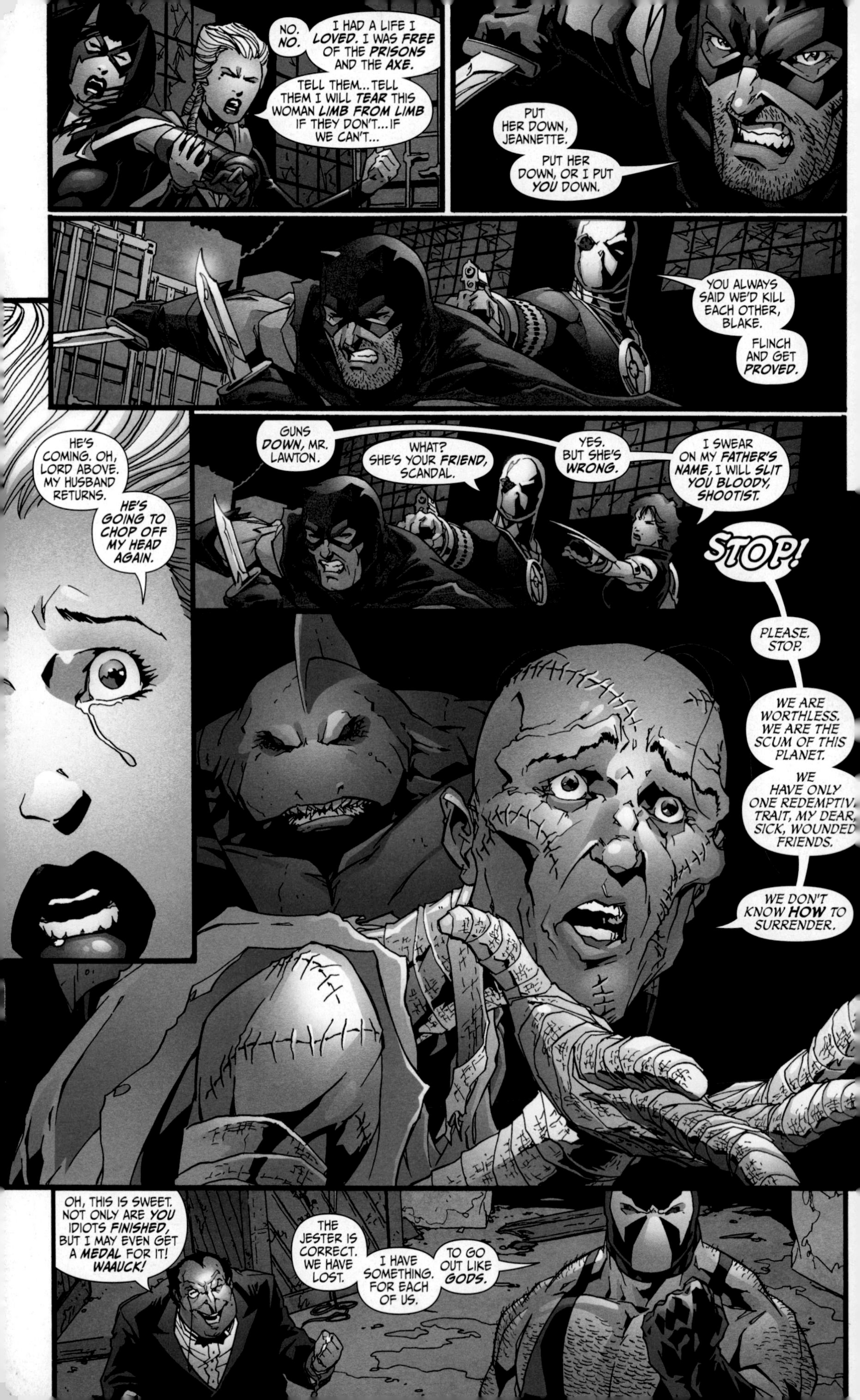
NO. NO.
I HAD A LIFE I LOVED. I WAS FREE OF THE PRISONS AND THE AXE.
TELL THEM...TELL THEM I WILL TEAR THIS WOMAN LIMB FROM LIMB IF THEY DON'T...IF WE CAN'T...
PUT HER DOWN, JEANNETTE.
PUT HER DOWN, OR I PUT YOU DOWN.
YOU ALWAYS SAID WE'D KILL EACH OTHER, BLAKE.
FLINCH AND GET PROVED.
HE'S COMING. OH, LORD ABOVE. MY HUSBAND RETURNS.
HE'S GOING TO CHOP OFF MY HEAD AGAIN.
GUNS DOWN, MR. LAWTON.
WHAT? SHE'S YOUR FRIEND, SCANDAL.
YES. BUT SHE'S WRONG.
I SWEAR ON MY FATHER'S NAME, I WILL SLIT YOU BLOODY, SHOOTIST.
STOP!
PLEASE. STOP.
WE ARE WORTHLESS. WE ARE THE SCUM OF THIS PLANET.
WE HAVE ONLY ONE REDEMPTIV TRAIT, MY DEAR, SICK, WOUNDED FRIENDS.
WE DON'T KNOW HOW TO SURRENDER.
OH, THIS IS SWEET. NOT ONLY ARE YOU IDIOTS FINISHED, BUT I MAY EVEN GET A MEDAL FOR IT! WAAUCK!
THE JESTER IS CORRECT. WE HAVE LOST.
I HAVE SOMETHING. FOR EACH OF US.
TO GO OUT LIKE GODS.

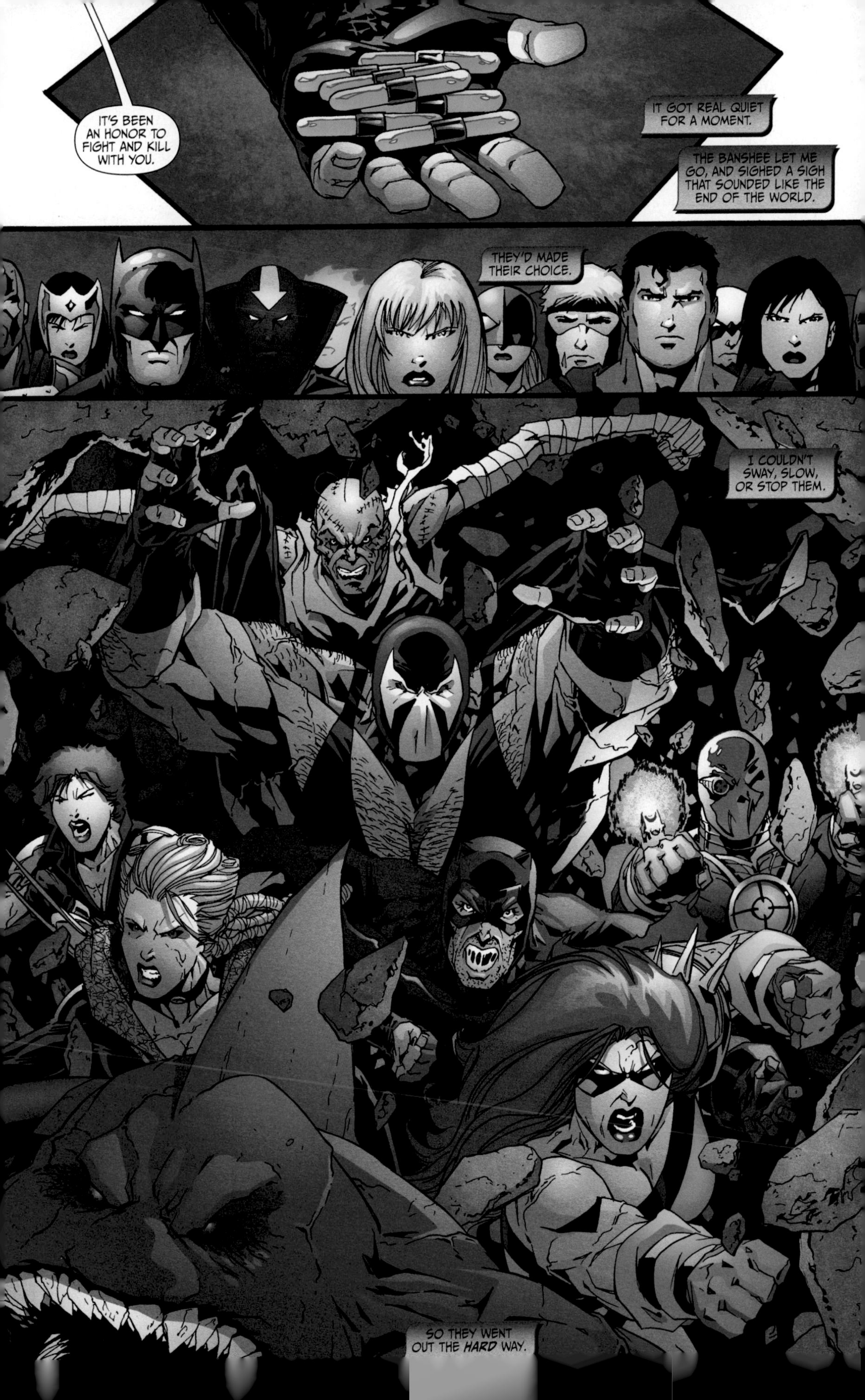
IT'S BEEN AN HONOR TO FIGHT AND KILL WITH YOU.
IT GOT REAL QUIET FOR A MOMENT.
THE BANSHEE LET ME GO, AND SIGHED A SIGH THAT SOUNDED LIKE THE END OF THE WORLD.
THEY'D MADE THEIR CHOICE.
I COULDN'T SWAY, SLOW, OR STOP THEM.
SO THEY WENT OUT THE HARD WAY.

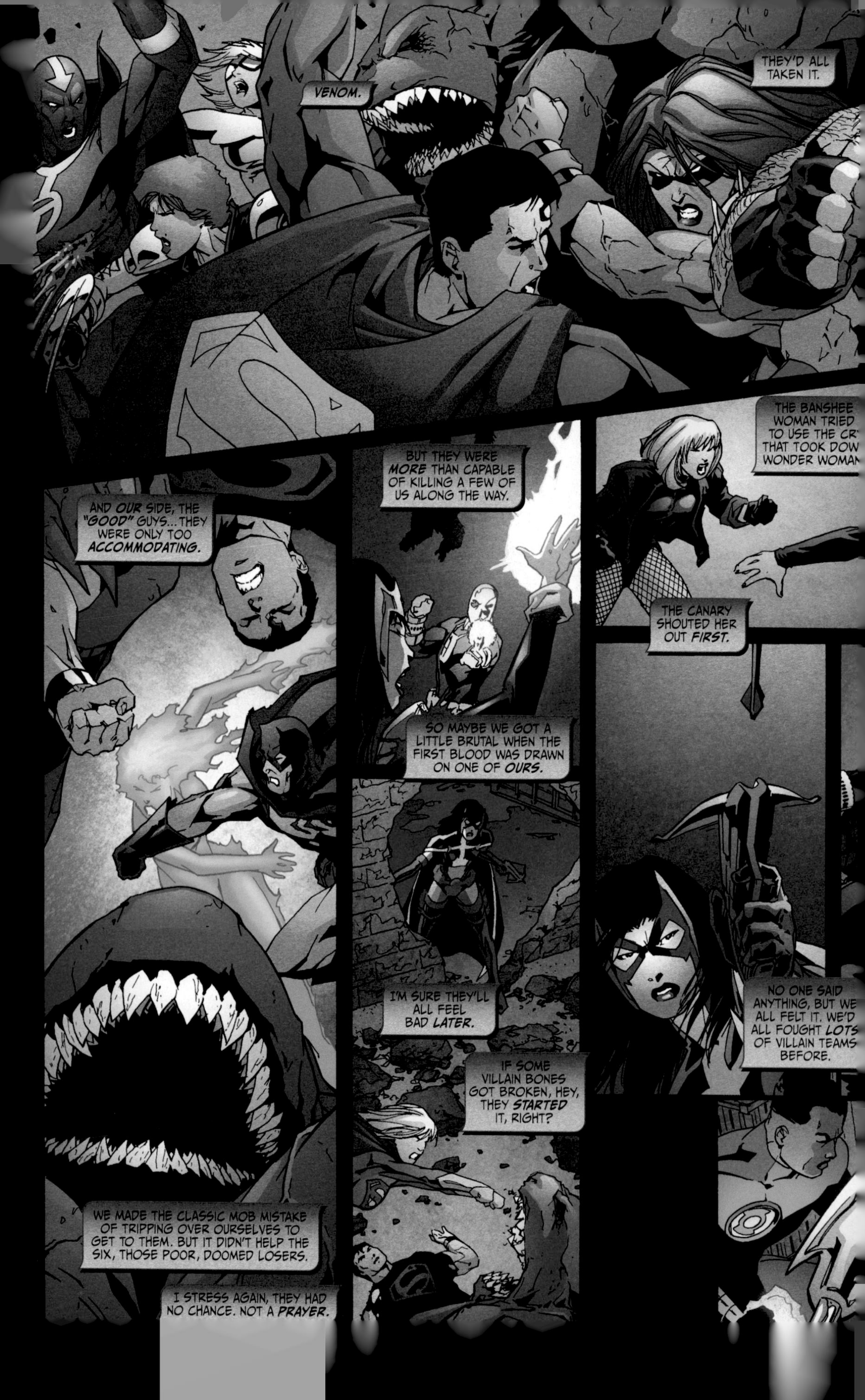
VENOM.
THEY'D ALL TAKEN IT.
AND OUR SIDE, THE "GOOD" GUYS... THEY WERE ONLY TOO ACCOMMODATING.
WE MADE THE CLASSIC MOB MISTAKE OF TRIPPING OVER OURSELVES TO GET TO THEM. BUT IT DIDN'T HELP THE SIX, THOSE POOR, DOOMED LOSERS.
I STRESS AGAIN, THEY HAD NO CHANCE. NOT A PRAYER.
BUT THEY WERE MORE THAN CAPABLE OF KILLING A FEW OF US ALONG THE WAY.
SO MAYBE WE GOT A LITTLE BRUTAL WHEN THE FIRST BLOOD WAS DRAWN ON ONE OF OURS.
I'M SURE THEY'LL ALL FEEL BAD LATER.
IF SOME VILLAIN BONES GOT BROKEN, HEY, THEY STARTED IT, RIGHT?
THE BANSHEE WOMAN TRIED TO USE THE CR
THAT TOOK DOW
WONDER WOMAN
THE CANARY SHOUTED HER OUT FIRST.
NO ONE SAID ANYTHING, BUT WE
ALL FELT IT. WE'D ALL FOUGHT LOTS
OF VILLAIN TEAMS BEFORE.

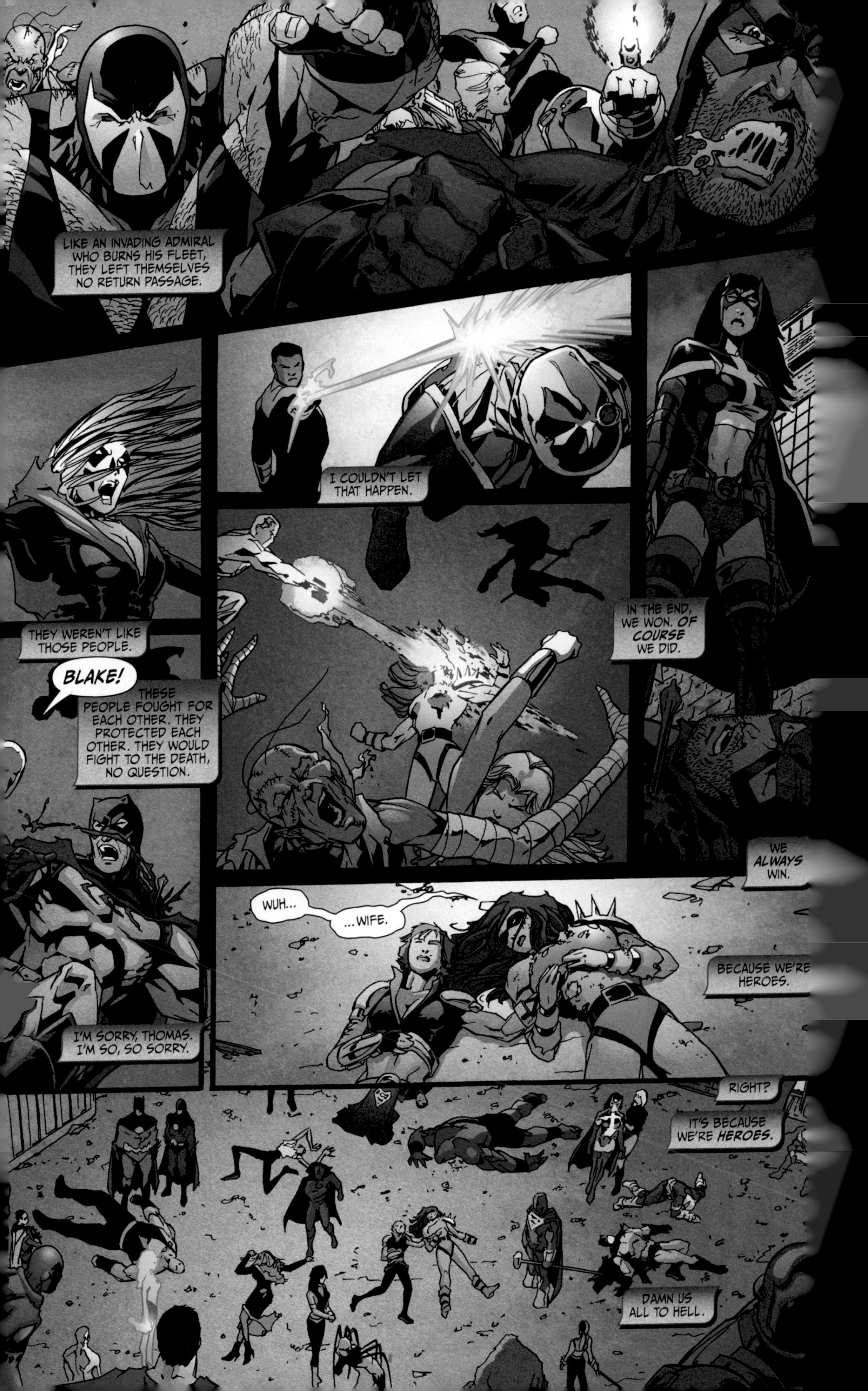
LIKE AN INVADING ADMIRAL WHO BURNS HIS FLEET, THEY LEFT THEMSELVES NO RETURN PASSAGE.
I COULDN'T LET THAT HAPPEN.
THEY WEREN'T LIKE THOSE PEOPLE.
BLAKE!
THESE PEOPLE FOUGHT FOR EACH OTHER. THEY PROTECTED EACH OTHER. THEY WOULD FIGHT TO THE DEATH, NO QUESTION.
I'M SORRY, THOMAS. I'M SO, SO SORRY.
IN THE END, WE WON. OF COURSE WE DID.
WE ALWAYS WIN.
WUH...
...WIFE.
BECAUSE WE'RE HEROES.
RIGHT?
IT'S BECAUSE WE'RE HEROES.
DAMN US ALL TO HELL.

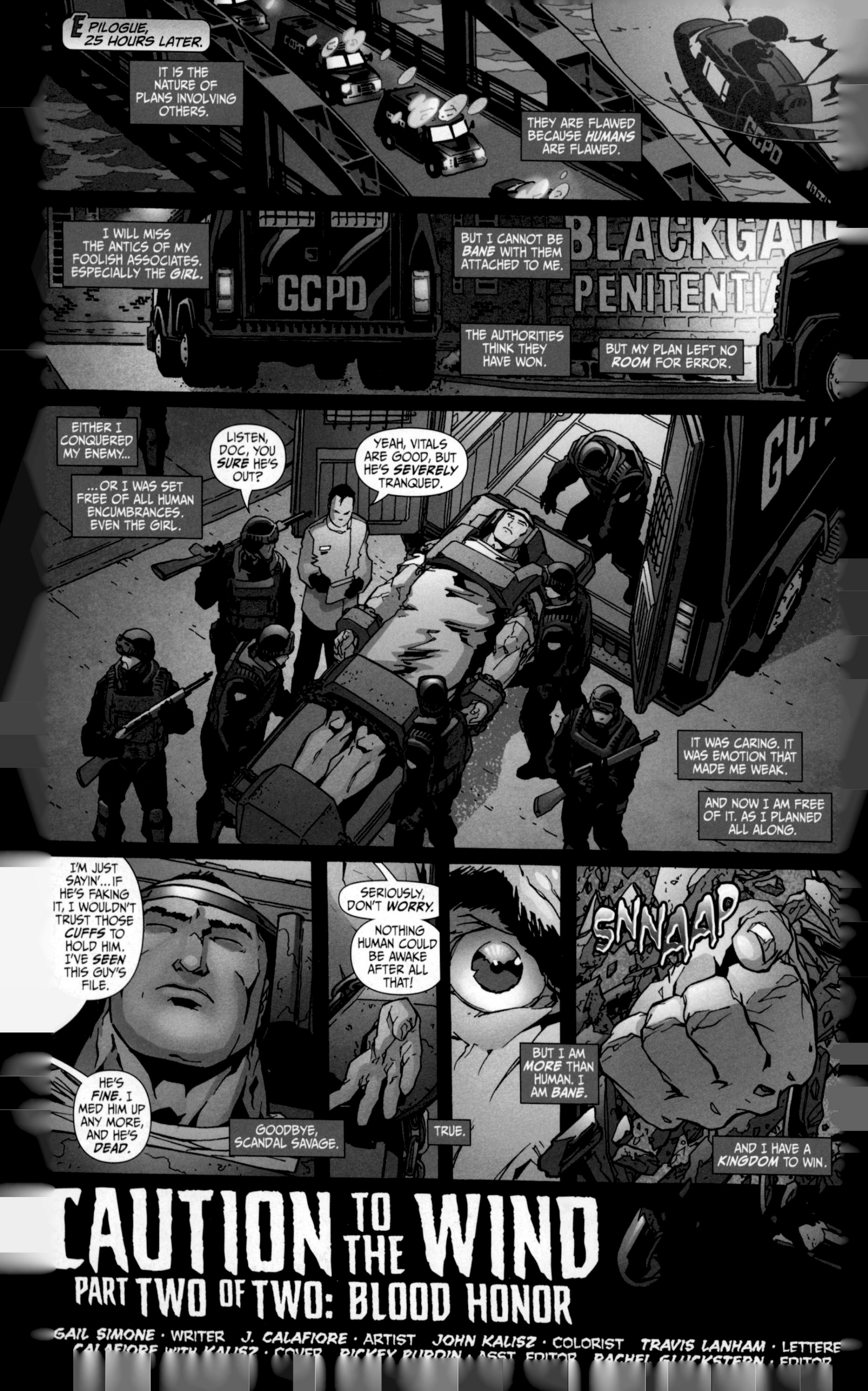
EPILOGUE, 25 HOURS LATER.
IT IS THE NATURE OF PLANS INVOLVING OTHERS.
THEY ARE FLAWED BECAUSE HUMANS ARE FLAWED.
GCPD
I WILL MISS THE ANTICS OF MY FOOLISH ASSOCIATES. ESPECIALLY THE GIRL.
GCPD
BUT I CANNOT BE BANE WITH THEM ATTACHED TO ME.
BLACKGA
PENITENTI
THE AUTHORITIES THINK THEY HAVE WON.
BUT MY PLAN LEFT NO ROOM FOR ERROR.
EITHER I CONQUERED MY ENEMY...
...OR I WAS SET FREE OF ALL HUMAN ENCUMBRANCES. EVEN THE GIRL.
LISTEN, DOC, YOU SURE HE'S OUT?
YEAH, VITALS ARE GOOD, BUT HE'S SEVERELY TRANQUED.
IT WAS CARING. IT WAS EMOTION THAT MADE ME WEAK.
AND NOW I AM FREE OF IT. AS I PLANNED ALL ALONG.
I'M JUST SAYIN'...IF HE'S FAKING IT, I WOULDN'T TRUST THOSE CUFFS TO HOLD HIM. I'VE SEEN THIS GUY'S FILE.
HE'S FINE. I MED HIM UP ANY MORE, AND HE'S DEAD.
GOODBYE, SCANDAL SAVAGE.
SERIOUSLY, DON'T WORRY.
NOTHING HUMAN COULD BE AWAKE AFTER ALL THAT!
TRUE.
BUT I AM MORE THAN HUMAN. I AM BANE.
SNNAAP
AND I HAVE A KINGDOM TO WIN.
CAUTION TO THE WIND
PART TWO OF TWO: BLOOD HONOR
GAIL SIMONE · WRITER J. CALAFIORE · ARTIST JOHN KALISZ · COLORIST TRAVIS LANHAM · LETTERE
CALAFIORE WITH KALISZ · COVER RICKEY PURDIN · ASST. EDITOR RACHEL GLUCKSTERN · EDITOR

"A pretty irresistible hook. What if the good guys assembled a bunch of bad guys to work as a Dirty Dozen-like superteam and do the dirty work traditional heroes would never touch (or want to know about)?"—THE ONION/AV CLUB

START AT THE BEGINNING!

SUICIDE SQUAD
VOLUME 1: KICKED IN THE TEETH

**SUICIDE SQUAD
VOL. 2: BASILISK
RISING**

**SUICIDE SQUAD
VOL. 3: DEATH IS FOR
SUCKERS**

**DEATHSTROKE VOL. 1:
LEGACY**

ADAM **GLASS** FEDERICO **DALLOCCHIO** CLAYTON **HENRY**